ANNUAL REVIEW OF ANTHROPOLOGY

EDITORIAL COMMITTEE (1996)

ANNUAL REVIEW OF ANTHROPOLOGY

VOLUME 25, 1996

WILLIAM H. DURHAM, *Editor*
Stanford University

E. VALENTINE DANIEL, *Associate Editor*
University of Michigan

BAMBI B. SCHIEFFELIN, *Associate Editor*
New York University

http://annurev.org   science@annurev.org   415-493-4400

ANNUAL REVIEWS INC.   4139 EL CAMINO WAY   P.O. BOX 10139   PALO ALTO, CALIFORNIA 94303-0139

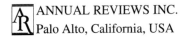 ANNUAL REVIEWS INC.
Palo Alto, California, USA

International Standard Serial Number: 0084-6570
International Standard Book Number: 0-8243-1925-7
Library of Congress Catalog Card Number: 72-821360

Annual Review and publication titles are registered trademarks of Annual Reviews Inc.

The paper used in this publication meets the minimum requirements of American National Standards for Information Sciences—Permanence of Paper for Printed Library
Materials, ANZI Z39.48-1984

Annual Reviews Inc. and the Editors of its publications assume no responsibility for
the statements expressed by the contributors to this *Review.*

Typesetting by Ruth McCue Saavedra and the Annual Reviews Inc. Editorial Staff

PRINTED AND BOUND IN THE UNITED STATES OF AMERICA

PREFACE

Readers of the *Annual Review of Anthropology* often ask, How do we choose the topics and authors that appear in a volume such as the one before you? The answer is relatively simple, for there are but two main pathways to the publication of a chapter. The first and most common pathway is by invitation. Once each year, we take a poll of the members of the Editorial Committee (whose names are listed here opposite the title page), asking for a list of topics that would be especially appropriate to review at this time and for the names of the best authors working in the area. It is not unusual for Committee members, in turn, to take their own informal polls of colleagues and acquaintances before compiling their lists. In recent years, we have also asked Committee members for suggestions of subjects that warrant treatment as "special themes," thus to include simultaneous related contributions by a number of authors. The replies from Committee members are then compiled in the agenda for the annual meeting, together with similar responses from local guests who join us for the occasion.

The second, and more unusual, pathway to publication in the *ARA* is by volunteering. Although we do not actively seek topics and authors via this path, we do consider each one we receive, again at the annual meeting of the Committee. For this purpose we require the proposed title of a volunteered contribution, a one- or two-page outline or précis, and a copy of the author's recent CV. The volunteered proposals are then reviewed together in a preliminary session at the start of the annual meeting, and a selected sample are then forwarded to the agenda for the main planning session. Whether from nomination or the volunteer path, all candidate topics and authors are then discussed, debated, and voted on by the Committee as a whole. These are lively and stimulating discussions, you may be sure. Eventually, we come up with a final list to whom we mail invitations for the next volume. (Let me leave to next year's Preface a discussion of the editorial process that is then set in motion once an author accepts our invitation.)

In the volume before you, this procedure has resulted in a collection of 19 review chapters, ranging in topics from the ethnography of Amazonia to the epidemiology of zoonoses. The volume includes two in our continuing series of theme sections, "Environmental Issues" and anthropological studies of "Childhood," with additional chapters on these themes expected for Volume 26 as well. During the development of this volume, as well as the previous four, we were fortunate indeed to have the help of Louise Lamphere (New Mexico) on the Editorial Committee. We will all miss Louise's steadfast commitment to timely topics, awesome authors, and abundant good cheer. I am happy to report that her fine work will now be carried forward by Faye Harrison (Kentucky). This year we have also welcomed Tamotsu Aoki (Osaka

University) as a new International Correspondent. As always, my colleagues and I on the Editorial Committee of the *ARA* would be more than happy to hear readers' suggestions for improving the content and coverage of this publication.

William H. Durham

Editor

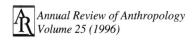Annual Review of Anthropology
Volume 25 (1996)

CONTENTS

SOME RELATED ARTICLES IN OTHER *ANNUAL REVIEWS*

From the *Annual Review of Psychology,* Volume 47 (1996)

Cross-Cultural Social and Organizational Psychology, M. H. Bond and P. B. Smith
Environmental Psychology 1989–1994, E. Sundstrom, P. A. Bell, P. L. Busby, and C. Asmus

From the *Annual Review of Sociology,* Volume 22 (1996)

Comparative Medical Systems, D. Mechanic and D. A. Rochefort
Cultural and Social Structural Explanations of Cross-National Psychological Differences, C. Schooler
Law and Inequality: Race, Gender... and, Of Course, Class, C. Seron and F. Munger

From the *Annual Review of Nutrition,* Volume 16 (1996)

Dietary Change and Traditional Food Systems of Indigenous Peoples, H. V. Kuhnlein and O. Receveur

From the *Annual Review of Public Health,* Volume 17 (1996)

Population and Women's Reproductive Health: An International Perspective, K. Miller and A. Rosenfield
Racial Differences in Health: Not Just Black and White, But Shades of Gray, M. Lillie-Blanton, P. E. Parsons, H. Gayle, and A. Dievler

From the *Annual Review of Genetics,* Volume 30 (1996)

Phylogenetic Analysis in Molecular Evolutionary Genetics, M. Nei

From the *Annual Review of Energy and the Environment,* Volume 21 (1996)

Global Change and Human Susceptibility to Disease, G. C. Daily and P. R. Ehrlich
Rural Energy in Developing Countries: A Challenge for Economic Development, D. F. Barnes and W. M. Floor

Paul T Baker

Annu. Rev. Anthropol. 1996. 25:1–18

ADVENTURES IN HUMAN POPULATION BIOLOGY

Paul T. Baker

47-450 Lulani Street, Kaneohe, Hawaii 96744

KEY WORDS: high altitude, human adaptability, Quechua, Samoans

ABSTRACT

In this professional memoir I trace my career and the changes that occurred after World War II in the biological anthropology studies of human populations. I describe my academic training at the University of New Mexico and Harvard University and my research training at the US Climatic Research Laboratory. During my academic career at The Pennsylvania State University, I directed two multidisciplinary research efforts as part of the International Biological Programme and Man in the Biosphere Program. These were the high-altitude studies in Nunoa, Peru, and the migration and modernization studies of Samoan communities. I describe my participation in the development of these international science programs as well as the effects on the discipline of biological anthropology. In conclusion, I reflect on the growth and development of biological anthropology, particularly in human population biology.

INTRODUCTION

Physical anthropology and to some extent all anthropology in the United States was substantially altered by World War II and its subsequent impact on science. During the war, physical anthropologists became involved in surveys of the body dimensions of military personnel for use in uniform sizing, airplane cockpit design, and even the fitting of gas masks. After the war, government sources of funding for research grew rapidly and the GI Bill produced a flood of undergraduate and graduate students. In reading previous volumes of the *Annual Review of Anthropology,* I noted that I am the first to reflect on the impact of the postwar environment on biological anthropology.

0084-6570/96/1015-0001$08.00

1

With all of today's media attention to human fossil finds and human variability, it is difficult to realize how little the public knew about anthropology fifty years ago. As a youthful veteran of World War II, I entered the University of Miami in Florida with a curiosity about where people came from and what made them behave as they did. A major in psychology seemed a likely source of answers, but aside from providing me with the opportunity to meet Thelma, my wife and intellectual mentor, the subject proved unsatisfactory. The single course in anthropology at the University suggested a more exciting view of our species, and we were off to the University of New Mexico for enlightenment.

EARLY DAYS IN PHYSICAL ANTHROPOLOGY

The New Mexico department was a stimulating environment with a group of completely involved undergraduate and graduate students. It was also a department that, at that time, expected its PhD students to have true depth in all four subfields. Such a requirement may explain why so few students completed PhDs there in the early 1950s. Personally, I found the material of cultural anthropology exciting but too speculative. Furthermore I could see few ways to test the validity of its postulates. Paul Reiter, who had been trained as an archeologist, taught physical anthropology, and his introductory course inspired me to pursue the study of human evolution as a career. I would have been content to stay at New Mexico, but Reiter decided I should not. Instead, he told me he would recommend me to EA Hooton if I promised to buy a suit before the Harvard interview, become a used car salesman for the summer, and above all rise when ladies entered the room. He thereby changed my life. I did buy the suit and after warning me that rebels weren't very successful in the program, Hooton admitted me to Harvard.

My acquaintance with Hooton was limited to his famous teas and his classic one-year course in physical anthropology. I found it informative and fun in spite of the fact that he was adamant that the Piltdown specimen was a human ancestor. As other students of Hooton have noted, he was a pleasant and very supportive mentor. Of greater significance to my development as an anthropologist were Stanley M Garn and Edward E Hunt, both of whom not only taught me the biological anthropology of the living but remained for me advisors and friends throughout my career. WW Howells replaced Hooton and acted as my final savior at Harvard. I proceeded with him through the necessary oral exams and my dissertation, a manuscript that he noted initially contained over 100 "howevers" and "therefores." This is a problem that continues to plague me as a writer and a thinker.

With very little financial support available for anthropology graduate students in the early 1950s, economic necessity forced many of us to find part-time work. My good fortune was to be hired by Russell W Newman, then head of the Anthropology section of the US Army Climatic Research Laboratory. During the war, physical anthropology was useful to the army because it initially furnished information on the measurements of soldiers so that clothing and equipment could be designed in appropriate sizes and quantities. After the war, this section became integrated with the Quartermaster (QM) unit concerned with environmental protection as it is today. Newman had decided that human body composition was related to the objectives of the unit and initially hired me to measure how three months of an exercise regimen in the hot desert of Yuma, Arizona, would affect the weight and body composition of soldiers.

This was a time of change in the anthropological studies of living populations. A number of specific genes had been identified from blood, and it was possible to show some examples of natural selection in human populations. Furthermore, mechanical computers could perform analysis based on sophisticated statistical techniques. Derek F Roberts (41) and others had shown that human populations conformed to Allen & Bergmann's rule on how climate characteristics related to body size and shape in mammals. Marshall Newman (39) suggested that the body dimensions and climate association found in the Americas might be partially related to nutritional differences in populations. On a worldwide basis the relationships appeared to be better correlated to climatic characteristics.

The emphasis of the laboratory on human performance in extreme environments encouraged me to examine some of the relationships between environment and human population morphology. With the aid and advice of Farrington Daniels, Jr, and Ellsworth R Buskirk, I tested how individual and population differences in morphology affected physiological performance in extreme environments. Most of the positive results from these studies remain unchallenged today (1, 23). Some findings on population differences seem debatable to me now because of uncontrolled sampling variables (2).

Undertaking these studies taught me the practicalities of conducting field research. For three summers I worked in the Yuma desert with groups of soldiers who marched around carefully laid out desert tracks in temperatures up to 120°F. Interesting senior colleagues were also present on the various summer field trips. Perhaps the most unusual was Sir Hubert Wilkinson, the first man to take a submarine under the Arctic ice cap. Sir Hubert arrived one summer to test his conviction that desert attire should include a sweat barrier, in this instance a kind of sponge rubber jacket designed for Arctic use. It did not prove to be a successful idea, although he bravely wore one while he was in the desert. A field study conducted during the month of February in Fort Churchill, Canada, did suggest that sweating when exercising in heavy clothing could create serious heat loss. Work outside in the Arctic winter also dissuaded me later in my career from joining faculties either at the University of Alaska or the University of Minnesota.

My final field trip for the QM was a three-month stay at the Army's war dead identification laboratory in Kokura, Japan. The objective was to study the relationship of living body weight to bone weight (14). It was not a type of research I enjoyed, but it gave me the opportunity to become friends with T Dale Stewart and Ellis Kerley, both of whom were also working at the laboratory. We had interesting times together, but I must admit that on a hike through the surrounding hills T Dale, who was then 55 years old, left Ellis and me far behind though we were still in our 20s.

Five years with the QM research unit afforded me an excellent education in human biology, research design, and scientific writing. Russell Newman demanded a careful scientific approach and interpretation but supported some of my more eccentric ideas. He was definitely one of my most significant educators.

BACK TO ACADEMIA

In 1957, I was offered a research position at The Pennsylvania State University and decided it was an opportunity to rejoin academia. The position, in a biophysics laboratory, involved research on the measurement of bone density in living people. At this time X-ray was the only technique known for measuring bone density. The results were very imprecise. I attempted for a year to determine how density measured with focused X-rays at several sites related to total human bone mass and density. The results were not very satisfactory (15). Following the first year, I was happy to move into a position in the Department of Sociology and Anthropology. Here I continued some research on human bone structure in collaboration with Larry Angel but abandoned it in the mid-1960s (10).

As was true of many state universities at that time, there was no undergraduate major or graduate program in anthropology, but there was an administrative intent to establish one. Between 1957 and 1959 Louis Dupree, William T Sanders, and I joined Frederick R Matson and Maurice Mook in the Department. Bachelor's and master's programs in anthropology were rapidly instituted, and by 1963 we had convinced the dean of the Graduate School that anthropology was indeed a suitable discipline for a PhD. Our first PhD to graduate was Michael A Little, whose degree was conferred in 1968. We became a separate department in 1979, where I remained until retirement.

Several developments in the early 1960s further expanded and altered the future directions of physical anthropology research on living populations.

Among these were Fred Hulse's textbook of physical anthropology, *The Human Species* (30), arguably the first comprehensive text since Hooton's *Up from the Ape* (29), which emphasized living populations. The advanced text *Human Biology* (28) increased the emphasis on studies of human genetics, selection, and responses to the environment. Gabriel Lasker's expansion of the journal *Human Biology* from the Raymond Pearl tradition had also encouraged the study of living populations.

When I started to teach anthropology in the late 1950s, I developed an advanced course where I presented some of my ideas on how the interaction of human biological characteristics, the natural environment, and culture produced the biology and behavior of human populations. I called it Human Ecology and, surprisingly, it attracted many students who have now become well-known professionals in biological anthropology and related disciplines. For reasons I no longer remember, I also organized a symposium on anthropological ecology for the AAAS in 1960 (3). Perhaps because of its reasonably good reception and the later Nuñoa project (described below), I was invited to join the long-term ecological program being planned by the International Council of Scientific Unions (ICSU) (44).

THE HUMAN ADAPTABILITY PROJECT

This program, which was called the International Biological Programme (IBP), included a project in human ecology because human interaction with the natural environment was considered an essential component of the overall program. Joseph S Weiner organized this under the title Human Adaptability (HA) (42). He remained the coordinator of the project for the duration of the research effort and the subsequent publication of synthesis volumes. Joe was an unusually gifted scholar who knew the world of arts and literature as well as human physiology and physical anthropology. His skill in organizing and managing the project was a major reason for its success.

My own participation in the HA project included some of the planning for the overall research program. I now find it difficult to recapture in words the excitement I felt about the ideas, the people, and the potential scientific results of the HA effort. My initial involvement was at the 1964 Wenner-Gren Foundation meeting at their conference center in Burg Wartenstein, Austria, where we developed a basic structure for the HA project (16). Lita F Osmundsen, then president of the foundation, had great talent in organizing meetings and structuring professional interactions. The small group size, the isolation, and the long duration of Wenner-Gren conferences combined to produce an optimum learning environment. It also encouraged the best possible situation for groups of scientists from diverse academic and cultural backgrounds to reach agreements. The research and internationalization of anthropology during the 1960s and 1970s were greatly enhanced by her skills. Over the 10-year life of the HA project, six conferences related to it were held in the Burg Wartenstein castle. I believe these were crucial to the success of the HA program.

During the 1964 planning conference, we agreed that there would be two strategies for research on human populations that could fit the ecological theme of the IBP. The first was studies of how specific environmental conditions related to population differences in traits such as growth, adult size, disease patterns, gene frequencies, etc. The second was the development of a few in-depth studies of traditional populations to explore how specific populations had adapted and survived in extreme physical environmental conditions of cold, altitude, heat, and aridity.

In the United States, the National Academy of Sciences formed a National Research Council committee to oversee the US efforts in the program. The Human Adaptability section of the program consisted of two parts. The first was the designation of four in-depth studies of traditional populations: the Aleut study directed by William Laughlin, the Eskimos of northwest Alaska study directed by Frederick Milan, the Quechua study that I directed, and the Yanomama project directed by James Neel (38). There were also several affiliated projects. The one best known to most physical anthropologists was the Solomon Islanders project directed by Al Damon. During the final years of the US effort, a coordinating office was established at Penn State that over its lifetime had three directors, Joel M Hanna, Michael A Little, and Paul L Jamison.

Nuñoa Project

The Nuñoa project was my major research contribution to the Human Adaptability studies. It had its origin in a series of unplanned events. In 1961, at the suggestion of Gabriel Lasker, I applied for a Fulbright Research fellowship in Peru. Funded by a variety of small grants, four Penn State graduate students worked with me in Peru at various periods. Thelma and our four young children also served as unpaid members of the field team. With the help of A Roberto Frisancho and Julio Sotomayor, then students at the University of Cuzco, we arranged studies of bone density and cold tolerance in Quechua men. We also conducted a month-long study comparing the heat tolerance of Shipibo and mestizo men in the tropical forest near Pucallpa (25).

Along with almost all the anthropologists who worked in Peru during the 1950s and 1960s, we stayed at the Pension Morris when we were in Lima. It was operated by Signora Nora Andrade and her daughter Olga. They were truly magnificent hostesses and even provided perfect care for the six of us who returned from the Shipibo with the usual intestinal nasties. The first trip to

Peru ended with a brief lecture tour in Brazil, which provided us the opportunity to meet several future participants in the IBP.

Our stay in Cuzco, along with reading the research of Carlos Monge (37) and Alberto Hurtado (31), convinced me that the Quechua did indeed have a remarkable altitude tolerance compared with lowlanders. Even those lowlanders who had spent extended periods at high altitude showed reduced work capacity. While the traditional research on altitude tolerance relied on anatomy and physiology, I wanted to go beyond this approach to develop an integrated analysis of how the native Quechua coped with the gamut of environmental stresses found in the altiplano. Through Peruvian colleagues we had been introduced to the Nuñoa district, which is one of the highest and most isolated districts on the Peruvian altiplano. Nuñoa also contained a variety of social and settlement patterns including a town, haciendas, and a self-governing Quechua rural community. Thus the district, with a minimum altitude of 4000 m, seemed ideal for an in-depth study of the population's adaptive response to the environment. The drawback was that the town lacked such simple requirements as electricity and an appropriate building for a laboratory. We subsequently built a laboratory that contained testing rooms, controlled temperature chambers, and living quarters for most of the investigators. Fortunately for the project, my former associate in the Climatic Research Laboratory, ER Buskirk, had moved to Penn State as the director of the Human Performance Laboratory and joined the research effort.

The choice of a high-altitude population for study was at the time fortuitous since the developing high-altitude confrontation between China and India on the Himalayan ridges made the topic of hypoxia interesting to the Quartermaster Climatic Research group. They provided research support during the first three years of the project. For the remaining years, Buskirk and I obtained funds from several sources including an NIGMS training grant. The original project in Nuñoa ended in 1970. In the 1980s, R Brooke Thomas and his students were able to conduct a partial restudy of the population (32).

Of the many professionals who contributed to the project, several were particularly critical to its success. These included three Peruvian professionals: Tulio Velasquez, Director of the Instituto de Estudios Andinas; Emilio Picon-Reatigeau, Professor of Nutrition at the University of San Marcos, Peru; and Professor Gabriel Escobar, who later joined the Penn State faculty in cultural anthropology. Thelma developed the survey questionnaires and conducted infant growth and development and socialization studies, while Buskirk trained the students in human physiology and directed the testing of hypoxic tolerance at high altitude. More than 20 graduate students participated in the study, and 11 developed their dissertations from various parts of the overall program. In many graduate anthropology programs the tradition has been to require the student to develop his or her own project. This is, of course, in the tradition of the English and European scientific communities, but it had almost disappeared in scientific fields in the United States by the early 1970s. The PhD completion rate was quite high in the Peru project, and many graduates have since made major contributions to biological anthropology and human biology. From my experience with graduate students who pursued independent projects vs those who joined faculty in research, I am convinced that the latter not only provided them a better education but better motivation.

In biological anthropology such large-scale research attempts to link the biological and behavioral variations of human populations to ecological factors were generally well accepted. However, some cultural anthropologists in the United States rejected research based on biological aggregates, which included, of course, races, subraces, and populations. They believed that research based on these units supported racism and discrimination. I encountered the strength of these views while presenting an invited paper at an AAAS meeting in the 1970s. During my presentation on classificatory systems, including race as research tools, Margaret Mead kept pounding her house post at the speakers' table and shouting her disagreement (4).

Near the end of the Nuñoa project we decided to write a synthesis volume for the US IBP series. Six senior professionals who helped plan and carry out various aspects of the program and nine young professionals who had participated as graduate students in fieldwork and analysis contributed chapters. The resulting book summarizing the project bore the unfortunate title "Man in the Andes" (13), which reflected my admiration of brevity and precision in book titles. It was, however, prepared in the midst of significant linguistic changes in the United States. We did, of course, conduct a number of studies involving women but not the critical ones involving altitude tolerance. In retrospect, I wish we could have conducted the total repertoire of physiological studies on women as well as men. Given the techniques used in exercise physiology, it would have been very difficult to obtain cooperation from the population even with women professionals conducting the research.

A major justification for the project was to determine how well the traditional population was adapted to the low oxygen pressure. The Quechua did show maximal oxygen consumption capacities that matched the values of fit young men at sea level, which indicated little if any hypoxic-related reduction in work capacity (5). However, one might also consider the results of an unusual bicycle race in Nuñoa equally good evidence of the Quechua's impressive adaptation. As part of a research project for the Mexico City Olympics, Buskirk brought six of Penn State's best runners for a six-week period of training and acclimatization at altitude. The acclimatization added little to their oxygen consumption capacity, but at the end of their stay they arranged a bicycle race with some of the local young men. Only one of Penn State's best racers managed even a tie for first place.

The studies reinforced the idea that birth and development at high altitude were a necessary part of achieving sea-level work capacities at the 3000–4000 m level. Even so, it was not possible to prove whether there was also a specific genetic component in the Quechua's performance at altitude. Buskirk believed there was (18), I believed the evidence was very suggestive but not conclusive, and most of the graduate students did not believe it was genetic. Recent research seems to confirm that both Andean high-altitude people (24) and the Tibetan populations (17) have genetic adaptations to hypoxia. Interestingly, the two groups may not have the same genetic adaptations.

Joe Weiner asked me to coordinate the various IBP studies of high-altitude peoples. During the IBP, altitude research expanded rapidly. Genetic and growth projects were initiated among the Quechua and Aymara in Bolivia and Chile as well as in Peru (21). A British study used an interesting migrant-re-search design to examine the effects of altitude on growth and health of the Amhara in Ethiopia (19, 27). Studies of growth, physiology, and demography were conducted in Nepal (43). In the Soviet Union, work capacity and growth studies were completed in the Pamir and Tien Shan mountains (36). At the end of the IBP, I edited a book that summarized and integrated the major findings from all the high-altitude studies (7). Many of the professionals who worked on the projects contributed chapters. I do not remember how the reviewers appraised the resulting volume, but I do value the Russian translation.

ENVIRONMENTAL CHANGE AND HEALTH

With the completion of the Nuñoa project and the IBP (20), two similar paths led me to the rest of my professional career. The first was a growing interest in how environmental and cultural change affected the biology of a human population. During the Peruvian research, establishing a design that would allow the partition of the effects of varying natural and cultural conditions became of increasing concern. G Ainsworth Harrison had, at the beginning of IBP planning, suggested how one might simulate controlled experiments by using naturally occurring contrasts in environmental variables (26). This approach could be extended to populations and socioeconomic variables. Thus, we decided to mount a study in a community comparable to Nuñoa in socioeconomic level but at low altitude. It had to contain migrants from high altitude, permanent residents, and migrants from low altitude. Ideally, this would allow some conclusions on the relative effects of altitude and migration on the biology of the population. For this problem we selected the District of Cocachacra, an isolated district on the southern coast of Peru. The project proved productive in understanding how growth, development, and socialization in one environment affect the health of migrants in a new physical environment. However, involvement in the more modern society of the coast had a great effect on the migrants. This made it difficult to distinguish the changes related to the natural environment from those that were culturally mediated (11).

It was not apparent to me how the migrant research could be furthered in Peru. I thought that studies of biologically and culturally different populations would inspire new insights into migrant research. Joel M Hanna, who had been part of the high-altitude project had later conducted, as a faculty member of the University of Hawaii, Manoa, some growth research on the Samoans. Considering this experience he suggested that an in-depth study of Samoans in various settings would be worthwhile. He pointed out that lifestyles of Samoans varied from the traditional in some villages in Western Samoa to total integration in some urban settings in Oahu.

Samoan Project

I thought such a project was a good idea and decided to consult with Ian Prior, an epidemiologist in New Zealand, who was directing a long-term study of Tokelau islanders (40). His comprehensive study was designed to examine the health of the Tokelauans on their islands and as migrants to New Zealand. The research group included professionals from social anthropology, medical sociology, and human genetics. The results of the studies at that time encouraged me to believe that a study that traced the human biology and behavior of the Samoans from the most traditional villages of Western Samoa to the more economically prosperous life of American Samoa and Hawaii would produce a better understanding of how changes in environment and culture affected the biology, health, and behavior of a population. Hanna and I agreed to start the project in 1975. A group of graduate students and two postdoctoral trainees in human biology from Penn State University joined Hanna and his associates for initial studies on Samoan migrants in Hawaii.

The research efforts in the project gradually expanded despite a chronic shortage of funds. Attempts to obtain substantial funding for the project were never successful. Instead, the research was supported for 10 years by a combination of graduate assistantships, NIGMS training grants at Penn State, and an NIMH grant at the University of Hawaii. Work-study programs and odd small grants helped too. Perhaps the most important gap in the total project was caused by the lack of funding for a detailed study of Samoans in the San Francisco area. IG Pawson, who directed this part of the study, was able to conduct a small survey and obtain some information from the California census. These studies made clear that the Samoans in California were showing the greatest health effect from the change in cultural environment, but the data were too sparse for detailed analyses.

Outside of some archeology and fossil research, integrated long-term research efforts have been scarce in our discipline. Partially as a consequence of this tradition, very limited research funds were made available to anthropology by the National Science Foundation. NIMH training grants were possible but difficult to obtain, and special health studies on minorities required that the minorities were so identified in the census. Our final problem was that Samoans at that time were not enumerated separately in the US decennial census and were not considered a large enough minority to qualify. The problem was resolved in the 1990 census, too late for the necessary major funding.

The lack of central funding was partially mitigated by data from other sources. The directors of the LBJ Tropical Medical Center and the Samoan Health Planning and Development Agency in American Samoa generously made available to us a wealth of birth, child development, health, and mortality data. Equally important was the high level of Samoan public interest and participation in the work. The medical and census data available from the independent country of Western Samoa was more limited, but intensive studies on the population characteristics in the most traditional villages provided an adequate baseline for comparison with the more urban populations and other Samoan groups.

The field research projects continued through the early 1980s, and Thelma and I continued to direct the survey work carried out by junior graduate students in the Samoas. The Samoan people were a pleasure to know and work with. However, at the end of one field session we decided we no longer had the endurance to direct junior graduate students in the field. Furthermore, it was time to put the pieces together in a book synthesis. This was more difficult to do than the Nuñoa volume because professionals and former students from three geographically dispersed universities were involved. The final synthesis volume was authored by 8 senior professionals and 15 young professionals who had been students during the research (12). Not surprisingly, agreement on the interpretation of some of the results was not achieved. Even so, it remained removed from the "Mead in Samoa" controversy.

For me there were several unexpected scientific results. In particular I was surprised that unlike most traditional populations moving to a modern society, the children did not grow faster in height or as adults end up taller than the previous generation. More striking was the people's rapid gaining of massive amounts of weight when they moved from the traditional village way of life to more affluent lifestyles. We could find no evidence that this was related to a change in the composition of the diet (12). In Pacific populations, the massive weight gain tendency seems to be primarily a Polynesian and secondarily a

Micronesian trait. Continuing studies show that the average weights have continued to increase in younger adults but not in older ones (35). Of the Pacific populations that show massive increases in average weight, the Samoans currently have the largest body mass indices. I suggested that this tendency for rapid weight gain in both Polynesians and Micronesians may be another example of the selective process known as the thrifty genotype. In this instance the cold of voyaging and typhoon damage to food supply would have acted as the selective force (9). Such large body weights have been associated with increased cardiovascular disease (CVD) mortality and rapidly increased rates of non-insulin-dependent diabetes mellitus (NIDDM) in some Pacific populations (45). However, at the time of our study the Samoans still showed only modest frequencies of CVD mortality and levels of NIDDM.

I previously noted that graduate students involved in the Nuñoa project had a high rate of degree completion and professional success. Most of those students entered academia, but the Samoan studies' group found the academic market in anthropology more limited. A higher percentage successfully found careers in medically related research. The ability of these PhDs to obtain good research positions suggests that human population biology may be able to grow as a field because of its applicability to health problems.

MAN AND THE BIOSPHERE PROGRAM

Before I begin this section on my last experiences as an administrator, I must state that I never was enthusiastic about the job of administration. Even so, I was willing to try for the sake of expanding anthropological knowledge about what makes us appear and behave the way we do. The early 1980s reinforced my belief that, while necessary, administration in scientific endeavors is often limited in its rewards.

As the IBP continued, it was fairly obvious that ICSU would end it on schedule in 1975 and not replace it with a similar program. Staff in the UNESCO Biology Division decided that the potential gap should be filled and started a program in the early 1970s called Man and the Biosphere, or MAB in government jargon. I was invited to serve for three months as a staff consultant to the program in Paris. My nominal duty was to develop a UNESCO MAB technical note on research strategies and designs for ecological research involving human populations (6). In retrospect, I doubt this document had much impact because the examples required such large studies that resources for them were never available. While there, I also found that I was frequently the only UNESCO-related participant with any background in the social sciences at regional planning conferences. The potential benefits of such a massive ecological program to our understanding of how populations acquired their general biology and behavior seemed substantive, and I was highly impressed with the UNESCO staff directing the program. In my opinion, one factor that reduced the program's effectiveness was the fact that the Social Science section of UNESCO would not join the effort. I believe that my attempt to help fill the gap was inadequate, and today the program remains less effective than it could be. I continued over the next few years to accept short consulting requests, including acting as the series editor for a four-volume series on Andean ecological problems (8). The difficulties of involvement in government-related programs such as MAB became increasingly apparent to me in the late 1980s.

Meanwhile, I was asked to chair the US National Academy of Sciences subcommittee on UNESCO. This gave me an opportunity to promote international research programs including the Man and the Biosphere program. We held a meeting on the topic and were able to incorporate some participants from the newly developing human ecology group within anthropology. However, the subcommittee did not last long, and instead I became chair of the US MAB committee, which was supervised by the US Commission for UNESCO. The possibility of incorporating a strong anthropological human ecology existed, and I was optimistic for the first year. Unexpectedly, there was a sudden political impetus for the United States to withdraw from UNESCO. I joined a movement to try to prevent the withdrawal, lobbying Congressmen and testifying before the House Committee on Science. Of course, the United States did withdraw and the UNESCO commission was dissolved, but funding for coordinating the US MAB program and some other international research programs was saved by using dues formerly contributed to UNESCO. Control of the MAB program was shifted directly to a branch of the State Department. It took until the late 1980s for me to realize that the position of chairman was by then primarily symbolic, at which time I resigned.

REFLECTIONS ON RETIREMENT

In 1985, I completed five years as department head at Penn State, and the synthesis volume on the Samoan project was finished. At this time, Thelma and I decided to retire in 1987. Because I was only 60, many colleagues and former students found it somewhat of an odd decision. Actually the reasons were rather simple. The excitement of anthropology for me had been in developing new knowledge. It also included helping interested graduate students develop scientific skills as well as learning from and interacting with people from other cultures. Most importantly, I enjoyed unraveling some of the complexity of the environmental, genetic, and cultural interactions that determine our biology and behavior. To do so properly required graduate students and financial resources, both of which had become by this time scarce for anthropology. Finally, the pursuit of funding, teaching, and the training of graduate students in fieldwork required personal effort somewhat beyond my and Thelma's aging abilities.

Retirement has not meant a complete withdrawal from anthropology. In fact, I read more on the subject now than I had time for in the 10 years before retirement. My major efforts have been in aiding some of the professional associations in anthropology. From my past experience with attempts to obtain project funding, I realize that the backing of a well-organized scientific organization is of great value in the promotion and funding of a given discipline and particular type of research. It is, of course, necessary for members of an organization to agree on what kinds of research are desirable and then to show why it is important. Anthropological organizations in the United States have not been very successful in reaching such unity or in forming joint objectives. The international organizations have been somewhat more successful.

For example, the International Association of Human Biologists (IAHB), founded in 1967 during the IBP, soon became affiliated with the International Union of Biological Sciences (IUBS), as a consequence of Joe Weiner's efforts. In 1980, Derek Roberts became the Secretary General, and I became president of the organization. Derek was very active in the organization and was able to incorporate anthropologists and human geneticists in an IUBS research program focusing on ecological studies in the tropics. There are also possibilities for major involvement by anthropologists in the Human Genome Project, but in the United States there appear to be more cultural anthropologists opposing such involvement than supporting it.

The International Union of Anthropological and Ethnological sciences became a full member of the ICSU in 1994, a recognition that I strongly supported as one of its vice presidents. This recognition provided anthropology with political representation in international science. However, the Union cannot use this position very effectively at present because it lacks significant funding. Many US anthropologists do not realize the importance of involvement in national or international scientific structures or the necessity of going beyond individual research for the future survival of the field.

Evidence supporting the importance of internationally organized science for the development of knowledge in anthropology is provided by the Little et al (34) examination of recent multidisciplinary research on human biology and behavior. In this article, 17 major projects between the early 1960s and 1992 were examined. Of these 17 projects, nine were designated IBP projects and two MAB-affiliated. All are now completed except for the final publications of the Turkana project.

These projects are the major source of information about how the biology and behavior of human populations from traditional hunters and gatherers to modern migrants relate to their physical and cultural environments. Unfortunately, no new projects of these dimensions are in progress. I do hope some of the new generation in our field will realize that the days of Darwin and Einstein are past. Perhaps regrettably, scientific discovery now requires group efforts.

HUMAN BIOLOGY AND ANTHROPOLOGY

It still surprises me that the field of physical anthropology is less than two generations old. Obviously our future as a professional species is doubtful, but then science in general resembles the Eocene's disruptive punctuated equilibrium. In 1952 when I joined the American Association of Physical Anthropologists there were only about 150 members. This venerable organization has now reached over 2000. This increase occurred in spite of the rapid development of five or six academic subspecies, races, populations, or yet-to-be-designated taxons. Like the horseshoe crab, the parent may well survive, but the taxonomy is changing, and perhaps a majority of the species now call themselves biological anthropologists.

I must admit a certain paternal involvement in one offspring—the Human Biology Association. In the early 1970s the Society for the Study of Human Biology, based in the United Kingdom, decided to publish its own journal, thus withdrawing some support from the journal *Human Biology*. Gabriel Lasker, the editor, asked if I would help found a US-based society called the Human Biology Council to help the journal and topic. Of course, I agreed and helped to send out the original solicitation for members. There was strong national interest and the membership grew rapidly. The organization now has 450 members and holds two-day meetings. Still further fission occurred in organization, and there are now three original research journals published with the words Human Biology in the title: *American Journal of Human Biology, Annals of Human Biology,* and *Human Biology*. Last year, this trio produced over 2600 pages.

There was and still remains a place for another focus in biological anthropology. Such a program would include a strong applied aspect. Al Damon saw the need clearly in the early 1970s and felt it should be called physiological anthropology. In one sense this name was appropriate because groups in Germany and Japan had and still do have professional societies called Physiological Anthropology. At the time, I agreed with the need for such an applied orientation, but to me the title implied too much specialization (22).

Human biology or human population biology (33), a nomenclature that I prefer, appeals to me because in its breadth of conceptual framework one returns to what I consider a basic anthropological tenet. Namely, it is not possible to explain any specific aspect of human behavior or biology without realizing its origin was the result of past genetic selection and the specific natural and human environment in which individuals develop. The human environment of course includes the symbolic as well as the material.

It is obviously impossible for an individual or group of scientists to study all these aspects simultaneously. It is also impossible to train the individual in the total breadth of knowledge in anthropology. Some of my training in the broad aspects of the field has encouraged me to remember that nothing about our biology or behavior is caused simply by a gene, a physical environment, or a cultural tradition. There are now many specialties in biological anthropology of which I know very little that range from primate anatomy to the new methods of human fossil dating. However, I can read and understand the pertinent literature as I can in most of archeology. At one time, I thought I even understood descriptive ethnology. The ecological and sociobiological views of human behavior also make sense to me. Now I find that many professionals with positions in anthropology have views that seem to me more philosophical or social-reform oriented than scientific. As a result, in recent years when asked my profession, I often mumble "medical researcher" or "human biologist."

Despite these disclaimers, I realize that anthropology was for me not only a profession but an avocation and a style of life. Thelma and I have pursued common professional lives from the first hand calculation of a Pearson r on a large paper matrix through complementary bachelor's, master's, and doctorate degrees to the preparation of this memoir. We once calculated that as a family we had spent over five years of our joint lives outside of the United States. Consequently, our children now remember such exotic experiences as using the llama pen in Nuñoa as a toilet and departing each morning in elegant uniforms for school in Cuzco and Oxford. In their maturity, all of them remember the experiences as exciting and fun. I recently received a request for information from one of our children who had been telling childhood stories about Peru to one of our granddaughters. The child asked why we had all been there, and I have been asked to respond. Hopefully these reflections on my career will also answer her question.

Literature Cited

1. Baker PT. 1958. The biological adaptation of man to hot deserts. *Am. Nat.* 92:337–57
2. Baker PT. 1958. Racial differences in heat tolerance. *Am. J. Phys. Anthropol.* 16:287–306
3. Baker PT. 1962. The application of ecological theory to anthropology. *Am. Anthropol.* 64:15–22
4. Baker PT. 1968. The biological race concept as a research tool. In *Science and the Concept of Race,* ed. M Mead, T Dobzhansky, E Tobach, R Light, pp. 94–102. New York: Columbia Univ. Press
5. Baker PT. 1969. Human adaptation to high altitude. *Science* 163:1149–56
6. Baker PT, ed. 1977. Human population problems in the biosphere: some research strategies and designs. *MAB Tech. Notes 3.* Paris: UNESCO
7. Baker PT, ed. 1978. *The Biology of High-Altitude Peoples.* Cambridge: Cambridge Univ. Press
8. Baker PT, ed. 1982. *State of Knowledge Report on Andean Ecosystems,* Vols. 1–4. Boulder, CO: UNESCO, Int. Mt. Soc.
9. Baker PT. 1984. Migrations, genetics, and the degenerative diseases of South Pacific islanders. In *Migration and Mobility: Biosocial Aspects of Human Movement,* ed. AJ Boyce, pp. 209–39. London: Taylor & Francis
10. Baker PT, Angel JL. 1965. Old age changes in bone density: sex and race factors in the United States. *Hum. Biol.* 37:104–21
11. Baker PT, Beall CM. 1982. The biology and health of Andean migrants: a case study in south coastal Peru. See Ref. 8, 2:81–95
12. Baker PT, Hanna JM, Baker TS, eds. 1986. *The Changing Samoans: Behavior and Health in Transition.* New York: Oxford Univ. Press
13. Baker PT, Little MA, eds. 1976. *Man in the Andes: A Multidisciplinary Study of High-Altitude Quechua.* Stroudsburg, PA: Dowden, Hutchinson, Ross
14. Baker PT, Newman RW. 1957. The use of bone weight for human identification. *Am. J. Phys. Anthropol.* 15:601–18
15. Baker PT, Schraer H, Yalman RG. 1959. The accuracy of human bone composition determination from roentgenograms. *Photogramm. Eng.* June:455–60
16. Baker PT, Weiner JS, eds. 1967. *The Biology of Human Adaptability.* New York: Clarendon
17. Beall CM, Blangero J, Williams-Blangero S, Goldstein M. 1994. Major gene for percent of oxygen saturation of arterial hemoglobin in Tibetan highlanders. *Am. J. Phys. Anthropol.* 95:271–76
18. Buskirk ER. 1978. Work capacity of high-altitude natives. See Ref. 7, pp. 173–87
19. Clegg EJ, Pawson IG, Ashton EH, Flinn RM. 1972. The growth of children at different altitudes in Ethiopia. *Philos. Trans. R. Soc. London Ser. B* 264:403–37
20. Collins KJ, Weiner JS. 1977. *Human Adaptability: A History and Compendium of Research in the International Biological Programme.* London: Taylor & Francis
21. Cruz-Coke R. 1978. A genetic description of high-altitude populations. See Ref. 7, pp. 47–63
22. Damon A, ed. 1975. *Physiological Anthropology.* New York: Oxford Univ. Press
23. Daniels FR Jr, Baker PT. 1961. Relationship between body fat and shivering in air at 15°C. *J. Appl. Phys.* 16:421–25
24. Frisancho AR, Frisancho HG, Milotich M, Brutsaert T, Albalak R, et al. 1995. Developmental, genetic, and environmental components of aerobic capacity at high altitude. *Am. J. Phys. Anthropol.* 96:431–42
25. Hanna JM, Baker PT. 1974. Comparative heat tolerance of Shibipo Indians and Peruvian mestizos. *Hum. Biol.* 46:69–80
26. Harrison GA. 1967. Human adaptability with reference to the IBP proposals for high altitude research. See Ref. 7, pp. 509–19
27. Harrison GA, Kuchemann CF, Moore MAS, Boyce AJ, Baju T, et al. 1969. The effects of altitudinal variation in Ethiopian populations. *Philos. Trans. R. Soc. London Ser. B* 256:147–82
28. Harrison GA, Weiner JS, Barnicot NA, Tanner J. 1964. *Human Biology.* Oxford: Oxford Univ. Press
29. Hooton EA. 1931. *Up from the Ape.* New York: Mcmillan
30. Hulse FS. 1964. *The Human Species: An Introduction to Physical Anthropology.* New York: Random House
31. Hurtado A. 1964. Animals in high altitudes: resident man. In *Handbook of Physiology,* ed. DB Dill, EF Adolf, CG Wilber, pp. 843–60. Washington, DC: Am. Phys. Assoc.
32. Leatherman TL, Carey JW, Thomas RB. 1995. Socioeconomic change and patterns of growth in the Andes. *Am. J. Phys. Anthropol.* 97:307–21
33. Little MA, Haas JD, eds. 1989. *Human Population Biology: A Transdisciplinary Science.* New York: Oxford Univ. Press
34. Little MA, Leslie PW, Baker PT. 1991. Multidisciplinary studies of human adaptability: twenty-five years of research. *J. Indian Anthropol. Soc.* 26:9–29
35. McGarvey ST, Levinson PD, Bausserman L, Galanis DJ, Hornick CA. 1993. Popula-

tion change in adult obesity and blood lipids in American Samoa from 1976–1978 to 1990. *Am. J. Hum. Biol.* 5:17–30
36. Mirrakhimov MM. 1978. Biological and physiological characteristics of the high-altitude natives of Tien Shan and the Pamirs. See Ref. 7, pp. 299–315
37. Monge C. 1973. *Acclimatization in the Andes.* Detroit: Blaine Ethridge-Books
38. Neel JV, Layrisse M, Salzano FM. 1967. Man in the tropics: the Yanomama Indians. See Ref. 16, pp. 109–42
39. Newman MT. 1953. The application of ecological rules to the racial anthropology of the aboriginal New World. *Am. Anthropol.* 55:311–27
40. Prior IAM, Hooper A, Huntsman JW, Stan-hope JM, Salmond CE. 1967. The Tokelau migrant study. See Ref. 16, pp. 165–86
41. Roberts DF. 1953. Body weight, race and climate. *Am. J. Phys. Anthropol.* 11:533–58
42. Weiner JS. 1977. The history of the human adaptability section. See Ref. 20, pp. 1–23
43. Weitz CA. 1973. *The effects of aging and habitual activity pattern on exercise performance among a high altitude Nepalese population.* PhD thesis. Pa. State Univ., University Park
44. Worthington EB. 1975. *The Evolution of IBP.* Cambridge: Cambridge Univ. Press
45. Zimmet P, Dowse G, Finch C, Sargentson S, King H. 1990. The epidemiology and natural history of NIDDM: lessons from the South Pacific. *Diabetes/Metab. Rev.* 6:91–124

Annu. Rev. Anthropol. 1996. 25:19–43

NARRATING THE SELF

Elinor Ochs and Lisa Capps

Department of TESL and Applied Linguistics, 3300 Rolfe Hall, University of California, Los Angeles, Los Angeles, California 90095-1531; e-mail: ochs@humnet.ucla.edu

KEY WORDS: narrative, self, coauthorship, discourse, temporality

ABSTRACT

Across cultures, narrative emerges early in communicative development and is a fundamental means of making sense of experience. Narrative and self are inseparable in that narrative is simultaneously born out of experience and gives shape to experience. Narrative activity provides tellers with an opportunity to impose order on otherwise disconnected events, and to create continuity between past, present, and imagined worlds. Narrative also interfaces self and society, constituting a crucial resource for socializing emotions, attitudes, and identities, developing interpersonal relationships, and constituting membership in a community. Through various genres and modes; through discourse, grammar, lexicon, and prosody; and through the dynamics of collaborative authorship, narratives bring multiple, partial selves to life.

NARRATIVE HORIZONS

Narrative is a fundamental genre in that it is universal and emerges early in the communicative development of children (4, 19, 152, 157, 164, 182, 209). This review focuses on narratives of personal experience, defined here as verbalized, visualized, and/or embodied framings of a sequence of actual or possible life events.

Personal narratives comprise a range of genres from story (60, 135, 147, 175, 177, 207) to novel (11, 38, 39, 132, 188), diaries (239) and letters (21) to memoirs (100), gossip (20, 28, 101, 160) to legal testimony (10, 165), boast (207) to eulogy (29, 30), troubles talk (119) to medical history (49), joke (191) to satire (132, 183), bird song (65, 202) to opera (40), etching to palimpsest (150), and mime (5, 233) to dance (93, 205). Counter to a prevalent ideology of disembodied objectivity (98), even scientific narratives can be personal in tone. Scientists, for example, routinely construct oral narratives of procedures and interpretations, casting themselves and others as protagonists (136, 137, 169, 170).[1] Culture and gender studies scholars have advocated written scientific narratives with subjects who reflexively situate and resituate themselves with respect to the objects they are visualizing (51, 98, 149). While differing in complexity and circumstance, narratives transform life's journeys into sequences of events and evoke shifting and enduring perspectives on experience.

Echoing Aristotle, Kenneth Burke deems ritual drama "the *Ur*-form" of narrative (39:103), and Victor Turner (233:154) proposes that enacted social drama is "the experiential matrix from which…oral and literary narrative have been generated." This perspective parallels the ontogenesis of narrative, wherein embodied enactments of experiences anticipate verbal accounts (33, 181, 234).

Narratives are not usually monomodal, but rather they integrate two or more communicative modes. Visual representation, gesture, facial expression, and physical activity, for example, can be combined with talk, song, or writing to convey a tale (43, 85, 88, 91, 102, 103, 167, 170). These blendings characterize narratives in a wide array of settings and communities. Conversational narratives told during American family dinners, for instance, can involve dramatic enactments of past and present problematic events (167, 227). Ceremonial narratives of personal experience among the Xavante (93) and Kaluli (205) blend song and dance. Courtroom testimonial (88) relies heavily on pictorial renderings such as photographs, drawings, diagrams, models, and graphs.[2] Novels and other written accounts evoke orality by incorporating reported speech (11). Visual art forms tell a story along a continuum of condensation and abstraction (1, 16, 150). A story may be told across a sequence of pictures, as in cave art, or condensed into a single frame, which can be unpacked using a particular form of narrative literacy. Paintings and sculptures may similarly detail a narrative through realistic representations or may minimalistically evoke a narrative through metaphor and juxtaposition of shape, texture, and color (41).

THE NARRATED SELF

Personal narrative simultaneously is born out of experience and gives shape to experience. In this sense, narrative and self are inseparable. Self is here

---

[1] Members of a physics laboratory used the term "story" throughout their collaborations to describe what they were constructing (79). Further, the physicists stated that their experimental narratives were highly personal in that they spent their days building equipment, running experiments, and relating results to theory.

[2] Similarly, scientific narratives blend linguistic and visual representation (22, 141, 211).

broadly understood to be an unfolding reflective awareness of being-in-the-world, including a sense of one's past and future (62, 106). We come to know ourselves as we use narrative to apprehend experiences and navigate relationships with others.

The inseparability of narrative and self is grounded in the phenomenological assumption that entities are given meaning through being experienced (106, 110, 155, 208) and the notion that narrative is an essential resource in the struggle to bring experiences to conscious awareness. At any point in time, our sense of entities, including ourselves, is an outcome of our subjective involvement in the world. Narrative mediates this involvement. Personal narratives shape how we attend to and feel about events. They are partial representations and evocations of the world as we know it.

From this perspective, narratives are versions of reality. They are embodiments of one or more points of view rather than objective, omniscient accounts (76, 178, 219, 240). While some narrators emphasize the truth of a narrated text (83, 105, 120, 127, 136, 203, 229), others grapple with the fragility of memory and the relativity of point of view (7, 54, 126, 130, 131, 238). A leitmotif running through the writings of Milan Kundera is the paradoxical relationship between remembering and forgetting. While warning us that "the struggle of man against power is the struggle of memory against forgetting" (130:3), Kundera despairs that memory never captures authentic experience. "We immediately transform the present moment into its abstraction. We need only recount an episode we experienced a few hours ago: the dialogue contracts to a brief summary, the setting to a few general features.... Remembering is not the negative of forgetting. Remembering is a form of forgetting" (132:128). An important challenge to humanity is to recognize that lives are the pasts we tell ourselves.

Narratives are tales that tellers and listeners map onto tellings of personal experience. In this sense, even the most silent of listeners is an author of an emergent narrative (11, 60, 85). A particular telling inspires distinct and only partially overlapping narratives, as interlocutors link the telling to their particular lived and imagined involvements in the world. Among the Kaluli of Papua New Guinea, for example, performers of the Gisaro ceremony motivate listeners to recall experiences through reference to significant places in their lives: "Framed in sentiments of loneliness or abandonment, the mention of particular trees, hills, and other details of the locality evoke for the listeners particular times and circumstances" (205:181). Regardless of their elaborateness, tellings of personal experience are always fragmented intimations of experience. While telling surely assists the construction of a tale, the tale necessarily lies beyond the telling (242).

Every telling provides narrators and listener/readers with an opportunity for fragmented self-understanding. Each telling of a narrative situated in time and space engages only facets of a narrator's or listener/reader's selfhood in that it evokes only certain memories, concerns, and expectations (41, 126, 162). In this sense, narratives are apprehended by *partial* selves, and narratives so apprehended access only fragments of experience. Marcel Proust captures this insight in writing, "it is only in one small section of the complete idea we have of [a person] that we are capable of feeling any emotion; indeed it is only in one small section of the complete idea he has of himself that he is capable of feeling any emotion either" (185:91).

Narratives situate narrators, protagonists, and listener/readers at the nexus of morally organized, past, present, and possible experiences (95, 106). For example, narrators and listener/readers exist in the here-and-now world of the telling/reading as they are drawn into the multiple worlds of emergent, apprehended narratives (37, 242). Narrators may cast protagonists as aware of their past, present, and possible moral selves (78). In *The Man Without Qualities,* for example, Robert Musil casts the protagonist Ulrich as two selves: "At this moment there were two Ulrichs, walking side by side. One took in the scene with a smile....[T]he other had his fists clenched in pain and rage" (163:164). Similarly, in *Remembrance of Things Past,* Marcel Proust portrays the young Gilberte as throwing a ball not to the present "me" who loves her but to the past "me" who was merely a friend of hers (185).

In these ways, narratives have the potential to generate a *multiplicity* of partial selves. Selves may multiply along such dimensions as past and present (11, 106, 130, 131, 185, 188); subject and object (98, 100, 106, 149, 163, 169); male and female (73, 98, 107, 113, 121, 163); id, ego, and superego (70); good and evil (as in the biblical tale of Adam and Eve); normal and aberrant (7, 43, 46, 67, 73, 113, 225); and public and private (79, 81, 82, 101, 159, 239). A narrator may first present partial selves in the form of distinct protagonists and then recognize them as facets of a single being. Such recastings are common in psychoanalysis, as analysts and patients interpret figures in narratives as facets of the patient's psyche (70). Theological narratives also present deities as distinct and at the same time treat them as parts of one being and one's self. For example, the Christian Bible holds that God the Father, the Son, and the Holy Spirit are at once a trinity of distinct entities and a unity and that this trinity/unity inhabits the souls of followers.

As narratives are apprehended, they give rise to the selves that apprehend them. Nobel Laureate Toni Morrison (161:22) noted, "Narrative is radical, creating us at the very moment it is being created." As narratives reach out to tap a preexisting identity, they construct a fluid, evolving identity-in-the-making (54, 117, 139). Spinning out their tellings through choice of words, degree of elaboration, attribution of causality and sequentiality, and the foregrounding and backgrounding of emotions, circumstances, and behavior, narrators build novel understandings of themselves-in-the-world. In this manner, selves evolve in the time frame of a single telling as well as in the course of the many tellings that eventually compose a life (78, 197). It may be that novel self-understandings are attributable to hearing or telling novel accounts of events. However, like the protagonist in *Remembrance of Things Past,* whose memories are evoked through reexperiencing the moist crumbs of a madeleine, one may return to a known account, rereading or relistening to it utilizing a different facet of one's self. This self may construe new narrative readings, which in turn alter one's sense of being-in-the-world.

Self-understandings do not always take the form of soothing narrative solutions to life's dilemmas. Rather, narratives may illuminate life as we know it by raising challenging questions and exploring them from multiple angles (100, 132). Although they sometimes deceive, narrators may also probe beneath the surface of phenomena and take interlocutors on "an adventurous journey toward a deeper understanding, or rather to a new and deeper question, of ourselves in the world" (100:252). While narrative does not yield absolute truth, it can transport narrators and audiences to more authentic feelings, beliefs, and actions and ultimately to a more authentic sense of life.

TWO DIMENSIONS OF PERSONAL NARRATIVE

Scholars of narrative highlight two basic dimensions of narrative: temporality and point of view (5, 38, 39, 82, 133, 135, 177, 184, 188, 192).

Temporality

Narratives depict a temporal transition from one state of affairs to another. Paul Ricoeur referred to this as the "chronological dimension" of narrative (188). Temporality is a cornerstone of William Labov and Joshua Waletsky's linguistic definition of narrative as two or more temporally conjoined clauses that represent a sequence of temporally ordered events (135). The Kaluli mythic tale "The Boy Who Became a Muni Bird," for example, begins as follows (202:113):

> Once there was a boy and his older sister; they called each other *adε.* One day they went off together to a small stream to catch crayfish. After a short while the girl caught one; the brother as yet had none. Looking at the catch, he turned to her, lowered his head, and whined, "*adε, ni galin andoma"—"adε,* I have no crayfish."

This passage lays out a narrative setting ("Once there was a boy and his older sister; they called each other *adε*") then presents a sequence of events, which includes going off to catch crayfish, the sister but not the brother catching one, the brother's gaze at the catch, and subsequent whining.

The chronological dimension offers narrators a vehicle for imposing order on otherwise disconnected experiences. That is, chronology provides a coherence that is reassuring. Robert Musil captured this aspect of narrative in depicting the reflections of the man without qualities (163:709):

> It struck him that when one is overburdened and dreams of simplifying one's life...the law one longs for is nothing other than that of narrative order, the simple order that enables one to say: "First this happened and then that happened...." Lucky the man who can say "when," "before," and "after"! Terrible things may have happened to him, he may have writhed in pain, but as soon as he can tell what happened in chronological order he feels as contented as if the sun were warming his belly.

Narratives often do not unfold parallel to the chronological ordering of events. Rather, narrators may shift back and forth in time as bits and pieces of a tale and the concerns they manifest come to the fore, as in the following conversation in which a white working-class American mother recounts an episode about her daughter (Beth) and niece (Edith) to the researcher (157:299):

> Mother: Beth won't hit a little baby back. I told her that. But she did—Edith must've hurt her on her hair or something. And she bit her.

Here the narrator recounts that Beth hit Edith, then goes back in time to identify a possible event that precipitated this action ("Edith must've hurt her on her hair or something"), and then shifts forward in time again to recount that Beth subsequently bit Edith.

Sometimes chronology is artfully altered for rhetorical purposes, as when a narrator uses flashbacks or slow disclosures to enhance the dramatic effect (212). As Goffman noted, a narrative "falls flat if some sort of suspense cannot be maintained" (82:506). At other times, the telling lurches forward and back in time, as interlocutors recall or dispute various details, some of which may have been buried or skewed in an attempt to portray a protagonist in a particular light (91, 172).

Predominantly, narratives of personal experience focus on past events, i.e. they are about "what happened" (82, 135, 177, 188). However, such narratives link the past to present and future life worlds. The myth of "The Boy Who Became a Muni Bird" relates to a multiplicity of enduring cultural themes, especially expectations of reciprocity between older sisters and younger brothers. Similarly, in the above excerpt Beth's mother situates a past episode with respect to a present desirable trait ("Beth won't hit a little baby back"). When young Xavante men of Brazil publicly narrate dream-songs, their form and

composition link them to the past of their elders, while their collective performance links them to a present cohort of peers and ultimately legitimizes
them to transmit dream-songs to future generations (93).

Personal narratives about the past are always told from the temporal perspective of the present. Narrators linguistically shape their tellings to accommodate circumstances such as the setting as well as the knowledge, stance, and
status of those in their midst (14, 148). Zuni storytellers, for example, code-
switch from Zuni to English to mark a story's transition from past to present
relevance (229). Peruvian Quechua storytellers personalize mythic tales by
situating them in local places, thereby linking those present to a moral past
(148). Moreover, the most fundamental linguistic marking of the past, namely
the past tense, implies a time closer to the present (19). It is also common for
narrators in many speech communities to shift into present tense, called the
historical present, in referring to past events. In these cases, narrators move the
deictic locus of a story from there and then to here and now, a process Karl
Buhler calls "transposition" (37). This rhetorical strategy renders narrated
events vivid and captivating. The use of the present tense to relate past events
may indicate a continuing preoccupation; the events are not contained in the
past but rather continue to invade a narrator's current consciousness. This is
the case in an agoraphobic woman's narrative about an anxiety-provoking
experience (42:420):

> Meg: I felt real *help*less. I thought here I *a::m.* (.2) I'm so *damn mad* I could
> just storm outa here in the car but? (.2) (.hhh) I can't *le:ave*

In this passage the narrator casts temporally and spatially remote events and
emotions as present time phenomena. The narrated experience is upsetting
now, as it was then.

In this manner, the telling of past events is intricately linked to tellers' and
listeners' concerns about their present and their future lives (91, 106, 167).
Even a toddler lying in her crib uses narrative to forge understandings of
unsettling events that remain puzzling (66). The narrated past matters because
of its relation to the present and the future. Interlocutors tell personal narratives about the past primarily to understand and cope with their current concerns. Thus, narratives are often launched in response to current worries,
complaints, and conflicts (91, 167). In a reciprocal way, in the course of their
telling, portions of narratives may provoke interlocutors' concerns about the
present and future. For example, among the Weweya of Indonesia, clients'
present concerns about a past misfortune lead them to diviners, who exhort
spirits to tell the tale of misfortune, delineating who is to blame, how to atone,
and who should do so (129).

Point of View

A narrative of personal experience is far more than a chronological sequence of events. In his *Poetics,* Aristotle discerned that narratives have a thematically coherent beginning, middle, and end (5). As Goffman noted, every tale is told from a particular vantage point (82). Ricoeur referred to the configurational dimension of narrative, which "construes significant wholes out of scattered events" (187:174), and Labov (133) stressed that narratives of personal experience have a point to make, which is linguistically realized through phonological, lexical, morpho-syntactic, and discursive evaluative devices.

While point of view may be explicitly conveyed through soliloquies, asides, idioms, and other predications (82, 157), it is implicitly realized through the structuring of narrative plots. Aristotle used the term *mythos* to characterize how events and emotions form a coherent narrative (5). Interweaving human conditions, conduct, beliefs, intentions, and emotions, it is the plot that turns a sequence of events into a story or a history (71, 184, 188, 232).

The proclivity to organize experience in terms of plots is characteristically human, a point that has recently garnered the attention of cognitive psychologists (9, 19, 34–36). Jerome Bruner has propelled this orientation by hypothesizing that narrative is one of two fundamental modes of cognitive functioning. In contrast with paradigmatic thinking, which emphasizes formal categorization, narrative thinking emphasizes the structuring of events in terms of a human calculus of actions, thoughts, and feelings. In recounting their tales, narrators construct a dual landscape, one of action and one of consciousness (34). The landscape of action focuses on what a protagonist does in a given circumstance; the landscape of consciousness focuses on what protagonist and narrator believe and feel. William Hanks (97:324) illuminated how a Mayan shaman, for example, recounted the experience that instilled his shamanic powers in terms of actions ("I entered the woods...I disappeared from among the people, from my family") and interior changes that altered his consciousness ("My *nà'at* 'understanding' was lost, taken away. I didn't know anything at that time, because everything was lost, everything was forgotten to me"). The landscape of consciousness categorizes and rationalizes protagonists' actions, beliefs, and emotions in relation to norms. It is the landscape of consciousness that socializes narrators and audiences into local understandings of events (34, 35, 97, 157, 168, 202, 204). Singly, each plot attempts to illuminate an experience. Pieced together over time, narrative plots attempt to illuminate a life.

Narratives of personal experience display a discursive syntax or story grammar that binds narrative (146, 220). While linguistic, psychological, and literary treatments of narrative identify somewhat different narrative elements, they all stress that narratives of personal experience characteristically revolve around an unexpected or troubling turn of events. In "The Boy Who Became a Muni Bird," the narrative initially centers around the troubling predicament of the younger brother who catches no crayfish to eat. Similarly, in the narrative about Beth and Edith, Beth's mother recounts a probable trouble source for Beth, namely that "Edith must've hurt her on her hair or something." For the Mayan shaman, the narrative trouble hinges on the meaning of being lost.

Narrative activity attempts to resolve the discrepancy between what is expected and what has transpired (38). In the Muni bird myth, the discrepancy is between the Kaluli expectation that an older sister be generous toward her younger brother and the sister's withholding of food that transpires later as the myth unfolds. In the Beth and Edith story, Beth's mother tries to reconcile how she hopes her daughter will behave with how her daughter acted. The Mayan shaman uses narrative to explain the unexpected disappearance of body and consciousness during a routine walk in the woods.

Referred to as the complication (5), complicating action (133), trouble (38), the inciting event (212), the initiating event (220, 221), or the problematic event (34, 42), the discrepant event is contextualized and partly defined by story *settings*. Such settings include not only time and place but also psychological dispositions, historical precedent, and other domains of background knowledge. A narrator may thus frame an event as problematic by drawing upon listeners' commonsense knowledge of what is expected in particular circumstances (73, 76). Or a narrator may render the event problematic in light of a protagonist's emotional predisposition, as in the following (43:88):

> Meg: And I *remember* (.6) not really *wanting* to go (.3) that morning, feeling
> some *foreboding,* some feeling that um (.4). For one thing I had a lot on
> my *mind.*

Alternatively, a narrator may frame an event as problematic through detailing one or more distressing *responses* to that event (43). Thus, when the narrator reveals the whining response of the boy who became a Muni bird, we learn that not catching a crayfish is distressing to him. Similarly Beth's mother casts Edith's conduct as distressing in part by recounting Beth's angry response: Beth hit and bit Edith.

In forging story elements into a plot, narrators build a theory of events (15, 66, 175, 240). Narrators attempt to identify life problems, how and why they emerge, and their impact on the future. As such, narrative allows narrators to work through deviations from the expected within a conventional structure. As mentioned, the conventionality of narrative structure itself normalizes life's unsettling events.

In addition to the discursive structuring of the plot, narrative point of view is realized through a community's linguistic repertoire, including its set of languages, dialects, and registers (103, 153, 160). Guugu Yimidhirr co-narrators, for example, piece together shards of experience through a mosaic of codes (103). The juxtaposition of English, mission language, and a six-year-old's version of Guugu Yimidhirr captures the "confusion of tongues and selves in modern Hopevale" (103:345). As narrators shift between codes they iconically represent the radical displacements that define their life history.

Within each code, point of view is further realized through lexical, morpho-syntactic, and phonological forms (42, 43, 134, 171). Invoking the linguistic relativity hypothesis, psycholinguists in recent studies point out how languages offer narrators different resources for parsing and constructing experience (19, 47). In their introduction to a cross-linguistic, developmental study of narrative, Ruth Berman and Dan Slobin articulated a Filtering Principle: "The world does not present 'events' to be encoded in language. Rather, experiences are filtered—(a) through choice of perspective and (b) through the set of options provided by a particular language—into verbalized events" (19:9).

While the grammatical repertoires of languages vary, the following morpho-syntactic forms are widely used in shaping point of view: word order (19, 202), tense-aspect marking (3, 13, 18, 202, 210), case marking (2, 34, 35, 42, 43, 58, 228), verb voice (134, 171), evidentials (12, 21, 23, 48, 89, 102, 108, 127, 148, 203), deictic adverbs (42, 43, 96), and pronouns (2, 31, 50, 56, 122, 202, 217). Phonological resources for conveying point of view include primarily suprasegmental features such as loudness, pitch height, stress, sound stretches, pacing, and voice quality (21, 27, 42, 55, 74, 93, 102, 114, 138, 156, 160, 199, 200, 229). These linguistic forms depict actions and stances and in so doing cast protagonists, narrators, and listeners in a certain light (54, 166, 189).

Penetrating the use of discursive and grammatical forms illuminates *how* narrative creates us at the moment it is being created. While difficult to apprehend, narrativization of the self is not entirely mystical. Rather, the process can be understood in part in terms of linguistic tools and resources for painting selves in the world. Each person draws from community repertoires of codes, genres, lexicons, and grammars in a more or less different way to render self and other in a particular evaluative hue.

BOUNDARIES OF THE SELF

The notion of a narrative of personal experience implies that a person has his or her own experiences, that selves are ultimately discrete entities. At the same time, the unfolding narrative defines selves in terms of others in present, past, and imagined universes.

Developing a sense of one's self as separate from others is considered a cornerstone of human cognition and well-being (143, 159, 176, 222). The inability to differentiate objects in the world marks an infantile state of being, which gives way to the recognition that people and things exist as discrete entities (object permanence). This intelligence hinges on the development of memory, i.e. apprehending the continuity between past and present experience. From 8 to 18 months, the normally developing child gains a sense of "me" as a coherent, continuous, and discrete being over time.

This view of human development and the invention of referential forms such as personal names and pronouns imply a unified self. In its simplest form, this perspective contrasts with the view that the self comprises multiple, partial selves in flux. A protean world view of person has been linked to small-scale, non-European societies (57, 109, 123, 189, 195, 213), as in Michele Rosaldo's account of the Ilongot (189:146): "Ilongot hearts are not fixed entities....Personal names may change when one contracts disease, moves to a new locale, makes friends, or marries." Yet notions and realizations of self as fragmented and fluid are much at home in the postmodern Western world (54, 82, 100, 106, 132, 139, 190, 241). Scholars and artists emphasize that selves are not necessarily the same across time and place nor do they necessarily cohere. As Havel (100:155) commented, "I exist...as the tension between all my 'versions,' for that tension, too (and perhaps that above all), is me." Narrative is born out of such tension in that narrative activity seeks to bridge a self that felt and acted in the past, a self that feels and acts in the present, and an anticipated or hypothetical self that is projected to feel and act in some as yet unrealized moment—any one of which may be alienated from the other (42, 43, 94, 132). It is in this sense that we actualize our selves through the activity of narrating. We use narrative as a tool for probing and forging connections between our unstable, situated selves. Narrative activity places narrators and listener/readers in the paradoxical position of creating coherence out of lived experience while at the same time reckoning with its impossibility. The struggle to reconcile expectation with experience is particularly salient in the narratives of sufferers of mental and physical illness (6, 42, 43, 46, 77, 111, 112, 158) and political repression (51, 67–69, 94, 98, 100, 132, 161).

Whether or not a narrative offers a resolution for a particular predicament, all narratives, through dialogue, action, and reflection, expose narrators and listener/readers to life's potentialities for unanticipated pain and joy. Herein lies the spiritual and therapeutic function of narrative activity. Artists and healers alike use narrative to confront audiences with unanticipated potentialities, by either (a) laying bare the incommensurabilities of a particular lived situation, (b) luring the audience into an imaginary, even shocking, realm where prevailing moral sentiments do not apply, or (c) improvising a form of narrative expression that unsettles status quo principles of a genre. Kundera articulated how the modern novel in particular carries out this mission: "A novel's value is in the revelation of previously unseen possibilities of existence as such: in other words, the novel uncovers what is hidden in each of us" (132:264).

Narrative activity is crucial to recognizing and integrating repressed and alienated selves. Posttraumatic stress disorder, for example, arises when an experience is too devastating to incorporate into one's life story. Such experiences invade present lives in the form of somatic sensations or fragmented memories, i.e. flashbacks, but are not narrativized into a coherent sequence of events and reactions associated with a past self (216, 230). In the most extreme form, a traumatic event too threatening to make explicit through narrative may lead to dissociated selves, as in multiple personality disorder (186, 218, 236). In these cases, individual personalities have different names and may not even know of one another. One personality may begin a narrative from a particular perspective only to have this narrative abruptly circumvented by the intrusion of another personality, who has another narrative to relate, and so on and so on. Many therapeutic interventions strive to develop a narrative that articulates the dissociated events and reconciles them with subsequent past, present, and future selves. Clinical cases help to illuminate dynamics characteristic of all human beings. While people do not usually abandon and start new narratives in midstream, they do display multiple selves as a narrative unfolds and use narrative as a forum for dialogue among them. The struggle for everyone is to cultivate both diversity and coherence among potential and actual selves.

Although many societies celebrate the notion of an individual thinking ego, the development of self-awareness in all human beings is inextricably tied to an awareness of other people and things (100, 106, 154, 176, 222, 237). From this perspective, we define our selves through our past, present, future, and imagined involvements with people and things; our selves extend into these worlds, and they into us. One of the most important functions of narrative is to situate particular events against a larger horizon of what we consider to be human passions, virtues, philosophies, actions, and relationships. As the late poet James Merrill commented in an interview, "Don't you think there comes a time when everyone, not just a poet, wants to get beyond the self" (153:59). As narrators, we evaluate specific events in terms of communal norms, expectations, and potentialities; communal ideas of what is rational and moral; communal senses of the appropriate and the esthetic. In this way, we affiliate with other members of society both living and dead. We come to understand, reaffirm, and revise a philosophy of life. Merrill once responded to a protégé's account of his troubled love affair (153:60):

I read your last letter…with pangs of recognition….You won't be ready yet to *like* the fact of belonging to a very large group who've all had—allowing for particular differences—the same general experience. Later on, when your sense of humor and proportion returns, that fact ought rather to please you: to have so shared in the—or at least *a*—human condition.

The power to interface self and society renders narrative a medium of socialization par excellence. Through narrative we come to know what it means to be a human being.

Not only narrative content but also words, grammar, reported speech, and conventions of narrative genre join narrators and listener/readers with historical communities (11, 132, 142). Bahktin (11:283) explained that "Prior to the moment of appropriation, words do not exist in a neutral and impersonal language, but in other people's mouths, in other people's contexts." When we use linguistic forms, we materialize and blend others' voices with our own.

The boundaries between selves and other entities are porous. In their problem-solving narratives, physicists, for example, produce utterances like "When I come down, I'm in a domain state" as they gesture a path through a graphic representation. In so doing, these problem-solvers forge a hybrid identity that fuses scientific investigators and the entities they are trying to understand (169, 170). That is, the physicists take an imaginative, liminal journey with the objects of their inquiry. These narrative journeys are prosaic complements to artistic and mystical fusions of self and the world. Theater, for example, provides a lush context for merging selves into communities (100:255):

> In the theater, the work we are watching is not finished, but instead is being born before our eyes, with our help, so that we are both witnesses to its birth and, in a small sense, its cocreators as well….An immediate existential bond is created between the work and we who perceive it….Seeing it is more than just an act of perception, it is a form of human relationship.

A similar point has been made for rites of passage and other rituals wherein participants forge a collective identity (30, 93, 99, 224). Communion with others, elusive and fleeting though it may be, constitutes the greatest potentiality of narrative.

Self-world fusions fall along a continuum of perceived completeness. Past and present company can play a significant role in authoring a person's self-identity. As noted, voices of the past enter into narrated experience in the form of reported speech, words, idioms, and narrative style. Young children as well as adults may also incorporate stories they have heard into a present telling (157, 167, 172, 182, 201). Further, those present contribute to one's life history by co-telling the evolving story through verbal comments and questions, gestures, eye gaze, facial expression, and other modes of body comportment (15, 57, 60, 61, 84, 85, 86, 90, 103, 104, 116, 118, 125, 192, 198, 199,

229, 231). Co-telling can be elicited through a narrator's forgetfulness (20, 87), teasing (206), or blaming (91, 145), among other narrative provocations, and it can be as fine-grained as syllable by syllable (138, 199, 235). If we develop our selves through the stories we tell and if we tell them with others, then we are a complex, fluid matrix of coauthored selves.

Members of some social groups worry that sociability can define and override the needs and desires of a vulnerable "private" self (159). Indeed, such fear of fusion can lead to hatred of both those one perceives as radically different and those one perceives as almost the same (17). Ethnographic accounts suggest, however, that the concern for a unique, autonomous, private self is culture specific (213, 215). Further, phenomenologists and hermeneuticians consider the fusing of self and other an impossibility, given that one person cannot completely enter into the experience of another person (72, 208). Co-narrators may *attempt* to establish intersubjectivity or empathy with one another or with protagonists in their tales but can only partially achieve this goal. This accounts for the multiplicity of narratives that are mapped onto a single telling and for the isolation that persons may suffer upon realizing that their narrative has not been heard.

NARRATIVE ASYMMETRIES

Whether in the courtroom, workplace, scientific laboratory, classroom, athletic field, or simply in the course of conversing with family and friends, narrative activity challenges participants to make sense of enigmatic and frustrating situations. Faced with such a challenge, narrators alternate between two fundamental tendencies—either to cultivate a dialogue between diverse understandings or to lay down one coherent, correct solution to the problem. The first tendency is associated with relativistic and the second with fundamentalistic perspectives (44, 51, 75, 98, 105, 151, 203). These two polarities are present (to varying extents) in all human beings as they struggle to narrate lives (43).

The relativistic tendency offers a potentially infinite range of interpretive frames for organizing experience and promotes alterity and relative openness to new ideas. However, it can also lead to a paralyzing sense of indeterminacy. The fundamentalistic tendency lends consistency to otherwise fragmented experiences and allows us to assess what is happening in an expedient manner. Adherence to a dominant narrative is also community-building in that it presumes that each member ascribes to a common story. Reliance solely on a dominant narrative, however, may lead to oversimplification, stasis, and irreconcilable discrepancies between the story one has inculcated and one's encounters in the world. As noted earlier, psychological disorders such as posttraumatic stress, depression, and anxiety involve silencing would-be narratives that deviate from the dominant story by which one lives (42, 43, 112, 115, 186, 215). Silencing is a product of internal and interactional forces in that a person may repress and suppress emotions and events, but these processes are linked to external circumstances, including others' expectations and evaluations. Silencing takes many forms, most of which do not lead to severe psychopathology. Silencing is part of the fabric of culture in that it is critical to socializing prevailing ideologies. Assuming one's expected place in society entails conforming to and telling stories that reinforce social order.

To varying degrees, the silencing of alternative stories is a form of linguistic oppression. Dominating stories that preserve the status quo can estrange and muffle alternative perspectives. In Morrison's words, such stories can "sanction ignorance and preserve privilege." She likened them to "a suit of armor, polished to shocking glitter, a husk from which the knight departed long ago...exciting reverence in schoolchildren, providing shelter for despots, summoning false memories of stability, harmony among the public" (161:14). Morrison's point that dominant stories yield a false stability in communities is analogous to the psychodynamics of posttraumatic stress, in which a false sense of psychological stability is attained by muffling inconsistencies. In both cases, the roar of countervalent stories is ever present, on the edge of recognition.

Institutionalized master storylines prevail in educational, military, religious, legal, and medical settings (7, 49, 51, 63, 67, 68, 69, 88, 98, 136, 140, 149, 203, 225, 227). Foucault, for example, has detailed how legal and religious institutions organize moralizing narratives that define world views of criminality, sanity, and sexuality (67–69). Religious narratives have been institutionalized and missionized for centuries, reconfiguring communities worldwide. Missionized, legitimized storylines can extend beyond matters of the spirit to matters of health and the body. Bambi Schieffelin's analysis of missionization in Papua New Guinea indicates how pictures and factualizing grammatical forms can imbue a narrative text with authority. These rhetorical strategies are also used by scientists to render scientific narratives accurate and factual (98, 136, 141). Similarly, storylines promulgated by defense intellectuals use statistics, technical terms, and impersonalization to authorize and sanitize the stockpiling and testing of nuclear weapons (51). These narratives become all the more powerful when domestic metaphors are used to depict deadly weapons. On a seemingly more benign but nonetheless consequential level, parental accounts of family incidents often carry more legitimacy than those told by children (6, 227). Family therapy involves bringing children's versions to the fore as viable counterpoints to adult renderings of reality (6).

Narrative asymmetries lie in the values assigned not only to different versions of experience but also to different ways of recounting experience. Universally, families and schools socialize novices into prevailing conventions for narrating events (26, 45, 105, 156, 157, 175, 226, 227). While family norms organize personal narration in the early period of life, schools may disfavor family-preferred narrative styles and resocialize children into teacher-preferred ways of narrating. The personal storytelling style of African American children, for example, during so-called sharing time periods at school, are often radically reconfigured in terms of the genre conventions favored by the teacher (74, 156).

Yet another manifestation of narrative asymmetry involves entitlement to narrate. Who can tell a story? What role can one play in the course of a storytelling interaction? In many communities, those who have participated or otherwise witnessed an event have priority to tell the story of what happened (145, 192). However, there are circumstances that disqualify central participants as storytellers. Among the Australian Aborigines of Darwin fringe camps, for example, those who have suffered illness or accident do not have rights to narrate the tale of that experience (194). Rather, such rights are allocated to those who nursed the sick back to health. In these communities, when one is sick, one is not oneself and therefore not able to access what happened.

But curtailing narrative rights of parties central to an event is more pervasive than may seem to be the case. In many societies, children are deemed less than competent tellers of their experiences. The right to tell can be contingent upon a formal rite of passage into adolescence, as in the Xavante mandate that adolescent males be ceremonially initiated to recount dream narratives (93). In other cases, adults may preempt children's tellings of their experiences (8, 25, 157, 173, 174, 214, 226, 227). During visits to pediatricians in Sweden, for example, children are rarely asked to describe their own conditions; more often doctor and parent co-narrate a child's situation (8). Similarly, at the dinner tables of many mainstream American families, children rarely initiate stories about themselves; rather, such stories tend to be introduced by mothers (e.g. "Chuck went to gymnastics today? 'n he *swam* a lot?"), which renders children overhearers of their own experiences (173, 174, 227). Criminal suspects also have diminished rights to recount their version of what happened. In Western Samoa, suspects' accounts are recouched by orators as they announce the topic of the day at juridical decision-making assemblies (58, 59). In Sweden and in other countries, suspects' stories are told to police, who transform them into official, much modified written reports (140).

Narrative asymmetry also involves curtailment of the rights to decide when to narrate. When parents elicit a narrative from their child (e.g. "Tell Dad what you thought about gymnastics and what you did"), they attempt to determine the timing, content, and teller of narrative topics. The child, however, may not want to tell that narrative at that time or to have it told at all. Forced confessions represent a more extreme form of curtailment of such narrative rights. Confession is predicated on the principle that human beings must divulge their sinful acts and thoughts to avoid damnation (69:79).

In addition to entitlements to determine the content, shape, and timing of a story, there is the entitlement to hear a story. Within this entitlement, there is a further privileging of primary recipiency of a telling. A primary recipient is the party to whom talk is principally addressed (86, 144). Thus while a story may be overheard by some persons, it is directed to particular recipients. Institutional settings such as courtrooms closely regulate and linguistically mark who is the authorized primary recipient and who are authorized overhearers of narratives (10, 82).

Given that narrative mediates self-understanding and that narratives are interactional achievements, the role of primary recipient can be highly consequential (60). The primary recipient is positioned to provide feedback on a narrative contribution, for example, to align and embellish; to question, tease, and refute; or to ignore. Ignoring can lead the narrator to revise the story content to secure acknowledgment if not support from the intended recipient or search for another, more responsive primary recipient (84–86, 104, 179, 180, 193). Insufficient feedback from a designated recipient can lead a narrator to amplify volume, pitch range, and/or the scope of a claim. If even this fails to secure feedback, the narrator may suffer loss of validation as narrator and protagonist. This dynamic characterizes the narrative interactions between some sufferers of mental disorders and those around them when they relate upsetting experiences. Sufferers can become ensnared in a catch-22 situation when interlocutors withhold feedback, perhaps to contain intense emotions; but, paradoxically, such withholding often leads to escalation of displayed distress (42, 43, 80).

At American family dinner tables, narratives tend to be told by mothers and children and directed primarily to fathers. Fathers, in turn, may exploit this position to pass judgment on mothers and children as protagonists and narrators (173, 174). Children in these families, however, are rarely selected as primary recipients of narratives about parents. In contrast, in Japanese families mothers and children tend to select each other as primary recipients, while fathers are much less involved in family narrative interactions (223).

Differential control over narrative content, genre, timing, and recipiency is central to the constitution of social hierarchies. Narrative practices reflect and establish power relations in a wide range of domestic and community institutions. Differential control over content, genre, timing, and recipiency is also critical to the selves that come to life through narrative.

NARRATIVE RESISTANCE

Narrative asymmetries do not preclude narrative acts of resistance. Narratives are coauthored and as such allow for the possibility that particular contributions will be challenged. Such challenges require positive uptake to successfully neutralize the status quo. Reestablishing asymmetries in the face of narrative challenges demands effectively issuing a counterchallenge or otherwise managing dissent through minimization or suppression.

Resistance to dominant narratives is salient among academics, politicians, and artists. Challenge is central, for example, to the evolution of scientific paradigms in Western societies, especially to the social perception of an idea as distinct and novel (128). It is a routine and expected practice when scientists deliberate the meaning and reliability of scientific accounts of events (136, 141). The to-and-fro of challenges and counterchallenges also characterizes narrative-laden political discourse; for example, that between American pro-choice and prolife supporters (78) or between Ecuadorian advocates of and objectors to commodification of peasant labor (53). The emergence of new genres within artistic communities can be understood in terms of dialogic resistance to the status quo. Indeed, refusals, contradictions, and rejections are among the earliest speech acts to develop, and across many communities and languages the expression of negation is a hallmark of social growth (24, 32, 52, 202). Negation marks children's increasing autonomy and awareness of self and other. Although children are not universally entitled to protest narrative renderings of experience (92, 105), developmental studies indicate that they are capable of doing so.

Resistance to narratives of experience assumes many forms, including minimal feedback, ridicule, denial, and counterversion. We illustrated how a husband's minimal feedback to his anxious wife's tales of panic implicitly undermines her point of view. Minimal feedback also characterizes many white middle-class American children's responses to parental castings of experience; these children often provide only one-word responses or ignore altogether their parents' persistent attempts to elicit narratives (173, 227). Ridicule in the form of teasing, insult, and mockery is also woven into narrative interactions, as in the following exchange between a white middle-class American couple (175:53):

> Jon: ('f) Janie had come out and said to me—"Dad will you tell M:ommy
>   where the films- are from the pic?tures," I would have said "Yes? Janie"
> Marie: Well when she's about eight or nine I bet she'll be able to do that...
> Jon: YOU: are over eight or nine are you not?

A third form of resistance, denials (e.g. "NO I'M NOT!"), are usually coupled with counterversions, as in the elaborate challenges posed by African American children to "he-said-she-said" narratives about their wrong-doing (91:200):

> Barb: They say y'all say I wrote everything over there.
> Bea: UHUH. =THAT WAS VINCENT SAID.

Counterversions may arise in the immediate aftermath of a telling, as in the above excerpt. They may also emerge long into the future—even after generations of alignment or silence (64, 98, 124, 161). Further, counternarratives do not necessarily involve overt reference to a prevailing narrative world view. It is the voicing of a disjunctive reality itself that constitutes the counterpoint. Indeed, the posing of an alternative account may be more effective in dismantling the status quo perspective than overt critiques. In making reference to them, critiques perpetuate the salience of the dominant discourses they otherwise aim to uproot.

CONCLUSION

Through its various genres and modes; through discourse, grammar, lexicon, and prosody; and through the dynamics of collaborative authorship; narrative brings multiple, partial selves to life. Universally, tellers grapple with the inconsistencies between expectation and experience through narrative. Each narrative organizes a vector of experience along a temporal horizon that spans past, present, and possible realms. Each imbues the past with significance—both personal and collective—and, in so doing, constructs present and projected life worlds. Subject to challenge both from without (i.e. others) and from within (i.e. multiple, conflicting selves), these worlds are not fully coherent and are ever evolving. Whenever narrators launch a story, they open themselves to reconstrual. For better and for worse, everyday narrative practices confront interlocutors with unanticipated emotions and ideas and ultimately with unanticipated selves.

Literature Cited

1. Adorno T. 1984. *Aesthetic Theory*. London: Routledge & Paul
2. Agha A. 1993. Grammatical and indexical convention in honorific discourse. *J. Linguist. Anthropol.* 3:131–63
3. Aksu-Koç A. 1994. See Ref. 19, pp. 329–88
4. Applebee AN. 1978. *The Child's Concept of a Story: Ages Two to Seventeen*. Chicago: Univ. Chicago Press
5. Aristotle. 1962. *Poetics*. New York: Norton
6. Aronsson K, Cederborg A-C. 1994. Co-narration and voice in family therapy: voicing, devoicing, and orchestration. In *Family Therapy as Collaborative Work*, ed. AC Cederborg. Linköping: Linköping Univ. Stud. Arts Sci.
7. Aronsson K, Cederborg A-C. 1996. A love story retold: moral order and intergenera-

tional negotiations. In *Moral Dimensions in Dialogue*, ed. J Bergmann, P Linell. In press

8. Aronsson K, Rundstrom B. 1988. Child discourse and parental control in pediatric consultations. *Text* 8:159–89

9. Astington J. 1990. Narrative and the child's theory of mind. In *Narrative Thought and Narrative Language*, ed. BK Britton, AD Pellegrini, pp. 151–72. Hillsdale, NJ: Erlbaum

10. Atkinson JM, Drew P. 1979. *Order in Court: The Organization of Verbal Interaction in Judicial Settings*. London: Macmillan

10a. Atkinson M, Heritage J, eds. 1984. *Structures of Social Action*. Cambridge: Cambridge Univ. Press

11. Bakhtin MM. 1981. *The Dialogic Imagination: Four Essays*, ed. M Holquist. Transl. C Emerson, M Holquist. Austin: Univ. Tex. Press (From Russ.)

12. Bakhtin MM. 1986. *Speech Genres and Other Late Essays*. Transl. VW McGee. Austin: Univ. Tex. Press. (From Russ.)

13. Bamberg M. 1994. Development of linguistic forms: German. See Ref. 19, pp. 189–238

14. Bauman R. 1986. *Story, Performance, and Event: Contextual Studies of Oral Narrative*. Cambridge: Cambridge Univ. Press

15. Beals DE, Snow CE. 1994. "Thunder is when the angels are upstairs bowling": narratives and explanations at the dinner table. *J. Narrat. Life Hist.* 4:331–52

16. Berger J. 1972. *Ways of Seeing*. London: BBC/Penguin

17. Berman P. 1994. The other and the almost the same. *New Yorker Magazine*, Feb. 18, pp. 61–71

18. Berman RA, Neeman Y. 1994. Development of linguistic forms: Hebrew. See Ref. 19, pp. 285–28

19. Berman RA, Slobin DI, eds. *Relating Events in Narrative: A Crosslinguistic Developmental Study*. Hillsdale, NJ: Erlbaum

20. Besnier N. 1989. Information withholding as a manipulative and collusive strategy in Nukulaelae gossip. *Lang. Soc.* 18:315–41

21. Besnier N. 1995. *Literacy, Emotion, and Authority: Reading and Writing on a Polynesian Atoll*. Cambridge: Cambridge Univ. Press

22. Biagoli M. 1993. *Galilieo Courtier: The Practice of Science in the Culture of Absolutism*. Chicago: Univ. Chicago Press

23. Biber D, Finegan E. 1989. Styles of stance in English: lexical and grammatical marking of evidentiality and affect. *Text* 9: 93–124

24. Bloom LM. 1970. *Language Development: Form and Function in Emerging Grammars*. Cambridge: MIT Press

25. Blum-Kulka S. 1994. The dynamics of family dinner talk: cultural contexts for children's passages to adult discourse. *Res. Lang. Soc. Interact.* 27:1–50

26. Blum-Kulka S, Snow CE. 1992. Developing autonomy for tellers, tales, and telling in family narrative events. *J. Narrat. Life Hist.* 2:187–218

27. Bolinger D. 1972. *Intonation*. Baltimore: Penguin

28. Brenneis D. 1984. Grog and gossip in Bhatgaon: style and substance in Fiji Indian conversation. *Am. Ethnol.* 11:487–506

29. Briggs CL. 1992. "Since I am a Woman, I will Chastise my Relatives": gender, reported speech, and the (re)production of social relations in Warao ritual wailing. *Am. Ethnol.* 19:337–61

30. Briggs CL. 1993. Personal sentiments and polyphonic voices in Warao women's ritual wailing: music and poetics in a critical and collective discourse. *Am. Anthropol.* 95: 929–57

31. Brown P, Levinson SC. 1987. *Politeness: Some Universals in Language Usage*. Cambridge: Cambridge Univ. Press

32. Brown R. 1973. *A First Language: The Early Stages*. Cambridge: Harvard Univ. Press

33. Bruner J. 1983. *Child's Talk*. New York: Basic

34. Bruner J. 1986. *Actual Minds, Possible Worlds*. Cambridge: Harvard Univ. Press

35. Bruner J. 1990. *Acts of Meaning*. Cambridge: Harvard Univ. Press

36. Bruner J. 1991. The narrative construction of reality. *Crit. Inq.* 18:1–21

37. Buhler K. 1934. *Sprachtheorie: Die Darstellungsfunktion der Sprache*. Jena, Ger: Fischer

38. Burke K. 1962. *A Grammar of Motives and a Rhetoric of Motives*. Cleveland/New York: Meridian

39. Burke K. 1973. *The Philosophy of Literary Form*. Berkeley: Univ. Calif. Press

40. Calkowski M. 1991. A day at the Tibetan opera: actualized performance and spectacular discourse. *Am. Ethnol.* 18: 643–57

41. Capps L, Bjork R, Siegel D. 1993. The meaning of memories. *UCLA Mag.* 4(4): 8–10

42. Capps L, Ochs E. 1995. Out of place: narrative insights into agoraphobia. *Discourse Process.* 19:407–40

43. Capps L, Ochs E. 1995. *Constructing Panic: The Discourse of Agoraphobia*. Cambridge: Cambridge Univ. Press

44. Capps WH. 1990. *The New Religious Right: Piety, Patriotism, and Politics*. Columbia: Univ. South Carol. Press

45. Cazden C, Hymes D. 1978. Narrative thinking and storytelling rights: a folklor-

ist's clue to a critique of education. *Keyst. Folk.* 22(1–2):21–35
46. Cederborg AC. 1994. *Family therapy as collaborative work*. PhD thesis. Linköping Univ., Swed.
47. Chafe W, ed. 1980. *The Pear Stories: Cognitive, Cultural, and Linguistic Aspects of Narrative Production*. Norwood, NJ: Ablex
48. Chafe W, Nichols J. 1986. *Evidentiality: The Linguistic Coding of Epistemology*. Norwood, NJ: Ablex
49. Cicourel AV. 1992. The interpenetration of communicative contexts: examples from medical encounters. See Ref. 61, pp. 291–310
50. Clancy P. 1980. Referential choice in English and Japanese narrative discourse. See Ref. 47, pp. 127–202
51. Cohn C. 1987. Sex and death in the rational world of defense intellectuals. *Signs* 12: 687–718
52. Cole M, Cole S. 1989. *The Development of Children*. New York: Sci. Am.
53. Crain MM. 1991. Poetics and politics in the Ecuadorian Andes: women's narratives of death and devil possession. *Am. Ethnol.* 18:67–89
54. Crapanzano V. 1992. *Hermes' Dilemma and Hamlet's Desire*. Cambridge: Harvard Univ. Press
55. Crystal D, Davy D. 1969. *Investigating English Style*. Bloomington: Indiana Univ. Press
56. Duranti A. 1984. The social meaning of subject pronouns in Italian conversation. *Text* 4:277–311
57. Duranti A. 1984. Intentions, self, and responsibility: an essay in Samoan ethnopragmatics. In *Responsibility and Evidence in Discourse*, ed. J Hill, J Irvine, pp. 24–47. Cambridge: Cambridge Univ. Press
58. Duranti A. 1990. Politics and grammar: agency in Samoan political discourse. *Am. Ethnol.* 17:646–66
59. Duranti A. 1994. *From Grammar to Politics: Linguistic Anthropology in a Western Samoan Village*. Berkeley/Los Angeles: Univ. Calif. Press
60. Duranti A, Brenneis D. 1986. The audience as co-author. *Text* 6(3):239–347
61. Duranti A, Goodwin C, eds. 1992. *Rethinking Context: Language as an Interactive Phenomenon*. Cambridge: Cambridge Univ. Press
62. Edelman G. 1989. *The Remembered Present: A Biological Theory of Consciousness*. New York: Basic
63. Ehrenhaus P. 1993. Cultural narratives and the therapeutic motif: the political containment of Vietnam veterans. In *Narrative and Social Control: Critical Perspectives*, ed.

DK Mumby, pp. 77–98. Newbury Park, CA: Sage
64. Etter-Lewis G. 1991. Standing and speaking out: African American women's narrative legacy. *Discourse Soc.* 2:425–38
65. Feld S. 1982. *Sound and Sentiment: Birds, Weeping, Poetics, and Song in Kaluli Expression*. Philadelphia: Univ. Pa. Press
66. Feldman C. 1989. Monologue as problem-solving narrative. See Ref. 164, pp. 98–119
67. Foucault M. 1965. *Madness and Civilization: A History of Insanity in the Age of Reason*. New York: Pantheon
68. Foucault M. 1979. *Discipline and Punish: The Birth of the Prison*. New York: Random House
69. Foucault M. 1990. *The History of Sexuality: An Introduction*. New York: Random House
70. Freud S. 1933/1965. *New Introductory Lectures on Psychoanalysis*. New York: Norton
71. Frye N. 1957. *The Anatomy of Criticism*. Princeton: Princeton Univ. Press
72. Gadamer H-G. 1976. *Philosophical Hermeneutics*. Berkeley: Univ. Calif. Press
73. Garfinkel H. 1967. *Studies in Ethnomethodology*. Englewood Cliffs, NJ: Prentice-Hall
74. Gee JP. 1986. Units in the production of narrative discourse. *Discourse Process.* 9: 391–422
75. Geertz C. 1973. *The Interpretation of Cultures*. New York: Basic
76. Geertz C. 1983. *Local Knowledge: Further Essays in Interpretive Anthropology*. New York: Basic Books
77. Gerhardt J, Stinson C. 1994. The nature of therapeutic discourse: accounts of the self. *J. Narrat. Life Hist.* 4:151–92
78. Ginsberg F. 1987. Procreation stories: reproduction, nurturance, and procreating in life narratives of abortion activists. *Am. Ethnol.* 14:623–36
79. Goffman E. 1959. *The Presentation of Self in Everyday Life*. Garden City, NY: Doubleday
80. Goffman E. 1961. *Asylums: Essays on the Social Situation of Mental Patients and Other Inmates*. Garden City, NY: Anchor/Doubleday
81. Goffman E. 1963. *Behavior in Public Places: Notes on the Social Organization of Gathering*. New York: Free Press
82. Goffman E. 1974. *Frame Analysis: An Essay on the Organization of Experience*. New York: Harper & Row
83. Goodman N. 1978. *Ways of Worldmaking*. Indianapolis, IN: Hackett
84. Goodwin C. 1981. *Conversational Organization: Interaction Between Speakers and Hearers*. New York: Academic

85. Goodwin C. 1984. Notes on story structure and the organization of participation. See Ref. 10a, pp. 225–46
86. Goodwin C. 1986. Audience diversity, participation and interpretation. *Text* 6(3): 283–316
87. Goodwin C. 1987. Forgetfulness as an interactive resource. *Soc. Psychol. Q.* 50: 115–30
88. Goodwin C. 1994. Professional vision. *Am. Anthropol.* 96(3):606–33
89. Goodwin C. 1996. Transparent vision. See Ref. 170a, In press
90. Goodwin C, Duranti A. 1992. Rethinking context: an introduction. See Ref. 61, pp. 1–42
91. Goodwin MH. 1990. *He-Said-She-Said: Talk as Social Organization among Black Children.* Bloomington: Indiana Univ. Press
92. Goody E. 1978. *Questions and Politeness: Strategies in Social Interaction.* Cambridge: Cambridge Univ. Press
93. Graham LR. 1994. Dialogic dreams: creative selves coming into life in the flow of time. *Am. Ethnol.* 21:723–45
94. Gramsci A. 1971. *Selections from the Prison Notebooks.* New York: Internal
95. Guignon C. 1993. *The Cambridge Companion to Heidegger.* Cambridge: Cambridge Univ. Press
96. Hanks WF. 1990. *Referential Practice: Language and Lived Space Among the Maya.* Chicago: Univ. Chicago Press
97. Hanks WF. 1993. The five gourds of memory. In *Mémoires de la Tradition,* ed. AB Monod, AM Fioravanti, pp. 319–45. Nanterres, Fr: Soc. Ethnol.
98. Haraway DJ. 1991. *Simians, Cyborgs, and Women: The Reinvention of Nature.* New York: Routledge
99. Harris GG. 1989. Concepts of individual, self, and person in description and analysis. *Am. Anthropol.* 91:599–612
100. Havel V. 1983. *Letters to Olga.* New York: Holt
101. Haviland JB. 1977. *Gossip, Reputation, and Knowledge in Zinacantan.* Chicago: Univ. Chicago Press
102. Haviland JB. 1989. "Sure, Sure": Evidence and affect. *Text* 9:27–68
103. Haviland JB. 1991. "That Was the Last Time I Seen Them, and No More": Voices Through Time in Australian Aboriginal Autobiography. *Am. Ethnol.* 18:331–61
104. Heath C. 1984. Talk and recipiency: sequential organization in speech and body movement. See Ref. 10a, pp. 247–66
105. Heath SB. 1983. *Ways with Words: Language, Life and Work in Communities and Classrooms.* Cambridge: Cambridge Univ. Press
106. Heidegger M. 1962. *Being and Time.* New York: Harper & Row
107. Herdt G, ed. 1994. *Third Sex, Third Gender: Beyond Sexual Dimorphism in Culture and History.* New York: Zone Books
108. Hill JH, Irvine JT, eds. 1992. *Responsibility and Evidence in Oral Discourse.* Cambridge: Cambridge Univ. Press
109. Holland D. 1992. Cross-cultural differences in the self. *J. Anthropol. Res.* 48(4): 283–300
110. Husserl E. 1913/1931. *Ideas: General Introduction to Pure Phenomenology.* New York: Collier
111. Hyden L-C. 1995. In search of an ending: narrative reconstruction as a moral quest. *J. Narrat. Life Hist.* 5:67–84
112. Hyden M, McCarthy IC. 1994. Woman battering and father-daughter incest disclosure: discourses of denial and acknowledgment. *Discourse Soc.* 5:543–65
113. Hymes D. 1971. The "wife" who "goes out" like a man: re-interpretations of a Clackamas Chinook myth. In *Structural Analyses of Oral Traditions,* ed. P Maranda, EK Maranda, pp. 173–99. Philadelphia: Univ. Pa. Press
114. Hymes D. 1981. *"In Vain I Tried to Tell You": Essays in Native American Ethnopoetics.* Philadelphia: Univ. Pa. Press
115. Jack DC. 1991. *Silencing the Self: Women and Depression.* Cambridge: Harvard Univ. Press
116. Jacoby S, Ochs E. 1995. Co-construction: an introduction. *Res. Lang. Soc. Interact.* 28(3): 171–84
117. James W. 1902/1958. *The Varieties of Religious Experience.* New York: Mentor
118. Jefferson G. 1978. Sequential aspects of storytelling in conversation. See Ref. 201a, pp. 219–48
119. Jefferson G. 1984. On the organization of laughter in talk about troubles. See Ref. 10a, pp. 346–69
120. Jonsson L, Linell P. 1991. Story generations: from dialogical interviews to written reports in police interrogations. *Text* 11: 419–40
121. Jung CG. 1973. *Four Archetypes.* Princeton: Bollingen
122. Karmiloff-Smith A. 1979. *A Functional Approach to Child Language.* Cambridge: Cambridge Univ. Press
123. Keenan EO. 1974. Conversational competence in children. *J. Child Lang.* 1:163–83
124. Keesing RM. 1985. Kwaio women speak: the micro-politics of autobiography in a Solomon Island society. *Am. Anthropol.* 87: 27–39
125. Kendon A. 1983. Gesture and speech: how they interact. In *Nonverbal Interaction, Sage Annual Reviews of Communication,*

ed. JM Wiemann, R Harrison, 11:13–46. Beverly Hills, CA: Sage

126. Kramer J. 1995. The politics of memory. *New Yorker,* Aug. 14, pp. 48–65

127. Kroskrity PV. 1993. *Language, History, and Identity: Ethnolinguistic Studies of the Arizona Tewa.* Tucson: Univ. Ariz. Press

128. Kuhn T. 1962. *The Structure of Scientific Revolutions.* Chicago: Univ. Chicago Press

129. Kuipers JC. 1986. Talking about troubles: gender differences in Weyewa speech use. *Am. Ethnol.* 13:448–62

130. Kundera M. 1981. *The Book of Laughter and Forgetting.* Harmondsworth, UK: Penguin

131. Kundera M. 1985. *The Unbearable Lightness of Being.* New York: Harper & Row

132. Kundera M. 1995. *Testaments Betrayed.* New York: Harper Collins

133. Labov W. 1972. *Language in the Inner City: Studies in the Black English Vernacular.* Philadelphia: Univ. Pa. Press

134. Labov W. 1984. Intensity. In *Meaning, Form, and Use in Context: Linguistic Applications, GURT '84,* ed. D Schiffrin, pp. 43–70. Washington, DC: Georgetown Univ. Press

135. Labov W, Waletzky J. 1968. Narrative analysis. In *A Study of the Non-Standard English of Negro and Puerto Rican Speakers in New York City,* ed. W Labov, pp. 286–338. New York: Columbia Univ.

136. Latour B. 1987. *Science in Action.* Cambridge: Harvard Univ. Press

137. Latour B, Woolgar S. 1979. *Laboratory Life: The Social Construction of Scientific Facts.* London: Sage

138. Lerner GH. 1991. On the syntax of sentences-in-progress. *Lang. Soc.* 20:441–58

139. Lifton RJ. 1993. *The Protean Self: Human Resilience in an Age of Fragmentation.* New York: Harper & Row

140. Linell P, Jonsson L. 1991. Suspect stories: on perspective-setting in an asymmetrical situation. In *Asymmetries in Dialogue,* ed. I Markova, K Foppa, pp. 75–100. Savage, Md: Barnes & Noble

141. Lynch M, Woolgar S. 1988. *Representation in Scientific Practice.* Cambridge: MIT Press

142. Macaulay R. 1987. Polyphonic monologues: quoted direct speech in oral narratives. *Pap. Pragmat.* 1(2):1–34

143. Mahler M, Pine F, Bergman A. 1975. *The Psychological Birth of the Human Infant.* New York: Basic Books

144. Mandelbaum J. 1987. *Recipient-driven storytelling in conversation.* PhD thesis. Univ. Tex., Austin

145. Mandelbaum J. 1993. Assigning responsibility in conversational storytelling: the in-

teractional construction of reality. *Text* 13: 247–66

146. Mandler JH, Johnson NS. 1977. Remembrance of things parsed: story structure and recall. *Cogn. Psychol.* 9:111–51

147. Mandler JH, Johnson NS. 1977. Remembrance of things parsed: story structure and recall. *Cogn. Psychol.* 9:111–51

148. Mannheim B. 1991. After dreaming: image and interpretation in southern Peruvian Quechua. *Etnofoor* 4:43–79

149. Marcus G. 1995. *Technoscientific Imaginaries: Conversations, Profiles, and Memoirs.* Chicago: Univ. Chicago Press

150. Marsack A. 1991. *The Roots of Civilization.* Mt. Kisco, NY: Moyer Bell

151. Marty M, Appleby S, eds. 1995. *Fundamentalism Comprehended.* Chicago: Univ. Chicago Press

152. McCabe A, Peterson C, eds. 1991. *Developing Narrative Structure.* Hillsdale, NJ: Erlbaum

153. McClatchy JD. 1995. James Merrill. *New Yorker,* March 27, pp. 49–61

154. Mead GH. 1934. *Mind, Self, and Society.* Chicago: Univ. Chicago Press

155. Merleau-Ponty M. 1945/1967. *Phenomenologie de la Perception.* Paris: Editions Gallimard

156. Michaels S. 1981. 'Sharing time': children's narrative styles and differential access to literacy. *Lang. Soc.* 10:423–42

157. Miller PJ, Potts R, Fung H, Hoogstra L, Mintz J. 1990. Narrative practices and the social construction of self in childhood. *Am. Ethnol.* 17:292–311

158. Mishler EG. 1995. Models of narrative analysis: a typology. *J. Narrat. Life Hist.* 5:87–124

158a. Mitchell WJT, ed. 1981. *On Narrative.* Chicago: Univ. Chicago Press

159. Modell A. 1993. *The Private Self.* Cambridge: Harvard Univ. Press

160. Morgan M. 1996. Conversational signifying: grammar and indirectness among African American women. See Ref. 170a, In press

161. Morrison T. 1994. *The Nobel Lecture in Literature, 1993.* New York: Knopf

162. Munn ND. 1992. The cultural anthropology of time: a critical essay. *Annu. Rev. Anthropol.* 21:93–123

163. Musil R. 1995. *The Man Without Qualities.* Transl. S. Wilkins. New York: Knopf (From Ger.)

164. Nelson K, ed. 1989. *Narratives from the Crib.* Cambridge: Harvard Univ. Press

165. O'Barr WM, Conley JM. 1985. Litigant satisfaction versus legal adequacy in small claims court narratives. *Law Soc. Rev.* 19(4):661–701

166. Ochs E. 1993. Constructing social identity:

a language socialization perspective. *Res. Lang. Soc. Interact.* 26:287–306

167. Ochs E. 1994. Stories that step into the future. In *Perspectives on Register: Situating Register Variation within Sociolinguistics,* ed. D Finegan, F Biber, pp. 106–35. Oxford: Oxford Univ. Press

168. Ochs E. Narrative. 1996. In *Discourse: A Multidisciplinary Introduction,* ed. T Van Dijk. London: Sage. In press

169. Ochs E, Gonzales P, Jacoby S. 1996. "When I come down, I'm in the domain state": talk, gesture, and graphic representation in the interpretive activity of physicists. See Ref. 170a, In press

170. Ochs E, Jacoby S, Gonzales P. 1994. Interpretive journeys: how physicists talk and travel through graphic space. *Configurations* 2:151–72

170a. Ochs E, Schegloff EA, Thompson SA, eds. 1996. *Interaction and Grammar.* Cambridge: Cambridge Univ. Press. In press

171. Ochs E, Schieffelin BB. 1989. Language has a heart. *Text* 9:7–25

172. Ochs E, Smith R, Taylor C. 1989. Dinner narratives as detective stories. *Cult. Dyn.* 2:238–57

173. Ochs E, Taylor C. 1992. Family narrative as political activity. *Discourse Soc.* 3: 301–40

174. Ochs E, Taylor C. 1994. Mothers' role in the everyday reconstruction of "Father Knows Best." In *Locating Power: Proc. 1992 Berkeley Women Lang. Conf.,* ed. K Hall, pp. 447–62. Berkeley: Univ. Calif. Press

175. Ochs E, Taylor C, Rudolph D, Smith R. 1992. Story-telling as a theory-building activity. *Discourse Process.* 15:37–72

176. Piaget J, Inhelder B. 1969. *The Psychology of the Child.* London: Routledge, Kegan & Paul

177. Polanyi L. 1989. *Telling the American Story: A Structural and Cultural Analysis of Conversational Storytelling.* Cambridge: MIT Press

178. Polkinghorne DE. 1988. *Narrative Knowing and the Human Sciences.* Albany: State Univ. NY

179. Pomerantz A. 1978. Compliment responses: notes on the co-operation of multiple constraints. See Ref. 201a, pp. 79–112

180. Pomerantz A. 1984. Agreeing and disagreeing with assessments: some features of preferred/dispreferred turn shapes. See Ref. 10a, pp. 57–101

181. Preece A. 1985. *The development of young children's productive narrative competence in conversational contexts: a longitudinal investigation.* PhD thesis. Univ. Victoria, Can.

182. Preece A. 1992. Collaborators and critics: the nature and effects of peer interaction on children's conversational narratives. *J. Narrat. Life Hist.* 2:277–92

183. Preziosi D. 1989. *Rethinking Art History: Meditations on a Coy Science.* New Haven: Yale Univ. Press

184. Propp V. 1968. *The Morphology of the Folktale.* Transl. T Scott. Austin: Univ. Tex. Press. (From Russ.) 2nd ed.

185. Proust M. 1989/1913. *Swann's Way.* New York: Random House

186. Putnam F. 1989. *Diagnosis and Treatment of Multiple Personality Disorder.* New York: Guilford

187. Ricoeur P. 1981. Narrative time. See Ref. 158a, pp. 165–86

188. Ricoeur P. 1988. *Time and Narrative.* Chicago: Univ. Chicago Press

189. Rosaldo M. 1984. Toward an anthropology of self and feeling. See Ref. 215a, pp. 137–57

190. Rymes B. 1996. Naming as social practice: the case of little creeper from Diamond Street. *Lang. Soc.* 25(2):In press

191. Sacks H. 1978. Some technical considerations of a dirty joke. See Ref. 201a, pp. 249–69

192. Sacks H. 1992. *Lectures on Conversation,* Vol. 2. Cambridge, MA: Blackwell

193. Sacks H, Schegloff EA, Jefferson G. 1974. A simplest systematics for the organization of turn-taking for conversation. *Language* 50:696–735

194. Sampson B. 1982. The sick who do not speak. In *Semantic Anthropology,* ed. D Parkin, pp. 183–95. New York: Academic

195. Sankoff G. 1980. *The Social Life of Language.* Philadelphia: Univ. Pa. Press

196. Sarbin T. 1995. A narrative approach to "repressed memories." *J. Narrat. Life Hist.* 5:51–66

197. Schafer R. 1992. *Retelling a Life.* New York: Basic Books

198. Schegloff EA. 1984. On some gestures' relation to talk. See Ref. 10a, pp. 266–96

199. Schegloff EA. 1996. Turn organization: one intersection of grammar and interaction. See Ref. 170a, In press

200. Schegloff EA, Ochs E, Thompson S. 1996. Introduction. See Ref. 170a, In press

201. Schenkein J. 1978. On the achievement of a series of stories. See Ref. 201a, pp. 113–32

201a. Schenkein J, ed. 1978. In *Studies in the Organization of Conversational Interaction.* New York: Academic

202. Schieffelin BB. 1990. *The Give and Take of Everyday Life: Language Socialization of Kaluli Children.* Cambridge: Cambridge Univ. Press

203. Schieffelin BB. 1996. Creating evidence: making sense of written words in Bosavi. See Ref. 170a, In press

204. Schieffelin BB, Ochs E. 1986. Language

socialization. *Annu. Rev. Anthropol.* 15: 163–91

205. Schieffelin EL. 1976. *The Sorrow of the Lonely and the Burning of the Dancers.* New York: St. Martin Press

206. Schieffelin EL. 1985. Performance and the cultural construction of reality. *Am. Ethnol.* 12:707–24

207. Schiffrin D. 1984. How a story says what it means and does. *Text* 4:313–46

208. Schutz A. 1967/1932. *The Phenomenology of the Social World.* Evanston, IL: Northwest. Univ. Press

209. Scollon R, Scollon SBK. 1981. *Narrative, Literacy, and Face in Interethnic Communication.* Norwood, NJ: Ablex

210. Sebastian E, Slobin DI. 1994. Development of linguistic forms: Spanish. See Ref. 19, pp. 239–84

211. Shapin S. 1994. *The Social History of Truth: Civility and Science in Seventeenth-Century England.* Chicago: Univ. Chicago

212. Sharff S. 1982. *The Elements of Cinema: Toward a Theory of Cinesthetic Impact.* New York: Columbia Univ. Press

213. Shore B. 1982. *Sala'ilua: a Samoan mystery.* New York: Columbia Univ. Press

214. Shuman A. 1986. *Storytelling Rights: The Uses of Oral and Written Texts by Urban Adolescents.* Cambridge: Cambridge Univ. Press

215. Shweder R, Bourne E. 1984. Does the concept of the person vary cross-culturally? See Ref. 215a, pp. 158–99

215a. Shweder R, LeVine R, eds. 1984. *Culture Theory: Essays on Mind, Self, and Emotion.* Cambridge: Cambridge Univ. Press

216. Siegel D. 1995. Memory, trauma, and psychotherapy. *J. Psychother. Pract. Res.* 4: 93–119

217. Silverstein M. 1976. Shifters, linguistic categories, and cultural description. In *Meaning in Anthropology,* ed. KH Basso, HA Selby, pp. 11–56. Albuquerque: Univ. N. M. Press

218. Spanos NP. 1994. Multiple identity enactments and multiple personality disorder: a socio-cognitive perspective. *Psychol. Bull.* 116:143–65

219. Spence DP. 1982. *Narrative Truth and Historical Truth.* New York: Norton

220. Stein N, Glenn CG. 1979. An analysis of story comprehension in elementary school children. In *New Directions in Discourse Processing,* ed. RO Freedle, pp. 53–120. Norwood, NJ: Ablex

221. Stein N, Policastro M. 1984. The concept of a story: a comparison between children's and teacher's viewpoints. In *Learning and Comprehension of Text,* ed. H Mandl, N Stein, T Trabasso, pp. 113–58. Hillsdale, NJ: Erlbaum

222. Stern D. 1977. *The First Relationship: In-*

fant and Mother. London: Fontana/Open Books

223. Steveron MT. 1995. *The mother's role in Japanese dinnertime narratives.* PhD thesis. Univ. Hawaii

224. Stromberg PG. 1990. Ideological language in the transformation of identity. *Am. Anthropol.* 92:42–56

225. Szasz T. 1974. *The Myth of Mental Illness.* New York: Harper & Row

226. Taylor CE. 1995. "You think it was a fight?" Co-constructing (the struggle for) meaning, face, and family in everyday narrative activity. *Res. Lang. Soc. Interact.* 28:283–317

227. Taylor CE. 1995. *Child as apprentice-narrator: socializing voice, face, identity, and self-esteem amid the narrative politics of family dinner.* PhD thesis. Univ. South. Calif.

228. Taylor C. 1989. *Sources of the Self.* Cambridge: Harvard Univ. Press

229. Tedlock D. 1983. *The Spoken Word and the Work of Interpretation.* Philadelphia: Univ. Pa. Press

230. Terr L. 1994. *Unchained Memories.* New York: Basic

231. Testa R. 1991. Negotiating stories: strategic repair in Italian multi-party talk. *Pragmatics* 1:345–70

232. Toolan MJ. 1988. *Narrative: A Critical Linguistic Introduction.* New York: Routledge

233. Turner V. 1981. Social dramas and stories about them. See Ref. 158a, pp. 137–64

234. Umiker-Sebeok DJ. 1979. Preschool children's intraconversational narratives. *J. Child Lang.* 6:91–109

235. Urban G. 1991. *A Discourse-Centered Approach to Culture: Native South American Myths and Rituals.* Austin: Univ. Tex. Press

236. Van der Kolk BA, Van der Hart O. 1989. The failure of adaptation to trauma. *Am. J. Psychiatr.* 146:1530–40

237. Vygotsky LS. 1978. *Mind in Society: The Development of Higher Psychological Processes.* Cambridge: Harvard Univ. Press

238. Watson-Gegeo K, White G, eds. 1990. *Disentangling: Conflict Discourse in Pacific Societies.* Stanford: Stanford Univ. Press

239. Weisner MJ. 1991. Mario M. Cuomo decides to run: the construction of a political self. *Discourse Soc.* 2:85–104

240. White H. 1981. The value of narrativity in the representation of reality. See Ref. 158a, pp. 1–24

241. Wittgenstein L. 1980. *Remarks on the Philosophy of Psychology,* Vol. 1. Chicago: Univ. Chicago Press

242. Young KG. 1987. *Taleworlds and Story realms: The Phenomenology of Narrative.* Dordrecht: Nijhoff

Annu. Rev. Anthropol. 1996. 25:45–61

ARCHAEOLOGICAL APPROACHES TO THE ORGANIZATION OF DOMESTIC LABOR: Household Practice and Domestic Relations

Julia A. Hendon

Department of Sociology and Anthropology, Gettysburg College, Gettysburg, Pennsylvania 17325

KEY WORDS: gender, specialization, microscale, Mesoamerica, Neolithic

ABSTRACT

The household has emerged as a focus of archaeological inquiry over the past decade. This review summarizes issues raised by economic and feminist anthropologists about the meaning of the terms *household* and *domestic* and then considers research on household archaeology, craft specialization, and gender relevant to the study of the organization of domestic labor. It is argued that the common functional definition of the household as an adaptive mechanism reacting to environmental and social conditions underconceptualizes the household and renders its study unlikely to contribute to our understanding of economic and social processes in past societies. Studies of craft specialization and women's economic production that emphasize what members of the domestic group do and how that action is valued are more successful in demonstrating the dynamic interaction between household and society.

INTRODUCTION

Archaeological interest in the household and domestic relations has evolved with attempts to develop cross-culturally valid approaches to these issues in cultural anthropology. Anthropological studies of modern and historic domestic groups emphasize the importance of activities and their culturally constructed meaning, rather than kinship norms or family composition, in defining the household. The activities considered to be the "culturally recognized tasks" (19:47) of the household vary cross-culturally. Thus, what households do becomes a matter to be investigated rather than assumed a priori. However, it is not enough to focus on activities alone. Of equal importance is the symbolic dimension, what we might call the "idea" of the household (see 102). It is the practice [in Bourdieu's (10) sense of the term] of the household—what people do as members of a domestic group and the meaning assigned to their actions—that is critical to an understanding of household dynamics (19, 83, 110, 114, 122).

What is the nature of the relations among household members? Feminist and economic anthropologists have questioned the household as an undifferentiated and homogenous social entity (46, 80, 111, 122). All households in a society may be charged with the same basic tasks and interact with the same physical and social environment. But they do not necessarily respond in the same way to external conditions nor organize themselves in the same way. Wilk (111:25), writing about the Kekchi Maya of Belize, noted that "[h]ouseholds that may look the same, with the same number of members and the same kinship structure, at the same stage of the developmental cycle, can have very different economic structures." Moreover, differences in class or wealth must be considered. Although the members of the domestic group are clearly interdependent, they are not a cooperative unit in which individual members automatically subordinate their wishes to the larger good of the group. Nor are decisions always made at the level of the household as a whole (with the implication that there is one member whose decisions carry the greatest weight). The domestic group consists of social actors differentiated by age, gender, role, and power whose agendas and interests do not always coincide.

Consideration of the internal differences in power and function has led to a recognition of the importance of gender as a culturally constructed ideology that structures women's and men's roles, relationships, access to resources, and opportunities for control both within the household and in society as a whole. Emphasis on the role of individuals, or of categories of people determined, for example, by gender and age, forces us "to engage directly with questions of ideology and the construction of meaning, and recognize how struggles over resources and labor are simultaneously struggles over meaning" (46:121). The household is, in effect, politicized in that its internal relations are inextricable from the larger economic and political structure of society (46, 80, 122).

The contested and dynamic nature of domestic relations requires a reevaluation of the folk concept domestic as linked exclusively to the home, women, and subsistence, and therefore not relevant to the production of surplus or wealth (6, 14, 78, 102, 104, 118, 122). Cross-cultural studies of gender have undermined the domestic/public opposition as universal or even particularly meaningful (19, 46, 75, 80, 94, 95, 114, 121). The household's role in social reproduction is as culturally constructed as its economic role (122), and the relationship between child rearing and women's economic activities is not everywhere the same (20, 78, 87). Domestic action and relations, defined as those that occur within the household, are of larger political and economic significance precisely because they are not separable from the relationships and processes that make up the "public domain." "[D]omestic relationships are often so inextricably intermeshed with relationships of political alliance that to separate the domestic aspects from the political aspects is to misconstrue these relationships" (122:191). Household relations and actions are not isolated from society as a whole nor do they merely react passively to changes imposed from outside.

In this review I consider recent archaeological research on the domestic group. I discuss the degree to which this research has dealt with household practice and the political nature of domestic relations as important to an understanding of social and economic processes in past societies. I pay particular attention to how relations among household members and the organization of domestic labor have been modeled by this research. I discuss briefly household archaeology to illustrate why little of this work has come to grips with these issues. I then turn to studies of craft specialization and the role of women that have been more successful.

Although the studies reviewed here use data from a range of time periods and geographic regions, a good many of them deal with pre-Columbian New World or Neolithic European societies. Research on pre-Columbian Latin American households has been informed by assumptions of long-term cultural continuity allowing the use of regional ethnohistorical and ethnographic data as sources for models (3, 5, 25, 36, 41, 54, 55, 61, 62, 100). Study of Neolithic Period European households is more recent and demonstrates how ideas about household organization and change are developed in the absence of such a rich culturally specific record (1, 2, 9, 102–108). In the review, I use *household* and *domestic group* interchangeably to refer to the task-oriented, coresident, and symbolically meaningful social group that forms "the next bigger thing on the social map after an individual" (45:40–41), a group that archaeologists have tried to study based on the remains of houses, or other sorts of living space, and the traces of activities associated with this space. Although ethnographic research shows that coresidence, domestic activities, and the household are not necessarily isomorphic (6), they often are. The assumption is a practical necessity for archaeology and is accepted here.

HOUSEHOLD ARCHAEOLOGY

Research identifying itself as "household archaeology" has increased greatly over the past fifteen years since Wilk & Rathje (114) first introduced the term in their 1982 publication (71, 72, 89, 92, 96, 113, 115). Wilk & Rathje noted that a definition of the household as a task-focused group that conducts many of its activities within a specific kind of physical setting—what they call a dwelling unit, or the indoor and outdoor space in which people live—renders the household susceptible to study using archaeological data (see also 5).

The household has been called the "level at which social groups articulate directly with economic and ecological processes" (114:618) and the "fundamental unit of organization" (56:21). Studies of the household that focus on identifying activities and their location within dwelling units have illuminated some of the culturally recognized tasks that domestic groups perform in particular societies (1, 2, 7, 30, 34, 36, 43, 44, 48–52, 61, 70, 73, 92, 93, 100, 106–108). By looking at the distribution, nature, scale, and technology of these activities within and between dwelling units, this research has the potential to reveal internal and external economic and social relations through the traces of people's actions. The participation of households, as both consumers and producers, in long-distance exchange networks has been demonstrated through the presence of imported materials and evidence for craft production. The occurrence of food preparation areas has been used to reconstruct social relations within the household. The use of material culture and the built environment to mark differences in wealth or status among households has been discussed. The ritual life of the household has also been considered.

Household archaeology's focus on the dwelling unit reveals much of what households did but has not contributed as much as it should to our understanding of who did what. When considering social relations, household archaeology too often elides the household with the family, taking the reconstruction of kinship organization as its goal, and assumes that domestic relations are uncontested and stable. This approach loses sight of the household as a symbolic construct defined and contested through practice. The variation in the actions and relations of people in domestic groups needs to be considered more fully (96, 102).

Defining the household as an adaptive mechanism renders it an irreducible entity whose structure and activities are the result of external environmental and social conditions (56, 92). Although all households may share a common goal of survival, in both a physical and social sense they do not all necessarily follow the same strategy or have the same degree of success. Even within the confines of a subsistence economy, room exists for different decisions on the allocation of time and labor and the use of resources (9, 111).

DOMESTIC ACTION AND SOCIAL RELATIONS WITHIN THE HOUSEHOLD

The most productive archaeological studies of the household have focused on gender as a symbolic system that structures social and economic relations within the household and the larger community. Among the challenges faced by this research is the need to disentangle conceptually gender from biological sex to deal with gender as a social construct. Another challenge is to consider how gender, like other social constructs such as rank or wealth, may be reflected in and constructed through material culture. Studies that have attempted to connect sets of activities carried out in dwelling units with different social actors have proved particularly productive in disaggregating the undifferentiated concept of the household and its domestic action (13, 20, 22, 29, 37, 38, 40, 41, 47, 59, 62, 63, 81, 102–105). Consideration of gender's role has also contributed to studies of specialized craft production (13, 15–17a, 23, 25, 26, 39, 53, 55, 63, 69, 74, 76, 79, 88, 97–99, 117).

Much of the research on gender has concentrated on women's contributions to household economies to highlight the importance of their labor. Archaeologists have traditionally been most interested in specialized production by households or the production of things for exchange outside the producer's domestic group (21, 24). Brumfiel & Earle (18) distinguished specialization in subsistence goods from that in wealth or status goods. The latter type of goods are seen to matter most to the development and maintenance of political control and social hierarchies because they are "primitive valuables used in display, ritual, and exchange" (18:4). Although political leaders cannot ignore subsistence goods, they are generally more interested in, and more successful at, controlling the production or distribution of wealth (12, 16, 25, 26). The role of the production of wealth in the political economy of complex societies has predominated in recent studies of craft specialization (but see 28). It is part of the long-standing interest in archaeology in the evolution from simple to complex forms of political organization marked by inequalities in power, status, and wealth, and by a diversity in occupation and role. Household-focused production, where the household supplies itself through the labor of its members (3, 4), has been seen as less important to processes of social evolution. One of the challenges facing an archaeology of the household that is cognizant of gender is to find ways of reconstructing household practice that illuminate the interaction between these two kinds of production.

Gender and Household Production: The Case of Cooking and Eating

What kinds of things households produce for themselves vary and depend on particular circumstances. One problem encountered by archaeologists who study production is how to decide whether the ceramic vessels, stone tools, or other artifacts found in dwelling units were manufactured there and, if so, whether for internal use or external distribution (for reviews, see 3, 21, 24, 101). Therefore, I use a different example to discuss the importance of household-focused production for the organization of domestic labor. I examine the acquisition, processing, and cooking of food, that is, food preparation. Food preparation, broadly defined, is a set of tasks often assumed to be an essential function of the domestic group, if not its primary reason for existing (6, 56, 92, 122).

In societies where the household is responsible for food preparation, it inevitably affects the way household members allocate their time and divide up work. Like many other household-focused activities, food preparation has not figured much in archaeological discussions of household organization or function. I presume this is because it is seen as unrelated to issues of specialized production or wealth acquisition that contribute to differential control of resources within society. Food preparation and some of its production is in many cultures the responsibility of women and therefore seems to have been regarded as an unproblematic domestic chore (78, 83). But acquiring, processing, and cooking food requires the acquisition of certain kinds of knowledge, skills, utensils, and materials. Many food preparation activities consume hours of work each day, which reduces the time some household members have to spend on other activities.

Several studies ask what effects do processing techniques, cooking technology, types of food, and the social importance of eating have on the people responsible for food preparation (13, 20, 29, 37, 38, 40, 41, 47, 81). These studies, which use archaeological data from indigenous New World societies, postulate that women bore primary responsibility for cooking and processing. These hypotheses are based either on ethnohistorical or ethnographic sources that discuss the particular group studied or on cross-cultural analogies drawn from societies with similar socioeconomic structures and forms of subsistence economy (e.g. 82).

Despite its seemingly mundane status, food preparation takes on a political dimension because women's ability to produce food and drink becomes critical to a household's ability to fulfill its obligations to society, often in the form of ritual feasts or tribute owed to political leaders (37, 38, 40, 41). Brumfiel (13) has looked at how food habits changed in the Valley of Mexico under Aztec rule (after AD 1430) as tribute demands increased. She argued that tortillas became relatively more important in the daily diet at the expense of stews or corn porridge. This change in food habits increased work for women because tortillas take much longer to prepare and cook. But the end results were foods that were more transportable, allowing household members to work away from home more easily (see also 8, 33, 57, 86). Women also changed their activities in the Mantaro Valley, Peru, as independent groups came under Inca control in the fifteenth century AD. Hastorf (47) drew on paleoethnobotanical remains to argue that after the Inca conquest women spent more time making corn beer, which was used as a social emollient in the feasts sponsored by the state to feed its subjects paying their tribute in the form of labor. Stable isotope analysis of skeletons, however, indicates that during this same period women's diet was lower in corn than men's, which suggests that they were less likely to participate in these feasts.

Food preparation has also been seen as having implications for the development of ceramic technology. In considering the development of pottery containers, attention has been drawn to the association between the increasing importance of fired clay vessels and changes in cooking styles and food storage needs. Research on the Archaic period in the American Southwest (29) and pre-Harappan to Harappan occupation in South Asia (117) suggests that women were involved in the invention and production of fired clay containers because of their role in food preparation, their familiarity with food preparation techniques that were applicable to clay processing and firing, and their interest in improving cooking and storage technology. However, the association of food preparation needs and the impetus to create fired clay containers are the result of particular social circumstances, rather than the acting out of some universal law. Vitelli (109) has argued that women were the first potters in Greece during the Neolithic period, but she noted that their pottery does not seem to have been used for cooking or food storage. The possibility that women were directly involved with making pots raises questions of how they adjusted their schedules to fit in this task and what other tasks, such as other kinds of production or farming, might have been reallocated to other household members.

Claassen (20) and Moss (81) have addressed the relationship between cultural notions of value and food sources. Shellfish represents a heavily used and reliable resource for many native North American societies. Yet, paradoxically, ethnohistorical or ethnographic descriptions of groups who eat a lot of shellfish either make little mention of this food source or downplay its importance. Claassen has argued that the denigration of or inattention to shellfishing relates to its status as women's work, which makes it less visible and less interesting to outside researchers. Moss elucidated how shellfishing, as a gendered domestic task, becomes a focus of social tensions and constructions of value for the Tlingit of the Pacific Northwest. She discussed how Tlingit attitudes toward shellfish are shaped by concepts of appropriate male and female behavior, social status, purity, and danger, as well as by shellfish abundance and relative ease of acquisition.

Claassen explored this relationship for a prehistoric population based on data from Shell Mound Archaic sites in the Southeastern United States dating to ca 5500–3000 years ago (20). These sites consist of mounds of shells, animal and plant remains, floors, hearths, and tools. The sites also contain burials in which shells are used as offerings. Assuming that women did the collecting, Claassen suggested that we may infer the value of this labor to society by the occurrence of objects of ceremonial use in women's graves and the comparable health of men and women. She further suggested that the shift away from shellfish as a major food resource some time around 3500 years ago may have as much to do with decisions by women to concentrate on other kinds of food producing tasks or a change in the symbolic importance of shell as with any sort of environmental stress on shellfish beds.

Craft Specialization at the Household Level

Efforts to categorize craft specialization have tended to focus on the producer and the production process. Common elements in various typologies are how much time the producer spends on the craft, where the production occurs, how much is produced, and the kind of consumers at which production is aimed. Is the work part-time or full? Does it occur at home or in a separate location? Are the producers working at the behest of specific patrons who provide support or in response to the perceived needs or wants of a pool of potential consumers—are they, in Brumfiel & Earle's (18) terminology, attached or independent specialists? Costin (24) has systematized these elements into four variables—context, concentration, scale, and intensity—which she argues should be treated separately and viewed as continua.

The household figures in typologies of craft specialization as a place where production occurs, as a means of organizing production, and as a level of output. Membership in the household, or in some kinship group assumed to be equivalent to the household, determines choice of craft and access to the necessary training. Home-based craft specialization is seen as more likely to be part-time and on a relatively small scale (21, 24, 90, 101, but see 79).

By focusing on the craft specialist as the primary social actor and on the household as only one of several modes of production, we run the risk of overlooking the effects of such production on the domestic group. Any change in the occupation of some members of the household will have an impact on the household as a whole (79). As with food preparation and other forms of household-focused production, incorporating specialized production into the household's definition of its appropriate and necessary tasks must result in reallocations of time and responsibility for specialists and other household members alike. It may also change the balance of power among household members and how certain tasks are valued.

Both Wright (117) and Mills (79) have discussed the problem of "invisible" or "hidden" producers. They detail how aspects of the production process may be assigned to different people as a way of facilitating the work. The idealized categories of "artisan" and "rest of the household" break down in practice. "[A] common pattern is for other members of the household to help....Many of these 'assistants' are not credited when the products reach the market, but they are 'hidden producers' whose work is important to the overall income of the household" (79:160). Such task assignment often organizes itself by gender, age, or skill. In her research on the origins of pottery technology in South Asia, Wright points to the association between pottery production and dwelling units at such sites as Mehrgarh, Pakistan, to argue that multiple members of the household may have been assigned specific tasks in the production process.

Research on the production of obsidian tools at the site of Tula in Hidalgo, Mexico, suggests that skill is one factor in organizing production (48). Grinding obsidian cores to produce a striking platform—the less skilled work—occurs in and around houses. Striking prismatic blades off these cores, which requires more skill, is concentrated in an area away from the houses. Healen concluded that two kinds of people, novices and experts, were part of the specialized manufacture of blades.

Nor is the level of participation stable within the household. Through her study of modern and historic craft specialization among the Zuñi Indians of New Mexico, Mills (79) has demonstrated how more household members become involved in various kinds of production, such as potting, jewelry making, weaving, and fetish carving, as demand grows and other sources of income become less viable. She also notes that, contrary to the assumptions of many archaeological typologies, the manufacture of silver jewelry moves from a few workshops located outside the home into the home itself as more households concentrate on this type of specialized production. Thus the spatial distribution of specialized production increases rather than decreases in this particular case, which suggests that we need to consider the interplay of technology, economic organization, and level of production when evaluating the scale or type of production. The problems posed by the need to balance specialized work and household-focused production hold regardless of where the production occurs, how it is remunerated, at what scale it operates, the nature of the craft, or the degree of sociopolitical complexity achieved by society (3, 4, 11, 13, 15, 28, 79, 117).

Specialization in the form of women's production of cloth in New World societies has been the focus of several studies (13, 15–17a, 25, 26, 41, 53, 55, 62, 63, 65). Spinning and weaving in pre-Columbian Mesoamerican and Andean societies emerge from ethnohistorical sources, myth, and indigenous imagery as female gendered work imbued with a rich symbolism (41, 67, 77). Although cloth rarely preserves, certain elements of the technology, such as spindle weights and sewing implements, do survive. Much of this particular form of wealth was produced by women working part-time in a household setting. Only during the period of Inca rule in the Andes did significant numbers of full-time cloth producers, both male and female, emerge (25), and even then they only augmented the continuing production within the household. In considering the Andean data, Costin (25, 26) and Gero (41) have focused on what they see as an increasing loss of control by women over the products of their own labor under Inca rule. They see the transition from "kinship" to state institutions as detrimental to women's status and power both within the household and in society as a whole (but see 94, 95).

Joyce (62, 63, 65) considered the way the Maya represent cloth and women in two different kinds of visual imagery—monumental art and clay figurines. She contrasted the symbolic language of monuments, which are carved for the political leaders and serve to commemorate their power, with that of figurines, which are used mainly in household-level rituals. She argued that figurines celebrate women's productive action by depicting them actively engaged in weaving and food preparation. The association between women and cloth continues in monumental art through the depiction of richly dressed elite women. These images and the general frequency of cloth in these scenes as offerings, however, downplay the act of production in a household setting in favor of images of control by elite men and women of the product itself. Joyce ties the differences in imagery to tensions centering on issues of power, control, and gender. Figurines of active, productive women become one way that households contest or resist the consolidation of political power into the hands of a set of elite families. Joyce is also one of the few scholars to discuss the interplay of social rank and gender in ancient complex societies. Discussions of the household would benefit from greater attention to this issue (e.g. 92).

Brumfiel (13, 16–17a) has considered the impact of increased demands for cloth by the Aztec Empire on women's labor. As with food preparation, weaving comes to occupy more of women's time. Despite the greater output required of women, the quality of the cloth may actually have improved, based on the preference for smaller and lighter spindle whorls from Aztec period contexts. Brumfiel (16) argued that this change reflects the imposition of coercive forces on a system that already strongly associated women's social identity with weaving and spinning. Looking at another category of material culture, figurines, Brumfiel (17, 17a) also argued for different levels of meaning between official and popular images of women. Brumfiel, like Joyce, sees figurines as a medium through which households could express their desire to resist political domination and changes in economic relations.

QUESTIONS OF PURPOSE AND SCALE

The majority of the research reviewed here is oriented toward issues of women's economic production. It is, in a sense, remedial in that it seeks to redress a lack of interest in women and to articulate implicit assumptions about gender that have informed archaeological research (22, 23, 120, 121). It is, however, also progressive in that it suggests how much more complex our understanding of economic and social relations becomes if we begin to think in terms of social actors rather than abstract entities such as adaptive mechanisms. By focusing on women's action, research on household-focused and specialized production makes clearer the complexity of what the domestic group does, thus making the household a much more interesting object of study.

Tringham has argued for what she calls a "microscale" approach in which the "richness of the variability of the social context of domestic action" (102: 101) would be elucidated. In this view, the domestic group becomes the focus of research in its own right because it is the social group best represented in the archaeological record whose practice relates directly to the economy, political organization, and social structure (see also 32). That is, the prehistoric and ancient household must be seen as politicized as the modern one. As I have tried to show with the studies in this review, it is artificial to separate what occurs within and outside the household, or to treat specialized and domestic tasks in isolation from one another. While Aztec imperial tribute demands affected the domestic group by requiring women to reallocate their time and shift to cooking different foods, women's ability to weave cloth for tribute and for their household and to spend more time preparing food influenced the amount of tribute the empire could extract. Although not discussed by Brumfiel, new responsibilities for women must have affected what other household members—children and adults—did.

Interest in the household should not become merely a convenient justification for excavation of houses, as Smith (96) argued has too often occurred in Mesoamerican archaeology. The functional orientation of most current research in household archaeology does not provide a compelling reason for why the domestic group should matter to our reconstructions of the past, especially since much of this research has not even done a particularly good job of establishing what households do. Too often, the vast majority of household-level action is categorized as domestic, which is taken as a self-evident set of activities and relationships. Treating a few dwelling units as representative of a time period and region begs the issue of household variability.

Studying the household as an arena of social and economic relations that interacts dynamically with the larger society requires us to deal with the domestic group as a set of social actors. In the research on gender and craft specialization I discuss, the household is not the focus of study. It appears because it is seen as one of the primary settings of women's action and as a locus of specialized production. To complete our picture of the importance of women's production, in particular, or household-based specialized production, in general, we need to consider the consequences of particular kinds of production for the group as a whole. Crown & Wills (29), for example, postulated that women in Southwestern United States Archaic Period society were responsible for food production and preparation, the production of all sorts of "soft" goods, while also becoming the primary producers of pottery. They further suggest that one effect of ceramic cooking pots was to allow women to cook food that could be eaten by quite young children, which allowed weaning to occur at an earlier age. What then were the social consequences for the domestic group as an economic unit and for relations among men and women?

We also need to think more about the household as practice. The gender and craft specialization research reviewed here, and some household archaeology, has gone a great way toward identifying what domestic groups do but has made less progress in conceptualizing the meaning of that action. Rather than continuing to view the archaeological record as a passive reflection of people's activities, we need to consider technology as a social process and material culture as an active component in the constitution of social relations (32, 60, 63, 102, 104, 105). This brings us directly to Cowgill's (27) call for better social theory in archaeology that relies less on artificial simplifying assumptions about human behavior. A greater sensitivity to the variation in material culture is needed that acknowledges that many of its characteristics represent choices by people who made or used it (60, 109). Thus, Joyce's and Brumfiel's discussions of Maya and Aztec figurines recognize that the content of the imagery is not random but rather the result of how they are to be used and by whom. Through figurines, households and the state engage in a dialogue, expressed through visual imagery, over how women's labor is to be valued and controlled.

Methodological issues centering on problems of data recovery and interpretation, context, and temporal relations among dwelling units have been raised in the literature reviewed here (52, 56, 68, 90, 91) and should be addressed. Modeling the relationship between material culture and social construction, however, represents the most serious challenge for archaeology. Where should we look for analogies to help us interpret our archaeological remains? Archaeologists able to draw on visual imagery or historically specific written documentation have been readiest to talk about social actors such as male and female, adult and child, and to interpret the culturally constructed system of value that informs domestic relations (13, 15–17a, 23, 25, 26, 40, 41, 53, 55, 62–65, 69, 76, 81, 97–99). The benefits of these sources are not unalloyed, however, and must be used critically (62, 66, 69, 95, 97). The lack of such sources must not discourage archaeologists from dealing with issues of practice and meaning. Claassen (20), Crown & Wills (29), Wright (117), and especially Tringham (102–105) have discussed ways of using cross-cultural analogy in the interpretation of material culture and social relations.

Tringham (102–105) has perhaps gone farthest in exploring how to connect archaeological remains and the people who produced them in the absence of direct-historical sources. She has worked at reconfiguring household archaeology by emphasizing the importance of social relations within the household, especially those defined by gender. Drawing on data from the fifth millennium BC Late Neolithic/Early Eneolithic Vinča culture settlement of Opovo-Ugar Bajbuk, Serbia (106, 107), she has looked for ways to connect the built environment to the organization of domestic action. She considers architecture an active element in the constitution of social relations rather than as merely the setting in which such relations are acted out. Tringham draws on an eclectic array of research on the social meaning of space, gender, and social organization to present possible reconstructions of how male and female household members interacted (see also 98, 99). Her efforts are important because they make the connections between assumptions and explanation explicit and refuse to simplify the past any more than necessary. It is, in fact, only through a greater willingness to examine the complexity and variability of human relations that we can hope to develop intellectually satisfying approaches to the household.

Literature Cited

1. Ammerman AJ. 1988–1989. Towards the study of Neolithic households. *Origini* 14: 73–82
2. Ammerman AJ, Shaffer GD, Hartmann N. 1988. A Neolithic household at Piana di Curinga, Italy. *J. Field Archaeol.* 15: 121–40
3. Arnold PJ III. 1991. *Domestic Ceramic Production and Spatial Organization.* Cambridge: Cambridge Univ. Press
4. Arnold PJ III, Santley RS. 1993. Household ceramics production at Middle Classic Period Matacapan. See Ref. 89, pp. 227–48
5. Ashmore W, Wilk RR. 1988. Household and community in the Mesoamerican past. See Ref. 113, pp. 1–27
6. Bender DR. 1967. A refinement of the concept of household: families, co-residence, and domestic functions. *Am. Anthropol.* 69: 493–504

7. Bermann M, Estévez Castillo J. 1995. Domestic artifact assemblages and ritual activities in the Bolivian Formative. *J. Field Archaeol.* 22:389–98

8. Blanton RE, Kowalewski SA, Feinman G, Appel J. 1982. *Ancient Mesoamerica: A Comparison of Change in Three Regions.* Cambridge: Cambridge Univ. Press

9. Bogucki P. 1993. Animal traction and household economies in Neolithic Europe. *Antiquity* 67:492–503

10. Bourdieu P. 1977. *Outline of a Theory of Practice.* Cambridge: Cambridge Univ. Press.

11. Brumfiel EM. 1986. The division of labor at Xico: the chipped stone industry. See Ref. 58, pp. 245–79

12. Brumfiel EM. 1987. Consumption and politics at Aztec Huexotla. *Am. Anthropol.* 89: 676–86

13. Brumfiel EM. 1991. Weaving and cooking: women's production in Aztec Mexico. See Ref. 42, pp. 224–51

14. Brumfiel EM. 1992. Distinguished lecture in archeology: breaking and entering the ecosystem—gender, class, and faction steal the show. *Am. Anthropol.* 94:551–67

15. Brumfiel EM. 1995. *The social identity of Aztec craft specialists.* Presented at Annu. Meet. Am. Anthropol. Assoc., 94th, Washington, DC

16. Brumfiel EM. 1996. Tribute cloth production and compliance in Aztec and Colonial Mexico. *Mus. Anthropol.* In press

17. Brumfiel EM. 1996. Figurines and the Aztec state: testing the effectiveness of ideological domination. See Ref. 119. In press

17a. Brumfiel EM. 1996. The quality of tribute cloth: the place of evidence in archaeological argument. *Am. Antiq.* 61:In press

18. Brumfiel EM, Earle TK. 1987. Specialization, exchange, and complex societies: an introduction. In *Specialization, Exchange, and Complex Societies,* ed. EM Brumfiel, TK Earle, pp. 1–9. Cambridge: Cambridge Univ. Press

19. Carter AT. 1984. Household histories. See Ref. 84, pp. 44–83

20. Claassen CP. 1991. Gender, shellfishing, and the Shell Mound Archaic. See Ref. 42, pp. 276–300

21. Clark JE. 1986. From mountains to molehills: a critical review of Teotihuacan's obsidian industry. See Ref. 58, pp. 23–74

22. Conkey MW, Gero JM. 1991. Tensions, pluralities, and engendering archaeology: an introduction to women and prehistory. See Ref. 42, pp. 3–30

23. Conkey MW, Spector JD. 1984. Archaeology and the study of gender. *Adv. Archaeol. Method Theory* 7:1–38

24. Costin CL. 1991. Craft specialization: issues in defining, documenting, and explaining the organization of production. *Archaeol. Method Theory* 3:1–56

25. Costin CL. 1993. Textiles, women, and political economy in late Prehispanic Peru. *Res. Econ. Anthropol.* 14:3–28

26. Costin CL. 1996. Exploring the relationship between gender and craft in complex societies: methodological and theoretical issues of gender attribution. See Ref. 119, In press

27. Cowgill GL. 1993. Distinguished lecture in archeology: beyond criticizing New Archeology. *Am. Anthropol.* 95:551–73

28. Cross JR. 1993. Craft specialization in nonstratified societies. *Res. Econ. Anthropol.* 14:61–84

29. Crown PL, Wills WH. 1995. The origins of Southwestern ceramic containers: women's time allocation and economic intensification. *J. Anthropol. Res.* 51:173–86

30. Diamanti M. 1991. *Domestic organization at Copan: reconstruction of elite Maya households through ethnographic models.* PhD thesis. Pa. State Univ., State College

31. di Leonardo M, ed. 1991. *Gender at the Crossroads of Knowledge: Feminist Anthropology in the Postmodern Era.* Berkeley: Univ. Calif. Press

32. Dobres M-A, Hoffman CR. 1994. Social agency and the dynamics of prehistoric technology. *J. Archaeol. Method Theory* 1:211–58

33. Feinman G. 1986. The emergence of specialized ceramic production in Formative Oaxaca. See Ref. 58, pp. 347–73

34. Flannery KV. 1976. The early Mesoamerican house. See Ref. 35, pp. 16–24

35. Flannery KV, ed. 1976. *The Early Mesoamerican Village.* New York: Academic

36. Flannery KV, Winter MC. 1976. Analyzing household activities. See Ref. 35, pp. 34–47

37. Fung CD. 1993. *Gender, power, and domestic labour on the Mesoamerican frontier.* Presented at Annu. Chacmool Conf., 26th, Calgary

38. Fung CD. 1995. *Domestic labor, gender, and social power: household archaeology in Terminal Classic Yoro, Honduras.* PhD thesis. Harvard Univ., Cambridge

39. Gero JM. 1991. Genderlithics: women's roles in stone tool production. See Ref. 42, pp. 163–93

40. Gero JM. 1991. Who experienced what in prehistory? A narrative explanation from Queyash, Peru. In *Processual and Postprocessual Archaeologies: Multiple Ways of Knowing the Past,* ed. RW Preucel. *Occas. Pap.* 10:126–39. Carbondale: Cent. Archaeol. Invest., South. Ill. Univ.

41. Gero JM. 1992. Feasts and females: gender ideology and political meals in the Andes. *Nor. Archaeol. Rev.* 25:15–30

42. Gero JM, Conkey MW, eds. 1991. *Engendering Archaeology: Women and Prehistory*. Oxford: Blackwell
43. Gonlin N. 1993. *Rural household archaeology at Copan, Honduras*. PhD thesis. Pa. State Univ., State College
44. Grygiel R. 1984. The household cluster as a fundamental social unit of the Brześć Kujawski group of the Lengyel culture in the Polish lowlands. *Pr. Mater. Muz. Archeol. Etnogr. Łodzi Ser. Archeol.* 31: 43–270
45. Hammel EA. 1984. On the *** of studying household form and function. See Ref. 84, pp. 29–43
46. Hart G. 1992. Imagined unities: constructions of "the household" in economic theory. See Ref. 85, pp. 111–29
47. Hastorf CA. 1991. Gender, space, and food in prehistory. See Ref. 42, pp. 132–59
48. Healen DM. 1986. Technological and nontechnological aspects of an obsidian workshop excavated at Tula, Hidalgo. See Ref. 58, pp. 133–52
49. Healen DM, ed. 1989. *Tula of the Toltecs: Excavations and Survey*. Iowa City: Univ. Iowa Press
50. Healen DM. 1993. Urbanism at Tula from the perspective of residential archaeology. See Ref. 89, pp. 105–19
51. Hendon JA. 1989. Elite household organization at Copan, Honduras: analysis of activity distribution in the Sepulturas zone. See Ref. 71, pp. 371–80
52. Hendon JA. 1991. Status and power in Classic Maya society: an archeological study. *Am. Anthropol.* 93:894–918
53. Hendon JA. 1992. Hilado y tejido en la época prehispánica: tecnología y relaciones sociales de la producción textil. In *La Indumentaria y el Tejido Mayas a Través del Tiempo*, ed. L Asturias de Barios, D Fernández García, pp. 7–16. Guatemala City: Mus. Ixchel de Traje Indígena
54. Hendon JA. 1996. The Pre-Classic Maya compound as the focus of social identity. In *Social Patterns in Pre-Classic Mesoamerica*, ed. D Grove, RA Joyce. Washington, DC: Dumbarton Oaks. In press
55. Hendon JA. 1996. Women's work, women's space, and women's status among the Classic Period Maya elite of the Copan Valley, Honduras. In *Case Studies in the Archaeology of Women: North America and Mesoamerica*, ed. CP Claassen, RA Joyce. Philadelphia: Univ. Pa. Press. In press
56. Hirth KG. 1993. The household as an analytical unit: problems in method and theory. See Ref. 89, pp. 21–36
57. Isaac BL. 1986. Introduction. See Ref. 58, pp. 1–19
58. Isaac BL, ed. 1986. *Economic Aspects of Prehispanic Highland Mexico. Research in Economic Anthropology Supplement 2*. Greenwich, CT: JAI
59. Jackson TL. 1991. Pounding acorns: women's production as social and economic focus. See Ref. 42, pp. 301–25
60. Johnson MH. 1989. Conceptions of agency in archaeological interpretations. *J. Anthropol. Archaeol.* 8:189–211
61. Joyce RA. 1991. *Cerro Palenque: Power and Identity on the Maya Periphery*. Austin: Univ. Tex. Press
62. Joyce RA. 1992. Images of gender and labor organization in Classic Maya society. In *Exploring Gender through Archaeology: Selected Papers from the 1991 Boone Conference*, ed. C Claassen. *Monogr. World Archaeol.* 11:63–70. Madison: Prehistory Press
63. Joyce RA. 1993. Women's work: images of production and reproduction in Pre-Hispanic southern Central America. *Curr. Anthropol.* 34:255–74
64. Joyce RA. 1995. *Making men and women of children: the construction of gender in Mesoamerican society*. Presented at Annu. Meet. Am. Anthropol. Assoc., 94th, Washington, DC
65. Joyce RA. 1996. The construction of gender in Classic Maya monuments. See Ref. 119. In press
66. Kellogg S. 1993. The social organization of households among the Tenochca Mexica before and after conquest. See Ref. 89, pp. 207–24
67. Klein CF. 1982. Woven heaven, tangled earth: a weaver's paradigm of the Mesoamerican cosmos. *Ann. NY Acad. Sci.* 385: 1–35
68. Leventhal RM, Baxter KH. 1988. The use of ceramics to identify the function of Copan structures. See Ref. 113, pp. 51–71
69. Linnekin J. 1988. Who made the feather cloaks? A problem in Hawaiian gender relations. *J. Polyn. Soc.* 97:265–80
70. Lucero LJ. 1994. *Household and community integration among hinterland elites and commoners: Maya residential ceramic assemblages of the Belize River area*. PhD thesis. Univ. Calif., Los Angeles
71. MacEachern S, Archer DJW, Garvin RD, eds. 1989. *Households and Communities: Proc. 21st Annu. Chacmool Conf.* Calgary: Archaeol. Assoc., Univ. Calgary
72. Manzanilla L, ed. 1986. *Unidades habitacionales mesoamericanos y sus áreas de actividad. Ser. Antropol. 76*. Mexico City: Univ. Nac. Autón. Méx.
73. Manzanilla L, Barba L. 1990. The study of activities in Classic households: two case studies from Coba and Teotihuacan. *Anc. Mesoam.* 1:41–49

74. Marshall Y. 1985. Who made the Lapita pots? A case study in gender archaeology. *J. Polyn. Soc.* 94:205–33
75. Marti J. 1993. Introduction. In *The Other Fifty Percent: Multicultural Perspectives on Gender Relations,* ed. M Womack, J Marti, pp. 179–83. Prospect Heights, IL: Waveland
76. McCafferty GG. 1992. *The material culture of Postclassic Cholula, Puebla: contextual interpretations of the UA-1 domestic compounds.* PhD thesis. State Univ. NY, Binghamton
77. McCafferty SD, McCafferty GG. 1991. Spinning and weaving as female gender identity in Postclassic Mexico. In *Textile Traditions of Mesoamerica and the Andes,* ed. MB Schevill, JC Berlo, EB Dwyer, pp. 19–44. New York: Garland
78. McGaw JA. 1996. Reconceiving technology: why feminine technologies matter. See Ref. 119. In press
79. Mills BJ. 1995. Gender and the reorganization of historic Zuni craft production: implications for archaeological interpretation. *J. Anthropol. Res.* 51:149–72
80. Moore HL. 1992. Households and gender relations: the modelling of the economy. See Ref. 85, pp. 131–48
81. Moss ML. 1993. Shellfish, gender, and status on the Northwest Coast: reconciling archeological, ethnographic, and ethnohistorical records of the Tlingit. *Am. Anthropol.* 95:631–52
82. Murdock GP, Provost C. 1973. Factors in the division of labor by sex: a cross-cultural analysis. *Ethnology* 12:203–25
83. Netting RM, Wilk RR, Arnould EJ. 1984. Introduction. See Ref. 84, pp. xiii–xxxviii
84. Netting RM, Wilk RR, Arnould EJ, eds. 1984. *Households: Comparative and Historical Studies of the Domestic Group.* Berkeley: Univ. Calif. Press
85. Ortiz S, Lees S, eds. 1992. *Understanding Economic Process. Monogr. Econ. Anthropol. 10.* Lanham: Univ. Press Am., Soc. Econ. Anthropol.
86. Patterson TC. 1990. Processes in the formation of ancient world systems. *Dialect. Anthropol.* 15:1–18
87. Peacock NR. 1991. Rethinking the sexual division of labor: reproduction and women's work among the Efe. See Ref. 31, pp. 339–60
88. Rice PM. 1991. Women and prehistoric pottery production. In *The Archaeology of Gender: Proc. 22nd Annu. Chacmool Conf.,* ed. D Walde, ND Willows, pp. 430–43. Calgary: Archaeol. Assoc., Univ. Calgary
89. Santley RS, Hirth KG, eds. 1993. *Prehispanic Domestic Units in Mesoamerica:*
Studies of the Household Compound and Residence. Boca Raton, FL: CRC
90. Santley RS, Kneebone RR. 1993. Craft specialization, refuse disposal, and the creation of spatial archaeological records in Prehispanic Mesoamerica. See Ref. 89, pp. 37–63
91. Schortman EM, Urban PA. 1995. Late Classic society in the Rio Ulua drainage, Honduras. *J. Field Archaeol.* 22:439–57
92. Sheets PD. 1992. *The Ceren Site: a Prehistoric Village Buried by Volcanic Ash in Central America.* Fort Worth, TX: Harcourt Brace Coll.
93. Sheets PD, Beaubien HF, Beaudry M, Gerstle A, McKee B, et al. 1990. Household archaeology at Cerén, El Salvador. *Anc. Mesoam.* 1:81–90
94. Silverblatt I. 1991. Interpreting women in states: new feminist ethnohistories. See Ref. 31, pp. 140–71
95. Silverblatt I. 1995. Lessons of gender and ethnohistory in Mesoamerica. *Ethnohistory* 42:639–50
96. Smith ME. 1993. New World complex societies: recent economic, social, and political studies. *J. Archaeol. Res.* 1:5–41
97. Spector JD. 1983. Male/female task differentiation among the Hidatsa: toward the development of an archeological approach to the study of gender. In *The Hidden Half: Studies of Plains Indian Women,* ed. P Albers, B Medicine, pp. 77–99. Washington, DC: Univ. Press Am.
98. Spector JD. 1991. What this awl means: toward a feminist archaeology. See Ref. 42, pp. 388–406
99. Spector JD. 1993. *What This Awl Means: Feminist Archaeology at a Wahpeton Dakota Village.* St. Paul: Minn. State Hist. Soc. Press
100. Stanish C. 1989. Household archeology: testing models of zonal complementarity in the south central Andes. *Am. Anthropol.* 91:7–24
101. Stark BL. 1985. Archaeological identification of pottery production locations: ethnoarchaeological and archaeological data in Mesoamerica. In *Decoding Prehistoric Ceramics,* ed. BA Nelson, pp. 158–94. Carbondale: South. Ill. Univ. Press
102. Tringham R. 1991. Households with faces: the challenge of gender in prehistoric architectural remains. See Ref. 42, pp. 93–131
103. Tringham R. 1991. Men and women in prehistoric architecture. *Traditional Dwell. Settl. Rev.* 3(1):9–28
104. Tringham R. 1994. Engendered places in prehistory. *Gend. Place Cult.* 1:169–203
105. Tringham R. 1995. Archaeological houses, households, housework, and the home. In *The Home: Words, Interpretations, Mean-*

ings, and Environments, ed. DN Benjamin, pp. 79–107. Aldershot, Engl: Avebury

106. Tringham R, Brukner B, Kaiser T, Borojević K, Bukvić L, et al. 1992. Excavations at Opovo, 1985–1987: socioeconomic change in the Balkan Neolithic. *J. Field Archaeol.* 19:351–86

107. Tringham R, Brukner B, Voytek B. 1985. The Opovo project: a study of socioeconomic change in the Balkan Neolithic. *J. Field Archaeol.* 12:425–44

108. Tringham R, Krstić D, eds. 1990. *Selevac: a Neolithic Village in Yugoslavia. Monum. Archaeol. 15.* Los Angeles: Inst. Archaeol., Univ. Calif.

109. Vitelli KD. 1989. Were pots first made for foods? Doubts from Franchthi. *World Archaeol.* 21:17–29

110. Weismantel M. 1989. Making breakfast and making babies: the Zumbagua household as constituted process. See Ref. 112, pp. 55–72

111. Wilk RR. 1989. Decision making and resource flows within the household: beyond the black box. See Ref. 112, pp. 23–52

112. Wilk RR, ed. 1989. *The Household Economy: Reconsidering the Domestic Mode of Production.* Boulder: Westview

113. Wilk RR, Ashmore W, eds. 1988. *House-hold and Community in the Mesoamerican Past.* Albuquerque: Univ. N. M. Press

114. Wilk RR, Netting RM. 1984. Households: changing forms and functions. See Ref. 84, pp. 1–28

115. Wilk RR, Rathje WL. 1982. Household archaeology. See Ref. 116, pp. 617–39

116. Wilk RR, Rathje WL, eds. 1982. *Archaeology of the Household: Building a Prehistory of Domestic Life. Am. Behav. Sci.* 25

117. Wright RP. 1991. Women's labor and pottery production in prehistory. See Ref. 42, pp. 194–223

118. Wright RP. 1996. Introduction: gendered ways of knowing in archaeology. See Ref. 119, In press

119. Wright RP, ed. 1996. *Gender in Archaeology: Essays in Research and Practice.* Philadelphia: Univ. Pa. Press. In press

120. Wylie A. 1991. Gender theory and the archaeological record: why is there no archaeology of gender? See Ref. 42, pp. 31–54

121. Wylie A. 1992. Feminist theories of social power: some implications for a processual archaeology. *Nor. Archaeol. Rev.* 25:51–68

122. Yanagisako SJ. 1979. Family and household: the analysis of domestic groups. *Annu. Rev. Anthropol.* 8:161–205

Annu. Rev. Anthropol. 1996. 25:63–79

NATIVE AMERICANS AND THE PRACTICE OF ARCHAEOLOGY

T. J. Ferguson

5000 W. Placita de los Vientos, Tucson, Arizona 85745

KEY WORDS: American Indians, theory, ethics, repatriation, cultural resources management

ABSTRACT

Archaeologists are in the midst of restructuring their relationship with Native Americans. The legal, political, social, and intellectual ramifications of this process are reviewed to examine the fundamental changes occurring in the way archaeology is conducted in the Americas. Much of the impetus for this change resulted from the criticism of archaeology by Native Americans, which led to passage of the Native American Graves Protection and Repatriation Act of 1990 (NAGPRA). NAGPRA has indelibly changed how archaeologists will work in the United States. The issues raised by Native Americans about why and how archaeological research is conducted, however, go beyond NAGPRA to the paradigmatic basis of archaeology. Archaeologists will have new opportunities available to them if they work in partnership with Native Americans in studying the rich archaeological record in the Americas.

INTRODUCTION

Archaeologists and Native Americans are in the midst of restructuring their relationship in ways that are exciting to some archaeologists, frustrating to others. Regardless of how archaeologists feel about the process, fundamental changes are occurring in the way archaeology is conducted in the Americas. Much of the impetus for this change resulted from the criticism of archaeology by Native Americans, which, coupled with political activism, led to the passage of Public Law 101-601, the Native American Graves Protection and Repatriation Act of 1990 (NAGPRA). There is no doubt that NAGPRA has indelibly changed how archaeologists will work in the United States. The issues raised by Native Americans about why and how archaeological research is conducted, however, go beyond NAGPRA to the paradigmatic basis of archaeology. This review explores the new opportunities available to archaeologists if they work in partnership with Native Americans in studying the rich archaeological record of the Americas.

The term Native American refers to the indigenous populations of Canada, the United States, Mexico, and Central and South America, including a variety of Indians, Eskimos, Native Alaskans, and Native Hawaiians. Native Americans do not constitute a single, monolithic cultural or ethnic group. There are more than 550 recognized tribes in the United States alone, with additional Indian groups not formally recognized by the US government. Each group or tribe of Native Americans in North and South America has unique cultural characteristics. The great variation in cultures should be kept in mind when generalizations are made about Native Americans. Native Americans have a wide range of opinions, approaches, and solutions to the issues concerning archaeology.

Americanist archaeology is closely tied to Native Americans because many, perhaps most, archaeologists investigate an archaeological record formed by the ancestors of contemporary Native Americans. A random survey of almost 550 archaeologists in the United States indicated that 38% of them had conducted research on lands belonging to Native Americans (151). Even more archaeologists have investigated archaeological sites on public or private lands ancestral to Native Americans.

A BRIEF HISTORY OF ARCHAEOLOGICAL RESEARCH RELATED TO NATIVE AMERICANS

The practice of archaeology occurs in a social context, and interpretations of the archaeological record have been and continue to be used for political purposes whether or not archaeologists recognize this (37). Early archaeology in the Americas was essentially a colonialist endeavor, part of an intellectual development that occurred in many places where native populations were replaced or dominated by European colonists. Native peoples were denigrated by a colonialist belief that native societies lacked the initiative and capacity for development. The interpretation of the archaeological record was inextricably linked to the political and cultural processes entailed in taking land from Native Americans for incorporation into expanding nation states (18, 53, 81, 87, 131, 135, 145). This history is reviewed in a series of publications by Trigger (131–136) and McGuire (86, 87).

The concepts of unilinear evolution in nineteenth-century archaeological theory characterized Indian societies as static cultures at a relatively primitive stage of development compared with European civilizations (59, 102, 135).

Native Americans were dehumanized and objectified when the remains of their ancestors were collected for craniology, which was undertaken to prove that Native Americans were racially inferior and naturally doomed to extinction (87, 90, 112, 137). These ideas were incorporated into the "Vanishing Red Man" theory that influenced government policy as a scientific justification for the relocation of Indian tribes, establishment of reservations, and other acts that some Native Americans now characterize as genocide.

As scholars became more familiar with the archaeological record in the twentieth century, the cultural development of native peoples was recognized, as was the historical continuity between ancient and contemporary Native Americans (131, 135, 145). Archaeologists concentrated on the development of chronological techniques and temporal sequences, and interest in reconstructing prehistoric lifeways waned. Consequently, archaeology became less integrated with ethnology, and this weakened the social and intellectual interaction between archaeologists and Native Americans. Americanist archaeologists who worked in Central and South America allied themselves with the ruling elites and state bureaucracies in the countries where they worked rather than with indigenous peoples. This supported the status quo of social inequalities in the host countries (102).

The processual archaeology that developed in the 1960s and 1970s focused explanations of change in Native American societies on internal sociocultural developments and ecological variables. This was positive because Native American cultures were considered as creative as European cultures (132). However, the nomothetic goals of this paradigm denied the validity of studying the specific development of Native American peoples as an important end in itself. This affected how Native Americans viewed archaeology, because archaeological findings were presented in universal terms that had no relevance to specific tribal peoples. Archaeologists gave little thought to the feelings of native peoples about the excavation of the graves of their ancestors and how their past was represented in archaeological interpretations. These developments were significant because they coincided with Native Americans increasingly asserting control over their cultural affairs (134).

The history of archaeological research in the United States and other countries in relation to Native Americans has been largely characterized by ineffective communication and a lack of mutual respect (53, 90). There have been a few notable exceptions, of course, in particular archaeologists who have testified for Native Americans in land claims (52).

The development of cultural resources management (CRM) since the 1970s has greatly increased the amount of knowledge about Native American archaeological sites threatened by development (11, 42, 74, 109). CRM has commodified knowledge about the past by removing archaeology from the

realm of universities into the commercial arena of contracts and private consulting companies. As Spriggs (121) observed in Hawaii, Native Americans
often act on the knowledge amassed in CRM, which moves archaeology more
clearly into the political domain. This trend exists wherever Native Americans
perceive archaeological sites as an essential part of their heritage needing
protection.

FEDERAL, STATE, AND TRIBAL REGULATION OF ARCHAEOLOGICAL RESEARCH IN THE UNITED STATES

It is incumbent upon all archaeologists to read and understand the laws regulating archaeology in the jurisdictions where they work. The legal regulation of
archaeology is highly developed in the United States, where archaeological
research on Federal lands, including Indian reservations, has been regulated by
Federal legislation since the passage of the Antiquities Act of 1906 (P. L.
59-209). The complex of laws that regulate archaeology and historic preservation in the United States are summarized elsewhere (53, 58, 74, 77, 78, 104,
125). Because these laws are periodically amended, archaeologists need to
follow new developments as they occur.

Of particular note is that the Archaeological Resources and Protection Act
of 1979 (P. L. 96-95) requires that the consent of Indian tribes be obtained
before the issuance of federal permits for the excavation or removal of archaeological materials from Indian lands. NAGPRA gives Native Americans property rights in grave goods and cultural patrimony, as well as the right to
repatriate human remains from federal and Indian lands (90, 125, 137). Archaeological resources on private land, however, are still treated as private
property, which is vexing for Native Americans (10). Virtually all archaeological investigations conducted on federal or tribal lands in the United States now
require consultation with Native Americans (27, 74, 90). The review of archaeological research designs by Native Americans gives them a new opportunity
to communicate with archaeologists.

NAGPRA has fundamentally changed the way American archaeology is
practiced in the United States. The identification of cultural affiliation following NAGPRA is becoming a research question of legal import, forcing archaeologists to think about old classifications in new ways. Many Indian tribes and
Native American groups will not allow excavation or investigation of human
remains unless those remains are threatened, e.g. by land development. Some
archaeologists excavating sites for research not related to the mitigation of
adverse impacts are now required to cease excavation of archaeological features or units that expose human remains. The profession is adjusting to
NAGPRA, and new ways to collect and analyze archaeological data about
human remains and grave goods are being developed and institutionalized.

A majority of states have also adopted some form of repatriation or reburial statute specifically relating to Native Americans or have adopted general laws that protect graves and cemeteries (103, 140, 150). As Price (104) noted, the practical impact of these state laws can't be assessed until they have been implemented for a number of years. Some of the constitutional issues raised by state laws may need to be decided by the US Supreme Court.

The National Historic Preservation Act of 1966 (P. L. 74-292, NHPA), as amended, is currently responsible for most of the research conducted on Native American archaeological sites in the United States. Many archaeologists are employed by federal and state agencies as cultural resource managers to administer the Act. Even more archaeologists work under contract to provide the inventories of archaeological and historical sites required to implement the NHPA, or to undertake data recovery programs to mitigate adverse impacts on sites eligible for the National Register of Historic Places. Amendments in 1992 to Section 101 of the NHPA require that Native American values be considered in the management of archaeological sites and historic properties. They also establish that properties of traditional religious and cultural importance to an Indian tribe or Native Hawaiian organization may be eligible for the National Register of Historic Places. These traditional cultural properties include sacred sites, natural resource collection areas, and occasionally archaeological sites ancestral to contemporary Native Americans.

The management of traditional cultural properties as historic sites creates new issues for archaeologists engaged in CRM, including the integration of ethnographic and ethnohistoric data into archaeological reports, and negotiations with Native Americans about maintaining the confidentiality of findings (7, 29, 41, 51, 101). The inability to mitigate adverse impacts to many traditional cultural properties, especially sacred sites, results in a management quandary for many Native Americans and the archaeologists who work with them.

The 1992 amendments to the NHPA allow tribes to implement tribal historic preservation programs and assume the management and compliance responsibilities exercised by State Historic Preservation Officers on their lands. Many tribes concerned with sovereignty are currently working to do this and are enacting tribal historic preservation legislation (10, 27, 40, 66, 73–75, 90). Some tribes are proposing to manage cultural resources by preserving them as they are and keeping archaeologists away (99). Other tribes are opting to establish their own tribal archaeology or historic preservation programs modeled after existing federal programs. In the United States, these developments make it possible for Indian tribes to regulate archaeological research on their land.

CHALLENGES TO THE PROFESSION AND ORGANIZATIONAL RESPONSES

In the 1960s and 1970s, Native Americans began to actively protest archaeological research, especially the excavation of burials. In the 1970s, the Society for American Archaeology (SAA) recognized that the relationship between archaeologists and Native Americans needed improvement (3, 70, 85, 120). Native American concerns were deemed legitimate, and the SAA recommended that archaeologists communicate more effectively with Native Americans and find ways to increase their participation in archaeological research. In the 1980s, Native American concerns in the United States and Canada were focused on repatriation. The contentious history and resolution of the reburial issue is reviewed in numerous publications (4, 13, 14, 22, 30, 38, 46, 56, 57, 60, 67, 69, 74, 76, 86, 87, 90, 97, 103, 112, 113, 125, 127, 128, 137-138, 142, 152–155). The objections to repatriation raised by some archaeologists (92–94) have been made moot in the United States by the passage of NAGPRA, although a number of issues remain to be worked out, including exactly what under the law constitutes human remains (21).

Most archaeologists have come to respect Native American concerns about the remains of their ancestors, even while working outside the United States. McGuire & Villalpando (88) have demonstrated that archaeologists can effectively consult about reburial of human remains even when an international border separates part of a contemporary group of Native Americans from their ancestors in another country.

The reburial of human remains entails a loss of potential new data because reanalysis is no longer possible (26, 140). However, NAGPRA has not halted the excavation and analysis of human remains. Many Native American archaeological graves and cemeteries are still investigated when they are threatened by development (64, 108, 109, 122, 125). Reburial makes it incumbent upon archaeologists to develop cumulative research designs oriented toward the collection of new data rather than the reanalysis of curated human remains.

Even before the passage of NAGPRA, many archaeologists began to work to ameliorate the problems Native Americans had with how archaeology was conducted (1, 2, 9, 50, 61–63, 108, 120, 114, 146, 156). In 1990, the SAA responded to the challenges raised by Native Americans by establishing a task force to advise the society on how to develop a better relationship with Native Americans. This task force was made into a standing committee in 1995, and the committee is now working to establish a liaison with Native American organizations, define the responsibilities of archaeologists to Native American communities, develop the means for Native Americans and archaeologists to cooperate in the protection of cultural resources, and prepare guidelines concerning repatriation by Indian tribes and groups that are not federally recognized (117). Many state archaeological organizations have established similar committees to work on improving relations with Native Americans at the local level.

The SAA also identified Native American outreach and public education as important professional activities to improve communication with Native Americans. Many archaeologists in North and South America are now working to meet this challenge (6, 19, 20, 36–38, 47, 56, 68, 78, 89, 91, 124).

INCREASED PARTICIPATION OF NATIVE AMERICANS IN PROFESSIONAL ACTIVITIES

The participation of Native Americans in archaeological activities has dramatically increased in the past twenty years. Native Americans now regularly participate in national and regional meetings, opening new avenues of dialog with archaeologists (15, 35, 110, 116). Archaeologists who work for Indian tribes have provided on-the-job training so Native Americans can be employed in professional positions (11, 50, 72), and many private archaeological contractors regularly employ Native Americans in field and laboratory research. Northern Arizona University, through cooperative programs with the Navajo Nation and the Hopi Tribe, is pioneering work-study programs where tribal members can earn income and gain experience while pursuing undergraduate and graduate degrees in anthropology and related fields (139).

Many tribes now operate historic preservation programs, including the Colville Confederate Tribes (54), the Confederated Tribes of the Umatilla Reservation (27), the Hopi Tribe (51), the Mashantucket Pequot (84), the Mohegan Nation (49), the Navajo Nation (16, 42), and the Pueblo of Zuni (10–12, 50). Several tribes also operate CRM firms to undertake contracted archaeological research, including the Gila River Indian Community (109); a consortium of the Klamath, Modoc, and Yaahooskin tribes (7); the Navajo Nation (72); and the Pueblo of Zuni (11). In addition to providing needed archaeological services, these tribally based historic preservation programs and contract archaeology businesses provide substantial economic benefits to Indian tribes.

Many Native Americans have successfully collaborated with archaeologists to manage cultural resources or undertake archaeological research, including the Bannock-Shoshone (45), the Catawba (130), the Chugach (71), the Dakota (119), the Kodiak Area Native Association (105) and other Native corporations in Alaska (32, 115), the Narragansetts (84, 114), the Mashantucket Pequot and Gay Head Wampanoag (84), and the Northern Cheyenne and Crow (33). Several tribes, including the Makah (55), the Blackfoot (23), and the Cree (48), have worked with archaeologists to establish museums that bring Native

American heritage into sharper focus by situating it in the present. One group of Native Americans investigates archaeological sites using an educational program similar to Earthwatch (5).

NEW DEVELOPMENTS IN ARCHAEOLOGICAL THEORY AND PRACTICE

Criticism by Native Americans has caused archaeologists to examine the epistemological basis of their discipline (110). Scholars who recognize that archaeologists and Native Americans view the past in fundamentally different ways call for the application of cultural relativism in archaeological research (17, 153). Thomas (129) accomplished this in compiling studies of the consequences of European contact by applying a "cubist" perspective that incorporates multiple viewpoints of the past at the same time, drawing upon narrative history, historical archaeology, Native American studies, historical demography, and ethnohistory.

Archaeologists have become more reflexive. Wylie (149) and Handsman (61) have written about the political nature of archaeological studies of Native Americans. Wilk (144) analyzed the dual nature of archaeological discourse about the ancient Maya, which reflects political and philosophical debates in contemporary society as it pursues knowledge about the past. Leone & Preucel (82) applied critical theory to the dialog between archaeologists and Native Americans concerning the reburial issue. In so doing, they moved beyond the specifics of the reburial debate to a greater understanding of the underlying issue, which is how opposing scientific and Native American worldviews can be reconciled through negotiation.

Postprocessual archaeologists concerned with the political implications of research are working to develop a multitiered methodology that incorporates the use of several paradigms. Duke (43) suggested that reconstructing past events as well as processes allows Native Americans to use this knowledge in tandem with their own oral traditions to create a past relevant to themselves. However, postprocessual approaches create a "two-edged sword" in that they call for a renewed interest in Native American religion, power, authority structures, gender roles, and treatment of the dead at a time when many Native Americans are unsure whether these are appropriate research topics.

Zimmerman (155) and Anyon (10) consider the relation between concepts of time, politics, and archaeology in the construction of the past, noting that while archaeologists use time as a linear framework to give meaning to their observations, many Native Americans perceive time differently. For Native Americans, the past can and does exist in the present, and it can therefore be known through contemporary oral traditions, rituals, and spiritual activities

(39). Zimmerman (155) concluded that archaeologists don't have to give up their point of view but they do need to share with Native Americans the power archaeology can bring to constructing the past.

With respect to multiple pasts, Trigger (136) noted that the archaeological record constitutes evidence that was created independently of any archaeological interpretation. This independence constrains the subjectivity of archaeologists and facilitates the search for new data that can convince other people that a particular interpretation is correct. Archaeological data thus continue to play an important role in forcing people to revise their outmoded views about Native Americans. More archaeologists consider the study of Native American cultures to be a valid goal in itself, and the move toward more holistic investigations entails a closer working relationship with contemporary native peoples.

Archaeologists who recognize that many archaeological sites are also sacred places for Native Americans have addressed a number of issues, including who "owns" sacred sites, who has a right to study them, and how they should be managed (28). Research and management of sacred sites is difficult because many Native Americans think information about them should be kept secret, and decisions about their protection entail political issues about the power relations between dominant and indigenous cultures.

NATIVE AMERICAN PERSPECTIVES ON ARCHAEOLOGY AND THE PAST

Archaeology has benefited from what Native Americans and the archaeologists who work for them have written about the discipline. While most archaeologists firmly believe that archaeology is a beneficial activity, some Native Americans mistrust archaeology because of its historical association with the desecration of graves and removal of cultural property. Some Native Americans also take exception to archaeological theories that conflict with traditional history, such as the Bering land bridge migration and the conventional depiction of Native Americans primarily according to extinct lifeways, a convention that works to divorce contemporary people from their heritage (24, 36, 37).

Klesert & Holt (75), however, suggested that archaeologists may be overly cautious about what Native Americans think about archaeology. In a survey of 64 Indian tribes, Klesert & Holt found that more than half of the respondents considered archaeology to be beneficial because it helped to preserve Native American culture. Although some Indians thought archaeology stimulated interference and trespass by outsiders, the political leaders of tribes did not consider archaeology to be an impediment to their people or culture. It may be, as Reid (111) suggested, that many archaeologists think the rift between Native Americans and their discipline is larger than it really is.

Nevertheless, Deloria (35) noted that many Native Americans resent the attitude of some archaeologists who think they have a privileged view of the past because it is scientific and therefore superior to the traditional views of Native Americans. Many Native Americans have residual hard feelings that stem from the arrogant attitudes of archaeologists expressed during discussion of the reburial issue. Deloria suggested one way to improve the situation is for archaeologists and Native Americans to cooperate in reworking and restating the major findings of archaeology using plain language that eliminates cultural bias while accurately summarizing what is known.

Some Native Americans who were initially antagonistic toward archaeology report they now realize that working with archaeologists provides an effective means to attain legal and managerial goals relating to cultural resources management (60, 155). Other Native Americans report that they had little interest in archaeology until recently. The Inuit, for instance, gained an interest in archaeology when they realized it had utility for Canadian land claims, as well as an economic benefit related to tourism (8).

Many Native Americans in South America think archaeology is still used for colonialist ends that alienate them from their past by appropriating their archaeological heritage to construct national identities (31, 65, 83). Condori (31) added that the practice of renaming archaeological sites whose names have long been preserved in oral traditions is offensive because it dispossess Indians from their identity.

Condori (31) and Echo-Hawk (44) criticized the concept of "prehistory," noting that in popular usage this term implies that Native Americans have not maintained a legitimate form of history in their oral traditions, or worse, that Native Americans had no history at all until Europeans arrived in their land. This devalues Native American concepts of their own history and is perceived as an attempt by archaeologists to displace Native American historians as experts on the ancient past. In fact, Native American oral traditions provide a historiographic basis for historical thought and interpretation. Condori (31) thinks that the development of a Native American archaeology, using native concepts of time and space, has the potential to help Native Americans understand their historical development and thus attain their goals.

Rappaport (107) noted that traditional Native American knowledge about the past is sometimes embedded in a conceptual framework that is spatial rather than temporal. This is the case with the Páez Indians of Colombia, where historical knowledge is transmitted orally in fragments that allow listeners to construct a history based on their spatial knowledge of geographical referents. There is thus not one history but multiple histories.

Naranjo (98) pointed out that much of Native American traditional knowledge is axiomatic rather than hypothetical. Truth is something that is known within individuals and communities, not something external to a person as it is for most archaeologists. Truth is thus multiversal rather than universal, and one person's truth does not invalidate another's. In applying this perspective to the ancestral migration of Santa Clara Pueblo, Naranjo concluded it is the overall conceptual framework of movement that is the most important idea, not the specific sites, dates, and places that preoccupy the attention of archaeologists.

Riding In (112) provided a harsh critique of the history of archaeology as an imperialistic and racist endeavor, concluding that the reburial of Native American human remains is a fundamental human right that must take legal, moral, and ethical precedence over scientific research. While many archaeologists have come to agree with this basic position, Riding In extended the argument by suggesting that scholars should not use data obtained from "immoral" forms of archaeological inquiry, and most disturbingly, that universities and libraries should remove from circulation all works that contain references to "immoral" archeological research.

ETHICS AND GUIDELINES FOR RESEARCH

Ethics are the rules or standards of behavior that govern how a profession is practiced. The American Anthropological Association, the Society for American Archaeology, the American Society for Conservation Archaeology, the Society of Professional Archaeologists, the World Archaeological Congress, and various state associations have all promulgated ethical codes or position papers that relate to the conduct of archaeological research. These are reviewed in several publications (58, 76, 118, 143, 147, 148, 154). Although not specifically directed toward archaeologists, Mihesuah (96) provided a set of general guidelines useful for all scholars conducting research on Native Americans. Every archaeologist should review these ethical codes and implement them in archaeological research.

Archaeologists should consider the financial gain they earn from their work and share this with Native Americans as appropriate. The SAA dedicated the royalties from the three-volume *Columbian Consequences* series to a Native American Scholarship Fund (129), and other archaeologists are beginning to donate all or part of the royalties from their works to the tribes they study. An increasing number of Native Americans expect this sort of reciprocity (34).

Several archaeologists have observed that the current problems between Native Americans and archaeologists are due to cultural conflicts stemming from different systems of ethics (56, 57, 142). Recognizing that Native Americans have valid ethical principles that archaeologists need to consider does not mean that archaeologists should ignore their own system of ethics. Archaeologists have an ethical responsibility to their profession as well as to the people they study, and they need to be willing and able to explain their positions and research in dialog with Native Americans.

THE FUTURE OF ARCHAEOLOGICAL RESEARCH

Archaeologists and Native Americans are moving beyond the contentious rhetoric of the 1970s and 1980s. Together, they are forging new partnerships to change archaeology so it is more acceptable and relevant to the descendants of the people who produced the archaeological record many archaeologists study. People who espoused radical views on both sides of the repatriation issue have gravitated more toward a centrist position. This is good because in the post-NAGPRA era archaeologists will pay a severe price for not doing a better job of sharing their work with Native Americans (89).

Native Americans have diverse uses for archaeology. Some Native Americans find archaeology useful for learning about their past by using information that is not preserved in documentary records (106, 114, 131, 149, 152). Other Native Americans already know about their past through traditional means but still find a use for archaeology in managing their heritage resources (74). By establishing and building on cooperative relationships, archaeologists and Native Americans can be powerful allies in efforts to preserve archaeological resources from looting or development (30, 48, 100).

Archaeologists are realizing that the archaeological record has power in the present because it is used to construct knowledge of the past (87). Archaeologists are beginning to use their discipline to address issues that Native Americans identify as important, which adds a humanistic dimension to their scientific research and yields new ways to think about the past (155). It is now common for Native Americans to consult on archaeological and cultural resource management projects (17, 51, 126). Many archaeologists have committed themselves to developing long-term research projects with Native Americans, which creates a foundation for the mutual trust that is needed to make archaeological research work in a contemporary setting.

Universities are beginning to teach the ethics and broad anthropological skills that archaeologists need to successfully interact with Native Americans (87). Additional change is still needed in the profession. As Brumfiel (25) noted, the didactic generalization entailed in public education and Native American outreach is not as favorably judged by peers as theoretically oriented publications. The profession needs to develop ways to recognize and reward archaeologists who share the results of their work with Native Americans in meaningful ways.

Native Americans are stewards of the archaeological record because it is an ancestral legacy (48). Archaeologists are stewards because they want to protect and use the archaeological record as a source of scientific data. If Native Americans and archaeologists continue to develop a close working relationship, all parties will benefit from a joint stewardship of the archaeological record and the past it represents (56). Each archaeologist bears a personal and professional responsibility to understand and act on the issues relating to Native Americans to transform archaeology into a discipline that is acceptable to its multiple constituencies.

Any *Annual Review* chapter, as well as any article cited in an *Annual Review* chapter, may be purchased from the Annual Reviews Preprints and Reprints service. 1-800-347-8007; 415-259-5017; email: arpr@class.org

---

Literature Cited

1. Adams E. 1984. Archaeology and the Native American: a case at Hopi. See Ref. 58, pp. 236–42
2. Adams E. 1989. The Homol'ovi research program. *Kiva* 54:175–94
3. Adams R. 1974. Report of the secretary. *Am. Antiq.* 39:666–68
4. Adams R. 1984. Annual report of the president. *Am. Antiq.* 49:214–16
5. Afognak Native Corporation. 1995. "Light the Past, Spark the Future, Dig Afognak" program outline. Kodiak, AK: Afognak Native Corp.
6. Ahler J. 1994. The benefits of multicultural education for American Indian schools: an anthropological perspective. See Ref. 124, pp. 453–59
7. Allison J. 1995. Letter to the editor. *Cult. Resour. Manage.* 18(6):26–28
8. Anawak J. 1989. Inuit perceptions of the past. See Ref. 79, pp. 45–50
9. Anderson D, Finnegan M, Hotopp J, Fisher A. 1978. The Lewis Central School site (13PW5): a resolution of ideological conflicts at an Archaic ossuary in western Iowa. *Plains Anthropol.* 23:183–219
10. Anyon R. 1991. Protecting the past, protecting the present: cultural resources and American Indians. In *Protecting the Past,* ed. G Smith, J Ehrenhard, pp. 215–22. Boca Raton, FL: CRC Press
11. Anyon R, Ferguson T. 1995. Cultural resources management at the Pueblo of Zuni, New Mexico, USA. *Antiquity* 69:913–30
12. Anyon R, Zunie J. 1989. Cooperation at the Pueblo of Zuni: common ground for archaeology and tribal concerns. *Pract. Anthropol.* 11(3):13–16
13. Ayau E. 1992. Restoring the ancestral foundation of Native Hawaiians: implementation of the Native American Graves Protection and Repatriation Act. *Ariz. State Law J.* 24(1):193–216
14. Ayau E. 1995. Rooted in native soil. *Fed. Archeol. Rep.* 7(3):30–33
15. Barrios P. 1993. Native Americans and archaeologists working together toward common goals in California. *Soc. Am. Archaeol. Bull.* 11(3):6–7
16. Begay D. 1991. Navajo preservation: the success of the Navajo Nation historic preservation department. *Cult. Resour. Manage.* 14(4):1,3–4
17. Bielawksi E. 1989. Dual perceptions of the past: archaeology and Inuit culture. See Ref. 80, pp. 228–36
18. Blakeslee D. 1987. John Rowzée Peyton and the myth of the Mound Builders. *Am. Antiq.* 52:784–92
19. Blancke S, Slow Turtle C. 1990. The teaching of the past of the native peoples of North America in US schools. See Ref. 123, pp. 109–33
20. Blancke S, Slow Turtle C. 1994. Traditional American Indian education as a palliative to Western education. See Ref. 124, pp. 438–52
21. Bonnichsen R, Schneider AL. 1995. Roots. *Sciences* 35(3):26–31
22. Bray T, Killion T, eds. 1994. *Reckoning with the Dead: The Larson Bay Repatriation and the Smithsonian Institution.* Washington, DC: Smithson. Inst.
23. Brink J. 1992. Blackfoot and buffalo jumps: native people and the head-smashed-in project. In *Buffalo,* ed. J Foster, D Harrison, I MacLaren, pp. 19–43. Edmonton: Univ. Alberta Press
24. Brody H. 1981. *Maps and Dreams.* Harmondsworth: Penquin

25. Brumfiel E. 1994. Making history in Xal-tocan. *Soc. Am. Archaeol. Bull.* 12(4): 4–7,15

26. Buikstra JE. 1981. A specialist in ancient cemetery studies looks at the reburial issue. *Early Man* 3(3):26–27

27. Burney M. 1994. The emerging roles of American Indian consultation and coopera-tion in the management of cultural re-sources in Indian country. In *Proc. Rocky Mt. Symp. Environ. Issues Oil Gas Oper.: Soft Footprints for the 1990s,* ed. R Graves, J Rhett, pp. 139–55. Golden, CO: Colo. Sch. Mines

28. Carmichal D, Hubert J, Reeves B, Schanche A, eds. 1994. *Sacred Sites, Sa-cred Places.* London: Routledge

29. Chapman F. 1991. Native Americans and cultural resource management programs: the view from Wyoming. *Cult. Resour. Manage.* 15(4):19–21

30. Cheek A, Keel B. 1984. Value conflicts in osteoarchaeology. See Ref. 58, pp. 194–207

31. Condori C. 1989. History and prehistory in Bolivia: What about the Indians? See Ref. 80, pp. 46–59

32. Crozier S. 1991. Tribal cultural heritage programs in Alaska. *Cult. Resour. Manage.* 14(5):13–15

33. Deaver S, Tallbull B. 1988. Results: north-ern Cheyenne. In *Cultural Impacts to the Northern Cheyenne and Crow Tribes from Powder River I Federal Coal Leasing,* ed. S Deaver, pp. 20–38. Billings, MT: Eth-nosci. Bur. Land Manage.

34. Deloria V. 1991. Commentary: research, redskins, and reality. *Am. Indian Q.* 15: 457–69

35. Deloria V. 1992. Indians, archaeologists, and the future. *Am. Antiq.* 57:595–98

36. Devine H. 1991. The role of archaeology in teaching the native past: ideology or peda-gogy? *Can. J. Native Educ.* 18(1):11–22

37. Devine H. 1994. Archaeology, prehistory, and the native learning resources project: Alberta, Canada. See Ref. 124, pp. 478–94

38. Dincauze D. 1985. Report on the confer-ence on reburial issues. *Bull. Soc. Am. Ar-chaeol.* 3:1–3

39. Dongoske K, Jenkins L, Ferguson T. 1993. Understanding the past through Hopi oral tradition. *Native Peoples* 6(2):24–31

40. Downer A. 1990. Tribal sovereignty and historic preservation, Native American par-ticipation in cultural resource management on Indian lands. See Ref. 74, pp. 67–91

41. Downer A, Roberts A. 1993. Traditional cultural properties and consultation with traditional communities. *Cult. Resour. Manage.* 16:12–14

42. Downer A, Roberts A. 1996. The federal historic preservation program and the pres-ervation of tribal cultural resources: the Navajo experience. *Nat. Resour. Environ.* 10(3):39–42, 78–79

43. Duke P. 1995. Working through theoretical tensions in contemporary archaeology: a practical attempt from southwestern Colo-rado. *J. Archeol. Method Theory* 2:201–29

44. Echo-Hawk R. 1993. Exploring ancient worlds. *Soc. Am. Archaeol. Bull.* 11(4):5–6

45. Edmo J. 1972. The Bannock-Shoshone project. In *The American Indian Reader,* ed. J Henry, pp. 170–74. San Francisco: Indian Hist.

46. Emerson T, Cross P. 1990. The sociopoli-tics of the living and the dead: the treatment of historic and prehistoric remains in con-temporary midwest America. *Death Stud.* 14:555–76

47. Fagan B. 1984. Archaeology and the wider audience. See Ref. 58, pp. 175–83

48. Fagan B. 1995. Perhaps we may hear voices. In *Save the Past for the Future II,* pp. 25–30. Washington, DC: Soc. Am. Ar-chaeol.

49. Fawcett M. 1995. Shantok: a tale of two sites. *Cult. Resour. Manage.* 18(7):8–10

50. Ferguson T. 1984. Archaeological ethics and values in a tribal cultural resource man-agement program at the Pueblo of Zuni. See Ref. 58, pp. 224–35

51. Ferguson T, Dongoske K, Jenkins L, Yeatts M, Polingyouma E. 1993. Working to-gether: the roles of archeology and ethno-history in Hopi cultural preservation. *Cult. Resour. Manage.* 16:27–37

52. Ford R. 1973. Archaeology serving human-ity. In *Research and Theory in Current Archaeology,* ed. C Redman, pp. 83–93. New York: Wiley

53. Fowler D. 1986. Conserving American ar-chaeological resources. See Ref. 95, pp. 135–62

54. Fredin A. 1990. Colville confederated tribes. See Ref. 74, pp. 289–99

55. Friedman R. 1995. Return to Ozette. *Fed. Archeol. Rep.* 7(4):16–19

56. Goldstein L. 1992. The potential for future relationships between archaeologists and Native Americans. See Ref. 141, pp. 59–71

57. Goldstein L, Kintigh K. 1990. Ethics and the reburial controversy. *Am. Antiq.* 55: 585–91

58. Green E, ed. 1984. *Ethics and Values in Archaeology.* New York: Free Press

59. Gruber J. 1986. Archaeology, history, and culture. See Ref. 95, pp. 163–86

60. Hammil J, Cruz R. 1989. Statement of American Indians against desecration be-fore the world archaeological congress. See Ref. 80, pp. 46–59

61. Handsman R. 1989. Native Americans and an archaeology of living traditions. *Arti-facts* 17(2):3–5

62. Handsman R. 1989. *The Fort Hill Project, Native Americans in Western Connecticut and an Archaeology of Living Traditions.* Washington, CT: Res. Manuscr. Ser. Am. Indian Archaeol. Inst.

63. Handsman R. 1990. The Weantinock Indian homeland was not a "desert." *Artifacts* 18(2):3–7

64. Herrman N, Ogilvie M, Hilton C, Brown K. 1993. *Across the Colorado Plateau: Anthropological Studies for the Transwestern Pipeline Expansion Project,* Vol. 27, *Human Remains and Burial Goods.* Albuquerque: Off. Contract Archeol. Maxwell Mus. Anthropol. Univ. N. M.

65. Holland L. 1990. Whispers from the forest: the excluded past of the Aché Indians of Paraguay. See Ref. 123, pp. 134–51

66. Holt B. 1990. Tribal sovereignty over archaeology, a practical and legal fact. See Ref. 74, pp. 9–14

67. Hubert J. 1989. A proper place for the dead: a critical review of the 'reburial' issue. See Ref. 80, pp. 131–66

68. Jamieson J. 1994. One view of native education in the Northwest Territories, Canada. See Ref. 124, pp. 495–510

69. Johnson B. 1977. The cultural and ethical aspects of archaeology in Canada: an Indian point of view. In *New Perspectives in Canadian Archaeology,* ed. A McKay, pp. 173–75. Ottawa: R. Soc. Can.

70. Johnson E. 1973. Professional responsibilities and the American Indian. *Am. Antiq.* 38:129–30

71. Johnson J. 1993. In search of a legacy. *Fed. Archeol. Rep.* 5(2):3–4

72. Klesert A. 1992. A view from Navajoland on the reconciliation of anthropologists and Native Americans. *Hum. Organ.* 51(2): 17–22

73. Klesert A, Andrews M. 1988. The treatment of human remains on Navajo lands. *Am. Antiq.* 53:310–20

74. Klesert A, Downer A, eds. 1990. *Preservation on the Reservation, Native Americans, Native American Lands, and Archaeology.* Navajo Nation Pap. Anthropol. 26. Window Rock, AZ: Navajo Nation Archaeol. Dept. Navajo Nation Hist. Preserv. Dept.

75. Klesert A, Holt H. 1990. Archaeology and the contemporary American Indian. See Ref. 74, pp. 247–64

76. Klesert A, Powell S. 1993. A perspective on ethics and the reburial controversy. *Am. Antiq.* 58(2):348–54

77. Knudson R. 1986. Contemporary cultural resource management. See Ref. 95, pp. 395–414

78. Knudson R, Keel B, eds. 1995. *The Public Trust and the First Americans.* Corvallis: Or. State Univ. Press

79. Layton R, ed. 1989. *Who Needs the Past?*

Indigenous Values and Archaeology. London: Unwin Hyman

80. Layton R, ed. 1989. *Conflict in the Archaeology of Living Traditions.* London: Unwin Hyman

81. Lekson S. 1988. The idea of the kiva in Anasazi archaeology. *Kiva* 53:213–34

82. Leone M, Preucel R. 1992. Archaeology in a democratic society: a critical theory perspective. See Ref. 141, pp. 115–35

83. Males A. 1989. Past and present of Andean Indian society: the Otavalos. See Ref. 79, pp. 95–104

84. McBride K. 1995. CRM and Native Americans, an example from the Mashantucket Pequot reservation. *Cult. Resour. Manage.* 18(3):15–17

85. McGimsey C, Davis H. 1977. *The Management of Archeological Resources, The Airlie House Report.* Washington, DC: Soc. Am. Archaeol.

86. McGuire R. 1989. The sanctity of the grave: white concepts and American Indian burials. See Ref. 80, pp. 167–84

87. McGuire R. 1992. Archeology and the first Americans. *Am. Anthropol.* 94:816–36

88. McGuire R. 1995. Working together on the border. *Soc. Am. Archaeol. Bull.* 13(5):8–9

89. McManamon F. 1991. The many public faces of archaeology. *Am. Antiq.* 56:121–30

90. McManamon F. 1994. Changing relationships between Native Americans and archaeologists. *Hist. Preserv. Forum* 81(2): 15–19

91. McManamon F. 1994. Presenting archaeology to the public in the USA. See Ref. 124, pp. 61–81

92. Meighan C. 1984. Archaeology: science or sacrilege? See Ref. 58, pp. 208–23

93. Meighan C. 1992. Some scholars' views on reburial. *Am. Antiq.* 57:704–10

94. Meighan C. 1995. Burying American archaeology. *Archaeology* 47(6):64,66,68

95. Meltzer D, Fowler D, Sabloff J, eds. 1986. *American Archaeology Past and Future: A Celebration of the Society for American Archaeology, 1935–1985.* Washington, DC: Smithson. Inst.

96. Mihesuah D. 1993. Suggested guidelines for institutions with scholars who conduct research on American Indians. *Am. Indian Cult. Res. J.* 17(3):131–39

97. Moore S. 1989. Federal Indian burial policy: historical anachronism or contemporary reality? See Ref. 80, pp. 200–10

98. Naranjo T. 1995. Thoughts on migration by Santa Clara Pueblo. *J. Anthropol. Res.* 14: 247–50

99. National Park Service. 1990. *Keepers of the Treasures: Protecting Historical Properties and Cultural Traditions on Indian Lands.* Washington, DC: Gov. Print. Off.

100. Nichols D, Klesert A, Anyon R. 1989. An-

cestral sites, shrines, and graves: Native American perspectives on the ethics of collecting cultural properties. In *The Ethics of Collecting Cultural Property: Whose Culture? Whose Property?* ed. P Messenger, pp. 25–38. Albuquerque: Univ. N. M. Press

101. Othole A, Anyon R. 1993. A tribal perspective on traditional cultural property consultation. *Cult. Resour. Manage.* 16:42–45

102. Patterson T. 1986. The last sixty years: toward a social history of Americanist archeology in the United States. *Am. Anthropol.* 88:7–26

103. Powell S, Garza C, Hendricks A. 1993. Ethics and ownership of the past, the reburial and repatriation controversy. In *Archaeological Method and Theory,* ed. M Schiffer, 5:1–42. Tucson: Univ. Ariz. Press

104. Price H. 1991. *Disputing the Dead, U. S. Law on Aboriginal Remains and Grave Goods.* Columbia: Univ. Mo. Press

105. Pullar G. 1990. The Kodiak Island archaeological project. See Ref. 74, pp. 269–74

106. Purdy B. 1988. American Indians after A. D. 1492: a case study of forced culture change. *Am. Anthropol.* 90:640–55

107. Rappaport J. 1989. Geography and historical understanding in indigenous Columbia. See Ref. 79, pp. 84–94

108. Ravesloot J. 1990. On the treatment and reburial of human remains: The San Xaxier Bridge project. *Am. Ind. Q.* 14(1):35–50

109. Ravesloot J. 1995. The road to common ground. *Fed. Archeol. Rep.* 7(3):36–40

110. Reid J. 1992. Editors corner: recent findings on North American prehistory. *Am. Antiq.* 57:195–96

111. Reid J. 1992. Editors corner: quincentennial truths and consequences. *Am. Antiq.* 57:583

112. Riding In J. 1992. Without ethics and morality: a historical overview of imperial archaeology and American Indians. *Ariz. State Law J.* 24(1):11–34

113. Rosen L. 1980. The excavation of American Indian burial sites: a problem in law and professional responsibility. *Am. Anthropol.* 82(1):5–27

114. Rubertone P. 1989. Archaeology, colonialism and 17th-century native America: towards an alternative interpretation. See Ref. 80, pp. 32–45

115. Schaaf J. 1992. The shared Beringian heritage program. *Fed. Archeol. Rep.* 5(2): 1,4–5

116. Schwab D. 1993. Continuing cooperation between archaeologists and Native Americans in Montana. *Soc. Am. Archaeol. Bull.* 11(5):5–6

117. Society for American Archaeology. 1995. *Final Report on the Native American/SAA Relations Task Force.* Washington, DC: Soc. Am. Archaeol.

118. Society of Professional Archaeologists. 1981. Code of ethics and standards of performance. In *Directory of Professional Archaeologists,* pp. 3–6. St. Louis, MO: Soc. Prof. Archaeol.

119. Spector J. 1994. Collaboration at *Inyan Ceyaka Atonwan* (Village of the Rapids). *Soc. Am. Archaeol. Bull.* 12(3):8–10

120. Sprague R. 1974. American Indians and American archaeology. *Am. Antiq.* 39(1): 1–2

121. Spriggs M. 1990. God's police and damned whores: images of archaeology in Hawaii. In *The Politics of the Past,* ed. P Gathercole, D Lowenthal, pp. 118–29. London: Unwin Hyman

122. Spurr K. 1993. *NAGPRA and Archaeology on Black Mesa, Arizona.* Navajo Nation Pap. Anthropol. 30. Window Rock, AZ: Navajo Nation Archaeol. Dept.

123. Stone P, Mackenzie R, eds. 1990. *The Excluded Past: Archaeology in Education.* London: Unwin Hyman

124. Stone P, Molyneaux B, eds. 1994. *The Presented Past, Heritage, Museums, and Education.* London: Routledge

125. Stumpf G. 1992. A federal land management perspective on repatriation. *Ariz. State Law J.* 24(1):303–20

126. Sullivan A, Hanson A, Hawkins R. 1994. Active anthropological archeology. *Cult. Resour. Manage.* 17(9):30–31

127. Swinton G. 1977. Archaeology as a concern of the Inuit community. In *New Perspectives in Canadian Archaeology,* ed. A McKay, pp. 163–71. Ottawa: R. Soc. Can.

128. Talmage V. 1982. The violation of sepulture: Is it legal to excavate human burials? *Archaeology* 35(6):11–49

129. Thomas D. 1992. A retrospective look at *Columbian Consequences. Am. Antiq.* 57: 613–16

130. Tippitt V, Haire W. 1993. Tradition and innovation: preserving the Catawba's cultural heritage. *Fed. Archeol. Rep.* 6(2): 1,6–7

131. Trigger B. 1980. Archaeology and the image of the American Indian. *Am. Antiq.* 45:662–76

132. Trigger B. 1984. Alternative archaeologies: nationalist, colonialist, and imperialist. *Man* 19:355–70

133. Trigger B. 1985. The past as power: anthropology and the North American Indian. In *Who Owns the Past?* ed. I McBryde, pp. 49–74. Oxford: Oxford Univ. Press

134. Trigger B. 1986. Prehistoric archaeology and American society. See Ref. 95, pp. 187–216

135. Trigger B. 1989. *A History of Archaeological Thought.* Cambridge: Cambridge Univ. Press

136. Trigger B. 1990. The 1990s: North Ameri-

can archaeology with a human face? *Antiquity* 64:778–87

137. Trope J, Echo-Hawk W. 1992. The Native American graves protection and repatriation act: background and legislative history. *Ariz. State Law J.* 24(1):35–77

138. Turner E. 1989. The souls of my dead brothers. See Ref. 80, pp. 189–94

139. Two Bears D. 1995. A Navajo student's perception: anthropology and the Navajo Nation archaeology department student training program. *Soc. Am. Archaeol. Bull.* 13(1):4–6

140. Ubelaker D, Grant L. 1989. Human skeletal remains: preservation or reburial? *Yearb. Phys. Anthropol.* 32:249–87

141. Wandsnider L, ed. 1992. *Quandaries and Quests: Visions of Archaeology's Future.* Cent. Archaeol. Invest. Occas. Pap. 20. Carbondale: South. Ill. Univ.

142. Watkins J. 1994. *Ethics and value conflicts: analysis of archeologists' responses to questionnaire scenarios concerning the relationship between American Indians and archaeologists.* PhD thesis. South. Methodist Univ., Dallas

143. Watkins J, Goldstein L, Vitelli K, Jenkins L. 1995. Accountability: responsibilities of archeologists to other interest groups. In *Ethics in American Archaeology: Challenges for the 1990s,* ed. M Lynott, A Wylie, pp. 33–37. Washington, DC: Soc. Am. Archaeol.

144. Wilk R. 1985. The ancient Maya and the political present. *J. Anthropol. Res.* 41: 307–26

145. Willey G, Sabloff J. 1980. *A History of American Archaeology.* London: Thames & Hudson

146. Winter J. 1980. Indian heritage preservation and archaeologists. *Am. Antiq.* 45: 121–31

147. Wood J, Powell S. 1993. An ethos for archaeological practice. *Hum. Organ.* 52: 405–13

148. World Archaeological Congress. 1991. World Archaeological Congress first code of ethics (members' obligations to indigenous peoples). *World Archaeol. Congr. Bull.* 5:22–23

149. Wylie A. 1992. Rethinking the quincentennial: consequences for past and present. *Am. Antiq.* 57:591–94

150. Yalung C, Wala L. 1992. A survey of state repatriation and burial protection statutes. *Ariz. State Law J.* 24(1):419–33

151. Zimmer J, Wilk R, Pybum A. 1995. A survey of attitudes and values in archaeological practice. *Soc. Am. Archaeol. Bull.* 13(5): 10–12

156. Zimmerman L, Alex R. 1981. Digging ancient burials: the Crow Creek experience. *Early Man* 3(3):3–6,8–10

152. Zimmerman L. 1989. Made radical by my own. See Ref. 80, pp. 60–67

153. Zimmerman L. 1989. Human bones as symbols of power: aboriginal American belief systems towards bones and "grave-robbing" archaeologists. See Ref. 80, pp. 211–16

154. Zimmerman L. 1992. Archaeology, reburial, and a discipline's self-delusion. *Am. Indian Cult. Res. J.* 16(2):37–56

155. Zimmerman L. 1995. We do not need your past: politics, Indian time and plains archaeology. In *Beyond Subsistence: Plains Archaeology and the Postprocessual Critique,* ed. P Duke, M Wilson, pp. 28–45. Tuscaloosa: Univ. Ala. Press

Annu. Rev. Anthropol. 1996. 25:81–103

NAGPRA IS FOREVER: Osteology and the Repatriation of Skeletons

Jerome C. Rose,[1] Thomas J. Green,[2] and Victoria D. Green[3]

[1]Department of Anthropology, University of Arkansas, Fayetteville, Arkansas 72701
[2]Arkansas Archeological Survey, University of Arkansas, Fayetteville, Arkansas 72701
[3]Geo-Marine, Inc., 550 East Fifteenth Street, Plano, Texas 75074

KEY WORDS: bioarcheology, Native Americans, federal regulations, reburial, skeletons

ABSTRACT

The 1990 Native American Graves Protection and Repatriation Act requires universities, museums, and federal agencies to inventory their archeological collections to prepare for the repatriation of skeletons to their Native American descendants. The loss of these collections will be a detriment to the study of North American osteology, but the inventory and repatriation process has increased the number of skeletons studied from about 30% to nearly 100%. The availability of funds stimulated by this law produced osteological data collection and systematization unprecedented in the history of osteology. The possibility of forming partnerships between Native Americans and osteologists has the potential of producing a vibrant future for North American osteology and the new bioarcheology.

INTRODUCTION

In 1971, archeologists excavating near Glenwood, Iowa, decided to rebury 26 European American skeletons and curate two Native American skeletons in a local museum (61). The Native American community was upset. Subsequently, confrontations between Native Americans and archeologists in Iowa, California, and the Dakotas contributed to the formation of several organizations such as American Indians Against Desecration and the Native American Rights Fund, among others. Two decades of lobbying efforts by Native American groups resulted in passage of the Native American Graves Protection and Repatriation Act (NAGPRA) in 1990 (PL 101-601). This fed-

0084-6570/96/1015-0081$08.00

eral legislation propelled the archeological and museum professions into a national inventory process to prepare vast collections of Native American skeletons and specific types of cultural items for repatriation.

The passage of NAGPRA has ushered in a period of change and uncertainty for scholars who study human skeletal remains, namely osteologists (bone experts) and bioarcheologists (those who study adaptation through bones—see below). The new law raises important questions. Does NAGPRA and the ongoing process of repatriation and reburial ring the death knell for bioarcheology as a research paradigm and profession? Will we lose the capability of discerning, for instance, the reasons for the development of agriculture and its impact upon the health and longevity of the adopting populations? The answer to these questions is no. On the contrary, NAGPRA will allow bioarcheology to emerge as a vigorous and possibly more publicly relevant and responsible profession. What we must understand is that NAGPRA is not an event. There is no post-NAGPRA. "NAGPRA is forever" (MK Trimble, personal communication).

To establish this conclusion we examine the condition or quality of osteology and bioarcheology before NAGPRA. To understand NAGPRA we must know where skeletons came from, how many there are, and what osteologists have been doing with them. After this brief history we describe the most salient portions of the law. Finally, we describe the ongoing NAGPRA compliance efforts and attempt to predict the future of North American bioarcheology.

OSTEOLOGY BEFORE NAGPRA

Origin of the Skeletons

Nineteenth- and early twentieth-century archeological excavations are the foundation of the large museum skeleton collections of today. For example, CB Moore, sponsored by the Philadelphia Academy of Science, cruised the southeastern rivers on his steamboat excavating hundreds of large mortuary sites to obtain museum-quality artifacts. He succeeded in collecting 12 skulls and a number of pathological bones from the 1908 excavation of two sites along the Arkansas River. The skulls were sent to Aleš Hrdlička at the US National Museum (Smithsonian Institution), and the pathological specimens were sent to the US Army Medical Museum (Armed Forces Institute of Pathology). The bones were analyzed and a report included as an appendix in CB Moore's (36) publication of his excavations. So begins the history of bioarcheology in the state of Arkansas.

Simply by changing names and dates in this story one can describe the early history of osteology anywhere in the United States (2, 10, 60). In most cases, archeologists simply selected some of the skeletal material for shipment to museums, while in other cases osteologists requested the skeletons for use in teaching and research, as did Samuel Morton in the mid-nineteenth century (13). In Arkansas and Louisiana, 41.6% of the 4759 documented skeletons were collected between 1880 and 1919 (51).

The history of archeology and osteology elsewhere is the same as it is in North America. In Egypt, Flinders Petrie excavated hundreds of tombs during most field seasons at the turn of the century, keeping only some of the skulls for craniometric analysis. When the statistician Karl Pearson needed skulls for his mathematical treatment of evolution (43), Petrie, his next door neighbor, excavated several hundred from the Giza plateau adjacent to the pyramids (17).

The Great Depression contributed significantly to the collection of human osteological remains. Works Progress Administration (WPA) funds were used to hire unemployed archeologists and local laborers to excavate on a "heroic" scale (24, 50). Thousands of human skeletons were excavated from hundreds of mortuary sites. In Arkansas and Louisiana, for example, 22.2% of the excavated skeletons were acquired during the Depression (51). Few osteological analyses were conducted by WPA personnel. A rare example is Goldstein's (21) publication on cranial deformation in the *American Journal of Physical Anthropology*.

After World War II, the military engaged in massive flood-control projects. Salvage excavations organized as River Basin Survey projects (Inter-Agency Archaeological Salvage Program) produced thousands of skeletons—23.4% of the Arkansas and Louisiana collections (49–51). William Bass was hired by the River Basin Survey to study the Missouri River skeletons (4), which began the long-term Plains osteology studies by Bass and his students at the Universities of Kansas and Tennessee that continue to this day [for a review, see Bass (5)].

There was an almost seamless transition of personnel and activities from reservoir salvage to highway salvage excavations needed to build the interstate system conceived by the Eisenhower administration, which was eventually funded with passage in 1966 of PL 89-670, or the Department of Transportation Act (19). The highway salvage programs provided the context for development of national conservation legislation, modern cultural resource management (CRM) practices (19), and continued growth of skeletal collections. At this time, professional archeologists were also excavating skeletons as part of their academic research, but the number of skeletons they produced is dwarfed by the number excavated in the federally funded projects.

Although most archeology involved Native American skeletons, those of other peoples were not neglected. Shapiro's (55) excavation and analysis of "Old New Yorkers," whose cemetery was being destroyed by subway construction, is just one example (see 41). Historic cemetery excavations increased after publication of the June 1982 *National Register,* which clarified the status of historic cemeteries within CRM procedures (33). Analysis of historic skeletons and cemeteries has been prolific during the past two decades (22, 41, 52).

Number of Skeletons Excavated

We will probably never know precisely how many skeletons have been excavated by archeologists, and we will almost certainly never know the number of graves opened by looters and "pot hunters," which may number two, three, or more times those excavated by archeologists. However, the number of excavated skeletons can be estimated from an archeological and bioarcheological overview conducted for the Southwestern Division of the US Army Corps of Engineers (referred to here as the southern overview) that covers Arkansas, Louisiana, Texas, Oklahoma, New Mexico, and portions of Missouri, Kansas, and Colorado (1). In 1988, when data collection for the overview ceased, 142,202 archeological sites were reported, of which 2205 had produced 26,823 individual human skeletons. An ongoing overview funded by the Department of Defense Legacy Program and conducted by the Arkansas Archeological Survey (referred to here as the northern overview) covers Wisconsin, Iowa, Missouri, North Dakota, South Dakota, Nebraska, Kansas, Montana, Wyoming, and the portion of Colorado not covered in the previous overview. A total of 2919 mortuary sites have been identified to date by the overview and have produced 25,717 skeletons. Although the vast majority of the skeletons are Native American, those of European, African, and Asian descent are well represented.

In summary, between the Mississippi River and the Continental Divide and the Canadian and Mexican borders, 5124 excavated mortuary sites have so far produced the remains of 52,540 individuals. Until overviews are conducted of the remaining 45% of the continental United States we do not have comprehensive figures for total excavated skeletons. Because these are conservative figures and only report clearly identified skeletons, the total number of individuals actually excavated is certainly larger, and the total for the United States will probably be more than four times larger.

Number of Skeletons Curated

According to a questionnaire survey conducted by El-Najjar (18), museum skeleton collections include 14,150 Native American skeletons from the continental United States. A comparison of El-Najjar's (18) figures with those in the two overviews shows that only 7.8% (4124) are in museums. We know this inventory is incomplete, but it is the only one extant. There are many estimates, e.g. 600,000 curated skeletons (66), but none are based on inventories. We will know the total number of curated Native American skeletons in three to five years when the results of the NAGPRA compliance inventories are definitively tallied.

Progress in Osteological Research

Archeologists have spent more than a century accumulating skeletal remains because they were an important source of knowledge, and osteologists have been busy studying what they have found. The full history of osteological and paleopathological research has been discussed elsewhere (2, 10, 12, 29, 60), but a couple of recent retrospective studies provide revealing evidence of its impact. Lovejoy et al (34) performed a content analysis of the *American Journal of Physical Anthropology* published between 1930 and 1980 and reported that 44.4% of the 2239 articles therein concern osteology. The percentages vary little over time and range between 33.7% and 51.3% by decade.

Buikstra & Gordon (13) performed a content analysis of *American Journal of Physical Anthropology*, *American Antiquity*, and *Human Biology* between 1950 and 1980 to establish the importance of curated skeletal collections for research. They noted that skeletons collected before 1930 were used more during the 1970s than in the past and that older skeletal series appear to be just as useful for technical research as those collected more recently. They also reported that 32% of the analyses went back to skeletal collections that had already been studied, and that in 62% of these cases the investigators reached new or different conclusions from those previously published. 25.8% of the studies employed new techniques unavailable when the skeletons were excavated.

These two studies clearly demonstrate four important points: (*a*) osteology is a popular research endeavor; (*b*) skeleton collections have contributed significantly to the total research effort of biological anthropologists; (*c*) skeleton collections have current research value regardless of excavation date; and (*d*) skeleton collections are repeatedly restudied, especially when new techniques become available.

Modern bioarcheology, a new subfield derived from these earlier osteological efforts, is concerned with reconstructing dietary and activity patterns, estimating genetic affiliation, and employing demography and paleopathology to evaluate the adaptive success of particular cultures to their environments. It builds specifically on two other research paradigms, paleoepidemiology and paleodemography, each with its own relatively recent origins. Paleoepidemiology arose from the slow transformation of paleopathology from a descriptive to an analytical orientation. A critical event was the paleopathology conference convened on January 14, 1965 by Jarcho (29), where the idea to use the frequency of pathological lesions in skeletal samples to infer the degree of adaptive success was discussed (for bibliography, see 12). Interpretive analysis of demographic data had an early beginning, but its widespread integration into archeological and osteological research stems from a 1973 *Society for American Archaeology Memoir* by Weiss (64) and a later memoir edited by Swedlund (56).

Bioarcheology itself began with a key symposium of the 1976 annual meeting of the Southern Anthropological Society, at which the importance of regional research designs and area studies, ecology- and population-based research, and most importantly the collaborative development of research designs by osteologists and archeologists was espoused (6). Transformed from a descriptive endeavor, osteology hereby joined the rest of biological anthropology in adopting an evolutionary framework. An evaluation almost 13 years after the 1976 conference indicated an increase in successful collaborations between archeologists and bioarcheologists (11).

Bioarcheology has made significant progress in producing so-called processual research. In fact, the literature has exploded. Researchers have used skeletal data to explore such fundamental research questions as the origins of agriculture (16) and the impact of European conquest upon Native Americans (32, 63). Regional syntheses of skeletal data are being produced, such as *Skeletal Biology in the Great Plains* (42). Edited monographs detailing new osteological methodologies are rapidly emerging (20, 28, 53, 65, to list just a few).

Quality of Osteological Research

Any examination of the quality of osteological research by individual researchers shows it to be very good, especially with theoretically important issues. Individual researchers select a problem, set up testable hypotheses, select suitable skeletal samples, and then design data collection protocols for hypothesis testing (2, 12, 13, 60).

However, a quality examination from a regional perspective yields entirely different conclusions. In particular, we mean an examination of our knowledge base for all time periods, cultures, and ecological zones within a particular region such as the Lower Mississippi Valley, without regard to specific research paradigms and investigators. The southern overview (exclusive of New Mexico) indicates that 20,947 skeletons were excavated but that 64% have not been studied even to determine age and sex. Of 10,896 skeletons from Arkansas and Louisiana, 70.3% of the skeletons have not been analyzed at all, only 23.4% have been analyzed beyond age and sex, and even then the data usually consist only of gross pathological lesion descriptions. This record is poor and clearly indicates that our bioarcheological knowledge of these states is deficient.

Owing to lack of time and funds, many skeletons in the southern overview remain unstudied. Funding agencies, including those available in the CRM process, did provide resources for excavation, but they expected that anthropology students would analyze the skeletons for theses and dissertations. Some of this did occur, but there were never enough students to keep up with the huge quantity of curated skeletons. To show how extensive osteological analyses can be, the approximately 1050 skeletons excavated from the Dickson Mounds site located in Fulton County, Illinois, have been the subject of at least 57 theses, dissertations, meeting papers, and publications (14).

In the northern overview area the situation is slightly better: Only 37.3% of the 25,717 skeletons have ever been analyzed. When examined by state the percentages of analyzed skeletons range from 16.4% in Missouri to 97.9% for Iowa, which has the oldest state reburial law. These data are complete up to early 1995 and clearly reflect the ongoing analyses associated with the earliest phases of the repatriation movement.

Switching from numbers of skeletons to the bioarcheological history of specific regions, we find additional problems. Two bioarcheological overviews of the Mississippi Valley in the states of Missouri, Arkansas, and Louisiana (24, 39) reveal large gaps in our knowledge of the temporal trends. Certain sites were never excavated because skeletal preservation was poor, the culture was considered impoverished, or the artifacts were too mundane (37, 38). In addition, many skeletons were never included in problem-oriented osteological research. Today, analysis of biocultural processes—such as infectious-disease trends with the adoption of agriculture—is often impossible because osteological data sets and scoring methodologies differ from study to study. Sometimes the number of skeletons examined was simply not recorded, so that rates cannot be calculated. At other times, two, three, or more data-recording protocols were used by different investigators. Thus, even when the skeletons were analyzed, the data could not be used to compare skeletal series with one another.

Ethics of Osteology

Osteological research has mostly been ethical, and there is no difference in the treatment of prehistoric skeletons and modern forensic or medico-legal analyses. However, treatment of skeletons is not always controlled during and after excavation. Treatment is often determined by archeological customs, museum or repository policies, various state and national laws, and even the whims of politicians.

Western bioarcheologists cite numerous advances in knowledge obtained from the study of human remains and claim that this knowledge is useful and beneficial to the living, especially Native Americans (7, 30, 61). However, bioarcheology, like all other academic research, is driven by the pursuit of knowledge and truth for its own sake. Recent years have seen the advent of rules and regulations about the use of human beings and other organisms in research that require all research proposals to be examined by review committees. It has also been argued that anthropologists must conduct their activities within the best interests and beliefs of those under study and that this ethic should be extended to past cultures and the ancient deceased (for discussion and references, see 30).

Control of the historical record is an important component of the political process and though hard to understand at first glance, the dead can be used to harm the living. At present, bioarcheologists control the record of biological history of Native Americans. Meanwhile, some Native Americans contend that their oral histories contain all the relevant knowledge of their past and that they do not need the information provided by skeletal analysis (61). This situation might change on both sides if Native Americans were able to participate in the design and content of research (see also accompanying chapter by TJ Ferguson, this volume).

NAGPRA: THE LAW

History of Repatriation Legislation

On November 16, 1990, George Bush signed the Native American Graves Protection and Repatriation Act, the culmination of over two decades of lobbying effort by Native American groups for the return of human remains and objects of cultural and religious significance. This event was preceded by numerous state laws and considerable federal activity (58, 61, 66).

As Native Americans' lobbying efforts for repatriation of skeletal remains increased, many states enacted laws that included protection for unmarked grave sites. These laws afforded prehistoric graves protection similar to the type granted to marked cemeteries. In general, state unmarked-burial laws created guidelines to be followed when burial sites were discovered and further disturbance was required by construction. Permit systems and burial boards were established to notify and involve Native American descendants in the disposition of the human remains and grave goods from burial sites. In almost every state, reburial laws pertained to current or future excavations (61). Several states recently extended these laws to include repatriation of previously excavated skeletons. An example of this is Nebraska's 1989 Unmarked Human Burial Sites and Skeletal Remains Protection Act, which requires state-recognized museums to repatriate, upon request, reasonably identifiable human remains and grave goods to the related tribes (58, see also 45).

In 1987, public reporting of the many Native American remains held at the Smithsonian Institution served as a catalyst for passage of federal repatriation legislation (27). Hearings held by the Select Committee on Indian Affairs revealed that 42.5% of the 34,000 human remains at the Smithsonian are of Native American ancestry, and an additional 11.9% are individuals of Aleut, Eskimo, or Koniag heritage (27). A year later, testimony heard by the Select Committee on Indian Affairs concerning Senate Bill 187 prompted a decision to create a discussion forum for Native American representatives, museums, and scientific communities concerning the appropriate disposition and treatment of human remains and cultural artifacts (58). A year-long dialogue in 1989, hosted by the Heard Museum in Arizona, resulted in the drafting of recommendations for the Select Committee that included a call for developing "judicially-enforceable standards for repatriation" and repatriation policies.

Also in 1989, Senator Inouye of Hawaii introduced Senate Bill 978, The National Museum of the American Indian Act, which addresses the proper treatment and repatriation process for human remains and funerary objects at the Smithsonian Institution. The substance of PL 101-185, signed November 21, 1989, was combined with recommendations from the Panel for a National Dialogue on Museum/Native American Relations to become the framework for the Native American Graves Protection and Repatriation Act. This law effectively extended the provisions of the National Museum of the American Indian Act to include all federal agencies and other institutions receiving federal funds.

NAGPRA: Requirements of the Law

NAGPRA extends to Native American and Native Hawaiian graves of any age the general principles of American common law, namely, that human remains do not belong to individuals or to governmental or institutional organizations and that artifacts placed in human graves as funerary offerings belong to the deceased (66). Following American common law, NAGPRA asserts that descendants have the right to determine the disposition of the human remains and associated funerary objects (66) and hence can claim custody of these items. Because of the sanctity of private property in the United States, the law applies only to Native American and Hawaiian skeletons and funerary objects excavated on federal and tribal land or currently housed in museums that receive federal money. It does not apply to private collections. Following the NAGPRA implementing regulations (62), 43 CFR Part 10, all institutions with Native American skeletons and funerary objects that receive federal funds or are part of an institution receiving federal funds are considered museums. This definition includes all universities in the United States and all state and local governmental museums.

NAGPRA does not prohibit archeological excavation of or scientific research on Native American skeletons. NAGPRA does require, as well as do the 1992 amendments to the National Historic Preservation Act of 1966 and many state grave protection laws, consultation with Native Americans concerning the excavation, treatment, and disposition of Native American skeletons. Through the consultation process, agreements concerning scientific analysis can be reached. Many tribes and Native Hawaiian organizations will prohibit and have prohibited any scientific research on skeletons (3), but many have also consented (8). Osteologists seeking permission to conduct scientific research on Native American skeletons must now follow procedures analogous to those required of biologists and social scientists conducting human-subject research in a university setting (i.e. review by committee) and show evidence of consent by the descendants of the skeletal populations they wish to study.

NAGPRA does not require the reburial of Native American or Hawaiian skeletons, although reburial is the expected outcome of the repatriation process by most tribes.

Because the descendants have the right to determine treatment and disposition of Native American skeletons and cultural items, NAGPRA sets forth detailed procedures to determine custody of these items. Determining which tribe (the National Park Service compiled a list of 759 Native American tribes, Native Alaskan entities, and Native Hawaiian organizations) is the appropriate custodian of any human remains and cultural items recovered from federal or tribal land is no easy task. The law, however, does provide criteria to aid in this determination. Direct lineal descendants are given first priority. If a skeleton is found on tribal land and lineal descendants cannot be found, then the tribe receives custody. If a skeleton is found on federal land and lineal descendants cannot be found, then the tribe with the closest cultural affiliation assumes custody. If cultural affiliation cannot be determined and if the human remains were discovered inadvertently—that is, accidentally through construction or by exposure by natural forces—on federal land, and if the federal land was determined by the Indian Claims Commission to be the aboriginal land of a particular tribe, then that aboriginal tribe has custody, unless another tribe can demonstrate a stronger cultural relationship with the human remains. This last section applies only to inadvertent discoveries; lineal descendants or cultural affiliation is used to assign custody for intentional excavations.

The law and the implementing regulations also specify a process to determine which tribe should have custody of existing skeletal collections and cultural items now housed in museums and federal agency repositories. All federal agencies and museums must prepare a detailed inventory listing each and all human remains and associated artifacts curated by an institution. This inventory was due November 16, 1995. This report is to be submitted to lineal descendants, if known, and to tribes thought to be culturally affiliated with any of the human remains. If any of the human remains, funerary objects, sacred objects, or objects of cultural patrimony are claimed by lineal descendants or culturally affiliated tribes, the law prescribes a very detailed repatriation process including notification of the Departmental Consulting Archeologist in the Department of Interior and publication of intent to repatriate in the Federal Register (for examples, see 40). After the notification procedures are completed, repatriation can proceed.

The determination of which tribe or tribes are culturally affiliated with the skeletal remains and associated artifacts is the most difficult problem for both institutions and tribes. Cultural affiliation is defined in the regulations as "a relationship of shared group identity which can reasonably be traced historically or prehistorically between members of a present-day Indian tribe or Native Hawaiian organization and an identifiable earlier group" (62). Evidence for this relationship can be based on geography, kinship, biology (osteology), archeology, linguistics, folklore, oral tradition, historical evidence, or other information. The theoretical and methodological issues associated with identifying archeological cultures are enormous. In addition, the need to operationalize, in an applied sense, the vagaries of archeological cultural typologies to identify relationships with present-day tribes makes the identification of cultural affiliation a monumental task in most parts of the United States. Fortunately, the law does permit an institution to list cultural affiliation of specific skeletons or collections as "unknown" when circumstances demand. Scientific certainty is not required in the determination of cultural affiliation, a "preponderance of the evidence" is the legal test, and biological (genetic or osteological) information can be used and gathered to help determine the cultural affiliation of human remains. A section of NAGPRA's implementing regulations is reserved for the disposition of human remains and cultural items where cultural affiliation cannot be determined.

To mediate disputes between institutions and tribes or between tribes about aspects of NAGPRA, the law established a seven-member review committee composed of Native Americans, Hawaiians, and representatives from the archeological and museum community (for the current list, see 35). The recommendations of the review committee are not binding, but the records and findings of the committee can be used in federal courts as evidence. To date, the committee's recommendations have been followed by the disputing parties (35). These procedures can also be used by tribes that share a common cultural affiliation to claim groups of skeletons or artifacts that cannot be associated with any one present-day tribe.

While NAGPRA permits future scientific excavation and analysis of Native American skeletons, it establishes stringent requirements for intentional excavation of Native American graves on federal or tribal land. Before a permit for archeological excavation is issued, as required by the Archeological Resource Protection Act, the federal agency must notify in writing the Native American tribes or Hawaiian organizations culturally affiliated with the skeletons or the archeological site. This notice must describe the site, the excavations, and the reasons for believing human remains will be found; identify the likely tribe who will be custodians of the remains; and propose a time and place to discuss in person the excavations, treatment, and disposition of human remains. Although the law and the implementing regulations are silent on this point, agreements on what scientific analyses will be allowed would presumably be settled before permits are issued. If the excavations are on tribal land, consent of the tribe is required. If the excavations are on federal land, consultation is required but not the consent of the culturally affiliated tribes.

NAGPRA's requirements for intentional excavation apply to federal and tribal land, which is approximately one third of the United States. Excavations on state and private lands are regulated by state laws. Thirty-two states have laws protecting in some manner Native American or Hawaiian unmarked graves. Most of these laws require consultation, but not necessarily consent, with tribal authorities before intentional excavation of Native American skeletons is permitted, and most require repatriation of the skeletons to the appropriate tribes (54). Even in those states that do not have laws requiring consultation with tribes before excavation or scientific analysis is permitted, once the skeletons and associated funerary objects are excavated they will most likely be transferred to an institution receiving federal money and hence will come under the provisions of NAGPRA. The law is unclear about what will happen to these collections, but the regulations do have a section entitled Future Applicability (62) that will address treatment and disposition of future acquisitions. Currently, there are very few situations where the excavations of Native American skeletons are permitted without consultation with Indian tribes.

NAGPRA AND OSTEOLOGY

Methodological Syntheses and Data Standardization

Osteologists responded to the threat of repatriation by publicizing the utility of their profession and the knowledge it provides archeologists, government officials, the general public, and Native Americans. These efforts included methodological syntheses by Huss-Ashmore et al (26), Larsen (31), and Buikstra & Cook (12). Ubelaker (59) prepared a pamphlet for the Interagency Archeological Service describing what osteology can offer the archeologist. Even avocational archeologists were being informed of the importance of bioarcheology to archeology (44). All these efforts contributed significantly to an overall improvement in the quantity and quality of bioarcheological analyses, especially those conducted as CRM mitigation projects.

The threat of repatriation provided the motivation and financial resources for osteologists to resolve problems of data incompatibility and noncomprehensive analyses of excavated skeletal remains. In 1988, the Paleopathology Association directed an ad hoc committee to develop osteological data collection standards to ensure that a minimum set of essential data categories were collected and that the data were collected using the same protocols from all skeletal series. After debate and approval by the Paleopathology Association membership, the *Skeletal Database Committee Recommendations* (referred to here as the *Paleopathology Standards*) were published as a supplement to the *Paleopathology Newsletter* (46) and widely distributed to archeologists in various state and federal agencies. Subsequent translation and publication in both Spanish and French (47, 48) enabled international distribution. Shortly after, these recommendations were included (or cited) in federal CRM "scopes of work" as the procedures that must be followed for osteological analyses.

In 1989, the Field Museum of Natural History in Chicago was actively negotiating with the Blackfeet tribe over the disposition of the Blackfeet skeletal remains. The Museum's Vice President for Collections and Research, Jonathan Hass, obtained funding from the National Science Foundation to design a minimum set of osteological data collection standards (15). With Buikstra and Ubelaker, Hass organized a workshop to develop a comprehensive set of data collection recommendations (referred to here as the *Skeletal Standards*), which include detailed definitions, instructions, illustrations, data codes, and recording forms, subsequently published in 1994 (15). It is doubtful whether the NSF would have funded such an endeavor if national legislation enabling repatriation of human skeletal remains had not existed. These new unified standards have gone through two printings, which demonstrates that they are being used, and university bookstore orders indicate their use as a textbook (ML Kennedy, personal communication). They appear to have replaced the *Paleopathology Standards* as the data collection standards for NAGPRA skeletal inventory contracts.

With the regular use of computers by osteologists since the 1970s, there have been frequent attempts to convince osteologists to adopt one or another of the many database systems designed by various osteologists. Unfortunately, the great variation in both hardware and software made widespread adoption of any particular database financially impossible for poorly funded osteologists in anthropology departments. The passage of the National Museum of the American Indian Act required the Smithsonian Institution to inventory its skeletal collections in preparation for potential repatriation. Funds provided along with this directive enabled the Repatriation Office (Museum of Natural

History, Smithsonian Institution) under the direction of John Verano to complete a computerized osteological database system that follows the *Skeletal Standards*.

Development of the *Skeletal Standards* and the passage of NAGPRA encouraged the Center for Advanced Spatial Technologies of the University of Arkansas to obtain funding from NSF to develop a "stand-alone" computerized osteological database titled *Standardized Osteological Database* (referred to here as *SOD*) that follows the *Skeletal Standards* in virtually all respects (25). Cooperation by the Smithsonian Repatriation Office (sharing of their file codes and structures) ensured that the two databases are as compatible as possible despite their having been written with different software. None of this progress toward standardization of osteological data would have been possible without extensive funding, which would not have been available without the stimulation of required inventories and potential repatriation.

The Skeletal Inventory Process

NAGPRA requires federal agencies and other institutions receiving federal funds to conduct inventories of their curated Native American skeletal collections and to consult with the appropriate descendants about their ultimate disposition. The sources of funding and procedures for conducting the inventories have varied considerably, and specific cases from federal agencies, CRM contracting firms, and universities are used to illustrate this range of variation.

FEDERAL AGENCIES   The combined branches of the Department of Defense have the largest aggregate skeletal collection in the United States, and the US Army Corps of Engineers' Mandatory Center for Expertise for Archeological Curation and Collections Management is responsible for meeting the NAGPRA requirements (MK Trimble, personal communication). Inventories of the relatively small Army, Navy, and Air Force collections are being conducted with in-house staff that includes four osteologists. The US Army Corps of Engineers, with its 36 districts, has the largest skeletal collections. Twelve of the districts, using their own funds, had completed a significant portion of their inventories before the Corps was provided NAGPRA funds, and they will continue this process while compliance will be centralized for the remaining districts.

For example, the Tulsa district let a competitive contract in 1994 to a private CRM firm to conduct its inventory. Its NAGPRA coordinator identified the skeletal collections housed throughout the region under various curation contracts, and teams from Geo-Marine Inc. performed the inventories and analyses. This process identified a number of skeletal collections that had neither curation agreements nor an official listing about their locations. These collections were located and retrieved, thus illustrating a benefit of NAGPRA—the relocation of "missing" skeletal collections.

The other 24 Corps districts will be inventoried through a centralized process. The United States was divided into three regions (east, central, west) and six-year competitively-bid blanket contracts for total collections management, including NAGPRA inventories, were let for each region. The inventory and recording protocols (*Skeletal Standards* and *SOD* software) will be standardized for the entire country. The coordinating office in St. Louis has two or three coordinators for each of the three regions who will accompany the recording teams provided by the contracting firms. The use of these standardized protocols and their own coordinators will guarantee that all data collected during the inventory process will be consistent and compatible. Other federal agencies such as the Park Service have taken a decentralized approach. The Mesa Verde National Park, for example, has contracted out its inventory as a competitive bid (D Martin, personal communication). The *Skeletal Standards* and *SOD*, with modification, were employed.

CRM CONTRACTING FIRMS   Geo-Marine Inc., Cultural Resources Division of Plano, Texas, won contracts from both the Tulsa and Fort Worth districts of the US Army Corps of Engineers that include the NAGPRA compliance efforts of taking inventory of human remains and artifacts recovered during Corps mitigation projects. This required Geo-Marine personnel to visit multiple repositories, conduct collection and site documentary research, and inventory identified collections. Geo-Marine added one master's level project manager with several years experience as a bioarcheological specialist at Zuni Pueblo for these projects. Additional personnel were hired for the Tulsa district NAGPRA contract. This included one full-time master's level osteologist, one temporary (project-specific) master's level osteologist, one temporary master's level archeologist, and one temporary bachelor's level osteologist. These individuals were all experienced in NAGPRA and other repatriation efforts.

Before Geo-Marine's efforts, these two districts' skeletal collections had received varying levels of osteological analysis ranging from comprehensive to none. The Fort Worth district's collections had been the subject of substantial and extensive examinations, while the Tulsa district's collections had received relatively little analytical attention.

The Fort Worth contract required Geo-Marine to follow the *Paleopathology Standards*, but when the *Skeletal Standards* was published the Fort Worth district permitted a change in the data collection protocol. A portion of the osteological inventory was subcontracted to the University of Arkansas anthropology department and the *Skeletal Standards* and *SOD* database were specified as the required protocols. The Tulsa district inventory was performed by Geo-Marine staff, which employed the *Skeletal Standards* and *SOD* database. In this case, the protocol was abbreviated to comply with contract specifications and Native American concerns. In all, 17 repositories in Kansas,

Oklahoma, and Texas were visited by Geo-Marine staff. The end result was an expanded and standardized database for both districts' collections. New or refined techniques, specified in the protocols, used to reexamine previously documented mortuary samples improved the identification and documentation of individuals. The reanalysis permitted recording of these collections in a manner more appropriate for complying with the reporting procedures specified in the proposed NAGPRA Regulations (62) and section 5 of NAGPRA.

UNIVERSITIES AND MUSEUMS   Many institutions expected that federal funding would be available for complying with NAGPRA requirements. The first round of NAGPRA competition produced 107 proposals from Native American tribes and 113 from museums and other institutions worth a total of $23 million. Only 41 grants worth $2.14 million were awarded (35). A second competition funded approximately the same proportion of proposals. The Arkansas Archeological Survey completed its inventory with NAGPRA funding, while the Research Laboratories of Anthropology at the University of North Carolina at Chapel Hill used a NAGPRA grant to finish phase two of its compliance. With federal government funding only 10% of the perceived need, most institutions were left to their own resources.

A description of how the summaries and inventories were put together in Arkansas provides an illustration of variation in funding and staffing during university compliance activities. The majority of the archeological and osteo logical collections in Arkansas are curated by the University Museum and Department of Anthropology at the University of Arkansas, Fayetteville, and by the Arkansas Archeological Survey, a separate and independent unit of the University of Arkansas system. The three units curate 2700 Native American skeletons and thousands of other cultural items subject to NAGPRA. These items were collected over the past 65 years through academic and CRM archeological excavations, purposeful collection, and donations from the public.

The inventory of Native American skeletons and associated artifacts required considerable resources to accomplish. The University Museum received financial support from the vice-chancellor's office to prepare its inventory. This permitted hiring two half-time experienced undergraduate osteology students and purchasing osteometric equipment and laptop computers. Funds for additional personnel and equipment were diverted from other Museum budgetary categories. The department of anthropology used one graduate assistant diverted from teaching duties, unreleased faculty time, and some part-time student help. The Arkansas Archeological Survey received a NAGPRA grant to prepare its inventory and develop a guide for identifying cultural affiliation of skeletons in Arkansas. This grant funded hiring of one full-time master's level osteologist, two half-time experienced undergraduate osteology students, and various part-time undergraduate students. All three units used the same inventory process. Each skeleton was analyzed using the *Skeletal Standards* and was then entered into the *SOD* database. Individuals analyzing the collections were trained by the same individual, and thus the descriptions are highly consistent and comparable. Because it is the intent of the tribes affiliated with this material to rebury the skeletons, this database will be the basic research tool for future research.

The NAGPRA grant to the Arkansas Archeological Survey was intended for the development of a biological system of indicators for identifying Caddo skeletal remains. The identification of Caddo skeletons was initially based on funerary pottery and other cultural traits in southwestern Arkansas, where there is established cultural continuity since AD 1000. While the core of the Caddo cultural tradition is easily identifiable, the geographical limits of the tradition are difficult to determine, and it was thought that osteological analysis would provide the key for determining the cultural affiliation of skeletons on the fringes of Caddo territory (up to half the state of Arkansas). In the core territory, Caddo skeletons are characterized by high percentages of unique characteristics such as extra teeth, failure of teeth to develop, depressed occipital bones of the skull, and depressions on the clavicles. These features were recorded during the inventory process for all skeletons from Arkansas. This constellation of traits does distinguish groups who are most closely related to those from the Caddo core area from those who probably have a stronger genetic affiliation elsewhere. The most important aspect of this project was its support by the Caddo and Quapaw tribes of Oklahoma. These two groups, along with the Tunica-Biloxi, are the most likely cultural affiliates for the majority of the Arkansas collections.

The complexity of funding, staffing, and conducting these inventories can be further illuminated by the osteological activities at the University of North Carolina at Chapel Hill. The Georgia state legislature appropriated funds for the osteological inventory and analysis of the University of Georgia skeletal collections, and this competitively bid project was completed by Larsen (personal communication). In addition, Larsen obtained a contract to inventory collections for the Universities of South Alabama and Auburn. However, the first phase of the University of North Carolina inventory was funded by the University and completed with a NAGPRA grant. In total, one PhD in osteology, three half-time osteology graduate students, and two half-time undergraduates were employed during these various inventory activities. A modification of the *Paleopathology Standards* were employed in these projects, which produced a large, internally consistent, osteological database.

New Alliances and Opportunities

NAGPRA has produced alliances between Native American tribes and osteologists that have stimulated innovative research and provided a source of funding previously unavailable. At the request of the Omaha tribe, Reinhard and others (45) conducted extensive analyses of Omaha and Ponca skeletal remains for assessing the impact of trade and European contact on the health of women dying between 1780 and 1820. In addition to paleoepidemiological analysis of degenerative joint diseases and trauma, extensive dietary reconstruction using stable isotopes was initiated. Elemental analysis was used to assess the impact of toxic metals such as lead. Dietary reconstructions provided by stable isotope analysis were used in NAGPRA compliance determination of tribal affiliation. Having completed the dietary reconstructions for burials of known cultural affiliation, stable isotope data were used to distinguish Omaha from non-Omaha burials (primarily prehistoric Woodland) so that only Omaha skeletons would be repatriated to the Omaha (57). Funding for these analyses was provided first by the Vice Chancellor for Research at the University of Nebraska–Lincoln, and subsequently as part of the University of Nebraska–Lincoln's NAGPRA effort to determine cultural affiliation of burials with no or nondiagnostic grave furniture. These destructive analyses were conducted at the request of the Omaha.

An example of consultation under state law is the Buhl burial case from Idaho (23). In 1989, a well-preserved Indian skeleton was encountered in a gravel pit near Buhl, Idaho. The geomorphological setting of the burial indicated an extreme age, and following Idaho's grave protection act (1984), permission was requested of the Shoshone-Bannock Tribes of Fort Hall to use a portion of the humerus and ribs to obtain a radiocarbon date. Permission was granted by the tribal council, and it was dated to 10,675 radiocarbon years, which made it one the best-preserved early skeletons from the Americas (23). In 1991, requests were made for additional bone for chemical and DNA analysis, to complete a comprehensive osteological analysis and for casting the artifacts found associated with the skeleton. The Shoshone-Bannock Tribes approved the additional analysis and casting of artifacts but denied further destructive analysis of bone. In addition, they requested that the skeleton be repatriated as soon as possible for reburial on the reservation. After analysis, the skeleton was returned in December 1991 and reburied.

Future Skeletal Excavations and Osteological Analyses

Clearly the vast majority of skeletal collections will be repatriated and most probably reburied. NAGPRA and most of the state laws require consultation concerning excavation, scientific analysis, and ultimate disposition of skeletons. They do not prohibit traditional bioarcheological or osteological research, and hence, consultation is the key to future research.

In Arkansas, agreements with tribes in advance of specific archeological excavations are becoming common. A written agreement with the Quapaw Tribe of Oklahoma was reached in 1991 over how to treat the excavation of human skeletons at Parkin State Archeological Park. The site is owned by the State of Arkansas, and excavations of Native American skeletons are regulated by Act 753 of 1991, which requires consultation with appropriate tribes and a permit from the State Historic Preservation Office. Skeletal research is an important part of the overall research design at this late prehistoric site and because of the spatial patterning of burials it is impossible to excavate without encountering a human skeleton. The agreement specifically allows osteological analysis and specifies reburial at the Park.

In contrast, an agreement was reached with the Caddo Tribe not to excavate any burials at the 1995 annual Arkansas Archeological Society training excavations. These excavations were held at five prehistoric and historic sites on the Little Missouri River on the Ouachita National Forest. NAGPRA provisions for intentional excavations applied. The agreement was based on the expectation that domestic features, the main focus of research, could be excavated without encountering burials. It is planned that programmatic agreements will be negotiated with tribes culturally affiliated with Arkansas archeological sites to cover a variety of excavation and research situations.

NAGPRA: ITS CONTRIBUTIONS TO OSTEOLOGY

The repatriation movement and most recently NAGPRA have made significant positive contributions to osteology as a research enterprise and to the bioarcheology of North America. This is not to say that there are no negative aspects, but we are confident that time will show the overall results to be positive.

First, the inventory process is eliminating gaps in our knowledge of specific time periods and geographic areas. Skeletons untouched for decades are now being studied. NAGPRA funding has come from federal, state, and institutional sources, many of which had not previously considered osteology within their funding domain. A side benefit of the entire inventory process is that the location of all skeletal collections will be recorded and it will be possible for the first time to locate skeletal collections necessary for solving particular research problems.

Second, osteological analyses are more comprehensive in their data collection efforts than ever before. CRM "scopes of work" have most recently required comprehensive analysis of excavated skeletal remains. Osteologists no longer collect only a select series of observations when doing a study but feel compelled to collect a broad range of data because they may not be able to return for reanalysis. More importantly, osteological studies are using uniform data collection protocols, and various funding agencies are specifying that standardized methods be used. The field is moving toward developing uniform, possibly even a national, osteological database system. This should make it possible for the first time to integrate and interpret osteological data produced by different researchers.

Third, rather than showing a decrease, osteological analyses and the development of new methodologies will increase. Very few of the skeletal collections have obvious relationships with specific Native American tribes, and osteological analysis will be required for determining which will have custody of the remains. This identification process will require the development of new techniques, the use of analytical methods in new ways, and the acquisition of additional data (for examples, see 40).

Fourth, certainly curation facilities for skeletons, never a high priority, will improve. The Army Corps of Engineers has instituted a uniform process for curation management, curation facility design, and a uniform inventory process for its collections. Institutions wishing to continue archeological research will not risk the unflattering publicity of having "disrespectful" curation facilities. Native American organizations may wish to have their collections curated, and institutions wishing to perform this service must offer a situation that meets established conservation standards.

Fifth, the bioarcheological process will become more ethical and fair to the dead. NAGPRA essentially requires the same consultation processes for the excavation, analysis, and disposition of prehistoric remains that are required for the relocation of historic cemeteries. Provisions of national and state laws regarding the study of human skeletal remains will eventually be incorporated within the human subjects review process of universities and research organizations. Thus, as Klesert & Powell (30) recommended, anthropology will have a uniform set of standards for the study of human subjects, and osteologists will follow the same procedures for the prehistoric dead as are now required for research on the living and the recently dead (e.g. autopsy studies).

On the negative side, these improvements in ethics will not remove osteological data from the political process but may increase the politicization of osteology. Disputes between curatorial organizations and various ethnic groups as well as between ethnic organizations themselves will increase, and the federal advisory committee will be occupied for decades resolving these. Not only will the custody of skeletons be important, but control over data and interpretations will be important as well. If identification of the skeletal remains has implications for the ownership or control over resources, then financial considerations resulting from the past destruction of so many skeletons will be brought to bear upon the actual process of osteological research. Sixth, the excavation and analysis of human skeletons will continue. Massive construction projects will increase in the face of a growing population, and skeletons will be uncovered. Whenever this happens during the CRM process, state laws and ultimately NAGPRA will come into force. Despite the fact that the inventory deadlines have passed, the inventory and tribal affiliation identification process will continue for years into the future. This has been clearly recognized by the Army Corps of Engineers, which has let its regional collections management contracts for a six-year period and by CRM firms that are adding osteologists as permanent members of their staffs. In short, NAGPRA is forever!

Any *Annual Review* chapter, as well as any article cited in an *Annual Review* chapter, may be purchased from the Annual Reviews Preprints and Reprints service. 1-800-347-8007; 415-259-5017; email: arpr@class.org

Literature Cited

1. Arkansas Archeological Survey. 1990. *Southwestern Division Overview,* 11 Vols. (RS031–38). Fayetteville: Ark. Archeol. Surv.
2. Armelagos GJ, Carlson DS, Van Gerven DP. 1982. The theoretical foundations and development of skeletal biology. See Ref. 55a, pp. 305–28
3. Ayau EH. 1995. Rooted in native soil. *Fed. Archeol. Rep.* 7(3):30–33
4. Bass WM. 1964. The variation in physical types of the prehistoric plains Indians. *Plains Anthropol.* 9:65–145
5. Bass WM. 1981. Skeletal biology on the United States plains: a history and personal narrative. *Plains Anthropol.* 26:3–18
6. Blakely RL, ed. 1977. *Biocultural Adaptations in Prehistoric America.* Athens: Univ. Ga. Press
7. Brenton BP. 1994. Paleonutrition: implications for contemporary Native Americans. In *Paleonutrition: The Diet and Health of Prehistoric Americans,* ed. KD Sobolik, pp. 294–305. Carbondale: South. Ill. Univ.
8. Brooks ST, Haldeman MB, Brooks RH. 1988. *Osteological Analyses of the Stillwater Skeletal Series in Stillwater Marsh, Churchill County, Nevada.* US Fish Wildl. Reg. 1, Cult. Resour. Ser. No. 2, Portland, OR
9. Buikstra JE. 1977. Biocultural dimensions of archeological study: a regional perspective. See Ref. 6, pp. 67–84
10. Buikstra JE. 1979. Contributions of physical anthropology to the concept of Hopewell: a historical perspective. In *Hopewell Archaeology: The Chillicothe Conference,* ed. DS Brose, N Greber, pp. 220–33. Kent, OH: Kent State Univ. Press
11. Buikstra JE. 1991. Out of the appendix and into the dirt: comments on thirteen years of bioarchaeological research. In *What Mean These Bones?* ed. ML Powell, PS Bridges, AMW Mires, pp. 172–88. Tuscaloosa: Univ. Ala. Press
12. Buikstra JE, Cook DC. 1980. Paleopathology: an American account. *Annu. Rev. Anthropol.* 9:433–70
13. Buikstra JE, Gordon CC. 1981. The study and restudy of human skeletal series: the importance of long term curation. *Ann. NY Acad. Sci.* 376:449–65
14. Buikstra JE, Milner GR. 1989. *The Dickson Mounds Site: An Annotated Bibliography.* Springfield: Ill. State Mus.
15. Buikstra JE, Ubelaker DH. 1994. Standards for data collection from human skeletal remains. *Proc. Sem. Field Mus. Nat. Hist. Organ. Jonathan Haas.* Fayetteville: Ark. Archeol. Surv.
16. Cohen MN, Armelagos GJ. 1984. *Paleopathology at the Origins of Agriculture.* Orlando, FL: Academic
17. Drower MS. 1985. *Flinders Petrie: A Life in Archaeology.* London: Gollancz
18. El-Najjar MY. 1977. The distribution of

skeletal material in the continental United States. *Am. J. Phys. Anthropol.* 46(3): 507–12

19. Fowler DD. 1982. Cultural resources management. See Ref. 54a, 5:1–40

20. Gilbert RI Jr, Mielke JH. 1985. *The Analysis of Prehistoric Diets.* New York: Academic

21. Goldstein MS. 1940. Cranial deformation among Texas Indians. *Am. J. Phys. Anthropol.* 27:312–14

22. Grauer AL. 1995. *Bodies of Evidence: Reconstructing History Through Skeletal Analysis.* New York: Wiley-Liss

23. Green TJ, Cochran B, Davis MA, Fenton T, Miller S, et al. 1992. *The Buhl burial: the recovery and reburial of a Paleoindian from southern Idaho.* Presented at Annu. Meet. Great Basin Anthropol. Conf., 23rd, Boise, ID

24. Harmon AM, Rose JC. 1989. Bioarcheology of the Louisiana and Arkansas study area. See Ref. 29a, pp. 323–54

25. Harris R, Rose JC. 1995. *Standardized Osteological Database.* Fayetteville: Cent. Adv. Spat. Technol., Univ. Ark. (Comput. Softw.)

26. Huss-Ashmore R, Goodman AH, Armelagos GJ. 1982. Nutritional inference from paleopathology. See Ref. 54a, 5: 395–474

27. Inouye DK. 1990. Providing for the protection of Native American graves and the repatriation of Native American remains and cultural patrimony. *Rep. 101st Congr. No. 101–473.* Washington, DC: US Govt. Print. Off.

28. İşcan MY, Kennedy KAR. 1989. *Reconstruction of Life from the Skeleton.* New York: Liss

29. Jarcho S. 1966. *Human Paleopathology.* New Haven: Yale Univ. Press

29a. Jeter MD, Rose JC, Williams GI Jr, Harmon AM, eds. 1989. *Archeology and Bioarcheology of the Lower Mississippi Valley and Trans-Mississippi South.* Fayetteville: Ark. Archeol. Surv.

30. Klesert AL, Powell S. 1993. A perspective on ethics and the reburial controversy. *Am. Antiq.* 58(2):348–54

31. Larsen CS. 1987. Bioarchaeological interpretations of subsistence economy and behavior from human skeletal remains. See Ref. 54a, 10:339–443

32. Larsen CS, Milner GR, eds. 1994. *In the Wake of Contact: Biological Responses to Conquest.* New York: Wiley-Liss

33. Limp WF, Rose JC. 1986. The relocation of the historical cemetery at Cedar Grove. *J. Field Archeol.* 13:339–42

34. Lovejoy CO, Mensforth RP, Armelagos GJ. 1982. Five decades of skeletal biology as reflected in the *American Journal of Physical Anthropology.* See Ref. 55a, pp. 329–36

35. McKeown CT. 1995. Confessions of a bureaucrat. *Fed. Archeol. Rep.* 7(3):13–19

36. Moore CB. 1908. Certain mounds of Arkansas and Mississippi. *J. Acad. Nat. Sci. Phila.* 13(2):279–97

37. Moore CB. 1910. Antiquities of the St. Francis, White and Black Rivers, Arkansas. *J. Acad. Nat. Sci. Phila.* 14:255–364

38. Moore CB. 1912. Some aboriginal mounds on Red River. *J. Acad. Nat. Sci. Phila.* 14:481–644

39. Murray KA, Rose JC. 1995. Bioarcheology of Missouri. In *Holocene Human Adaptations in the Missouri Prairie-Timberlands,* ed. WR Wood, MJ O'Brien, KA Murray, JC Rose, pp. 112–47. Fayetteville: Ark. Archeol. Surv.

40. National Park Service. 1995. Special report: the Native American Graves Protection and Repatriation Act. *Fed. Archeol. Rep.* 7(3):1–44

41. Owsley DW. 1990. The skeletal biology of North American historical populations. In *A Life in Science: Papers in Honor of J. Lawrence Angel,* ed. JE Buikstra, pp. 171–90. Evanston, IL: Cent. Am. Archeol.

42. Owsley DW, Jantz RL. 1994. *Skeletal Biology in the Great Plains: Migration, Warfare, Health, and Subsistence.* Washington, DC: Smithson. Inst.

43. Pearson K. 1896. VII. Mathematical contributions to the theory of evolution. III. Regression, heredity, and panmixia. *Philos. Trans. R. Soc. Ser. A* 187:253–318

44. Rathbun TA. 1981. Human remains as an archeological resource. *J. Archaeol. Soc. S. C.* 13:12–34

45. Reinhard KJ, Tieszen L, Sandness KL, Beiningen LM, Miller E, et al. 1994. Trade, contact, and female health in northeast Nebraska. See Ref. 32, pp. 63–74

46. Rose JC, Anton S, Aufderheide A, Buikstra JE, Eisenberg L, et al. 1991. *Paleopathology Association Skeletal Database Committee Recommendations.* Detroit: Paleopathol. Assoc.

47. Rose JC, Anton S, Aufderheide A, Buikstra J, Eisenberg L, et al. 1994. *Asociación de Paleopatologia Recomendaciónes del Comité para la Base de Datos de Restos Oseos.* Bogotá, Columbia: Centro Estud. Bioantropol., Univ. Andes

48. Rose JC, Anton S, Aufderheide A, Buikstra J, Eisenberg L, et al. 1994. Recommandations du Comité 130es Squelettiques en Paléopathologie. In *Lésions Ostéo-Archéologiques Recueil et Identification,* ed. PL Thillaud, P Charon, pp. 67–79. Paris: Kronos B. Y.

49. Rose JC, Burnett BA. 1990. Part 1: Bio archeology of the eastern portion of the gulf

coastal plain. In *The Archeology and Bioarcheology of the Gulf Coastal Plain,* ed. DA Story, JA Guy, BA Burnett, MD Freeman, JC Rose, et al, 1:132–48. Fayetteville: Ark. Archeol. Surv.

50. Rose JC, Harcourt JP, Burnett BA. 1988. Bioarcheology of the OAO study area. In *Human Adaptation in the Ozark-Ouachita Mountains,* ed. G Sabo, AM Early, pp. 171–92. Fayetteville: Ark. Archeol. Surv.

51. Rose JC, Harmon AM. 1989. History of bioarcheology and bioarcheological resources. See Ref. 29a, pp. 291–322

52. Saunders SR, Herring A. 1995. *Grave Reflections: Portraying the Past Through Cemetery Studies.* Toronto: Can. Scholar's Press

53. Saunders SR, Katzenberg MA. 1992. *Skeletal Biology of Past Peoples: Research Methods.* New York: Wiley-Liss

54. Schamel K, Schaefer J, Neumann L. 1993. Compilation of state repatriation, reburial, and grave protection laws. USDA Soil Cons. Serv. by CEHP Inc.

54a. Schiffer MB, ed. 1982. *Advances in Archaeological Method and Theory.* New York: Academic

55. Shapiro HL. 1930. Old New Yorkers: a series of crania from the Negel burying ground, New York City. *Am. J. Phys. Anthropol.* 14(3):379–404

55a. Spencer F, ed. 1982. *A History of American Physical Anthropology, 1930–1980.* New York: Academic

56. Swedlund AC. 1975. Population studies in archaeology and biological anthropology: a symposium. *Am. Antiq.* 40(2):iii–133

57. Tieszen LL, Reinhard K Jr, Forshoe DL. 1995. Application of stable isotopes in analysis of dietary patterns. Ark. Archeol. Surv., Fayetteville

58. Trope JF, Echo-Hawk WR. 1992. The Native American Graves Protection and Repatriation Act: background and legislative history. *Ariz. State Univ. Law Rev.* 24: 35–77

59. Ubelaker DH. 1980. *Human Bones and Archeology.* Washington, DC: US Gov. Print. Off.

60. Ubelaker DH. 1982. The development of American paleopathology. See Ref. 55a, pp. 337–56

61. Ubelaker DH, Grant LG. 1989. Human skeletal remains: preservation or reburial? *Yearb. Phys. Anthropol.* 32:249–87

62. United States Government. 1995. Native American Graves Protection and Repatriation Regulations. *Fed. Reg.* 60(22): 62158–69

63. Verano JW, Ubelaker DH. 1992. *Disease and Demography in the Americas.* Washington, DC: Smithson. Inst.

64. Weiss KM. 1973. Demographic models for anthropology. *Am. Antiq.* 38(2):iii–186

65. Wing ES, Brown AB. 1979. *Paleonutrition.* New York: Academic

66. Winski JB. 1992. There are skeletons in the closet: the repatriation of Native American human remains and burial objects. *Ariz. Law Rev.* 34:187–214

Annu. Rev. Anthropol. 1996. 25:105–26

HOLOCENE BIODIVERSITY: An Archaeological Perspective from the Americas

Peter W. Stahl

Department of Anthropology, Binghamton University, State University of New York, Binghamton, New York 13902-6000

KEY WORDS: archaeology, holocene, biodiversity, prehistoric ecology, anthropogenic environments

ABSTRACT

Any understanding of contemporary biodiversity change in the Americas is likely to be uninformative and misleading if it employs a prehistoric baseline imbued with pristine characteristics. Archaeological evidence clearly displays a protracted history of environmental transformations at varying geographical and temporal scales throughout the Holocene (that is, the past 10,000 years). Because of problems inherent to the interpretation of the archaeological record, the genesis of these transformations often can only be ambiguously attributed to environmental and/or anthropogenic origins. However, at any given time or place, both the distribution of the numbers of different kinds of organisms and their relative abundances were in a constant state of flux since the retreat of glacial cover some 10,000 years ago. Here I review archaeological evidence to illustrate the dynamism of prehistoric biodiversity, which can be attributed to environmental events, to anthropogenic causation, or as a response of these to each other.

If travellers, the moment they set foot in a tropical region, and even while on islands, in the vicinity of the sea coast, imagine that they are within the precincts of a primeval forest, the misconception must be ascribed to their ardent desire of realizing a long-cherished wish. Every tropical forest is not *primeval* forest. I have scarcely ever used the latter term in the narrative of my travels....

A Von Humboldt (229:193)

0084-6570/96/1015-0105$08.00

INTRODUCTION

Writing at the turn of the nineteenth century, Baron Von Humboldt chose these words to address certain misconceptions resulting from generalizations commonly used in his time to describe natural history. He reserved the special appellation *primeval* (primitive) to describe the South American forests of the Orinoco and Amazon basins that he and his contemporaries Bonpland, Martius, Pöppig, and the Schomburgks explored in such detail. In this quote, written nearly 200 years ago, the Baron equated *primeval* with *impenetrability,* a description he "scarcely ever" used to describe the forests of his travels. We would do well today to remember his caution. All too often the pre-Columbian condition of the Americas is explicitly or implicitly assumed to be a "pristine" or "natural" baseline for comparing contemporary ecosystemic alteration.

The current explosion of interest in global biodiversity issues is spurred in large part by dramatic ecosystemic transformations, developments that can now be publicly observed through a range of media from television to interactive games. Perhaps nowhere are these transformations more dramatic than in the tropics, particularly the immense Amazonian forest, where recent estimates have projected staggering rates of biodiversity loss measured in hectares or acres per minute (157, 226). Moreover, the recent Columbian quincentenary has kindled a renewed evaluation of the historic encounter between hemispheres, once isolated by vast expanses of ocean (e.g. 25, 216, 224, 227).

Whenever we invoke concepts of biodiversity change, we imply that it can be somehow measured or estimated against a standard. The comparative yardstick we choose is usually arbitrary and often imbued with stable attributes, much like a homeostatic "climax" community that had gradually and inevitably achieved equilibrium with its surroundings. In this instance, any subsequent ecosystem disturbance could then be comfortably observed, measured, and hopefully understood. Although we could place our baseline anywhere along a continuum of time—for example, before the appearance of agriculture and urban centers, or after the recession of glaciers—a popular point is the historic encounter between hemispheres in AD 1492.

Much has been written, most notably by Crosby (42–45), about dramatic transformations and the exchange of organisms between East and West. While conquering Europeans set out diligently to re-create familiar landscapes, they also unintentionally introduced organisms previously unknown in their new habitats. However, ample evidence suggests that a large portion of the Americas was also transformed by humans long before the arrival of Columbus. Therefore, we must proceed with caution when applying "pristine," "virgin," or "natural" as attributes of a pre-Columbian America (9, 28, 40, 50, 56, 200,

202, 207, 237) and take great care to avoid excess when uniformly ascribing "environmentalist," "conservationist," or "ecological" ethics to its inhabitants (see arguments in 3–6, 23, 29, 31, 85, 99, 103, 120, 137, 170, 180, 182, 204, 209, 225, 237).

Lingering notions that indigenous Americans passively languished in a pristine *Urwald* both mislead us and denigrate native achievement. Botkin (20a) has explored how divine and, later, mechanical models have historically shaped the views of environmentalists about nature and the role of humans therein. Each scenario presumes that nature attains "on its own" a constant and stable order that we can either perfect or disrupt. Alteration of natural order is generally viewed as bad, or at least unwise. However, "natural humans" can play a good role by living in harmony with nature and by leaving their surroundings essentially intact. Although this scenario has strong psychological appeal, Botkin forcefully argues that the biosphere is not a steady state machine but a dynamic organism with a constantly evolving history in which all humans play an important and dramatic role.

Botkin's argument is highly amenable to the so-called long view in archaeology, which clearly detects a protracted history of environmental transformation in the Americas. This history includes events at different levels of geographic and time scales, whose genesis can be attributed with varying ambiguity to environmental and/or anthropogenic processes. These ongoing events can dramatically affect the temporal and spatial diversity of life-forms by modifying the distribution of different kinds of organisms (richness) and their relative abundances (evenness). "Biodiversity" is a vaguely defined and often abused concept. However, by exploring these two components we may heuristically illustrate time and space variations that conform to recently proposed definitions (222a). Nevertheless, unlike contemporary ecological field study, which can estimate the richness and evenness of a community with some accuracy, retrodiction (inferring past conditions from present observations) of similar measurements from the buried record is confounded by the nature of archaeological data and interpretation.

This review employs an archaeological perspective to explore various issues related to Holocene biodiversity in the Americas. It briefly reviews the nature of available data and discusses its limitations, specifically for the retrodiction of biological richness and evenness. Subsequent sections review environmental and anthropogenically implicated ecosystem alterations during the Holocene epoch and emphasize their effects on biological diversity since the end of the Pleistocene epoch some 10,000 years ago. Owing to the size and scope of the subject, the bibliography is limited to recent discussions, reviews, and summaries.

THE ARCHAEOLOGICAL RECORD

Archaeologists unearth various kinds of direct and indirect evidence pertinent to assessing biodiversity before the advent of written accounts and scientific observation. Principal among this evidence are preserved plant and animal remains recovered from secure temporal contexts. Additional adjuncts as diverse as phytoliths, landscape modifications, architectural features, and artistic depictions can have important implications to our understanding of past biodiversity. Nevertheless, inferences based on the buried record are often frought with difficulties.

Difficulties associated with logistics and visibility can render the simple location of preserved items highly problematic. Ironically, surviving evidence is often discovered through destruction. Depositional contexts that foster preservation can be detected as a by-product of diverse erosive forces such as wind, water, and treasure hunting. In those fortuitous situations where preserved remains are located and excavated for scientific purposes, we usually take a sample from the deposits, often with relatively crude technology. Even when the most sophisticated recovery techniques are employed, there remains a complex relationship between a recovered object's relative durability and its local burial conditions. Items originally accumulated in discrete episodes often tend to be compacted into time-averaged contexts that obscure temporal resolution. Of course, archaeologists are primarily interested in archaeological sites, which are assumed to be spatially discrete refuse deposits initially created by past human activity. But surely, these targets of study are not unbiased samplings of local paleoenviroments. Further, it can be as difficult to firmly identify the mechanism responsible for initial accumulation as it is to control for what was accumulated and in what amount. Finally, the many factors that can numerically and spatially modify aspects of the buried record, both before and after burial, must be critically assessed.

Retrieving reliable information about past species richness and evenness from archaeological data can be highly problematic; therefore, any clear resolution of former biodiversity most often escapes the archaeologist's trowel. Numbers, particularly relative abundances, can be highly unreliable (91–93). Retrodiction of past species richness from the buried record must be undertaken cautiously because archaeologists cannot control for initial accumulation and subsequent survivorship of buried materials. In this sense, it is wiser to emphasize presence over absence in archaeological contexts, because the former is verifiable and the latter is not. Retrodiction of past evenness is even more difficult because archaeologists can neither control the amount and rate of initial deposition nor accurately factor in the subsequent loss. Therefore, archaeologists often end up with qualitative estimations understood in broad temporal blocks, poorly defined spatial units, and ambiguous accumulation histories. Despite these inherent problems, archaeological evidence reveals dynamic changes in the Western Hemisphere that can be attributed to environmental and/or anthropogenic events in the prehistoric past.

A VIEW THROUGH THE ARCHAEOLOGICAL WINDOW

In his seminal article on New World landscapes before Columbus, Denevan (50) compelled us to consider the temporal duration and size of native human populations when assessing their impact on prehistoric American environments. The issues of duration and size are not resolved. In fact, there is sufficient latitude in each to accommodate polar viewpoints. Timing of the earliest human arrivals is clouded by historically competing perspectives, disputes over terminology, and a general lack of agreement on the validity, nature, pertinence, and adequacy of the data. These problems divide opinion about whether the earliest New World inhabitants entered over a connecting land bridge or by other means, long before or shortly after 12,000 BP (19, 59–61, 96, 132, 145, 146, 233). Although many of the vectors responsible for population decrease after contact are well known, accurate estimation of native population size remains elusive. Retrodiction of prehistoric figures is usually based on some combination of early historical testimony, backward projection of contemporary demographic data, extrapolation from archaeological and ecological evidence, reconstruction of social structure based on modern analogues, and informed guesswork. Population estimates for the entire hemisphere at the time Columbus arrived have ranged from just a few million to well over one hundred million inhabitants (52, 62, 116, 159, 179, 216, 217, 222, 224, 244).

Even if we choose conservative estimates, we would still need to appreciate the cumulative environmental impact of millions of humans over more than 10,000 years. Resolving causation archaeologically can be very difficult. What was environmental? What was anthropogenic? Which of these was a response to the other? Data from the buried record make it possible to infer major environmental changes at varying temporal and spatial scales since the retreat of the Pleistocene ice cover. This Holocene record suggests a dynamic ecological history that impacted plants, animals, and native human populations on a hemispheric scale. Occasionally the buried record yields considerable evidence of human impact on the pre-Columbian environment. This includes dramatic anthropogenic alterations at varying temporal and spatial scales, from short-term localized impact to the construction of long-term regional landscapes.

Holocene Biodiversity and Environmental Change

The boundary between the Pleistocene and Holocene is conventionally placed at 10,000 BP. Although decidedly arbitrary, this date broadly separates two epochs in the earth's geological history in which environmental conditions were markedly different from each other. Interpretation of the paleobiological record suggests that with gradual and oscillating climatic amelioration during the end of the Pleistocene, previously equable climatic conditions were eventually replaced with greater seasonal extremes in temperature and moisture. The Pleistocene fossil evidence appears to support the existence of "disharmonious" or "intermingled" faunal and floristic communities for whom no contemporary analogue exists. It is suggested that these diverse assemblages of now allopatric taxa once existed in environments characterized by a low climatic variability that could support relatively high biodiversity. The onset of warming produced greater climatic extremes that facilitated increased environmental homogeneity. Local community composition then changed as various species of flora and fauna suffered subsequent ecological incompatibility or "misadaptation." Community change was particularly pronounced in continental land masses at higher latitudes, whereas refugia could exist in lower latitudinal lands (79, 89, 90, 95, 100, 130, 230, 242). Not only were extant ice-free habitats continuously altered, but the recession of glacial cover and increased availability of waters melting from glaciers exposed new land while inundating littorals.

How did faunistic and floristic communities react to these changing habitats? Communities did not migrate as single organisms. Rather, each taxon responded individually to habitat change in time and space (90, 130). In this scenario, local richness and evenness of any biota would be in a state of constant spatial and temporal flux as each component acted and reacted according to its own ecological needs depending upon changing circumstances.

However, stable conditions did not necessarily begin at the onset of the Holocene (15, 87, 101, 109, 136, 171, 223). All available evidence points to variability in the climatic record as it set out on a long cooling trend toward another glaciation. At different times throughout the Holocene, different areas experienced warmer and drier conditions. These events were variably associated with geographical and elevational shifts of floral and faunal taxa over periods as long as many millennia. Various refugia throughout the Holocene have been postulated, particularly at higher elevations in the Northern Hemisphere and throughout tropical basins in the Southern. Apparently within the past 4000 to 5000 years climate has been unsteadily growing colder and wetter, interrupted by oscillations referred to as the "little ice age cycle" (87). At various times in the recent past, a set of "little" climatic optima and at least one "little ice age" have been interpreted for the entire Western Hemisphere on the basis of assorted data.

Certain periodic and localized events connected with long-term and continuous processes can have profound impacts on regional biodiversity. The combined forces of earthquakes, tsunamis (giant sea waves produced by undersea earth movement), and volcanoes have played a constant and relentless role in shaping the landscapes of tectonically active areas throughout the Western Hemisphere. Largely concentrated along the boundaries of crustal plates, most earthquake activity has been recorded around the margin of the Pacific Ocean Basin, which defines the westernmost edge of the New World. Through subsidence and uplift, earthquakes can cause changes in land levels, which have been implicated in the appearance and subsequent demise of vegetation formations (71). Tectonically produced alteration of surface hydrology has been connected with prehistoric agrarian collapse (150). Ground movement, e.g. earthquake-associated liquefaction and faulting, has also been detected in the prehistoric past (162, 187, 241). Fault-induced seafloor displacement or undersea landslides are prevalent in the Pacific Basin and are directly responsible for tsunamis, which have been implicated in pre-Columbian settlement shifts in western South America (17).

Volcanic activity is found where geological plates subduct, e.g. around the Pacific Ring of Fire, which includes 75% of the world's active volcanoes. Resultant magma flows, escaping gases, airborne and waterborne ash and dust, fast-moving glowing ash clouds, falling rocks, and mudslides can combine and cause massive landscape transformations. The effects can include fires, hydrological alterations, reduced solar radiation, increased erosion, and defoliation or destruction of plants and animals. Long-term benefits include the release of fertilizers, which can support a rich and abundant flora and fauna (161, 193, 211, 240). The archaeologically visible evidence of Holocene volcanic activity and its possible effects have been recorded for various periods throughout the tectonically active zones of North and South America (35, 115, 193, 194, 214).

Cyclical and roughly predictable climatic perturbations can produce short-term and potentially reversible changes. On a global level, the well-studied El Niño/Southern Oscillation (ENSO) event periodically reappears with variable "teleconnections" (different events in widely dispersed areas that are caused by the same initiating event) lasting from one to three years. Past Super-ENSO and Mega-ENSO events may have lasted from a decade to even a millennium. Torrential rains and flooding on the western coast of South America can be associated with droughts, wildfires, storm activity, flooding, and heavy snows at different latitudes and elevations throughout the hemisphere. ENSO events often affect surface hydrology, assist erosion, originate beach ridge formation and dune encroachment, and strongly modify animal and plant life both on land and in water. In the buried record, evidence of paleo-ENSOs has been found in ice cores, tree rings, marine invertebrates, fossil diatoms, and palaeolandforms. These events have been implicated in prehistoric agrarian collapse and large-scale population displacements. However, their buried signatures are potentially similar to those of annual or seasonal storms, floods, and droughts (58, 134, 149, 151, 154, 155, 166, 184, 196, 206, 231).

Against this backdrop of environmental fluctuation over vast areas, we must also consider the effects of isolated and sporadic phenomena on past biodiversity. Fire is a major agent in ecosystemic alteration and was undoubtedly important throughout the Holocene. With current global estimates of as many as 100 cloud-to-ground discharges per second, lightning is a regular and significant cause of fire, except in moist tropical and ice-covered areas (88, 178). Fire is an important instrument in shaping ecosystems and determining the distribution of species, particularly through the creation of vegetative mosaics and increased heterogeneity. Fire facilitates nutrient recycling; alters seed beds; controls parasites; and assists in the flowering, germination, and seed dispersal of many plants while directly or indirectly devastating others (81, 88, 126, 178). Vertebrate communities tend to exhibit greater stability in the face of conflagration. Taxon diversity remains fairly constant through replacement, though with a proportionate increase in ground dwellers (14).

Various forms of aeolian or waterborne deposition may also be archaeological proxies for the destructive forces of seasonal storms, tornadoes, hurricanes, or floods (47, 74, 102, 123, 163, 169, 213, 220). The archaeological record can also register capricious hazards such as ice overrides (49) and mudslides (80). Any way we approach it, the accumulated evidence clearly supports Goudie's (87:94) observation that "the concept of a stable Holocene environment is quite untenable." This position is further justified when we consider humans as active participants in continuous landscape transformation.

Holocene Biodiversity and Anthropogenic Change

One of the most popular and controversial topics in American archaeology involves the concurrent appearance of Clovis hunters and disappearance of megafauna at the close of the Pleistocene. Proponents of a "prehistoric overkill" hypothesis argue that this apparent coincidence is the result of the arrival and rapid advance, or "blitzkrieg," of skilled human hunting populations specializing on large mammalian prey. Proceeding as a wave or front, an initially small group of hunters quickly exterminated its quarry on both continents over a few generations. The patterns of sudden large mammalian extinctions without species' replacement, the time-transgressive span of these global events after the appearance of human populations, and the survival of small continental faunas into the Holocene support overkill and undermine hypotheses invoking "natural change" (138–140, 156).

However, numerous problems, many of them methodological, weaken the overkill hypothesis (e.g. 89, 90, 94, 95, 165, 230, 233). In particular, a chronology of sudden extinction events at the time of the appearance of humans has been questioned, as has the actual extent of taxa involved. Not only is it claimed that most extinction events had occurred by 12,000 BP, but there appears to be little consensus about when humans first arrived in the Western Hemisphere. However, Guthrie (100:290) has cogently stated that "It is possible to argue that both the megafaunal extinctions and the expansion of humans are features of the same climatic event, an event that opened the door in the Arctic to human expansion while at the same time bringing the environmental changes that led to the extinctions." Seen in this light, we should perhaps be more cautious than to blame a new and highly ingenious predator with the full extinction of Pleistocene mega-fauna in a changing environment (98, 108, 230).

Prehistoric faunal depletion by overhunting has been suggested elsewhere in the archaeological record (110, 120, 200, and see 117, 131). However, the establishment of causation remains enigmatic for reasons already discussed. Diamond (57) has elucidated this problem with a clever analogy to the extirpation of Southeast Asian tigers. Although we know that these felines were pushed toward extinction through hunting, harassment, and habitat destruction, future archaeologists would likely seek and find other reasons, i.e. environmental change and volcanic catastrophe, owing to the paucity of direct evidence for causation (e.g. skeletons with mortal bullet wounds). Contemporary examples suggest that both habitat alteration and the introduction by humans of other animals are likely more important in extinctions. Diamond suggested that extinction is more plausibly the outcome of a "sitzkrieg," or slow war of attrition, rather than a "blitzkrieg" of rapidly advancing hunters (57; see also 88, 181). Many examples of extensive and intensive habitat alterations by humans creating favorable conditions for themselves are evident in the prehistoric archaeological record.

Consider first the intentional use of fire by prehistoric Americans. How much native peoples used fire has been widely documented and debated (40, 88, 127, 178, 185, 236), but it appears to have been a regular resource and important tool for hunting, gathering, horticulture, herding, fuel, and general landscape management. Except in very specific contexts, the identification of an anthropogenic origin for any fire is usually approached through historical documents because it is difficult to establish human causation based on archaeological evidence (13). However, there are important data on ancient anthropogenic fires in the tropical forests of Central and South America. Despite the greatest magnitude of thunderstorms, natural conflagration was likely rare in these areas as evidenced by lengthy fire return intervals and the apparent absence of evolved adaptations among forest flora to the ravages of fire (118, 125). However, evidence does indicate that fires occurred over large areas of the northern tropics from Panama to the Amazon basin during much of the Holocene (173, 174, 186, 188). Some events are associated with evidence of human presence, and others may correspond to periods of drought. It is also possible that their origin lies in a combination of both.

Fire and deforestation are interrelated processes. Humans use fire to remove trees and underbrush for landscape management and crop these plants principally for fuel, building, and tool manufacture. Widespread deforestation has been documented at various times in the New World archaeological record (2, 16, 24, 27, 30, 74, 78, 109, 124, 129, 158, 173, 174, 210, 223). While fire can be used to remove forest trees and understory, deforestation also augments the likelihood of fire. Fuel loads, temperature, wind speed, vapor pressure, and the quantity of ignition sources are increased as ambient humidity decreases (118, 119). Forest removal can also increase the rate and degree of erosion and sedimentation and affect local faunal communities by eliminating established habitats and creating new ones. Certain requirements for larger herbivorous browsers and grazers, often the desired prey of humans, can be notably improved.

The geologically recent *grasslands,* including various North American prairies and steppes and South American pampas and campos, are interesting cases in point. Contemporary landscape studies, bolstered by historical accounts, connect the important role of anthropogenic fire with the extension and management of grassland habitats, particularly for improving wildlife and—later—livestock rangeland (63, 86, 88, 97, 106, 121, 168, 178, 228). This has led to speculation about an anthropogenic origin for assorted grassland habitats. However, palynological and ecological evidence suggests that these formations were naturally established at various times, with some predating the arrival of humans (21, 37, 105, 144, 223). Of course, this does not rule out human agency in the prehistoric extension and subsequent maintenance of local natural grasslands (24, 86, 122, 223).

The high-altitude Andean puna grasslands appear to have been the setting for early exploitation, management, and domestication of native camelids. Archaeological evidence indicates a proportionate shift in dependence upon camelid resources as early as 5000 BC, which suggests the appearance of domesticated taxa. Whereas llamas can adapt to various settings but thrive on the dry forage of unmanaged puna, alpacas are best suited to high-altitude landscapes and need natural or artificial wetlands (bofedales). Dated evidence in the form of bones, corral structures, and pottery depictions successfully document the time-transgressive movement of domesticated camelid stock outward from their heartland to areas throughout the prehistoric Andean world. Analyses of mummified remains suggest greater anthropogenic control of breeding stocks, and early documents record expansive imperial herds before the arrival of Europeans (11, 26, 77, 142a, 197, 205, 232, 238). Certainly since the early arrival of domesticated dogs into the New World, native peoples had been manipulating, deliberately transporting, and inadvertently introducing animals throughout the hemisphere. These included domesticates such as dogs (36), muskovy duck, guinea pigs (209, 238), and turkeys (175), as well as captive or transported macaws and parrots (39, 148), wild jays (7), island foxes (34), tinamous, and various rodents (239).

The local distribution and relative abundance of various animal taxa were further manipulated as a direct consequence of habitat alteration for plant management. The success of "garden hunting" of desired game animals in anthropogenic habitats, ranging from manipulated stands of useful plants to horticultural clearings and house gardens, is a function of increased foraging opportunity created by habitat disturbance and the additional lure of edible plants. Of particular note is the increase of large browsers such as white-tail deer, whose bones are ubiquitous in archaeological deposits on both continents. Indeed, Linares (128) suggested that garden hunting may have been the neotropical counterpart of prehistoric animal domestication. The vicinity of native anthropogenic clearings is usually characterized by high overall species diversity (10, 215), and we must also consider the wide range of indigenous silvicultural management techniques documented at different times throughout the hemisphere (9, 12, 20, 40, 53, 70a, 82, 83, 127, 176, 177, 234). Recently, Balée (9, and see 70a) estimated that at least 11.8% of *terra firme* forest in Brazilian Amazonia is anthropogenic.

The actual magnitude of prehistoric forest clearance dedicated to prototypical *slash-and-burn horticulture* is open to question on technological and analogical grounds (51, 65). However, we are certain about the great antiquity and geographical extension of genetically transformed plant cultivars throughout the hemisphere (38, 70a, 189). Native peoples actively encouraged increased crop yields and expanded growing ranges for their domesticates using genetic manipulation and highly sophisticated agricultural techniques. After 1492, improved New World plant stocks spread rapidly worldwide and are today responsible for feeding much of the planet (142b). Remnants of impressive native agricultural infrastructure, which aided the expansion of plant cultivation into areas normally too cold, wet, steep, and/or dry remain observable in the archaeological record.

In its many forms, indigenous *raised field agriculture* involved the artificial elevation of cultivation surfaces, usually in association with contiguous water conduits. This technique effectively increased the geographic range and/or intensity of crop yields, especially in marginal agricultural lands. Natural wetlands and periodically inundated areas could be fashioned into productive agricultural lands through the removal and subsequent control of standing water. Artificially raised surfaces also increased soil depth and quality, while facilitating weed control. Adjacent canals and ditches expedited water management and helped to regulate microclimate, while also serving as compatible sites for nutrient cycling and intensive aquaculture. Documented at various times in low elevations and high-altitude environments throughout northeastern, midwestern, and southeastern North America, Mexico, Central America, Colombia, Venezuela, the West Indies, Surinam, Ecuador, Peru, Bolivia, and northeastern Argentina (24, 46, 54, 65, 67, 68, 70, 76, 84, 176, 191, 198, 203, 212, 221, 235, 243), remnant prehistoric fields represent significant regional-scale human landscape modifications.

The prehistoric *terracing* of naturally sloping surfaces has left its mark on the contemporary landscape. Highland bench terraces were used on the steep slopes of elevated terrain to increase the horizontal and vertical extent of agricultural growing surfaces. Various forms of weir, barrage, pit, and sloping terraces primarily improved growing conditions in less steep topography. Over time, especially where aridity or seasonal water shortage was a concern, prehistoric terracing appears to have approached the latitudinal limits of aboriginal agriculture from southern Utah and Colorado through Mexico, Central America, and the Andes to Chile and Argentina. Most agricultural slope modifications were primarily directed at some form of water management, such as drainage or equitability of water distribution. These were often supplemented by artificial irrigation and sustained by check dams or reservoirs that could effectively control and store surface runoff. Terracing also deepened planting substrates, improved soil qualities while arresting erosion, and controlled microclimatic conditions for non–frost-resistant crops such as maize that would normally suffer in high-altitude valley basins (e.g. 55, 63, 65, 66, 69, 75, 176, 191, 201, 218, 235).

Massive networks of prehistoric *canal irrigation* spanned huge tracts of arid land throughout the American Southwest and northern Mexico and stretched along the coastal plains lying to the west of the Andes. Predictable sources of water were controlled and redirected into these and other regularly or periodically arid regions through a variety of irrigation projects. Availability of cultivable land and intensification of crop yield were greatly augmented by systems linking ingeniously engineered water catchment and control features with expansive redistributive mechanisms. These systems incorporated a wide array of technological sophistication and employed natural and artificial impoundments, wells, filter galleries, cisterns, channelized streams, dikes, weirs, dams, gates, canals, ditches, furrows, berms, and terraces. Archaeology has documented the great antiquity, evolution, and sophisticated engineering prowess involved in a host of prehistoric water redistribution schemes, ranging from smaller localized systems to monumental infrastructure and massive intervalley efforts. Careful study of the surviving evidence has also revealed episodes of construction, continuous remodeling, and innovation in response to dynamic conditions. Expensive irrigation systems certainly reduced short-term risk, yet they remained vulnerable to natural flooding and tectonic activity that could have also led to eventual collapse and abandonment (64, 72, 74, 112, 143, 153, 160, 166, 167, 190, 198, 199, 235).

Finally, we must consider extensive landscape modification through the steady accretion of *human communities* ranging from isolated encampments to immense pre-Columbian cities. The substantial impact of prehistoric settlements is recorded even in settings where structural remains rarely survive. Amazonian soil taxonomy recognizes a separate and extensive *terra preta do indio* anthrosol, found in an assortment of geomorphological contexts and isomorphic with former human settlement (202). Throughout the Western Hemisphere, it is often difficult to find areas where the imprint of previous habitation is lacking. However, the overall magnitude of environmental transformation is most spectacularly confronted in the pre-Columbian city. Beginning at least in the millennium before Christ, permanent and densely settled communities began to appear on the American landscape. Over the ensuing millennia, large settlements grew, evolved, and collapsed long before invading Europeans described the immense and magnificent cities that awaited their arrival. The archaeological legacy of these great pre-Columbian settlements extends southward from the impressive Cahokia Mounds to the vast Andean cities of South America (8, 28, 33, 104, 114, 152, 172, 192, 195).

The massive scale of landscape modification motivated by large and densely populated centers can be estimated according to labor cost involved in monumental architectural construction (1). Similar expenditures were required for expansive public spaces (111), domestic dwellings, and other infrastructural demands (11) needed by a heterogenous populace not directly involved in subsistence production. Analogous to the tip of an iceberg, most large centers had numerous minor centers, each with their own sustaining hinterland. Linking structures such as simple trails to sophisticated road networks interconnected each system with itself and its neighbors, which resulted in a complex communication network whose imprint also remains etched into the landscape of the Americas (113, 183, 219). In placing heavy demands on local surroundings for food, water, fuel, construction material, and waste disposal, pre-Columbian cities were plagued by an assortment of environmental dilemmas not unlike those of their contemporary counterparts (48).

Summary and Conclusion

Without doubt the rapid and massive transformations of global biodiversity caused by contemporary human populations will have serious repercussions for this and future generations. Habitat degradation, destruction, and the dramatic loss of species richness and overall ecosystemic health are events that can be recorded and compared on a scale of seconds—with the passing of a bulldozer's blade—and on a scale of years—with the chronic abuse and mismanagement of natural capital. The scale we choose is arbitrary, but the popular comparative yardstick of an assumed "pristine" or "natural" pre-Columbian America is both uninformative and misleading.

The often ambiguous archaeological record clearly demonstrates a protracted history of environmental transformations at different temporal and spatial scales throughout the Holocene. At any given time and place, environmentally and/or anthropogenically induced alteration set both the numbers of different kinds of species and their respective proportions into a continuous flux. Individual taxa responded to changing conditions according to their unique demands, such that a dynamic patchwork was the norm and not the exception. Similarly, the protracted imprint of substantial pre-Columbian human populations variably increased and decreased the temporal and spatial parameters of biological richness and evenness, according to particular strategies or circumstances.

Whatever the prehistoric magnitude of human impact on Holocene landscapes and biodiversity in the Western Hemisphere, that impact was surely less profound than many of the dramatic changes wrought since Columbus. Nevertheless, it is important not to paint the resource utilization practices of native American peoples, both past and present, with a broad ecological brush. Some groups likely approached a "conservation" ethic, but others likely did not. Regardless, as long as we pigeonhole native deeds into opposing dichotomies our representations will likely be uninformative and misleading. For contemporary native peoples who view themselves as integral parts of nature, the Western idea of conservation as a strategy of short-term restraint for long-term sustainability (6) and the opposing notion of ecosystemic devastation are inherently flawed. Either concept implies that an ecosystem can be potentially ruined by one of its elements, a position that must be somewhat foreign to peoples who view themselves as living within nature.

Enormous biodiversity change resulted from the hemispherical turf war that raged after the arrival of Columbus. In this new arena, the Bible (Genesis 1:28) had ordained that nature could be dominated, and fixed ownership in a market-based economy eventually secured its treatment as property. The introduced notion of land as the essential commodity ensured further biodiversity loss. Resources were purchased, sold, conserved, or depleted by burgeoning populations, according to the whims of an extractive global economy. Native peoples were drawn into this battle over land rights from its inception. Rushing to seize their piece of America, resource-starved newcomers projected stereotypes of "savage" and "uncivilized" Indians to justify their appropriation of land. Today, the struggle over real estate continues as natives and newcomers compete for land and resources and in how they are to be utilized—concepts that are inextricably bound into notions of entitlement and identity. This relationship is eloquently described by Cronon et al, who wrote (41:15):

> The more settlers invested their labors and their dreams in the land, the more they belonged to that land and the more the land belonged to them. Indeed, the longer they (and their children and their grandchildren) perceived themselves in such terms, the less one could call them invaders. Before very many years had passed, they too were defending the homes of their ancestors. 'Europeans' and 'Africans' and 'Asians' had become 'Americans.'

ACKNOWLEDGMENTS

For their valued input and help with references, I thank Donald Chrisman, Charlie Cobb, Al Dekin, Clark Erickson, Paul Fish, Suzy Fish, John Isaacson, Dan Janzen, Bill Isbell, Michael Little, Randy McGuire, Mike Muse, Ann Stahl, Andrea Wiley, and Jim Zeidler. Deepest thanks are extended to Michael, Clark, and Ann for reading an earlier version of this manuscript, and for their protracted support and enthusiasm in this and related projects; however, I alone must remain responsible for the contents of this paper.

Literature Cited

1. Abrams EM. 1994. *How the Maya Built Their World: Energetics and Ancient Architecture.* Austin: Univ. Tex. Press. 176 pp.
2. Abrams EM, Rue DJ. 1988. The causes and consequences of deforestation among the prehistoric Maya. *Hum. Ecol.* 16:377–95
3. Alcorn JB. 1993. Indigenous peoples and conservation. *Conserv. Biol.* 7:424–26
4. Alvard MS. 1993. Testing the "ecologically noble savage" hypothesis: interspecific prey choice by Piro hunters of Amazonian Peru. *Hum. Ecol.* 21:355–87
5. Alvard MS. 1994. Conservation by native peoples: prey choice in a depleted habitat. *Hum. Nat.* 5:127–54

6. Alvard MS. 1995. Intraspecific prey choice by Amazonian hunters. *Curr. Anthropol.* 36:789–818
7. Anawalt PR. 1992. Ancient cultural contacts between Ecuador, west Mexico, and the American southwest: clothing similarities. *Lat. Am. Antiq.* 3:114–29
8. Andrews GF. 1975. *Maya Cities: Placemaking and Urbanization.* Norman: Univ. Okla. Press. 468 pp.
9. Balée W. 1989. The culture of Amazonian forests. *Adv. Econ. Bot.* 7:1–21
10. Balée W. 1994. *Footprints of the Forest: Ka'apor Ethnobotany: The Historical Ecology of Plant Utilization by an Ama-*

zonian People. New York: Columbia Univ. Press. 396 pp.

11. Bawden G. 1982. Galindo: a study in cultural transition during the middle horizon. See Ref. 152, pp. 285–320

12. Bean LJ, Lawton HW. 1993. Some explanations for the rise of cultural complexity in native California with comments on proto-agriculture and agriculture. See Ref. 18, pp. 27–54

13. Bellomo RV. 1993. A methodological approach for identifying archaeological evidence of fire resulting from human activities. *J. Archaeol. Sci.* 20:525–53

14. Bendell JF. 1974. Effects of fire on birds and mammals. See Ref. 126, pp. 73–138

15. Berger WH, Labeyrie LD, eds. 1987. *Abrupt Climatic Change: Evidence and Implications.* Dordrecht: Reidel. 425 pp.

16. Bettancourt JL, Van Devender TR. 1981. Holocene vegetation in Chaco Canyon, New Mexico. *Science* 214:656–58

17. Bird RM. 1987. A postulated tsunami and its effects on cultural development in the Peruvian early horizon. *Am. Antiq.* 52: 285–303

18. Blackburn TC, Anderson K, eds. 1993. *Before the Wilderness: Environmental Management by Native Californians.* Menlo Park, CA: Ballena. 476 pp.

19. Bonnichsen R, Steele DG, eds. 1994. *Method and Theory for Investigating the Peopling of the Americas.* Corvallis, OR: Cent. Stud. First Am. 264 pp.

20. Boom BM. 1989. Use of plant resources by the Chácabo. *Adv. Econ. Bot.* 7:78–96

20a. Botkin DB. 1990. *Discordant Harmonies: A New Ecology for the Twenty-First Century.* New York: Oxford Univ. Press. 241 pp.

21. Bourlière F, ed. 1983. *Ecosystems of the World.* Vol. 13: *Tropical Savannas.* Amsterdam: Elsevier Sci. 730 pp.

22. Bourlière F, Hadley MA. 1983. Present-day savannas: an overview. See Ref. 21, pp. 1–17

23. Bowden MJ. 1992. The invention of American tradition. *J. Hist. Geogr.* 18:3–26

24. Bray W. 1995. Searching for environmental stress: climatic and anthropogenic influences on the landscape of Colombia. See Ref. 208, pp. 96–112

25. Bray W, ed. 1993. The meetings of two worlds: Europe and the Americas 1492–1650. *Proc. Br. Acad., 81st.* Oxford: Oxford Univ. Press. 336 pp.

26. Browman DL. 1989. Origins and development of Andean pastoralism: an overview of the past 6000 years. See Ref. 32, pp. 256–68

27. Bush MB, Colinvaux PA. 1988. A 7000-year pollen record from the Amazon lowlands, Ecuador. *Vegetatio* 76:141–54

28. Butzer KW. 1990. The Indian legacy in the American landscape. In *The Making of the American Landscape,* ed. MP Conzen, pp. 27–50. Boston: Unwin Hyman

29. Callicott JB. 1989. American land wisdom? Sorting out the issues. *J. For. Hist.* 33: 35–42

30. Chapman J, Delcourt PA, Cridlebaugh PA, Shea AB, Delcourt HR. 1982. Man-land interaction: 10,000 years of American Indian impact on native ecosystems in the lower Little Tennessee River Valley, eastern Tennessee. *Southeast. Archaeol.* 1: 115–21

31. Clad J. 1984. Conservation and indigenous peoples. *Cult. Surviv. Q.* 8:68–73

32. Clutton-Brock J, ed. 1989. *The Walking Larder: Patterns of Domestication, Pastoralism, and Predation.* London: Unwin Hyman. 368 pp.

33. Collins JM, Chalfant ML. 1993. A Second-terrace perspective on Monks Mound. *Am. Antiq.* 58:319–32

34. Collins PW. 1991. Interaction between island foxes (*Urocyon littoralis*) and Indians on islands off the coast of southern California. *J. Ethnobiol.* 11:51–81

35. Cordova F de AC, Martin del Pozzo AL, López Camacho J. 1994. Palaeolandforms and volcanic impact on the environments of prehistoric Cuicuilco, southern Mexico City. *J. Archaeol. Sci.* 21:585–96

36. Cordy-Collins A. 1994. An unshaggy dog story. *Nat. Hist.* 2/94:34–41

37. Coupland RT, ed. 1992. *Ecosystems of the World.* Vol. 8A: *Natural Grasslands: Introduction and Western Hemisphere.* Amsterdam: Elsevier. 401 pp.

38. Cowan CW, Watson PJ, eds. 1992. *The Origins of Agriculture: An International Perspective.* Washington, DC: Smithson. Inst. Press. 224 pp.

39. Creel D, McKusik C. 1994. Prehistoric macaws and parrots in the Mimbres area, New Mexico. *Am. Antiq.* 59:510–24

40. Cronon W. 1983. *Changes in the Land: Indians, Colonists, and the Ecology of New England.* New York: Hill & Wang. 241 pp.

41. Cronon W, Miles G, Gitlin J. 1992. Becoming west: toward a new meaning for western history. In *Under an Open Sky: Rethinking America's Western Past,* ed. W Cronon, G Miles, J Gitlin, pp. 3–27. New York: Norton

42. Crosby AW. 1972. *The Columbian Exchange: Biological and Cultural Consequences of 1492.* Westport, CT: Greenwood. 268 pp.

43. Crosby AW. 1986. *Ecological Imperialism: The Biological Expansion of Europe, 900–1900.* Cambridge: Cambridge Univ. Press. 368 pp.

44. Crosby AW. 1991. Metamorphosis of the Americas. See Ref. 227, pp. 70–89
45. Crosby AW. 1994. *Germs, Seeds, and Animals: Studies in Ecological History.* Armonk, NY: Sharpe. 214 pp.
46. Darch JP, ed. 1983. Drained field agriculture in Central and South America. *Br. Archaeol. Rep. Int. Ser. 189.* Oxford. 263 pp.
47. Davis RA Jr, Knowles SA, Bland MJ. 1989. Role of hurricanes in the Holocene stratigraphy of estuarines: examples from the gulf coast of Florida. *J. Sediment. Petrol.* 59:1052–61
48. Deevey ES, Rice DS, Rice PM, Vaughan HH, Brenner M, Flannery MS. 1979. Mayan urbanism: impact on a tropical karst environment. *Science* 206:298–306
49. Dekin AA. 1987. Sealed in time: Ice entombs an Eskimo family for five centuries. *Nat. Geogr. Mag.* 171:825–36
50. Denevan WM. 1992. The pristine myth: the landscape of the Americas in 1492. *Ann. Assoc. Am. Geogr.* 82:396–85
51. Denevan WM. 1992. Stone vs metal axes: the ambiguity of shifting cultivation in prehistoric Amazonia. *J. Steward Anthropol. Soc.* 20:153–65
52. Denevan WM, ed. 1992. *The Native Population of the Americas in 1492.* Madison: Univ. Wis. Press. 353 pp. 2nd ed.
53. Denevan WM, Padoch C, eds. 1987. Swidden-Fallow agroforestry in the Peruvian Amazon. *Adv. Econ. Bot. 5.* Bronx: NY Bot. Gard. 107 pp.
54. Denevan WM, Mathewson K, Knapp G, eds. 1987. Prehispanic agricultural fields in the Andean region. *Br. Archaeol. Rep. Int. Ser. 359.* UK: Oxford. 504 pp.
55. Di Peso CC. 1984. The structure of the 11th century Casas Grandes agricultural system. See Ref. 73, pp. 261–69
56. Diamond JM. 1988. The golden age that never was. *Discover* 9(12):70–79
57. Diamond JM. 1989. Quaternary megafaunal extinctions: variations on a theme by Paganini. *J. Archaeol. Sci.* 16:167–75
58. Diaz HF, Markgraf V, eds. 1992. *El Niño: Historical and Paleoclimatic Aspects of the Southern Oscillation.* Cambridge: Cambridge Univ. Press. 476 pp.
59. Dillehay TD, Meltzer DJ, eds. 1991. *The First Americans: Search and Research.* Boca Raton, FL: CRC Press. 310 pp.
60. Dillehay TD, Calderón GA, Politis G, Beltrão M da C de MC. 1992. Earliest hunters and gatherers of South America. *J. World Prehist.* 6:145–204
61. Dixon EJ. 1993. *Quest for the Origins of the First Americans.* Albuquerque: Univ. N. M. Press. 156 pp.
62. Dobyns HF. 1983. *Their Numbers Became Thinned: Native American Population Dynamics in Eastern North America.* Knoxville: Univ. Tenn. Press. 378 pp.
63. Donkin RA. 1979. *Agricultural Terracing in the Aboriginal New World. Viking Fund Publ. Anthropol., No 56.* Tucson: Univ. Ariz. Press. 196 pp.
64. Doolittle WE. 1990. *Canal Irrigation in Prehistoric Mexico: The Sequence of Technological Change.* Austin: Univ. Tex. Press. 205 pp.
65. Doolittle WE. 1992. Agriculture in North America on the eve of contact: a reassessment. *Ann. Assoc. Am. Geogr.* 82:386–401
66. Dunning NP, Beach T. 1994. Soil erosion, slope management, and ancient terracing in the Maya lowlands. *Lat. Am. Antiq.* 5:51–69
67. Erickson CL. 1994. Methodological considerations in the study of ancient Andean field systems. See Ref. 147, pp. 111–52
68. Erickson CL. 1995. Archaeological methods for the study of ancient landscapes of the Llanos de Mojos in the Bolivian amazon. See Ref. 208, pp. 66–95
69. Evans ST. 1990. The productivity of maguey terrace agriculture in Central Mexico during the Aztec period. *Lat. Am. Antiq.* 1:117–32
70. Farrington IS, ed. 1985. Prehistoric intensive agriculture in the tropics. *Br. Archaeol. Rep. Int. Ser. 232(1).* UK: Oxford. 434 pp.
70a. Fedick SL. 1995. Indigenous agriculture in the Americas. *J. Archaeol. Res.* 3:257–303
71. Ferdon EN Jr. 1981. Holocene mangrove formation on the Santa Elena Peninsula, Ecuador: pluvial indicators or ecological response to physiographic changes. *Am. Antiq.* 46:619–26
72. Fish PR, Fish SK. 1994. Southwest and northwest: recent research at the juncture of the United States and Mexico. *J. Archaeol. Res.* 2:3–44
73. Fish SK, Fish PR, eds. 1984. Prehistoric agricultural strategies in the southwest. *Anthropol. Res. Pap. No. 33.* Tempe: Ariz. State Univ. Press. 387 pp.
74. Fish SK, Fish PR. 1994. Prehistoric desert farmers of the southwest. *Annu. Rev. Anthropol.* 23:83–108
75. Fish SK, Fish PR, Downum C. 1984. Hohokam terraces and agricultural production in the Tucson basin. See Ref. 73, pp. 55–71
76. Flannery KV, ed. 1982. *Maya Subsistence: Studies in Memory of Dennis E. Puleston.* New York: Academic. 368 pp.
77. Flannery KV, Marcus J, Reynolds RG. 1989. *The Flocks of the Wamani: A Study of Llama Herders on the Punas of Ayacucho, Peru.* San Diego: Academic. 239 pp.
78. Flenley JR. 1979. *The Equatorial Rain Forest: A Geological History.* London: Butterworths. 162 pp.

79. Gingerich PD. 1984. Pleistocene extinctions in the context of origination-extinction equilibria in Cenozoic mammals. See Ref. 141, pp. 211–22

80. Gleeson P, Grosso G. 1976. Ozette site. In *The Excavation of Water-Saturated Archaeological Sites (Wet Sites) on the Northwest Coast of North America,* ed. DR Croes, pp. 13–44. Ottawa: Archaeol. Surv. Can.

81. Goldammer JG, ed. 1990. *Fire in the Tropical Biota: Ecosystem Processes and Global Challenges.* Berlin: Springer-Verlag. 497 pp.

82. Gómez-Pompa A, Kaus A. 1990. Traditional management of tropical forests in Mexico. In *Alternatives to Deforestation: Steps Toward Sustainable Use of the Amazon Rain Forest,* ed. AA Anderson, pp. 45–64. New York: Columbia Univ. Press

83. Gómez-Pompa A, Salvador Flores J, Aliphat Fernández M. 1990. The sacred cacao groves of the Maya. *Lat. Am. Antiq.* 1: 247–57

84. González CJ, ed. 1992. *Chinampas Prehispánicas.* Mexico: Inst. Nac. Antropol. Hist. 285 pp.

85. González N. 1992. We are not conservationists. *Cult. Surviv. Q.* Fall:43–45

86. Gordon BL. 1957. *Human Geography and Ecology in the Sinú Country of Colombia.* Ibero-Americana 39. Berkeley: Univ. Calif. 136 pp.

87. Goudie A. 1977. *Environmental Change.* Oxford: Clarendon. 244 pp.

88. Goudie A. 1990. *The Human Impact on the Natural Environment.* Oxford: Blackwell. 388 pp. 3rd ed.

89. Graham RW. 1979. Paleoclimates and late Pleistocene faunal provinces in North America. In *Pre-Llano Cultures of the Americas: Paradoxes and Possibilities,* ed. RL Humphrey, D Stanford, pp. 49–69. Washington, DC: Anthropol. Soc. Wash.

90. Graham RW, Lundelius EL Jr. 1984. Coevolutionary disequilibrium and Pleistocene extinctions. See Ref. 141, pp. 223–49

91. Grayson DK. 1979. On the quantification of vertebrate archaeofaunas. In *Advances in Archaeological Method and Theory,* ed. MB Schiffer, 2:199–237. New York: Academic

92. Grayson DK. 1981. A critical view of the use of archaeological vertebrates in paleoenvironmental reconstruction. *J. Ethnobiol.* 1:28–38

93. Grayson DK. 1984. *Quantitative Zooarchaeology.* Orlando, FL: Academic. 202 pp.

94. Grayson DK. 1989. The chronology of North American late Pleistocene extinctions. *J. Archaeol. Sci.* 16:153–65

95. Grayson DK. 1991. Late Pleistocene mammalian extinctions in North America: taxonomy, chronology, and explanations. *J. World Prehist.* 5:193–231

96. Grayson DK. 1993. *The Desert's Past: A Natural Prehistory of the Great Basin.* Washington, DC: Smithson. Inst. Press. 356 pp.

97. Grimm EC. 1984. Fire and other factors controlling the big woods vegetation of Minnesota in the mid-nineteenth century. *Ecol. Monogr.* 54:291–311

98. Guilday JE. 1967. Differential extinction during late-Pleistocene and recent times. See Ref. 142, pp. 121–40

99. Guthrie DA. 1971. Primitive man's relationship to nature. *BioScience* 21:721–23

100. Guthrie RD. 1984. Mosaics, allochemics and nutrients: an ecological theory of late Pleistocene megafaunal extinctions. See Ref. 141, pp. 259–98

101. Haffer J. 1987. Quaternary history of tropical America. In *Biogeography and Quaternary History in Tropical America,* ed. TC Whitmore, GT Prance, pp. 1–18. Oxford: Clarendon

102. Hajic ER. 1990. Koster site archeology 1: stratigraphy and landscape evolution. *Res. Ser. 8.* Kampsville, IL: Cent. Am. Archaeol. 99 pp.

103. Hames R. 1987. Game conservation or efficient hunting? In *The Question of the Commons: The Culture and Ecology of Communal Resources,* ed. B McCay, J Acheson, pp. 97–102. Tucson: Univ. Ariz. Press

104. Hardoy JE. 1973. *Pre-Columbian Cities.* New York: Walker. 602 pp.

105. Harris DR. 1980. Tropical savanna environments: definition, distribution, diversity and development. See Ref. 106, pp. 3–27

106. Harris DR, ed. 1980. *Human Ecology in Savanna Environments.* London: Academic

107. Harrison PD, Turner BL Jr, eds. 1978. *Pre-Hispanic Maya Agriculture.* Albuquerque: Univ. N. M. Press. 414 pp.

108. Haynes CV. 1991. Geoarchaeological and paleontological evidence for a Clovis-age drought in North America and its bearing on extinction. *Quat. Res.* 35:438–50

109. Heine K. 1987. Anthropogenic sedimentological changes during the Holocene in Mexico and Central America. *Striae* 26: 51–63

110. Hildebrandt WR, Jones TL. 1992. Evolution of marine mammal hunting: a view from the California and Oregon coasts. *J. Anthropol. Archaeol.* 11:360–401

111. Holley GR, Dalan RA, Smith PA. 1993. Investigations in the Cahokia site grand plaza. *Am. Antiq.* 58:306–19

112. Howard JB. 1993. A paleohydraulic approach to examining agricultural intensifi-

cation in Hohokam irrigation systems. See Ref. 191, pp. 263–324.

113. Hyslop J. 1984. *The Inka Road System.* Orlando, FL: Academic. 377 pp.

114. Hyslop J. 1990. *Inka Settlement Planning.* Austin: Univ. Tex. Press. 377 pp.

115. Isaacson JS. 1994. Volcanic sediments in archaeological contexts from western Ecuador. In *Regional Archaeology in Northern Manabí, Ecuador. Environment, Culture Chronology, and Prehistoric Subsistence in the Jama River Valley,* ed. JA Zeidler, DM Pearsall, 1:131–40. Univ. Pittsbg. Mem. Lat. Am. Anthropol. No. 8. Pittsburgh: Univ. Pittsbg. Press

116. Johansson SR. 1982. The demographic history of the native peoples of North America: a selective bibliography. *Yearb. Phys. Anthropol.* 25:133–52

117. Jones TL, Hildebrandt WR. 1995. Reasserting a prehistoric tragedy of the commons: reply to Lyman. *J. Anthropol. Archaeol.* 14:78–98

118. Kauffman JB, Uhl C. 1990. Interactions of anthropogenic activities, fire and rain forests in the Amazon basin. See Ref. 81, pp. 117–34

119. Kauffman JB, Uhl C, Cummings DL. 1988. Fire in the Venezualan Amazon 1: fuel biomass and fire chemistry in the evergreen rainforest of Venezuela. *Oikos* 53:167–75

120. Kay CE. 1994. Aboriginal overkill: the role of Native Americans in structuring western ecosystems. *Hum. Nat.* 5:359–98

121. Kayll AJ. 1974. Use of fire in land management. See Ref. 126, pp. 483–511

122. Kellman M. 1975. Evidence for late glacial age fire in a tropical montane savanna. *J. Biogeogr.* 2:57–63

123. Kochel RC, Baker VR. 1982. Paleoflood hydrology. *Science* 215:353–61

124. Kohler TA, Mathews MH. 1988. Longterm Anasazi land use and forest reduction: a case study from southwest Colorado. *Am. Antiq.* 53:537–64

125. Koonce AL, González-Cabán A. 1990. Social and ecological aspects of fire in Central America. See Ref. 81, pp. 135–58

126. Kozlowski TT, Ahlgren CE, eds. 1974. *Fire and Ecosystems.* New York: Academic. 542 pp.

127. Lewis HT. 1993. Patterns of indian burning in California: ecology and ethnohistory. See Ref. 18, pp. 55–116

128. Linares OF. 1976. "Garden hunting" in the American tropics. *Hum. Ecol.* 4:331–49

129. Lopinot NH, Woods WI. 1993. Wood overexploitation and the collapse of Cahokia. In *Foraging and Farming in the Eastern Woodlands,* ed. CM Scarry, pp. 206–31. Gainesville: Univ. Fla. Press

130. Lundelius EL Jr. 1989. The implications of disharmonious assemblages for Pleisto-

cene extinctions. *J. Archaeol. Sci.* 16: 407–17

131. Lyman RL. 1995. On the evolution of marine mammal hunting on the west coast of America. *J. Anthropol. Archaeol.* 14:45–77

132. Lynch TF. 1990. Glacial-age man in South America? A critical review. *Am. Antiq.* 55: 12–36

133. Deleted in proof

134. Macharé J, Ortlieb L, eds. 1993. Registros del fenómeno El Niño y de eventos ENSIO en América del sur. *Bull. Inst. Fr. Etud. Andines* 22(1). 408 pp.

135. Deleted in proof

136. Markgraf V, Bradbury JP. 1982. Holocene climatic history of South America. *Striae* 16:40–45

137. Martin C. 1981. The American Indian as miscast ecologist. *Hist. Teach.* 14:243–52

138. Martin PS. 1967. Prehistoric overkill. See Ref. 142, pp. 75–120

139. Martin PS. 1984. Prehistoric overkill: the global model. See Ref. 141, pp. 354–403

140. Martin PS. 1990. 40,000 years of extinction on the "Planet of Doom." *Palaeogeogr. Palaeoclimatol. Palaeoecol.* 82:187–201

141. Martin PS, Klein RG, eds. 1984. *Quaternary Extinctions: A Prehistoric Revolution.* Tucson: Univ. Ariz. Press. 892 pp.

142. Martin PS, Wright HE Jr, eds. 1967. *Pleistocene Extinctions: The Search for a Cause.* New Haven, CT: Yale Univ. Press. 453 pp.

142a. McGreevy T. 1989. Prehispanic pastoralism in northern Peru. See Ref. 32, pp. 231–39

142b. McNeill WH. 1991. American food crops in the old world. See Ref. 227, pp. 42–59

143. Matheny RT. 1978. Northern Maya lowland water control systems. See Ref. 107, pp. 185–210

144. Medina E. 1980. Ecology of tropical American savannas: an ecophysiological approach. See Ref. 106, pp. 297–319

145. Meltzer DJ. 1989. Why don't we know when the first people came to North America? *Am. Antiq.* 54:47–90

146. Meltzer DJ. 1995. Clocking the first Americans. *Annu. Rev. Anthropol.* 24:21–45

147. Miller NF, Gleason KL, eds. 1994. *The Archaeology of Garden and Field.* Philadelphia: Univ. Pa. Press. 228 pp.

148. Minnis PE, Whalen ME, Kelley JH, Stewart JD. 1993. Prehistoric macaw breeding in the North American southwest. *Am. Antiq.* 58:270–76

149. Moore JD. 1991. Cultural responses to environmental catastrophes: post-El Niño subsistence on the prehistoric north coast of Peru. *Lat. Am. Antiq.* 2:27–47

150. Moseley ME. 1983. The good old days *were* better: agrarian collapse and tectonics. *Am. Anthropol.* 85:773–99

151. Moseley ME. 1987. Punctuated equilibrium: searching the ancient record for El Niño. *Q. Rev. Archaeol.* 8:7–10

152. Moseley ME, Day KC, eds. 1982. *Chan Chan: Andean Desert City.* Albuquerque: Univ. N. M. Press. 373 pp.

153. Moseley ME, Deeds EE. 1982. The land in front of Chan Chan: agrarian expansion, reform and collapse in the Moche valley. See Ref. 152, pp. 25–53

154. Moseley ME, Feldman RA, Ortloff CR. 1981. Living with crises: human perception of process and time. In *Biotic Crises in Ecological and Evolutionary Time,* ed. MH Nitecki, pp. 231–67. New York: Academic

155. Moseley ME, Richardson JB III. 1992. Doomed by natural disaster. *Archaeology* 45(6):44–45

156. Mosimann JE, Martin PS. 1975. Simulating overkill by Paleo-Indians. *Am. Sci.* 63: 304–13

157. Myers N. 1991. Tropical deforestation. *BioScience* 41:282

158. Neitzel RS. 1981. A suggested technique for measuring landscape changes through archaeology. *Geosci. Man* 22:57–70

159. Newson LA. 1993. The demographic collapse of native peoples of the Americas, 1492-1650. See Ref. 25, pp. 247–88

160. Nicholas L, Neitzel J. 1984. Canal irrigation and sociopolitical organization in the lower Salt River valley: a diachronic analysis. See Ref. 73, pp. 161–78

161. Oakeshott GB. 1976. *Volcanoes and Earthquakes: Geologic Violence.* New York: McGraw-Hill. 143 pp.

162. Obermeier SF, Bleuer NR, Munson CA, Munson PJ, Martin WS, et al. 1991. Evidence of strong earthquake shaking in the lower Wabash Valley from prehistoric liquefaction feature. *Science* 251:1061–63

163. O'Connor JE, Ely LL, Wohl EE, Stevens LE, Melis TS, et al. 1994. A 4500-year record of large floods on the Colorado River in the Grand Canyon, Arizona. *J. Geol.* 102:1–9

164. Deleted in proof

165. Olsen SJ. 1990. Was early man in North America a big game hunter? In *Hunters of the Recent Past,* ed. LB Davis, BOK Reeves, pp. 103–10. London: Unwin Hyman

166. Ortloff CR. 1988. Canal builders of pre-Inca Peru. *Sci. Am.* 259(6):100–7

167. Ortloff CR. 1993. Chimu hydraulic technology and statecraft on the north coast of Peru, A.D. 1000-1470. See Ref. 191, pp. 327–67

168. Parsons JJ. 1980. Europeanization of the savanna lands of northern south America. See Ref. 106, pp. 267–89

169. Patton PC, Dibble DS. 1982. Archeologic and geomorphic evidence for the paleohydrologic record of the Pecos River in west Texas. *Am. J. Sci.* 282:97–121

170. Peres CA. 1994. Indigenous reserves and nature conservation in Amazonian forests. *Conserv. Biol.* 8:586–88

171. Pielou EC. 1991. *After the Ice Age: The Return of Life to Glaciated North America.* Chicago: Univ. Chicago Press. 366 pp.

172. Piña Chan R. 1963. *Ciudades Arqueológicas de México.* Mexico: Inst. Nac. Antropol. Hist. 152 pp.

173. Piperno DR. 1990. Aboriginal agriculture and land usage in the Amazon basin. *J. Archaeol. Sci.* 17:665–77

174. Piperno DR. 1995. Plant microfossils and their application in the new world tropics. See Ref. 208, pp. 130–53

175. Pohl M, Feldman LH. 1982. The traditional role of women and animals in lowland Maya economy. See Ref. 76, pp. 295–311

176. Puleston DE. 1978. Terracing, raised fields, and tree cropping in the Maya lowlands: a new perspective on the geography of power. See Ref. 107, pp. 225–45

177. Puleston DE. 1982. The role of ramón in Maya subsistence. See Ref. 76, pp. 353–66

178. Pyne SJ. 1982. *Fire in America: A Cultural History of Wildland and Rural Fire.* Princeton, NJ: Princeton Univ. Press. 654 pp.

179. Ramenofsky AF. 1987. *Vectors of Death: The Archaeology of European Contact.* Albuquerque: Univ. N. M. Press. 300 pp.

180. Redford KH. 1991. The ecologically noble savage. *Cult. Surviv. Q.* 15(1):46–48

181. Redford KH. 1992. The empty forest. *Bio Science* 42:412–22

182. Redford KH, Stearman AM. 1993. Forest-dwelling native Amazonians and the conservation of biodiversity: interests in common or in collision? *Conserv. Biol.* 7: 248–55

183. Redmond EM, Spencer CS. 1994. Pre-Columbian chiefdoms. *Nat. Geogr. Res. Explor.* 10:422–39

184. Rollins HB, Sandweiss DH, Richardson JB III. 1986. The birth of El Niño: geoarchaeological evidence and implications. *Geoarchaeology* 1:17–28

185. Russell EWB. 1983. Indian-set fires in the forests of the northeastern United States. *Ecology* 64:78–88

186. Saldarriaga J, Clark DC. 1986. Holocene fires in the northern Amazon basin. *Quat. Res.* 26:358–66

187. Sandweiss DH, Rollins HB, Anderson TH. 1981. A single large magnitude uplift in the Holocene record of the Peruvian north coast. *Geol. Soc. Am. Abstr.* 13:545

188. Sanford RL, Saldarriaga J, Clark KE, Uhl C, Herrera R. 1985. Amazon rain-forest fires. *Science* 227:53–55

189. Sauer JD. 1993. *Historical Geography of*

Crop Plants: A Select Roster. Boca Raton, FL: CRC Press. 309 pp.
190. Scarborough VL. 1994. Maya water management. Natl. Geogr. Res. Explor. 10: 184–99
191. Scarborough VL, Isaac BL, eds. 1993. Economic aspects of water management in the Prehispanic New World. Res. Econ. Anthropol., Suppl. 7. Greenwich, CT: JAI Press. 471 pp.
192. Schaedel RP, Hardoy JE, Kinzer NS, eds. 1978. Urbanization in the Americas from Its Beginnings to the Present. The Hague: Mouton. 676 pp.
193. Sheets PD, Grayson DK, eds. 1979. Volcanic Activity and Human Ecology. New York: Academic. 644 pp.
194. Sheets PD, McKee BR, eds. 1994. Archaeology, Volcanism, and Remote Sensing in the Arenal Region, Costa Rica. Austin: Univ. Tex. Press. 350 pp.
195. Shimada I. 1994. Pampa Grande and the Mochica Culture. Austin: Univ. Tex. Press. 323 pp.
196. Shimada I, Schaaf CB, Thompson LG, Mosley-Thompson E. 1991. Cultural impacts of severe droughts in the prehistoric Andes: application of a 1500-year ice core precipitation record. World Archaeol. 22: 247–70
197. Shimada M, Shimada I. 1985. Prehistoric llama breeding and herding on the north coast of Peru. Am. Antiq. 50:3–26
198. Siemens AH. 1982. Prehispanic agricultural use of the wetlands of northern Belize. See Ref. 76, pp. 205-25
199. Siemens AH. 1988. El papel de las tierras inundables en la subsistencia de los habitantes prehistóricos en el suroeste de Ecuador. In Orígenes del Hombre Americano, ed. A González, pp. 275–303. Mexico: Secr. Educ. Públ.
200. Simms SR. 1992. Wilderness as a human landscape. In Wilderness Tapestry: An Eclectic Approach to Preservation, ed. SI Zeveloff, LM Vause, W McVaugh, pp. 183–201. Reno: Univ. Nev. Press
201. Sluyter A, Siemens AH. 1992. Vestiges of Prehispanic, sloping-field terraces on the piedmont of central Veracruz, Mexico. Lat. Am. Antiq. 3:148–60
202. Smith NJH. 1980. Anthrosols and human carrying capacity in Amazonia. Ann. Assoc. Am. Geogr. 70:553–66
203. Spencer CS, Redmond EM, Rinaldi M. 1994. Drained fields at La Tigra, Venezuelan llanos: a regional perspective. Lat. Am. Antiq. 5:119–43
204. Sponsel LE. 1995. Relationships among the world system, indigenous peoples, and ecological anthropology in the endangered Amazon. In Indigenous Peoples and the Future of Amazonia: An Ecological Anthropology of an Endangered World, ed. LE Sponsel, pp. 263–93. Tucson: Univ. Ariz. Press
205. Stahl PW. 1988. Prehistoric camelids in the lowlands of western Ecuador. J. Archaeol. Sci. 15:355–65
206. Stahl PW. 1991. Arid landscapes and environmental transformations in ancient southwestern Ecuador. World Archaeol. 22: 346–59
207. Stahl PW. 1994. The significance of anthropogenic landscapes in prehistoric South America to studies of biodiversity. Biol. Int. Spec. Issue 32:3–11
208. Stahl PW, ed. 1995. Archaeology in the Lowland American Tropics: Current Analytical Methods and Recent Applications. Cambridge: Cambridge Univ. Press. 312 pp.
209. Stahl PW, Norton P. 1987. Precolumbian animal domesticates from Salango, Ecuador. Am. Antiq. 52:382–91
209a. Stearman AM. 1994. "Only slaves climb trees": revisiting the myth of the ecologically noble savage in Amazonia. Hum. Nat. 5:339–57
210. Steet-Perrott FA, Perott RA, Harkness DD. 1989. Anthropogenic soil erosion around Lake Pátzcuaro, Michoacán, Mexico, during the preclassic and late postclassic-Hispanic periods. Am. Antiq. 54:759–65
211. Steinbrugge KV. 1982. Earthquakes, Volcanoes, and Tsunamis: An Anatomy of Hazards. New York: Scand. Am. Group. 392 pp.
212. Stemper DM. 1993. The Persistence of Prehispanic Chiefdoms on the Río, Daule Coastal Ecuador. Mem. Lat. Am. Archaeol. 7. Pittsburgh: Univ. Pittsbg. Press. 212 pp.
213. Stewart RM. 1983. Soils and the prehistoric archaeology of the Abbott farm. North Am. Archaeol. 4:27–49
214. Sullivan AP III, Downum CE. 1991. Aridity, activity, and volcanic ash agriculture: a study of short-term prehistoric cultural-ecological dynamics. World Archaeol. 22: 271–87
215. Taylor KI. 1988. Deforestation and Indians in Brazilian Amazonia. In Biodiversity, ed. EO Wilson, pp. 138–44. Washington, DC: Natl. Acad. Press
216. Thomas DH, ed. 1991. Columbian Consequences. Vol. 3: The Spanish Borderlands in Pan-American Perspective. Washington, DC: Smithson. Inst. Press. 559 pp.
217. Thornton R. 1987. American Indian Holocaust and Survival: A Population History Since 1492. Norman: Univ. Okla. Press. 292 pp.
218. Treacy JM, Denevan WM. 1994. The creation of cultivable land through terracing. See Ref. 147, pp. 91–110
219. Trombold CD, ed. 1991. Ancient Road Net-

works and Settlement Hierarchies in the New World. Cambridge: Cambridge Univ. Press. 277 pp.

220. Turnbaugh WA. 1978. Floods and archaeology. *Am. Antiq.* 43:593–607

221. Turner BL II, Harrison PD, eds. 1983. *Pulltrouser Swamp: Ancient Maya Habitat Agriculture, and Settlement in Northern Belize.* Austin: Univ. Tex. Press. 294 pp.

222. Ubelaker DH. 1988. North American Indian population size, A.D. 1500 to 1985. *Am. J. Phys. Anthropol.* 77:289–94

222a. US Congress Office of Technology Assessment. 1987. *Technologies to Maintain Biological Diversity.* Washington, DC: US Congr. Off. Technol. Assess. 334 pp.

223. Van der Hammen T. 1983. The palaeoecology and palaeogeography of savannas. See Ref. 21, pp. 19–35

224. Verano JW, Ubelaker DH, eds. 1992. *Disease and Demography in the Americas.* Washington, DC: Smithson. Inst. Press. 294 pp.

225. Vickers WT. 1994. From opportunism to nascent conservation: the case of the Siona-Secoya. *Hum. Nat.* 5:307–37

226. Viola HJ. 1991. See Ref. 227, pp. 11–15

227. Viola HJ, Margolis C, eds. 1991. *Seeds of Change: A Quincentennial Commemoration.* Washington, DC: Smithson. Inst. Press. 278 pp.

228. Vogl RJ. 1974. Effects of fire on grasslands. See Ref. 126, pp. 139–94

229. Von Humboldt A. 1850/1807. *Views of Nature: Or Contemplations on the Sublime Phenomena of Creation.* Transl. EC Otté, HG Bohn. London: Bohn. 452 pp. (From German)

230. Webb SD. 1984. Ten million years of mammal extinction in north America. See Ref. 141, pp. 189–210

231. Wells LE. 1990. Holocene history of the El Niño phenomenon as recorded in flood sediments of northern coastal Peru. *Geology* 18:1134–37

232. Wheeler JC, Russel AJF, Redden H. 1995. Llamas and alpacas: pre-conquest breeds and post-conquest hybrids. *J. Archaeol. Sci.* 22:833–40

233. Whitely DS, Dorn RI. 1993. New perspectives on the Clovis vs pre-Clovis controversy. *Am. Antiq.* 58:626–47

234. Wilken GC. 1971. Food-producing systems available to the ancient Maya. *Am. Antiq.* 36:432–48

235. Wilken GC. 1987. *Good Farmers: Traditional Agricultural Resource Management in Mexico and Central America.* Berkeley: Univ. Calif. Press. 302 pp.

236. Williams M. 1989. *Americans and Their Forests: A Historical Geography.* Cambridge: Cambridge Univ. Press. 599 pp.

237. Wilson SM. 1992. "That unmanned wild country." *Nat. Hist.* 5/92:16–17

238. Wing ES. 1986. Domestication of Andean mammals. In *High Altitude Tropical Biogeography,* ed. F Vuilleumier, M Monasterio, pp. 246–64. New York: Oxford Univ. Press

239. Wing ES. 1993. The realm between wild and domestic. In *Skeletons in Her Cupboard: Festschrift for Juliet Clutton-Brock,* ed. A Clason, S Payne, H-P Uerpmann, pp. 243–50. *Oxbow Monogr. 34.* UK: Oxford

240. Wood RM. 1987. *Earthquakes and Volcanoes.* New York: Weidenfeld & Nicolson. 160 pp.

241. Wood WR, Johnson DL. 1978. A survey of disturbance processes in archaeological site formation. In *Advances in Archaeological Method and Theory,* ed. MB Schiffer, pp. 315–81. New York: Academic

242. Wright HE. 1991. Environmental conditions for paleoindian immigration. See Ref. 59, pp. 113–35

243. Zier CJ. 1992. Intensive raised-field agriculture in a posteruption environment, El Salvador. In *Gardens of Prehistory: The Archaeology of Settlement Agriculture in Greater Mesoamerica,* ed. TW Killion, pp. 217–33. Tuscaloosa: Univ. Ala. Press

244. Zubrow E. 1990. The depopulation of native America. *Antiquity* 64:754–65

Annu. Rev. Anthropol. 1996. 25:127–51

"THE POPULAR" IN AMERICAN CULTURE

Elizabeth G. Traube

Anthropology Department, Wesleyan University, Middletown, Connecticut 06459

KEY WORDS: popular culture, mass culture, hegemony theory, domination and resistance, identity formation

ABSTRACT

This review contrasts the relative lack of interest in "popular culture" within anthropology with the close, increasingly critical attention this concept has received within cultural studies. Rejecting both a production-oriented model of a manipulative mass culture imposed from above and a reception-oriented model of an expressive culture of the people, cultural studies scholars broke with essentialized conceptions and redefined the popular in Gramscian terms, as a zone of contestation, a site where the struggle for hegemony unfolds. The review uses this approach to relate the production of popular culture to class formation in the United States. Against overemphasis on the ideological effectivity of popular culture and a revisionist tendency to redefine it in affirmative, politically essentialized terms, the review suggests that contradictions and instabilities characterize all stages of the popular cultural circuit: commodity, text, and lived culture.

INTRODUCTION

Since intellectuals invented "popular culture" in the eighteenth century (13, 146), they have never been more attentive to it than they are today. In the United States, until recently interest in the heterogeneous space of texts and practices variously known as popular, mass, or commercial culture was largely confined to communications researchers and folklorists. Now, stimulated in great part by the retheorization of "the popular" undertaken in British cultural studies (7, 68, 83), the study of popular culture is a growth industry in the American academy, energetically pursued in literary and film studies, history, sociology, and communications, as well as American Studies, African American Studies, ethnic studies, and women's studies.

0084-6570/96/1015-0127$08.00

Anthropology, however, remains ambivalent toward cultural studies (138) and reluctant to legitimize popular culture as an object of study, especially in its domestic forms. Almost ten years have passed since George Marcus and Michael Fischer (105:153) singled out mainstream popular culture as a critical area for a "repatriated anthropology" to explore, yet the response has been modest, at best. Even using a broad definition of the popular, only a few anthropologists (16, 44, 45, 61, 76, 97, 103, 104, 122, 137, 155) have addressed its manifestations in the United States. Moreover, that most of these studies were written by already established scholars rather than recent PhDs suggests that work on American popular culture cannot be relied on to certify professional anthropologists.[1] In contrast, in American Studies, studies of popular culture have played an important role since the 1980s in the formation of the field and its scholars. A sampling of recent work would include a number of anthologies (12, 14, 47, 108, 117), various monographs and essay collections (31, 93, 95, 98, 99, 101, 126, 130, 141, 142, 148, 149, 152)—many of which have already achieved the status of classics—and recent works by junior scholars (81, 102, 139, 145).

American Studies had previously concentrated on validated literary texts, and research on popular culture promised to expand the field in two ways. First, it was perceived as a means of moving from the "high-cultural" preferences of elites to the tastes of "ordinary people" (132). Second, popular cultural texts were thought to be so enmeshed in their social conditions of production and reception that, according to George Lipsitz (100), investigators had to understand them in relation to wider social processes. Ironically, a new emphasis on popular culture was associated with the emergence of an anthropological approach within American Studies, whereas anthropologists, who compare the popular to the lived cultures of social groups, have tended to regard it as an impoverished object.

What inhibits anthropology from productively engaging with American popular culture is the exoticism inscribed in the anthropological culture concept and reproduced in classical ethnographic writing. From this perspective, the rethinkings of the popular reviewed in this essay bear on a sense among many anthropologists that neither the traditional culture concept nor the forms of research and writing it animated are adequate for the analysis of cultural processes in a world of advanced capitalism. As it has been redefined in cultural studies, the concept of the popular breaks with the model of culture as a unified, expressive totality organically linked to social groups. Together with

---

[1] In an interdisciplinary 1991 volume on popular culture (115), the three anthropology entries are all 1970s essays by well-known scholars. Only one addresses American culture, and all construct their objects as "folk" rather than "popular" culture.

concepts such as borders, transnationalism, and diaspora, it is a valuable resource for an anthropology that attempts to think of cultures as fragmented, hybrid, deterritorialized, and mutually entangled.

THE "POPULAR" AND THE "OTHER"

It is now widely acknowledged (2, 5, 22, 39, 136, 153, 154) that modern anthropology constructs its object as the Other. The critical point is not that anthropologists have generally studied cultures other than their own, but that they have produced what Nicholas Thomas (153:3) calls a "discourse of alterity" that distances what it studies from the fictional self it constructs. Using a set of binary contrasts (myth/history, gift/commodity, hierarchy/equality, ritual/politics, etc), this discourse sorts human diversity into opposed spheres, which derive their appearance of unity from the opposition. An effect of the dichotomizing is to emphasize differences between the cultures of observers and observed, suppressing what connects them to one another and neglecting intracultural forms of difference.

If difference tends to be seen in terms of cultures, relativist culture is defined according to difference and provides "the essential tool," Lila Abu-Lughod (2:143) observes, "for making other." Using the relativist culture concept, anthropologists reorganized the hierarchical field constructed by universalizing discourses into a plurality of separate, self-contained, integrated cultural wholes, all available to be understood in their own terms, as sources of meaning, value, and coherence for those who live within them. Cultural relativism encourages accounts that focus on single systems, and until recently, the great majority of anthropologists have constructed their authority ethnographically, by thickly exploring the distinctive features of a people and "their" culture. Ethnographic representations of cultures as socially grounded, expressive totalities reinforce the model they presuppose of a plurality of unique, unitary, self-contained cultures, linked to one another through their common difference from an imagined Western Self.

Because exoticism is not an inherent attribute of certain cultures but a discursive operation, nothing prevents its transposition from foreign to domestic phenomena. Indeed, Abu-Lughod (2:130) suggests that anthropologists working "at home" may exoticize their subjects to reassure themselves and others that their disciplinary identities remain intact. Those who began to study the United States in the 1970s, Sherry Ortner (125) observes, tended to reproduce the basic structure of otherness, whether by studying marginal communities (gangs, ethnic minorities, students, the elderly); by concentrating on beliefs, values, rituals, and other cultural phenomena; or by combining these strategies to represent marginal groups as unusually rich in culture, thereby reinforcing a correlation of cultural visibility with subordinate status (137). Still more pervasive was what Ortner calls the tendency to ethnicize whatever unit was studied, treating privileged and disadvantaged groups alike as autonomous meaning-making communities.[2]

To maintain such fictions of autonomy required excluding or discounting some very unexotic signs of entanglement, such as the everyday consumption of a commercial popular culture that was not made by its consumers but produced in centralized industries, much like any other consumer good, and distributed to national markets.[3] Outside of anthropology, postwar intellectuals had initiated a debate on this mass-produced popular culture (140). Opinion in the 1970s remained sharply divided between pessimistic and optimistic views, neither of them calculated to encourage an anthropology of commercially provided cultural forms.

The "mass culture debate," as it was known, was informed by a discourse on the popular with close connections to the discourse on the primitive. Since the sixteenth century, European elites had used the concept of the popular to distance and disqualify specific beliefs and practices of the lower classes (19, 133). Popular culture was an idea that emerged in the late eighteenth century, in association with a shift in attitude that left the structure of otherness intact. The phrase popular culture was coined by Herder to represent the expressive forms preserved among rural people as comprising an integrated, organic whole.[4] Herder used the categories "low" and "high" to distinguish this "culture of the people" from "learned culture," constructing and valorizing the new object of study as Reason's domestic Other. Like the primitive, popular culture was associated with irrationality, emotionality, traditionalism, communality—everything that the intellectuals who invented it thought they themselves were not (13:9).

What held traditional popular culture together in this construction was an essentialized idea of its folk creators on the one hand and its exclusion from elite cultural institutions on the other. Throughout the nineteenth century, however, the term began to be applied to precisely what had been viewed as a threat to popular culture in its "folk" inflection, the commercially provided culture consumed by the urban working classes. As the referents of the discourse shifted from the rural folk to the urban masses, from a culture made by the people to one made for and merely consumed by them, the popular lost its

---

[2] Or see an earlier study (129) of the motion picture industry as an exotic tribe.

[3] Although global markets are increasingly important for the US culture industries, this review focuses on domestic consumption.

[4] Through Boas, the romantic concept of popular culture would help to shape the modern anthropological culture concept.

moorings in an organic, culture-generating community. In its "mass" inflection, as an artificial commercial culture imposed from the outside, the primary question popular culture raised for intellectuals was that of its "effects" upon consumers. These were overwhelmingly judged to be negative, an evaluation that the term mass culture has come to convey.

A long tradition of conservative cultural criticism links mass culture to moral decadence and the decline of civilization (see 6, 11), but the postwar debate in the United States was shaped by criticism from the left. Paradigmatically articulated in the Frankfurt School critique of the "culture industry" (77), left-wing cultural pessimism takes as its starting point the increasing integration of culture into commodity production brought about by the development of new mass media of communication, the expansion of the entertainment industry, and the intensification in the commercialization of leisure. According to the Frankfurt School theorists (who had originally coined the phrase mass culture to describe the Nazi propaganda machine), the American culture industry had transformed culture from a potentially liberating process of self-creation into an instrument of social control, a manipulative force that blocked class consciousness, stifled or deformed individuality, and assimilated passive receivers to the homogeneous mass.

What effected this transformation was a rationalized process of commodity production, which Frankfurt theorists defined by a double opposition. On one axis, the mass-produced cultural commodity is opposed to a preindustrial commercial popular culture in which consumers are thought to have participated more actively and directly. But the primary axis constructs a mass-produced low culture as Other to a high culture that supposedly transcends commodity production (53:13). On this axis, the standardized goods produced in the culture industry and governed by the "external" demands of profit realization are opposed to art, which derives a critical potential from an "internal" aesthetic process. Mass culture's supposed aesthetic poverty is thus a function of its production as a market value and also the source of its ideological effect: In opposition to art, mass culture is defined as a form that systematically blocks vision of alternatives to the established order.

The elitism of the mass culture critique has provoked a variety of reactions from the left, which I discuss in the next section. But optimistic counter-assertions of the positive value of mass culture came initially from the center. While sympathetic to what they generally call popular culture, these liberal-pluralist approaches are functionalist rather than populist, asserting the educational value of popular culture to consumers (55, 134) and/or its functional value to the system (147). What redeems popular culture, that is, is neither aesthetic worth (treated with typical functionalist disregard) nor oppositional potential (ruled out by the pluralist assumption of unity), but its role in expressing a "consensus" of values that binds diverse interest groups into a whole.[5]

Against the pessimistic emphasis on cultural production, liberals assumed what Andrew Ross (142:53) describes as a two-sided consumptionist perspective. On the one hand, liberal sociologists equated the educational value of popular culture with the training it provided for life in a consumer society. On the other hand, they took up a position developed in mainstream mass communications audience research over the 1940s (92) that defined media consumption as an active, variable process. According to proponents of what has become known as the "uses and gratification" approach to media audiences (96), audiences do not passively absorb media texts, as cultural pessimists believe, but actively and selectively use them to fulfill subjective needs.

None of these approaches to mass-popular culture gave much attention to cultural diversity. Empirical audience research was framed in terms of a psychological model of variation (114:52), whereas cultural pessimists and optimists alike were primarily concerned with what linked Americans together, whether negatively (as "homogenization") or positively (as "consensus"), at a time when anthropologists were most concerned with what kept them apart. Between the ethnicizing tendency of the 1970s anthropology of the United States and the available constructions of the popular, it is not surprising that mass-produced popular culture received little attention from anthropologists. Tightly confined between the poles of an opposition between productionist pessimism and consumptionist optimism, the study of popular culture reached an impasse in the late 1970s. The field has shifted since then, although whether the opposition has been transcended (32) or displaced (20, 110) remains to be seen. Nevertheless, the rethinking of the popular undertaken in British cultural studies has stimulated new and productive approaches to historical and contemporary cultural processes in the United States.

POPULAR CULTURE AND HEGEMONY THEORY

Rethinking the concept of popular culture was part of a wider effort undertaken by Marxist theorists to understand the relationship between culture and class in nonreductive terms, while also attending to the cultural politics of nonclass divisions. The primary resource in this endeavor was the Gramscian (64) concept of hegemony, leadership, or rule, which describes the production of consent to alternative versions of social reality as a diffuse process of cultural struggle. In influential essays, Stuart Hall (68) and Tony Bennett (7) used a Gramscian framework to define popular culture as a site where the

---

[5] Hall (69) notes that the pluralist model of an expressive consensus can be recast as the imposition of "dominant" values.

struggle for hegemony unfolds, the terrain of an uneven, continually shifting engagement between dominant and subordinate forces. Popular culture, in this conception, was not reducible to a form of social control imposed from above, but neither could it be understood as a purely expressive culture emergent from below. More precisely, specific forms of popular culture had to be grasped according to the opposed poles the concept united, as both ideological constraint and expressive process.

On the one hand, this was to refuse the pessimistic left critique of popular culture as a manipulative mass culture. On the other hand, it was to reject the pluralist construction of mass culture as an expression of consensus, while also renouncing a lingering, left-populist nostalgia for a more authentic "culture of the people," which mass culture was thought to have destroyed. Whereas pluralism is content with the existing mass culture, both left-pessimism and left-populism, as Bennett (7:15) observed, represent "the current and actual forms of 'the people's' culture" as wholly corrupt and in need of replacement. In contrast, the Gramscian concept of a zone or terrain structured by multiple conflicts has the advantage for Marxist intellectuals of constructing popular culture as a site of positive political engagement (7:xii; 68:239).

This is, of course, a highly politicized conception of popular cultural value. However, asserting the political centrality of culture against sociologism on the one hand and literary aestheticism on the other was a key move in the cultural studies project (32:5). The theoretical consequences of the Gramscian turn are to define culture according to relations between groups, rather than as a possession or expression of any unified social totality. The term indicates forms and practices rooted in the experiences of diverse subordinate groups, which acquire a hybrid, contradictory character from being worked over by the dominant culture. Hybridity is attributed a subversive potential, which may be realized in certain conjunctures. Popular culture is where a struggle over identities is lost or won, a site where, in the progressive outcome, diverse oppressed groups divided from one another by culture as much as any other factor unite as "the people" against "the power-bloc" (7:20; 68:238–39).

Drawn from the cultures of subordinates, popular culture is also understood as a subordinated cultural formation, constituted by opposition to a "nonpopular" or "high" culture, which Hall (68:235) referred to (with some imprecision) as the "dominant culture." Hall's purpose was to identify both high and popular culture as historical realizations of a structuring opposition rather than as essentialized domains. What is constant, he argued, is not the contents of the categories, which vary from one period to another, but "the relations of power which are constantly punctuating and dividing the domain of culture into its preferred and its residual categories" (68:234). The argument bears implicitly on the Frankfurt School's affirmation of art against mass culture. For Hall, at least, the response to the mass culture critique is not to reverse its terms and valorize what it devalorizes but rather to expose the power that is exercised in polarizing a cultural field.

The emphasis on struggle, hybridity, and contradiction was also intended as a modification of the structuralist model of ideological domination, which had governed film and to a lesser extent television studies throughout the 1970s (84, 116; see also 114, 150). Known as *Screen* theory, after the journal that promoted it, this melding of Althusserian with Lacanian concepts defines mass culture as the carrier of dominant ideology and assigns it a crucial role in the formation of capitalist-patriarchal subjects. Critics (1) have questioned the degree of difference between the so-called dominant ideology thesis and hegemony theory, pointing out that both attribute ideological force to commercial popular culture. There is, however, a considerable difference in the respective models of the ideological process.

The model in *Screen* theory is of a textually encoded capitalist-patriarchal ideology that imposes itself on spectators in the act of reception, replacing any alternative or oppositional forms of subjectivity. Because subjectivity is represented in the model entirely as an effect of textual structures, it is only in a formal sense that one can speak of anything being replaced. An assumption of this particular mode of textual analysis is that the text governs its readings, interpellating readers to the subject positions it constructs. The critic's task is then to expose the process of textual positioning. Attention to production is limited to the assumption that monolithically capitalist-patriarchal institutions reproduce dominant ideology, while *Screen* theory's textual determinism precludes interest in the social reception of media texts (85). Hegemony theory begins with an alternative understanding of cultural relations and arrives at a different model of the production and reception of popular cultural forms. Viewed according to a struggle for hegemony, popular culture involves a complex, power-laden circuit of appropriations, transformations, and reappropriations. The popular is not produced by imposing a dominant onto a subordinate culture, but by the dominant reaching into the cultural formations of subordinate groups, selectively appropriating elements, and stitching them into new discourses. Those discourses in turn become resources for still other groups to use in negotiating identities and meanings, and they may also be distributed to the groups whose cultural forms were initially appropriated. Indeed, a characteristic of the production of a national-popular culture under advanced capitalism is the increasingly complex character of its circuits, as the culture industries incorporate the popular commercial entertainments of subordinate groups into new, mass-marketed commodities (21).

One result of these processes of "cultural ventriloquism" [Hall (68:233)] is that mass-produced popular culture neither confronts its consumers as an alien, external force nor reflects their lived reality. Elements rooted in diverse experiences of subordination, resentment, and struggle or, more precisely, in the cultural discourses that mediate such experiences are continually appropriated by the culture industries, reprocessed, partially absorbed into hegemonic frameworks, and circulated to socially differentiated receivers. Reception or consumption initiates a process of reappropriation, which has received close attention in cultural studies. Against both the productionism of the Frankfurt mass culture critique and the textual determinism of *Screen* theory, reception is understood as a process of negotiation in which people actively engage with mass-produced cultural forms, producing meanings informed by their lived experience (59, 114).

Initially, what was emphasized in cultural studies was the inherently unstable character of a dominant ideology constructed out of a mobile, contradictory ensemble of cultural elements drawn from diverse social locations. If the culture industries contribute to the production of dominant forms of subjectivity, the argument goes, at the same time, by relaying the discourses of the disadvantaged, even in highly contained and fragmented forms, they also provide potential resources for sundry forms of cultural resistance. The latter have figured ever more prominently in cultural studies, as the field drifted throughout the 1980s from hegemony theory to the consumptionist perspective of what critics call the "new revisionism" (27, 60). Characterized by an ethnographic sensibility if not by a fully ethnographic method (119), this new version of cultural optimism focuses on creative appropriations of cultural commodities by consumers (160). Jim McGuigan (110) associates the trajectory with the embrace by left-liberal intellectuals of an "uncritical populism," which constructs popular culture as a positive value for consumers. According to McGuigan and other critics (20, 21, 62, 114), while the focus on situated everyday processes is valuable, it has encouraged a tendency to detach consumption from production, to overstate the control exercised by consumers, and to romanticize consumption practices as "resistance."

Revisionist analyses of "cultural resistance" claim to show how social subjects refuse the ideological meaning of cultural commodities and use them instead to differentiate themselves from or resist assimilation to some dominant identity or norm. Phenomena of popular resistance that have been recuperated as popular resistance include the use of commercial leisure and subcultural styles to preserve or reformulate working-class identities (18, 74, 75, 159), contesting patriarchal codes of femininity and negotiating a feminine individuality through commodity consumption (111, 113, 150, 161), and oppositional readings of mainstream media texts.

The main proponent of media consumption as resistance is John Fiske (41–43). In Fiske's extreme revisionism, the concept of popular culture undergoes a double reduction. First, it is detached from the cultural circuit and redefined in purely consumptionist terms, as what people make out of the cultural commodities produced by the culture industry. Second, only certain ways of using cultural commodities count as popular in Fiske's model—those formed in reaction to textually encoded forces of domination. According to Fiske, the various, putatively oppositional subjectivities formed in this way are articulations of "the people," or the "popular subject position," but the populist theory (91) he invokes would distinguish such local forms of difference as the "democratic subject position."

Hall and Bennett had stressed the potential of popular culture for constructing the popular subject position, an alliance of the people against "the power-bloc." Resistance, that is, had less to do with the privatized local forms of dissent recuperated by the new revisionism than with the possibility of building a broad oppositional coalition. While it was thought that the former might provide resources for the latter, it was also assumed that mobilization would require additional cultural resources, which the culture industries were unlikely to provide (see 20). Nor was there any guarantee that mobilization would take a progressive form. The increased interest of the left in neo-Gramscian hegemony theory was partly a response to the rise of New Right political coalitions in Britain and the United States and the apparent effectiveness of their ideological appeals. While the extent of New Right hegemony can be debated, its rhetoric of conservative populism has articulated the people in what is proving to be a politically efficacious way: as hard-working, independent consumers united by their antagonism to an oppressive, profligate social-democratic or liberal state (see 89).

It is one thing, however, to look at how particular discursive constructions of the people circulated in political discourses may be reproduced, transformed, or contested in popular fictional forms, as Bennett & Woollacott (9) do with respect to the James Bond novels and films. It is another to define popular culture as the site where political subjects are constructed either for or against a represented power-bloc. The overpoliticization of popular culture entailed in this latter view (17) may have contributed to the drift from hegemony theory to the new revisionism, with its scaled-back, romanticized focus on local subjectivities, amplified in Fiske's rhetoric into "the people."

In an important critique of the concept of the popular, John Frow (52, 53) argues that its coherence depends on a populist model of the people that is flawed in several respects. According to Frow: the model rests on an implicitly economistic and reductionist conception of class as a function of the technical division of labor. Its top-down conception of power leaves no room for the complexities and ambiguities of hegemonic struggle, such as the rivalries among subordinate groups comprising the people. Populist discourses, whether of the right or the left, are demonological, which is to say, they can construct "the people" only by imagining the political enemy as an absolute Other, a "structure of feeling" ill-suited to socialist politics.

Frow's argument is part of his wider critique of the coherence of the category of popular culture. Although he regards the Gramscian concept of a contested terrain as a significant break from essentialized conceptions of popular culture, he is concerned with how revisionists such as Fiske have used the figure of the people to reessentialize popular culture as the expression of a homogeneous, politically virtuous will.

If popular culture has no unitary source (the fundamental point of the hegemony approach), it is only held together by exclusion from high culture, which, as Hall argued, is a dynamic, power-laden process. It is no longer accurate, however, to represent popular culture as a peripheral, marginalized, subordinate formation. Hall acknowledges this in a later essay, where he notes that "the cultural dominant" has shifted over the twentieth century from high culture to mainstream popular culture and "its mass-cultural, image-mediated, technological forms" (70:21–22). Yet high and popular culture have not simply exchanged places and values. Rather, as Frow (53) and others (24, 50, 120) argue, the binary division of the cultural field has broken down. In the next section I trace the formation and erosion of the high/popular split in the history of the United States.

CULTURE AND CLASS FORMATION IN THE UNITED STATES

Between the 1830s and the 1890s, the American cultural field was organized into a hierarchical structure that correlated roughly with social class. This was the period of the so-called great divide (78), the separation of high from popular culture, or more precisely, their articulation as opposed, mutually conditioned spheres (80). Historian Lawrence Levine (95) and sociologist Paul DiMaggio (33) have emphasized the organizational dimension of this process. Both point to a distinction created during the last quarter of the nineteenth century between the commercial culture industry and a new organizational form, the nonprofit cultural institution. Founded and controlled by urban social elites, private organizations such as city-based symphony orchestras and fine arts museums provided the base for high culture, sacralizing the cultural forms they isolated and restricting their distribution on class lines. The mechanism of restriction was cultural as well as economic. What excluded working-class people from the new venues was not only high admissions prices but the escalating cultural resources or "cultural capital" (10) required to appropriate what was displayed. Conversely, social elites invoked their appreciation for high culture to reinforce or enhance their social status.

Levine and DiMaggio rely on a functionalist version of hegemony theory that reduces the creation of high culture to a mechanism of social control used by elites for the purpose of status distinction (72). However, the reorganization of the cultural field can be understood as part of what historians (63, 71, 82, 135, 158) have analyzed as a process of class formation in the United States, which gave rise to distinctive, relationally constructed working-class, middle-class, and elite cultures. I focus on two aspects of this larger process: the implications for working-class formation of the culture industries that emerged in the urban Northeast in the 1830s (31, 102, 126, 141, 148) and the transformation of middle-class culture associated with the turn-of-the-century expansion of the culture industries (14, 36, 87, 88, 118, 123, 127, 149).

Even before high culture was marked off as a separate domain, commercial popular culture split into sensational and genteel or respectable forms. The distinction both reflected and promoted a growing separation of social classes. Genteel popular culture included magazines, sentimental fiction, and the respectable theater, and it was consumed primarily by the middle classes. What distinguished genteel culture were not only the forms themselves but its primarily domestic mode of consumption, which was ideally characterized by the disciplined self-restraint that became the badge of middle-class identity. In contrast, a "sensational" popular culture, comprising such forms as dime novels, the penny press, Barnum's American Museum, blackface minstrelsy, and melodramatic theater, was consumed predominantly, though never exclusively, by the emerging industrial working class. Whereas middle-class leisure was centered around the home, an array of popular commercial amusements constructed an urban public sphere, where a rowdy style of consumption and the forms consumed gave expression to a version of working-class identity.

One index of the class character of popular entertainments is the anxiety they aroused among the emergent middle classes. Intellectuals attacked sensational commercial culture as immoral and demoralizing, a potentially dangerous influence on so-called savage immigrant workers (148). Michael Denning (31) emphasized in his pathbreaking study of the dime novel how genteel reformers repeatedly intervened in sensational fiction over the latter half of the nineteenth century, seeking to appropriate what they could not abolish and to enlist it in uplifting the working classes. Denning's larger argument is that dime novels were a contradictory formation, a site, as he puts it, where the signs of class were spoken in multiple, conflicting, ambiguous "accents." These derived from subordinate as well as from dominant social discourses and included the "mechanic accents" of the novels' primary intended readers. Reading involved a struggle over meaning, its outcome dependent on the cultural resources brought to bear. Although workers, according to Denning, were not uniformly resistant readers, they could and often did draw on particular interpretive strategies and ideological discourses to activate the texts in ways that affirmed a subordinated conception of the social world.

Like Denning, Eric Lott (102) uses hegemony theory to explore working-class consumption of a popular cultural form. In a stunning interpretation of one of the earliest culture industries in the United States, Lott showed how blackface minstrelsy absorbed elements of black culture into an idiom of class dissent. Lott's study is a valuable reminder that cultural resistance may have its own oppressive dynamic. Thus, while interpreting blackface as a form of working-class resistance, he also focuses on the interracial relations of power that gave white men control over the means of racial representation, authorizing them to produce "blackness" for white consumption.

Lott's main argument, however, is that neither minstrelsy's white middle-class creators nor its white, mostly male working-class audiences could fully contain the fantasies that cross-racial impersonation unleashed. There were conflicting racial impulses at work, he argues, not only in minstrelsy but in the everyday lives of its audiences. Their own racial status disputed from above (79, 135), newly proletarianized ethnic workers lived their whiteness in contradictory ways, in fear of becoming "black," yet also fascinated by that prospect. In blackface minstrelsy, Lott argues, these racialized fears and desires were expressed through cross-racial impersonation, and they were disavowed through racial ridicule and derision.

Disavowal was to be the predominant social realization. The possibility of suspending racial boundaries was largely exiled into fantasy, as an imaginary blackness was enlisted in the construction of a white class identity. Nevertheless, Lott's emphasis is on the equivocal, potentially subversive character of the fantasy formation and the hybridity of the class-cultural formation. Even minstrelsy's highly managed and disavowed cross-racial identification, he argues, disturbed dominant constructions of racial identities as biologically fixed, while the cultural exchange it set in motion implicitly challenged the idea of culture as an essence lodged in separate human groups.

Lott also elucidates minstrelsy's gendered character. That what was desired from blackness was an imagined form of masculine power suggests that proletarianization was lived at one level as a threat to traditional ethnic masculinities. Not only minstrelsy but the larger sphere of urban popular entertainment constituted a masculinized, largely misogynistic field of sociality, where a sense of manhood that neither industrial work nor domestic life could be counted on to provide found enactment in consumption. At the same time, as feminist historians Christine Stansell (151) and Kathy Peiss (126) have argued, the new space of urban leisure offered opportunities to young, single, working-class women, from the Victorian rowdy girls who strolled along the Bowery to the urban working girls who sampled the "cheap amusements" on sale in turn-of-the-century New York.

Both Stansell and Peiss are alert to the contradictions of consumption for women. On the one hand, it can be argued (38) that in consuming fashion, make-up, and style, working-class women reinforced their own objectification. One may also note how limited material means made female pleasure seekers dependent on male favors. On the other hand, as Stansell and Peiss insist, dressing up flamboyantly and participating in urban nightlife were outrageously expressive practices, which contributed to a new sense of feminine autonomy, independence, and individuality. Subjects as well as objects of consumer discourses, working-class women differentiated themselves from the bourgeois ideal of true womanhood and from traditional ethnic femininities. In the process, they pioneered a sexually expressive, heterosocial culture that, in absorbed form, would transform the gender-segregated orders of genteel as well as local ethnic cultures.

Beginning around the turn of the century, local entrepreneurs who catered to class-specific urban markets gave way to oligopolistic corporations producing for national markets (14, 118). These processes of centralization and expansion engendered modern "mass culture," efficiently defined by Simon Frith (50:108) as "the culture made possible by technological change, by the use of the means of mass cultural production." With its emphasis on circulation and availability, this formulation avoids fictions such as "the people" (106). In addition, mass culture, Frith continues, "has always been a form of middle-class culture, characterized by middle-brow concerns."

More specifically, the emergence of modern mass culture was part of a challenge launched from within the middle class to the hegemony of genteel Victorian culture. Over the next decades, commercial entertainment became one site of a struggle for cultural leadership between the older middle class, who continued to espouse a producer-ethic based on work and self-denial, and a new urban middle class, who valued work but also promoted an emergent ethic of consumption. Leisure entrepreneurs in various fields mediated the cultural transition. Alert to the potential for profit in a shifting public mood, they aimed what John Kasson (87:35) describes as a "respectable alternative" to genteel culture at those who belonged or aspired to the new urban middle class. Amusement parks (87), nightclubs and cabarets (36, 37, 127), vaudeville (118), magazines and popular literature (123), spectator sports (124), and Hollywood movies (107) began to hold out a new promise of sensory excitement, sexual expressiveness, and emotional release, all available for consumption in basically safe and respectable environments.

As Simon Frith (50) and John Clarke (21) emphasize, the "loosening" of nineteenth-century respectable culture entailed both a direct and indirect "tightening" of nineteenth-century so-called unrespectable culture: direct, because the promotion of middle-class consumption coincided then, as it does today (see 30, 143), with assaults on the lack of discipline of the poor, whose "disorderly" entertainments were condemned by progressives and evangelicals alike (90, 126); indirect, in that the culture industries promoted middle-class consumption by drawing on mutually entangled working-class and black popular forms.

This latter process, which Clarke (21:99) characterizes as "appropriation of the vernacular," is a central dynamic of industrial cultural production, as understood by hegemony theory. It implies a tension, Clarke continues, between the economic and ideological logics of the culture industries, between borrowing from vernaculars to revitalize cultural production in the pursuit of markets and conventionalizing and containing what is borrowed. Cultural borrowing in the United States over the twentieth century has meant, on the one hand, that the middle classes, and especially postwar middle-class youth, have been provided with hybrid resources for identity formation, sometimes with unintended effects (48, 65, 66, 98). On the other hand, as Clarke (21:93) observes, it meant that when consumer culture was extended after World War I to subordinate groups (23), these groups had to negotiate its distorted version of their own lives (68, 70).

The formation of mass audiences in the twentieth century has eroded the nineteenth-century correlation of high and popular with social class. Once associated primarily with the working classes, commercial popular culture is now consumed at comparable rates by all social classes (26, 34). The movie and television industries, in particular, tailor many of their products for large heterogeneous audiences, although heightened competition (especially in television) has lately encouraged a subsidiary strategy of appealing to more homogeneous, fragmented markets.[6] The point, however, is not that everyone consumes the same cultural forms or consumes them in the same way, but that consumption of low culture is no longer a subordinated class practice and, argues John Frow (53:25), lacks the sense of cultural inferiority that characterizes it in other regimes. Conversely, high culture is neither the dominant culture nor the culture of the dominant class. Its exclusiveness was undercut by the modern culture industries, which were often promoted as a means of access to "serious" culture (49, 51). Within the contemporary cultural market, Frow argues, high culture forms a specific niche market, related primarily to middle-class intellectuals and able to assimilate heterogeneous aesthetic texts. As Frith (50:109) points out, the high/low distinction is now located within mass cul-

---

[6] My understanding of this dual strategy draws on interviews with media professionals conducted at Wesleyan University from 1993 to 1994. I am indebted to a paper by Michael Curtin.

ture, "produced by the commercial process itself at *all* 'levels' of cultural expression." Used by the culture industries to market such products as movies (121), television (40), rock music (48), and children's toys (144), it provides cultural producers and consumers alike with a flexible idiom for constructing social identities. To study the popular in contemporary American culture is to investigate a historically constructed ideological category that operates within a decentered cultural field. In the final section, I review some recent approaches.

"THE POPULAR" IN CONTEMPORARY CULTURAL FORMS AND PRACTICES

The primary analytical challenge is to preserve rather than dissolve the tension between production and reception that constitutes popular culture as a distinctive theoretical object. To avoid reducing popular culture to a manipulative mass culture, controlled by its producers, reception needs to be understood as an active, socially differentiated process of negotiation. To keep from collapsing the popular into a folk culture, expressive of its receivers, commodity production needs to be acknowledged as an active force in shaping what is made available to be received. A second challenge is to see both production and reception as mixed, uncertain, contradictory processes, unstable blendings of domination and resistance.

Whereas revisionists attributed oppositional meaning to the reception of mainstream popular culture, the aesthetic productions of marginal groups have been associated with a form of resistance to cultural assimilation. A sophisticated instance of this approach is Jose Limón's (97) analysis of a Mexican ballad tradition and its appropriation by Chicano poets. Originally produced along the territorial South Texan border, the ballads, or corridos, were fostered by and expressed the prolonged struggle waged by Mexican workers against Anglo-American domination. Transposed to urban settings in the 1930s, this oppositional musical culture was incorporated by the music industry, a process that Limón represents as the dilution of a folk tradition. However, the heroic version of the corrido lived on as a residual form, largely through oral transmission in the cantina, the barroom, and other masculine spaces of consumption. In the 1960s, according to Limón, the corrido became a resource for a new creative process, also associated with a borderland. Chicano intellectuals, he argues, occupying a deterritorialized cultural space, mixed the patriarchal corrido with subordinated feminine discourses from the folk tradition and with elements of high modernism to create a new political art.

Commercial culture occupies a minor place in Limón's narrative. Focused on how subordinates mix their own vernaculars into hybrid formations rather than on the appropriation of those vernaculars by the culture industries, his

study leaves questions of cultural markets largely unaddressed. The commodification and marketing of ethnic culture figures more prominently in George
Lipsitz's (99) use of the border model, although I think the relationship of
ethnic artists to the culture industry is misrepresented.

Lipsitz's approach is informed by a version of postmodern theory that sees
popular culture as a site for the formation of hybrid, plural identities (74, 75,
112). To this largely affirmative construction of the popular, Lipsitz adds the
"border" proposition that living between different cultural systems gives ethnic minorities a heightened tolerance for irony and ambiguity (4, 137). Between the 1950s and 1980s, he argues, Chicano rock musicians in East Los
Angeles put those capacities to creative use, mixing their own folk traditions
with musical forms and styles borrowed from other minority as well as mainstream traditions. Lipsitz understands their aesthetic practice as an attempt to
manage "the anguish of invisibility" (99:151), a demand to be seen, which he
codes as resistance. Potentially accessible to white, middle-class youth searching for ways to express their own alienation, hybrid cultural forms such as
Chicano rock, Lipsitz suggests, enable a minority group to make itself visible
to the mainstream in a form that challenges dominant constructions of ethnic
difference.

The claim that the artists refuse both assimilation and ghettoization is
persuasive. What is misleading is the suggestion that those alternatives are
imposed by the music industry. It presupposes a neo-Frankfurt construction of
the culture industries as routinely producing standardized, homogenized products for a uniform mass taste, while Chicano musicians are cast as artists of the
people, who contest the rigid commercial marketing structure imposed by the
industry (99:152) but nevertheless achieve commercial success. However,
rather than popular art against the market, this is a case of a market for popular
art. Lipsitz's mistake is to apply a Fordist model of production to an industrial
cultural system that, as I have already noted, has become considerably more
flexible in its strategies as it pursues an increasingly fragmented market. In
short, the culture industries today (and the rock industry, in particular) are
more interested in incorporating and marketing diversity than in limiting or
suppressing it (51, 94).

This is not to deny that commercial culture circulates varying constructions
of ethnic, racial, and gendered difference, many with far less progressive
potential than Los Lobos (157). But it is to challenge a construction of "the
dominant," common to the border model of ethnic identity, postmodern cele-
brations of transgressive popular styles, and reception models of "resistant"
readers who refuse dominant norms. As Steven Connor (25:195) argues, the
"politics of difference" entailed in such theoretical schemes presupposes a
dominant culture that seeks to keep invisible what it subordinates:

> In fashion, in music, in art, in writing, the obvious way to resist this condemnation to invisibility has seemed to be for the marginal group to insist on *being seen* (and heard)....Such an analysis encounters difficulties when faced with the fact that this visibility of diverse and stylistically distinct groups is part of the official or dominant mode of advertising and media in the West....Under these circumstances, visibility and self-proclamation may have become a market requirement rather than a mode of liberation.

Connor gets at a fundamental problem with romantic affirmations of "popular resistance." These assume that the project of the culture industries is to assimilate subalterns to a dominant, unified bourgeois norm, whereas their primary modern project has been to promote middle-class consumption, which has always involved making cultural difference visible in incorporated forms. However, against Connor and other similarly pessimistic assessments of contemporary consumer culture (38, 44, 57), I would argue that if the increasingly frenetic marketing of cultural diversity is not liberatory in itself, neither is it inherently or inevitably repressive.

Rather, in their ideologically and economically driven efforts to absorb, rework, and market the progressive as well as the reactionary discourses of the past decades, the culture industries and their products have become a site of deepening contradictions. The mobile perspective it takes to represent the contradictory workings of the cultural system is exemplified in Andrew Goodwin's (62) study of music television, which shifts fluidly between levels, without unilaterally condemning popular culture as domination or celebrating it as resistance. Goodwin also displays a methodological eclecticism that is preferable, in my view, to a simple intensification of ethnographic method.

The latter strategy has been recommended for the analysis of reception, in acknowledgment of the doubtful ethnographic character of most audience research (114, 119, 150). As a fiction constructed in discourses of cultural producers rather than a commonly used self-representation, the very concept of "audience" is ethnographically suspect (73). Janice Radway (131, 132), for example, now sees her work on romance readers as too narrow in focus and advocates more fully ethnographic accounts of cultural consumption as an array of mixed, shifting subject positions. Valuable as such perspectives are, the problem is to connect an ethnography of everyday life with studies of how culture is produced and made available to be consumed.

Research on production and circulation recovers the enduring insight of the Frankfurt School that the culture industries are concentrations of economic and cultural power. In recent depictions (40, 54, 58, 62, 103), however, production is a less seamless, more conflictual process than cultural pessimism had anticipated. Julie D'Acci's (29) excellent study of the television series *Cagney & Lacey,* for example, shows how a contested process of production both enables and limits possibilities for critical readings. Focusing on prime-time television's role in constructing gender, D'Acci analyzes the production of the show as a struggle over the meanings of woman, women, feminism, and femininity. Prompted by commercial logic to try to build an audience defined as upscale working women, network executives and advertisers clashed repeatedly throughout the show's run with the production team, journalists, feminist activists, and ordinary viewers over the definition of this particular audience fiction. Although the network exerted a conservative influence, it did not go unchallenged. Discourses generated by the women's movement were selectively incorporated into the program and partially disrupted the patriarchal conventions of the police genre, while the contradictory character the program took on from multiple interventions, D'Acci argues, may have increased its potential to disturb dominant constructions of gender difference.

From an institutional perspective, D'Acci's study suggests that while corporate control over cultural production is extensive and materially grounded, it is not absolute. In this regard, more work needs to be done on media professionals as middle-class intellectuals with structurally ambivalent relations to the dominant class (35, 53, 56). From a textual perspective, which D'Acci also assumes, popular culture appears as a site where ideological discourses are not merely reproduced but are subjected to a work of transformation, where they undergo what Michael Denning (31) calls the "dreamwork of the social."

In a compelling analysis of a crisis of hegemony in the United States produced by the postwar economic transformation, Roger Rouse (143) makes a powerful case for treating the popular media as an instrument of hegemonic influence. Working in broad but deft strokes, Rouse isolates from media texts (primarily movies and television) a set of discursive strategies that, he argues, either shape dispositions adapted to an emerging post-Fordist system or model the class system in ways that generate consent to specific coalitions. While conceding that the analysis might be enhanced by attention to "people's varied forms of challenge and resistance" (143:398), Rouse argues that one needs to know how discursive forms of power operate to challenge them. I agree, and I think that Rouse skillfully isolates the discourses of power currently in operation. However, I question how isolated those discourses are in popular fictions. Forms of challenge, I suggest, may be at work within media texts as well as within what Rouse calls the "corporate-controlled media." Because my own work (155, 156) on popular movies and television has focused on texts, I end with a few remarks on textual processes, using Fred Pfeil's (128) remarkable new study of contemporary popular cultural constructions of masculinity to complicate rather than to refute Rouse's version of mass-mediated hegemonic influence.

Pfeil, like Rouse, reads popular culture against an ongoing transition to a post-Fordist system. For both, economic transformation has produced massive shifts in the gender system, feminizing the workplace—both literally and categorically—and undermining the traditional masculine role of provider, though Pfeil also regards feminism as a cause and effect of those shifts. White middle-class and working-class men, Pfeil argues, live this moment, from their different positions, as one of indeterminacy and flux. While the conditions for them to securely inhabit the provider role are no longer in place, neither are the conditions for undoing its gender coding. In popular culture, Pfeil argues, the desires and anxieties aroused by flux are reprocessed and rechanneled. Through close readings of movies, rock music, detective fiction, and the New Age Men's movement, he traces the emergence of various "wild masculinities," hybrid structures in which features associated with femininity and non-white or non-Western masculinities are appropriated and condensed with white straight masculinity.

We may see this as yet another stage in popular culture's historic mission of "loosening" white middle-class identities, adapting subjects to what has been coded as the feminine and/or ethnic province of consumer desire, as well as to increasingly flexible postindustrial workplaces. What Pfeil stresses, however, is a fundamental tension, embodied in various ways in different texts, between the feminine-ethnic qualities of emotional openness, nurturance, sensuality, and connection attributed to the new heroes and their hypermasculine inwardness, violence, invulnerability, and detachment. Simultaneously celebrating the mobility and flexibility required by post-Fordist workplaces and nostalgic for a more autonomous, self-contained, residual "Fordist" masculinity, popular cultural fictions, in Pfeil's analysis, symptomatically shift between accommodation and resistance to the new postindustrial order.

I linger over Pfeil's interpretations to make one last point about the place of textual analysis in the study of popular culture. Between a justifiable reaction to the excesses of *Screen* theory and an overvaluation of ethnographic research on reception, the close reading of popular cultural texts has acquired a bad name in some circles. The sound argument that the formal features of texts do not in themselves validate particular meanings (9) is sometimes taken to mean that texts have no formal features and that either producers or audiences are the sole arbiters of their meaning. With Pfeil, I believe that to refuse textual criticism is to risk losing the complex, contradictory character of popular cultural forms. A poetics is a necessary resource in understanding popular cultural forms and appreciating the shifting, uncertain politics of their pleasures.

ACKNOWLEDGMENTS

I am grateful to Karen Bock, who provided encouragement when it was most needed; to all the members of the Wesleyan media studies group; to Louise

Lamphere for helpful comments on an outline of this paper; and to John Frow, for making this paper so much harder than I had thought it would be.

Any *Annual Review* chapter, as well as any article cited in an *Annual Review* chapter, may be purchased from the Annual Reviews Preprints and Reprints service.
1-800-347-8007; 415-259-5017; email: arpr@class.org

Literature Cited

1. Abercrombie N. 1990. Popular culture and ideological effects. In *Dominant Ideologies,* ed. N Abercrombie, S Hill, B Turner, pp. 199–228. London: Unwin Hyman
2. Abu-Lughod L. 1991. Writing against culture. See Ref. 46, pp. 137–62
3. Angus I, Jhally S, eds. 1989. *Cultural Politics in Contemporary America.* New York/ London: Routledge
4. Anzaldúa G. 1987. *Borderlands/La Frontera: The New Mestiza.* San Francisco: Spinsters/Aunt Lute
5. Appadurai A. 1988. Putting hierarchy in its place. *Cult. Anthropol.* 3:36–49
6. Bennett T. 1982. Theories of the media, theories of society. See Ref. 67, pp. 30–55
7. Bennett T. 1986. Introduction: popular culture and 'the turn to Gramsci': the politics of 'popular culture'. See Ref. 8, pp. xi–xix, 6–21
8. Bennett T, Mercer C, Woollacott J, eds. 1986. *Popular Culture and Social Relations.* Philadelphia: Open Univ. Press
9. Bennett T, Woollacott J. 1987. *Bond and Beyond: The Political Career of a Popular Hero.* New York: Methuen
10. Bourdieu P. 1984. *Distinction: A Social Critique of the Judgment of Taste.* Transl. R Nice. Cambridge: Harvard Univ. Press
11. Brantlinger P. 1983. *Bread & Circuses: Theories of Mass Culture as Social Decay.* Ithaca: Cornell Univ. Press
12. Buhle P, ed. 1987. *Popular Culture in America.* Minneapolis: Univ. Minn. Press
13. Burke P. 1978. *Popular Culture in Early Modern Europe.* London: Temple Smith
14. Butsch R, ed. 1990. *For Fun and Profit: The Transformation of Leisure into Consumption.* Philadelphia: Temple Univ. Press
15. Butsch R. 1990. Introduction: leisure and hegemony in America. See Ref. 14, pp. 3–27
16. Canaan J. 1990. Passing notes and telling jokes: gendered strategies among American middle school teenagers. In *Uncertain Terms: Negotiating Gender in America,* ed.

F Ginsburg, AL Tsing, pp. 215–31. Boston: Beacon
17. Caughie J. 1986. Popular culture: notes and revisions. In *High Theory/Low Culture: Analyzing Popular Culture and Film,* ed. C MacCabe, pp. 156–71. New York: St. Martin's
18. Chambers I. 1986. *Popular Culture: The Metropolitan Experience.* London: Methuen
19. Chartier R. 1984. Culture as appropriation: popular cultural uses in early modern France. See Ref. 86, pp. 229–53
20. Clarke J. 1990. Pessimism versus populism: the problematic politics of popular culture. See Ref. 14, pp. 28–44
21. Clarke J. 1991. *New Times and Old Enemies: Essays on Cultural Studies and America.* London: Harper Collins
22. Clifford J. 1988. *The Predicament of Culture: Twentieth-Century Ethnography, Literature, and Art,* pp. 255–76. Cambridge: Harvard Univ. Press
23. Cohen L. 1993. The class experience of mass consumption. In *The Power of Culture,* ed. RW Fox, TJJ Lears, pp. 135–60. Chicago: Univ. Chicago Press
24. Collins J. 1989. *Uncommon Cultures: Popular Culture and Postmodernism.* London: Routledge
25. Connor S. 1989. *Postmodernist Culture: An Introduction to Theories of the Contemporary.* Oxford: Blackwell
26. Crane D. 1992. *The Production of Culture: Media and the Urban Arts.* London: Sage
27. Curran J. 1990. The "new revisionism" in mass communications research. *Eur. J. Commun.* 5:2–3
28. Curran J, Gurevitch M, eds. 1991. *Mass Media and Society.* London: Edward Arnold
29. D'Acci J. 1994. *Defining Women: The Case of Cagney & Lacey.* Chapel Hill/London: Univ. N. C. Press
30. Davis M. 1992. *City of Quartz: Excavating the Future in Los Angeles.* New York: Vintage
31. Denning M. 1987. *Mechanic Accents:*

Dime Novels and Working-Class Culture in America. London: Verso

32. Denning M. 1990. The end of mass culture. *Int. Labor Working Class Hist.* 37:4–18

33. DiMaggio P. 1982. Cultural entrepreneurship in nineteenth-century Boston: the creation of an organizational base for high culture in America. *Media Cult. Soc.* 4: 33–50

34. DiMaggio P, Useem M. 1978. Social class and arts consumption. *Theory Soc.* 5(2): 141–61

35. Ehrenreich B. 1989. *Fear of Falling: The Inner Life of the Middle Class.* New York: Pantheon

36. Erenberg L. 1981. *Steppin' Out: New York Nightlife and the Transformation of American Culture, 1890–1930.* Westport: Greenwood

37. Erenberg L. 1986. From New York to Middletown: repeal and the legitimization of nightlife in the great depression. *Am. Q.* 38(5):761–78

38. Ewen S, Ewen E. 1982. *Channels of Desire: Mass Images and the Shaping of American Consciousness.* New York: McGraw-Hill

39. Fabian J. 1983. *Time and the Other: How Anthropology Makes Its Object.* New York: Columbia Univ. Press

40. Feuer J, Kerr P, Vahimagi T, eds. 1984. *MTM 'Quality Television.'* London: BFI

41. Fiske J. 1989. *Understanding Popular Culture.* Boston: Unwin Hyman

42. Fiske J. 1989. *Reading the Popular.* London: Verso

43. Fiske J. 1993. *Power Plays, Power Works.* London: Verso

44. Fjellman S. 1992. *Vinyl Leaves: Walt Disney World and America.* Boulder: Westview

45. Foley D. 1990. *Learning Capitalist Culture: Deep in the Heart of Tejas.* Philadelphia: Univ. Pa. Press

46. Fox RG, ed. 1991. *Recapturing Anthropology: Working in the Present.* Santa Fe, NM: School Am. Res.

47. Fox RW, Lears TJJ, eds. 1983. *The Culture of Consumption: Critical Essays in American History 1880–1980.* New York: Pantheon

48. Frith S. 1983. *Sound Effects: Youth, Leisure, and the Politics of Rock.* London: Constable

49. Frith S. 1988. *Music for Pleasure.* New York: Routledge

50. Frith S. 1991. The good, the bad, and the indifferent: defending popular culture from the populists. *Diacritics* 21(4): 102–15

51. Frith S. 1992. The industrialization of popular music. In *Popular Music and Social Communication,* ed. J Lull, pp. 49–74. Newbury Park, CA: Sage

52. Frow J. 1992. The concept of "the popular." *New Form.* 18:25–38

53. Frow J. 1995. *Cultural Studies and Cultural Value.* Oxford: Clarendon

54. Gamson J. 1994. *Claims to Fame: Celebrity in Contemporary America.* Berkeley: Univ. Calif. Press

55. Gans H. 1974. *Popular Culture and High Culture.* New York: Basic Books

56. Garnham N. 1995. The media and narratives of the intellectual. *Media Cult. Soc.* 17(3):359–84

57. Giroux HA. 1994. *Disturbing Pleasures: Learning Popular Culture.* New York: Routledge

58. Gitlin T. 1983. *Inside Prime-Time.* New York: Pantheon

59. Gledhill C. 1988. Pleasurable negotiations. In *Female Spectators: Looking at Film and Television,* ed. ED Pribram, pp. 64–89. London: Verso

60. Golding P, Murdock G. 1991. Culture, communication, and political economy. See Ref. 28, pp. 15–32

61. Goldstein J. 1993. The female aesthetic community. *Poet. Today* 14(1):143–63

62. Goodwin A. 1992. *Dancing in the Distraction Factory: Music Television and Popular Culture.* Minneapolis: Univ. Minn. Press

63. Gordon D, Edwards R, Reich M. 1982. *Segmented Work, Divided Workers: The Historical Transformation of Labor in the United States.* Cambridge: Cambridge Univ. Press

64. Gramsci A. 1971. *Selections from the Prison Notebooks.* Ed./Transl. Q Hoare, G Nowell-Smith. New York: Int. Publ.

65. Grossberg L. 1992. Rock and roll in search of an audience. In *Popular Music and Social Communication,* ed. J Lull, pp. 152–75. Newbury Park, CA: Sage

66. Grossberg L. 1994. The political status of youth and youth culture. In *Adolescents and Their Music: If It's Too Loud, You're Too Old,* ed. JS Epstein, pp. 25–46. New York: Garland

67. Gurevitch M, Bennett T, Curran J, Woollacott J, eds. 1982. *Culture, Society, and the Media.* London: Arnold

68. Hall S. 1981. Notes on deconstructing 'the popular'. In *People's History and Socialist Theory,* ed. R Samuel, pp. 227–40. London: Routledge/Kegan Paul

69. Hall S. 1982. The rediscovery of "ideology": return of the repressed in media studies. See Ref. 67, pp. 56–90

70. Hall S. 1992. What is this "black" in black popular culture? In *Black Popular Culture,* ed. G Dent, pp. 21–33. Seattle: Bay Press

71. Halttunen K. 1982. *Confidence Men and Painted Women: A Study of Middle-Class*

Culture in America, 1830–1870. New Haven, CT: Yale Univ. Press
72. Handler R. 1992. High culture, hegemony, and historical causality. *Am. Ethnol.* 19(4): 818–24
73. Hartley J. 1992. *Tele-ology: Studies in Television.* London: Routledge
74. Hebdige D. 1979. *Subculture: The Meaning of Style.* London: Methuen
75. Hebdige D. 1988. *Hiding in the Light: On Images and Things.* London: Comedia
76. Holland DC, Eisenhart MA. 1990. *Educated in Romance: Women, Achievement, and College Culture.* Chicago: Univ. Chicago Press
77. Horkheimer M, Adorno TW. 1972. *The Dialectic of Enlightenment,* pp. 120–67. New York: Seabury Press
78. Huyssen A. 1986. *After the Great Divide: Modernism, Mass Culture, Postmodernism.* Bloomington: Indiana Univ. Press
79. Jacobson M. 1995. *Special Sorrows: Irish-, Polish-, and Jewish-American Nationalism and the Diasporic Imagination.* Cambridge: Harvard Univ. Press
80. Jameson F. 1979. Reification and utopia in mass culture. *Soc. Text* 1:130–48
81. Jenkins H. 1992. *Textual Poachers: Television Fans and Participatory Culture.* New York: Routledge
82. Johnson PE. 1978. *A Shopkeeper's Millennium: Society and Revivals in Rochester, New York, 1815–1837.* New York: Hill & Wang
83. Johnson R. 1986–1987. What is cultural studies anyway? *Soc. Text* 16:38–80
84. Kaplan EA. 1983. *Women and Film: Both Sides of the Camera.* New York: Methuen
85. Kaplan EA. 1987. *Rocking Round the Clock: Music, Television, Postmodernism and Consumer Culture.* New York: Methuen
86. Kaplan SL, ed. 1984. *Understanding Popular Culture: Europe from the Middle Ages to the Nineteenth Century.* Berlin: Mouton
87. Kasson JF. 1978. *Amusing the Million: Coney Island at the Turn of the Century.* New York: Hill & Wang
88. Kasson JF. 1990. *Rudeness and Civility: Manners in Nineteenth Century Urban America.* New York: Hill & Wang
89. Kazin M. 1995. *The Populist Persuasion: An American History.* New York: Basic Books
90. Kunzel RG. 1993. *Fallen Women, Problem Girls: Unmarried Mothers and the Professionalization of Social Work, 1890–1945.* New Haven, CT: Yale Univ. Press
91. Laclau E, Mouffe C. 1985. *Hegemony & Socialist Strategy: Towards a Radical Democratic Politics.* London: Verso
92. Lazarsfeld PF, Berelson B, Gaudet H.

1944. *The People's Choice.* New York: Duell, Sloan & Pearce
93. Lears TJJ. 1981. *No Place of Grace: Antimodernism and the Transformation of American Culture.* New York: Pantheon
94. Lee MJ. 1993. *Consumer Culture Reborn: The Cultural Politics of Consumption.* London/New York: Routledge
95. Levine L. 1988. *Highbrow/Lowbrow: The Emergence of Cultural Hierarchy in America.* Cambridge, MA: Harvard Univ. Press
96. Liebes T, Katz E. 1990. *The Export of Meaning: Cross-Cultural Readings of Dallas.* New York: Oxford Univ. Press
97. Limon J. 1992. *Mexican Ballads, Chicano Poems: History and Influence in Mexican-American Social Poetry.* Berkeley: Univ. Calif. Press
98. Lipsitz G. 1981. *Class and Culture in Cold War America.* New York: Praeger
99. Lipsitz G. 1990. *Time Passages: Collective Memory and American Popular Culture.* Minneapolis: Univ. Minn. Press
100. Lipsitz G. 1990. Listening to learn and learning to listen: popular culture, cultural theory, and American studies. *Am. Q.* 42(4):615–36
101. Long E. 1985. *The American Dream and the Popular Novel.* Boston: Routledge & Kegan Paul
102. Lott E. 1993. *Love and Theft: Blackface Minstrelsy and the American Working Class.* New York: Oxford Univ. Press
103. Lutz CA, Collins JL. 1993. *Reading National Geographic.* Chicago: Univ. Chicago Press
104. MacAloon J. 1987. Missing stories: American politics and Olympic discourse. *Gannett Cent. J.* 1:111–42
105. Marcus G, Fischer MJ. 1986. *Anthropology as Cultural Critique: An Experimental Moment in the Human Sciences.* Chicago: Univ. Chicago Press
106. Martin A. 1993. In the name of popular culture. In *Australian Cultural Studies,* ed. J Frow, M Morris, pp. 133–45. Urbana: Univ. Ill. Press
107. May L. 1980. *Screening Out the Past: The Birth of Mass Culture and the Motion Picture Industry.* New York: Oxford Univ. Press
108. May L, ed. 1989. *Recasting Postwar America.* Chicago: Univ. Chicago Press
109. Deleted in proof
110. McGuigan J. 1992. *Cultural Populism.* London: Routledge
111. McRobbie A. 1991. *Feminism and Youth Culture: From 'Jackie' to 'Just Seventeen.'* Boston: Unwin Hyman
112. McRobbie A. 1994. *Postmodernism and Popular Culture.* London: Routledge
113. McRobbie A, Nava M, eds. 1984. *Gender and Generation.* London: Macmillan

114. Morley D. 1992. *Television, Audiences and Cultural Studies*. London: Routledge
115. Mukerji C, Schudson M, eds. 1991. *Rethinking Popular Culture: Contemporary Perspectives in Cultural Studies*. Berkeley: Calif. Univ. Press
116. Mulvey L. 1975. Visual pleasure and narrative cinema. *Screen* 16(3):6–18
117. Naremore J, Brantlinger P, eds. 1991. *Modernity and Mass Culture*. Bloomington: Indiana Univ. Press
118. Nasaw D. 1993. *Going Out: The Rise and Fall of Public Amusements*. New York: Basic Books
119. Nightingale V. 1993. What's "ethnographic" about ethnographic audience research? In *Nation, Culture, Text: Australian Cultural and Media Studies,* ed. G Turner, pp. 164–77. London: Routledge
120. Nowell-Smith G. 1987. Popular culture. *New Form.* 2:79–90
121. Nowell-Smith G. 1991. On Kiri te Kanawa, Judy Garland, and the culture industry. See Ref. 117, pp. 70–79
122. O'Barr WM. 1994. *Culture and the Ad: Exploring Otherness in the World of Advertising*. Boulder, CO: Westview
123. Ohmann R. 1996. *Selling Culture: Magazines, Markets, and Class Around the Turn of the Century*. London: Verso
124. Oriard M. 1993. *Reading Football: How the Popular Press Created an American Spectacle*. Chapel Hill: Univ. N. C. Press
125. Ortner SB. 1991. Reading America: preliminary notes on class and culture. See Ref. 46, pp. 163–89
126. Peiss K. 1986. *Cheap Amusements: Working Women and Leisure in Turn-of-the-Century New York*. Philadelphia: Temple Univ. Press
127. Peiss K. 1990. Commercial leisure and the "woman question." See Ref. 14, pp. 105–17
128. Pfeil F. 1995. *White Guys*. London: Verso
129. Powdermaker H. 1950. *Hollywood, The Dream Factory: An Anthropologist Looks at the Movie Makers*. Boston: Little Brown
130. Radway J. 1984. *Reading the Romance: Women, Patriarchy and Popular Literature*. Chapel Hill: Univ. N. C. Press
131. Radway J. 1988. Reception study: ethnography and the problems of dispersed audiences and nomadic subjects. *Cult. Stud.* 2(3):359–76
132. Radway J. 1993. Reading *Reading the Romance*. In *Studying Culture,* ed. A Gray, J McGuigan, pp. 62–79. London: Arnold
133. Revel J. 1984. Forms of expertise: intellectuals and "popular culture" in France (1650–1800). See Ref. 86, pp. 255–73
134. Riesman D. 1950. *The Lonely Crowd: A Study of the Changing American Character*. New Haven, CT: Yale Univ. Press

135. Roediger DR. 1991. *The Wages of Whiteness: Race and the Making of the American Working Class*. London: Verso
136. Rosaldo R. 1989. *Culture & Truth: The Remaking of Social Analysis*. Boston: Beacon
137. Rosaldo R. 1989. Border crossings. See Ref. 136, pp. 196–217
138. Rosaldo R. 1994. Whose cultural studies? *Am. Anthropol.* 96(3):524–29
139. Rose T. 1994. *Black Noise: Rap Music and Black Culture in Contemporary America*. Hanover, NH: Wesleyan Univ. Press
140. Rosenberg B, Manning DM, eds. 1957. *Mass Culture: The Popular Arts in America*. New York: Free Press
141. Rosenzweig R. 1983. *Eight Hours for What We Will: Workers and Leisure in an Industrial City, 1870–1920*. Cambridge: Cambridge Univ. Press
142. Ross A. 1989. *No Respect: Intellectuals and Popular Culture*. New York: Routledge
143. Rouse R. 1995. Thinking through transnationalism: notes on the cultural politics of class relations in the contemporary United States. *Public Cult.* 7(2):353–402
144. Seiter E. 1995. *Sold Separately: Parents and Children in Consumer Culture*. New Brunswick, NJ: Rutgers Univ. Press
145. Shank B. 1994. *Dissonant Identities: The Rock'n'roll Scene in Austin, Texas*. Hanover, NH: Wesleyan Univ. Press
146. Shiach M. 1989. *Discourse on Popular Culture: Class, Gender and History in Cultural Analysis, 1730 to the Present*. Stanford: Stanford Univ. Press
147. Shils E. 1972. Mass society and its culture. In *The Intellectuals and the Powers and Other Essays,* pp. 229–47. Chicago: Univ. Chicago Press
148. Slotkin R. 1985. *The Fatal Environment: The Myth of the Frontier in the Age of Industrialization, 1800–1890*. Middletown, CT: Wesleyan Univ. Press
149. Slotkin R. 1992. *Gunfighter Nation: The Myth of the Frontier in Twentieth-Century America*. New York: Atheneum
150. Stacey J. 1994. *Star Gazing: Hollywood Cinema and Female Spectatorship*. London: Routledge
151. Stansell C. 1987. *City of Women: Sex and Class in New York, 1789–1860*. Urbana: Univ. Ill. Press
152. Susman W. 1984. *Culture as History: The Transformation of American Society in the Twentieth Century*. New York: Pantheon
153. Thomas N. 1991. *Entangled Objects: Exchange, Material Culture, and Colonialism in the Pacific*. Cambridge: Harvard Univ. Press
154. Thomas N. 1991. Against ethnography. *Cult. Anthropol.* 6(3):306–22
155. Traube EG. 1992. *Dreaming Identities:*

Class, Gender, and Generation in 1980s Hollywood Movies. Boulder, CO: Westview

156. Traube EG. 1993. Family matters: post-feminist constructions of a contested site. Vis. Anthropol. 9(1):57–73

157. Wallace M. 1990. Invisibility Blues: From Pop to Theory. London: Verso

158. Wilentz S. 1984. Chants Democratic: New York City and the Rise of the American Working Class, 1788–1850. New York: Oxford Univ. Press

159. Willis P. 1981/1977. Learning to Labor: How Working Class Kids Get Working Class Jobs. New York: Columbia Univ. Press. Morningside ed.

160. Willis PE. 1990. Common Culture: Symbolic Work at Play in the Everyday Cultures of the Young. Boulder, CO: Westview

161. Winship J. 1987. Inside Women's Magazines. London: Pandora

Annu. Rev. Anthropol. 1996. 25:153–78

THE ANTHROPOLOGY OF PHARMACEUTICALS: A Biographical Approach

Sjaak van der Geest,[1] *Susan Reynolds Whyte,*[2] *and Anita Hardon*[1]

[1]Medical Anthropology Unit, University of Amsterdam, Oudezijds Achterburgwal 185, 1012 DK Amsterdam, The Netherlands

[2]Institute of Anthropology, University of Copenhagen, Frederikholms Kanal 4, 1220 Copenhagen, Denmark

KEY WORDS: medical anthropology, pharmaceuticals, drugs, applied anthropology

ABSTRACT

This review discusses pharmaceuticals as social and cultural phenomena by following their "life cycle" from production, marketing, and prescription to distribution, purchasing, consumption, and finally their efficacy. Each phase has its own particular context, actors, and transactions and is characterized by different sets of values and ideas. The anthropology of pharmaceuticals is relevant to medical anthropology and health policy. It also touches the heart of general anthropology with its long-time interest in the concepts of culture vs nature, symbolization and social transformation, and its more recent concerns with the cultural construction of the body and processes of globalization and localization. The study of transactions and meanings of pharmaceuticals in diverse social settings provides a particularly appropriate empirical base for addressing these new theoretical issues.

Introduction

Throughout human history and across cultures, people have attributed special transformative powers to material substances. A love medicine turns the world upside down in Shakespeare's *A Midsummer Night's Dream,* and in Burgess's *A Clockwork Orange,* the main character is treated with medicine to cure him of his violent behavior. Abu-Lughod (3) recounted a Bedouin legend about a man who took his wife's fertility medicine, became pregnant, and gave birth to

0084-6570/96/1015-0153$08.00

153

a daughter. Keller (95) reported that women in Zambia have ingenious medicines to prevent their husbands from engaging in extramarital sex, and Sacks (172) described how a medicine awakened patients from a thirty-year lethargy. The Jesuit missionary Alexandre de Rhodes, who visited Vietnam in the first half of the seventeenth century, wrote in his diary: "They have such reverence for holy water....They give it to all the sick to drink, with marvelous results. Every Sunday I was obliged to bless at least 500 jars of this sacred water to satisfy their pious desires" (39a).

By definition medicines are substances that have the capacity to change the condition of a living organism—for better or, in the case of sorcery medicines, for worse. The prototype of medicines are the materia medica that alleviate ill health, and the significance of medicines for most people lies in their curative efficacy. What makes medicines so popular as solutions in moments of distress? What gives them the potency to become candidates for "tournaments" in which the central tokens of value are at stake, as Tan (195) suggested, using a term from Appadurai (10)? The secret of their attributed power lies primarily in their concreteness (218). Their "thinginess" provides patients and healers with a means to deal with the problem at hand. Medicines are tangible, usable in a concrete way: They can be swallowed, smeared on the skin, or inserted into orifices—activities that hold the promise of a physical effect. By applying a "thing," we transform the state of dysphoria into something concrete, into some thing to which the patient and others can address their efforts. Medicines thus fit logically into biomedicine and most other medical traditions. Practicing medicine, after all, is the art of making dis-ease concrete.

The cultural (symbolic) logic of medicines was discerned by early anthropologists in so-called primitive societies. They called it magic, fetishism, or animism: the belief in the immanence of forces that people attempt to possess, control, and manipulate to their own advantage. Until recently, however, few anthropologists extended that cultural perspective to pharmaceuticals—the synthesized, manufactured, and commercially distributed therapeutic substances that constitute the hard core of biomedicine. With the exception of a few pioneers (8, 38, 117), anthropologists did not begin systematically to examine pharmaceuticals as social and cultural phenomena until the 1980s. By then it was abundantly clear that biomedicine, and particularly "biomedicines," were genuinely popular and heavily used in many societies of Africa, Asia, and Latin America (57, 74, 210). Moreover, radical critiques of the pharmaceutical invasion of the Third World (23, 29, 63, 125, 139, 182, 183) had caught the attention of some academics. Illich's (83) attack on biomedicine's expropriation of health in Western society sparked critical studies about medicalization and overconsumption of medical services, including pharmaceuticals. It was also in the 1980s that the concept of essential drugs—inexpensive and safe medications for the most common diseases—gained attention worldwide, mainly through promotion by the World Health Organization (93, 120). Policymakers as well as anthropologists concerned with the policy implications of their work increasingly attended to the ways that drugs were provided and used in settings of the South.

Thus health-care issues constituted one setting antecedent to the rise of anthropological interest in pharmaceuticals, although in the North the relation between medicines and society became primarily the province of social pharmacy (115, 191, 192). Researchers documented the local realities in which medicines were actually made available and used. They showed the significance of the transaction of medicines through commercial and informal channels and emphasized that most pharmaceuticals, even regulated "prescription-only" drugs, were taken as self-medication, that is, without the supervision of a formally trained health worker. Some researchers examined the often capricious transactions involving pharmaceuticals; others explored the meanings that people attached to Western medicines. Anthropologists emphasized what Kleinman (98) called the "folk" and the "popular" sectors of health care. Only a few researchers focused primarily on the transaction of pharmaceuticals within professional settings (168, 171, 209, 224).

Another setting antecedent to the increased interest in pharmaceuticals laid within anthropology itself. Greater interest in Western culture and products led to greater interest in biomedicine as a cultural phenomenon worthy of study. As the "exotic bias" diminished, more anthropologists from both the North and South undertook fieldwork in their own societies. Capsules, tablets, and hypodermic syringes were no longer taken for granted and ignored by researchers. They could be defamiliarized (denaturalized) and analyzed according to their attributed meanings. It is striking, however, that sociocultural research on pharmaceuticals has been far less common in societies of the North than in those of the South (223). Apparently, the deexoticization of (medical) anthropology is still incomplete.

A renewed interest by anthropologists in material objects (130) cast older Marxist approaches to commodities and fetishism in a new light and provided a bridge between culture and economy (10, 40, 42, 55, 197). The "thinginess" of medicines and their use as commodities suit them extremely well to this theoretical development (15, 109). The new approach to cultural economy fits with the study of processes of globalization and localization. As older paradigms of modernization and development were supplemented by analyses of transnational cultural flows (11, 70), it became evident that political ideals, entertainment, institutional forms, fashions, and commodities both transformed and were transformed by the contexts through which they moved. Biomedicine is one of the best examples of globalization. It is truly cosmopolitan—not Western—medicine (111). Biomedical technology in diverse social settings provides a particularly appropriate empirical base for addressing newer theoretical issues concerning cultural globalization (154).

The Biography of Pharmaceuticals

By following the transactions of pharmaceuticals, one may discern a biographical order in their "social life" (101). First, they are prepared, usually in a technologically advanced setting, and marketed to wholesale suppliers such as ministries of health and private firms, as well as to retailers (hospitals and clinics, pharmacists, storekeepers, and medical practitioners). Next, they are distributed to consumers, either by prescription or direct sale. The prescription is an intermediate phase. It provides the patient only with a piece of paper that eventually leads to purchase of the medicine. After the pharmaceutical has come into the hands of a consumer, it will reach the final stage of its life: Someone will use the medicine with the purpose of restoring, improving, or maintaining his or her health. The way in which a medicine is taken constitutes a crucial moment in its life. "Wrong use" may render its entire life meaningless. Finally, pharmaceuticals have, as it were, a life after death. The fulfillment of their life purpose lies in their effect on the well-being of the person who took them. The pharmaceutical's efficacy is its ultimate and decisive life stage.

Each life stage is characterized by a specific context and particular actors. In the production and marketing phase, the primary social actors are scientists and businesspeople working for pharmaceutical companies. The prescription phase mainly involves health professionals and their patients in the context of a medical practice. Distribution is carried out mostly by sellers such as pharmacists, storekeepers, drug pedlars, and their customers in a market-type setting. Use occurs mostly in a household setting, away from medical professionals, as does the final phase: efficacy.

Each stage has a "regime of values" (10), expressed in distinctive sets of ideas about medicines. In the production and marketing phase, concepts of scientific research, market commodity, and commercial competition are dominant. Medical practitioners see pharmaceuticals as indispensible in their encounters with the sick. Pharmacists and other sellers regard pharmaceuticals as commodities, while patients and their relatives expect medicines to solve their problems.

Of course, a "biography" of pharmaceuticals is a metaphor. Through manufacturing, trading, prescribing, buying, and consuming, people give these substances a history. As powerful technical devices and cultural symbols (136), medicines acquire a status and force in society. As medical technology, pharmaceuticals are not only products of human culture, but producers of it. As vehicles of ideology, facilitators of self-care, and perceived sources of effi-cacy, they direct people's thoughts and actions and influence their social life. The availability of medicines affects how practitioners and patients deal with sickness. They move people into establishing, avoiding, and breaking off social relationships. To say in Lévi-Strauss's well-known words that medi-cines are "good to think" (and act) with, renders them insufficient justice. Their role in human life extends much farther, for they use people as much as people use them. A biography of pharmaceuticals is an apt metaphor because it puts order in their social and cultural vagaries and casts light on their complex-ity. Furthermore, we may distinguish five research themes that coincide with the five biographical life stages mentioned above.

Production and Marketing

Social scientists were first drawn to pharmaceuticals by critical studies of dubious practices by the pharmaceutical industry such as bribery, fraud in safety testing, dumping, and misinformation (24, 29, 32, 123, 124, 139, 182–184). These studies set the tone for a rather uneasy, if not hostile, relation-ship between the industry and anthropologists, who traditionally chose the side of the weaker party. This animosity may have been a reason why anthropolo-gists failed to study the production and marketing of pharmaceuticals as social and cultural phenomena. Additional reasons might have been the reluctance of the industry to allow researchers to observe their practices, as well as the exotic bias of anthropologists. Capturing the manufacturer's point of view, to paraphrase Malinowski, still needs to be put on the agenda of anthropological research.

There are many questions for anthropologists about pharmaceutical produc-tion and marketing. What beliefs do laboratory scientists and drug manufactur-ers hold about health, disease, and medicine? How is their knowledge of pharmaceuticals produced in concrete industrial activities and social relation-ships? What are their daily routines in the production and marketing of phar-maceuticals? How are claims about safety and efficacy of medicines con-structed? How are such claims used to justify registration and marketing of medicines? How are marketing strategies developed for maximum effect on prescribing and use?

One of the few examples of an anthropological (participant observation) study of the production of scientific knowledge is by Latour & Woolgar (108), although the study does not include pharmaceuticals. A recent study by Abra-ham (2) that does focus on medicines is a rare attempt at opening the black box of industrial production and marketing of new pharmaceuticals as well as state regulation. The study shows how industry presents biased safety data to drug regulatory bodies to register new products and get them on the market. Reviewing a number of case studies, the author states that manufacturers were protected by government drug regulators and that the interests of patients in having adequate information were compromised.

It is no coincidence that the little research undertaken on pharmaceutical production and marketing pertains to their more accessible and visible aspects such as production and sales figures (32), advertisements (64, 137, 198), drug information on inserts (153, 182, 183), drug compendia (157), and attempts by political authorities to curb the influence of pharmaceutical companies (93, 105). Nor is it a coincidence that most of these studies were undertaken by nonanthropologists. An exception is a study of advertisements with telling images of the reinterpretation of pharmaceuticals according to local cultures (136). Drug commercials on TV reflect and produce popular perceptions of pharmaceuticals (72, 88, 148, 193, 219).

It is also striking that the sales representatives of the pharmaceutical industry ("reps") have attracted so little attention from anthropologists (exceptions are 113; VR Kamat & M Nichter, unpublished manuscript). Reps are usually only mentioned in passing (54, 145, 233). Production and marketing still constitute the most conspicuous gap in the anthropological study of pharmaceuticals.

Anthropologists' failure to study the pharmaceutical industry does not mean that the industry has failed to study anthropology. While the industry first ignored critiques blaming it for neglecting the social, cultural, and economic conditions in developing countries (124, 125), it now tends to follow another line. Claiming openness to local variations in cultural concepts of health, illness, and medicine, the industry asserts that it supplies what people welcome as useful and effective. In doing so, the industry argues, they are culturally more sensitive than critics who demand that pharmaceutical firms apply the same standards of practice worldwide, thus imposing Western criteria upon non-Western people. The anthropological perspective is congenial to market research. Ironically, pharmaceutical companies delivering products that, from a biomedical perspective, are dubious, useless, or dangerous, can defend their practice thanks to anthropological studies that show that people cherish vitamins, blood tonics, antidiarrhea medicines, and hormonal preparations.

Prescription

Prescribing a medication is much more than meets the eye. Smith (185) in a now classic article lists 27 "latent functions" of the prescription, some of which are discussed below. A prescription has psychological effects, it is a means of communication, it shows power and facilitates social control, it produces income, and it has symbolic (metonymic) significance. We address five questions about prescribing medicines: Who prescribes? What is being prescribed? Why do prescribers prescribe as they do or what does prescribing mean to them? What does the prescription mean to the client? And what are the consequences of overprescribing?

Not only medical doctors write prescriptions or instruct people on what medicines they should take. In many societies nurses and other health workers perform this role. Sciortino (175) reported that nurses in rural health centers in Java routinely take over most activities that are the responsibility of doctors. This occurs widely where doctors are scarce. Pharmacists, who are supposed to fill doctors' prescriptions, often skip the doctor (or other health worker) and prescribe medicines themselves (68, 88, 91, 116, 132, 150, 199, 232). Although this practice is particularly likely to develop in societies where medical doctors are difficult to reach, pharmacists are also consulted for medical advice in Western societies (177, 223).

Storekeepers and drug peddlers also prescribe medicines (though not in writing), especially in societies with defective health-care systems (49, 81, 107, 178, 210, 215). These medicine sellers are closer to their customers than doctors and pharmacists geographically, financially, and socially. Whyte (229) called them "folk healers" (98) and noted that they treat their customers with more respect than formal health-care professionals and that they adjust their "prescriptions" to the purses of their clients. Medicines may also be purchased by proxy, another advantage. A last category of prescribers are traditional healers, who have integrated Western pharmaceuticals into their practice (30, 145, 233).

The quality of prescribing is often criticized by biomedical observers. The most common critique refers to overprescribing: too many medicines, too many varieties, unnecessary antibiotics and/or injections, too expensive medicines (22, 66, 84, 102, 104, 162, 164, 180, 198, 221)—in all countries, but particularly in the South. Overprescribing can be the result of poor or biased information disseminated to prescribers (198, 234), profit making (97, 114, 125), or the simple fact that it is easier to satisfy patients with drugs than with words (127).

Faulty prescribing raises the question of the rationality of prescribers. That unqualified dispensers prescribe wrongly can be explained by their lack of biomedical knowledge. However, why do trained physicians and pharmacists prescribe in contradiction with their own professional directives? Sachs & Tomson (170, 171) identified several types of "rationality" in medical practice. What from a biomedical perspective appears irrational and objectionable may make good sense for social, cultural, or other reasons.

Innovative work on how physicians prescribe has been done by Haaijer-Ruskamp (67) and Denig (39). In a series of studies, these authors attempted to develop a model to understand physician prescribing behavior. The studies show that knowledge about biomedical treatment outcomes determines drug choices only in part. Especially in cases that do not seem serious, doctors tend to resort to simplified strategies in which they do not compare different treatment options. Such routines are sometimes learned or copied from others without conscious deliberation.

Prescribing is a social act. It demonstrates the physician's concern (155, 185). Through prescriptions, doctors show their patients that they recognize their complaints and are trying to help them. The concreteness of the prescription paper presages the concreteness of the medicine. Where medication is seen as the essence of medical practice, prescribing is the main thing expected from a physician. A nonprescribing doctor presents a contradiction. Not prescribing, which might be preferable on biomedical grounds, would then be irrational by cultural criteria. Numerous authors noted that doctors attempt to increase their good reputation by prescribing profusely (90). Conversely, where people are more critical of prescribing and may regard it as avoiding the real issue (25, 220), doctors are more parsimonious in prescribing medicines. In both cases, the doctor is complying with patient demands (75, 90). Schwartz et al (174) mentioned patient demands as one of the three main reasons for "nonscientific" prescribing in the United States (The other two are are the wish to give a placebo, which is also a form of compliance, and clinical experience).

Prescribing, finally, is as much a matter of the doctor solving his own problems as solving those of the patient (34, 126, 127, 185, 219). The doctor's problems are: how to react satisfactorily to the patient's request, how to conceal his uncertainty about cause and cure of the sickness, and how to dispose of the patient in an acceptable manner. The prescription comes to his rescue, as Pellegrino suggests (155:627):

> The medication indicates the doctor's concern; it enables him to communicate with patients with lesser education, different values, or different socioeconomic status; it can forestall lengthy discussion of symptoms and their meaning…it is an effective device for parcelling out the limited time a physician can alot to a patient.…Giving a prescription is also a major source of satisfaction to the physician, since it may be the only way he can 'do' something for the patient.

Even when practitioner and patient do not understand each other, the prescribed medicines give them the illusion that they are in agreement about the best therapy (168). The leading role of pharmaceuticals in clinical practice is nowhere more convincing: The available medicines create the possibility of the doctor's most therapeutic act—writing a prescription—and urge him to perform it. Pellegrino (155) called it the doctor's "benediction."

The wholesome effect the prescription has on the doctor—and any other prescriber—is not lost on the patient. With the prescription as a kind of written contract, the healer and the person to be healed unite to undertake a common action. The prescription is an "offshoot" of the doctor, his metonymic representation. Taking along the prescription is like taking along the doctor himself with his knowledge and good advice, his concern, and his access to medication.

The prescription is not yet the medication, but for many it nearly is (61, 107, 155). Samuel Butler wrote in one of his Notebooks: "I read once of a man who was cured of a dangerous illness by eating his doctor's prescription." The man's fortunate mistake parallels a common therapy in Islamic medicine, that of drinking the sacred words of the Koran after their ink has dissolved in water (43).

For the patient, a prescription also functions as a legitimation of sickness. It proves to the environment that he is indeed sick and entitles him to the privileges and roles reserved for the sick. A refusal to give a prescription would cast doubt over the genuineness of the patient's complaint. In cultures where the prescription of medicines is less well appreciated, a written referral to a medical specialist will have the same effect.

Liberal prescribing may serve a social and cultural logic, but biomedical observers emphasize that it also causes considerable problems. One concern is that it leads to erratic buying of medicines when poor patients are unable to buy all the medicines on the prescription and choose arbitrarily (e.g. the first on the list, the cheapest, the one that happens to be in stock) (96, 180). Another problematic consequence of bad prescribing is that people tend to imitate doctors' prescriptions in self-medication (71, 148, 194).

Distribution

Anthropologists studying health-care practices in cultures of the South long ignored the widespread distribution of pharmaceuticals. Buying so-called modern drugs in local stores and market booths had already become established practice while anthropologists continued to write exclusively about ritual treatments and medicinal herbs. One of the first to draw attention to the sale of "patent medicines" was Geertz (62) in his study of religion in Java. Geertz included an extensive field note about a man dressed in Western-style clothes selling a medicine in the town square. He claims that the medicine is good for everything, from heart trouble, cough, and stomachaches to insanity. The medicine is used with great success in America and Jakarta. During his talk he shows pictures from *Life* magazine and some glossy medical journals and mentions the name of President Eisenhower. In another early observation, Bleek (21) reported how young people in a rural town of Ghana buy injections,

Nivaquine tablets, laxatives, and various other pharmaceuticals to cause abortion.

The first reaction to the news that Western pharmaceuticals were not different from Coca-Cola in that they were offered for sale everywhere in the world, without professional medical supervision, was concern about their health consequences (e.g. 13, 49, 119, 122). At the same time, anthropologists set out to study their ubiquitous availability as an integral part of changing culture.

Reviewing the work to date we may distinguish (*a*) contextual descriptions of drug selling and more analytical studies that (*b*) contrast and compare private/public and formal/informal distribution, (*c*) view distribution in the light of state policy, and (*d*) discuss commoditization and commercial aspects.

Most descriptions focus on pharmacies (54, 68, 81, 82, 88–91, 99, 100, 116, 132, 142, 161, 198, 199, 219, 232, 233). A common observation is that pharmacy customers do not always need a doctor's prescription to purchase "prescription-only" medicine. Officially, pharmacies are managed by qualified pharmacists, but especially in countries of the South this is often not the case. Trained pharmacists sometimes are put in charge of several pharmacies but cannot be found in any of them. The actual work of dispensing medicines is done by untrained assistants without supervision (81, 90, 91).

As noted above, pharmacy personnel often give advice to customers and act as doctors (54, 68, 100, 116, 132, 161, 225). Pharmacies are mainly found in urban centers. For people who live near them, they are often the first choice of therapeutic action (116, 219). Several authors point out that prescription habits by pharmacy personnel leave much to be desired (198) and that profit motives largely determine their practices (82). Others, however, emphasize their closeness to the people and their concern (91, 116, 219).

The most detailed and informative study of pharmacies is by Kamat (89). He carried out research in 75 pharmacies in Bombay and gave a rich account of their functioning. He described pharmacies as extremely lucrative and versatile business enterprises and discussed some views of pharmacists about their profession. They believe that the professional competence of a pharmacist has lost much of its significance because most medicines are now prepacked. He also described in detail how customers buy their medicines and how they interact with the pharmacy workers (cf 91).

Another category of medicine distributors is health workers in clinics and hospitals (20, 87, 209, 229) of the South. They usually do not own the medicines they distribute and are thus able to dispense them more freely. They may sell medicines under the counter or "out the back door," and they are likely to treat medicines as gifts to friends and relatives (209). Health workers distribute pharmaceuticals both within the institutions where they work and outside them from their homes and in informal practices (229).

There are a variety of informal and untrained vendors of medicines. Pharmaceuticals are sold in shops that can be either specialized drugstores (85, 99, 145, 149, 152, 212) or general stores (72, 163, 212). Pharmaceuticals are also sold in markets and by itinerant hawkers (52, 53, 158, 159, 212, 215). Increasingly popular places for medicine hawkers are lorry stations, taxi parks, and buses (7, 122). In West Africa, it is now common to see a medicine seller entertaining the passengers in a bus with a mixture of religious preaching and commercial drug selling. The Nigerian novelist Ben Okri gives a hilarious account of this practice in his story "Stars of the New Curfew" (151). Two final categories of drug distributors are traditional healers (16, 30, 145, 233), who demonstrate the dynamic character of tradition and passing tourists (188).

Very few of the above studies are truly ethnographic in the sense that they are "thick descriptions," rich in context and with an emphasis on symbol and cognition. Most attention is given to a few transactions and questions that are relevant from a medical perspective. Which pharmaceuticals are being purchased for what type of sickness? Are prescriptions used? Are customers informed about correct use? How much is being paid? But for a few exceptions (30, 215), the conceptual world of medicine providers is hardly discussed.

The public-vs-private and formal-vs-informal status of drug distribution has received much attention, no doubt because it has policy implications. Several authors have contrasted public and private distribution, pointing out the inefficiency of the public system (58, 79, 214, 222). Some suggested that the drug supply system is likely to fail where economic incentives are missing altogether (209), while others criticized the "commerciogenic" nature of private distribution, which leads to severe inequity in health care (54). At the same time, it is noticed that private and public can only be distinguished and contrasted formally. At an informal level, the two "systems" are tightly intertwined and keep each other alive (214). Some examples of informal practices within the formal system have already been mentioned: health workers clandestinely sell medicines (209, 229) and state-registered pharmacies function as informal drugstores where medicines can be purchased without a prescription and untrained assistants act as prescribing doctors.

Closely connected to the articulation of formal and informal distribution channels is the discussion about the place of medicine distribution in state policy. Several authors explain the large-scale informal and uncontrolled distribution of pharmaceuticals in developing countries as the result of a failing health-care policy. The state's failure is threefold. Inability to make professional health workers (doctors and nurses) accessible to the entire population makes it impossible for many to obtain an official prescription. Continuous drug shortages in state health institutions mean that people cannot get what they regard as the essence of health care. Inadequate wages require health workers to supplement their incomes, often by informal practices. The failures of the state's policy force people into a self-help culture of medicine and create space for the development of an informal medicine market (9, 107, 120, 189, 213, 228, 229).

The commodification of health and health care through the buying and selling of medicines has given rise to some lively debates in medical anthropology. The most prominent critic is Nichter (146) who, on the basis of research in South and Southeast Asia, remarked that there is a growing tendency to see health as something one can obtain through the consumption of pharmaceuticals. He calls this trend "defective modernization" and rejects it because it impoverishes the concept of health and gives a "false sense of health security" (see also 173, 187). Fifteen years earlier, Ferguson (54) had also criticized the "pharmaceuticalization" of health care.

Other authors have a more optimistic view. Plattner's (156) article on the social character of face-to-face market transactions is seminal. Commercial activities do not necessarily destroy social relationships. Money also creates interaction and confidence beween people. Uncertainty about the quality of a product encourages customers to buy from someone who is reliable, and conversely a seller will keep his customers if his products are good. In such a situation, buying implies mutual trust. The seller is accountable to the client while a free health-care system may lead to a loss of accountability.

Arguing from this perspective, some (14, 216) plead for a certain degree of privatization in the distribution of pharmaceuticals. Whyte (SR Whyte, unpublished manuscript) observed that commodification of health care through the sale of medicines is a creative grass-roots response to difficult conditions in Uganda. Local users and providers of drugs are pleased that they can meet their needs when the formal system has failed them. Reeler (163) also takes a positive attitude toward commercialization trends. She regarded "negotiating as a customer" as a form of "empowerment" through which urban people in Thailand are better able to put pressure on health-care providers. She wrote: "The commodification of the popular and the folk sector has turned the patient into a customer who can refuse a treatment or puchase exactly what he wants."

Use of Medicines

The previous stages in the pharmaceutical's biography prepare it for use. Only when it is consumed does the substance become a medicine. "Wrong use" may render the best medicine useless or dangerous. Three topics in the literature on use of pharmaceuticals include self-medication, compliance and noncompliance, and conceptual aspects. Self-medication is a natural, self-evident act. It is by far the most common medical action (1, 5, 36, 37, 56, 59, 60, 71, 72, 98, 106, 116, 119, 131, 138, 142, 146, 181, 190, 212, 223, 228). Its self-evidence is why it initially received little attention from anthropologists, mainly interested in more spectacular medical practices. It is usually practiced with minor ailments, which, according to a founding father of medical anthropology, "are not important enough to theorize about" (4).

Self-medication is "natural" because it is convenient and economical. In addition, availability makes self-medication easy. Almost everywhere pharmaceuticals have replaced herbal medicines. They are available "around the corner" in local shops and kiosks. Even in small villages people can buy painkillers, broad-spectrum antibiotics, and medicines against malaria, worms, and diarrhea. Studies that have documented drug-use patterns in households systematically reveal that people self-medicate common health problems with a limited range of medicines that are easily accessible in the local health-care context (68, 72, 109a). Treatment strategies in these health problems are fixed. They have become routines that are not easily changed. Many people, moreover, store some medicines at home (72, 208, 212).

Self-medication is "natural" in another sense. Because medicines are the essence of medicine, why visit a doctor or nurse when one can get the "thing" directly? Only when the problem remains should one consult an expert. In the Third World, experts may not be available, so self-medication is imperative.

In the North, self-medication is encouraged in reaction to overdependence on medical services. For consumers, it is a movement to assume greater responsibility over their own health. For the state it is a welcome opportunity to economize on health care (223). It also benefits the pharmaceutical industry (78, 186).

By definition, self-medication is practiced outside the control of medical professionals, usually at home. Not surprisingly, biomedical observers are concerned about the risks of self-medication (e.g. 1, 49, 119). There is only a thin line between self-medication and prescribed medication, and a doctor or nurse can never be sure patients will take medicines exactly as they were instructed. Thus, every medication is to some extent self-medication, unless the health worker administers it (e.g. an injection).

Hundreds of studies have been published about compliance in taking medication. In nearly all of them, compliance is viewed from a medico-centric perspective, and noncompliance—not following professional instructions about medication—is considered a problem. These studies have been undertaken to investigate the causes of noncompliance to improve compliance. Conrad (35) and others (77, 148, 204) have argued, however, that noncompliance needs to be studied from the patient's point of view. Patients may have good reasons for taking their medicines in a way other than that indicated by the prescriber. Conrad reported that epileptics may follow their own ideas of self-medication to test how long they can stay without medication, to gain more control over their situation, to escape the stigmatization associated with medication, or for practical reasons.

Rarely is noncompliance the result of patients misunderstanding the doctor's information, but it is the result of patients having different ideas and, in particular, different interests. Compliance, wrote Trostle (202), is an ideology that justifies the physician's authority. Understanding noncompliance requires an anthropological approach to capture the patient's viewpoint. In noncompliance, patients express their rationality vis-à-vis the doctor's. That rationality includes not only medical considerations but also social, political, and economic ones. This applies to mothers in Ecuador (56) as well as to women in the United States who want to control the symptoms of their illness within the constraints of their daily routine of life (80).

In most cases, however, other conceptions of health, illness, and medicine affect the way people take medicines in both Western (26, 61, 75, 76) and, in particular, non-Western societies, where pharmaceuticals are often recast in another knowledge system and used very differently from the way they were intended in the "regime of value" where they were produced (17, 20, 69, 103, 131, 226).

One of the first to draw attention to this phenomenon of cultural reinterpretation was Logan (117), who showed that Guatemalan villagers categorized Western medicines as "hot" or "cold" according to their own illness classification. Acceptance or rejection of a particular medication depended on this classification and not on biomedical knowledge (see also 86, 128). Color is also related to use. Especially in African cultures, illness and healing are often linked to color symbolism (20, 143, 178), and notions of color qualities relevant to traditional medicines may guide preferences for pharmaceuticals.

In some societies, notions of "compatibility" are used to steer drug use. Hardon (73), for example, heard from her informants in Manila that a medicine must fit the person using it (in the local language, the medicine must be *hiyang*). People believe that a drug that is good for one person can be bad for another. When individuals conclude that a medicine is bad they refuse to take it, even if the drug seems medically suitable . For the same reason, they could decide to take a medicine considered "wrong" by the doctor. An interesting variation occurs in Sri Lanka (147). Sinhalese people believe that an effective medicine must not only fit the patient, the therapeutic capacity of the practitioner administering it should also accord with the patient's constitution.

Other ideas that influence people's consumption of pharmaceuticals are concepts of pathological process and etiology. Etkin et al (46), who studied the use of plant medicine among the Hausa in Northern Nigeria, noticed that people view illness as a process. A tenet in their selection of medicines was "the understanding that symptoms of a disease—or even different diseases—develop sequentially, one eventuating from another" (46:921). They therefore used different medicines at different stages of the disease. Each medicine had specific qualities to fight the symptoms at that particular stage. This idea was also applied in their use of Western pharmaceuticals. Their use was stopped as soon as their target symptom had been resolved. In terms of etiology, their conviction that dirt is the dominant cause of sickness, for example, encourages people to use laxatives frequently (143, 179).

Popular concepts in countries of the North affect medicine use too. Vuckovic & Nichter (223) describe two contradictory trends in the way Americans think about pharmaceuticals. There is, on the one hand, the impatience with pain and illness, which results in an attitude of "more is better" and overconsumption. On the other hand, people are increasingly suspicious of medicines and doubt their safety and efficacy. Pharmaceuticals are poison to be avoided (26, 50, 171).

Efficacy

Only after it has "died" can a medicine accomplish its mission. Its final stage is the "hereafter" or "great beyond" when it takes effect. The efficacy of a pharmaceutical is not limited to the medical domain, however. Its power extends far beyond physical and mental well-being. The effects of medication are also social, cultural, psychological, and even metaphysical.

Opinions differ about the source of therapeutic potency in medicines. Biopharmacologists hold that their healing power is an inherent part of their substance, an opinion that is widespread in other medical cultures as well. For many, that innate capacity is the great blessing of pharmaceuticals because it enables people to find a therapy without becoming dependent on others (discussed below). Often it is argued that medicines derive their power from what the healer puts into them. Yoruba practitioners make their medicines effective by singing to them (28), and healers in Burundi claim that it does not make a difference which herbs they use because it is their personal power added to the herbs that makes them work (12).

The idea of added potency may also be applied to pharmaceuticals believed to be more effective if given by a good hand or accompanied by the right words (18, 19, 147).

Anthropologists, balancing between emic and etic, lie between these two poles. They see efficacy as a cultural construction with both biological and social dimensions (cf 44, 195). Efficacy is brought about in a context of belief and expectation and through social communication and interaction. It has a processual nature and is initiated by preparatory activities like prescribing, buying, collecting, and preparing the medicine. Therefore, the therapeutic effect of a medicine cannot be reduced to its chemical substance. Its "total drug effect" (33) depends also on nonchemical attributes of the drug such as its color, name, and provenance; on properties of the recipient and prescriber; and on the situations in which the medicine is delivered and consumed. The placebo effect—some prefer the term nonspecific effect—is now almost universally accepted as inherent in medicine, responsible for 10–90% of its efficacy (133–135, 160, 167, 206). "Meaning mends" and "metaphors heal," as Moerman remarked. However, if efficacy is culturally constructed, then so are side effects (148). Etkin (45) noted, moreover, that what is considered a side effect in one culture may be intended in another. The appearance of side effects is often regarded as a sign that the medicine is strong (171).

One attribute of a medicine, its provenance, is particularly interesting with regard to the construction of efficacy. The belief that medicines that come from afar are stronger than native ones is present in many cultures (48, 110, 178, 227). Pharmaceuticals from Switzerland and Sweden are metonymically endowed with the prestige of these countries' advanced technology (218). This foreign aura is dexterously exploited in drug advertisements (193).

The social efficacy of pharmaceuticals is manifold. Medicines mark people's identity, as do other material goods (10). Pharmaceuticals affect people as intimately as food and body decorations and seem particularly well designed to shape people's sense of being (148) and belonging. Reeler (163) noted that Thai labor migrants write for medicines to be sent from home, even though pharmaceuticals are readily available where they are working. Nichter & Nichter (146) reported a similar example in India of people trying to obtain medicines from their home area. In addition, pharmaceuticals serve as ritual objects facilitating transitions from one phase to another, from health to sickness and back (206). That ritual effect is particularly strong in the social handling of sickness in children (31, 169, 200, 201). For many people, medicines mark the passage from being awake to sleep (61).

Medicines can be used to facilitate, mark, and reinforce social relationships. They can be given in friendship or controlled restrictively in order to maintain authority. As noted above, in the communication between a patient and practitioner, or between a patient and his environment, a medicine—even before it is used—can be more convincing and more effective than words in communicating knowledge and emotion (166, 168, 185).

Just as medicines can serve to facilitate, they can also be used to obviate social relations. With their perceived innate healing power, pharmaceuticals can have a liberating effect on people. Purchasing such a powerful object enables sick people to evade obligations and entanglements with significant social others and solve their problems privately (227). For problems that involve shame (e.g. sexually transmitted diseases, tuberculosis, or unwanted pregnancy), such an alternative solution is particularly welcome (21, 148, 218).

The cultural efficacy of pharmaceuticals lies primarily in their capacity to carry meanings. As we indicated above, pharmaceuticals are not only applied after a disease has been diagnosed. They may also play a crucial role in identifying and interpreting illness and thus contribute to its cultural construction. The character and gravity of sickness are often expressed in terms of kind and quantity of medicines (68, 146, 148). Even the concept of risk may be reified as a phenomenon that can be managed through pharmaceuticals (223). Medicines taken by women in the Philippines signal the image of women as weak and feeble (196).

Pharmaceuticals carry many other messages. They are vehicles of ideologies and fashions and are thus convenient means by which globalization runs its course. If industrial goods spread the commodity ethic (40, 130), pharmaceuticals do so par excellence, as they are the commodities most urgently needed and most invasive, especially in countries of the South (146, 148). If health can be bought, then anything must be for sale.

The psychological efficacy of pharmaceuticals was indicated above in the section on Prescription. The concreteness of the medicine fills the patient with confidence that something is being done about his health problem. Likewise, the person who prescribes or dispenses the medicine feels satisfied that he has been able to reassure the patient. Pharmaceuticals free both patients and doctors from their anxieties (34, 126, 155, 185, 219).

Pharmaceuticals may even have metaphysical efficacy. The fact that they work confirms to those who prescribe and consume them that their beliefs about reality are correct. To most, the "miracles" of pharmaceuticals prove that natural science is the right "religion." To others, who have integrated pharmaceuticals into their own explanatory models, those miracles are taken as proofs of the correctness of their model. The therapeutic efficacy of pharmaceuticals establishes belief in beings that have never been seen, like bacteria, and dogmas that are unintelligible, such as theories of infection and immunity.

Conclusion

In closing, we indicate issues for future research in the anthropology of pharmaceuticals and in applied health research, as well as suggest some areas in which pharmaceutical anthropology can contribute to theory building in the discipline as a whole.

Because they are manufactured commodities, pharmaceuticals present problems for research that have been little explored in medical anthropology. The cultures of commercial scientific research and development and of industrial production are ethnographically unknown areas. We also know little about the mass marketing of health products from the perspective of advertisers and distributors. To date, research has focused on the "reinterpretation" of pharmaceuticals (20, 45) as they are localized. It is well established that the biomedical meaning of drugs is transformed through "indigenization" (46, 69). But the dichotomy between biomedical and local conceptions is a simplification. There are contexts of meaning and regimes of value in factories, advertising companies, and the practices of traveling sales reps as well.

The neglect of these ethnographic research sites may partly be due to the continuing interest of anthropologists in geographically delimited communities and exotic cultures. The fieldwork tradition is more oriented to communities of neighbors than to multinational communities of interest. Nor have the majority of anthropologists who come from societies of the North sufficiently explored the patterns of value and dynamics of meaning construction characteristic of these mass-media consumer cultures.

Pharmaceuticals constitute a perfect opportunity for the study of the relation between symbols and political economy. On one hand, they are a part of the international flow of capital and commerce. On the other, they are symbols of hope and healing and of the promise of advanced technology. They are more thoroughly incorporated than blue jeans and popular music, and they are more desperately sought than Coca-Cola and videos. They allow individuals and peripheral communities to exercise more autonomy in health care but also create dependence on distant markets.

Medical anthropologists have been working in close cooperation with global and local public health officials involved in attempts to regulate and control the distribution of medicines, and in efforts to enhance the safe and effective use of drugs. Although anthropological studies have pointed to public health problems that need to be addressed, they have done little toward solving the problems in culturally appropriate ways. More knowledge is needed about how local self-care regimes are constructed and how they change over time in response to changes in international, national, and local drug distribution and health interventions aimed at making drug-use patterns safer and more effective (27). Such studies can show how people learn about medicines and evaluate their safety and efficacy, how they choose between available health-care options and drug distribution channels, and how these patterns change over time.

As things, pharmaceuticals move easily from one regime of value and knowledge to another. They can be separated from the expertise that developed, produced, and prescribed them. At the same time, consumers often express a desire to learn about their qualities and potentials (147). How is knowledge about drugs actually disseminated and/or constructed? To what extent does it carry over from one context of social life to another? We mentioned the paucity of studies on the worldviews of drug providers. There is also a lack of understanding of the differential distribution of knowledge among users and of the channels through which information flows in the popular sector. Such research would be relevant to essential drugs and primary health programs that aim at improving the use and distribution of drugs, providing insight into the effects of the existing programs, and offering alternative ways to achieve their aims. It would be especially useful in the design of health education that takes local knowledge and experience as its starting point (5, 14, 41, 116, 118, 140, 141, 146, 207, 216).

Research on pharmaceuticals is central to several areas of theory in anthropology. One of these is the anthropology of the body. Because of their intimate application, pharmaceuticals directly affect our conception and experience of our bodies. Through their concreteness, they help to make dis-ease tangible and manageable, as we have suggested. In the long run, they may facilitate greater sensitivity to symptoms and a lower threshold of discomfort (148).

Pharmaceuticals provide an eminent example of processes of globalization and localization, and they reveal the insufficiencies and paradoxes of some of the models we have for analyzing cultural complexity. Pharmaceuticals and indigenous medicines take on meaning in contrast with one another (146, 190) and thus appear distinctive. At the same time, pharmaceuticals provide a prototype in terms of packaging and marketing for indigenous medicines, so that the difference between them is diminished (6, 112, 205). Pharmaceutical specialists appear who belong neither to the tradition of biomedicine as practiced in formal health institutions nor to the tradition of indigenous medicine. These quacks or charlatans or bush doctors, as they are called by professionals, provide examples of creolization (70, 231) or counterwork (51) in that they creatively rework forms and ideas.

We have used Appadurai's notion of the social life of things and Kopytoff's biographical framework to organize this review of the literature. As commodities, pharmaceuticals have lives and "deaths" far more significant than their shelf lives and expiration dates. Like other commodities, they are subject to enclaving (attempts to restrict their commonality) and diversion (10, 101). However, in certain respects, pharmaceuticals are not common things that move lightly from one meaning to another. In situations of suffering, they have a potential that may well not be realized if they are not attached to a certain kind of knowledge. As special kinds of commodities, pharmaceuticals may contribute to refining theories about the social life of things.

Literature Cited

1. Abosede OA. 1984. Self-medication: an important aspect of primary health care. *Soc. Sci. Med.* 19(7):699–703
2. Abraham J. 1995. *Science, Politics and the Pharmaceutical Industry: Controversy and Bias in Drug Regulation.* London: Univ. College Press
3. Abu-Lughod L. 1986. *Veiled Sentiments: Honor and Poetry in a Bedouin Society.* Berkeley: Univ. Calif. Press
4. Ackerknecht EH. 1946. Natural diseases and rational treatment in primitive medicine. *Bull. Hist. Med.* 19:467–97
5. Adams DL. 1994. *Self-medication among urban residents of Salvador, Bahia, Brazil.* PhD thesis. Univ. Calif., Los Angeles. 332 pp.
6. Afdhal AF, Welsch RL. 1988. The rise of the modern *jamu* industry in Indonesia: a preliminary overview. See Ref. 217, pp. 149–72
7. Akubue PI, Mbah CJ. 1989. Drugs and treatment in streetmarkets and buses. See Ref. 159, pp. 33–42
8. Alland A Jr. 1970. *Adaptation in Cultural Evolution: An Approach to Medical Anthropology.* New York: Columbia Univ. Press
9. Alubo SO. 1987. Drugging the Nigerian people: the public hazards of private profits. See Ref. 86a, pp. 89–113
10. Appadurai A, ed. 1986. *The Social Life of Things: Commodities in Cultural Perspective.* Cambridge: Cambridge Univ. Press
11. Appadurai A. 1990. Disjuncture and difference in the global cultural economy. *Theory Cult. Soc.* 7:295–310
12. Baerts M, Lehmann J. 1993. *L'Utilisation de Quelques Plantes Médicinales au Burundi.* Tervuren: Mus. R. Afr. Cent.
13. Bagshawe AF, Maina G, Mngola EN, eds. 1974. *The Use and Abuse of Drugs and Chemicals in Tropical Africa.* Nairobi: East Afr. Lit. Bur.
14. Bennet FJ. 1989. The dilemma of essential drugs in primary health care. *Soc. Sci. Med.* 28(10):1085–90
15. Benoist J. 1989/1990. Le médicament, opérateur technique et médiateur symbolique. *Méd. Anthropol.* 1:45–50
16. Bhatia JC, Vir D, Timmappaya A, Chuttani CS. 1975. Traditional healers and modern medicine. *Soc. Sci. Med.* 9:15–21
17. Bierlich B. 1994. *The power of medicines: notions and practices of health and illness among the Dagomba of Northern Ghana.* PhD thesis. Cambridge Univ., Cambridge
18. Birungi H. 1994. Injections as household utilities: injection practices in Bugosa, Eastern Uganda. See Ref. 47, pp. 125–36
19. Birungi H. 1995. *The domestication of injections: a study of social relationships of health care in Busoga, Eastern Uganda.* PhD thesis. Univ. Copenhagen, Copenhagen. 158 pp.
20. Bledsoe CH, Goubaud MF. 1985. The reinterpretation of western pharmaceuticals among the Mende of Sierra Leone. *Soc. Sci. Med.* 21(3):275–82. Rev. version. See Ref. 217, pp. 253–76
21. Bleek W. 1976. *Sexual relationships and birth control in Ghana: a case study of a rural town.* PhD thesis. Univ. Amsterdam, Amsterdam. 343 pp.
22. Bloem M, Wolffers I, eds. 1993. *The Impact of Injections on Daily Medical Practice.* Amsterdam: Free Univ. Press
23. Blum R, Herxheimer A, Stenzl C, Wookcock J, eds. 1983. *Pharmaceuticals and Health Policy: International Perspectives on Provision and Control of Medicines.* London: Social Audit/IOCU
24. Braithwaite J. 1984. *Corporate Crime in the Pharmaceutical Industry.* London: Routledge & Kegan Paul
25. Britten N. 1994. Patient demand for prescriptions: a view from the other side. *Fam. Pract.* 11(1):62–66
26. Britten N. 1994. Patients' ideas about medicines: a qualitative study in a general practice. *Br. J. Gen. Pract.* 44:565–68
27. Brudon-Jacobowicz P. 1994. From research to practice: bridging the gap. See Ref. 47, pp. 9–14
28. Buckley AD. 1985. *Yoruba Medicine.* Oxford: Clarendon
29. Bühler M. 1982. *Geschäfte mit der Armut: Pharma-Konzerne in der Dritten Welt.* Frankfurt am Main: Medico Int.
30. Burghart R. 1988. Penicillin: an ancient Ayurvedic medicine. See Ref. 217, pp. 289–98
31. Bush PJ, Sanz EJ, Wirsing RL, Vaskilampi T, Trout A, eds. 1996. *Children, Medicines and Culture.* New York: Haworth Press
32. Chetley A. 1990. *A Healthy Business? World Health and the Pharmaceutical Industry.* London: Zed Books
33. Claridge G. 1970. *Drugs and Human Behaviour.* London: Lane
34. Comaroff J. 1976. A pill to swallow: placebo therapy in general practice. *Soc. Rev.* 24(1):79–96
35. Conrad P. 1985. The meaning of medications: another look at compliance. *Soc. Sci. Med.* 20(1):29–37
36. Cosminsky S. 1994. All roads lead to the pharmacy: use of pharmaceuticals on a Guatemala plantation. See Ref. 47, pp. 103–22

37. Cosminsky S, Scrimshaw M. 1980. Medical pluralism on a Guatemalan plantation. *Soc. Sci. Med. B* 14:267–78
38. Cunningham CE. 1970. Thai "injection doctors": antibiotic mediators. *Soc. Sci. Med.* 4:1–24
39. Denig P. 1994. *Drug choice in medical practice: rationales, routines and remedies.* PhD thesis. Univ. Groningen, Groningen. 206 pp.
39a. de Rhodes A. 1966. *Rhodes of Vietnam: The Travels and Missions of Father Alexandre de Rhodes in China and Other Kingdoms of the Orient.* Westminster: Newman
40. Douglas M, Isherwood B. 1979. *The World of Goods: Towards an Anthropology of Consumption.* London: Lane
41. Eisemon TO, Patel VL, Sena SO. 1987. Uses of formal and informal knowledge in the comprehension of instructions for ORT in Kenya. *Soc. Sci. Med.* 25(11): 1225–34
42. Ellen R. 1988. Fetishism. *Man* 23:213–35
43. El-Tom AO. 1985. Drinking the Koran: the meaning of Koranic verses in Berti erasure. *Africa* 55(4):414–31
44. Etkin NL. 1988. Cultural constructions of efficacy. See Ref. 217, pp. 299–326
45. Etkin NL. 1992. "Side Effects": cultural constructions and reinterpretations of western pharmaceuticals. *Med. Anthropol. Q.* 6:99–113
46. Etkin NL, Ross PJ, Muazzamu I. 1990. The indigenization of pharmaceuticals: therapeutic transitions in rural Hausaland. *Soc. Sci. Med.* 30:919–28
47. Etkin NL, Tan ML, eds. 1994. *Medicines: Meanings and Contexts.* Quezon City, Philipp: Health Action Inf. Netw.
48. Evans-Pritchard EE. 1937. *Witchcraft, Oracles and Magic among the Azande.* Oxford: Clarendon
49. Fabricant SJ, Hirschhorn N. 1987. Deranged distribution, perverse prescription, unprotected use: the irrationality of pharmaceuticals in the developing world. *Health Policies Plan.* 2(3):204–13
50. Fallsberg M. 1991. *Reflections on medicines and medication: a qualitative analysis among people on long-term regimes.* PhD thesis. Univ. Linköping, Linköping, Swed.
51. Fardon R. 1995. *Counterworks: Managing the Diversity of Knowledge.* London: Routledge
52. Fassin D. 1985. Du clandestin à l'officieux: les réseaux de vente illicite des médicaments au Sénégal. *Cah. Etud. Afr.* 25(2): 161–77
53. Fassin D. 1987. The illicit sale of pharmaceuticals in Africa: sellers and clients in the suburbs of Dakar. *Trop. Geogr. Med.* 39: 166–70

54. Ferguson AE. 1981. Commercial pharmaceutical medicine and medicalization: a case study from El Salvador. *Cult. Med. Psychiatry* 5(2):105–34. See Ref. 217, pp. 19–46
55. Ferguson J. 1988. Cultural exchange: new developments in the anthropology of commodities. *Cult. Anthropol.* 3:488–513
56. Finerman R. 1989. Tracing home-based health care change in an Andean Indean community. *Med. Anthropol. Q.* 3(2): 162–74
57. Foster GM. 1984. Anthropological research perspectives on health problems in developing countries. *Soc. Sci. Med.* 18(10):847–54
58. Foster S. 1991. Supply and use of essential drugs in sub-Saharan Africa: some issues and possible solutions. *Soc. Sci. Med.* 32(11):1201–18
59. Fryklöf LE, ed. 1990. Current trends in self-medication. *J. Soc. Adm. Pharm.* 7(4): 149–230
60. Fryklöf LE, Westerling R, eds. 1984. Self-medication. *J. Soc. Adm. Pharm.* 1984:1 (Suppl.)
61. Gabe J, ed. 1991. *Understanding Tranquilizer Use: The Role of the Social Sciences.* London: Tavistock & Routledge
62. Geertz C. 1976. *The Religion of Java.* Chicago: Univ. Chicago Press
63. Gish O, Feller LL. 1979. *Planning Pharmaceuticals for Primary Health Care: The Supply and Utilization of Drugs in the Third World.* Washington, DC: Am. Public Health Assoc.
64. Goldman R, Montagne M. 1986. Marketing 'mind mechanics': decoding antidepressant drug advertisements. *Soc. Sci. Med.* 22(10):1047–58
65. Deleted in proof
66. Greenhalgh T. 1987. Drug prescription and self-medication in India: an exploratory survey. *Soc. Sci. Med.* 25(3):307–18
67. Haaijer-Ruskamp FM. 1984. *Het voorschrijfgedrag van de huisarts.* PhD thesis. Univ. Groningen, Groningen
68. Haak H. 1988. Pharmaceuticals in two Brazilian villages: lay practices and perceptions. *Soc. Sci. Med.* 27(12):1415–27
69. Haak H, Hardon A. 1988. Indigenised pharmaceuticals in developing countries: widely used, widely neglected. *Lancet* 2: 620–21
70. Hannerz U. 1992. *Cultural Complexity: Studies in the Social Organization of Meaning.* New York: Columbia Univ. Press
71. Hardon A. 1987. The use of modern pharmaceuticals in a Filipino village: doctors' prescription and self-medication. *Soc. Sci. Med.* 25(3):277–92
72. Hardon A. 1991. *Confronting Ill Health: Medicines, Self-Care and the Poor in Ma-*

nila. Quezon City, Philipp: Health Action Inf. Netw.

73. Hardon A. 1994. People's understanding of efficacy for cough and cold medicines in Manila, the Philippines. See Ref. 47, pp. 47–67

74. Hardon A, van der Geest S, Geerling H. Le Grand A. 1991. *The Provision and Use of Drugs in Developing Countries: A Review of Studies and Annotated Bibliography.* Amsterdam: Spinhuis/HAI

75. Helman C. 1978. "Feed a cold, starve a fever": folk models of infection in an English suburban community, and their relation to medical treatment. *Cult. Med. Psychiatry* 2:107–37

76. Helman C. 1981. 'Tonic,' 'food,' and 'fuel': social and symbolic aspects of the long-term use of psychotropic drugs. *Soc. Sci. Med. B* 15:521–33

77. Homedes N, Ugalde A. 1993. Patients' compliance with medical treatments in the third world: What do we know? *Health Policies Plan.* 8(4):291–314

78. Höög S. 1992. The self-medication market: a literature study. *J. Soc. Adm. Pharm.* 9(3): 123–37

79. Hours B. 1985. *L'État Sorcier: Santé Publique et Société au Cameroun.* Paris: L'Harmattan

80. Hunt LM, Jordan B, Irwin S, Browner CH. 1989. Compliance and the patient's perspective: controlling symptoms in everyday life. *Cult. Med. Psychiatry* 13(3): 315–34

81. Igun UA. 1987. Why we seek treatment here: retail pharmacy and clinical practice in Maiduguri, Nigeria. *Soc. Sci. Med.* 24(8):689–95

82. Igun UA. 1994. Reported and actual prescription of oral rehydration therapy for childhood diarrheas by retail pharmacists in Nigeria. *Soc. Sci. Med.* 39(6): 797–806

83. Illich I. 1977. *Limits to Medicine. Medical Nemesis: The Expropriation of Health.* Harmondsworth: Penguin

84. Isenalumhe AE, Oviawe O. 1988. Poly pharmacy: its cost burden and barrier to medical care in a drug-orientated health care system. *Int. J. Health Serv.* 18(2): 335–42

85. Iweze EA. 1987. The patent medicine store: hospital for the urban poor. In *The Urban Poor in Nigeria*, ed. PK Makinwa, OA Oze, pp. 317–22. Ibadan: Evans Brothers

86. Iyun BF. 1994. Socio-cultural aspects of drug use in the treatment of childhood diarrhea in Oyo State Nigeria. See Ref. 47, pp. 33–46

86a. Jackson BE, Ugalde A, eds. 1987. *The Impact of Development and Modern Tech-*

nologies *in Third World Health.* Williamsburg, VA: Stud. Third World Soc.

87. Janzen JM. 1978. *The Quest for Therapy: Medical Pluralism in Lower Zaire.* Berkeley: Univ. Calif. Press

88. Kahane J. 1984. *The role of the 'western' pharmacist in rural Taiwanese culture.* PhD thesis. Univ. Hawaii, Honolulu. 230 pp.

89. Kamat VR. 1994. *Pharmacies, self-medication and pharmaceutical marketing in Bombay: an ethnographic case study.* PhD thesis. Univ. Ariz., Tucson

90. Kamat VR. 1995. Reconsidering the popularity of primary health centers in India: a case study from rural Maharashtra. *Soc. Med.* 41(1):87–98

91. Kamat VR, Nichter M. 1996. Pharmacies, self-medication and pharmaceutical marketing in India. *Soc. Sci. Med.* In press

92. Deleted in proof

93. Kanji N, Hardon A, Harnmeÿer JW, Mamdani M, Walt G. 1992. *Drugs Policy in Developing Countries.* London: Zed Books

94. Kapil I. 1988. Doctors dispensing medications: contemporary India and 19th century England. *Soc. Sci. Med.* 26(7):691–99

95. Keller BB. 1978. Marriage and medicine: women's search for love and luck. *Afr. Soc. Res.* 26:489–505

96. Kessels P, Sangare M. 1988. *Rapport d'une recherche exploratoire sur la prescription, l'achat, l'utilisation des médicaments dans le Cercle de Niono, Mali.* MA thesis. Univ. Amsterdam, Amsterdam. 68 pp.

97. Klass A. 1975. *There's Gold in Them Thar Pills: An Inquiry into the Medical-Industrial Complex.* Harmondsworth: Penguin

98. Kleinman A. 1980. *Patients and Healers in the Context of Culture.* Berkeley: Univ. Calif. Press

99. Kloos H. 1974. The geography of pharmacies, druggist shops and rural medicine vendors and the origin of customers of such facilities in Addis Ababa. *J. Ethiop. Stud.* 12:77–94

100. Kloos H, Getahun B, Teferi A, Gebre Tsadik K, Belay S. 1988. Buying drugs in Addis Ababa: a quantitative analysis. See Ref. 217, pp. 81–106

101. Kopytoff I. 1986. The cultural biography of things: commoditization as process. See Ref. 10, pp. 64–91

102. Krishnaswamy K, Dinesh Kumar B, Radhaiah G. 1985. A drug survey: precepts and practices. *Eur. J. Clin. Pharmacol.* 29(3): 363–70

103. Ladinsky JL, Volk ND, Robinson M. 1987. The influence of traditonal medicine in shaping medical care practices in Vietnam today. *Soc. Sci. Med.* 25(10):1105–10

104. Laing R. 1990. Rational drug use: an unsolved problem. *Trop. Dr.* 20:101–3

105. Lall S, Bibile S. 1978. The political economy of controlling transnationals: the pharmaceutical industry in Sri Lanka,
1972–1976. *Int. J. Health Serv.* 8:299–328

106. Lapido PA, Balogun EK. 1978. Sources of
medical care in the Isoya Project villages
(NS). *Odu* 17:100–11

107. Lasselain J. 1987. *Médicaments Inessen-
tiels, Consommation Pharmaceutique d'un
Département Peruvien.* Paris: L'Harmattan

108. Latour B, Woolgar S. 1979. *Laboratory
Life.* Princeton, NJ: Princeton Univ. Press

109. Lefèvre F. 1991. *O Medicamento como
Mercadoria Simbolica.* São Paulo: Cortez
Editoria

109a. le Grand A, Sri-ngeryuang L. 1989.
*Herbal Drugs in Primary Health Care.
Thailand: The Impact of Promotional Ac-
tivities on Drug Consumption, Drug Provi-
sion and Self-Reliance.* Amsterdam: R.
Trop. Inst.

110. Lepowsky M. 1990. Sorcery and penicillin:
treating illness on a Papua New Guinea
island. *Soc. Sci. Med.* 30(10):1049–63

111. Leslie C, ed. 1976. *Asian Medical Systems:
A Comparative Study.* Berkeley: Univ.
Calif. Press

112. Leslie C. 1989. Indigenous pharmaceuticals, the capitalist world and civilization.
Kroeger Anthropol. Soc. Pap. 69/70:23–31

113. Lexchin J. 1989. Doctors and detailers:
therapeutic education or pharmaceutical
promotion? *Int. J. Health Serv.* 19(4):
663–79

114. Lexchin J. 1992. Pharmaceutical promotion in the Third World. *J. Drug Issues*
22(2):417–54

115. Lilja J. 1988. *Theoretical Social Pharmacy: The Drug Sector from a Social Science Perspective.* Kuopio, Finl: Dep. Soc.
Pharm.

116. Logan K. 1983. The role of pharmacists
and over-the-counter medications in the
health care system of a Mexican city. *Med.
Anthropol.* 7(3):68–89 Rev. version. See
Ref. 217, pp. 107–30

117. Logan M. 1973. Humoral medicine in Guatemala and peasant acceptance of modern
medicine. *Hum. Org.* 32(4):385–95

118. MacCormack C, Draper A. 1988. Cultural
meanings of oral rehydration salts in Jamaica. See Ref. 217, pp. 277–88

119. Maitai CK, Guantai A, Mwangi JM. 1981.
Self-medication in management of minor
health problems in Kenya. *East Afr. Med. J.*
58(8):593–600

120. Mamdani M, Walker G. 1985. *Essential
Drugs and Developing Countries: A Re-
view and Selected Annotated Bibliography.*
London: Sch. Hyg. Trop. Med.

121. Mapes R, ed. 1980. *Prescribing Practice
and Drug Usage.* London: Croom Helm

122. McEvoy J. 1976. The bus-stop dispenser.
East Afr. Med. J. 53(3):193–95

123. Medawar C. 1979. *Insult or Injury? An
Enquiry into the Marketing and Advertising of British Food and Drug Products in
the Third World.* London: Social Audit

124. Medawar C, Freese B. 1982. *Drug Diplo-
macy.* London: Social Audit

125. Melrose D. 1982. *Bitter Pills: Medicines
and the Third World Poor.* Oxford: OX-
FAM

126. Melville A. 1980. Reducing whose anxiety? A study of the relationship between
repeat prescribing of minor tranquillisers
and doctors' attitudes. See Ref. 121, pp.
100–18

127. Melville A, Johnson C. 1982. *Cured to
Death: The Effects of Prescription Drugs.*
London: Secker & Warburg

128. Messer E. 1981. Hot-cold classification:
theoretical and practical implications of a
Mexican study. *Soc. Sci. Med. B* 15:
133–45

129. Michel JM. 1985. Why do people like
medicines? A perspective from Africa.
Lancet 11(1):210–11

130. Miller D. 1987. *Material Culture and Mass
Consumption.* Oxford: Blackwell

131. Mitchell MF. 1983. Popular medical concepts in Jamaica and their impact on drug-
use. *West. J. Med.* 139:841–47

132. Mitchell MF. 1988. Pharmacists in Jamaica: health care roles in a changing society. In *Black Folk Medicine: The Therapeutic Significance of Faith and Trust,* ed. WH
Watson. New Brunswick, NY: Transaction
Books

133. Moerman DE. 1979. Anthropology of symbolic healing. *Curr. Anthropol.* 20(1):
59–80

134. Moerman DE. 1983. General medical effectiveness and human biology: placebo
effects in the treatment of ulcer disease.
Med. Anthropol. Q. 14(4):13–16

135. Moerman DE. 1992. Minding the body: the
placebo effect unmasked. In *Giving the
Body Its Due,* ed. M Sheets-Johnstone, pp.
69–84. New York: State Univ. NY Press

136. Montagne M. 1988. The metaphorical nature of drugs and drug taking. *Soc. Sci.
Med.* 26: 417–24

137. Montagne M, ed. 1992. Drug advertising
and promotion. *J. Drug Issues* 22(2):
195–480

138. Moshaddeque Hossain M, Glass RI, Khan
MR. 1982. Antibiotic use in a rural community in Bangladesh. *Int. J. Epidemiol.* 11(4):
402–5

139. Muller M. 1982. *The Health of Nations: A
North-South Investigation.* London: Faber
& Faber

140. Ngoh LN. 1992. *The comprehension of antibiotic prescription instructions and their*

utilization in three primary health care settings in Cameroon, West Africa. PhD thesis. Univ. Tex., Austin

141. Ngoh LN, Shepherd MD. 1994. The effect of visual aids and advanced organizers on improving the use of antibiotics in rural Cameroon. See Ref. 47, pp. 243–63

142. Ngokwey N. 1995. Home remedies and doctors' remedies in Feira (Brazil). *Soc. Sci. Med.* 40(8):1144–53

143. Ngubane H. 1977. *Body and Mind in Zulu Medicine: An Ethnography of Health and Disease in Nyuswa-Zulu Thought and Practice.* London: Academic

144. Nichter M. 1980. The layperson's perception of medicine as perspective into the utilization of multiple therapy systems in the Indian context. *Soc. Sci. Med. B* 14: 225–33

145. Nichter M. 1983. Paying for what ails you: sociocultural issues influencing the ways and means of therapy payment in South India. *Soc. Sci. Med.* 17(14):957–65

146. Nichter M, Nichter M. 1996. *Anthropology and International Health: Asian Case Studies.* Amsterdam: Breach & Gordon

147. Nichter M, Nordstrom C. 1989. A question of "medicine answering": health commodification and the social relations of healing in Sri Lanka. *Cult. Med. Psychiatry* 13(4): 367–90

148. Nichter M, Vuckovic N. 1994. Agenda for an anthropology of pharmaceutical practice. *Soc. Sci. Med.* 39(11):1509–25

149. Nordberg E. 1974. Self-portrait of the average rural drug shop in Wollega province, Ethiopia. *Ethiop. Med. J.* 12(1):25–32

150. Nyamwaya D. 1987. A case study of the interaction between indigenous and western medicine among the Pokot of Kenya. *Soc. Sci. Med.* 25(12):1277–87

151. Okri B. 1988. *Stars of the New Curfew.* London: Secker & Warburg.

152. Oshiname FO, Brieger WR. 1992. Patent medicine stores: necessary evil? See Ref. 159, pp. 27–32

153. Osifo NG. 1983. Overpromotion of drugs in international product package inserts. *Trop. Dr.* 13(1):5–8

154. Parkin D. 1995. Latticed knowledge: eradication and dispersal of the unpalatable in Islam, medicine and anthropological theory. See Ref. 51, pp. 143–63

155. Pellegrino ED. 1976. Prescribing and drug ingestion: symbols and substances. *Drug Intell. Clin. Pharm.* 10:624–30

156. Plattner S. 1983. Economic custom in a competitive marketplace. *Am. Anthropol.* 85:848–58

157. Pleil AM, Pathak DS. 1988. Commercial drug compendium information: a First World/Third World comparison. *Int. J. Health Serv.* 18(4):587–602

158. Pole D, ed. 1988. *La Distribution de Médicaments sans Ordonnance en Côte d'Ivoire, Particulièrement les Hypnotiques/Sedatifs et Tranquillisants.* Basel: Inst. Med. Inform.

159. Pole D, ed. 1989. *Drug Distribution and Fake Drugs in Nigeria. Proceedings of an International Workshop.* Basel: Inst. Med. Inform.

160. Price L. 1984. Art, science, faith and medicine: the implications of the placebo effect. *Soc. Health Illn.* 6(1):61–73

161. Price L. 1989. In the shadow of biomedicine: self medication in two Ecuadorian pharmacies. *Soc. Sci. Med.* 28(9):905–15

162. Reeler AV. 1990. Injections: a fatal attraction? *Soc. Sci. Med.* 31(10):1119–25

163. Reeler AV. 1995. *Patient, friend or customer? Modes of empowerment in health care.* PhD thesis. Univ. Copenhagen, Copenhagen. 221 pp.

164. Reeler AV, Hematorn C. 1994. *Injection Practices in the Third World: A Case Study of Thailand.* Geneva: WHO

165. Deleted in proof

166. Rhodes L. 1984. "This will clear your mind": the use of metaphors for medication in psychiatric settings. *Cult. Med. Psychiatry* 8:49–70

167. Roberts AH. 1995. The powerful placebo revisited: the magnitude of nonspecific effects. *Mind/Body Med.* 1(1):1–10

168. Sachs L. 1989. Misunderstanding as therapy: doctors, patients, and medicines in a rural clinic in Sri Lanka. *Cult. Med. Psychiatry* 13:335–49

169. Sachs L. 1990. The symbolic value of drugs in the socialization of illness behaviour among Swedish children. *Pharm. Weekbl.* 12(3):107–11

170. Sachs L, Tomson G. 1992. Medicines and culture: a double perspective on drug utilization in a developing country. *Soc. Sci. Med.* 34(3):307–15

171. Sachs L, Tomson G. 1994. Brokers, medicines, and rationality: mirroring health centers in Sri Lanka and Sweden. See Ref. 47, pp. 265–83

172. Sacks O. 1976. *Awakenings.* Harmondsworth: Penguin

173. Scheper-Hughes N. 1992. *Death without Weeping: The Violence of Everyday Life in Brazil.* Berkeley: Univ. Calif. Press

174. Schwartz RK, Soumerai SB, Avorn J. 1989. Physician motivations for nonscientific drug prescription. *Soc. Sci. Med.* 28(6): 577–82

175. Sciortino R. 1992. *Care-Takers of Cure: A Study of Health Centre Nurses in Rural Central Java.* Amsterdam: Spinhuis

176. Seligman S. 1927. *Die Magischen Heilund Schutzmittel der Unbelebte Natur.* Stuttgart: Strecker & Schröder

177. Selya RM. 1988. Pharmacies as alternative sources of medical care: the case of Cincinnati. *Soc. Sci. Med.* 26(4):409–16

178. Senah KA. 1994. "Blofo Tshofa": local perceptions of medicines in a Ghanaian coastal community. See Ref. 47, pp. 83–101

179. Senah KA. 1996. *"Money be man": the perception and use of medicines in a Ghanaian rural community.* PhD thesis. Univ. Amsterdam, Amsterdam

180. Shatrughna V. Nd. Drug prescription: service to whom? In *Health Care: Which Way to Go,* ed. A Bang, AJ Pate, pp. 25–29. Pune, India: Medico Friend Circle

181. Silva KT, Amarasiri de Silva MW, Wijekoon Banda TM. 1994. Access to western drugs, medical pluralism and choice of therapy in an urban low income community in Sri Lanka. See Ref. 47, pp. 185–208

182. Silverman M. 1976. *The Drugging of the Americas.* Berkeley: Univ. Calif. Press

183. Silverman M, Lee PR, Lydecker M. 1982. *Prescriptions for Death: The Drugging of the Third World.* Berkeley: Univ. Calif. Press

184. Silverman M, Lee PR, Lydecker M. 1992. *Bad Medicine: The Prescription Drug Industry in the Third World.* Stanford, CA: Stanford Univ. Press

185. Smith MC. 1980. The relationship between pharmacy and medicine. See Ref. 121, pp. 157–200

186. Sorofman B. 1992. Drug promotion in self-care and self-medication. *J. Drug Issues* 22(2):377–88

187. Stoker A, Jeffery R. 1988. Pharmaceuticals and health policy: an Indian example. *Soc. Sci. Med.* 27(5):563–67

188. Streefland PH. 1985. The frontier of modern western medicine in Nepal. *Soc. Sci. Med.* 20(11):1151–59

189. Streefland PH. 1994. Shaping the context of drug use: availability of pharmaceuticals at the frontier of cosmopolitan medicine. See Ref. 47, pp. 209–24

190. Sussman LK. 1988. The use of herbal and biomedical pharmaceuticals on Mauritius. See Ref. 217, pp. 199–216

191. Svarstadt BL. 1979. Pharmaceutical sociology. *Am. J. Pharm. Educ.* 43(3):252–57

192. Svarstadt BL. 1981. The sociology of drugs. In *Pharmacy Practice: Social and Behavioral Aspects,* ed. AI Wertheimer, MC Smith. Baltimore: Univ. Park Press

193. Tan ML. 1989. *Dying for Drugs: Pill Power and Politics in the Philippines.* Quezon City, Philipp: Health Action Inf. Netw.

194. Tan ML. 1989. Traditional or transitional medical systems? Pharmacotherapy as a case for analysis. *Soc. Sci. Med.* 29(3): 301–7

195. Tan ML. 1994. The meaning of medicines: examples from the Philippines. See Ref. 47, pp. 69–81

196. Tan ML. 1996. *Magalin na Gamot: pharmaceuticals and the construction of knowledge and power in the Philippines.* PhD thesis. Univ. Amsterdam, Amsterdam

197. Thomson N. 1991. *Entangled Objects: Exchange, Material Culture and Colonisation in the Pacific.* Cambridge, MA: Harvard Univ. Press

198. Tomson G. 1990. *Drug utilization studies in Sri Lanka: towards an understanding of medicines in society.* PhD thesis. Karolinska Inst., Stockholm

199. Tomson G, Sterky G. 1986. Self-prescribing by way of pharmacies in three Asian developing countries. *Lancet* 2:620–21

200. Trakas DJ. 1990. Greek children's perception of illness and drugs. *Pharm. Weekbl.* 12(6):247–51

201. Trakas DJ, Sanz EJ, eds. 1992. *Studying Childhood and Medicine Use: A Multidisciplinary Approach.* Athens: 'Zhta' Med. Publ.

202. Trostle JA. 1988. Medical compliance as an ideology. *Soc. Sci. Med.* 27(12):1299–308

203. Trostle JA. 1996. Introduction. Inappropriate distribution of medicines by professionals in developing countries. *Soc. Sci. Med.* 42(8):1117–20

204. Trostle JA, Hauser WA, Susser IS. 1983. The logic of noncompliance: management of epilepsy from the patient's point of view. *Cult. Med. Psychiatry* 7(1):35–56

205. Tuchinsky C. 1991. *Produktion, Handel und Konsumption nicht-westlicher Medikamente in Südost-Asien: Malaiische Jamu in Singapore.* Münster: Lit Verlag

206. Uddenberg N. 1990. Medicines as cultural phenomenon. *J. Soc. Adm. Pharm.* 7(4): 179–83

207. Ugalde A, Homedes N. 1988. Medicines and rural health services: an experiment in the Dominican Republic. See Ref. 217, pp. 57–80

208. Ugalde A, Homedes N. 1994. Household storage of pharmaceuticals in Costa Rica. See Ref. 47, pp. 165–83

209. van der Geest S. 1982. The efficiency of inefficiency: medicine distribution in South Cameroon. *Soc. Sci. Med.* 16:2145–53

210. van der Geest S. 1982. The illegal distribution of western medicines in developing countries. *Med. Anthropol.* 6(4):197–219

211. van der Geest S. 1984. Anthropology and pharmaceuticals in developing countries. *Med. Anthropol. Q.* 15(3):59–62, 15(4): 87–90

212. van der Geest S. 1987. Self-care and the informal sale of drugs in South Cameroon. *Soc. Sci. Med.* 25(3):293–306

213. van der Geest S. 1987. Unequal access to pharmaceuticals in Southern Cameroon:

the context of a problem. See Ref. 86a, pp. 141–66

214. van der Geest S. 1988. The articulation of formal and informal medicine distribution in South Cameroon. See Ref. 217, pp. 131–48

215. van der Geest S. 1991. Marketplace conversations in South Cameroon: how and why popular medical knowledge comes into being. *Cult. Med. Psychiatry* 15(1): 69–90

216. van der Geest S. 1992. Village health workers as medicine sellers? *Health Plan. Manage.* 7(3):185–97

217. van der Geest S, Whyte SR, eds. 1988. *The Context of Medicines in Developing Countries: Studies in Pharmaceutical Anthropology.* Dordrecht: Kluwer

218. van der Geest S, Whyte SR. 1989. The charm of medicines: metaphors and metonyms. *Med. Anthropol. Q.* 3(4):345–67

219. Van Staa A. 1993. *Myth and metronidazole in Manila: the popularity of drugs among prescribers and dispensers in the treatment of diarrhoea.* MA thesis. Univ. Amsterdam, Amsterdam

220. Verbeek-Heida PM. 1993. How patients look at drug therapy: consequences for therapy negotiations in medical consultations. *Fam. Pract.* 10:326–29

221. Victora CG, Facchini LA, Filho MG. 1982. Drug usage in southern Brazilian hospitals. *Trop. Dr.* 12:231–35

222. Vogel RJ, Stephens B. 1989. Availability of pharmaceuticals in sub-Saharan Africa: roles of the public, private and church mission sectors. *Soc. Sci. Med.* 29:479–86

223. Vuckovic N, Nichter M. 1996. Changing patterns of pharmaceutical practice in the United States. *Soc. Sci. Med.* In press

224. Waddington C, Enyimayew KA. 1989/ 1990. A price to pay: the impact of user charges in Asanti-Akim District, Ghana. *Int. J. Health Manage.* 4:17–47; 5:287–312

225. Weisberg DH. 1982. Northern Thai health care alternatives. *Soc. Sci. Med.* 16(16): 1507–17

226. Whyte SR. 1982. Penicillin, battery acid and sacrifice: cures and causes in Nyole medicine. *Soc. Sci. Med.* 16(23):2055–64

227. Whyte SR. 1988. The power of medicines in East Africa. See Ref. 217, pp. 217–34

228. Whyte SR. 1991. Medicines and self-help: the privatization of health care in eastern Uganda. In *Changing Uganda: Dilemmas of Structural Adjustment and Revolutionary Change,* ed. HB Hansen, M Twaddle, pp. 130–48. London: Currey

229. Whyte SR. 1992. Pharmaceuticals as folk medicine: transformations in the social relations of health care in Uganda. *Cult. Med. Psychiatry* 16(2):163–86

230. Deleted in proof

231. Whyte SR, van der Geest S. 1994. Injections: issues and methods for anthropological research. See Ref. 47, pp. 137–61

232. Wolffers I. 1987. Drug information and sale practices in some pharmacies of Colombo, Sri Lanka. *Soc. Sci. Med.* 25(3):319–21

233. Wolffers I. 1988. Traditional practitioners and western pharmaceuticals in Sri Lanka. See Ref. 217, pp. 47–56

234. Wolf-Gould CS, Taylor N, McCue Horwitz S, Barry M. 1991. Misinformation about medications in rural Ghana. *Soc. Sci. Med.* 33(1):83–89

Annu. Rev. Anthropol. 1996. 25:179–200

IMAGES OF NATURE AND SOCIETY IN AMAZONIAN ETHNOLOGY

Eduardo Viveiros de Castro

Departamento de Antropologia, Museu Nacional, 20940-040 Rio de Janeiro RJ, Brazil

KEY WORDS: Amerindians, society and nature, ecological anthropology, social anthropology

ABSTRACT

This review discusses changes in Amazonian indigenous anthropology since the synthesis presented in the *Handbook of South American Indians*. The past few years have seen the emergence of an image of Amazonia characterized by a growing emphasis on the complexity of indigenous social formations and the ecological diversity of the region. This new image of society and nature is taking shape in a theoretical context characterized by the synergistic interaction between structural and historical approaches, by an attempt to go beyond mono-causal explanatory models (whether naturalistic or culturalistic) in favor of a dialectical view of the relations between society and nature, and by hopes of a "new synthesis" that could integrate the knowledge accumulated in the fields of human ecology, social anthropology, archeology, and history.

INTRODUCTION

When the *Annual Review of Anthropology* last published an overall review of the field in 1975 (70), Amazonian anthropology was entering a period of unprecedented growth: In comparative terms, this literature seems to have increased more than that of any other region over the past twenty years. This phenomenon has been celebrated by various commentators (40, 61, 117, 140, 151), who often mention a preboom collection of texts subtitled *The Least Known Continent* (87), and then add how fortunate the situation has changed.

The optimism is justified. If, as Taylor (140) observed, there were no more than 50 monographs about indigenous Amazonia before the 1970s, then the subsequent explosion at least quadrupled this figure. In the past twenty years, many societies have been described for the first time according to modern standards of ethnographic writing; some have been studied by successive waves of researchers with different theoretical backgrounds; and for certain geographical areas the bibliography has since achieved an impressive density. During the same period, ecology, history, and archeology have made equally remarkable advances. This coming of age may be evaluated in five recently published compilations—Descola & Taylor (41), Roosevelt (127), Carneiro da Cunha (23), Viveiros de Castro & Carneiro da Cunha (157), and Sponsel (134)—all of whom present a good sample of research developments in different areas of knowledge about Amazonia, as well as various critical and comparative overviews.

The following review focuses exclusively on the more general changes in regional anthropology. The past few years have seen the emergence of an image of Amazonia characterized by a growing emphasis on the complexity of indigenous social formations and the ecological diversity of the region. This new image of society and nature is taking shape in a theoretical context characterized by the synergistic interaction between structural and historical approaches, by an attempt to go beyond monocausal explanatory models (whether naturalistic or culturalistic) in favor of a dialectical apprehension of the relations between society and nature, and by hopes of a "new synthesis" (126) that could integrate the knowledge accumulated by the various disciplines.

THE STANDARD MODEL

The calls for a new synthesis point to the obsolescence of the image of Amazonia derived from the monumental *Handbook of South American Indians* edited by Julian Steward from 1946 to 1950 (135) and from the digest of this work published by Steward & Faron in 1959 (137). Combining a schema of cultural areas, a typology of "levels of sociocultural integration," and a theory of the determining action of the environment over a society's "cultural core," the picture of indigenous Amazonia that emerged from the synthesis presented by Steward and his collaborators became deeply rooted in the ethnological tradition.

This model presented the societies of slash-and-burn horticulturalists of the "Tropical Forest" as typological hybrids occupying an intermediate evolutionary position. Similar to the circum-Caribbean chiefdoms (from whom they were supposed to have borrowed a number of traits) in technology, from a sociopolitical angle, the Tropical Forest cultures differed little from the "Marginal Tribes" of hunters-gatherers of Central Brazil and Patagonia (136, 137).[1]

---

[1] The Gê and Bororo of Central Brazil—"Marginals" in the *Handbook*—were reclassified as "hunters and gatherers turned farmers" by Steward & Faron (137) and placed closer to the Tropical Forest type.

The typical Tropical Forest "tribe" was organized in autonomous and egalitarian villages, which were limited in their size and permanence by both a simple technology and an unproductive environment, and were thus unable to produce the requisite economic surplus to allow the rise of the craft specialization, social stratification, and political centralization that had developed in other areas of South America. Steward recognized the existence of ecological differences between the riverine and interfluvial environments, as well as a certain variety in the Tropical Forest type due to different local conditions and to the relations with the centers of cultural diffusion. However, the overall impression was one of a largely uniform Tropical Forest: an environment hostile to civilization and of comparatively recent settlement, sparsely populated, sociologically stunted, and culturally dependent on more advanced areas. Native societies that had stuck to their traditional ways were seen as moving fast toward assimilation into national populations.

At the time this synthesis was produced, Amazonian ethnology was dominated by a blend of diffusionism and geographical determinism, following the German historicocultural tradition under whose influence it had been formed. Adding to the mix a theory of social evolution, Steward transformed this tradition into the new discipline of "cultural ecology," which was to have a large progeny in North American anthropology and which has wielded considerable influence in Amerindian studies ever since. The heirs of Steward's cultural ecology (and of Leslie White's neoevolutionism) continued with Amazonia as their choice field for speculation. An example is the heated debate on the "limiting factors" responsible for the region's sociopolitical landscape, which was to monopolize the attention of researchers of this persuasion at least until the 1980s (see 59, 133).

European anthropology began, with Lévi-Strauss (81–85), to break the hegemony of this paradigm before the 1950s were over, but it was with the publication particularly of his *Mythologiques* in the 1960s that structuralism became influential in regional ethnology. It proposed an analytical style and, above all, a thematic agenda that was to have far-reaching repercussions. Lévi-Strauss emphasized the cognitive and symbolic value of the material dimensions of social life studied by cultural ecologists from an adaptive viewpoint—relations with animals, origin of cultivated plants, diet, technology. Thus the conceptual opposition between "nature" and "culture," which had underlain the deterministic theories of Steward's heirs, Lévi-Strauss made internal to indigenous cosmologies.

The late 1960s saw the first ethnographies derived from British social anthropology, which until then had been absent from studies of tropical America. The landmark monographs of Maybury-Lewis (88) and Rivière (113), both clearly influenced by Lévi-Strauss, opened the contemporary phase of

Amazonian ethnology. In the United States, ethnoscience and symbolic anthropology—complementary transformations of Boasian culturalism having certain affinities with some aspects of structuralism—had come to share the limelight with Steward's and White's cultural materialism. The wave of monographs on Amazonian sociocosmological systems that began in the 1970s (e.g. 22a, 28, 103, 129, 131, 154, 155) shows a combination of influences of European schools and North American neoculturalism, but no perceptible trace, except in the form of a hostile silence, of cultural ecological approaches.

Thus there was increasing polarization over the following two decades. On one side were the descendants of Steward and White, who adopted a four-field approach, were interested in great historicocultural syntheses and macrotypologies, and were guided by an adaptationist and energetic conception of culture that underscored its material ordering by nature and privileged the technological interface. On the other side were the anthropologists who followed a structural-functionalist or "structural-culturalist" orientation. They were interested in the synchronic analysis of particular Amerindian groups and in the institutional and ideological dimensions of the societies they studied, thus privileging the symbolic ordering of nature by culture (and thereby the cognitive interface).

Despite this polarization, certain aspects of the picture generated by the *Handbook* were common to both camps. Amazonia was still seen as the habitat of small, dispersed, isolated groups that were autonomous and self-contained, egalitarian, and technologically austere. Cultural ecologists tried to discover which environmental determinants accounted for this "simple" sociopolitical profile—that is, to what scarce natural resource (fertile soils, animal protein) it was an adaptation. Social anthropologists saw this situation as a nonproblematic given and attempted instead to describe the complex and specific cultural contents they saw as associated with this material simplicity. When they did try to generalize [for instance, Clastres (25, 26) and, on occasion, Lévi-Strauss (81)], they traced the autonomy, egalitarianism, and minimalistic economy of contemporary societies not to negative environmental limitations but to positive sociocultural ones—ideological denial of historical change, social resistance to political centralization, and cultural impediments to economic accumulation.

THE PASSING OF THE STANDARD MODEL

The elements that contributed to the progressive demise of the situation outlined above have been gathering for a long time. They derive first from a revision of the received ideas about the ecology and the cultural history of Amazonia. In fact, this revision is part of a general revaluation of pre-Columbian America, which has consistently tended to (*a*) raise the estimated Amerindian population in 1492; (*b*) argue for earlier archeological datings; (*c*) attribute greater complexity to the social formations outside the Andean and Meso-American areas, upgrading various "tribes" to the category of "middle-range societies"; (*d*) underscore the importance of regional systems articulating ecological zones and heterogeneous sociopolitical types; and (*e*) emphasize the action of long-distance societal influences.

The other element responsible for the reformulation of the traditional image of Amazonia has been the consolidation of a theoretically renovated anthropology of indigenous social formations. Here, too, much derives from broader intellectual reorderings, notably (*a*) the critique of the classical paradigms of kinship theory, seen as relying on a regulative and mechanistic conception of social life; (*b*) more generally, the critique of the concept of society as a bounded and structured entity; and (*c*) the attempt to escape the classical dichotomies, from the "Great Divide theories" to the nature-culture opposition, from the antagonism between "materialist" and "mentalist" positions to the antinomy between structure and process.

What follows is an outline of the most important instances of these points in recent anthropological literature on Native Amazonia.

Human Ecology

The most significant change in the field of ecology has to do with the growing emphasis on the environmental diversity of Amazonia and on the correlations between this diversity and human activity. For a long time it has been known (74, 92) that there is a difference between the *várzea,* the floodplains of the white-water rivers that receive sediments from the Andes, and the *terra firme,* the uplands of poorer soil drained by black- or clear-water rivers. However, as Moran (97, 98) and others (107) have insisted, the region's pedological, botanical, and zoological variety do not fit into this simple opposition. In particular, it is not possible to continue subsuming profoundly different ecosystems into the blanket category terra firme (about 98% of Amazonia).

In addition, there is more and more evidence that in several areas outside the várzea the soil is not as poor as was once thought, and that in some areas there was intense and prolonged prehistoric occupation, indicated by the fact that anthropogenic forests cover at least 12% of the terra firme in Brazilian Amazonia (8). These forests tend to be favored by contemporary populations because of their high fertility. In addition, they support vegetational associations of great importance to indigenous economies, such as palm forests, Brazil-nut forests, and others, which should thus be seen as "arrested successional forest on archeological sites, including prehistoric swiddens as well as settlements and camps" (8:6). That is, much of the distribution of forest types and vegetation of the region is the product of millennia of human manipulation.[2] Balée, who has drawn the most insightful conclusions from these findings, observed that Amazonian "nature" is therefore a part of and a result of a long cultural history, and that indigenous economies previously seen as instances of "adaptive responses" (58) to a pristine and transcendent environment are actually meta-adaptations to culture, or to the historical result of a cultural transformation of nature (5a–11). Incidentally, contrary to what one might imagine, Balée has found that anthropogenic forests have more biodiversity than undisturbed forests (12, 13).

The adaptationist outlook dominant in ecological anthropology has led to valuable studies of certain quantitative dimensions of the subsistence practices of Amazonian groups. However, there has been very little interchange between ecological anthropology and social anthropology; the two approaches are as incommensurable as neoclassical economics and political economy (56). This is no mere analogy. Adaptationist theories take for granted the marginalist postulates of resource scarcity and optimization of yield-to-effort ratios and assume an immanent rationality of an evolutionary kind, governed by thermodynamic parameters, whereas social anthropologists working in Amazonia have tended to underscore the structural constraints of socioeconomic regimes founded on reciprocity and symbolic exchange and have tended to emphasize the historical, socially determined nature of interaction with the physical environment (although, as shown below, some forms of nonenvironmental scarcity have been suggested as explanations of Amazonian social morphologies). In any case—after the vogue of the "limiting factor" and then the "optimal foraging" theories (for evaluations internal to the tradition, see 59, 119, 133; for a critique informed by a different paradigm, see 31, 33)—the gap between ecological and social anthropology has been considerably narrowed by the advent of studies of "resource management strategies" of indigenous populations (e.g. 106), which give pride of place to native conceptualizations of ecosystems (11) and allow "cultural ecology" to mean not only "ecologically caused aspects of culture" but also "culturally created aspects of ecology." There are pending empirical and theoretical problems in this approach—for instance, the degree and nature (whether intentional or not) of human environmental shaping—but nevertheless it suggests a welcome general tendency of ecological anthropologists to acknowledge the formal causality of culture [or to use more updated language, the capacity for "cultural self-selection" (43)]. This seems to be part of a wider shift away from the view of societies as isolates in an adaptive tête-à-tête with nature toward an essentially historical

---

[2]   Some, such as Denevan (29), have claimed that there were no longer any "virgin" tropical forests in 1492, which seems unrealistic.

conception of human ecology, which is beginning to bear fruit in Amazonia (15, 60).

Prehistory

It was in the very camp of cultural materialism that there arose the most current and widely publicized reaction against the view of Amazonia as a region unpropitious to social complexity. This is Roosevelt's theory concerning the várzea societies (119, 120, 123–125), which is essentially a reaction to Meggers's thesis on the environmental limitations of cultural development in Amazonia that she originally formulated in the 1950s (90–93). Confronted with the sophistication of the cultures that left the archeological remains of the lower Amazon and with early chroniclers' descriptions of the societies they found in the várzea, Meggers tried to salvage the theory that the region could not support, let alone generate, a stratified and politically complex society by attributing these archeological complexes to Andean influence, or even to Andean migration.

Opposing this view, Roosevelt argued that the várzea was able to support very dense populations with maize and other seed crops (119) or by means of a general intensification of production (123). She suggested that maize, rather than having been diffused from the Andes or Meso-America to Amazonia, may have been domesticated independently in the latter region and that, more generally, the Andes were not a factor of cultural diffusion for Amazonia but that the opposite was true. Although the várzea societies took far longer than the Andes to reach a high level of complexity, certain pan-American cultural features (pottery, sedentariness, agriculture) first appeared there. The late prehistoric societies of the floodplain, in particular the social formation that once flourished on Marajó island (400–1300 AD), were, according to Roosevelt, complex chiefdoms or even states of autochthonous origin that featured social stratification, specialized manufactures, priests, ancestor worship, and other so-called advanced characteristics.

Roosevelt concluded that the contemporary societies are "geographically marginal remnants of the peoples that survived the decimation which took place in the várzea during the European conquest" (124:57; cf also 122:130), having involuted to a level earlier to that of the agricultural chiefdoms after they came to the unproductive upland environment. Thus one should avoid the "ethnographic projection" (121) practiced by those ecological anthropologists who see the regressive simplicity characterizing the situation of Amerindian societies in the present as representative of the inexorable limits of Amazonian nature.

Roosevelt's studies gave much impetus to regional archeology; her view of late-prehistoric Amazonian chiefdoms is the most sophisticated to date and has been successfully received even by anthropologists who are distant from the theoretical context in which it was produced.[3] However, Roosevelt was not the first to break the traditional continuity between approaches that attribute to the physical environment a causal value in the interpretation of Amazonian social forms and the naturalizing ideology that since the sixteenth century has depicted the inhabitants of the New World—particularly the peoples of the tropical forest—as prime representatives of "Natural Man," unable to attain civilizational autonomy because of their adaptive subjection to a hostile, restricting nature (31). Lathrap had already proposed the idea of Amazonia as the cradle of complex societies and a focus of cultural diffusion and formulated the argument against "ethnographic projection" (74, 75). Carneiro (for a recapitulation, see 24) had already contested Meggers's notions about Amazonia's agricultural limitations and offered a theory of the emergence of political centralization, which in fact is adapted and used by Roosevelt. And as early as 1952, Lévi-Strauss had mentioned the "centers of civilization" in Amazonia and discussed the "false archaism" of several present-day peoples (82, 86). As Carneiro observed, Roosevelt indulged in not a few self-serving anachronisms when she treated the Steward-Meggers model as if it had survived unscathed to the present.

Moreover, these theses face a number of problems. The central role assigned in *Parmana* (119) to the theory of technological change and to the cultivation of maize in the evolution of chiefdoms disappeared in Roosevelt's later work on Marajó (123). The later work is thus left without any specific causal hypothesis, a weakness she herself had criticized ten years earlier in the work of other authors. In its insistence on a generic contrast between várzea and terra firme as the determining factor of Amazonian cultural evolution (119, 124), her model is outdated in relation to the more differentiated and less negative view of terra firme mentioned above and is a traditional example of "ecological determinism" (history seems to come into the picture only after the European conquest). At times the model seems to incorrectly assume that the uplands were uninhabited before the European invasion (24), or else that all groups that happened (or still happen) to live there were marginal peoples cast out from the alluvial paradise, as if there were an irresistible tropism in every society, whatever its regime of social production and reproduction, toward abstractly more fertile areas. The model also reifies the distinction between riverine chiefdoms [which Roosevelt compared to the Indus valley, the Minoan and Mycenaean city-states, and the Ashanti (124)] and the social systems

---

[3] See, for instance, S Hugh-Jones (66) and Rivière (118), who mentioned Roosevelt's theses about the várzea in order to suggest that the clan hierarchies of the Northwestern Amazon had a much more marked socioeconomic significance in the past.

of the uplands, past or present. It would be more reasonable, considering the cultural substratum common to all of Amazonia, to imagine a *gumsa/gumlao*-type dynamics (80; see 130:226 for this analogy in present-day Amazonia) subject to conjunctural contractions and expansions that articulated populations of the várzea and the terra firme in ecologically and sociopolitically heterogeneous regional systems.

The presence of "complex" developments inland from the alluvial areas, based on bitter manioc cultivation, is beginning to be substantiated by archeological evidence (60).[4] If this supports the picture of a pre-Columbian Amazonia sociopolitically quite different from that of the present, it also minimizes the contrast between várzea and terra firme and undermines the simple deterministic ecological model. It seems increasingly evident that the emergence and persistence of "simple" or "complex" social structures—for whatever these characterizations are worth (smacking as they do of the old social evolutionism)—cannot be explained by environmental factors considered without taking into account large-scale historical dynamics and social interactions, as well as processes of political decision-making guided by value systems that respond to much more than extrinsically defined environmental challenges or problems.

As to her attacks on "ethnographic projection," note that Roosevelt often—and naively—used ethnographic analogy in her own reconstructions (123), resorting to contemporary literature to suggest, for instance, that Marajoara society came close to being a matriarchy, which may be ideologically pleasing but [pace Whitehead (163)] is theoretically problematic and ethnologically improbable.

Social Anthropology

The major contribution of the anthropology of contemporary peoples has been in the area of social organization, which is given short shrift in the typological tradition derived from the *Handbook*. Steward (136, 137) attributed a central role to unilineal descent and believed Amazonia was filled with single- or multilineage villages. Lévi-Strauss, in turn, could not say much about South American kinship systems in the book that launched the theory of matrimonial exchange (85). At the time, they were little known and would have furnished him with more puzzles than solutions (83, 84). By the mid-1970s there was enough ethnographic evidence to warrant an evaluation of the "descent" and "alliance" paradigms in the South American context (99, 104). The reexamina-

---

[4] Alternatively, we know of terra firme economies based on maize cultivation, though these cases, curiously, seem to be the outcome of processes of "agricultural regression" rather than of technological progress (see 10).

tion of Central Brazilian societies (89) undermined or qualified their earlier characterization according to descent groups and simultaneously minimized the matrimonial implications of their pervasive dualism: Uxorilocality replaced descent as an explanatory principle, and moieties were seen as regulating onomastic and ceremonial—rather than matrimonial—transactions. In Guiana, Rivière (113) and Overing (103) identified a combination of symmetric alliance, local endogamy, and cognatic kinship that turned out to be widely diffused throughout Amazonia. Symmetric alliance came to be suggested as an invariant feature of social organization in the whole region (114). Relying on Dumont's work on Dravidian systems, Overing, with much theoretical success, dissociated marriage alliance from any descent construct and from the segmentary society prototype. Later developments in this field (117) were marked by the exploration of the cultural idioms that counted as organizational principles of indigenous societies (105, 132), by local and regional comparative syntheses (4, 64, 115), by attempts to describe in detail the formal features and sociological implications of Amazonian alliance regimes (61a, 139, 143, 156, 158), and by the exploration of new analytic categories that might replace the notion of unilineal descent for true segmentary societies such as the Gê and the Tukanoans (66, 67, 77, 78).

For a long time, ethnologists tended to consider the village or local community as the most comprehensive unit of analysis. The need to describe practically unknown societies imposed this limitation at first, when it was not the simple result of an objective situation (because various contemporary native peoples have been reduced to a single village). In other cases, the view of the local community as a microcosm encapsulating the social structure of the people under examination seems to have derived from a reliance on native ideologies, if not from an explicit theoretical-philosophical position (25, 26). However, it has become increasingly common to emphasize the significance of supralocal networks of trade and politico-matrimonial alliance and to adopt a perspective centering on regional systems (for Guiana, see 21, 22; for the Vaupés, see 65, 71, 72; for the Upper Xingu, see 17, 94, 96; for Panoans, see 46; for the sub-Andean Arawak, see 110). The political picture associated with the *Handbook*'s ecological necessitarianism and Clastres's philosophical voluntarism has also been subjected to severe revision (34).

There are three major analytical styles in contemporary studies of Amazonian societies. This classification highlights only theoretical emphases within a widely shared thematic field, and various ethnologists (including some of those mentioned below) combine more than one. The first is the "political economy of control," developed by Turner for Central Brazil (145, 146) and Rivière for Amazonia proper (115, 116), which shows the influence of the structural-functionalist distinction between the jural-political and the domestic "domains." The ethnologists of Central Brazil (89) have denied the ethnographic relevance of the concept of descent but have nonetheless preserved the analytical substratum of the classical Fortesian model, attributing to communal institutions (moieties, age classes) the function of mediating between the domestic and public domains.[5] To this, Turner added the uxorilocal control of older over younger men through women, seeing the wife's father/daughter's husband relation as the structural axis of Central Brazilian social dynamics and elaborating a complex theory of the recursive dialectics that generates the domestic (natal and conjugal households) and communal (moieties, age-sets) domains and hierarchically articulates them. Rivière generalized the model by proposing (in opposition to the limiting factor theories) that the crucially scarce resource in Amazonia is human labor, which generates a political economy of people based on the distribution and control of women. From this he proceeded to explain the morphological variations present in tropical lowlands by examining the correlation between the ways of managing human resources and the presence or absence of supradomestic institutions.

The second style is the "moral economy of intimacy" found in the recent work of Overing and her former students (53, 54, 100–102, 129). Influenced by the feminist critique of the domestic/public opposition (in particular by the ideas of M Strathern), this tendency has produced stimulating work on the social philosophy and the practice of everyday sociability in Amazonia, emphasizing the egalitarian complementarity between genders and the intimate character of native economies and rejecting a sociology of objective (natural or social) scarcity in favor of a phenomenology of desire as intersubjective demand. This style tends to privilege the local group's internal relationships—defined by sharing and caring between relatives—at the expense of interlocal relationships, conceived by native ideologies as defined by a reciprocity always on the verge of the predatory violence that also characterizes the relations between society and nature. It theoretically values production over exchange, practices of mutuality over reciprocity structures, and the morals of consanguinity over the symbolics of affinity. Although it rejects the notion of "society" as a totality embodying a transcendent, a priori structural rationality, this model, with its essentially moral view of "sociality," nevertheless presents curious analogies with the Fortesian conception of kinship as "Amity." In addition, in a certain way its critique of the public/domestic opposition leads to the reduction of society to the domestic level.

---

[5] Note also the influence of the "developmental cycle of the domestic group" theme as well as the influence of a famous article by Leach (79) on these researchers' interpretations of the Gê kinship systems.

The third style is the "symbolic economy of alterity" of structuralist-inspired ethnologists (1, 22a, 32, 36, 45, 73, 95, 144, 154, 155). It has produced analyses of complex multicommunity systems such as that of the Yanomami [thanks to the outstanding work of Albert (1)] or of the Jívaro (30, 141), which by working with a strategic distinction between local endogamous networks and the politico-ritual structures of interlocal articulation, provided an Amazonian version of the two-dimensional conception of social structure present in Central Brazilian ethnology.[6] However, the group's orientation is clearly Lévi-Straussian. Interested in the interrelations between native sociologies and cosmologies, these researchers have concentrated on processes of symbolic exchange (war and cannibalism, hunting, shamanism, funerary rites) that cross sociopolitical, cosmological, and ontological boundaries, thereby playing a constitutive role in the definition of collective identities. This has led to a critique of the notion of Society as a closed, self-sufficient unit or monad, counterposed to analogous monads that serve them as sociological mirrors (156) or to a Nature that functions as a transcendental Other (39)—two recurring images in regional ethnography. This trend has explored the multiple meanings of the category of affinity in Amazonian cultures (a theme that also appears in the writings of such authors as Rivière or Overing, but in an emically "negative" form), indicating its value as a central sociocosmological operator (156) and emphasizing the dialectics between identity and alterity that is thought to be at the root of Amazonian sociopolitical regimes.

The most consistent attempt to confront the ecological and sociological views of the relation between nature and society in Amazonia comes from a representative of the latter—Descola. In his painstaking studies of the ecology and economy of the Achuar Jívaro (32, 37), who definitely cannot be seen as regressive survivors of the European conquest, the author challenged several theses that are dear to cultural materialism, demonstrating on the one hand that the difference between the productive potentials of the riverine and interfluvial habitats occupied by the Achuar is not economically or politically relevant and on the other that sociocultural limits on the duration of labor expenditure, as well as on the general forms of social organization and the conceptions of the relations with the natural world, lead to a homeostasis of the productive forces on a "low" level of operation, which is nevertheless sufficient to keep the group in nutritionally luxurious conditions. Elsewhere Descola has developed a general model of "symbolic ecology," which attempts to de-reify the nature/culture opposition by differentiating it into distinct practical-cognitive

---

[6] The similarities between the two-tiered models of social structure proposed by the ethnographers of Central Brazil and Amazonia should not be pushed too far; in the former case there is a noticeable concern with totalization that is lacking in the latter. In addition, the place and function of alterity in Central Brazilian and Amazonian social topologies are fundamentally different.

modes, according to the social regimes in which it is found (35, 39). In particular, he has contrasted the "naturalistic" mode that is characteristic of the Western tradition (where the relation between nature and society is metonymic and natural), the "totemic" mode privileged by classical structuralism (in which the relation is purely differential and metaphorical), and the "animic" mode of Amazonian cultures (where the relation is metonymic and social). The notion of an animic mode might illuminate some traditional ethnologic problems, such as the absence of animal domestication in Amazonia (38),[7] and it is generally very promising, though it remains to be more thoroughly tested in certain contexts where the totemic rendering of the nature/culture opposition seems to be quite powerful, as in the Central Brazilian cases [but see Seeger (131) and Crocker (28) for more nuanced views of Gê and Bororo nature/culture dualism]. Descola's theory dialogues with the ideas of Latour (76), and it shows possible convergences with the nonpositivistic ecological anthropology of Ingold (e.g. 68, 69), two authors whose presence in the theoretical context of Amazonian ethnology has yet to be felt more fully, and who offer interesting rephrasings of the shopworn antinomy between nature and culture that was for so long the hallmark of Amazonian ethnology.

History

The historiography of Amazonian peoples is a fast-growing area (161). This reflects a general theoretical tendency, though a more immediate cause is the soul-searching brought about by the fifth centennial of the invasion of America. Professional historians began to work on the region. Ethnologists found that secondary sources were no longer enough and resorted to the abundant archival material. In turn, ethnographic knowledge has been applied to historical sources, such that hypotheses are being advanced to clarify information often of a vague and contradictory nature. A consequence is the revaluation of the ethnographic content of old sources, no longer interpreted as mere records of European prejudices and interests. The interpenetration of anthropology and history has particularly benefited Guiana (5, 42, 47, 57, 159, 160, 162) and the pre-Andean region (27, 109, 111, 128, 142), but other areas are also being well examined for the first time, such as northwest Amazonia (164) and Central Brazil (153), not to speak of peoples who have long been the object of historical interest, such as the Guaraní.

---

[7] On the question of the relations with the animal world in Amazonia, see also the important work of Erikson (44). On the critique of the "totemizing" reading of Amazonian sociocosmologies, see also Viveiros de Castro (155).

The growth in the study of oral traditions has generated some works in ethnohistory proper (16, 50, 63) that demonstrate the importance of a specifically historical consciousness in Amazonian cultures, challenging the traditional vision that reduces Amerindian memory to the timeless world of myth. The relations between myth and history have been analyzed particularly in the context of the indigenous experience of the colonial situation (62). The implications of these relations for the wider cultural history of Amazonian peoples are yet to be explored.

The "historical turn" of regional ethnology has led to widespread interest in the interaction between native societies and Western sociopolitical structures. This theme, long favored by some local theoretical traditions (108), has been brought to the foreground by a metropolitan anthropology in the advanced stage of its postcolonial crisis. This change of analytical orientation reflects, in the case of Amazonia, objective historical changes: The massive incorporation of the region into the world economy that began in the 1970s has not resulted in the extinction or wholesale assimilation of native peoples, as was once feared. Rather, they are experiencing population growth, have preserved their sociocultural identity, and have emerged as political actors on the domestic and international spheres. Anthropology's response to this process has been a welcome breakdown of the traditional division of labor into specialists in "pure" and "acculturated" societies. That division of labor was characterized by an ahistorical approach, a view of native societies as passive or reactive entities, and by an orientation away from the present, whether toward a past of adaptive integrity or toward a future of disaggregation and anomie. We are finally giving up the conception of native societies as manifestations of timeless structural principles, which made social change a theoretical mystery, if not the exclusive result of determinant factors external to indigenous societies. The emergence of approaches that consider both local and global dynamics responsible for the trajectory of indigenous societies reveals an anthropology that both addresses contemporary ethnographic reality and the historical agency of native peoples. Examples of this new ability to articulate cosmology and history, ethnicity and ritual, political economy and symbolic analysis are the works of Turner (147–150), Albert (2, 3), Gow (54, 55), Gallois (51, 52), Brown & Fernandez (18–20), and Taussig (138), among many others.

Another factor responsible for the demise of the contrast mentioned above has been the progressive conviction that groups considered exemplary of a pristine condition when recently "contacted" by national societies have turned out to owe fundamental aspects of their demography, morphology, economy, and ideology to a long history of direct and indirect interaction with the colonial frontier (149, 160). The same may be said of the meaning and intensity of various practices seen as expressions of original environmental adaptations or immanent sociocultural principles, such as war (48, 49) or a foraging way of life (10). Alternatively, a theoretically sophisticated consideration of peoples that at first sight would seem irremediably acculturated has shown that they manage and preserve their identity by means of political strategies and cosmological categories that are very much similar to those described by ethnologists of "traditional" societies (54).

CONCLUSIONS

What are the theoretical and ideological implications of the new image of Amazonia as an originally populous area—with an ecology significantly changed by human intervention—and as sociopolitically "complex," a picture that makes the impact of European invasion and colonization all the more destructive? I accept practically all of its features but cannot avoid a certain feeling of discomfort caused by the excessive emphasis on the distance between the indigenous societies as they once were and as they are now. The revaluation of the impact of the conquest seems perfectly reasonable, but its implied greater victimization of native peoples might warrant a degeneration-istic view of present-day groups that would deny them any capacity for historical agency. Such a view would ultimately lead to the absurd conclusion (that of course none of us would subscribe to—but Amerindians have powerful enemies) that contemporary societies, since they do not represent the original wholeness, are expendable—that is, they may be assimilated into the national society. If "ethnographic projection" has its dangers, one should not underestimate the opposite danger of an "archeological perversion," particularly at a time when native peoples are using their historical continuity with the past as a means of legitimating their existence in the present world political context to ensure their future survival.

I believe also that we should think twice before attributing any problematic aspect of Amerindian societies—as a rule, any aspect that is difficult to reduce to adaptive explanations or that we find politically incorrect, such as war—to the devastating impact of Western civilization. This kind of explanation, for all its well-meaning radicalism, tends to treat native peoples as helpless play-things in the grip of the all-powerful logic of State and Capital—as, in another theoretical context, they are treated as puppets of ecological or sociobiological imperatives. Caught between European (or world) History and American (or human) Nature, indigenous societies are reduced to mere reflexes of a contingency and a necessity that are equally extrinsic. We should perhaps recall that the history of these peoples did not begin in 1492 (on the contrary, for many of them it ended then), just as it was not from 1492 on that adaptation *to* nature was replaced by adaptation *of* nature—even if the effects of human intervention on the Amazonian environment have undergone a dramatic change in scale and even more in direction [destroying biodiversity instead of stimulating it (12)] since national states were implanted. Above all, we should not reason as though up to that point the indigenous populations of Amazonia were following a "natural" evolutionary path, determined exclusively by the interaction among technology, demography, and environment, a trajectory then truncated by the irruption of History.

It seems quite clear that the várzea was a densely populated area at the time of the invasion, that this region is the most propitious for growing cereals, and that the várzea societies showed more political centralization and economic specialization than contemporary groups. Almost certainly some of these contemporary groups are descendants of the várzea peoples, who fled into the upland forests to escape disease, missionaries, and slave raiders. It is just as clear that many of the contemporary foraging societies were forced to give up agriculture because of direct or indirect pressures of the conquest (14), just as it is clear that activities such as war increased in intensity or changed direction as an effect of European invasion (149). However, if Amazonia can no longer be seen as the exclusive habitat of egalitarian hunters-horticulturalists living in small villages, it would be just as misguided to take for granted the vestigial, degenerative, and marginal condition of the terra firme peoples. Above all, it should be stressed that such phenomena as "agricultural regression"—or, more generally, present-day Amerindian ways of life—are not evolutionary events, but rather the consequence of political choices (112), historical decisions that privileged certain values (e.g. political autonomy) at the expense of others (e.g. access to commodities).

There is yet another intriguing problem with the picture of an Amazonia dominated by agricultural chiefdoms. Much of the available ethnographic evidence points to the overwhelming ideological importance assigned to hunting in contemporary indigenous cosmologies (even those present in full-blown horticultural societies), a view of the relations with nature that privileges social and symbolic interactions with the animal world and in which shamanism is the central institution—here the similarities between Amazonian cultures and the hunting populations of the North American Subartic and elsewhere are remarkable (39)—and a widespread ideology of ontological predation as a regime for the constitution of collective identities (156). All of this seems somewhat at odds with the ideological regimes associated with agriculture and/or political centralization in other parts of the world, and it would be insufficient to explain this away as a cognitive atavism manifested by societies in "regression." If this point is accepted, instead of evaluating the contemporary societies according to a standard defined by the intensive agriculture and political centralization in the past, it might be necessary to reconsider the effective sociopolitical expressions of these old chiefdoms in the light of a cultural horizon that is still present. Further, if we accept (as I do) that the state of productive homeostasis attributed by Descola to the Achuar is intrinsic to this society and owes nothing to any post-Columbian adaptive regression, and if we note how similar it is to what is known about other contemporary societies, we shall be forced to reopen the entire discussion about what type of extra-technological mutation might have led to the emergence of the várzea societies.

As to the hopes of a theoretical "new synthesis," I believe that any unification still lies somewhat ahead. Although researchers from opposite traditions, united by the unanimous desideratum of transcending the classical antinomies between nature and culture, history and structure, political economy of change and analysis of monads in cosmological equilibrium, "mentalism" and "materialism," and so on, are certainly—and auspiciously—edging closer, it is difficult not to see the persistence of attitudes that were characteristic of earlier phases of the discipline. For example, one cannot help but feel that "resource management" theories are themselves adaptations of the adaptationist viewpoint to an intellectual environment that favors the concepts of history and culture; that Roosevelt's critique (122) of Meggers's "ecological determinism" does no more than transform environmental factors from inhibitions into stimuli, preserving the same reactive view of indigenous societies; and that Descola's theses on the historical constraints of the Amerindian "animic" regime or on Jívaro homeostasis may not be all that different from Lévi-Strauss's rephrasing of the nature/society contrast as an internal feature of Amerindian cosmologies (totemism aside), or from Lévi-Strauss's and Clastres's ideas (metaphysics aside) of the structural self-limitation that kept Amazonian societies away from productivism and despotism. I am not quite sure that this is a pessimistic conclusion; it may be the case that "allopoietic" and "autopoietic" perspectives on the nature/society pair are alternative descriptions that imply each other (152)—and, accordingly, that any synthesis must begin by acknowledging their necessary complementarity.

Literature Cited

1. Albert B. 1985. *Temps du sang, temps des cendres: représentation de la maladie, système rituel et espace politique chez les Yanomami du sud-est (Amazonie brésilienne).* PhD thesis. Univ. Paris-X: Nanterre. 833 pp.

2. Albert B. 1988. La Fumée du métal: histoire et représentations du contact chez les Yanomami (Brésil). *L'Homme 106–107* 28(2–3):87–119

3. Albert B. 1993. L'Or cannibale et la chute du ciel: une critique chamanique de

l'économie politique de la nature. See Ref. 41, pp. 349–78

4. Århem K. 1981. *Makuna Social Organization: A Study in Descent, Alliance, and the Formation of Corporate Groups in the North-Western Amazon.* Stockholm: Almqvist & Wiksell. 379 pp.

5. Arvelo-Jiménez N, Biord H. 1994. The impact of the conquest on contemporary indigenous peoples of the Guiana Shield: the system of Orinoco regional interdependence. See Ref. 127, pp. 55–78

6. Balée WL. 1988. Indigenous adaptation to Amazonian palm forests. *Principes* 32(2): 47–54

7. Balée WL. 1989. Cultura e vegetação da Amazônia brasileira. In *Biologia e Ecologia Humana na Amazônia: Avaliação e Perspectivas,* ed. W Neves, pp. 95–109. Belém: Mus. Para. E Goeldi

8. Balée WL. 1989. The culture of Amazonian forests. See Ref. 106, pp. 1–21

9. Deleted in proof

10. Balée WL. 1992. Peoples of the fallow: a historical ecology of foraging in lowland South America. In *Conservation of Neotropical Forests: Working from Traditional Resource Use,* ed. K Redford, C Padoch, pp. 35–57. New York: Columbia Univ. Press

11. Balée WL. 1994. *Footprints of the Forest: Ka'apor Ethnobotany.* New York: Columbia Univ. Press. 396 pp.

12. Balée WL. 1993. Biodiversidade e os índios amazônicos. See Ref. 157, pp. 385–93

13. Balée WL. 1993. Indigenous transformation of Amazonian forests: an example from Maranhão, Brazil. See Ref. 41, pp. 231–54

14. Balée WL. 1995. Historical ecology of Amazonia. See Ref. 134, pp. 97–110

15. Balée WL, ed. 1996. *Advances in Historical Ecology.* In press

15a. Balée WL, Campbell DG. 1990. Evidence for the sucessional status of liana forest (Xingu River Basin, Amazonian Brazil). *Biotropica* 22(1):36–47

16. Basso EB. 1995. *The Last Cannibals: A South American Oral History.* Austin: Univ. Tex. Press. 319 pp.

17. Bastos RM. 1983. Sistemas políticos, de comunicação e articulação social no Alto Xingu. *Anu. Antropol.* 81:43–58

18. Brown MF. 1991. Beyond resistance: a comparative study of utopian renewal in Amazonia. *Ethnohistory* 38(4):388–413

19. Brown MF. 1993. Facing the state, facing the world: Amazonia's native leaders and the new politics of identity. See Ref. 41, pp. 307–26

20. Brown MF, Fernandez E. 1991. *War of Shadows. The Struggle for Utopia in Peru-* vian *Amazon.* Berkeley: Univ. Calif. Press. 280 pp.

21. Butt Colson A. 1983–1984. The spatial component in the political structure of the Carib speakers of the Guiana highlands: Kapon and Pemon. *Antropologica* 59–62: 73–124

22. Butt Colson A. 1985. Routes of knowledge: an aspect of regional integration in the circum-Roraima area in the Guiana highlands. *Antropologica* 63–64:103–49

22a. Carneiro da Cunha MM. 1978. *Os Mortos e os Outros.* São Paulo: Hucitec. 152 pp.

23. Carneiro da Cunha MM, ed. 1992. *História dos Indios no Brasil.* São Paulo: Cia. Letras/FAPESP/SMC. 611 pp.

24. Carneiro RL. 1995. The history of ecological interpretations of Amazonia: Does Roosevelt have it right? See Ref. 134, pp. 45–70

25. Clastres P. 1974. *La Société Contre l'État.* Paris: Minuit. 187 pp.

26. Clastres P. 1977. Archéologie de la violence: la guerre dans les sociétes primitives. *Libre* 1:137–73

27. Combes I, Saignes T. 1991. *Alter Ego: Naissance de l'Identité Chiriguano.* Paris: Éc. Hautes Étud. Sci. Soc. 153 pp.

28. Crocker JC. 1985. *Vital Souls: Bororo Cosmology, Natural Symbolism, and Shamanism.* Tucson: Univ. Ariz. Press. 380 pp.

29. Denevan WM. 1992. The pristine myth: the landscape of the Americas in 1492. *Ann. Assoc. Am. Geogr.* 82(3):369–85

30. Descola P. 1982. Territorial adjustments among the Achuar of Ecuador. *Soc. Sci. Inf.* 21(2):301–20

31. Descola P. 1985. De l'indien naturalisé à l'indien naturaliste: sociétés amazoniennes sous le regard de l'occident. In *Protection de la Nature: Histoire et Idéologie (de la Nature à l'Environnement),* ed. A Cadoret, pp. 221–35. Paris: Harmattan

32. Descola P. 1987. *La Nature Domestique: Symbolisme et Praxis dans l'Écologie des Achuar.* Paris: Maison Sci. Homme. 450 pp.

33. Descola P. 1988. L'explication causale. In *Les Idées de l'Anthropologie,* ed. P Descola, G Lenclud, C Severi, AC Taylor, pp. 12–59. Paris: Colin

34. Descola P. 1988. La chefferie amérindienne dans l'anthropologie politique. *Rev. Fr. Sci. Polit.* 38(5):818–27

35. Descola P. 1992. Societies of nature and the nature of society. In *Conceptualizing Society,* ed. A Kuper, pp. 107–26. London: Routledge

36. Descola P. 1993. Les affinités sélectives: alliance, guerre et prédation dans l'ensemble Jívaro. See Ref. 41, pp. 171–90

37. Descola P. 1994. Homeostasis as a cultural

system: the Jívaro case. See Ref. 127, pp. 203–24
38. Descola P. 1994. Pourquoi les Indiens d'Amazonie n'ont-ils pas domestiqué le pécari? Genéalogie des objets et anthropologie de l'objectivation. In *De la Préhistoire aux Missiles Balistiques: L'Intelligence Sociale des Techniques,* ed. B Latour, P Lemonnier, pp. 329–44. Paris: Découverte
39. Descola P. 1996. Constructing natures: symbolic ecology and social practice. In *Nature and Society: Anthropological Perspectives,* ed. P Descola, G Pálsson. In press
40. Descola P, Taylor A-C. 1993. Introduction. See Ref. 41, pp. 13–24
41. Descola P, Taylor A-C, eds. 1993. *La Remontée de l'Amazone: Anthropologie et Histoire des Sociétés Amazoniennes (Spec. ed. L'Homme 126–128).* Paris: Éc. Hautes Étud. Sci. Soc. 533 pp.
42. Dreyfus S. 1993. Os empreendimentos coloniais e os espaços políticos indígenas no interior da Guiana ocidental (entre o Orinoco e o Corentino) de 1613 a 1796. See Ref. 157, pp. 19–41
43. Durham WH. 1991. *Coevolution: Genes, Culture, and Human Diversity.* Stanford, CA: Stanford Univ. Press. 628 pp.
44. Erikson P. 1984. De l'approvisoisement à l'approvisionnement: chasse, alliance et familiarisation en Amazonie amérindienne. *Tech. Cult.* 9:105–40
45. Erikson P. 1986. Alterité, tatouage et anthropophagie chez les Pano: la belliqueuse quête de soi. *J. Soc. Am.* 72:185–210
46. Erikson P. 1993. Une Nébuleuse compacte: le macro-ensemble pano. See Ref. 41, pp. 45–58
47. Farage N. 1992. *As Muralhas dos Sertões: Os Povos Indígenas do Rio Branco e a Colonização.* Rio de Janeiro: Paz & Terra/ ANPOCS. 197 pp.
48. Ferguson RB. 1990. Blood of the Leviathan: Western contact and Amazonian warfare. *Am. Ethnol.* 17(2):237–57
49. Ferguson RB. 1995. *Yanomami Warfare: A Political History.* Santa Fe: Sch. Am. Res. 449 pp.
50. Franchetto B. 1993. A celebração da história nos discursos cerimoniais kuikúro (Alto Xingu). See Ref. 157, pp. 95–116
51. Gallois DT. 1987–1989. O discurso Waiãpi sobre o ouro: um profetismo moderno. *Rev. Antropol.* 30–32:457–67
52. Gallois DT. 1993. *Mairi Revisitada: A Reintegração da Fortaleza de Macapá na Tradição Oral dos Wayãpi.* São Paulo: Núcleo Hist. Indigena/Univ. São Paulo. 91 pp.
53. Gow P. 1989. The perverse child: desire in a native Amazonian subsistence economy. *Man* 24(4):567–82

54. Gow P. 1991. *Of Mixed Blood: Kinship and History in Peruvian Amazonia.* Oxford: Clarendon. 331 pp.
55. Gow P. 1994. River People: Shamanism and history in Western Amazonia. In *Shamanism, History and the State,* ed. C Humphrey, N Thomas, pp. 90–113. Ann Arbor: Univ. Mich. Press
56. Gregory C. 1982. *Gifts and Commodities.* London: Academic. 242 pp.
57. Grenand P. 1982. *Ainsi Parlaient Nos Ancêtres: Essai d'Etnohistoire Wayãpi.* Paris: Organ. Rech. Sci. Territ. Outre-Mer. 408 pp.
58. Hames RB, Vickers WT, ed. 1983. *Adaptive Responses of Native Amazonians.* New York: Academic. 516 pp.
59. Hames RB, Vickers WT. 1983. Introduction. See Ref. 58, pp. 1–26
60. Heckenberger MJ. 1996. *War and peace in the shadow of empire: sociopolitical change in the Upper Xingu of Southeastern Amazonia, A.D. 1250–2000.* PhD thesis. Univ. Pittsburgh, Pittsburgh
61. Henley P. 1996. Amazonian anthropology: the present state of the art. *Bull. Lat. Am. Res.* In press
61a. Henley P. 1996. *South Indian models in the Amazonian lowlands. Manch. Pap. Soc. Anthopol. No. 1.* Dep. Soc. Anthropol., Univ. Manchester.
62. Hill JD, ed. 1988. *Rethinking History and Myth: Indigenous South American Perspectives on the Past.* Urbana: Univ. Ill. Press. 337 pp.
63. Hill JD, Wright RM. 1988. Time, narrative, and ritual: historical interpretations from an Amazonian society. See Ref. 62, pp. 78–105
64. Hornborg A. 1988. *Dualism and Hierarchy in Lowland South America: Trajectories of Indigenous Social Organization.* Stockholm: Almqvist & Wiksell. 304 pp.
65. Hugh-Jones C. 1979. *From the Milk River: Spatial and Temporal Processes in Northwest Amazonia.* Cambridge: Cambridge Univ. Press. 302 pp.
66. Hugh-Jones S. 1993. Clear descent or ambiguous houses? A re-examination of Tukanoan social organization. See Ref. 41, pp. 95–120
67. Hugh-Jones S. 1995. Inside-out and back-to-front: the androgynous house in northwest Amazonia. In *About the House: Lévi-Strauss and Beyond,* ed. J Carsten, S Hugh-Jones, pp. 226–52. Cambridge: Cambridge Univ. Press
68. Ingold T. 1989. The social and environmental relations of human beings and other animals. In *Comparative Socioecology: The Behavioural Ecology of Humans and Other Mammals,* ed. V Standen, RA Foley, pp. 495–512. Oxford: Blackwell Sci.

69. Ingold T. 1992. Culture and the perception of the environment. In *Bush Base: Forest Camp. Culture, Environment and Development*, ed. E Croll, D Parkin, pp. 39–56. London: Routledge
70. Jackson JE. 1975. Recent ethnography of indigenous northern lowland South America. *Annu. Rev. Anthropol.* 4:307–40
71. Jackson JE. 1976. Vaupés marriage: a network system in the northwest Amazon. In *Regional Analysis. Social Systems*, ed. C Smith, 2:65–93. New York: Academic
72. Jackson JE. 1983. *The Fish People: Linguistic Exogamy and Tukanoan Identity in Northwest Amazonia*. Cambridge: Cambridge Univ. Press. 283 pp.
73. Keifenheim B. 1992. Identité et alterité chez les indiens Pano. *J. Soc. Am.* 78(2): 79–93
74. Lathrap D. 1970. *The Upper Amazon.* New York: Praeger. 256 pp.
75. Lathrap D. 1973/1968. The "hunting" economies of the tropical forest zone of the South America: an attempt at historical perspective. In *Peoples and Culture of Native South America*, ed. DRGross, pp. 83–95. New York: Doubleday
76. Latour B. 1991. *Nous n'Avons Jamais Été Modernes.* Paris: Découverte
77. Lea VR. 1992. Mebengokre (Kayapó) onomastics: a facet of houses as total social facts in Central Brazil. *Man* 27(1): 129–53
78. Lea VR. 1995. The houses of the Mebengokre (Kayapó) of Central Brazil: a new door to their social organization. In *About the House: Lévi-Strauss and Beyond*, ed. J Carsten, S Hugh-Jones, pp. 206–69. Cambridge: Cambridge Univ. Press
79. Leach ER. 1958. Concerning Trobriand clans and the kinship category Tabu. In *The Developmental Cycle in Domestic Groups*, ed. J Goody, pp. 120–45. Cambridge: Cambridge Univ. Press.
80. Leach ER. 1965/1954. *Political Systems of Highland Burma: A Study of Kachin Social Structure.* Boston: Beacon. 324 pp.
81. Lévi-Strauss C. 1955. *Tristes Tropiques.* Paris: Plon. 490 pp.
82. Lévi-Strauss C. 1958/1952. La Notion d'archaïsme en ethnologie. In *Anthropologie Structurale*, pp. 113–32. Paris: Plon
83. Lévi-Strauss C. 1958/1952. Les structures sociales dans le Brésil central et oriental. In *Anthropologie Structurale*, pp. 133–45. Paris: Plon
84. Lévi-Strauss C. 1958/1956. Les organisations dualistes existent-elles? In *Anthropologie Structurale*, pp. 147–80. Paris: Plon
85. Lévi-Strauss C. 1967/1949. *Les Structures Élémentaires de la Parenté.* Paris: Mouton. 591 pp. 2nd ed.
86. Lévi-Strauss C. 1993. Un autre regard. See Ref. 41, pp. 7–10
87. Lyon PJ, ed. 1974. *Native South Americans: Ethnology of the Least Known Continent.* Boston: Little, Brown. 433 pp.
88. Maybury-Lewis D. 1967. *Akwe-Shavante Society.* Oxford: Clarendon. 356 pp.
89. Maybury-Lewis D, ed. 1979. *Dialectical Societies: The Gê and Bororo of Central Brazil.* Cambridge, MA: Harvard Univ. Press. 340 pp.
90. Meggers BJ. 1954. Environmental limitations on the development of culture. *Am. Anthropol.* 56(4):801–41
91. Meggers BJ. 1957. Environment and culture in Amazonia: an appraisal of the theory of environmental limitations. In *Studies in Human Ecology (Soc. Sci. Monogr. 3)*, ed. A Palerm, pp. 71–89. Washington, DC: Panam. Union
92. Meggers BJ. 1971. *Amazonia: Man and Culture in a Counterfeit Paradise.* Chicago: Aldine-Atherton. 182 pp.
93. Meggers BJ, Evans C. 1973/1954. An interpretation of the cultures of Marajó Island. In *Peoples and Cultures of Native South America*, ed. DR Gross, pp. 39–47. Garden City, NY: Doubleday
94. Menget P. 1978. *Alliance and violence in the Upper Xingu.* Presented at Annu. Meet. Am. Anthropol. Assoc., 77th, Los Angeles
95. Menget P, ed. 1985. Guerres, sociétés et vision du monde dans les basses terres de l'Amérique du Sud. *J. Soc. Am.* 71: 129–208
96. Menget P. 1993. Les frontières de la chefferie: remarques sur le système politique du haut Xingu (Brésil). See Ref. 41, pp. 59–76
97. Moran EF. 1993. *Through Amazonian Eyes: The Human Ecology of Amazonian Populations.* Iowa City: Univ. Iowa Press. 230 pp.
98. Moran EF. 1995. Disaggregating Amazonia: a strategy for understanding biological and cultural diversity. See Ref. 134, pp. 71–95
99. Murphy RF. 1979. Lineage and lineality in lowland South America. In *Brazil: Anthropological Perspectives*, ed. M Margolis, W Carter, pp. 217–24. New York: Columbia Univ. Press
100. Overing J. 1992. Wandering in the market and the forest: an Amazonian theory of production and exchange. In *Contesting Markets*, ed. R Dilley, pp. 180–200. Edinburgh: Univ. Edinb. Press
101. Overing J. 1993. The anarchy and collectivism of the 'Primitive Other': Marx and Shalins in the Amazon. In *Socialism: Ideals, Ideologies, and Local Practice*, ed. C Hann, pp. 43–58. London: Routledge
102. Overing J. 1993. Death and the loss of

civilized predation among the Piaroa of the Orinoco Basin. See Ref. 41, pp. 191–211

103. Overing (Kaplan) J. 1975. *The Piaroa, A People of the Orinoco Basin.* Oxford: Clarendon. 236 pp.

104. Overing (Kaplan) J, ed. 1977. Social time and social space in lowland South American societies. In *Actes du XLII Congrès International des Américanistes,* II, pp. 7–394. Paris: Soc. Am.

105. Overing (Kaplan) J. 1981. Amazonian anthropology. *J. Lat. Am. Stud.* 13(1):151–64

106. Posey DA, Balée WL, eds. 1989. Resource management in Amazonia: indigenous and folk strategies. *Adv. Econ. Bot.* 7: 1–287

107. Prance GT, Lovejoy T, ed. 1985. *Key Environments: Amazonia.* New York: Pergamon. 442 pp.

108. Ramos AR. 1990. Ethnology Brazilian style. *Cult. Anthropol.* 5(4):452–72

109. Renard-Casevitz F-M. 1992. História Kampa, memória Ashaninca. See Ref. 23, pp. 197–212

110. Renard-Casevitz F-M. 1993. Guerriers du sel, sauniers de la paix. See Ref. 41, pp. 25–43

111. Renard-Casevitz FM, Saignes T, Taylor-Descola AC. 1986. *L'Inca, l'Espagnol et les Sauvages: Rapports Entre les Sociétés Amazoniennes et Andines du XVe au XVIIe siècle.* Paris: Rech. Civilis. 411 pp.

112. Rival L. 1996. Domestication as a historical and symbolic process: wild gardens and cultivated forests in the Ecuadorian Amazon. See Ref. 15. In press

113. Rivière P. 1969. *Marriage among the Trio: A Principle of Social Organisation.* Oxford: Clarendon. 353 pp.

114. Rivière P. 1973. *The lowlands South America culture area: towards a structural definition.* Presented at Annu. Meet. Am. Anthropol. Assoc., 72nd, New Orleans

115. Rivière P. 1984. *Individual and Society in Guiana: A Comparative Study of Amerindian Social Organization.* Cambridge: Cambridge Univ. Press. 124 pp.

116. Rivière P. 1987. Of women, men and manioc. In *Natives and Neighbours in South America,* ed. HO Skar, F Salomon, pp. 178–201. Göteborg: Göteborg Etnogr. Mus.

117. Rivière P. 1993. The Amerindianization of descent and affinity. See Ref. 41, pp. 507–16

118. Rivière P. 1995. Review of J. Chernela, *The Wanano Indians of the Brazilian Amazon.* *J. R. Anthropol. Inst.* 1(1):206–7

119. Roosevelt AC. 1980. *Parmana: Pre-historic Maize and Manioc Subsistence along the Amazon and the Orinoco.* New York: Academic. 320 pp.

120. Roosevelt AC. 1987. Chiefdoms in the Amazon and Orinoco. In *Chiefdoms in the Americas,* ed. RD Drennan, CA Uribe, pp. 153–85. Lanham, MD: Univ. Press Am.

121. Roosevelt AC. 1989. Resource management in Amazonia before the Conquest: beyond ethnographic projection. See Ref. 106, pp. 30–62

122. Roosevelt AC. 1991. Determinismo ecológico na interpretação do desenvolvimento social indígena na Amazônia. In *Origens, Adaptações e Diversidade Biológica do Homem Nativo da Amazônia,* ed. WA Neves, pp. 103–41. Belém: Mus. Para. E Gœldi

123. Roosevelt AC. 1991. *Moundbuilders of the Amazon: Geophysical Archaeology on Marajó Island, Brazil.* San Diego: Academic. 494 pp.

124. Roosevelt AC. 1992. Arqueologia Amazônica. See Ref. 23, pp. 53–86

125. Roosevelt AC. 1993. The rise and fall of Amazonian chiefdoms. See Ref. 41, pp. 255–83

126. Roosevelt AC. 1994. Amazonian anthropology: strategy for a new synthesis. See Ref. 127, pp. 1–29

127. Roosevelt AC, ed. 1994. *Amazonian Indians from Prehistory to the Present.* Tucson: Univ. Ariz. Press. 420 pp.

128. Santos Granero F. 1988. Templos y herrerías: utopia y re-creación cultural en la Amazonia Peruana, siglos XVIII-XIX. *Bull. Inst. Fr. d'Études Andines* 17(3–4): 1–22

129. Santos Granero F. 1991. *The Power of Love: The Moral Use of Knowledge amongst the Amuesha of Central Peru.* London: Athlone. 338 pp.

130. Santos Granero F. 1993. From prisoner of the group to darling of the gods: an approach to the issue of power in lowland South America. See Ref. 41, pp. 213–30

131. Seeger A. 1981. *Nature and Society in Central Brazil: The Suyá Indians of Mato Grosso.* Cambridge, MA: Harvard Univ. Press. 278 pp.

132. Seeger A, DaMatta RA, Viveiros de Castro EB. 1979. A Construção da pessoa nas sociedades indígenas brasileiras. *Bol. Mus. Nac.* 32:2–19

133. Sponsel LE. 1986. Amazon ecology and adaptation. *Annu. Rev. Anthropol.* 15: 67–97

134. Sponsel LE, ed. 1995. *Indigenous Peoples and the Future of Amazonia: An Ecological Anthropology of an Endangered World.* Tucson: Univ. Ariz. Press. 312 pp.

135. Steward JH, ed. 1946–1950. *Handbook of South American Indians,* Vols. 1–6. Washington, DC: Smithson. Inst.

136. Steward JH. 1948. South American cultures: an interpretative summary. In *Handbook of South American Indians,* ed. JH

Steward, 5:669–772. Washington, DC: Smithson. Inst.

137. Steward JH, Faron LC. 1959. *Native Peoples of South America.* New York: McGraw-Hill. 481 pp.

138. Taussig MT. 1987. *Shamanism, Colonialism, and the Wild Man: A Study in Terror and Healing.* Chicago: Univ. Chicago Press. 517 pp.

139. Taylor A-C. 1983. The marriage alliance and its structural variations in Jívaroan societies. *Soc. Sci. Inf.* 22(3):331–53

140. Taylor A-C. 1984. L'americanisme tropical: une frontière fossile de l'ethnologie? In *Histoires de l'Anthropologie: XVI-XIX siècles,* ed. B Rupp-Eisenreich, pp. 213–33. Paris: Klinksieck

141. Taylor A-C. 1985. L'art de la réduction. See Ref. 95, pp. 159–73

142. Taylor A-C. 1992. História pós-colombiana da Alta Amazônia. See Ref. 23, pp. 213–38

143. Taylor A-C. 1993. La parenté Jívaro: formules 'simples' et formules 'complexes'. Un groupe de transformation Dravidien. Presented at roundtable "Systèmes Dravidiens, Iroquois et Crow-Omaha," Paris: Maison Sci. Homme

144. Taylor A-C. 1993. Les bons ennemis et les mauvais parents: le traitement symbolique de l'alliance dans les rituels de chasse aux têtes des Jívaros de l'Equateur. In *Les Complexités de l'Alliance. Économie, Politique et Fondements Symboliques de l'Alliance,* ed. E Copet, F Héritier-Augé, 4:73–105. Paris: Arch. Contemp.

145. Turner TS. 1979. The Gê and Bororo societies as dialectical systems: a general model. See Ref. 89, pp. 147–78

146. Turner TS. 1984. Dual opposition, hierarchy, and value: moiety structure and symbolic polarity in Central Brazil and elsewhere. In *Différences, Valeurs, Hiérarchie: Textes Offerts à Louis Dumont,* ed. JC Galey, pp. 333–70. Paris: Éc Hautes Étud. Sci. Soc.

147. Turner TS. 1988. History, myth, and social counsciousness among the Kayapó of Central Brazil. See Ref. 62, pp. 195–213

148. Turner TS. 1991. Representing, resisting, rethinking: historical transformations of Kayapó culture and anthropological counsciousness. In *Colonial Situations: Essays on the Contextualization of Ethnographic Knowledge,* ed. GW Stocking, pp. 285–313. Madison: Univ. Wis. Press

149. Turner TS. 1992. Os Mebengokre Kayapó: história e mudança social, de comunidades

autônomas para a coexistência interétnica. See Ref. 23, pp. 311–38

150. Turner TS. 1993. De cosmologia a história: resistência, adaptação e consciência social entre os Kayapó. See Ref. 157, pp. 43–66

151. Urban G, Sherzer J. 1988. The linguistic anthropology of native South America. *Annu. Rev. Anthropol.* 17:283–307

152. Varela FJ. 1979. *Principles of Biological Autonomy.* New York: North Holland. 306 pp.

153. Verswijver G. 1992. *The Club-Fighters of the Amazon: Warfare among the Kayapó Indians of Central Brazil.* Gent: Rijksuniv. Gent

154. Vilaça AN. 1992. *Comendo como Gente: Formas do Canibalismo Wari'.* Rio de Janeiro: Ed. Univ. Fed. Rio de Janeiro. 363 pp.

155. Viveiros de Castro EB. 1992. *From the Enemy's Point of View: Humanity and Divinity in an Amazonian society.* Chicago: Univ. Chicago Press. 407 pp.

156. Viveiros de Castro EB. 1993. Alguns aspectos da afinidade no dravidianato amazônico. See Ref. 157, pp. 150–210

157. Viveiros de Castro EB, Carneiro da Cunha MM, eds. 1993. *Amazônia: Etnologia e História Indígena.* São Paulo: Núcleo Hist. Indigena/Univ. São Paulo. 431 pp.

158. Viveiros de Castro EB, Fausto C. 1993. La puissance et l'acte: la parenté dans les basses terres d'Amérique du Sud. See Ref. 41, pp. 141–70

159. Whitehead NL. 1988. *Lords of the Tiger Spirit: A History of the Caribs in Colonial Venezuela and Guyana, 1498–1820.* Dordrecht: Foris. 250 pp.

160. Whitehead NL. 1993. Ethnic transformation and historical discontinuity in Native Amazonia and Guayana, 1500–1900. See Ref. 41, pp. 285–305

161. Whitehead NL. 1993. Recent research on the native history of Amazonia and Guayana. See Ref. 41, pp. 495–506

162. Whitehead NL. 1994. The ancient Amerindian polities of the Amazon, the Orinoco, and the Atlantic Coast: a preliminary analysis of their passage from antiquity to extinction. See Ref. 127, pp. 33–53

163. Whitehead NL. 1995. The historical anthropology of text: the interpretation of Raleigh's *Discoverie of Guiana. Curr. Anthropol.* 36(1):53–74

164. Wright RM. 1992. História indígena do noroeste da Amazônia: hipóteses, questões e perspectivas. See Ref. 23, pp. 253–66

Annu. Rev. Anthropol. 1996. 25:201–16

SUDDEN INFANT DEATH SYNDROME IN CROSS-CULTURAL PERSPECTIVE: Is Infant-Parent Cosleeping Protective?

James J. McKenna

Department of Sociology and Anthropology, Pomona College, Claremont, California 91711

KEY WORDS: SIDS, child-care practices, epidemiology, evolution

ABSTRACT

This chapter reviews what is presently known about the sudden infant death syndrome (SIDS) and examines the role that infant sleeping arrangements may play in reducing SIDS risks. Alongside sleep laboratory–based experimental evidence comparing bedsharing and solitary sleeping mother-infant pairs, an evolutionary and cross-cultural framework is used to argue that infant-parent cosleeping is biologically, psychologically, and socially the most appropriate context for the development of healthy infant sleep physiology. It is also the context within which potentially more optimal breastfeeding activities for both the mother and infant are most likely to emerge. A survey of cross-cultural data and laboratory findings suggest that where infant-parent cosleeping and breast-feeding are practiced in tandem in nonsmoking households, and are practiced by parents specifically to promote infant health, the chances of an infant dying from SIDS should be reduced.

Introduction

Nowhere are the cultural values, expectations, and preferences of the Western industrial world more strongly reflected than in its clinical models of "normal" infant sleep and "normal" infant sleeping arrangements in the first year of life. From popular parenting books (18, 77) to the most widely respected scientific literature (2–4, 82) in the field of pediatric sleep medicine, cultural rather than biological understandings predominate, often without scientists' awareness (91). The nearly universal, species-wide pattern of infant sleep, which involves infants and parents sleeping within sensory proximity of one another (10, 36, 41, 44, 52, 89), is either ignored altogether or regarded as inherently unhealthful, psychologically damaging to the infant or child, and potentially threatening to the husband-wife relationship (14, 33, 69). Suffocation by overlying is considered an inevitable outcome of cosleeping, especially when bedsharing, and the ability to condition infants and children to sleep alone throughout the night, as early in life as possible, is a developmental goal around which both infant-child maturation and parenting skills are evaluated and rated (4, 12, 18, 63, 77, 88).

As Abbot (1) discussed, Western industrial values thus seem to favor early autonomy and individualism over familial interdependence (31). While this preference is not especially startling, given the apparent economic and professional needs of people whose lifestyles demand more and more time away from their infants and children, it has led scientists to define the best biological interests of infants and children according to the social interests of their parents. In so doing—and this is based on anthropological evidence—scientists push too far the notion of the infant's physiological independence from its caregivers, confusing the infant's preparedness to adapt with actual adaptation (50, 51), and confusing widespread underlying cultural assumptions with established scientific facts.

This review examines the sudden infant death syndrome (SIDS, cot or crib death), the leading cause of nonaccidental death in industrialized countries for infants younger than one year of age. SIDS is reviewed in the context of how Western cultural conceptualizations of infant sleep, rather than species-typical patterns, have influenced and constrained SIDS research. For example, measurements of so-called normal infant sleep physiology have been derived exclusively from studies of nonbreastfeeding, solitary-sleeping infants, a context that, for the species, is neither biologically nor socially normal at all. In addition, I explore SIDS rates cross-culturally to highlight how much childcare practices generally, and sleeping arrangements in particular, may potentially be linked to the ease by which certain types of infantile defects suspected to be involved in SIDS find expression. A laboratory-based study comparing physiological and behavioral differences between social- and solitary-sleeping mother-infant pairs is presented to illustrate the effect that "choice" of childcare practice has on factors that could potentially mitigate the suspected deficiencies of some SIDS victims.

One purpose of this review is to demonstrate just how powerful anthropological concepts can be in helping to reconceptualize fields of research, such as sleep, not traditionally within the discipline's purview. Unfortunately, few anthropologists are involved in SIDS or pediatric sleep research, and even fewer have considered, for example, the paleoecology of hominid sleep and its implications for the evolution of human sleep in general (19, 55). Perhaps this review will stimulate additional interest by anthropologists whose research knowledge and expertise are precisely relevant to these areas and demonstrate to nonanthropologists that their own research in sleep can benefit from evolutionary and cross-cultural perspectives.

What Is SIDS or Cot or Crib Death?

Responding to the increasing need for more in-depth, on-the-scene environmental data and family history as part of the pathologist's criteria for a SIDS diagnosis, the National Institutes of Child Health and Human Development (NICHD) recently modified the definition of SIDS to read as follows: "The sudden death of an infant under one year of age which remains unexplained after a thorough case investigation, including performance of a complete autopsy, examination of the death scene, and a review of the clinical history" (90). The most intriguing clue to understanding SIDS is the unique age distribution of its victims. No other human malady except infant botulism is so heavily concentrated around such a narrow developmental period. Ninety percent of SIDS deaths occur before six months of age, mostly between two and four months; rarely do such deaths occur beyond 12 months of age. In all societies studied to date, boys die more frequently from SIDS than girls (6).

What Are the Possible Causes of SIDS?

The primary causes of SIDS are still unknown, but the most compelling general hypothesis is that the fatal event is related to the control of breathing and/or arousal during sleep. As a result, the architecture of infant sleep, breathing patterns, and arousal have been intensely studied by SIDS researchers, as have the neurostructural, neurochemical, and physiological systems that underlie, influence, or control these activities. Researchers note that SIDS tends to occur after abnormalities of the cardiorespiratory control system have failed to monitor some combination of oxygen levels, breathing, heart-rate rhythmicity, body temperature, or the arousal responses needed to reinitiate breathing after a normal breathing pause or apnea. Essentially, the cardiorespiratory system is thought to collapse (26, 28, 32, 35, 49, 70, 72, 75).

The unfolding pattern of sleep itself, including how and when human infants arouse or awaken from sleep, is believed to be controlled by the primitive brain stem, located at the central base of the brain. This area is composed of clusters of differentiated cells that receive and send messages to and from the heart, hormonal centers, lungs, muscles surrounding the ribs, diaphragm, and airway passages, as well as structures that specifically help to balance the proper amounts of oxygen and carbon dioxide in the blood. Also controlled by the brain stem is the amount of time spent in various stages of sleep during any given sleep period—e.g. during light sleep (stages 1 or 2), deep sleep (stages 3 or 4), or rapid eye movement (REM), i.e. active sleep (26, 28). In addition, sleep architecture, including the form and timing of arousals, is also influenced by external stimuli such as feeding method and the presence of a cosleeping partner and must, therefore, be considered alongside internally based sleeping mechanisms (57).

Most recently, Kinney et al (35) studied an area of the brain, the arcuate nucleus, located on the ventral surface of the brain stem, an important area that monitors the proper balance of CO_2 and O_2. Recall that when CO_2 builds up in the blood, the respiratory neurons are activated to expel it, thereby causing fresh O_2 to be inhaled, reducing the acidity of the blood. A significant number of SIDS victims compared with control infants had fewer acethecoline-binding sites in this area of the brain. This suggests that in a variety of different circumstances, prone sleeping included, infants may not have the optimal or even minimal ability to arouse to reinitiate breathing following some type of apnea or exposure to their own exhaled CO_2 if it is trapped, for example, in a mattress as the baby lies face down, or if the infant is under thick blankets. Or it might mean that infants simply cannot arouse to breathe after particularly long breathing pauses or apneas. It is a promising clue.

Some SIDS victims may differ from surviving healthy babies not so much in kind as in degree (71). These SIDS infants appear to suffer from subtle deficits that develop during intrauterine life and are not apparent in the neonate (85, 86). Researchers believe that the actual expression of the fatal deficit is likely to be influenced by, if not dependent on, a number of cofactors that converge at a vulnerable moment in the infant's life (9, 70). Nobody can yet delimit all the appropriate SIDS cofactors or explain why cofactors seem to have differential effects on infants. However, it is extremely likely that certain factors are more relevant to some SIDS victims than to others. For example, for some infants a contributing SIDS risk factor might be the lack of breast-feeding (27), while for others it might be sleeping face down (prone) in the presence of an upper-respiratory infection that diminishes the potency (muscle tone) of airway passages (11). In certain predisposed infants, efficient respira-tory control might also be jeopardized by infantile hyperthermia, induced by atmospheric temperature, humidity, or too much bundling up (overheating) in cold weather (6, 7). One group of researchers suggests that between 28 and 52% of SIDS victims found "faces straight down" may have actually suffo-cated, especially those who were sleeping on beanbag cushions. Unable to dislodge themselves from the pockets formed by such cushions, the infants may have been forced to rebreathe lethal doses of their own expelled CO_2 (34).

Epidemiological Overview

Although this may be changing with recommendations to position infants in a supine position—on the back—for sleep, SIDS occurs most frequently in winter, and usually in the early morning or evening hours, when the infant is out of sight of the caregiver and presumably asleep. However, SIDS also occurs while babies are riding around in strollers, sitting in car seats, dozing in baby carriers, and even sleeping on their mother's chests following a breast-feeding episode (24, 50).

The SIDS population remains exceedingly heterogeneous. No single consistent criterion or pathological marker can be used to either predict potential SIDS victims or identify them upon postmortem autopsy. Nor is there an animal model of SIDS; it is not known to occur in any species other than human beings (70).

In the United States, SIDS rates are highest among both Native Americans and poor African Americans whose mothers are less than 20 years of age, smoke during their pregnancies, are unmarried, and lack access to prenatal care (27). SIDS rates are lowest in most Asian cultures, as well as Swedish, Finnish, Norwegian, English, and Israeli populations, where mothers tend to be a bit older, do not smoke during pregnancy, and place their infants in the supine or side position for sleep, and where parents, Asians especially, sleep either near or in contact with their infants during the first year of life and/or breastfeed intensively for the first six months of life (21, 87). SIDS is virtually unknown in China, although there could be serious reporting problems there, but it is as high as 9–15 per 1000 live births among impoverished Canadian Indians.

About 18% of all SIDS deaths involve premature infants. Low birthweight is a risk factor, as is the experience of one or more of an apparent life-threatening event (ALTE), which is characterized by a loss of muscle tone accompanied by gasping or choking, listlessness, color changes, or a cessation of breathing. Approximately 6% of infants who experience an ALTE die from SIDS (6).

Various studies report that before their deaths, some SIDS infants slept for longer periods, awoke less often, and had more difficulty awakening or arousing than healthy infants with whom they were compared (15, 26). At birth, some SIDS infants received lower Apgar scores and gained weight more slowly. Some exhibited less frequent but more sustained heart-rate variability and fewer but longer breathing pauses (apneas) (6).

In a major study funded by the National Institutes of Child and Maternal Health, 756 SIDS victims were compared with 1600 control infants. The research team found that many SIDS victims had had colds and bouts of diarrhea or vomiting within two weeks of death. A significant number had also exhibited droopiness, irritability, or some form of breathing distress involving a rapid heartbeat 24 h before they died. However, researchers believe that all these symptoms were acting in a secondary fashion rather than as primary causes of SIDS (27). As few as 10% of all SIDS victims have had any symptoms associated with a potential SIDS event before their deaths. This figure includes full-term infants with clinical histories of apneas as well as preterm underweight babies who experienced "apneas of prematurity" (6).

Only a relatively low number of symptomatic infants actually die of SIDS. As a result, the medical community is engaged in a volatile debate about whether infants with a history of repeated apneas should be sent home from the hospital with breathing monitors. At any given time, between 40,000 and 45,000 monitors are in use in the United States; yet no data indicate that monitors prevent SIDS deaths, and no data suggest how or under what circumstances infants die from SIDS when monitors are in use. At present, the effectiveness of home monitors in preventing SIDS deaths is highly questionable (6).

The Importance of Child-Care Practices: The Surprise of the Decade

In the past decade child-care practices have proven to be the single most important set of factors for reducing the chances of an infant dying of SIDS (25). The discovery that just by placing infants in the supine (back) rather than in the prone (belly) sleep position could cause a decline in SIDS rates by as much as 90% in some countries (Table 1) continues to astonish many SIDS researchers around the world. Many renowned investigators, including Johnson (29), now accept an idea suggested by some researchers nine years ago that the overall environment in which SIDS deficits find expression may be as important (to understanding SIDS) as the primary deficits themselves. Had researchers been asked just five years ago to prioritize SIDS research areas according to their likelihood in yielding clues about reducing SIDS risks quickly and significantly, child-care practices over which both parents and professionals assert control would not have been ranked very high. However, epidemiological findings across cultures now show consistently that, in the absence of maternal smoking, and where child-care patterns integrate the supine infant sleep position, breastfeeding, increased infant holding, maternal responsiveness, and cosleeping, SIDS rates are low compared with the rates in societies where mothers smoke, fail to breastfeed, infants sleep prone, and

Table 1 Reduction in SIDS rates per 1000 live births following public campaigns recommending the supine rather than prone infant sleep position.[a] *Before* campaign: prone position; *after* campaign: supine position

Country	Year: SIDS rate	Year: SIDS rate	Decline
Ireland	1986: 2.5	1993: 0.6	76%
Denmark	1991: 1.8	1993: 0.5	72%
Sweden	1991: 1.1	1993: 0.75	31%
New Zealand	1989: 4.0	1992: 2.2	45%
West Germany	1988: 1.8	1992: 1.2	33%
Great Britain	1989: 3.5	1992: 0.03	91%
Austria (Graz)	1990: 1.9	1994: 0.8	57%
Holland	1985: 1.07	1991: 0.44	58%

[a]Statistics reported at the Third International SIDS Conference, Stavanger, Norway, 1994.

early parent-infant separation, including solitary infant sleep, is encouraged (8, 13, 17, 21, 40, 80, 81).

From an anthropological perspective, it is not surprising that child-care practices in relationship to SIDS prevention should prove so important. Several different lines of evidence indicate that the social care of infants is practically synonymous with physiological regulation, since the infant's brain is only 25% of its adult brain weight, making the human infant the least neurologically mature primate of all primates and subject to the most extensive external regulation and support for the longest period. Hence for infants to survive, and for human (parental) reproductive success to be maximized, natural selection likely favored the coevolution of highly motivated caregivers on one hand and highly responsive infants on the other—infants designed to respond to and depend on external parental sensory signals and/or regulatory stimuli available in a microenvironment within which mothers and infants are almost always in contact. From both an evolutionary and developmental perspective, then, parental contact and proximity with infants (while awake and asleep) can be seen to represent a developmental bridge for the infant, extending into postnatal environments the role that the mother played prenatally in regulating important aspects of her infant's continuing development (53).

Recent laboratory studies corroborate the importance of maternal contact (42, 60, 65–68). Many studies show beneficial physiological effects of mothers holding their preterm and newborn infants using, for example, the kangaroo method of baby care, or skin-to-skin contact, which has the effects of increasing the infant's skin temperature, stabilizing heart rates, and reducing apneas and crying, all of which are consistent with an evolutionary perspective on how human infants develop optimally (5, 46–48). Years ago, Korner & Thoman (39) and Korner et al (38) demonstrated that vestibular (rocking) stimulation of neonates and infants could reduce infant crying and the number of apneas experienced during sleep. Laboratory studies also confirm that for slow-developing monkey and ape infants, even short-term separation from their mothers induces deleterious physiological consequences such as loss of skin temperature, cardiac arrhythmias, depressed immune responses, and increased stress involving adrenocorticotrophic hormone release and, in some cases, a reduction in the number of antibodies in the infants' blood (64, 66).

SIDS Rates in Cross-Cultural Perspective

If we assume, for the moment, that the most predominant known SIDS risk factors (maternal smoking, prone sleeping, not breastfeeding) can be held constant, and that no genetic factors predispose some populations more than others to SIDS, we should find lower SIDS rates in societies—or in segments within a society—in which maximum body contact between the mother and infant occurs. An evolutionary perspective on infants would suggest that intense and prolonged mother-infant contact evolved specifically to buffer infants from various kinds of environmental assaults, infantile vulnerabilities, or physiological deficiencies, including SIDS (43, 50, 78, 79).

Cross-cultural data from urban industrial Asian countries generally support aspects of this prediction, but such comparisons are, admittedly, difficult to make. In Japan, for example, where infant-mother cosleeping on futons remains the norm (74, 80), current published rates for SIDS are among of the lowest in the world: 0.15/1000 births in Tokyo in 1978; 0.053/1000 in Fukuoka in 1986; and 0.22/1000 births in Saga (81). The most recent estimate for the national SIDS rate in Japan is 0.3/1000 live births. These data do not, of course, prove that cosleeping is protective against SIDS. It may well be that SIDS is underreported in Japan, or that it is misdiagnosed as infantile suffocation. Japanese medical scientists have not participated in international SIDS research studies to the extent of American and European scientists, so the postmortem procedures they employ to identify SIDS may not be appropriate. Nevertheless, these low SIDS rates deserve explanation and further research.

In 1985, Davies (13) reported on the rarity of SIDS in Hong Kong. He used postmortem diagnostic protocols that, on review for a follow-up study by Lee et al (40), were judged comparative to Western diagnostic standards by John Emery (16), a renowned SIDS researcher from Great Britain. Davies found that even in a context of poverty and overcrowded conditions, where the incidence of SIDS should be high, the rates were 0.036/1000 live births, or approximately 50 to 70 times less common than in Western societies. This finding is even more surprising because breastfeeding is not common (of 175 infants at two, four, and six months of age, the percentage of infants nursing was 9, 4, and 2, respectively), although cosleeping and the supine sleep position for infants represent the cultural norm (13).

Davies proposed that proximity to the parent while the infant is asleep may be one reason why the rates are so low, as well as the typical (supine) sleeping position of Chinese infants. The author asked whether the possible influences of lifestyle and caretaking practices in cot death are being underestimated in preference for more exotic and esoteric explanations (13)—a viewpoint not unlike that of Emery (16), who also implicated, for some English infants, the importance of caregiving environments and other behavioral and socioeconomic factors. A follow-up on Davies' work by Lee et al (40) confirmed the relative rarity of cot deaths in Hong Kong, finding a slightly higher rate of deaths per 1000 live births (0.3, compared with 0.04/1000 reported by Davies).

A third study confirmed the rarity of SIDS in infants of Asian origin living in England and Wales, particularly infants of mothers born in India and Bangladesh but also infants of mothers with African origins. As the authors pointed out, Asian women have few illegitimate births and few births at younger ages, and few of them smoke (8), all of which seems to reduce the risks of infants dying of SIDS. No mention was made of any possible differences in sleeping patterns that could explain the lower SIDS rate among the Asian subgroup, although it is likely that these infants were sleeping near their parents.

These low SIDS rates continue in Asian ethnic groups even after they immigrate to Western (noncosleeping) cultures, where most continue their traditional care-giving practices, which include cosleeping (21). One study reports that among five Asian-American subgroups living in California, the incidence of SIDS ranged from a low of 0.9/1000 live births to a high of 1.5/1000. The variability was related directly to the duration of residence in the United States: The longer the group lived in the United States, the higher the SIDS rates (23), which leads us to ask whether the trend toward higher SIDS rates reflects the adoption of more "American" patterns of infant sleep management, i.e. solitary infant sleep, among other things.

Within Western societies it can be particularly difficult to show a correlation between cosleeping and reduced SIDS because usually the groups of people that practice bedsharing (or at least admit to practicing bedsharing) exhibit multiple risk factors for SIDS, much more so than do lower-risk groups. Consider, for example, the results of one of the very few studies of sleeping arrangements in the United States. In their study of parent-infant cosleeping among urban Americans in New York City, Lozoff et al (45) found that 35% of poor urban whites and 79% of poor urban blacks routinely slept with their children, who ranged in age from six months to four years (beyond the peak age for SIDS). If these data are representative of younger infants, why are the SIDS rates for black Americans in New York City higher rather than lower, since they bedshare? One reason could be that lower-risk groups underreport bedsharing because it violates the cultural norms. However, another more important factor has to do with the overall characteristics of the social and physical environment within which bedsharing is occurring. For African Americans the potential benefits of cosleeping may be overridden by the fact that black mothers ordinarily have their infants at a younger age (<20 years), smoke during their pregnancies, live in impoverished conditions, are less likely to be married, lack access to education on both parenting and prenatal care, and do not breastfeed (84). All these factors are known to increase the chances of an infant dying from SIDS (27, 59).

Physiological and Behavioral Studies of Infant-Parent Cosleeping: The Physiological Effects on Mother and Infant

My colleagues and I have attempted to understand infant-parent cosleeping by studying this behavior in a sleep laboratory, where differences between the solitary and bedsharing environments can be quantified and where both the behavioral and physiological findings can be interpreted in the context of known SIDS risk factors. We have hypothesized that under safe sleeping conditions, including those where mothers do not smoke, and for the vast majority of infants, infant-parent cosleeping should be inherently beneficial. More specifically, we suggest that the sensory-rich cosleeping microenvironment may change the sleep physiology and architecture of the human infant in ways helpful in resisting some types of SIDS (50, 53, 57, 58, 61, 62).

Two preliminary studies (56, 58, 61) and one more extensive NICHD-funded study have been completed to date. The most recent study included 35 healthy Latino mother-infant pairs (20 routine bedsharers and 15 routine solitary sleepers). All mothers and infants chosen for the study breastfed nearly exclusively, as determined by an analysis of logs kept by mothers at home and used to categorize them according to whether they routinely slept with their infants or routinely slept apart. Strict criteria were used to distinguish these two groups (57, 62). At the time of the study, the infants were approximately three months old (the peak age for SIDS vulnerability) and healthy. Once in the laboratory, and after retiring for bed, polysomnographic machines monitored all the relevant physiological variables of mother-infant pairs simultaneously, including EEG, eye movements, and breathing and heart rates. Among the infants, body temperatures, O_2 saturation levels, and nasal air flow rates were also monitored. The first night (the adaptation night) mothers and infants slept in their routine home condition (either in the same bed or in adjacent rooms). On the second and third nights (the order being randomly chosen) mother-infant pairs alternated between repeating their home (routine) condition and completing an experimental night wherein routine cosleepers slept in adjacent rooms, while routine solitary sleepers slept in the same beds. In addition to polysomnography, all behavioral interactions, including breastfeeding, were recorded throughout the nights for later analysis using infrared-sensitive audio/video camcorders.

Among other things discussed elsewhere, the data revealed that (a) bedsharing mothers and infants exhibit high levels of arousal overlap, both longer epochal and smaller physiologically defined transient arousals; (b) infants exhibit more frequent stage shifts, i.e. they move from one stage of sleep to another, or awaken more frequently, while bedsharing and spend more time, at the same time, in the same sleep stage (stages 1–2, 3–4, or REM) or awake condition as their mother, compared with when they sleep apart from their mothers; and (c) compared with when they sleep alone, bedsharing infants spend less time in deep stages of sleep (stage 3 or 4) (50, 56–58, 61, 62).

Behavioral analysis of the videotapes revealed that during the bedsharing night, infants faced toward their mothers for the vast majority of the night (between 72 and 100% of the time), and they almost doubled their number of breastfeeding episodes compared with what occurred on the solitary night. Also of importance is that on the bedsharing night the average breastfeeding interval was reduced by approximately one half, and the average total nightly duration of breastfeeding practically tripled compared with the solitary nights.

One additional observation is that when infants shared their mother's bed, almost always their mothers placed them in the safer supine position rather than in the prone or more risky infant sleep position. Watching our videos made it clear that if infants are breastfeeding they cannot get to or away from their mothers breasts and nipples or, indeed, suck milk if lying prone. Supine sleeping infants arouse more frequently, too, and in general they have far more control over their environment (throwing blankets off or awakening their mothers by arm movements to breastfeed) than prone sleeping infants. This is important because supine sleeping infants are at a significantly reduced risk of dying from SIDS (25), compared with prone sleeping infants. Prone sleeping is associated with infants being placed in a crib to sleep alone and not with bedsharing, according to our data.

Relevance of the Data to SIDS Prevention

At present, our laboratory is the only one in the world to have quantified both physiological and behavioral differences between bedsharing and solitary-sleeping mother-infant pairs. While this laboratory work does not prove that bedsharing protects infants from SIDS, several of our findings suggest that bedsharing, under safe environmental circumstances, could potentially reduce SIDS rates. For example, the finding that bedsharing mothers and infants exhibit synchronous, partner-induced physiological arousals, although not very surprising, is potentially important because of the suspected relationship between infantile arousal deficiencies and some cases of SIDS. As described earlier, Kinney et al (35) found that some SIDS victims had fewer neurotransmitter receptor sites in the brain stem, which suggests that arousals may be impaired in this group of SIDS infants. With increases in the type and number of arousals, bedsharing could potentially compensate for such a deficiency (62), possibly by providing the infant with more opportunities to practice arousing, thereby enabling it to become more proficient at it, or through its being closer to the mother, permitting her to intervene should she see or hear a distress signal from her infant.

Our finding that bedsharing infants spend less time in deep sleep—stages 3 and 4—and more time in light sleep—stages 1 and 2—is also potentially important. It is more difficult for infants to arouse to terminate apneas to reinitiate breathing from deep stages of sleep than it is for them to arouse from lighter stages. Arousals are protective responses required of the infant to terminate life-threatening, prolonged apneas. Solitary infant sleeping environments may accelerate, then, the maturation of deep sleep in infants prematurely before the infant's arousal mechanisms are able to effectively handle it. This problem could be exacerbated in infants born with arousal deficiencies.

Finally, that infants exhibit significantly more breastfeeding activities while bedsharing is potentially very important with respect to protection from SIDS. Two recent epidemiological studies suggested that breastfeeding lowers the risk of SIDS (27, 59), while two others suggested that the extent of protection may be dose specific, i.e. the more breastfeeding the greater the protection (20, 30). While a protective effect has not been found in every study (22), many international SIDS prevention campaigns, including those in the United States, encourage or recommend breastfeeding as a way to help reduce SIDS.

Note that in New Zealand, and among the Maori, a positive association has been found between bedsharing, maternal smoking, and increased risks of SIDS (73). This association is important and justifies a recommendation against Maori bedsharing in cases where mothers smoke. However, the special characteristics of the populations on which these findings are based do not justify the investigators' sweeping conclusion, namely, that under all circumstances and in all families and cultures, bedsharing in whatever form causes or necessarily increases the risk of SIDS and should therefore always be advised against. It is imperative that we reconceptualize, from a biological and not strictly a cultural point of view, the appropriateness of parents and infants sleeping alongside one another. The existence of dangerous cosleeping conditions is no more an argument against the potential benefits to infants and parents of sleeping together than the existence of dangerous solitary infant sleep environments constitutes a valid argument against the safety of all solitary infant sleep. No environment is risk free (53).

While recent cultural changes in Western societies stressing individualism over interdependence may help to support Mitchell & Scragg's recent suggestion that "cosleeping has outlived its historical usefulness" (59), the kinds of data being collected in our laboratory force us to ask whether cosleeping outlived its biological usefulness to the infant. We must conclude that it has not. In fact, there is far more evidence suggesting negative socioemotional and physiological consequences to infants sleeping socially distant from their parents than evidence suggesting inherent negative effects of increased contact or proximity (50). Moreover, not one scientific study documents the presumed socioemotional, psychological, or physiological benefits of solitary infant sleep, except where "benefits" are defined according to parental interests, other cultural values, or expectations, or where forms of social sleeping occur under unsafe conditions (53, 83).

If a valid understanding of the potential benefits or risks of cosleeping/bedsharing is ever to be achieved, anthropologists, forensic pathologists, and epidemiologists must work together. New ethnographically sensitive and appropriate epidemiological variables and categories must be defined that more precisely capture, describe, and classify the diverse social and physical environmental factors that characterize and differentiate cosleeping environments, as well as the social and physical characteristics of the participants.

Conclusion

The species-wide, "normal" context of maternal-infant sleep is social. In fact, so entwined is the biology of mother-infant cosleeping with nocturnal breastfeeding that any study that purports to understand biologically normal infant sleep without understanding how these two activities interrelate socially and biologically must be considered incomplete, inaccurate, or both (37, 54). That infant-parent cosleeping represents the evolutionarily stable and most adaptive context for the development of healthy infants is not to say that modern sleeping structures or conditions are always safe. However, it is important to differentiate between the act of mothers and infants sleeping in proximity and contact, which is adaptive, from the conditions within which they do so, which may not be. Much research is still needed to test the hypothesis that increased parental contact during the night reduces the chances of an infant dying of SIDS. Nevertheless, we must now recognize the legitimacy of diverse sleeping arrangements for infants, including diverse forms of cosleeping, in order to reach a complete understanding of SIDS and normal infant sleep.

Literature Cited

1. Abbott S. 1992. How can you expect to hold on to them in life if you push them away? *Ethos* 20(1):33–65
2. Adair R, Zuckerman B, Bauchner H, Philipp B, Levenson S. 1992. Reducing night waking in infancy: a primary care intervention. *Pediatrics* 89:585–88
3. Anders TF. 1979. Night-waking in infants during the first year of life. *Pediatrics* 63: 860
4. Anders TF. 1989. Clinical syndromes, relationship disturbances, and their assessments. In *Relationship Disturbances in Early Childhood: A Developmental Approach,* ed. A Sameroff, R Emde, pp. 145–65. New York: Basic Books
5. Anderson GC. 1991. Current knowledge about skin-to-skin (kangaroo) care for preterm infants. *J. Perinatol.* 11:216–26
6. Ariagno RL, Glotzbach SF. 1991. Sudden infant death syndrome. In *Pediatrics,* ed. AM Rudolph, pp. 850–58. Norwalk, CT: Appleton & Lange. 19th ed.
7. Azaz Y, Fleming PJ, Levine M, McCabe R, Stewart A, Johanson P. 1992. The relationship between environmental temperature, metabolic rate, sleep state and evaporative water loss in infants from birth to three months. *Pediatr. Res.* 32(4):417–23
8. Balarajan R, Raleigh VS, Botting B. 1989. Sudden infant death syndrome and postneonatal mortality in immigrants in England and Wales. *Br. Med. J.* 298: 716–20
9. Barnett H. 1980. *Sudden Infant Death Syndrome.* Child Health Hum. Dev., US Dept. Health Hum. Serv. Bull.
10. Barry H III, Paxson LM. 1971. Infancy and early childhood: cross-cultural codes. *Ethology* 10:466–508
11. Blackwell CC, Saadi AT, Raza MW, Weir DM, Busuttil A. 1993. The potential of bacterial toxins in sudden infant death syndrome (SIDS). *Int. J. Legal Med.* 105: 333–38
12. Cuthbertson J, Schevill S. 1985. *Helping Your Child Sleep Through the Night.* New York: Doubleday
13. Davies DP. 1985. Cot death in Hong Kong: a rare problem? *Lancet* 2:1346–48
14. Douglas J. 1989. *Behaviour Problems in Young Children.* London: Tavistock/Routledge
15. Einspieler C, Widder J, Holzer A, Kenner T. 1988. The predictive value of behavioral risk factors for sudden infant death. *Early Hum. Dev. 18:101–9*
16. Emery JL. 1983. A way of looking at the causes of crib death. In *Sudden Infant Death Syndrome,* ed. JT Tildon, LM Roeder, A Steinschneider, pp. 123–32. New York: Academic
17. Farooqi S, Perry IJ, Beevers DG. 1991. Ethnic differences in sleeping position and in risk of cot death. *Lancet* 338:1455
18. Ferber R. 1985. *Solve Your Child's Sleep Problem.* New York: Simon & Schuster
19. Foley R. 1992. *Another Unique Species: Patterns in Human Evolutionary Ecology.* Harlow: Essex
20. Fredrickson DD, Sorenson JF, Biddle AK. 1993. Relationship of sudden infant death syndrome to breast-feeding duration and intensity. *Am. J. Dis. Child.* 147:460
21. Gantley M, Davies DP, Murcott A. 1993. Sudden infant death syndrome: links with infant care practices. *Br. Med. J.* 306: 16–20
22. Gilbert RE, Wigfield RE, Fleming PJ. 1995. Bottle feeding and the sudden infant death syndrome. *Br. Med. J.* 310:88–90
23. Grether JK, Schulman J, Croen LA. 1990. Sudden infant death syndrome among Asians in California. *J. Pediatr.* 116(4): 525–28
24. Guntheroth WG. 1989. *Crib Death: The Sudden Infant Death Syndrome.* New York: Futura
25. Guntheroth WG, Spiers PS. 1992. Sleeping prone and the risk of sudden infant death syndrome. *JAMA* 267:2359–63
26. Harper RM, Leake B, Hoffman H, Walter DO, Hoppenbrouwers T, et al. 1981. Periodicity of sleep states is altered in infants at risk for the sudden infant death syndrome. *Science* 213:1030–32
27. Hoffman H, Damus K, Hillman L, Krongrad E. 1988. Risk factors for SIDS: results of the national institute of child health and human development SIDS cooperative epidemiological study. *Ann. NY Acad. Sci.* 533:13–30
28. Hoppenbrouwers T, Hodgman J, Arakawa K, Sterman MB. 1989. Polysomnographic sleep and waking states are similar in subsequent siblings of SIDS and control infants during the first six months of life. *Sleep* 12:265–76
29. Johnson P. 1995. Why didn't my baby wake up? See Ref. 70, pp. 218–25
30. Jura J, Olejar V, Dluholucky S. 1994. Epidemiological risk factors of SIDS in Slovakia, 1993, 1994 (Abstr.). In *Program and Abstr. 3rd SIDS Int. Conf.,* Stavenger, Norway, July 31-August 4, p. 98. Oslo: Holstad Grafisk
31. Kagan J. 1984. *The Nature of the Child.* New York: Basic Books
32. Kahn A, Picard E, Blum D. 1986. Auditory arousal thresholds of normal and near-miss

SIDS infants. *Dev. Med. Child Neurol.* 28: 299–302
33. Kaplan SL, Poznanski E. 1974. Child psychiatric patients who share a bed with a parent. *J. Am. Acad. Child Adolesc.* 13: 344–56
34. Kemp JS, Thach BT. 1991. Sudden death in infants sleeping on polystyrene-filled cushions. *N. Engl. J. Med.* 324(26): 1858–64
35. Kinney HC, Filiano JJ, Sleeper LA, Mandell F, Valdes-Dapena M, White WF. 1995. Decreased muscarinic receptor binding in the arcuate nucleus in sudden infant death syndrome. *Science* 269:1446–50
36. Konner MJ. 1981. Evolution of human behavior development. In *Handbook of Cross-Cultural Human Development,* ed. RH Munroe, RL Munroe, JM Whiting, pp. 3–52. New York: Garland STPM Press
37. Konner MJ, Worthman C. 1980. Nursing frequency, gonadal function and birth spacing among Kung hunter-gatherers. *Science* 207:788–91
38. Korner AF, Guilleminault C, Van den Hoed J, Baldwin RB. 1978. Reduction of sleep apnea and bradycardia in pre-term infants on oscillating waterbeds: a controlled polygraphic study. *Pediatrics* 61:528–33
39. Korner AF, Thoman EB. 1972. The relative efficacy of contact and vestibular-proprioceptive stimulation on soothing neonates. *Child Dev.* 43:443–53
40. Lee NY, Chan YF, Davies DP, Lau E, Yip DCP. 1989. Sudden infant death syndrome in Hong Kong: confirmation of low incidence. *Br. Med. J.* 298:721
41. LeVine R, Dixon S, LeVine S. 1994. *Child Care and Culture: Lessons from Africa.* Cambridge: Cambridge Univ. Press
42. Lipsitt LP. 1981. The importance of collaboration and developmental follow-up in the study of perinatal risk. See Ref. 76, pp. 135–50
43. Lozoff B. 1982. Birth in non-industrial societies. In *Birth, Interaction and Attachment,* ed. M Klaus, MO Robertson, p. 6. Johnson & Johnson Pediatr. Roundtable
44. Lozoff B, Brittenham G. 1979. Infant care: cache or carry. *J. Pediatr.* 95(3):478–83
45. Lozoff B, Wolf AW, Davis NS. 1984. Co-sleeping in urban families with young children in the United States. *Pediatrics* 74(2): 171–82
46. Ludington-Hoe SM. 1990. Energy conservation during skin-to-skin contact between premature infants and their mothers. *Heart Lung* 19:445–51
47. Ludington-Hoe SM, Hadeed AJ, Anderson GC. 1991. Physiological responses to skin-to-skin contact in hospitalized premature infants. *J. Perinatol.* 11:19–24
48. Ludington-Hoe SM, Hosseini RB, Ha-

shemi MS, Argote LA, Medellin G, Rey H. 1992. Selected physiologic measures and behavior during paternal skin contact with Colombian preterm infants. *J. Dev. Physiol.* 18:223–32
49. McCulloch K, Brouillette RT, Guzetta AJ, Hunt CE. 1982. Arousal responses in near-miss sudden infant death syndrome and in normal infants. *J. Pediatr.* 101:911–17
50. McKenna JJ. 1986. An anthropological perspective on the sudden infant death syndrome (SIDS): the role of parental breathing cues and speech breathing adaptations. *Med. Anthropol.* (special issue) 10(1): 9–53
51. McKenna JJ. 1991. *Researching the Sudden Infant Death Syndrome (SIDS): The Role of Ideology in Biomedical Science.* Stony Brook, NY: Res. Found. SUNY, New Liberal Arts Monogr. Ser.
52. McKenna JJ. 1992. Co-sleeping. In *Encyclopedia of Sleep and Dreaming,* ed. M Carskaden, pp. 143–48. New York: Macmillan
53. McKenna JJ. 1995. The potential benefits of infant-parent cosleeping in relation to SIDS prevention: overview and critique of epidemiological bed sharing studies. In *Sudden Infant Death Syndrome: New Trends in the Nineties,* ed. TO Rognum, pp. 256–65. Oslo: Scand. Univ. Press
54. McKenna JJ, Bernshaw N. 1995. Breastfeeding and cosleeping as adaptive strategies: Are they protective against SIDS? In *Biocultural Aspects of Breast Feeding,* ed. P Stuart-Macadem, K Dettwyler. New York: de Gruyter
55. McKenna JJ, Mack J. 1992. *The paleoecology of hominid sleep.* Presented at Soc. Cross-Cult. Res., Santa Fe, NM, February
56. McKenna JJ, Mosko S, Dungy C, McAninch J. 1990. Sleep and arousal patterns of co-sleeping human mother-infant pairs: a preliminary physiological study with implications for the study of sudden infant death syndrome (SIDS). *Am. J. Phys. Anthropol.* 83:331–47
57. McKenna JJ, Mosko S, Richard C. 1996. Bedsharing promotes breastfeeding among Latino mother-infant pairs. *Pediatr. Pulmonol.* 20:339
58. McKenna JJ, Thoman E, Anders T, Sadeh A, Schechtman V, Glotzbach S. 1993. Infant-parent co-sleeping in evolutionary perspective: imperatives for understanding infant sleep development and SIDS. *Sleep* 16:263–82
59. Mitchell EA, Stewart AW, Scragg R, Ford RPK, Taylor BJ, et al. 1992. Ethnic differences in mortality from sudden infant death syndrome in New Zealand. *Br. Med. J.* 306: S13–16

60. Montagu A. 1978. *Touching.* New York: Harper & Row
61. Mosko S, McKenna JJ, Dickel M, Hunt L. 1993. Parent-infant co-sleeping: the appropriate context for the study of infant sleep and implications for SIDS research. *J. Behav. Med.* 16:589–610
62. Mosko S, Richard C, McKenna JJ, Drummond S. 1996. Infant sleep and arousals during bedsharing. *Pediatr. Pulmonol.* 20: 349
63. Pinilla T, Birch LL. 1993. Help me make it through the night: behavioral entrainment of breast-fed infants' sleep patterns. *Pediatrics* 91(2):436–44
64. Reite M, Capitanio J. 1985. On the nature of social separation and social attachment. See Ref. 65, pp. 223–58
65. Reite M, Field T, eds. 1985. *The Psychobiology of Attachment and Separation.* New York: Academic
66. Reite M, Harbeck R, Hoffman A. 1981. Altered cellular immune response following peer separation. *Life Sci.* 29:1133–36
67. Reite M, Seiler C, Short R. 1978. Loss of your mother is more than loss of a mother. *Am. J. Psychiatr.* 135:370–71
68. Reite M, Snyder D. 1982. Physiology of maternal separation in a bonnet macaque infant. *Am. J. Primatol.* 2:115–20
69. Robertiello RC. 1985. *Hold Them Very Close: Then Let Them Go.* New York: The Dial Press
70. Rognum TO, ed. 1995. *SIDS in the 90's.* Oslo: Scand. Univ. Press
71. Schwartz PJ, Sagatini A. 1988. Cardiac innervation, neonatal electrocardiology, and SIDS: a key for a novel preventive strategy. *Ann. NY Acad. Sci.* 533:210–20
72. Schwartz PJ, Southall DP, Valdes-Dapena M. 1988. *The Sudden Infant Death Syndrome: Cardiac and Respiratory Mechanisms and Interventions. Ann. NY Acad. Sci.* 533
73. Scragg R, Stewart AW, Mitchell EA, Ford RPK, Thompson JMD. 1995. Public health policy on bed sharing and smoking in the sudden infant death syndrome. *NZ Med. J.* 108:218–22
74. Shand N. 1985. Culture's influence in Japanese and American maternal role perception and confidence. *Psychiatry* 48:52–67
75. Shannon DC, Kelly DH, O'Connell K. 1977. Abnormal regulation of ventilation in infants at risk for sudden-infant death syndrome. *N. Engl. J. Med.* 297:747–50
76. Smeriglio FL, ed. 1981. *Newborns and Parents: Parent-Infant Contact and New-born Sensory Stimulation.* Hillsdale, NJ: Erlbaum
77. Spock B, Rothenberg M. 1985. *Dr. Spock's Baby and Child Care.* New York: Pocket Books
78. Stewart MW, Stewart LA. 1991. Modification of sleep respiratory patterns by auditory stimulation: indications of a technique for preventing sudden infant death syndrome? *Sleep* 14(3):241–48
79. Super C, Harkness S. 1982. The infant's niche in rural Kenya and metropolitan America. In *Cross-Cultural Research at Issue,* ed. LL Adler, pp. 47–55. New York: Academic
80. Takeda KA. 1987. A possible mechanism of sudden infant death syndrome (SIDS). *J. Kyoto Prefect. Univ. Med.* 96:965–68
81. Tasaki H, Yamashita M, Miyazaki S. 1988. The incidence of SIDS in Saga Prefecture (1981–1985). *J. Pediatr. Assoc. Jpn.* 92: 364–68
82. Thoman EB. 1990. Sleeping and waking states in infants: a functional perspective. *Neurosci. Biobehav. Rev.* 14:93–107
83. Trevathan W, McKenna JJ. 1994. Evolutionary environments of human birth and infancy: insights to apply to contemporary life. *Child. Environ.* 11(2):88–104
84. US Government Printing Office. 1984. *Statistical Abstracts of the United States.* Washington, DC: USGPO. 104th ed.
85. Valdes-Dapena MA. 1980. Sudden infant death syndrome: a review of the medical literature, 1974–1979. *Pediatrics* 66(4): 567–614
86. Valdes-Dapena MA. 1988. A pathologist's perspective on possible mechanisms in SIDS. *Ann. NY Acad. Sci.* 533:31–37
87. Watanabe N, Yotsukura M, Kadoi N, Yashiro K, Sakanoue M, Nishida H. 1994. Epidemiology of sudden infant death syndrome in Japan. *Acta Pediatr. Jpn.* 36: 329–32
88. Weissbluth M, Liu K. 1983. Sleep patterns, attention span and infant temperament. *Dev. Behav. Pediatr.* 4:34–36
89. Whiting BB, Edwards C. 1988. *Children of Different Worlds: The Formation of Social Behavior.* Cambridge: Harvard Univ. Press
90. Willinger M. 1989. SIDS—a challenge. *J. Natl. Inst. Health NIH. Res.* 1:73–80
91. Wolfson A, Lacks P, Futterman A. 1992. Effects of parent training on infant sleeping patterns, parents' stress and perceived parental competence. *J. Consult. Clin. Psychol.* 60:41–48

Annu. Rev. Anthropol. 1996. 25:217–36

SOME RECENT TRENDS IN GRAMMATICALIZATION

Paul J. Hopper

Department of English, Carnegie Mellon University, Pittsburgh, Pennsylvania 15213

KEY WORDS: grammar, grammatical change, language change, emergent grammar, semantic change

ABSTRACT

Grammaticalization—the transformation of lexical items and phrases into grammatical forms—has been the focus of considerable study. Two chief directions can be identified. The first involves etymology and the taxonomy of possible changes in language, in which semantic and cognitive accounts of words and categories of words are considered to explain the changes. The second involves the discourse contexts within which grammaticalization occurs. Some researchers have questioned the standard idea of a stable synchronic a priori grammar in which linguistic structure is distinct from discourse, and have sought to replace this with the idea of "emergent grammar" in which repetitions of various kinds in discourse lead to perpetual structuration.

Amy manages to get a salary increase every year. When we study texts in English or any other language, we are struct by the fact that many ordinary, everyday words like *manage* can appear in contexts where their use is distinctly grammatical and quite different from their use in a full sense, such as *Amy manages the sales office of a large corporation.* The process whereby lexical forms such as the verb *to manage* are press-ganged into service as grammatical forms (in this case, as an auxiliary verb) is typical of "grammaticalization."

The concept of grammaticalization is a very old one (for history, see 55, 73, 82). But in recent years some linguists have come to see in it possibilities for an explanatory framework for the study of language universals and typology, and some have even looked to it for an alternative account of linguistic structure to that offered by synchronic formal grammar. Grammaticalization is

217

currently the focus of much research that, inevitably, comprises not only empirical studies but also internal debate over the content and limits of the term itself.

The term grammaticalization appears to have been first used by the French linguist Meillet (94), who coined the word to refer to the "attribution of a grammatical character to a formerly autonomous word." In his article "L'évolution des formes grammaticales" (94), Meillet described two processes by which grammatical forms come into being. One is *analogy,* the emergence of new forms through formal resemblance to already established ones, as when for some speakers *brang* replaces *brought* as the past tense of *bring* by analogy to *sing/sang, ring/rang,* etc. But analogy did not offer an explanation of the origins of the initial paradigm, and for this, Meillet named a second way in which new grammatical forms come into being: grammaticalization—"the passage of an autonomous word to the role of grammatical element" (94:131), "the progressive attribution of a grammatical role to autonomous words or to ways of grouping words" (94:132). In every case where certainty is possible, Meillet asserted, this is the origin of grammatical forms. Moreover, grammaticalization, in introducing new constructions, fundamentally changes the grammatical system. "Whereas analogy may renew forms in detail, usually leaving the overall plan of the system untouched, the 'grammaticalization' of certain words creates new forms and introduces categories which had no linguistic expression. It changes the system as a whole."

Not long after Meillet's introduction of the term grammaticalization, linguistics came to be dominated by Saussurean structuralism, a theory (or set of theories) founded on the synchronic perspective (30a), which had little time for the more diachronic fields. The study of grammaticalization remained an important tool in subdisciplines where change was a central fact, such as Indo-European linguistics (8, 79, 80, 95, 120), and was noted by a few linguists who had remained aloof from the mainstream (e.g. 3).

Especially in Romance linguistics, a field which had traditionally been hospitable to the study of variation, change, and grammaticalization, the study of the origins of and changes in grammatical forms was intensely pursued. Over the centuries of change since they emerged out of Latin, the Romance vernacular dialects, especially French, had changed in ways that made them bewilderingly different both from Latin and from the normative descriptions of the standard languages. Thus Bauche, in his description of Parisian French (7), by inverting some of the familiar analytic conventions of written French, revealed how an entirely new grammar had emerged. For example, obligatory subject pronouns were grammaticalized as prefixes on the verb in utterances such as *Le tramway il veut s'arrêter ici,* "The tram will stop here" (7:154) and *Moi j'aime pas le riz,* "I don't like rice" (7:107). Similarly, a number of researchers (4–6, 33, 49, 52, 81, 98, 99) noted the emergence of an "object conjugation" in vernacular French (and other Romance languages) whereby not only object pronouns but other relationships also could be "indexed" in the verb in a way that strikingly recalled more exotic languages. For example, in *Elle n'y a encore pas voyagé, ta cousine, en Afrique,* "Your cousin has never traveled to Africa" (7:154), the subject *ta cousine* and the locative *en Afrique* are referenced in the verbal expression with *elle* and *y* respectively. In fact, in this type of French, the corresponding sentence without "pronouns," i.e. **ta cousine n'a encore pas voyagé en Afrique,* would be quite impossible (81). The appearance is of a language that has reached an extreme stage of analytic structure and is, so to speak, collapsing in on itself by creating new synthetic structures through the grammaticalization of analytic elements (4, 104). Such developments have clear implications for typologies based on the degree of synthesis and for the historical development of inflections.

Outside the arenas of Indo-European and Romance linguistics, a renewed interest in grammaticalization began to awaken in the 1970s. Several factors underlay this resurgence. One was a growing interest in pragmatics and discourse, which probed at the interface between structure and use and in so doing revealed phenomena at the fraying edge of change. Another was the interest in language universals and the exploration of "naturalness" in language conceived in functionalist terms. The groundwork for this kind of study had been laid by Greenberg (42) in the 1950s with his cross-linguistic investigation of word order types. Greenberg established a typology based on the relative order of subject, verb, and object in the sentence and showed that other configurations appeared to be implicationally related to these. For example, in languages that placed the verb last in the sentence, speakers could be counted on to put the possessive before the possessed noun (*the conductor's baton* as opposed to *the baton of the conductor*), to indicate relationships with suffixes rather than prefixes, and to place verbal auxiliaries after, rather than before, the main verb. In his study of gender systems and their sources (43, 44), showing that the class markers of Bantu and other languages had their origins in articles that had themselves derived from demonstratives, Greenberg also identified the relationship between grammaticalization and typology.

By the 1970s, a number of researchers were seeing the advantages of combining Greenberg's typology with some long-standing observations of the Prague school of linguistics. (For a useful account of the syntactic theories of this school and for relevant literature, see 21.) The Prague school of linguists had noted the widespread tendency for newer and more prominent information to occur later in an utterance than older, more presupposed information. This work had formed part of the basis for a semantically based linguistic theory by Chafe (20). Li & Thompson (90) showed how the notion "subject of the sentence" could be understood as the outcome of a process that began as "topic of the discourse," a role which, in Chinese and certain other languages, remained the primary one. Li & Thompson also (89) showed how in Chinese the reanalysis of a serial verb as a preposition was resulting in the appearance of SOV (verb-final) sentences. [The phenomenon had been noted in African languages by Lord (91, 92).] Consider the following example, from an older period of Chinese:

> *zu   ba   zhu-ben-zi   xi   kan.*
> drunk BA   dogwood-tree careful look.

1. "While drunk, I took the dogwood tree and carefully looked at it" (*ba* 'take').
2. "While drunk, I carefully looked at the dogwood tree" (*ba* = accusative case preposition).

Here, *ba* is ambiguous between the older interpretation (statement 1) as a verb *take* and the newer interpretation (statement 2) as an accusative case marker. Synchronically, it is not clear how we should interpret *ba,* as a verb or as a case-marking preposition. Around this time, too, Haiman published an influential paper with the challenging title "Conditionals are Topics" (46), which showed that the relationship of the protasis (the *if*-clause) of a conditional to its main clause was essentially that of topic to comment. The idea that grammar could be understood as a historical process embedded in use rather than as a purely abstract synchronic state was in the air in the 1970s and was discussed in a number of studies in three volumes edited by Li (87–89). These volumes were the published proceedings of a series of annual or biennial symposia organized on the West Coast largely by Li, a series that has continued to the present. For other such volumes, see References 70 and 118.

An important figure in the development and popularization of the idea that grammar was a product of change and that its forms could be attributed to discourse functions was Talmy Givón. In an earlier paper (40), Givón had drawn attention to the origins of morphology in older syntactic patterns, and had explained the verbal prefixes of the Bantu languages as fossilized relics of older pronouns. The canonical word order of the modern Bantu languages is Subject-Verb-Object. However, the verbal prefixes, as in Swahili *ni-li-ki-vunja* (I-Past-it-break), "I broke it," appeared in the order Subject-Tense-Object-Verb because, Givón claimed, in Proto-Bantu that had been the original word order in the free sentence. Givón's assertion that "today's morphology is yesterday's syntax" (for a critique of this notion, see 25) became something of a slogan for the new functionalist linguistics that was now emerging around him. In his course at the Linguistics Institute in 1976 and in his book (41), Givón illustrated the discourse motivation of such linguistic parameters as reference, tense-aspect, word order, and patterns of negation. He spoke of the "syntacticization" of grammaticalized constructions out of autonomous elements and identified (41:223–31) a series of functional poles that were conducive to either a loose, unstructured or a tighter, grammaticalized formation:

Looser, pragmatic mode	Tighter, syntactic mode
Pidgin/Creole	Standard language
Child language	Adult language
Unplanned/oral discourse	Planned/written discourse

"Grammar" comprised a unidirectional movement from left to right along a structural continuum defined functionally by these poles. For example, a topic-comment structure typical of the pragmatic side develops into a subject-predicate structure of the syntactic side. On the pragmatic side, relationships among words in the pragmatic mode are inferred rather than explicitly indicated; on the syntactic side they are regulated by morphology and complex constructions, and so on. Givón also popularized among linguists the notion of grammaticalization itself, and he placed it in the context of typology. He pointed out numerous cross-linguistic consistencies in the ways that lexical items are pressed into service as grammatical categories; for example (41:222), typically tense, aspect, and modality markers derive from a rather small group of verbs:

want → FUTURE
go → IRREALIS → FUTURE
come → PERFECTIVE → PAST
have → PERFECTIVE → PAST
be → PROGRESSIVE → HABITUAL → FUTURE
know → can → HABITUAL-POSSIBLE-PERMISSIBLE
do → PERFECTIVE → PAST

Givón also argued that the meaning changes involved in such cases were to be characterized as "bleaching." In recent years, this characterization has been much disputed (see below). It was in any case a very old idea, although it is not clear where Givón found it since Meillet, Gabelentz, and Kurylowicz do not appear in his bibliography. While it is indisputable that many of these ideas were around in the 1970s, they were scattered and often unpublished, and this book as well as Givón's course on diachronic syntax at the 1976 Linguistics Institute were notable events in the blend of typology, grammaticalization, and discourse linguistics that has characterized much of linguistics since the 1970s. In *On Understanding Grammar,* Givón assembled a new and coherent picture of language out of the general interest in pragmatics, variation, change, and discourse, and thus laid the foundation of an entire subdiscipline, one that presented itself in conscious opposition to the prevailing Chomskian formalism.

In Europe, a group of linguists at the University of Cologne, working originally under the auspices of Hansjakob Seiler's Unityp (Universals and Typology) project, were developing a distinctive approach to grammaticalization both as an empirical tool in linguistic description and as a perspective on typology. Lehmann's (82) is perhaps the first full-length study of grammaticalization as a subdiscipline of linguistics, and it includes an important survey of its earlier history. It is, however, not easily available, having been published only as a working paper of the University of Cologne Project on Language Universals. Heine & Reh's *Grammaticalization and Reanalysis in African Languages* (59) presented an important survey of grammaticalization and laid out some of the principles that govern it [For a somewhat differently formulated set of principles, see Lehmann (83)]. By illustrating the way the term grammaticalization is used, I amplify some of these principles with familiar examples.

Heine & Reh (59:67) noted that the more a form is grammaticalized: (a) ...the more it loses in semantic complexity, functional significance, and/or expressive value. Comment: This idea of impoverishment has come to be disputed in more recent work, but it is a common feature of earlier studies. Taking the example of *to manage* mentioned above, the claim is that when the full word becomes an auxiliary (in *to manage to do something*) it loses the semantic richness and expressivity gained from all the contexts in which it appears, and is reduced to a small number of elementary features such as "ability."

(b) ...the more it loses in pragmatic and gains in syntactic significance. For example, the phrase *the fact that* normally requires that the following clause (known as the complement) be considered true by the speaker. *Bill was astonished at the fact that his wallet was still lying on the sidewalk* presupposes it to be true that the wallet was still lying on the sidewalk. The truth of the clause that follows *the fact that* is guaranteed by the presence of the word *fact*. But in some varieties of spoken English, the phrase *the fact that* is becoming grammaticalized as a simple complementizer. As a result, speakers of this variety of English are no longer constrained to presupposing the factual status of the complement and can freely say things like *My opponent has charged me with the fact that I used illegal campaign funds* (an utterance actually heard on the radio) without intending a confession. For such speakers, *the fact that* has only syntactic, no pragmatic significance.

(c) ...the more reduced is the number of members belonging to the same morphosyntactic paradigm. Comment: The history of negation in French nicely exemplifies this. In the modern standard language, the verb is preceded by *ne* and followed by a "reinforcer" *pas* or, rarely, *point*. At an earlier stage of the language (39:755), *ne* could be optionally reinforced by any of a number of more or less picturesque possible members of the category of reinforcers, including:

pas 'step, pace'	*amende* 'almond'
point 'dot, point'	*areste* 'fish-bone'
mie 'crumb'	*beloce* 'sloe'
gote 'drop'	*eschalope* 'pea-pod' (etc)

These may be compared to such colloquial English expressions as *not a drop, not a smidgen,* (British) *not a sausage,* etc. By the sixteenth century, a rather smaller number were possible:

pas 'step, pace'	*point* 'dot, point'
mie 'crumb'	*goutte* 'drop'

Today, in modern French, the field of reinforcers has narrowed to only two, *pas* and *point*. Of these, *point* is a rare and emphatic alternative that cannot appear in all contexts. For example, *pas beaucoup* 'not much' cannot as an isolated phrase be replaced with **point beaucoup*. Effectively, *pas* is now an obligatory concomitant of *ne,* and indeed in the spoken vernacular has supplanted *ne* altogether, as in *moi j'aime pas le riz,* "I don't like rice" (7:107). Note that both the category itself (the reinforcer of negation) *and* a specific exponent of it (*pas*) have become obligatory. See (*e*) below.

(*d*) ...the more its syntactic variability decreases; that is, its position in the clause becomes fixed. Comment: A prerequisite of grammaticalization is the fixing of a habitual order, a preference for one out of several possibilities. The predecessor of French *[je] chanterai une chanson,* "I will sing a song" would have been a Latin phrase *habeo canticulum cantare,* "I have a song to sing, I have to sing a song," whose component words could occur freely in any order (*canticulum cantare habeo,* etc). Even in Old and Middle French, some flexibility was possible between *cantar ayo* and *ayo cantar,* "I have to sing, I will sing" (4, 34, 35). But at the stage preceding the grammaticalization of *cantar ayo* as *chanterai* the order of the infinitive *cantar* and the auxiliary *ayo* has become fixed, and no variation is possible.

(*e*) ...the more its use becomes obligatory in some contexts and ungrammatical in others. Again, French negation supplies a good example, with the once optional reinforcer of negation *pas*—and its competitors—becoming increasingly obligatory and eventually supplanting the *ne* altogether in the spoken vernacular.

(*f*) ...the more it coalesces semantically, morphosyntactically, and phonetically with other units. Comment: Grammaticalization involves a collapsing and compacting of forms previously more distributed and separate. For example, English *I am going to buy a pig* in some registers becomes *I'm gonna buy a pig* and even *I ma buy a pig*.

(*g*) ...the more it loses in phonetic substance. Phonetic erosion is generally characteristic of change. It has been pointed out that in the spoken English phrase *Yes'm*, the *-m* is all that remains of the Latin *mea domina* 'my mistress' (> *ma dame* > *madam* > *ma'am* > *mum* >...). Grammaticalization often results in extreme erosion, even to the point where morphemes sometimes remain only as phonetic traces devoid of all meaning (67, 69). A familiar example is the history of the English negator *not*, originating from a reinforced negative in Old English *ná wiht* 'not a thing, no thing'. Here, *ná* is the simple negator and *wiht* an emphatic element meaning 'thing, creature'; compare present-day English *no way*. The history of *ná wiht* proceeds as follows: *ná wiht* > *nówiht*, *nówuht* > *noght* > *n't* > *t* (in *can't*).

A second direction of the Cologne linguists has been a strong empirical-descriptive project, centered around the Africanist Bernd Heine (beginning with 58, 59). The goals of this project have been:

1. The descriptive goal of using grammaticalization theory as a framework for the grammatical description of individual languages. Kilian-Hatz's grammar of Baka (75) stands as an excellent example of this direction, as do several book-length detailed investigations, such as C König's study of verbal aspect in Maa (77) and Claudi's studies of the rise of gender systems in Zande (22) and of word order in Mande (23). The approach in this work has been a conscious combining of synchronic and diachronic analyses (called panchronic in 55) that provides an unusually enlightening and novel perspective on the languages.
2. The empirical goal of identifying the characteristic trajectories of change. From the earliest work of Heine's group (e.g. 59), there has been a strong emphasis on an encyclopedic approach; cataloging in detail the types of changes that have been encountered, with a focus on African languages; and in particular aiming to identify the segments of the lexicon that are most likely to become grammaticalized. A recent result of this research has been the provisional version of an extensive index of grammaticalization phenomena in African languages (57). In one conclusion, Heine et al (55) discussed two models for starting points of prepositions, the body-part model (compare English *back of, ahead of*) and the landscape model. In the landscape model, the source of the preposition is a landscape feature such as *summit, sky,* etc (compare English *down,* originally *hill*). They noted

(55:125; see also 53) that in African languages the body-part model predominates, although both are found, as in Ewe (55:129):

é-le   βu-á   dzí
3sg-be   car-DEF   on
'It is on top of the car'

é-le   βu-á   tá-me
3sg-be   car-DEF   on
'It is on top of the car'

Here, *dzí* = 'sky', *tá-me* = 'head-in', and the two sentences are "largely synonymous."

3. The theoretical goal of generalizing the results into statements about the universal basis of these trajectories in human cognition. The hundreds of types of grammaticalization uncovered by linguists working in this area point to a small number of general principles that in turn suggest ways in which the linguistic forms used to talk about the world of ideas and to express grammatical relationships typically emerge out of words standing for presumably more concrete and more precisely contoured entities. In Reference 55:158, *topics*—things that need to be expressed—are matched with *vehicles*—corresponding linguistic formulations of the same reality (Table 1).

In Table 1, changes in the meanings of words predictably go from the left-hand to the right-hand column, never the other way around, and there is a common human propensity to manage the more diffuse and less tangible parameters in the right-hand column through linguistic forms appropriate to the concepts in the left-hand column. Thus, causation may be formulated in

Table 1 Linguistic coding of concepts[a]

	Vehicle	Topic
Ideational	Clearly delineated, compact	fuzzy, diffuse
	physical (visible, tangible, etc)	nonphysical, mental
	thing-like objects	qualities
	sociophysical interactions	mental processes
	space	time, cause, manner
Textual	"real world"	"world of discourse"
	less discourse-based	more discourse-based, or "speaker-based"
	referential	nonreferential
	central participant	circumstantial participant
	new	old
Interpersonal	expressive	nonexpressive

[a]From Reference 55:158.

terms of making, doing, and allowing. Notions of understanding and comprehension are expressed through physical acts like *see* and *grasp,* and obeying through *hear.* Words for *heart* and *man* come to stand for qualities like *courage.* Mental activities like thinking are "converted" into physical activities (to think *hard,* etc). The sociophysical act of making something real to others or to oneself comes to stand for a mental process of bringing something to consciousness in the verb *realize* (attested in this sense only since the end of the nineteenth century). Time concepts are typically expressed in terms of more readily apprehensible space concepts (a *long* time, a *short* time, etc) and so on. Language also adapts in consistent ways to the self-referential task of talking about speech. Demonstratives (*this* and *that*) are readily used to refer to things that have been said: *I have been home all evening, and that's the truth.* Concepts of the physical world come to be used as discourse markers (*next* originally meaning 'nearest', *after* originally meaning 'behind'). Referential markers whose primary sense was to indicate a specific entity come to be used for general, nonreferential ideas; for example, the English indefinite article *a(n)* was once used only for already identified particulars, as in *a (certain) man,* but later comes to stand for nonspecific, unidentified entities, as in *we called a taxi* (see 71). Similarly, Old English *sum* 'one, a certain' was used to introduce central participants into the discourse, but its Modern English descendent *some* can only refer to a circumstantial participant (*some official gave me permission*). The change from new to old mentioned in Table 1 is nicely exemplified in languages where a cleft construction, as in *It is John who is flying the plane,* has become a normal one (i.e. now means simply "John is flying the plane"). For example, in Teso (Eastern Nilotic) (55, 218) *mam Petero e-koto ekingok,* "Peter does not want a dog," the negative *mam* derives from a cleft clause *e-mam* 'it is not', following which the name *Petero* would originally have been new to the discourse. The reanalysis of *e-mam* as a simple negator *mam* has meant that the following noun is interpreted as the subject of the verb and is "old" to the discourse. The last item in Table 1, the interpretation of expressive value through nonexpressive forms, is seen in the common change of intensifiers such as *awfully, frightfully,* and *terribly* in *terribly nice of you,* etc. (A similar source underlies English *very* from an Old French word meaning 'truly'.)

An important question for many researchers has been whether typical relationships like these are driven by broader, still more general parameters. Earlier studies had referred to a change from "concrete" to "abstract" meanings. The idea of bleaching or loss of substantial meaning that had been introduced in the nineteenth century, e.g. by Bopp (9) and von der Gabelentz (119a), was revived for a time [e.g. by Givón (41:316–17)] to explain such changes as demonstratives becoming definite articles, and verbs with such meanings as 'stand', 'lie', 'stay' becoming copulas (e.g. Spanish *estar* 'to be' < Latin *stare* 'to stand'). It was challenged as a number of researchers began to point to compensatory strengthening of pragmatic implicatures that accompanied the supposed "weakening" (78, 116).

In the 1980s and 1990s, the nature of the semantic changes that accompany grammaticalization has been the subject of lively debate. After earlier statements (112, 113), Traugott identified the principal semantic development as being from propositional to textual (114). During grammaticalization, forms went from having meanings that could be identified autonomously to ones that contributed to wider discourse contexts. For example, a demonstrative like *this, that* with a deictic meaning ascertainable from its isolated propositional context changed into a definite article (*the*), whose interpretation required access to a more complex discourse environment. The earlier meaning was "less situated," that is, it required less discourse context; the later one was "more situated," that is, it required more discourse context (117). Traugott amplified and extended this idea, and identified three "Semantic-Pragmatic Tendencies" governing change of meaning (115:34–35):

1. "Meanings based in the external described situation > meanings based in the internal (evaluative/perceptual/cognitive) situation." For example, the Old English preposition *æfter* referred originally to a spatial situation, that is, 'behind', but came to have a temporal meaning 'later than'. The temporal meaning is, of course, an internal, cognitive one, while the earlier spatial meaning is objective.
2. "Meanings based in the described external or internal situation > meanings based in the textual situation." Meanings thus tend to become textual, and grammaticalized forms come to function as indicators of textual cohesion. To continue the same example (see also 118:208–9), *after,* because it is a temporal marker (*after he robbed the bank, he fled to Mexico*), enables arguments to be moved around the text without loss of coherence (e.g. *He fled to Mexico after he robbed the bank,* with the events narrated in the "wrong" temporal order).
3. "Meanings tend to become increasingly situated in the speaker's subjective belief-state/attitude toward the situation." Thus English *since,* from its earlier sense of 'after', is identified with a causal relationship. The speaker, that is, attributes subjectively a causal connection between events that are, objectively seen, only asserted in temporal succession. Similarly, *while* adds to its meaning of 'during' a concessive meaning equivalent to *although: While he is intelligent, he is often forgetful.*

Even more abstract characterizations of some of these processes have been discussed. Earlier work characterized the relationship between a lexical form and its grammaticalized counterpart as one of metaphor (24, 109, 110). For example, *ahead of* in *The Democrats are ahead of the Republicans in the polls* was said to be a metaphorical extension of the body-part noun *head*. This mode of explanation seemed unsatisfactory to many linguists, since it seemed to valorize an etymological method that compared single lexical items removed from contexts. Clearly what had happened was not a sudden replacement of one meaning by another—a metaphorical leap—but a reanalysis together with the extension of a meaning already implicit in the form. If metaphor is defined narrowly as the replacement of a present meaning by an absent one, grammaticalization must be seen as involving not, or not only, the "vertical," paradigmatic trope of metaphor but the "horizontal," syntagmatic trope of metonymy, which works through "contiguity" to exploit a secondary meaning already present in a primary one.

The mechanism by which this occurs must involve a horizontal (linear, syntagmatic) contiguity in the discourse situation. Traugott & König (119) identified three types of contiguity: contiguity in sociophysical or sociocultural experience, contiguity in utterance (collocation), and contiguity in part-whole relationship (synecdoche). They then extended the notion of metonymy to include the pragmatic step of inferencing, that is, of contiguity based in the discourse world (119:211). The temporal conjunction *since,* for example, acquires a causal meaning through the "post hoc ergo propter hoc" reasoning of speakers. Thus, in *Since it's going to rain tomorrow, we have canceled the picnic, since* is interpreted as 'because'. But historically, *since* was not causal but temporal, e.g. in *Since the army base was closed down the economy of the area has been depressed.* The shift of meaning, Traugott & König argued, is the metonymic one of conversational inference, a case of contiguity in discourse. The meaning change of *since* thus occurred through "abduction" (1), with the hearer choosing the most likely of competing analyses in a given context.

The difference between the two approaches has been stated as follows (119:212): "Metaphorical change involves specifying one, usually more complex, thing in terms of another not present in the context. Metonymic change involves specifying one meaning in terms of another that is present, even if only covertly, in the context."

The recent trend has been to see metaphor and metonymy not as mutually exclusive modes of explanation for the same phenomenon but as having their own roles in an overall explanatory schema. Thus Hopper & Traugott (73:87–90) see metonymy operating at earlier stages and being supplanted by metaphor later. They used as an example the grammaticalization of English *be going to* as a future tense. In accounting for the way that this expression is transformed between *I am going [in order] to buy a pig* and *I am going to need a bicycle,* for example, with the possibility of a nonaction verb such as *to need* in place of the action verb *to buy,* an intermediate stage is posited in which *[be going]* *[to buy a pig]* is reanalyzed as *[be going to]* *[buy a pig].* In this intermediate stage, the purpose expression *[be going]* *[to buy a pig]* is reanalyzed as a future tense *[be going to]* *[buy a pig],* but there is still a constraint that the verb that follows *be going to* must denote an activity of some sort, not a psychological state such as *to need.* This horizontal reanalysis along the syntagmatic axis involves a metonymic change. The extension of *be going to* to include all verbs rather than just activity verbs is an analogical one, a change down the vertical, paradigmatic axis, and therefore is considered metaphorical.

More than mere terminology is at stake here. There is a serious question of the kinds of data and the modes of explanation for the entire phenomenon. Is grammaticalization to be an etymological field concerned with the history of words, sustained by "cognitive" accounts of natural pathways of change in word semantics, as suggested by the title of Sweetser's 1990 book *From Etymology to Pragmatics: Metaphorical and Cultural Aspects of Semantic Structure* (110)? Or are explanations to be sought in the nature of human interaction and discourse, as insisted by Givón in his 1979 book (41) and by his successors?

Current research has moved fruitfully in both directions. The etymological project of discovering and classifying the possible sources and trajectories of grammatical forms has been the concern of a number of researchers (2, 22, 29, 50, 51, 54, 56–58, 85). Particularly important has been the "Gramcats" (grammatical categories) project of Bybee (11–17), whose goal is to uncover universal pathways of change and sources of grammatical markers. This project began with a carefully designed method of arriving at a representative sample of languages. [Greenberg (42) had also recognized the need to identify a sample of languages that would not be "contaminated" by mutual genetic or areal relationships, but his approach had been less systematic and less rigorous.] The Gramcats project has focused especially on the verb and has thus intersected with a similar project in Sweden conducted by Dahl (14, 29), as well as with the work of Heine, Claudi, and others in Germany. Bybee's group not only identified starting and ending points, such as the development of future tenses out of verbs of desiring and wanting (which had been noted by several researchers, e.g. 34, 35, 41), but described in some detail the characteristic intervening stages. For example, verbs denoting desire and ability assume meanings of intention and possibility, which in turn develop as futures. The change also involves the loss of the restriction to human subjects (*I will* > *I will, it will*).

The project of identifying paths of change on the basis of large samples necessarily meant a loss of detail in individual languages. However, the 1980s and 1990s saw numerous studies of grammaticalization phenomena in individual languages and in general. Although they are not addressed here, a sampling is listed in the bibliography (10, 18, 19, 26-28, 30, 32, 34, 47, 62, 63, 74, 76, 81, 84, 100, 101, 105, 106, 108). The edited collections (97, 118) contain a number of such studies.

In his 1991 paper, Hopper (68) attempted to pull together some of what had been learned in the form of some "principles" of grammaticalization. The goals of this article were to supplement earlier statements by Lehmann (83) and Heine & Reh (59; see above) by focusing on grammaticalization in its earliest stages, when obvious developments, such as the fusion of forms into stem + affix groups, had not yet occurred. The paper aimed to provide an empirical guide for identifying possible grammaticalization trends in discourse patterns. Moreover, by suggesting that the types of changes in question were not specifically "grammatical" ones, it endeavored to show that the border between lexical and grammatical phenomena was a very fuzzy one. The principles stated in this article are as follows.

1. *Layering.* Within a broad functional domain, new layers are continually emerging. As this happens, the older layers are not necessarily discarded but may remain to coexist with and interact with the newer layers.

    Layering points to something that had been noted by several researchers: Grammaticalization does not proceed by eliminating old forms and substituting new ones but by "crowding" the field with subtly differentiated forms all having approximately the same meaning (such as, for example, the many ways of expressing the future tense in English; see also 15).

2. *Divergence.* When a lexical form undergoes change to a clitic or affix, the original lexical form may remain as an autonomous element and undergo the same changes as ordinary lexical items.

    Divergence means that the grammaticalization of a form does not entail the disappearance of its lexical uses; rather, the grammaticalized form and its lexical counterpart may coexist, as in English *I've eaten it* (with *'ve* from *have* as an auxiliary verb) and *I have two of them* (with *have* as a main verb.)

3. *Specialization.* Within a functional domain, at one stage a variety of forms with different semantic nuances may be possible. As grammaticalization occurs, this variety of formal choices narrows and the smaller number of forms selected assume more general grammatical meanings.

    Specialization is a central aspect of grammaticalization, since it typically results in one form being singled out for a grammatical function, as in the example of French *pas* discussed above.

4. *Persistence.* When a form undergoes grammaticalization from a lexical to a grammatical function, so long as it continues to have a grammatical role,

some traces of its original lexical meanings tend to adhere to it, and details of its lexical history may be reflected in constraints on its grammatical distribution.

Persistence is characteristic of earlier stages, in which the original contextual meanings of forms continue as they move from lexical to grammatical functions. For example, the auxiliary use of *manage* mentioned in the first paragraph requires a main verb denoting an intentional action. *I managed to buy a pig* is possible but not **I managed to need a bicycle.* This restriction on the auxiliary use of *to manage* is an immediate consequence of its history as a volitional verb.

5. *De-categorialization.* Grammaticalization always involves a loss of categoriality and proceeds in the following direction: Noun or Verb → another category, never the reverse.

Thus adverbs, auxiliaries, prepositions, and other "minor" categories would always derive from the prime categories Noun and Verb, never the reverse (see also 72, where this idea is discussed from a discourse perspective).

It had been noted (e.g. 115) that semantic and pragmatic changes in general apply equally to lexical and grammatical elements. Indeed, the theory of grammaticalization would appear to deny any diachronic relevance to the grammatical-lexical distinction. And if these levels cannot be distinguished diachronically, it is hard to see how they could be unambiguously assigned to different "modules" synchronically. For some researchers in the 1980s and 1990's, this blurring of the distinction between grammar and lexicon added to a feeling that the concepts grammar and structure as applied to human language needed rethinking.

A discourse dimension to grammaticalization had been evident from Givón's work in the 1970s (see especially 41). Hopper (64) argued that the semantic category of perfective aspect identifiable in a variety of languages derived from the discourse function of event foregrounding. Other examples of a close relationship between discourse functions and grammaticalization were also proposed, including the English present perfect (18, 105–107, 111), the Cree definite article (27, 28), the "medial verb" morphology in Papuan (47), the ergative case in Sacapultec (31), the English indefinite article (71), anaphora (36), the marking of noun and verb morphology (72), aspect in Maa (77), topic and antitopic in French (81), relative clauses in the creole Tok Pisin (102) and in Tamil (60), English parenthetical evidentials (111), and subordinate clauses in general (93). Also in the 1980s, Hopper (65, 66) suggested that the study of grammaticalization tended to undermine the assumption of a preexistent a priori grammatical component that stood as a prerequisite to discourse and a precondition for communication, and he proposed instead that grammar was an emergent property of texts. "Structure" would then be an epiphenomenal by-product of discourse. The "emergent grammar" idea found parallels in the work of several linguists, such as Du Bois (31), Thompson (e.g. 111), and Himmelmann (61).

Perhaps some of the most important current empirical work on grammaticalization is that of Thompson, Fox, and others (e.g. 37) who are reevaluating grammar by working out the recurrent structures as they "emerge" in live conversation. Most studies of grammaticalization in its discourse context have involved written texts, distributed over longer historical periods. The newer work is in the Conversational Analysis paradigm and has depended crucially on "intonation units" [for the use and history of this term, see Chafe (21, especially pp. 53–70)]. Intonation units are the short bursts of speech of which spoken discourse naturally consists. Each unit, Chafe hypothesized, comprises a single event or state. Their internal structure and dialogic interrelationships are held to constitute the prototypes for clauses and hence for "grammatical" structure in general. The study of natural conversation, for a long time the province of sociologists and psychologists, has once again captured the interest of linguists whose goal is to explain grammatical structure through "real" data.

Of the two dimensions of research, or at least of their two poles—the lexical/etymological one and the discourse/textual one—it may be said that they complement each other in that the first explains *what* is grammaticalized and the second *how* this occurs. However, to the extent that these are competing rather than complementary views of grammaticalization, it seems likely that the richer discourse/textual direction will dominate and that studies of word histories will decline as the more important problems resolve. The discourse/textual direction that grammaticalization seems destined to take (see 55:20–21 and 55:238–43 for some discussion, though not fully sharing this view) may eventually bring mainstream linguistics into a long overdue contact with those neighboring disciplines such as anthropology, rhetoric, and literature, for which a preoccupation with texts is indispensable.

Literature Cited

1. Andersen H. 1973. Abductive and deductive change. *Language* 49:765–93
2. Anderson L. 1986. Evidentials, paths of change, and mental maps: typologically regular asymmetries. In *Evidentiality: The Linguistic Coding of Epistemology,* ed. W Chafe, J Nichols, pp. 273–312. Norwood, NJ: Ablex

3. Anttila R. 1980. *Historical and Comparative Linguistics.* Amsterdam: Benjamins
4. Ashby WJ. 1977. *Clitic Inflection in French: A Historical Perspective.* Amsterdam: Ed. Rodopi NV
5. Ashby WJ. 1980. Prefixed conjugation in Parisian French. In *Studies in Italic and Romance Linguistics Honoring Ernst Pulgram,* ed. H Izzo, pp. 195–208. Amsterdam: Benjamins
6. Bally C. 1966 (1932). *Linguistique Générale et Linguistique Française.* Berne: Francke. 4th ed.
7. Bauche H. 1928. *Le Langage Populaire: Grammaire, Syntaxe et Dictionnaire du Français tel qu'on le Parle dans le Peuple de Paris, avec Tous les Termes d'Argot Usuel.* Paris: Payot
8. Benveniste E. 1968. Mutations of linguistic categories. In *Directions for Historical Linguistics,* ed. WP Lehmann, Y Malkiel, pp. 85–94. Austin: Univ. Tex. Press
9. Bopp F. 1816. *Über das Conjugationssystem der Sanskritsprache in Vergleichung mit Jenem der Griechischen, Lateinischen, Persischen, und Germanischen Sprachen.* Frankfurt am Main: Andreäische Buchhandlung
10. Brinton L. 1988. *The Development of English Aspectual Systems.* Cambridge: Cambridge Univ. Press
11. Bybee JL. 1985. *Morphology: A Study of the Relation Between Meaning and Form.* Amsterdam: Benjamins
12. Bybee JL. 1988. Semantic substance vs. contrast in the development of grammatical meaning. *Berkeley Linguist. Soc.* 14: 247–64
13. Bybee JL. 1994. The grammaticalization of zero: asymmetries in tense and aspect systems. See Ref. 97, pp. 235–54
14. Bybee JL, Dahl Ö. 1989. The creation of tense and aspect systems in the languages of the world. *Stud. Lang.* 13:51–103
15. Bybee JL, Pagliuca W. 1985. Cross-linguistic comparison and the development of grammatical meaning. In *Historical Semantics: Historical Word Formation,* ed. J Fisiak, pp. 59–83. Berlin: Mouton de Gruyter
16. Bybee JL, Pagliuca W, Perkins RD. 1991. Back to the future. See Ref. 118, 2:17–58
17. Bybee JL, Pagliuca W, Perkins RD. 1994. *The Evolution of Grammar: Tense, Aspect, and Modality in the Languages of the World.* Chicago: Univ. Chicago Press
18. Carey K. 1994. The grammaticalization of the perfect in Old English: an account based on pragmatics and metaphor. See Ref. 97, pp. 103–18
19. Campbell L. 1991. Some grammaticalization changes in Estonian and their implications. See Ref. 118, 1:285–99

20. Chafe W. 1972. *Meaning and the Structure of Language.* Chicago: Univ. Chicago Press
21. Chafe W. 1994. *Discourse, Consciousness, and Time: The Flow and Displacement of Conscious Experience in Speaking and Writing.* Chicago: Univ. Chicago Press
22. Claudi U. 1985. *Zur Entstehung von Genussystemen: Überlegungen zu Einigen Theoretischen Aspekten, Verbunden mit einer Fallstudie des Zande.* Hamburg: Buske
23. Claudi U. 1994. Word order change as category change: the Mande case. See Ref. 97, pp. 191–231
24. Claudi U, Heine B. 1986. On the metaphorical base of grammar. *Stud. Lang.* 10: 297–335
25. Comrie B. 1980. Morphology and word order reconstruction: problems and prospects. In *Historical Morphology,* ed. J Fisiak, pp. 83–96. The Hague: Mouton de Gruyter
26. Craig C. 1991. Ways to go in Rama: a case study in polygrammaticalization. See Ref. 118, 2:455–92
27. Cyr D. 1993. Cross linguistic quantification: definite articles vs. demonstratives. *Lang. Sci.* 15:1–29
28. Cyr D. 1994. Discourse morphology: a missing link to cyclical grammatical change. See Ref. 97, pp. 171–90
29. Dahl Ö. 1985. *Tense and Aspect Systems.* Oxford: Blackwell
30. DeLancey S. 1991. The origins of verb serialization in modern Tibetan. *Stud. Lang.* 15:1–23
30a. de Saussure F. 1972. (1916). *Cours de Linguistique Générale.* Paris: Payot. 5th ed.
31. Du Bois JW. 1987. The discourse basis of ergativity. *Language* 63:805–55
32. Ebert K. 1989. Aspektmarkierung im Fering (Nordfriesisch) und verwandten Sprachen. In *Tempus—Aspekt—Modus: Die Lexikalischen und Grammatischen Formen in den Germanischen Sprachen,* ed. W Abraham, T Jensen, pp. 293–322. Tübingen: Niemeyer
33. Feldman DM. 1964. Analytic vs. synthetic: a problem in the Portuguese verbal system. *Linguistics* 10:16–21
34. Fleischman S. 1982. *The Future in Thought and Language: Diachronic Evidence from Romance.* Cambridge: Cambridge Univ. Press
35. Fleischman S. 1983. From pragmatics to grammar: diachronic reflections on complex pasts and futures in Romance. *Lingua* 60:183–214
36. Fox BA. 1987. *Discourse Structure and Anaphora.* Cambridge: Cambridge Univ. Press
37. Fox BA, Thompson SA. 1990. Relative

clauses in conversational English. *Language* 66:51–64

38. Deleted in proof

39. Gamillscheg E. 1957. *Historische Französiche Syntax.* Tübingen: Niemeyer

40. Givón T. 1971. Historical syntax and synchronic morphology: an archaeologist's field trip. *CLS* 7:394–415

41. Givón T. 1979. *On Understanding Grammar.* New York: Academic

42. Greenberg JH. 1966. Some universals of language, with particular reference to the order of meaningful elements. In *Universals of Language,* ed. JH Greenberg, pp. 73–113. Cambridge, MA: MIT Press. 2nd ed.

43. Greenberg JH. 1978. How does a language acquire gender markers? See Ref. 45, 3:4 7–82

44. Greenberg JH. 1991. The last stages of grammatical elements: contractive and expansive desemanticization. See Ref. 118, 1:301–14

45. Greenberg JH, Ferguson CA, Moravcsik E, eds. 1978. *Universals of Human Language,* 4 Vols. Stanford, CA: Stanford Univ. Press

46. Haiman J. 1978. Conditionals are topics. *Language* 54(3):564–89

47. Haiman J. 1987. On some origins of medial verb morphology in Papuan languages. *Stud. Lang.* 11:347–64

48. Haiman J. 1994. Ritualization and the development of language. See Ref. 97, pp. 3–28

49. Harris M. 1978. *The Evolution of French Syntax: A Comparative Approach.* London: Longman

50. Haspelmath M. 1989. From purposive to infinitive: a universal path of grammaticalization. *Folia Linguist. Hist.* 10:287–310

51. Haspelmath M. 1990. The grammaticization of passive morphology. *Stud. Lang.* 14:24–72

52. Heger K. 1966. La conjugaison objective en français et en espagnol. *Languages* 3: 19–39

53. Heine B. 1989. Adpositions in African languages. *Linguist. Afr.* 2:77–127

54. Heine B. 1993. *Auxiliaries: Cognitive Forces and Grammaticalization.* Oxford: Oxford Univ. Press

55. Heine B, Claudi U, Hünnemeyer F. 1991. *Grammaticalization: A Conceptual Framework.* Chicago: Univ. Chicago Press

56. Heine B, Claudi U, Hünnemeyer F. 1991. From cognition to grammar—evidence from African languages. See Ref. 118, 1: 149–87

57. Heine B, Güldeman T, Kilian-Hatz C, Lessau DA, Roberg H, et al. 1993. *Conceptual Shift: A Lexicon of Grammaticalization Processes in African Languages.* Cologne: Univ. Köln, Inst. Afr. (Afr. Arb.pap. 34/35)

58. Heine B, Reh M. 1982. *Patterns of Grammaticalization in African languages.* Cologne: Univ. Köln, Inst. Sprachwiss. (Arb. Kölner Univers. Proj. 47)

59. Heine B, Reh M. 1984. *Grammaticalization and Reanalysis in African Languages.* Hamburg: Buske

60. Herring SC. 1991. The grammaticalization of rhetorical questions in Tamil. See Ref. 118, 1:253–84

61. Himmelmann N. 1992. *Grammaticalization and Grammar.* Cologne: Univ. Köln, Inst. Sprachwiss. [Sprachwiss. Arb.pap. 16 (Neue Folge)]

62. Holland G. 1980. On the origin of the 3rd sg. -r in Old Norse. In *American Indian and Indoeuropean [sic] Studies, Pap. Honor Madison Beeler,* ed. K Klar, M Langdon, S Silver, pp. 347–55. The Hague: Mouton de Gruyter

63. Hook PE. 1991. The emergence of perfective aspect in Indo-Aryan languages. See Ref. 118, 2:59–89

64. Hopper PJ. 1979. Aspect and foregrounding in discourse. In *Discourse and Syntax,* ed. T Givon, pp. 213–41. New York: Academic

65. Hopper PJ. 1987. Emergent grammar. *Berkeley Linguist. Soc.* 13:139–57

66. Hopper PJ. 1988. Emergent grammar and the a priori grammar postulate. In *Linguistics in Context,* ed. D Tannen, pp. 117–34. Norwood, NJ: Ablex

67. Hopper PJ. 1990. Where do words come from? In *Studies in Typology and Diachrony (for Joseph Greenberg),* ed. W Croft, K Denning, S Kemmer, pp. 151–60. Amsterdam: Benjamins

68. Hopper PJ. 1991. On some principles of grammaticization. See Ref. 118, 1:17–35

69. Hopper PJ. 1991. Phonogenesis. See Ref. 97, pp. 29–45

70. Hopper PJ, ed. 1982. *Tense and Aspect: Between Semantics and Pragmatics.* Amsterdam: Benjamins

71. Hopper PJ, Martin J. 1987. Structuralism and diachrony: the development of the indefinite article in English. In *Pap. 7th Int. Conf. Hist. Linguist.,* ed. AG Ramat, O Carruba, G Bernini, pp. 295–304. Amsterdam: Benjamins

72. Hopper PJ, Thompson SA. 1984. The discourse basis for lexical categories in universal grammar. *Language* 60(4):703–83

73. Hopper PJ, Traugott EC. 1993. *Grammaticalization.* Cambridge: Cambridge Univ. Press

74. Keesing RM. 1991. Substrates, calquing and grammaticalization in Melanesian Pidgin. See Ref. 118, 1:315–42

75. Kilian-Hatz C. 1995. *Das Baka: Grundzüge einer Grammatik aus der Grammaticalisierungsperspektive.* Co-

logne: Univ. Köln, Inst. Afr. (Afr. Monogr. 6)

76. Kilroe P. 1994. The grammaticalization of French à. See Ref. 97, pp. 49–62

77. König C. 1993. *Aspekt im Maa.* Cologne: Univ. Köln, Inst. Afr. (Afr. Monogr. 3)

78. König E, Traugott EC. 1988. Pragmatic strengthening and semantic change: the conventionalizing of conversational implicature. In *Understanding the Lexicon: Meaning, Sense, and World Knowedge in Lexical Semantics,* ed. W Hüllen, R Schulze, pp. 10–24. Tübingen: Niemeyer

79. Kurylowicz J. 1972. The role of deictic elements in linguistic evolution. *Semiotica* 5:174–83

80. Kurylowicz J. 1975. (1965). The evolution of grammatical categories. In *Esquisses Linguistiques II,* pp. 38–54. München: Fink

81. Lambrecht K. 1981. *Topic, Antitopic and Verb Agreement in Non-Standard French.* Amsterdam: Benjamins

82. Lehmann C. 1982. *Thoughts on Grammaticalization: A Programmatic Sketch.* Cologne: Univ. Köln, Inst. Sprachwiss. (Arb. Kölner Univers. Proj. 48)

83. Lehmann C. 1985. Grammaticalization: synchronic variation and diachronic change. *Ling. Stile* 20(3):303–18

84. Lehmann C. 1991. Grammaticalization and related changes in contemporary German. See Ref. 118, 2:493–535

85. Lessau DA. 1994. *A Dictionary of Grammaticalization,* Vols. 1–2. Bochum: Univ. verl. Brockmeyer

86. Li CN, ed. 1975. *Word Order and Word Order Change.* Austin: Univ. Tex. Press

87. Li CN, ed. 1976. *Subject and Topic.* New York: Academic

88. Li CN, ed. 1977. *Mechanisms of Syntactic Change.* Austin: Univ. Tex. Press

89. Li CN, Thompson SA. 1974. An explanation of word order change SVO→SOV. *Found. Lang.* 12:201–14

90. Li CN, Thompson SA. 1989. Subject and topic: a new typology of language. See Ref. 93, pp. 457–90

91. Lord C. 1973. Serial verbs in transition. *Stud. Afr. Linguist.* 4:269–95

92. Lord C. 1982. The development of object markers in serial verb languages. In *Syntax and Semantics. Studies in Transitivity,* ed. PJ Hopper, SA Thompson, 15:277–300. New York: Academic

93. Matthiessen C, Thompson SA. 1989. The structure of discourse and 'subordination'. In *Clause Combining in Grammar and Discourse,* ed. J Haiman, SA Thompson, pp. 275–33. Amsterdam: Benjamins

94. Meillet A. 1958. (1912). L'évolution des formes grammaticales. In *Linguistique Historique et Linguistique Générale,* pp. 130–48. Paris: Champion

95. Meillet A. 1958. (1915–1916). Le renouvellement des conjonctions. In *Linguistique Historique et Linguistique Générale,* pp. 130–48. Paris: Champion

96. Mithun M. 1984. The evolution of noun incorporation. *Language* 60(4):847–94

97. Pagliuca W, ed. 1994. *Perspectives on Grammaticalization.* Amsterdam: Benjamins

98. Pulgram E. 1967. Trends and predictions. In *To Honor Roman Jakobson,* pp. 1634–49. The Hague: Mouton de Gruyter

99. Rothe W. 1966. Romanische objektkonjugation. *Romanische Forsch.* 78: 530–47

100. Rubba J. 1994. Grammaticalization as semantic change: a case study of preposition development. See Ref. 97, pp. 81–102

101. Rude N. 1991. Verbs to promotional suffixes in Sahaptian and Klamath. See Ref. 118, 2:185–99

102. Sankoff G, Brown P. 1976. The origin of syntax in discourse: a case study of Tok Pisin relatives. *Language* 52:631–66.

103. Deleted in proof

104. Schwegler A. 1990. *Analyticity and Syntheticity: A Diachronic Perspective with Special Reference to Romance Languages.* Berlin: Mouton de Gruyter

105. Schwentner SA. 1993. The grammaticalization of an anterior in progress: evidence from a Peninsular Spanish dialect. *Stud. Lang.* 18:71–111

106. Schwentner SA. 1994. 'Hot News' and the Grammaticalization of perfects. *Linguistics* 32:995–1028

107. Slobin DI. 1994. Talking perfectly: discourse origins of the present perfect. See Ref. 97, pp. 119–34

108. Stein D. 1990. *The Semantics of Syntactic Change: Aspects of the Evolution of 'Do' in English.* Berlin: Mouton de Gruyter

109. Sweetser E. 1988. Grammaticalization and semantic bleaching. *Berkeley Linguist. Soc.* 14:389–405

110. Sweetser E. 1990. *From Etymology to Pragmatics: Metaphorical and Cultural Aspects of Semantic Structure.* Cambridge: Cambridge Univ. Press

111. Thompson SA, Mulac A. 1991. A quantitative perspective on the grammaticization of epistemic parentheticals in English. See Ref. 118, 2:313–29

112. Traugott EC. 1978. On the expression of spatio-temporal relations. See Ref. 45, 3: 369–400

113. Traugott EC. 1980. Meaning change in the development of grammatical markers. *Lang. Sci.* 2:44–61

114. Traugott EC. 1982. From propositional to textual and expressive meanings: some semantic-pragmatic aspects of grammaticization. In *Perspectives in Historical Linguis-*

tics, ed. WP Lehmann, Y Malkiel, pp. 245–71. Amsterdam: Benjamins

115. Traugott EC. 1989. On the rise of epistemic meanings in English: an example of subjectification in language change. *Language* 65:31–55

116. Traugott EC. 1988. Pragmatic strengthening and grammaticalization. *Berkeley Linguist. Soc.* 14:406–16

117. Traugott EC. 1990. From less to more situated in language: the unidirectionality of semantic change. In *Pap. 7th Conf. Engl. Hist. Linguist.,* ed. S Adamson, V Law, N Vincent, S Wright, pp. 497–517. Amsterdam: Benjamins

118. Traugott EC, Heine B, eds. 1991. *Approaches to Grammaticalization,* Vols. 1, 2. Amsterdam: Benjamins

119. Traugott EC, König E. 1991. The semantics-pragmatics of grammaticalization revisited. See Ref. 118, 1:189–218

119a. von der Gabelentz G. 1891. *Die Sprachwissenschaft: Ihre Aufgaben, Methoden, und Bisherigen Ergebnisse.* Leibzig: Weigel

120. Watkins C. 1962. Preliminaries to the reconstruction of Indo-European sentence structure. In *Proc. 11th Int. Congr. Linguists,* ed. H Lunt, pp. 1035–45. The Hague: Mouton de Gruyter

Annu. Rev. Anthropol. 1996. 25:237–51

THE PARADOX OF CHILD LABOR AND ANTHROPOLOGY

Olga Nieuwenhuys

Institute for Development Research Amsterdam, University of Amsterdam, Plantage Muidergracht 12, 1018TV Amsterdam, The Netherlands

KEY WORDS: children's work, socialization, global childhood, girlhood, children's exploitation

---

ABSTRACT

In relating the child labor debate to the observed variety of children's work patterns, this review reveals the limits of current notions such as labor, gender, and exploitation in the analysis of this work. Particularly in the developing world, most work undertaken by children has for a long time been explained away as socialization, education, training, and play. Anthropology has helped disclose that age is used with gender as the justification for the value accorded to work. The low valuation of children's work translates not only in children's vulnerability in the labor market but, more importantly, in their exclusion from remunerated employment. I argue that current child labor policies, because they fail to address the exclusion of children from the production of value, reinforce paradoxically children's vulnerability to exploitation.

THE PARADOX OF CHILD LABOR

Irrespective of what children do and what they think of what they do, modern society sets children apart ideologically as a category of people excluded from the production of value. The dissociation of childhood from the performance of valued work is considered a yardstick of modernity, and a high incidence of child labor is considered a sign of underdevelopment. The problem with defining children's roles in this way, however, is that it denies their agency in the creation and negotiation of value. Illuminating the complexity of the work patterns of children in developing countries, recent anthropological research has begun to demonstrate the need to critically examine the relation between

0084-6570/96/1015-0237$08.00

the condemnation of child labor on the one hand and children's everyday work practice on the other. The emerging paradox is that the moral condemnation of child labor assumes that children's place in modern society must perforce be one of dependency and passivity. This denial of their capacity to legitimately act upon their environment by undertaking valuable work makes children altogether dependent upon entitlements guaranteed by the state. Yet we must question the state's role—as the evidence on growing child poverty caused by cuts in social spending has illuminated—in carrying out its mission.

This review is divided into three parts: (a) a discussion of the theoretical perspectives adopted by development theory as it has dealt with poverty and child labor, (b) an assessment of the contribution of anthropology to the child labor debate, and (c) a discussion of the need of future research based on the idea of work as one of the most critical domains in which poor children can contest and negotiate childhood. First, in the section on Approaches to Children's Work, I argue that from its inception the notion of child labor has been associated with factory work and hence was limited to Western countries. The interest in children's work in the developing world can be traced back to theories of socialization, a preoccupation with population growth, and unfair economic competition. The section on Children's Work and Anthropology probes the paradox of the market impinging upon locally accepted forms of child work without transforming it into "child labor." Here, I discuss how anthropologists have criticized the simplistic views of child labor espoused by Western development experts. Approaches to children's work undertaken from the anthropological perspective highlight the very complex interplay of gender and age in determining a child's work allocation. Third, in the section on The Negotiation of Childhood, I propose to enlarge the notion of children's exploitation to include the more mundane aspects of work. Finally, I outline the direction future research should take to enable us to understand not only how children's work is negotiated and acquires its meaning but children's own agency therein.

APPROACHES TO CHILDREN'S WORK

Recent concern with child labor draws on a shared understanding among development experts of how, from the mid-nineteenth century onward, Western industrial society began to eliminate through legislation the exploitation of children. However, historians still debate more deep-seated reasons for the nineteenth-century outcry in Western Europe and the United States against child labor, which is probably as old as childhood itself. For instance, Nardinelli (95) has questioned the assumption that this outcry was inspired, as some authors have argued (44, 117, 126), by the brutal treatment of children working in factories. Besides humanitarian reasons, Nardinelli argued that there was a desire to protect initiatives to mechanize the textile industry from the uncontrolled competition of a labor force composed almost entirely of children. Another equally important reason was the fear of political instability created by a youthful working class not to be disciplined by the army, schools, or the church (84, 95, 127, 128). While some believe compulsory education was the single most important instrument leading to the elimination of child labor (44, 127), others have argued that changes in the perceived roles of children (126, 135) and the increase in family income (95, 116) played a more decisive role.

Progressive state legislation has marked the major steps of child labor abolition in the West. However, while this legislation defined child labor as waged work undertaken by a child under a certain age, it also established the borderline between morally desirable and pedagogically sensible activities on the one hand, and the exploitation of children on the other. While condemning the relatively uncommon forms of waged labor as exploitation, it sanctioned a broad spectrum of other activities, including housekeeping, child minding, helping adults for no pay on the family farm and in small shops, domestic service, street selling, running errands, delivering newspapers, seasonal work on farms, working as a trainee in a workshop, etc. In contrast with child labor, these activities were lauded for their socializing and training aspects (26, 126).

The distinction between harmful and suitable—if not desirable—work as defined by Western legislation has become the main frame of reference of most contemporary governmental and bureaucratic approaches to children's work. Many countries in the world have now either ratified or adopted modified versions of child labor legislation prepared and propagated by the International Labor Organization (ILO) (55, 57). The implications are far reaching. Legislation links child labor quite arbitrarily to work in the factory and excludes a wide range of nonfactory work. It therefore sanctifies unpaid work in the home or under parental supervision, regardless of its implications for the child. In the words of an ILO report: "We have no problem with the little girl who helps her mother with the housework or cooking, or the boy or girl who does unpaid work in a small family business....The same is true of those odd jobs that children may occasionally take on to earn a little pocket money to buy something they really want" (see 58a). Many of the odd jobs mentioned here, as in the case of helping on the family farm or in shops and hotels, though strictly not prohibited, are felt by both children and the public at large to be exploitative. Legislation also selects chronological age as the universal measure of biological and psychological maturity, and it rejects cultural and social meanings attached to local systems of age ranking (67). More specifically, it denies the value of an early introduction to artisanal crafts or traditional occupations that may be crucial in a child's socialization (see section on The Negotiation of Childhood). Finally, legislation condemns any work undertaken by a child for his/her own upkeep—with the notable exception of work undertaken to obtain pocket money. The denial of gainful employment is the more paradoxical in that the family and the state often fail to provide children with what they need to lead a normal life (135). These are some of the reasons why the industrial countries, despite much lip service to the contrary, have not succeeded in eliminating all forms of child work (22, 51, 68, 69, 81, 133).

Given the factory origins of the notion of child labor, it is hardly surprising that children's work in the erstwhile colonies caused no concern. Most colonial administrations passed factory acts excluding children under 14 from the premises soon after they had been passed at home. However, these laws carried only a symbolic value: The colonies were merely seen as sources of cheap raw materials and semimanufactured goods produced by rural villagers, while the factory system of production was energetically discouraged. The administrations' main preoccupation was that the local rural population—men, women, and children—continue to find in the old forms of subsistence the means of surviving while delivering the agricultural goods necessary to maintain the colonial revenue (98, 129).

This may explain why in the West social activists expressed outrage about child labor at home, while anthropologists romanticized the work of rural children in the colonies as a form of socialization well adapted to the economic and social level of preindustrial society (78, 132; for a critique, see 54). Engrossed with the intricacies of age ranking and passage rites, anthropologists seldom hinted at what this meant in terms of work and services required by elders from youngsters (118). The high premium put on the solidarity of the extended family as the cornerstone of precapitalist society overshadowed the possibility of exploitation occurring within the family or the village.

This perception changed with the identification in postwar development theory of population growth as the main obstacle to the eradication of poverty in the new nations of the third world. Celebrated as an antidote to poverty during the colonial period, children's work contributions to the family economy came to be perceived as an indicator of poverty, if not its cause. In the 1960s and 1970s, a burgeoning literature on the "population explosion" tried to show that the fast-growing numbers of poor children—nonworkers with escalating expectations—were to be held responsible for consuming the developing world's scant resources (31, 34). These allegations often masked the fear that the mounting frustrations of youngsters would "fester into eruptions of violence and extremism" (77) and thereby threaten the stability of the postwar world order (82, 112). Large-scale foreign-funded research programs were introduced in high-fertility countries to induce poor couples to control births.

However, resistance to birth control was unexpectedly staunch. By the mid-1970s, research began to provide clues that the poor desired a large family because children represented an important source of free labor (82). Mamdani's seminal work on the importance of children's work contribution for the reproduction of the peasant household in the Green Revolution areas of the Punjab cast an entirely new light on high fertility by suggesting that India's peasants needed many children to meet their labor demands (71–73).

Mamdani's research inspired a fresh approach to children's work in terms of its utility to the peasant household. During the 1970s, anthropologists carried out extensive and painstaking time-allocation and family-budget studies to show that even young children were contributing to their own sustenance by undertaking a whole range of activities in the subsistence sphere of the peasant economy (53, 74, 89, 96, 131). The ensuing debate on the determinants of high fertility in peasant economies showed, however, that the claim that poor peasants' desire for children would be inspired by their value as workers was premature (25, 122–124, 130). Caldwell's work on Nigeria and India was particularly influential in mapping the wider setting of children's historical, social, and cultural roles (16–18). Research on intrahousehold relations also questioned the concept of the household as an unproblematic unit, highlighting the outspoken inequality that exists not only between males and females but between seniors and juniors (35, 39, 59, 110, 111). Another criticism of the "cost-benefit" analysis has been its exclusive focus on decision making at the level of the household; it ignores the larger context in which the actions of its members occur (46, 106, 125).

In spite of such criticism, the neoclassical belief that child labor is essentially a problem of household economics has continued to be espoused in the studies of child labor published under the auspices of national and international agencies such as UNICEF, WHO, and the ILO following the International Year of the Child in 1979 (7–9, 22, 44, 81, 93, 105). Similar views are expressed in the documents produced by the international charities devoted to the welfare of children, such as the International Catholic Bureau, Save the Children, Defence of Children International, Anti-Slavery International (for overviews, see 10, 14, 36). Typical of these publications is a moral preoccupation with abolition through legislation and a zealous belief in the desirability of extending Western childhood ideals to poor families worldwide. Their merit lies essentially in having staked out child labor as a new and legitimate field of global political and academic concern. As aptly put by Morice & Schlemmer, the continuous reference to (Western) moral values, however, all too often not only supplants scientific analysis but may at times mask its very need: The emerging picture is one of conceptual confusion, in which ill-grasped notions from diverse analytical fields are indiscriminately used (86). The most glaring confusion is undoubtedly the one between the moral oppression and the economic exploitation of children (86, 88, 97). Reference to broad and ahistorical causes of the oppression of children such as poverty, illiteracy, backwardness, greed, and cruelty fail to go beyond the mere description of oppression and ignore the historical and social conditioning of exploitation (107).

As a global solution to eliminate child labor, development experts are now proposing a standard based on the sanctity of the nuclear family on the one hand and the school on the other as the only legitimate spaces for growing up. If this becomes a universal standard, there is a danger of negating the worth of often precious mechanisms for survival, and penalizing or even criminalizing the ways the poor bring up their children (12, 24, 30). This criminalization is made more malevolent as modern economies increasingly display their unwillingness to protect poor children from the adverse effects of neoliberal trade policies (1, 23, 44, 90, 119).

CHILDREN'S WORK AND ANTHROPOLOGY

Children's lives have been a constant theme in anthropology. However, in-depth studies of their work remain few and have been inspired, as I argued, by a critical concern with the neoclassical approach to the value of children. Two main areas of research have elicited anthropologists' interest: the family context of work and the relation between socialization, work, and schooling.

One of the leading themes of economic anthropology has been the conceptualization of work and its cultural meanings. The growing numbers of publications on child labor in the developing world have invoked a renewed interest in the family context of work. Central to some of the most notable studies has been how children's work is constrained by hierarchies based on kinship, age, and gender, a constraint that results in its typically rural, flexible, and personalized character. Rather than a widespread form of exploitation, child employment is mostly limited by the free-labor requirement of families that is satisfied by giving children unremunerated and lowly valued tasks (21, 32, 76, 80, 104, 134).

Considering the low cost of children's labor, it is indeed surprising that employers do not avail themselves more fully of this phenomenal source of profit. Despite more than 100 million children in the age bracket 5 to 15 living in abject poverty in India, for example, a mere 16 million children are employed, the vast majority of whom are teenagers who work in agriculture. About 10% are employed by industries, largely producing substandard if not inferior products for the local market (48, 66, 98).

There is more and more evidence that poor children who are not employed perform crucial work, often in the domestic arena, in subsistence agriculture, and in the urban informal sector (20, 45, 74, 83, 85, 91, 98, 100, 104, 108). Theories explaining underdevelopment in terms of the persistence of precapitalist labor relations provide some clues about why these children are not employed (75, 79, 115). The crucial aspect of underdevelopment in these theories is the unequal exchange realized in the market between goods produced in capitalist firms, where labor is valued according to its exchange value, and goods produced by the peasantry and the urban informal sector, where the use value of labor predominates. The latter group is paid only a fraction of its real cost because households are able to survive by pooling incomes from a variety of sources, undertaking subsistence activities and using the work of women and children to save on the costs of reproduction (125). The unpaid work of children in the domestic arena, which turns them into "inactives," is seen as crucial for the developing world's low labor cost rationality.

The reasons children are more likely than adults to be allotted unpaid work in agriculture or the household can be gauged by the work of feminist researchers that highlights how ideologies of gender and age interact to constrain, in particular, girls to perform unpaid domestic work (28, 33, 98, 101, 104, 110, 111, 134). The ideology of gender permits the persistence of an unequal system in which women are excluded from crucial economic and political activities and their positions of wives and mothers are associated with a lower status than men (33, 39, 60, 109). The valuation of girls' work is so low that it has been "discovered" by feminist anthropologists making a conscious choice to include housework and child care in their definition of work (39, 59, 61, 110, 113). Girls are trained early to accept and internalize the feminine ideals of devotion to the family (6, 63). The role of caretaker of younger siblings has not only the practical advantage of freeing adult women for wage work, it also charges girls' work with emotional gratifications that can make up for the lack of monetary rewards (70, 92).

Elson has argued that seniority explains why children's work is largely valued as inferior: Inferiority is not only attached to the nature of the work but to the person who performs it as well. Poor children are not perceived as workers because what they do is submerged in the low status realm of the domestic (35). The effect of seniority is not limited to the control of children's work within the nuclear family. Anthropologists have also uncovered how children's work plays a cardinal role in the intricate and extensive kinship and pseudo-kinship patterns that are at the core of support systems in the developing world. While servicing the immediate household is young children's mandatory task, poor children coming of age may also be sent to work as domestics and apprentices for wealthier kin (17, 65, 87, 108). For the parent-employer, this is a source of status and prestige (17). The widespread African practice of fostering the children of poorer (pseudo-)relatives is just one example of the intricate way family loyalty and socialization practices combine to shape how poor children are put to work. Another example is the practice among the poor in some areas of India of pledging their children's work against a loan. Although the object of much negative publicity, the practice is seen by parents as a useful form of training, a source of security, and a way of cutting household expenditures (45, 58, 98). Old crafts such as carpet weaving, embroidery, silk reeling, artisanal fishing, metal work, etc, lend themselves to protracted periods of apprenticeship in which a child is made to accept long hours of work and ill pay in the hope of becoming master (64, 88, 120). While often exacting, children may experience apprenticeship or living in another household as valuable, particularly if it helps them learn a trade or visit a school. Children's valuation of the practice is nevertheless ambiguous, and they may prefer employment to servicing their kin (44, 69, 98, 108, 114, 129).

There is a persistent belief, which finds its origins in the neoclassical approach, that schooling is the best antidote to child labor (44, 127). However, one consequence of the personalized character of children's work patterns is that this work is often combined with going to school. Reynolds' study of the Zambezi Valley describes how Tonga children need to work in subsistence agriculture while attending school simply to survive (104). Insecurity about the value of diplomas and marriage strategies are among the reasons girls in Lagos, Nigeria spend much out-of-school time acquiring street-trading skills (100). In Kerala, India, where attending school is mandatory, children spend much time earning cash for books, clothes, and food (99). Around the world children undertake all kinds of odd jobs, not only to help their families but to defray the fast-rising costs of schooling, be it for themselves or for a younger sibling (5, 11, 50, 67). However, children may also simply dislike school and prefer to work and earn cash instead (64, 129).

Although to some extent schools and work can coexist as separate arenas of childhood, schooling is changing the world orientation of both children and parents. Among the most critical effects is the lowering of birth rates, which has been explained by the nonavailability of girls for child care (19, 92). Another explanation, inspired by the neoclassical approach of balancing children's costs against the returns, is related to what Caldwell has called the "intergenerational flow of wealth." This notion suggests that schooling increases the costs of child rearing while reducing children's inclination to perform mandatory tasks for the circle of kin. The traditional flow of wealth from juniors to seniors is thus reversed (16). Perhaps of greater importance, schooling—despite the heavy sacrifices it may demand—provides children with a space in which they can identify with the parameters of modern childhood. It makes possible negotiations with elders for better clothes and food; time for school, homework, and recreation; and often payment for domestic work (98). Proponents of compulsory education have also argued that literate youngsters are likely to be more productive later in life than uneducated ones, who may have damaged their health by an early entrance into the labor market (127). For Purdy, schooling reinforces the useful learning imparted by parents at home and may, for some children, be the only useful form of learning (103).

Schools are also said to have a negative impact. Illness, lack of support at home, or heavy work make poor children's performance often inadequate and repetition and dropping out common. Competition in the classroom helps breed a sense of inferiority and personal failure in poor children, turning their work assignments into a source of shame. The high costs of schooling, including the need to look respectable in dress and appearance, incites poor children to engage in remunerative work, which contradicts the belief that compulsory education would work as an antidote to child labor (15, 44, 77, 127).

In the past few years, nongovernmental organizations (NGOs) concerned with children have been encouraged to develop low-cost solutions to address the problem of child labor. The solutions are based on a combination of work and school and recognize the need of poor children to contribute to their own upkeep. The approach has gained support within the ILO, the organization that until recently was the most staunch defender of prohibition by legislation (10, 37, 43, 49, 56). The poor quality of the education imparted, the heavy demands of studying after work, and above all the fact that they leave untouched the unjust social system that perpetrates children's exploitation are among the most problematic aspects of the NGOs' interventions (13).

The articulation of gender, age, and kinship plays a cardinal role in the valuation of poor children's work and is instrumental in explaining why some work is condemned as unsuitable and some is lauded as salutary. Hierarchies based on gender, age, and kinship combine to define children's mandatory tasks as salutary work and condemn paid work. By legitimizing children's obligation to contribute to survival and denying them their right to seek personal gain, these hierarchies effectively constrain them to a position of inferiority within the family. It is then not so much their factory employment as their engagement in low-productivity and domestic tasks that defines the ubiquitous way poor children are exploited in today's developing world.

Anthropology has sought to explain the apparent inability of the market to avail itself more fully of the vast reservoir of cheap child labor by pointing out that the free-labor requirements of poor families are satisfied by giving children lowly valued tasks. This explanation questions child labor studies' conceptualization of the exploitation of poor children. Employment is clearly not the only nor the most important way children's work is exploited: Child work contributions to the family are instrumental to its subsistence and to the production of goods that reach the market at prices far below their labor value.

The moral assumption that poor children's socialization should occur through the performance of nonmonetized work excludes this work from the same economic realm that includes child labor; it is as much a part of children's exploitation. This fact seriously questions the premises of modern childhood discussed in the next section.

THE NEGOTIATION OF CHILDHOOD

Irrespective of what they do and what they think about what they do, the mere fact of their being children sets children ideologically apart as a category of people excluded from the production of value. The dissociation of childhood from the performance of valued work has been increasingly considered a yardstick of modernity. International agencies and highly industrialized countries now turn this yardstick into a tool to condemn as backward and undemocratic those countries with a high incidence of child labor (14). The problem with this way of defining the ideal of childhood, however, is that it denies children's agency in the creation and negotiation of value.

The view that childhood precludes an association with monetary gain is an ideal of modern industrial society (27, 135). Historians highlight the bourgeois origins of this ideal and question its avowed universal validity not only across cultures but across distinctions of gender, ethnicity, and class (3, 4, 24, 30, 52). Some have argued that this ideal is threatened at the very core of capitalism and may be giving way to more diversified patterns of upbringing or even to the "disappearance of childhood" (38, 102). The current debate over children's rights is symptomatic of the discredit bourgeois notions of parental rights and childhood incompetence seem to have suffered (2, 41, 42, 103, 121). The exposure of child abuse in the Western media during the 1980s and 1990s has, in this line, been explained as a display of excessive anxiety sparked by the growing fragility of personal relationships in late-modern society that cannot but also affect childhood. Late-modern experiences of childhood suggest that the basic source of trust in society lies in the child. Advances in children's rights or media campaigns against child labor or sex tourism would point to a growing sanctity of the child in late modernity (62). This sanctity, however, is essentially symbolic and is contradicted by actual social and financial policies, as borne out by the harshness with which structural adjustment programs have hit poor children in developing countries and caused a marked increase in child mortality, morbidity, illiteracy, and labor (1, 23, 40, 44, 47, 90). Under these conditions it is no wonder that, as noted by Jenks, late-modern visions of childhood are now increasingly split between "futurity" and "nostalgia" (62).

As childhood becomes a contested domain the legitimacy of directing children into economically useless activities is losing ground (135). The need to direct children into these activities is linked to a system of parental authority and family discipline that was instrumental in preserving established bourgeois social order. The price of maintaining this order is high, because it requires, among other commitments, money to support the institutions at the basis of the childhood ideal, such as free education, cheap housing, free health care, sport and recreation facilities, family welfare and support services, etc. Developing economies will unlikely be able to generate in the near future the social surplus that the maintenance of these institutions requires. As the neoliberal critique of the welfare state gains popularity, wealthy economies also become reluctant to continue shouldering childhood institutions. It is interesting to note that with the retreat of the state, the market itself has begun more and more to address children as consumers, explicitly linking their status to the possession of expensive goods, thereby inducing poor children to seek self-esteem through paid work (129). Working children find themselves clashing with the childhood ideology that places a higher value on the performance of economically useless work. Although working for pay offers opportunities for self-respect, it also entails sacrificing childhood, which exposes children to the negative stereotyping attached to the loss of innocence this sacrifice is supposed to cause (8, 10, 14, 22, 44, 93).

Rethinking the paradoxical relation between neoliberal and global childhood ideology is one of the most promising areas for research. Research should especially seek to uncover how the need of poor children to realize self-esteem through paid work impinges upon the moral condemnation of child labor as one of the fundamental principles of modernity. In stark contrast with what happened in the nineteenth-century West, the future may very well see employers, parents, children, and the state disputing the legitimacy of this moral condemnation. Women, in particular, as they expose the construction of gender roles as instrumental in their discrimination in the labor market, are likely to be girls' foremost allies in contesting modern childhood's ideal of economic uselessness (39, 40). The ways children devise to create and negotiate the value of their work and how they invade structures of constraint based on seniority are other promising areas of future anthropological research. This type of research is even more relevant in that it may not only enrich our knowledge of children's agency but may prove seminal in understanding the process by which work acquires its meaning and is transformed into value.

248 NIEUWENHUYS

Literature Cited

1. Amin AA. 1994. The socioeconomic impact of child labour in Cameroon. *Labour Cap. Soc.* 27(2):234–49
2. Archard D. 1993. *Children, Rights and Childhood.* London: Routledge
3. Ariès P. 1973. *L'Enfant et la Vie Familiale sous l'Ancien Régime.* Paris: Seuil
4. Ariès P. 1980. Motivation for declining birth rates in the West: the rise and fall of the role of the child. *Popul. Dev. Rev.* 6(4): 645–50
5. Bekombo M. 1981. The child in Africa: socialisation, education and work. See Ref. 106, pp. 113–30
6. Bellotti EG. 1981. *Dalla Parte delle Bambine, l'Influenza dei Condizionamenti Sociali nella Formazione del Ruolo Femminile nei Primi Anni di Vita.* Milano: Feltrinelli
7. Bequele A, Boyden J, eds. 1988. *Combating Child Labour.* Geneva: Int. Labor Organ.
8. Black M. 1995. *In the Twilight Zone: Child Workers in the Hotel, Tourism and Catering Industry.* Geneva: Int. Labor Organ.
9. Bouhdiba A. 1982. *Exploitation of Child Labour: Special Report of the Subcommittee on Prevention of Discrimination and Protection of Minorities.* New York: United Nat.
10. Boyd J. 1994. Introduction: child labour within the globalizing economy. *Labour Cap. Soc.* 27(2):153–61
11. Boyden J. 1991. Working children in Lima. See Ref. 93, pp. 24–46
12. Boyden J. 1990. Childhood and the policy makers: a comparative perspective on the globalization of childhood. In *Constructing and Reconstructing Childhood: Contemporary Issues in the Sociological Study of Childhood,* ed. A James, A Prout, pp. 184–215. London: Falmer
13. Boyden J, Myers WE. 1995. *Exploring Alternative Approaches to Combating Child Labour: Case Studies from Developing Countries.* Florence: UNICEF/Innocenti Occas. Pap. 8
14. Bureau of International Affairs, US Department of Labor. 1994. *By the Sweat and Toil of Children: The Use of Child Labor in American Imports.* Washington, DC: US Dept. Labor
15. Burra N. 1989. *Child Labour and Education: Issues Emerging from the Experiences of Some Developing Countries of Asia.* Paris: UNESCO-UNICEF
16. Caldwell JC. 1981. The mechanisms of demographic change in historical perspective. *Popul. Stud.* 35:5–27
17. Caldwell JC. 1982. *Theory of Fertility Decline.* London: Academic
18. Caldwell JC. 1976. Towards a restatement of demographic transition theory. *Popul. Dev. Rev.* 2(4):321–59
19. Caldwell JC, Reddy PH, Caldwell P. 1985. Educational transition in rural South India. *Popul. Dev. Rev.* 11(1):29–51
20. Campos R, Raffaelli M, Ude W. 1994. Social networks and daily activities of street youth in Belo Horizonte. *Child Dev.* 65: 319–30
21. Céspedes BS, Zarama MIV. 1994. Le travail des enfants dans la Colombie. *Trav. Cap. Soc.* 27(2):250–69
22. Challis J, Elliman D. 1979. *Child Workers Today.* Middlesex: Quartermaine
23. Cornia G, Jolly R, Stewart F, eds. 1987. *Adjustment with a Human Face,* Vol. 1, *Protecting the Vulnerable and Promoting Growth.* Oxford: Clarendon
24. Cunningham H. 1991. *The Children of the Poor: Representations of Childhood Since the Seventeenth Century,* Cambridge, MA: Blackwell
25. Datta SK, Nugent JB. 1984. Are old-age security and the utility of children in rural India really unimportant? *Popul. Stud.* 38: 507–9
26. Davin A. 1982. Child labour, the working class family, and domestic ideology in 19th-century Britain. *Dev. Change* 13(4): 663–52
27. De Mause L, ed. 1976. *The History of Childhood.* London: Souvenir
28. De Tray D. 1983. Children's work activities in Malaysia. *Popul. Dev. Rev.* 9(3):437–55
29. Deleted in proof
30. Donzelot J. 1977. *La Police des Familles.* Paris: Minuit
31. Dore R. 1982. *The Diploma Disease, Education, Qualification and Development.* London: Allen & Unwin
32. Dube L. 1981. The economic roles of children in India: methodological issues. See Ref. 106, pp. 179–213
33. Dube L. 1988. On the construction of gender in India, Hindu girls in patrilineal India. *Econ. Polit. Wkly.* April 30:WS11–24
34. Eisenstadt SN. 1956. *From Generation to Generation, Age Groups and Social Structure.* New York: Free Press
35. Elson D. 1982. The differentiation of children's labour in the capitalist labour market. *Dev. Change* 13(4):479–97
36. Ennew J. 1994. *Street and Working Children: a Guide to Planning.* London: Save Child.
37. Espinola B, Glauser B, Oriz RM, de Ortiz Cartzosa S. 1987. *In the Streets: Working Street Children in Asunciòn: A Book for Action.* Bogotà: UNICEF

38. Evans DT. 1994. Falling angels? The material construction of children as sexual citizens. *Int. J. Child. Rights* 2:1–33

39. Folbre N. 1986. Hearts and spades: paradigms of household economics. *World Dev.* 14(2):245–55

40. Folbre N. 1994. *Who Pays for the Kids?* London/New York: Routledge

41. Franklin B, ed. 1986. *The Rights of Children.* Oxford: Blackwell

42. Freeman MDA. 1983. *Rights and Wrongs of Children.* London/Dover: Pinter

43. Fyfe A. 1994. *Educational strategies for street and working children.* Presented at Conf. Street Child. Psychoact. Subst.: Innov. Coop., World Health Organ., Geneva

44. Fyfe A. 1989. *Child Labour.* Cambridge: Polity Press

45. Gangrade KD, Gathia JA, eds. 1983. *Women and Child Workers in the Unorganized Sector, NonGovernment Organization's Perspective.* Delhi: Concept

46. Goddard V, White B, eds. 1982. Child workers today. *Dev. Change* 13(4): 465–78

47. Graham-Brown S. 1991. *Education in the Developing World, Conflict and Crisis.* London/New York: Longman

48. Gulrajani M. 1994. Child labour and the export sector: a case-study of the Indian carpet industry. *Labour Cap. Soc.* 27(2): 192–215

49. Gunn SE, Ostas Z. 1992. Dilemmas in tackling child labour: the case of scavenger children in the Philippines. *Int. Labour Rev.* 131(6):629–46

50. Hallak J. 1990. Setting educational priorities in the developing world. In *Investing in the Future.* Paris: UNESCO/Int. Inst. Educ. Plan.

51. Herpen A. 1990. *Children and Youngsters in Europe: The New Proletariat? A Report on Child Labour in Europe.* Brussels: Cent. Eur. Stud./Eur. Trade Unions Comm.

52. Hoyles M, Evans P. 1989. *The Politics of Childhood.* London: Journeyman

53. Hull T. 1975. *Each Child Brings Its own Fortune: An Enquiry into the Value of Children in a Javanese Village.* Canberra: Aust. Natl. Univ.

54. Hull T. 1981. Perspectives and data requirements for the study of children's work. See Ref. 106, pp. 47–80

55. International Labor Organization. 1988. *Conditions of Work Digest: The Emerging Response to Child Labour,* Vol. 7(1). Geneva: Int. Labor Organ.

56. International Labor Organization/Government of Germany. 1991. *International Programme of the Elimination of Child Labour (IPEC).* Geneva: Int. Labor Organ.

57. International Labor Organization. 1991. *Conditions of Work Digest, Child Labour Law and Practice,* Vol. 10(1). Geneva: Int. Labor Organ.

58. International Labor Organization. 1992. *Children in Bondage: A Call for Action.* Geneva: Int. Labor Organ.

58a. International Labor Organization. 1993. *World of Work,* June 6–7. Geneva: Int. Labor Organ.

59. Jain D, Banerjee N, eds. 1985. *Tyranny of the Household: Investigative Essays on Women's Work.* Delhi: Shakti

60. Jain D, Chand M. 1979. Rural children at work: preliminary results of a pilot study. *Indian J. Soc. Work* 40(3):311–22

61. Jeffery P, Jeffery R, Lyon A. 1989. *Labour Pains and Labour Power, Women and Childbearing in India.* Delhi: Manohar

62. Jenks C. 1994. Postmodern child abuse. *Child. Glob. Perspect.* 2(3):111–21

63. Kakar S. 1981. *The Inner World, A Psycho-Analytic Study of Childhood and Society in India.* Delhi: Oxford Univ. Press

64. Kambargi R, ed. 1991. *Child Labour in the Indian Subcontinent, Dimensions and Implications.* Delhi: Sage

65. Kayongo-Male D, Walji P. 1984. *Children at Work in Kenya.* Nairobi: Oxford Univ. Press

66. Kothari S. 1983. There's blood on those matchsticks, child labour in Sivakasi. *Econ. Polit. Wkly.* 13(27):1191–202

67. La Fontaine JS. 1978. *Sex and Age as Principles of Social Differentiation.* London: Academic

68. Lavalette M. 1994. *Child Employment in the Capitalist Labour Market.* Aldershot, UK: Avebury

69. Lee-Wright P. 1990. *Child Slaves.* London: Earthscan

70. Leslie J, Paolosso M. 1989. *Women, Work and Child Welfare in the Third World.* Boulder, CO: Westview

71. Mamdani M. 1974. The ideology of population control. *Concerned Demogr.* 4: 13–22

72. Mamdani M. 1972. *The Myth of Population Control, Family, Caste and Class in an Indian Village.* New York: Monthly Rev. Press

73. Mamdani M. 1981. The ideology of population control. See Ref. 82, pp. 39–49

74. Marcoux R. 1994. Des inactifs qui ne chôment pas: une réflexion sur le travail des enfants en milieu urbain du Mali. *Trav. Cap. Soc.* 27(2):296–319

75. Martin WG, Beittel M. 1987. The hidden abode of reproduction: conceptualizing households in southern Africa. *Dev. Change* 18:215–34

76. McEwen SA. 1982. Changes in the structure of child labour under conditions of dualistic economic growth. *Dev. Change* 13(4):537–50

77. McNamara R. 1968. *The Essence of Security: Reflections in Office.* London: Hodder & Stoughton
78. Mead M, Wolfenstein M, eds. 1955. *Childhood in Contemporary Cultures.* Chicago: Univ. Chicago Press
79. Meillassoux C. 1983. The economic basis of demographic reproduction: from the domestic mode of production to wage earning. *J. Peasant Stud.* 11(1):50–61
80. Melhuus M. 1984. Cash crop production and family labour: tobacco growers in Corrientes, Argentina. In *Family and Work in Rural Societies: Perspectives on NonWage Labour.* London: Tavistock
81. Mendelievich E, ed. 1979. *Children at Work.* Geneva: Int. Labor Organ.
82. Michaelson KL, ed. 1981. *And the Poor Get Children: Radical Perspectives on Population Dynamics.* New York: Monthly Rev. Press
83. Mies M, Vandana Shiva. 1993. The impoverishment of the environment: women and children last. In *Ecofeminism,* ed. M Mies, Vandana Shiva, pp. 70–91. London: ZED
84. Minge-Kalman W. 1978. The industrial revolution and the European family: the institutionalization of childhood as a market for family labour. *Comp. Stud. Soc. Hist.* 20:456–63
85. Moerat F. 1989. *A Study of Child Labour with Regard to Newspaper Vendors in the Cape Peninsula.* Cape Town: Univ. Cape Town
86. Morice A, Schlemmer B. 1994. La mise au travail des enfants: une problématique à investir. *Trav. Cap. Soc.* 27(2):286–94
87. Morice A. 1982. Underpaid labour and social reproduction: apprenticeship in Koalack, Senegal. *Dev. Change* 13(4):515–26
88. Morice A. 1981. The exploitation of children in the "Informal Sector": proposals for research. See Ref. 106, pp. 131–58
89. Mueller E. 1975. *The economic value of children in peasant agriculture.* Presented at Conf. Popul. Policy, Resour. Fut.
90. Mundle S. 1984. Recent trends in the condition of children in India: a statistical profile. *World Dev.* 12(3):297–308
91. Mutiso R. 1989. *Housemaids in Nairobi: A Review of Available Documents on the Subject of Female Domestic Workers in Nairobi.* Nairobi: Undugu
92. Myers R. 1992. *The Twelve Who Survive: Strengthening Programmes of Early Childhood Development in the Third World.* London/New York: Routledge
93. Myers WE, ed. 1991. *Protecting Working Children.* London: ZED Books/UNICEF
94. Nag M, White B, Peet RC. 1978. An anthropological approach to the study of eco-

nomic value of children in Java and Nepal. *Curr. Anthropol.* 19(2):293–306
95. Nardinelli C. 1990. *Child Labour and the Industrial Revolution.* Bloomington, IN: Indiana Univ. Press
96. Nichols M. 1993. Third world families at work: child labor or child care? *Harvard Bus. Rev.* Jan./Feb.:12–23
97. Nieuwenhuys O. 1995. The domestic economy and the exploitation of children's work: the case of Kerala. *Int. J. Child. Rights* 3:213–25
98. Nieuwenhuys O. 1994. *Children's Lifeworlds: Gender, Welfare and Labour in the Developing World.* London/New York: Routledge
99. Nieuwenhuys O. 1993. To read and not to eat: South Indian children between secondary school and work. *Child. Glob. Perspect.* 1(2):100–9
100. Oloko BA. 1991. Children's work in urban Nigeria: a case study of young Lagos traders. See Ref. 93, pp. 24–45
101. Oppong C. 1988. Les femmes Africaines: des épouses, des mères et des travailleuses. In *Population et Sociétés en Afrique au Sud du Sahara.* Paris: Harmattan
102. Postman N. 1982. *The Disappearance of Childhood.* New York: Delacorte
103. Purdy L. 1992. *In Their Best Interests? The Case Against Equal Rights for Children.* Ithaca/London: Cornell Univ. Press
104. Reynolds P. 1991. *Dance Civet Cat: Child Labour in the Zambezi Valley.* London: ZED
105. Rimbaud C. 1980. *52 Millions d'Enfants au Travail.* Paris: Plon
106. Rodgers G, Standing G, eds. 1981. *Child Work, Poverty and Underdevelopment.* Geneva: Int. Labor Organ.
107. Sahoo UC. 1995. *Child Labour in Agrarian Society.* Jaipur/Delhi: Rawat
108. Salazar MC. 1991. Young workers in Latin America: protection of self-determination? *Child Welf.* 70(2):269–83
109. Scheper-Hughes N, ed. 1987. *Child Survival.* Dordrecht: Reidel
110. Schildkrout E. 1980. Children's work reconsidered. *Int. Soc. Sci. J.* 32(3):479–90
111. Schildkrout E. 1981. See Ref. 106, pp. 81–112
112. Schrijvers J. 1993. *The Violence of Development.* Utrecht: Int. Books; Delhi: Kali for Women (Inaug. address)
113. Sen A, Sengupta S. 1985. Malnutrition in rural children and the sex bias. See Ref. 59, pp. 3–24
114. Sinha SK. 1991. *Child Labour in Calcutta: A Sociological Study.* Calcutta: Naya Prokash
115. Southall A. 1988. On mode of production theory: the foraging mode of production

THE PARADOX OF CHILD LABOR   251

and the kinship mode of production. *Dialect. Anthropol.* 12:165–92
116. Stadum B. 1995. The dilemma in saving children from child labor: reform and casework at odds with families' needs. *Child Welf.* 74(1):20–33
117. Thompson EP. 1968. *The Making of the English Working Class.* Harmondsworth, UK: Penguin
118. Van Gennep A. 1960. (1908). *The Rites of Passage.* Chicago: Univ. Chicago Press
119. Verlet M. 1994. Grandir à Nima (Ghana): dérégulation domestique et mise au travail des enfants. *Trav. Cap. Soc.* 27(2):162–90
120. Vijayagopalan S. 1993. *Child Labour in the Carpet Industry: A Status Report.* Delhi: NCAER
121. Vittachi A. 1989. *Stolen Childhood: In Search of the Rights of the Child.* Cambridge: Polity Press
122. Vlassoff M. 1982. Economic utility of children and fertility in rural India. *Popul. Stud.* 36:45–60
123. Vlassoff M. 1979. Labour demand and economic utility of children: a case study in rural India. *Popul. Stud.* 33(3)
124. Vlassoff M, Vlassoff C. 1980. Old age security and the utility of children in rural India. *Popul. Stud.* 34(3):487–99
125. Wallerstein I, Martin WG, Dickinson T. 1982. Household structures and production processes: preliminary theses and findings. *Review* 5(3):437–58
126. Walvin J. 1982. *A Child's World: A Social History of English Childhood 1800–1914.* Harmondsworth, UK: Penguin
127. Weiner M. 1991. *The Child and the State in India: Child Labor and Educational Policy in Comparative Perspective.* Princeton, NJ: Princeton Univ. Press
128. Weissbach LS. 1989. *Child Labour Reform in Nineteenth Century France: Assuring the Future Harvest.* London: La. State Univ. Press
129. White B. 1994. *Children, Work and 'Child Labour': Changing Responses to the Employment of Children.* The Hague: Inst. Soc. Stud. (Inaug. address)
130. White B. 1982. Child labour and population growth in rural Asia. *Dev. Change* 13(4):587–610
131. White B. 1975. The economic importance of children in a Javanese village. In *Population and Social Organization,* ed. M Nag, pp. 127–46. The Hague: Mouton
132. Whiting BB, ed. 1963. *Six Cultures: Studies of Child Rearing.* New York: Wiley
133. Williams S. 1993. *Child Workers in Portugal.* London: Anti-Slavery Int.
134. Wyers J. 1986. Child labour in Brazilian agriculture. *Crit. Anthropol.* 6(2):63–80
135. Zelizer V. 1994. *Pricing the Priceless Child, The Changing Social Value of Children.* Princeton, NJ: Princeton Univ. Press

Annu. Rev. Anthropol. 1996. 25:253–74

MEDICAL ANTHROPOLOGY AND EPIDEMIOLOGY

James A. Trostle[1] *and Johannes Sommerfeld*[2]

[1]Five College Medical Anthropology Program, Mount Holyoke College, South Hadley, Massachusetts 01075

[2]Institute of Tropical Hygiene and Public Health, University of Heidelberg, Im Neuenheimer Feld 324, 69120 Heidelberg, Germany

KEY WORDS: interdisciplinary collaboration, methodology, risk, health, disease

ABSTRACT

Over the past decade anthropologists and epidemiologists have begun to move beyond the "benign neglect" that characterized their prior relationship. Some of the most important collaborations between these disciplines concern themes of culture change and stress, social stratification, and the unpacking of other social and cultural variables. Anthropologists have criticized and expanded epidemiological notions of risk and vulnerability. Multidisciplinary teams of anthropologists and epidemiologists have constructed new measures and used multiple methods to increase the validity of their results. Disputes about classification have also linked the two disciplines. Collaborative projects between anthropologists and epidemiologists are leading to more nuanced and accurate descriptions of human behavior and more appropriate and effective interventions. Epidemiological techniques and ideas are also being used for anthropological ends, because disease often spreads along the framework of social structure. These many forms of collaboration create the foundations of a cultural epidemiology.

INTRODUCTION

Medical anthropology is one of the fastest growing subfields of anthropology, and epidemiology—"the study of the distribution and determinants of disease" (132)—is the predominant mode of inquiry in public health. The relationship

0084-6570/96/1015-0253$08.00

253

between medical anthropology and epidemiology is important to contemporary health research because both fields address biological, social, and cultural causes and ramifications of sickness. Increasing amounts of theoretical and methodological attention are being invested in multisite, cross-disciplinary studies under rubrics of cultural studies of science and technology, health systems research, health services epidemiology, clinical medical anthropology, the anthropology of infectious diseases, and prevention research. Each of these cross-disciplinary fields has provided opportunities for exchange between anthropologists and epidemiologists.

The perspectives of anthropology and epidemiology are sometimes dichotomized into qualitative and interpretive vs quantitative and explanatory modes of inquiry. However, a closer look reveals a more complex picture. Medical anthropology uses a broad range of qualitative and quantitative research techniques to describe illness in biological and cultural contexts (76, 84, 220), and both disciplines debate the sources of their theories, the validity of their methods, and the utility of their findings (11, 15, 20, 34, 114, 118, 185, 201). Some epidemiologists have expressed interest in qualitative methods and interpretive modes of inquiry (13, 17, 21). Epidemiologists have written many articles reviewing the effects of culture on health (e.g. 10, 27, 28, 140, 141, 200, 209). They have also called for broader links between the liberal arts and epidemiology (158, 222). Epidemiology is not the unified and monolithic enterprise depicted by some anthropologists (e.g. 78, 153, 154, 221). Some specific areas within epidemiology offer many collaborative possibilities: social epidemiology (210) or behavioral epidemiology (89) and so-called historical materialist epidemiology (181). These domains contradict the polarized vision of a qualitative anthropology and a quantitative epidemiology.

This review examines theoretical descriptions of possible cross-disciplinary exchange and empirical examples of such exchange. We acknowledge fundamental differences between the cores of medical anthropology and epidemiology, but we also recognize the permeability of their borders. We explore this work at the margins, highlight its usefulness and even greater potential, and argue for more of it.

Ten years ago, one of us wrote that "the history of anthropology and epidemiology is neither one of antagonism nor one of close cooperation...it is rather a history of benign neglect" (215:80). Historical reviews (214, 215) and empirical as well as theoretical overviews published at that time (60, 106, 177) offered a variety of potential pathways toward productive collaboration, mutual criticism, and cross-disciplinary exchanges.

Much has changed in the decade since this statement about benign neglect was written. Contributors to the Society for Medical Anthropology column in the American Anthropological Association's *Anthropology Newsletter* have recommended that introductory and advanced epidemiology should form part of a core curriculum for graduate medical anthropology students (1a, 1b). At least 19 anthropologists are now employed at the Centers for Disease Control and Prevention (CDC) in Atlanta, the central epidemiological research agency for the US federal government (J Carey, personal communication, 1996). Since its beginning in 1951, 10 anthropologists or sociologists have enrolled in the Epidemic Intelligence Service, the primary postdoctoral training course for professionals interested in learning epidemiological field methods and joining the CDC. Five of these have enrolled in the past five years (R Hahn, personal communication, 1996).

Essays about these two disciplines over the past decade reveal many visions of anthropology and epidemiology as well as diverse opinions about whether there is merit in combining them. Sympathetic comparisons of anthropology and epidemiology have been cast according to direct and indirect collaboration (60), the utility for anthropology of the epidemiological attention to research questions and design (220), convergences and divergences of thought (99), and epistemology and underlying logic (84). Dunn & Janes (60) defined direct collaboration as involvement of anthropologists in the various phases of epidemiological research design. Indirect collaboration involves more distant cooperation including searching for correlates of epidemiological causal assemblages (e.g. links among malaria, sickle-cell trait and agriculture, or behavioral determinant studies); undertaking anthropological research on epidemiological problems (e.g. anthropological exploration of epidemiological linkages among poverty, acculturative stress, and disease outcomes such as hypertension and mental disorders); or collaborating with epidemiologists in prevention-related research. True (220) has paid closer attention to the structure of inquiry, giving various examples of differences and potential areas of collaboration between the two disciplines with respect to research questions, research designs, definitions of normality and abnormality, and assumptions about causation.

Inhorn (99) has discussed five areas of perceived divergence between anthropology and epidemiology and has explored their potential for convergence. She looked at complementarities in areas of study, breadth of causal framework, methods, focus on individual vs social responsibility for sickness, and contributions to prevention and the nature of risk. Hahn (84) concluded that anthropological and epidemiological epistemologies are fundamentally complementary even though the two disciplines differ dramatically in their objectives. He explored how each discipline uses context and contended that the anthropological creation of context requires epidemiological inferences while the epidemiological minimization of context requires anthropological inferences. Members of each discipline, he argued, have paid insufficient attention to the methods and sources they use to acquire information.

These accounts all necessarily mention the ongoing conflict within anthropology about the status of the discipline as a science (20, 25, 75). Our position is that both the scientific and the interpretive trends in anthropology can contribute to creating a productive relationship between anthropology and epidemiology. Exchanges can be critical or supportive, theoretical or applied. Data can be used to explain relationships or to create emotional responses in the reader. Anthropological methods can be used within epidemiological designs. For example, a qualitative preliminary stage can be added to an epidemiological study to improve measures or access to populations. Epidemiological methods can be added to anthropological designs, providing opportunities to test theories or measure prevalence of specific behaviors. Anthropological theory and method can be used to critique epidemiological measures and designs and vice versa. Such critiques may be designed with epidemiological or anthropological objectives in mind.

The broad scope of both anthropology and epidemiology leaves any review open to charges of selectivity. This review looks primarily at theoretical discourse and collaborative activities between medical or cultural anthropologists and epidemiologists. Separate reviews could be written of epidemiological explorations done by biological anthropologists (6, 233). Similarly, the interactions between psychological anthropologists and psychiatric epidemiologists have a long and important history (125, 130, 150). The role of cultural factors in disease causation could just as readily be reviewed from the perspectives of medical geography (147), biological anthropology (3, 97, 205, 231), behavioral epidemiology (89), demography (23), or medical sociology (194, 204).

Precursors of Contemporary Cross-fertilization

Before the mid-1980s, the literature on anthropology and epidemiology consisted primarily of notable exceptions to the tradition of benign neglect. Summaries of prior collaboration were included in a review of psychological anthropology and epidemiology (177) and in various chapters in an edited volume (106). Fleck & Ianni published an early paper on disciplinary collaboration in 1958 (68), and Scotch published a series of papers on sociocultural factors in epidemiology in the 1960s (182, 183). The epidemiologist John Cassel, anthropologist Ralph Patrick Jr, and psychologist David Jenkins cowrote an important paper differentiating social from cultural contributions to disease prevalence (28). Cassel followed this a few years later with a paper emphasizing the relevance of social science theory to epidemiological research (26).

The pace of collaborative research and interdisciplinary borrowing began to increase in the 1970s. Anthropologists began to examine the distribution of culture-bound syndromes (176) and the relevance of behavior to parasitic disease risk and prevalence (58). Although authors emphasized many different aspects of the behavioral sciences and epidemiology, programmatic calls for collaborative work became more frequent (27, 49, 57, 58, 206, 225). Some viewed social epidemiology as the bridging discipline between biomedical and behavioral disciplines (58), or between epidemiological and sociological approaches to understanding social conditions and disease processes (206). Others emphasized the common background among epidemiology, demography, sociology, and biostatistics and called for a common theoretical basis, common language, and set of exchangeable methods to support collaborative work (225). Partly because of increased funding for cross-disciplinary research and partly because of further disciplinary fragmentation, these programmatic calls for collaboration bore fruit in the 1980s and 1990s, as collaborative research efforts and sympathetic theories began to be developed.

RECENT EXCHANGES BETWEEN ANTHROPOLOGY AND EPIDEMIOLOGY

Factors Promoting and Impeding Collaboration

What drives current efforts to do more interdisciplinary work? Collaborative work in the 1950s and 1960s was pushed by epidemiologists' venturing into international studies and their domestic and international attention to human behavior as an etiologic variable. Anthropologists' involvement in medicine and public health was increasing at this same time, as the pace of human migration, and more generally of social and cultural change, began to quicken. The emerging domestic concern for chronic diseases and the growing importance of intervention campaigns combined to make funds available to support interdisciplinary exploration of these various themes (60, 84, 215).

External economic and political trends continue to influence these strivings for interdisciplinary collaboration. Sociologists' involvement with US epidemiologists in the 1960s and 1970s was supported largely by funding directed at cardiovascular diseases and cancer (215). Anthropologists' involvement with epidemiologists is supported today largely by domestic funding for particular chronic health risks, including cardiovascular diseases, hypertension, cancer, smoking, and alcohol abuse; domestic and international funding directed at AIDS and reproductive health; and at particular international child survival themes (diarrheal diseases, respiratory infections, and immunizations). As these themes change, so will the focus and breadth of interdisciplinary exchange.

The history of the development of professions in the United States has also contributed to the present separation between anthropology and epidemiology. In Latin America, a school of social medicine more supportive of linkages between anthropology and epidemiology has flourished for some time (16, 17, 70). A book entitled *Epidemiology Without Numbers* (1) has been published in Portuguese in Brazil, and a Spanish-language epidemiology methods text (17) published in Ecuador emphasizes the importance of qualitative research tools such as key informant interviewing and life histories.

French-speaking anthropologists and epidemiologists have highlighted the complementary role anthropology's community perspective could play in population-based epidemiological analyses of health (32, 41). Francophone researchers have called for an anthropological epidemiology of depression (12), cancer (94, 95), and schistosomiasis (173).

Modes of Contemporary Exchange

In the topical areas that follow, most collaboration between anthropology and epidemiology could be called "parallel," because researchers continue their disciplinary allegiance but work on a common project. Other patterns of collaboration can also be identified. Crossover collaboration is undertaken by particular individuals who make uncommon efforts within one discipline despite having primary identification within another discipline. This has far more often involved an anthropologist working in epidemiological projects than the reverse. Interdisciplinary foraging (see 197), wherein researchers borrow another discipline's concepts and methods, has become more common over the past decade (193). Finally, collaboration through merging involves deeper and more equal transfers between disciplines, combining method and theory.

Areas of Exchange

Both anthropology and epidemiology have appropriated and redefined key social and cultural concepts, including culture change, social stratification, various specific predictor and health outcome variables, and the concept of risk. Much of the collaborative work that has been undertaken focuses on methodological exchange, including processes of measurement and classification. Descriptive and intervention studies of human behavior are another important area of cross-disciplinary exchange. Anthropologists have used epidemiological concepts and techniques for social analysis. Each of these areas is reviewed in turn below.

CULTURE CHANGE AND STRESS   Epidemiological models often do not address how the sociocultural context mediates the relationship between psychosocial stressors and disease outcomes. Although measures of stress have persistently been associated with multiple disease outcomes, epidemiologists have devoted little attention to the role culture plays in this process. Some epidemiologists have used concepts and definitions of culture change and acculturation rejected by anthropologists. Important work on specific mediators has been undertaken by anthropologists; for example, on the significance of incongruities between life-style and status on depressive symptoms (52) and on hypertension (50). These and other studies (10, 103, 104, 107, 162) have hypothesized that stress is context dependent and that social support and coping strategies are unequally distributed across social groups.

SOCIAL STRATIFICATION Anthropologists view stratification as a key feature of complex societies, and thus they take it as given that health and disease will be differentially distributed among social groups. Epidemiologists have measured the effects of hierarchy on health since the mid-eighteenth century and, especially in the United Kingdom (43), have paid explicit attention to health differences based in class. Epidemiologists in the United States have been less concerned with class and power and more likely to treat class or race as confounding variables than as predictors (117, 131). There are hopeful signs of linkages between anthropologists and epidemiologists interested in looking at the health effects of stratification. For example, social epidemiologists have summarized the evidence about the health effects of social class and have described the many problems with how it has been conceptualized and measured (2, 14, 117, 131, 149, 207). Medical anthropologists, especially those concerned with political economic analyses, have done epidemiological studies of the health effects of poverty and social stratification in the United States (164, 187). Other anthropologists have produced broad reviews of the varied effects of stratification on health through time, drawing on both anthropological and epidemiological data (35, 142).

Race and ethnicity are also markers of social stratification that have received significant attention in health research. Much epidemiological research has been criticized for conflating social categories of hierarchy with perceptions of skin color, genetic inheritance, and biological difference (38, 116, 224). Anthropologists working in epidemiological settings have published important critiques of racial classifications within public health statistics. Hahn, for example (83), questioned many assumptions critical to the validity of race as a public health variable. His argument is particularly compelling because while it employs standard anthropological questions about the stability of racial categorizations over time, it uses epidemiological data to show how boundaries change and identities shift. Hahn et al (85) used birth and death certificates to show inconsistencies in racial codes for the same individuals over time. An issue of the CDC's *Morbidity and Mortality Weekly Report*

(30) followed these concerns, concluding that "Race and ethnicity are not risk factors—they are markers used to better understand risk factors." Pappas (163), who wrote about the differential rates of change in life expectancy between blacks and whites in the United States, presented a more nuanced picture of the meaning of race. He looked at living conditions, occupation, education, and income in addition to race and wrote about the permeability of social categories. Dressler has written a series of important papers on health-related effects of race and ethnicity, exploring the contribution of status incongruity to increasing hypertension (52). The journal *Ethnicity and Disease* specializes in articles on this topic (e.g. 42, 54). Some anthropologists have proposed that ethnicity is a more accurate and appropriate measure of social differentiation than race (83, 161). Physical anthropologists have contributed many important critiques of the use of race in epidemiology and public health research (80, 137).

UNPACKING OTHER SOCIAL AND CULTURAL VARIABLES   The anthropological critiques of standard epidemiological variables like race and socioeconomic status result in a type of "unpacking" of those variables. This unpacking involves identifying underlying assumptions in their development and use or demonstrating the contextual nature of their meanings (135, 217). Other variables have also received similar critical attention from anthropologists. These include religion (127), maternal education (134, 136), time (73, 90, 226), placebo effects (148), social support (103), stress (53, 230), and even behaviors like medication consumption (216), Type A behavior (90), and hyperactivity (178).

THE NATURE OF RISK AND VULNERABILITY   The concept of risk itself has been a fundamental topic for analysis by anthropologists interested in epidemiology (73, 74, 91). Some of this interest results from the large increase in the production of risk-related information in the medical literature (188) and the changing public perception of risk, exposure, and personal susceptibility (47, 48, 86). Danger and menace in modern Western cultures is increasingly expressed through an idiom of risk (79, 138). Anthropologists have compared lay, epidemiological, and clinical languages concerning the risks of childbirth (112) or the risks of infertility (101, 102).

Anthropologists have made important contributions to the epidemiology of AIDS by examining how individuals and groups perceive risk and how culture influences risk behaviors in a wide variety of settings (37, 66, 69, 81, 98, 110, 111, 139, 145, 146, 160, 166, 211). Anthropologists (73) and some epidemiologists (e.g. 141, 208) have been critical of epidemiological approaches that lead to individualized notions of risk. Such approaches postulate that ignorance of risk-enhancing behavior is the main cause of disease. They consequently have proposed individual educational interventions to increase knowledge of such risks. Anthropologists countered that social, cultural, political, and economic conditions place entire groups in positions more vulnerable to disease (64, 65, 77, 165, 166, 187) and that education is a necessary but not sufficient component of successful behavior-change campaigns (7).

METHODOLOGY AND MEASUREMENT   Medical anthropology began to confront questions about cross-cultural health research when international development, international health research, and funding for population research expanded in the 1950s and 1960s. Epidemiologists have been confronting these issues in the 1980s and 1990s as they receive funding for multinational clinical trials, prevalence studies, and intervention studies (56, 217). They have, by necessity, been publishing the differences between conceptual and semantic equivalence of interview schedules used in different cultures (54, 119, 120, 212). This issue occupied psychological anthropologists (31, 62) and cross-cultural psychiatrists (126) in prior decades.

Ethnographic methods have been used to construct scales of a variety of psychosocial phenomena, including life events, coping styles, and social support. For example, culture-specific notions of perceived stress were included in a life events scale looking at stress and hypertension in St. Lucia (50), and measures of perceived racism were used to look at coping, economic stress, and distress in a southern black community (51). Culture-specific measures of social support were used in a study of hypertension in Mexico (55). Ethnographic and observational techniques were used in AIDS research to formulate risk categories for use in epidemiological research (111, 191). Similar uses of ethnographic techniques for instrument development have been described in research on immunizations (39), diarrheal diseases (71, 108, 155), and hypertension (104).

The validity of various data collection techniques has also become an increasing focus of anthropological and epidemiological attention (11, 33, 93, 108, 172, 175, 190, 196, 198). Anthropological techniques and concerns can be seen in epidemiological articles about problems in patient recruitment and follow-up (159, 169) and the validity of cross-cultural comparison (63, 96).

The AIDS epidemic has created interest in and funding for a large series of research efforts on human sexual behavior. Anthropologists have helped to identify and overcome many of the measurement and selection biases inherent in such sensitive research within stigmatized or marginalized populations (29, 191, 228). AIDS has also been an important area where anthropologists and epidemiologists have collaborated in the design of effective intervention programs. Ethnographic research has been an important part of such intervention program development in various AIDS studies (23, 69, 98, 110, 139). Anthropologists and other social scientists have criticized the ways in which some epidemiologists have characterized both the nature of AIDS risk and the composition and behavior of specific "at risk" populations (73, 78, 111, 146, 157, 160, 187).

Some of these measurement issues have also been raised by US epidemiologists, who confront the challenges of working to determine the particular influences of culture and ethnicity on disease outcome. At times these explorations take quite different form than they might in anthropology. For example, epidemiologists have published papers about problems in using computerized algorithms to recognize "Hispanic" surnames (92), about the types of incentives people need to participate in research studies (180), or about differences in pregnancy reporting between husbands and wives (67). Medical historians have looked at these issues over longer periods, discussing, for example, how culture influences measurements of morbidity (109).

Bias, defined as effects "tending to produce results that depart systematically from the true values" (123), is a critical concept in epidemiological research. Epidemiologists have classified many different types of bias (179), but anthropologists reviewing the list will recognize many familiar research topics. What epidemiologists call "selection bias" is related to what anthropologists might call "health-seeking behavior"; what epidemiologists call "interview" or "recall" bias might be called "presentation of self," an "explanatory model," or an "illness narrative." Thus the same phenomena (e.g. incongruities between observed and reported behavior) are labeled, explained, and managed in very different ways. In epidemiology, bias is explored so that it can be minimized; in anthropology, it is explored so that it can be explained. Various authors have confronted these measurement issues and discussed them with reference to bias (11, 33, 67, 196, 198, 218).

Interdisciplinary foraging and borrowing increased in the mid-1970s as advocates called for multimethod research combining qualitative and quantitative methods, also known as triangulation (82, 152, 213). In addition to the uses (mentioned above) of ethnographic methods to refine epidemiological instruments, anthropologists and epidemiologists applied these methodologies for other purposes. For example, qualitative and quantitative methods were used in a study of health-care utilization for malaria and diarrhea in Rwanda (76), in a diarrheal disease control program in Papua New Guinea (71), in infant-feeding programs in Nigeria (9) and Egypt (129), and in a study of health resource utilization in Turkey (227).

ILLNESS CLASSIFICATION   Three areas of illness classification have prompted work by both anthropologists and epidemiologists.

Folk illness   Epidemiological work on so-called folk illnesses began in the mid-1960s (176) and became more popular a decade later (24, 124, 144, 168, 219, 223). Many of these studies used survey techniques to establish the prevalence of various nonbiomedical categories of illness. In this instance anthropologists were applying epidemiological techniques to symptom lists and illness categories they abstracted from traditional diagnoses and treatments.

Illness constructs in epidemiology   Critiques of the way epidemiologists construct and reify diseases and risk groups form another portion of the anthropological literature (73, 77, 151, 154). These works pay particular attention to the epidemiological concerns for modal behavior and central tendencies and binary separations into diseased vs disease-free. The anthropologists argue that such dichotomies both obscure the real truth about disease risk (that it is incremental rather than binary) and mislead those potentially at risk into believing that because they do not fall into an identified "risk group" for a disease, they are immune to that disease.

Folk taxonomy and lay epidemiology   Anthropological descriptions of disease taxonomy have been especially important in improving the accuracy of epidemiological assessments and the utility of prevention or treatment methods. Much of this work has been done on diarrheal diseases (44, 71, 121, 154, 155, 167, 229), but it has also been undertaken on the relationship between perceived season and susceptibility to malaria (226) and on respiratory infections (156).

Some epidemiologists have begun to explore the same idea, describing it as lay or popular epidemiology. Lay epidemiology describes the illness-related concepts of a population, as folk taxonomy does, but it is more often used for explorations of illness categories within developed countries, especially the United States and the United Kingdom (8, 19, 45, 72, 170).

DESCRIPTIVE AND INTERVENTION STUDIES OF BEHAVIOR   Human behavior is often incorporated as a variable in epidemiological studies, though usually as a predisposing or risk-enhancing factor between host and disease. Some epidemiologists have begun to confront the complexity of behavior and cognition in their modeling processes (18, 115). For example, the concept of "endogeneity" has been developed so that epidemiological models can account for the likelihood that awareness of health conditions and health risks will itself influence behaviors (18). Briscoe et al illustrated the idea by referring to women who have had past problems with pregnancy or who expect problems with a current pregnancy. They are more likely to seek prenatal care. If endogeneity is not considered in these circumstances, it can appear that prenatal care adversely affects child health, and its beneficial effects can be underestimated (18:150).

Important collaborative work between anthropologists and epidemiologists has focused on behavioral factors in disease transmission and production, yielding a refined description of behavioral pathways (58, 100, 174, 184, 195). Anthropological perspectives have been helpful in identifying behavioral pathways of infectious disease transmission such as water use or contact with feces, pathways often not easily included in epidemiological research designs (5, 36, 59). Ethnography has also been used to help explain causal assemblages of risk and disease in occupational health (105).

Much collaborative work between medical anthropology and epidemiology has focused on preventing and controlling diseases of populations. Epidemiology focuses on measurable behavior change. It tends to quantify and thus oversimplify behavioral and life-style factors involved in the transmission of infectious diseases and the production of chronic diseases. Medical anthropology contextualizes behavior and describes culture-specific life-styles. While epidemiologists begin with behavior-change objectives defined according to disease etiology, anthropologists have traditionally shown how behavior patterns are culturally mediated. Anthropologists have shown the changing meanings of the concept of life-style and how it is now used to encompass behavioral risk factors (40). Divergences between lay and professional ways of acquiring risk-related knowledge have been documented in anthropological studies of toxic waste contamination (8, 19) and health promotion campaigns (72).

Representatives of both disciplines have collaborated in recent years to develop more appropriate methods of disease prevention and control. The cultural construction of disease and its influence on the design of preventive programs have been documented for diarrheal diseases (44, 71, 108, 232), dysentery (155, 167), AIDS (69, 98), schistosomiasis (173), and parasitic diseases (58, 143). Epidemiologists and medical anthropologists have collaborated in a number of cross-disciplinary projects related to the control of tropical diseases (184) and health systems research (193). Examples include the development of interventions for the control of diarrheal diseases (232), malaria (36, 226), dengue fever (113), and Chagas' disease (5) and interventions to improve nutrition (9, 129) and pregnancy outcome (122). Attempts to control "posttransition" health problems (see 22) such as cancer (94, 95) and substance abuse (46, 186) have also benefited from this type of collaboration.

USING EPIDEMIOLOGY FOR SOCIAL ANALYSIS   An area of great potential for joint anthropological and epidemiological investigation falls within what Ralph Audy called "the epidemiology of ideas" (4, see also 193a, 193b). Audy & Dunn wrote that "ideas may be likened to infectious particles, transmitted among people who may be susceptible or who may also develop resistance (immunity)" (4:349). They provided an interesting metaphor, also used by Lindenbaum in *Kuru Sorcery* (133). In *Kuru Sorcery* Lindenbaum speaks of "an epidemiology of social relations," developing the notion in this way: "Chains of linkage transmit fashions and foods, agricultural technology, illness, and genetic material in small increments across vast regions. The limits and the vitality of particular networks may be defined by a language, a slow virus, or attitudes and concepts." (133:142). Disease can be analyzed as an insult to the social body, and epi demiological principles can be (at least metaphorically) applied to trace the ramifications of disease transmission across social networks. Related uses of the metaphor can be seen in the phrase "the epidemiology of functional apartheid and human rights abuses" (88) or in emerging studies of the epidemiology of violence (64).

Although the metaphor of an "epidemiology of ideas" has thus produced specific useful results in anthropology, the notion can be pushed farther. To date, epidemics of fainting or of other physical symptoms with no organic cause among predominantly school-age populations (87, 189) have excited little anthropological attention, despite their potential categorization as epidemics of pure ideas. In addition, the various epidemiological designations of risk and disease prevalence themselves are ideas, capable of their own spread and interpretation. Epidemiologists are beginning to recognize this, e.g. in an editorial entitled "Do epidemiologists cause epidemics?" (61). This editorial examined the social consequences of identifying disease trends and outlined how diagnostic practice sometimes shifts according to (mistaken) predictions about the onset of an epidemic.

DISEASE AS INDIVIDUAL VS POPULATION ATTRIBUTE   Ecological studies in epidemiology are those that use correlations between variables at the group level (e.g. national statistics on fat consumption correlated to national cancer rates) to substitute for risk measures at the individual level. Although epidemiologists long dismissed such studies as committing errors of inference, they have recently begun to reexamine the utility of ecological designs (e.g. 202, 203). These debates offer specific room for anthropological input. The issue within epidemiology is that some effects cannot be measured if social groups are seen only as collections of individuals (208). This is particularly important in prevention design, where much epidemiological and public health research has a limited vision of social change processes and too often focuses on change at the individual level (33, 45, 73, 84, 99, 171).

CONCLUSION

Although it was possible to speak of "benign neglect" between medical anthropology and epidemiology in the 1980s, the broad range of collaboration included in this review indicates the richness of this work today. Nevertheless, the collaboration between anthropology and epidemiology in the past decade has been uneven. Multimethod research is increasingly undertaken, but theoretical challenges and conceptual critiques are still relatively uncommon.

How then to achieve more fruitful exchanges, both critical and constructive? Many suggestions are obvious: better training in a broader range of methods and theories by both anthropologists and epidemiologists; fuller realization of the respective strengths and weaknesses of each discipline's contribution to research design; more attempts by each to recognize or create and take advantage of collaborative opportunities.

Because disciplinary exchanges are achieved through the concrete work of individuals, it is also important to undertake more studies of "anthropology in epidemiology," ethnographies (or even short reports) about collaborative or contested sites (e.g. 199), or epidemiological projects in communities (e.g. 7). Such studies can help illustrate new territory for productive exchanges between medical anthropology and epidemiology.

Many areas are left for those interested in exploring exchanges between anthropology and epidemiology. As epidemiology becomes more concerned with host factors in disease and more involved in prevention (a word only recently added to the title of the Centers for Disease Control and Prevention), anthropology becomes even more relevant. Themes likely to engage both disciplines more closely in the future include the interrelationship between environmental change and human health, the causes and prevention of antibiotic resistance, the causes and management of new and resurgent infectious disease epidemics from hantavirus to Lassa fever, tuberculosis to cholera (128, 192), and physical as well as structural violence and war as public health issues (64, 88).

We propose that some anthropological collaboration with epidemiology should be labeled as "cultural epidemiology" and that this area should be distinguished from the more common "social epidemiology." Cultural epidemiology should be preoccupied with cross-cultural analyses of the distribution and determinants of disease and illness and with unpacking variables (e.g. race, class, religion, time) to illustrate and specify their theoretical context and meaning. Various innovative methodological and theoretical opportunities await the cultural epidemiologist. Nesting anthropological studies within epidemiological samples can increase generalizability and improve estimates of nonresponse bias, both important barriers to the legitimacy of some anthropological conclusions. Anthropological knowledge of cross-cultural variability can be used to improve the development and measurement of epidemiological variables. Research results can be communicated more effectively to policymakers and to a public audience when both anthropological and epidemiological descriptions are employed. Conceptual and experimental work can be undertaken to determine the best measures of complex cultural and behavioral variables. Ethnographic and epidemiological information can be used to design health surveillance systems that return data to communities in more comprehensible forms, creating new meanings for the term "popular epidemiology."

Any *Annual Review* chapter, as well as any article cited in an *Annual Review* chapter, may be purchased from the Annual Reviews Preprints and Reprints service. 1-800-347-8007; 415-259-5017; email: arpr@class.org

Literature Cited

1. Almeida Filho N. 1989. *Epidemiologia Sem Numeros.* Rio de Janeiro: Campus
1a. American Anthropological Association. 1993. A proposed curriculum for the third decade of medical anthropology training. *Anthropol. Newsl.* 34(5):15-16
1b. American Anthropological Association. 1993. Commentaries on "A proposed curriculum for the third decade of medical anthropology training." *Anthropol. Newsl.* 34(9):41–42
2. Antonovsky A. 1967. Social class, life expectancy and overall mortality. *Milbank Mem. Fund Q.* 45:31–73
3. Armelagos GJ, Leatherman T, Ryan M, Sibley L. 1992. Biocultural synthesis in medical anthropology. *Med. Anthropol.* 14: 35–52
4. Audy JR, Dunn FL. 1974. Community health. In *Human Ecology,* ed. F Sargent, pp. 345–63. Amsterdam: North-Holland
5. Azogue E. 1993. Women and congenital Chagas' disease in Santa Cruz, Bolivia: epidemiological and sociocultural aspects. *Soc. Sci. Med.* 37:503–11
6. Baker PT. 1988. Human population biology: a developing paradigm for biological anthropology. *Int. Soc. Sci. J.* 40:255–63
7. Balshem M. 1993. *Cancer in the Community: Class and Medical Authority.* Washington, DC: Smithson. Inst. Press
8. Baxter J, Eyles J, Willms D. 1992. The Hagersville tire fire: interpreting risk through a qualitative research design. *Qual. Health Res.* 2:208–37
9. Bentley ME, Dickin KL, Mebrahtu S, Kayode B, Oni GA, Verzosa CC, et al. 1991. Development of a nutritionally adequate and culturally appropriate weaning food in Kwara state, Nigeria: an interdisciplinary approach. *Soc. Sci. Med.* 33: 1103–11
10. Berkman LF. 1980. Physical health and the social environment: a social epidemiological perspective. In *The Relevance of Social Science for Medicine,* ed. L Eisenberg, A Kleinman, pp. 51–75. Dordrecht: Reidel
11. Bernard RH, Killworth P, Kronenfeld D, Sailer L. 1984. The problem of informant accuracy: the validity of retrospective data. *Annu. Rev. Anthropol.* 13:495–517
12. Bibeau G. 1981. Préalables à une épidemiologie anthropologique de la dépression. *Psychopath. Afr.* 17:96–112
13. Black N. 1994. Why we need qualitative research. *J. Epidemiol. Comm. Health* 48: 425–26
14. Blane D. 1995. Editorial: social determinants of health: socioeconomic status, social class and ethnicity. *Am. J. Public Health* 87:903–5
15. Bolton J. 1995. Medical practice and anthropological bias. *Soc. Sci. Med.* 40: 1655–61
16. Breilh J. 1989. *Epidemiología: Economía, Medicina y Política.* Mexico City: Fontamara
17. Breilh J. 1994. *Nuevos Conceptos y Técnicas de Investigación: Guía Pedagógica para un Taller de Metodología.* Quito: Ed. Cent. Estud. Asesor. Salud
18. Briscoe J, Akin J, Guilkey D. 1990. People are not passive acceptors of threats to health: endogeneity and its consequences. *Int. J. Epidemiol.* 19:147–53
19. Brown P. 1992. Popular epidemiology and toxic waste contamination: lay and professional ways of knowing. *J. Health Soc. Behav.* 33:267–81
20. Browner CH, Ortiz de Montellano BR, Rubel AJ. 1988. A methodology for cross-cultural ethnomedical research. *Curr. Anthropol.* 29:681–89
21. Burrage H. 1987. Epidemiology and community health: a strained connection? *Soc. Sci. Med.* 25:895–903
22. Caldwell JC. 1993. Health transition: the cultural, social and behavioural determinants of health in the third world. *Soc. Sci. Med.* 36:125–35
22a. Caldwell JC, Findley S, Caldwell P, Santow G, Cosford W, et al, eds. 1990. *What We Know about Health Transition: The Cultural, Social and Behavioural Determinants of Health.* Canberra: Health Trans. Cent., Aust. Natl. Univ.
23. Caldwell JC, Orubuloye IO, Caldwell P. 1994. Methodological advances in study-

ing the social context of AIDS in West Africa. See Ref. 22a, pp. 1–12

24. Carey JW. 1993. Distribution of culture-bound illnesses in the southern Peruvian Andes. *Med. Anthropol. Q.* 7:281–300

25. Carrithers M. 1990. Is anthropology art or science? *Curr. Anthropol.* 31:263–72

26. Cassel JC. 1964. Social science theory as a source of hypotheses in epidemiological research. *Am. J. Pub. Health* 54:1482–88

27. Cassel JC. 1976. The contribution of the social environment to host resistance. *Am. J. Epidemiol.* 104:107–23

28. Cassel JC, Patrick RC, Jenkins CD. 1960. Epidemiologic analysis of the health implications of culture change: a conceptual model. *Ann. NY Acad. Sci.* 84:938–49

29. Catania JA, Gibson DR, Chitwood DD, Coates TJ. 1990. Methodological problems in AIDS behavioral research: influences on measurement error and participation bias in studies of sexual behavior. *Psychol. Bull.* 108:339–62

30. Centers for Disease Control and Prevention. 1993. Use of race and ethnicity in public health surveillance: summary of the CDC/ATSDR Workshop. *Morb. Mort. Weekly Rep.* 42:1–17

31. Chance N. 1965. Acculturation, self-identification, and personality adjustment. *Am. Anthropol.* 67:372–93

32. Chaperon J. 1987. Santé et sociétés: regards épidémiologique et anthropologique. In *Etiologie et Perception de la Maladie dans les Sociétés Modernes et Traditionelles*, ed. AR Laurentin, pp. 41–49. Paris: Harmattan

33. Chen KH, Murray GF. 1976. Truths and untruths in village Haiti: an experiment in third world survey research. See Ref. 141a, pp. 241–62

34. Chibnik M. 1985. The use of statistics in sociocultural anthropology. *Annu. Rev. Anthropol.* 14:135–57

35. Cohen MN. 1989. *Health and the Rise of Civilization.* New Haven, CT: Yale Univ. Press

36. Coimbra CE. 1988. Human factors in the epidemiology of malaria in the Brazilian amazon. *Hum. Organ.* 47:254–59

37. Cominos ED, Gottschang SK, Scrimshaw SC. 1989. Kuru, AIDS and unfamiliar social behaviour: biocultural considerations in the current epidemic. *J. R. Soc. Med.* 82:95–98

38. Cooper RA, David R. 1986. The biological concept of race and its application to public health and epidemiology. *J. Health Pol. Policy Law* 11:97–116

39. Coreil J. 1989. Use of ethnographic research for instrument development in a case-control study of immunization use in Haiti. *Int. J. Epidemiol.* 18:S33–37

40. Coreil J, Levin JS, Jaco EG. 1985. Life style: an emergent concept in the sociomedical sciences. *Cult. Med. Psychol.* 9: 423–37

41. Corin E. 1990. *Comprendre pour soigner autrement.* Montréal: Presses Univ. Montréal

42. Crews DE, Bindon JR. 1991. Ethnicity as a taxonomic tool in biomedical and biosocial research. *Ethnicity Dis.* 1:42–49

43. Davey Smith G, Bartley M, Blane D. 1990. The Black report on socioeconomic inequalities in health 10 years on. *Br. Med. J.* 301:373–77

44. Davey Smith G, Gorther A, Hoppenbrouwer J. 1993. The cultural construction of childhood diarrhea in rural Nicaragua: relevance for epidemiology and health promotion. *Soc. Sci. Med.* 36:1613–24

45. Davison C, Davey Smith G, Frankel SJ. 1990. Lay epidemiology and the prevention paradox: the implications of coronary candidacy for health education. *Soc. Health Illn.* 13:1–19

46. Delaney W, Ames GM. 1993. Integration and exchange in multidisciplinary alcohol research. *Soc. Sci. Med.* 37:5–13

47. Douglas M. 1986. *Risk Acceptability According to the Social Sciences.* London: Routledge & Kegan Paul

48. Douglas M, Wildavsky A. 1982. *Risk and Culture: An Essay on the Selection of Technical and Environmental Dangers.* Berkeley: Univ. Calif. Press

49. Dressler WW. 1982. *Hypertension and Culture Change: Acculturation and Disease in the West Indies.* South Salem, NY: Redgrave

50. Dressler WW. 1984. Hypertension and perceived stress: a St. Lucian example. *Ethos* 12:265–83

51. Dressler WW. 1985. The social and cultural context of coping: action, gender and symptoms in a southern black community. *Soc. Sci. Med.* 21:499–506

52. Dressler WW. 1988. Social inconsistency and psychological distress. *J. Health Soc. Behav.* 29:79–91

53. Dressler WW. 1990. Culture, stress, and disease. See Ref. 109a, pp. 248–67

54. Dressler WW. 1991. Social class, skin color, and arterial blood pressure in two societies. *Ethnicity Dis.* 1:60–77

55. Dressler WW, Mata A, Chavez A, Viteri FE, Gallagher P. 1986. Social support and arterial pressure in a central Mexican community. *Psychosom. Med.* 48:338–50

56. Dressler WW, Viteri FE, Chavez A, Grell GAC, Dos Santos JE. 1991. Comparative research in social epidemiology: measurement issues. *Ethnicity Dis.* 1:379–93

57. Dunn FL. 1975. *Causal assemblages in epidemiology as sources of hypotheses in*

anthropological research. Presented at Annu. Meet. Am. Anthropol. Assoc., 74th, San Francisco

58. Dunn FL. 1979. Behavioral aspects of the control of parasitic diseases. *Bull. World Health Organ.* 57:499–512

59. Dunn FL. 1990. Human behavior and the communicable diseases of childhood. *Am. J. Health* 80:141–42

60. Dunn FL, Janes CR. 1986. Introduction: medical anthropology and epidemiology. See Ref. 106, pp. 3–34

61. Editorial. 1993. Do epidemiologists cause epidemics? *Lancet* 341:993–94

62. Egerton RB. 1970. Method in psychological anthropology. In *A Handbook of Method in Cultural Anthropology*, ed. R Naroll, R Cohen, pp. 338–52. New York: Columbia Univ. Press

63. Eyton J, Neuwirth G. 1984. Cross-cultural validity: ethnocentrism in health studies with special reference to the Vietnamese. *Soc. Sci. Med.* 18:447–53

64. Farmer P. 1996. On suffering and structural violence: a view from below. *Daedalus* 125:261–83

65. Farmer P, Connors M, Simmons J, eds. 1996. *Women, Poverty, and AIDS: Sex, Drugs, and Structural Violence.* Monroe: Common Courage

66. Feldman DA, ed. 1990. *Culture and AIDS.* New York: Praeger

67. Fikree FF, Gray RH, Shah F. 1993. Can men be trusted? A comparison of pregnancy histories reported by husbands and wives. *Am. J. Epidemiol.* 138:237–42

68. Fleck AC, Ianni FAJ. 1958. Epidemiology and anthropology: some suggested affinities in theory and method. *Hum. Organ.* 16:38–40

69. Ford N, Koetsawang S. 1991. The sociocultural context of the transmission of HIV in Thailand. *Soc. Sci. Med.* 33:405–14

70. Franco S, Nunes E, Duarte E, Breilh J, Granda E, et al. 1991. *Debates en Medicina Social.* Serie Recursos Humanos, 92. Quito: Organ. Panam. Salud/Asoc. Latinoam. Med. Soc.

71. Frankel SJ. 1984. Oral rehydration therapy: combining anthropological and epidemiological approaches in the evaluation of a Papua New Guinea program. *J. Trop. Med. Hyg.* 87:137–42

72. Frankel SJ, Davison C, Davey Smith G. 1995. Lay epidemiology and the rationality of responses to health education. *Br. J. Gen. Pract.* 41:428–38

73. Frankenberg RJ. 1993. Risk: anthropological and epidemiological narratives of prevention. See Ref. 136a, pp. 219–42

74. Frankenberg RJ. 1994. Impact of HIV/AIDS on concepts relating to risk and culture within British community epidemiol-

ogy: candidates or targets for prevention. *Soc. Sci. Med.* 38:1325–35

75. Franklin S. 1995. Science as culture, cultures of science. *Annu. Rev. Anthropol.* 24: 163–84

76. Glik DC, Parker K, Muligande G, Hategikamana B. 1986–87. Integrating qualitative and quantitative survey techniques. *Int. Q. Community Health Educ.* 7:181–200

77. Glick Schiller N. 1992. What's wrong with this picture? The hegemonic construction of culture in AIDS research in the United States. *Med. Anthropol. Q.* 6:237–54

78. Glick Schiller N, Crystal S, Lewellen D. 1994. Risky business: the cultural construction of AIDS risk groups. *Soc. Sci. Med.* 38:1337–46

79. Gifford SM. 1986. The meaning of lumps: a case study of the ambiguities of risk. See Ref. 106, pp. 213–46

80. Goodman AH. 1995. The problematics of "race" in contemporary biological anthropology. In *Biological Anthropology: The State of the Science*, ed. NT Boaz, LD Wolfe, pp. 215–39. Bend, OR: Int. Inst. Evol. Res.

81. Gorman EM. 1986. The AIDS epidemic in San Francisco: epidemiological and anthropological perspectives. See Ref. 106, pp. 157–72

82. Greene J, McClintock C. 1985. Triangulation in evaluation: design and analysis issues. *Eval. Rev.* 9:523–45

83. Hahn RA. 1992. The state of federal health statistics on racial and ethnic groups. *J. Am. Med. Assoc.* 267:268–71

84. Hahn RA. 1995. Anthropology and epidemiology: one logic or two? In *Sickness and Healing: An Anthropological Perspective*, ed. RA Hahn, pp. 99–128. New Haven, CT: Yale Univ. Press

85. Hahn RA, Mulinare J, Teutsch S. 1992. Inconsistencies in coding race and ethnicity between birth and death in US infants. *J. Am. Med. Assoc.* 267:259–63

86. Hayes MV. 1992. On the epistemology of risk: language, logic and social science. *Soc. Sci. Med.* 35:401–7

87. Hefez A. 1985. The role of the press and the medical community in the epidemic of 'mysterious gas poisoning' in the Jordan West Bank. *Am. J. Psychiatr.* 142: 833–37

88. Heggenhougen HK. 1995. The epidemiology of functional apartheid and human rights abuses [editorial]. *Soc. Sci. Med.* 40: 281–84

89. Heggenhougen HK, Shore L. 1986. Cultural components of behavioural epidemiology: implications for primary health care. *Soc. Sci. Med.* 22:1235–45

90. Helman CG. 1987. Heart disease and the cultural construction of time: the Type A

behaviour pattern as a Western culture-bound syndrome. *Soc. Sci. Med.* 25:969–79

91. Helman CG. 1994. Cultural factors in epi demiology. In *Culture, Health, and Illness: Introduction for Health Professionals.* Oxford: Butterworth-Heinemann. 3rd ed.

92. Howard CA, Samet JM, Buechley RW, Schrag SD, Key CR. 1983. Survey research in New Mexico Hispanics: some methodological issues. *Am. J. Epidemiol.* 117: 27–34

93. Horwitz RI, Yu EC. 1985. Problems and proposals for interview data in epidemiological research. *Int. J. Epidemiol.* 14: 463–67

94. Hubert A. 1985. Epidémiologie et anthropologie: "La preuve du pudding c' est quand on le mange." *Sci. Soc. Santé* 3: 169–81

95. Hubert A. 1990. Applying anthropology to the epidemiology of cancer. *Anthropol. Today* 6:16–18

96. Hunt SM. 1986. Cross-cultural issues in the use of socio-medical indicators. *Health Pol.* 6:149–58

97. Huss-Ashmore R, Johnston FE. 1985. Bio anthropological research in developing countries. *Annu. Rev. Anthropol.* 14: 475–528

98. Ingstad B. 1990. The cultural construction of AIDS and its consequences for prevention in Botswana. *Med. Anthropol. Q.* 4: 28–40

99. Inhorn MC. 1995. Medical anthropology and epidemiology: divergences or convergences? *Soc. Sci. Med.* 40:285–90

100. Inhorn MC, Brown P. 1990. The anthropology of infectious disease. *Annu. Rev. Anthropol.* 19:89–117

101. Inhorn MC, Buss KA. 1993. Infertility, infection, and iatrogenesis in Egypt: the anthropological epidemiology of blocked tubes. *Med. Anthropol.* 15:217–44

102. Inhorn MC, Buss KA. 1994. Ethnography, epidemiology, and infertility in Egypt. *Soc. Sci. Med.* 39:671–86

103. Jacobson D. 1987. The cultural context of social support and support networks. *Med. Anthropol. Q.* 1:42–67

104. Janes CR. 1990. *Migration, Social Change and Health: A Samoan Community in Urban California.* Stanford, CA: Stanford Univ. Press

105. Janes CR, Ames GM. 1992. Ethnographic explanations for the clustering of attendance, injury, and health problems in a heavy machinery assembly plant. *J. Occup. Med.* 34:993–1003

106. Janes CR, Stall R, Gifford SM, eds. 1986. *Anthropology and Epidemiology: Interdisciplinary Approaches to the Study of Health and Disease.* Dordrecht: Reidel

107. Jenkins C, Dimitrakakis M, Cook I, Sand-ers R, Stallman N. 1989. Culture change and epidemiological patterns among the Hagahai, Papua New Guinea. *Hum. Ecol.* 17:27–57

108. Jenkins C, Howard P. 1992. The use of ethnography and structured observations in the study of risk factors for the transmission of diarrhea in highland Papua New Guinea. *Med. Anthropol.* 15:1–16

109. Johansson SR. 1992. Measuring the cultural inflation of morbidity during the decline of mortality. *Health Trans. Rev.* 2: 78–89

109a. Johnson TM, Sargent CF, eds. *Medical Anthropology: Contemporary Theory and Method.* New York: Praeger

110. Kane S. 1993. National discourse and the dynamics of risk: ethnography and AIDS intervention. *Hum. Organ.* 52:224–28

111. Kane S, Mason T. 1992. "IV drug users" and "sex partners": the limits of epidemiological categories and the ethnography of risk. In *The Time of AIDS,* ed. G Herdt, S Lindenbaum, pp. 199–222. Newbury Park, CA: Sage

112. Kaufert PA, O'Neil J. 1993. Analysis of a dialogue on risks in childbirth: clinicians, epidemiologists, and Inuit women. See Ref. 136a, pp. 32–54

113. Kendall C, Hudelson P, Leontsini E, Winch PJ, Lloyd L, et al. 1991. Urbanization, dengue, and the health transition: anthropological contributions to international health. *Med. Anthropol. Q.* 5:257–67

114. Kleinman A. 1994. An anthropological perspective on objectivity: observation, categorization, and the assessment of suffering. In *Health and Social Change in International Perspective,* ed. LC Chen, A Kleinman, Ware NC, pp. 129–38. Boston: Harvard Sch. Health

115. Krieger N. 1994. Epidemiology and the web of causation: Has anyone seen the spider? *Soc. Sci. Med.* 39:887–903

116. Krieger N, Fee E. 1994. Man-made medicine and women's health: the biopolitics of sex/gender and race/ethnicity. *Int. J. Health Serv.* 24:265–83

117. Krieger N, Fee E. 1994. Social class: the missing link in US health data. *Int. J. Health Serv.* 24:25–44

118. Krieger N, Zierler S. 1996. What explains the public's health? A call for epidemiologic theory. *Epidemiol.* 7:107–9

119. Kroeger A. 1983. Health interview surveys in developing countries: a review of the methods and results. *Int. J. Epidemiol.* 12: 465–81

120. Kroeger A. 1985. Response errors and other problems of health interview surveys in developing countries. *World Health Stat. Q.* 38:15–33

121. Kunstadter P. 1991. Social and behavioral

factors in transmission and response to shigellosis. *Rev. Inf. Dis.* 13:S272–78

122. Langer A, Victora C, Victora M, Barros F, Farnot U, et al. 1993. The Latin American trial of psychosocial support during pregnancy: a social intervention evaluated through an experimental design. *Soc. Sci. Med.* 36:495–507

123. Last JM, ed. 1983. *A Dictionary of Epi demiology.* New York: Oxford Univ. Press

124. Lefley HP. 1979. Prevalence of potential falling-out cases among the Black, Latin and NonLatin White populations of the city of Miami. *Soc. Sci. Med.* 12:89–97

125. Leighton AH. 1994. Social science and psychiatric epidemiology. a difficult relationship. *Acta Psychiatr. Scand.* 385:7–12

126. Leighton AH, Lambo TA, Hughes CC, Leighton DC, Murphy JM, et al. 1963. *Psychiatric Disorder among the Yoruba.* Ithaca, NY: Cornell Univ. Press

127. Levin JS. 1994. Religion and health: Is there an association, is it valid, and is it causal? *Soc. Sci. Med.* 38:1475–82

128. Levine MM, Levine OS. 1994. Changes in human ecology and behavior in relation to the emergence of diarrheal diseases, including cholera. *Proc. Natl. Acad. Sci.* 91: 2390–94

129. Lewando Hundt GA, Forman MR. 1993. Interfacing anthropology and epidemiology: the Bedouin Arab infant feeding study. *Soc. Sci. Med.* 36:957–64

130. Lewis-Fernandez R, Kleinman A. 1995. Cultural psychiatry: theoretical, clinical, and research issues. *Psychol. Clin. North Am.* 18:433–48

131. Liberatos P, Link BG, Kelsey J. 1988. The measurement of social class in epidemiology. *Epidemiol. Rev.* 10:87–121

132. Lilienfeld AM. 1976. *Foundations of Epidemiology.* New York: Oxford Univ. Press

133. Lindenbaum S. 1979. *Kuru Sorcery: Disease and Danger in the New Guinea Highlands.* Mountain View, CA: Mayfield

134. Lindenbaum S. 1990. Maternal education and health care processes in Bangladesh: the health and hygiene of the middle classes. See Ref. 22a, pp. 425–40

135. Lindenbaum S. 1990. Methodology, 4: The view from anthropology. See Ref. 22a, 2: 906–8

136. Lindenbaum S, Chakraborty M, Elias M. 1989. The influence of maternal education on infant and child mortality in Bangladesh. In *Selected Readings in the Cultural, Social and Behavioural Determinants of Health,* ed. JC Caldwell, G Santow, pp. 112–31. Canberra: Health Trans. Cent., Aust. Natl. Univ.

136a. Lindenbaum S, Lock M, eds. 1993. *Knowledge, Power and Practice: The An thropology of Medicine and Everyday Life.* Berkeley: Univ. Calif. Press

137. Littlefield A, Lieberman L, Reynolds LT. 1982. Redefining race: the potential demise of a concept in physical anthropology. *Curr. Anthropol.* 23:641–55

138. Lupton D. 1993. Risk as moral danger: the social and political functions of risk discourse in public health. *Int. J. Health Serv.* 23:425–35

139. MacQueen KM. 1994. The epidemiology of HIV transmission: trends, structure and dynamics. *Annu. Rev. Anthropol.* 23: 509–26

140. Marmot M. 1981. Culture and illness: epi demiological evidence. In *Foundations of Psychosomatics,* ed. MJ Christie, PG Mellett, pp. 323–40. Chichester: Wiley

141. Marmot M. 1994. Social differentials in health within and between populations. *Daedalus* 123:197–216

141a. Marshall JF, Polgar S, eds. 1976. *Culture, Natality and Family Planning.* Chapel Hill: Univ. NC Press

142. Mascie-Taylor CG, ed. 1990. *Biosocial Aspects of Social Class.* Oxford: Oxford Univ. Press

143. Mata L. 1982. Socio-cultural factors in the control and prevention of parasitic diseases. *Rev. Inf. Dis.* 4:871–79

144. McCombie SC. 1987. Folk flu and viral syndrome: an epidemiological perspective. *Soc. Sci. Med.* 25:987–93

145. McCombie SC. 1990. AIDS in cultural, historic, and epidemiologic context. See ref. 66, pp. 9–27

146. McGrath JW, Schumann DA, Pearson-Marks J, Rwabukwali CB, Mukasa R, et al. 1992. Cultural determinants of sexual risk behavior for AIDS among Baganda women. *Med. Anthropol. Q.* 6:153–61

147. Meade M. 1990. Epidemiological geography. In *Advances in Medical Social Science,* ed. JL Ruffini, 2:341–59. New York: Gordon & Breach

148. Moerman DE. 1991. Physiology and symbols: the anthropological implications of the placebo effect. In *The Anthropology of Medicine: From Culture to Method,* ed. L Romanucci-Ross, DE Moerman, LR Tancredi, pp. 129–43. New York: Bergin & Garvey

149. Morgenstern H. 1985. Socioeconomic factors: concepts, measurement, and health effects. In *Measuring Psychosocial Variables in Epidemiologic Studies of Cardiovascular Disease: Proceedings of a Workshop,* ed. AM Ostfeld, ED Eaker, pp. 3–35. Publ. No. 85–2270. Washington, DC: US Dept. Health Hum. Serv.

150. Murphy JM. 1994. Anthropology and psychiatric epidemiology. *Acta Psychiatr. Scand.* 385:48–57 (Suppl.)

151. Murray S, Payne K. 1989. The social classification of AIDS in American epidemiology. *Med. Anthropol.* 10:115–28

152. Myers V. 1977. Toward a synthesis of ethnographic and survey methods. *Hum. Organ.* 36:244–51

153. Myntti C. 1991. The anthropologist as storyteller: picking up where others leave off in public health research. In *The Health Transition: Methods and Measures,* ed. A Cleland, AG Hill, pp. 227–36. Canberra: Aust. Natl. Univ., Health Trans. Cent.

154. Nations MK. 1986. Epidemiological research on infectious disease: quantitative rigor or rigormortis? Insights from ethnomedicine. See Ref. 106, pp. 97–123

155. Nichter M. 1991. Use of social science research to improve epidemiologic studies of and interventions for diarrhea and dysentery. *Rev. Inf. Dis.* 13:S265–71

156. Nichter M. 1993. Social science lessons from diarrhea research and their application to ARI. *Hum. Organ.* 52:53–67

157. Oppenheimer GM. 1988. In the eye of the storm: the epidemiological construction of AIDS. In *AIDS: The Burdens of History,* ed. E Fee, DM Fox, pp. 267–300. Berkeley: Univ. Calif. Press

158. Oppenheimer GM. 1995. Comments: epidemiology and the liberal arts: toward a new paradigm? *Am. J. Health* 85:918–20

159. Oyejide CO, Fagbami AH. 1988. An epidemiological study of Rotavirus diarrhea in a cohort of Nigerian infants. I. Methodology and experiences in the recruitment and follow-up of patients. *Int. J. Epidemiol.* 17:903–7

160. Packard RM, Epstein P. 1991. Epidemiologists, social scientists, and the structure of medical research on AIDS in Africa. *Soc. Sci. Med.* 33:771–94

161. Palinkas LA. 1987. A longitudinal study of ethnicity and disease incidence. *Med. Anthropol. Q.* 1:85–108

162. Palinkas LA, Pickwell SM. 1995. Acculturation as a risk factor for chronic disease among Cambodian refugees in the United States. *Soc. Sci. Med.* 40:1643–53

163. Pappas G. 1993. Editorial: elucidating the relationships between race, socioeconomic status, and health. *Am. J. Health* 84:892–93

164. Pappas G, Queen S, Hadden W, Fisher G. 1993. The increasing disparity in mortality between socioeconomic groups in the United States, 1960 and 1986. *New Engl. J. Med.* 329:103–9

165. Parker RG. 1991. *Bodies, Pleasures, and Passions: Sexual Culture in Contemporary Brazil.* Boston: Beacon

166. Parker RG, Herdt G, Carballo M. 1991. Sexual culture, HIV transmission, and AIDS research. *J. Sex Res.* 28:77–98

167. Pelto GH. 1991. The role of behavioral research in the prevention and management of invasive diarrheas. *Rev. Inf. Dis.* 13: S255–58

168. Pfifferling J-H. 1975. Some issues in the consideration of non-Western and Western folk practices as epidemiologic data. *Soc. Sci. Med.* 9:655–58

169. Phillips DL. 1972. Data collection as a social process: its implications for "true prevalence" studies of mental illness. In *Medical Men and Their Work,* ed. E Freidson, J Lorber, pp. 453–72. Chicago: Aldine/Atherton

170. Popay J, Williams G. 1996. Public health research and lay knowledge. *Soc. Sci. Med.* 42:759–68

171. Ratcliffe JW. 1976. Analyst biases in KAP surveys: a cross-cultural approach. *Stud. Fam. Plan.* 7:322–30

172. Ricci JA, Jerome NW, Megally N, Galal O, Harrison GG, Kirksey AV. 1995. Assessing the validity of informant recall: results of a time use pilot study in peri-urban Egypt. *Hum. Organ.* 54:304–8

173. Robert C, Bouvier S, Rougemont A. 1989. Epidemiology, anthropology and health education. *World Health Forum* 10:355–64

174. Roizman B. 1995. *Infectious Diseases in an Age of Change: The Impact of Human Ecology and Behavior on Disease Transmission.* Washington, DC: Natl. Acad. Sci.

175. Ross DA, Vaughan JP. 1986. Health interview surveys in developing countries: a methodological review. *Stud. Fam. Plan.* 17:78–94

176. Rubel AJ. 1964. The epidemiology of a folk illness: *Susto* in Hispanic America. *Ethnology* 3:268–83

177. Rubinstein RA. 1984. Epidemiology and anthropology: notes on science and scientism. *Comm. Cogn.* 17:163–85

178. Rubinstein RA, Perloff J. 1986. Identifying psychosocial disorders in children: on integrating epidemiological and anthropological understandings. See Ref. 106, pp. 303–32

179. Sackett DL. 1979. Bias in analytic research. *J. Chron. Dis.* 32:51–63

180. Savitz DA, Hamman RF, Grace C, Strook K. 1986. Respondents' attitudes regarding participation in an epidemiologic study. *Am. J. Epidemiol.* 123:894–900

181. Schnall PL, Kern R. 1981. Hypertension in American society: an introduction to historical materialist epidemiology. In *The Sociology of Health and Illness: Critical Perspectives,* ed. P Conrad, R Kern, pp. 97–122. New York: St. Martin's

182. Scotch N. 1960. A preliminary report on the relation of sociocultural factors to hypertension among the Zulu. *Ann. NY Acad. Sci.* 84:1000–9

183. Scotch N. 1963. Sociocultural factors in the

epidemiology of Zulu hypertension. *Am. J. Health* 53:1205–13

184. Singer B. 1989. Social science and the improvement of tropical disease control programs. *Ann. NY Acad. Sci.* 569: 275–87

185. Singer M. 1992. The application of theory in medical anthropology: an introduction. *Med. Anthropol.* 14:1–8

186. Singer M. 1993. Knowledge for use: anthropology and community-centered substance abuse research. *Soc. Sci. Med.* 37: 15–25

187. Singer M. 1994. AIDS and the health crisis of the rural US urban poor: the perspective of critical medical anthropology. *Soc. Sci. Med.* 39:931–48

188. Skolbekken H-A. 1995. The risk epidemic in medical journals. *Soc. Sci. Med.* 40: 291–305

189. Small GW, Feinberg DT, Steinberg D, Collins MT. 1994. A sudden outbreak of illness suggestive of mass hysteria in schoolchildren. *Arch. Fam. Med.* 3:711–16

190. Smith SA, Radel D. 1976. The KAP in Kenya: a critical look at survey methodology. See Ref. 141a, pp. 263–88

191. Smith HL. 1993. On the limited utility of KAP-style survey data in the practical epidemiology of AIDS, with reference to the AIDS epidemic in Chile. *Health Trans. Rev.* 3:1–16

192. Sommerfeld J. 1994. Emerging epidemic diseases: anthropological perspectives. *Ann. NY Acad. Sci.* 740:276–84

193. Sommerfeld J. 1994. Medical anthropology and epidemiology in international health: towards cross-disciplinarity in health systems research. *Entwicklungsethnologie* 4:5–18

193a. Sperber D. 1985. Anthropology and psychology: towards an epidemiology of representations. *Man* (NS) 20:73–89

193b. Sperber D. 1990. The epidemiology of beliefs. In *The Social Psychology of Widespread Beliefs*, ed. C Fraser, G Gaskell, pp. 25–44. Oxford: Clarendon

194. Spruit I, Kromhout D. 1987. Medical sociology and epidemiology: convergences, divergences and legitimate boundaries. *Soc. Sci. Med.* 25:579–87

195. Stanley NF, Joske RA, eds. 1980. *Changing Disease Patterns and Human Behaviour.* London: Academic

196. Stanton B, Clemens JD, Aziz KMA. 1987. Twenty-four hour recall, knowledge-attitude-practice questionnaires, and direct observations of sanitary practices: a comparative study. *World Health Organ. Bull.* 65: 217–22

197. Stone DH, Lewando-Hundt GA. 1987. Interdisciplinary "foraging": a strategy for collaboration between epidemiologists and social scientists. *Health Pol. Plan.* 5:20–21

198. Stone L, Campbell JG. 1984. The use and misuse of surveys in international development: an experiment from Nepal. *Hum. Organ.* 43:27–37

199. Streefland P. 1995. Methodological and management issues in applied interdisciplinary AIDS research in developing countries. *Hum. Organ.* 54:335–39

200. Susser M. 1987. Social science and public health. In *Epidemiology, Health, and Society*, ed. M Susser, pp. 177–85. New York/ Oxford: Oxford Univ. Press

201. Susser M. 1989. Epidemiology today: "a thought-tormented   world." *Int. J. Epidemiol.* 18:481–88

202. Susser M. 1994. The logic in ecological. I. The logic of analysis. *Am. J. Pub. Health* 84:825–29

203. Susser M. 1994. The logic in ecological. II. The logic of design. *Am. J. Pub. Health* 84:830–35

204. Susser M, Watson W, Hopper K. 1985. *Sociology in Medicine.* New York: Oxford

205. Swedlund AC, Armelagos GJ. 1990. *Disease in Populations in Transition: Anthropological and Epidemiological Perspectives.* New York: Bergin & Garvey

206. Syme SL. 1974. Behavioral factors associated with the etiology of physical disease: a social epidemiological approach. *Am. J. Public Health* 64:1043–45

207. Syme SL. 1976. Social class, susceptibility and sickness. *Am. J. Epidemiol.* 104:1–8

208. Syme SL. 1986. Strategies for health promotion. *Preventive Med.* 15:492–507

209. Syme SL. 1992. Social determinants of disease. In *Maxcy-Rosenau-Last: Public Health and Preventive Medicine,* ed. JM Last, RB Wallace, pp. 687–700. Norwalk, CT: Appleton & Lange. 13th ed.

210. Syme SL. 1994. The social environment and health. *Daedalus* 123:79–87

211. Ten Brummelhuis H, Herdt G, ed. 1995. *Culture and Sexual Risk: Anthropological Perspectives on AIDS.* New York: Gordon & Breach

212. Thompson NJ, Snider J, Farrer LS. 1985. Variations in national health care practices and behaviors and their influence on international research. *Int. J. Epidemiol.* 14: 457–62

213. Trend MG. 1978. On the reconciliation of qualitative and quantitative analyses: a case study. *Hum. Organ.* 37:345–54

214. Trostle JA. 1986. Anthropology and epidemiology in the twentieth century: a selective history of collaborative projects and theoretical affinities, 1920 to 1970. See Ref. 106, pp. 59–94

215. Trostle JA. 1986. Early work in anthropology and epidemiology: from social medicine to the germ theory, 1840 to 1920. See Ref. 106, pp. 25–57

216. Trostle JA. 1988. Medical compliance as an ideology. *Soc. Sci. Med.* 27:1299–308

217. Trostle JA. 1992. Anthropology and epidemiology in public health programs. In *Dengue: A Worldwide Problem, A Common Strategy*, ed. SB Halstead, H Gomez-Dantes, pp. 107–16. Mexico City: Mex. Ministry Health, Rockefeller Found.

218. Trostle JA, Hauser WA, Sharbrough FW. 1989. Psychologic and social adjustment to epilepsy. *Neurology* 39:633–37

219. Trotter RT, Ortiz de Montellano B, Logan MH. 1989. Fallen fontanelle in the American Southwest: its origin, epidemiology, and possible organic causes. *Med. Anthropol.* 10:211–21

220. True WR. 1990. Epidemiology and medical anthropology. See Ref. 109a, pp. 298–318

221. Turshen M. 1984. *The Political Ecology of Disease in Tanzania.* New Brunswick, NJ: Rutgers Univ. Press

222. Weed DL. 1994. Epidemiology, the humanities, and public health. *Am. J. Pub. Health* 85:914–18

223. Weller SC, Ruebush TK, Klein RE. 1991. An epidemiological description of a folk illness: a study of empacho in Guatemala. *Med. Anthropol.* 13:19–31

224. Weissman A. 1990. "Race-ethnicity": a dubious scientific concept. *Pub. Health Rep.* 105:102–3

225. White K. 1974. Contemporary epidemiology. *Int. J. Epidemiol.* 3:295–303

226. Winch PJ, Makemba AM, Kamazima SR, Lwihula GK, Lubega P, et al. 1994. Seasonal variation in the perceived risk of malaria: implications for the promotion of insecticide impregnated bed nets. *Soc. Sci. Med.* 39:63–75

227. Wirsing R. 1992. *Gesundheits und Krankheitsverhalten und seine kulturelle Einbettung in einer Kleinstadt im Südosten der Türkei.* Köln: Böhlau

228. Wyatt GE. 1991. Examining ethnicity versus race in AIDS-related sex research. *Soc. Sci. Med.* 33:37–45

229. Yoder S. 1995. Examining ethnomedical diagnoses and treatment choices for diarrheal disorders in Lubumbashi Swahili. *Med. Anthropol.* 16:211–47

230. Young A. 1980. The discourse on stress and the reproduction of conventional knowledge. *Soc. Sci. Med.* 14B:133–46

231. Young TK. 1994. *The Health of Native Americans: Towards a Biocultural Epidemiology.* New York: Oxford Univ. Press

232. Zeitlyn S, Islam F. 1991. The use of soap and water in two Bangladeshi communities: implications for the transmission of diarrhea. *Rev. Inf. Dis.* 13:S259–64

233. Zhai S, McGarvey ST. 1992. Temporal changes and rural-urban differences in cardiovascular disease risk factors and mortality in China. *Hum. Biol.* 64:807–19

Annu. Rev. Anthropol. 1996. 25:275–301

THE FOSSIL EVIDENCE FOR HUMAN EVOLUTION IN ASIA

Dennis A. Etler

Laboratory for Human Evolutionary Studies, University of California, Berkeley, California 94720

KEY WORDS: human evolution, Asia, *Homo erectus*, premodern *H. sapiens*, modern *H. sapiens*, regional continuity

ABSTRACT

The past decade has seen a dramatic increase in the number of fossil human specimens discovered in China. A better understanding of the tempo and mode of human evolution in Asia during the Pleistocene can be gained as a result. This new evidence has important implications for understanding the course of human evolution not only in Asia but throughout the world. Major issues in human evolutionary studies such as the timing of the initial hominid dispersal event and the factors behind major transitions in the fossil record are addressed in light of these recent finds.

INTRODUCTION

The human fossil record in China has greatly expanded over the past decade, allowing for a new assessment of human evolution in East Asia throughout the Pleistocene. This reassessment must, however, consider current debates about the course of human evolution worldwide. Two such debates bear directly on interpretations of the Asian fossil record. The first revolves around acceptance or rejection of evidence for an early human presence in Eurasia during the late Pliocene and basal Pleistocene. The second concerns the question of modern human origins and whether archaic hominids in various regions of the Old World played a direct role in the genesis of living people. The human fossil record in China is of decisive importance for resolving both issues.

0084-6570/96/1015-0275$08.00

FOSSIL EVIDENCE FOR AN EARLY HUMAN PRESENCE IN ASIA

During the 1970s it was generally accepted that human ancestors had spread to Asia by the end of the Pliocene or the beginning of the Pleistocene, ~1.8–1.9 mya (16). Owing to the scarcity and fragmentary nature of early Asian human fossils, the questionable provenience of many fossil specimens, and differing interpretations of their geochronological age, this viewpoint was gradually abandoned. For the past decade the consensus has been that *Homo erectus* was the first hominid to enter Asia, approximately 1.0 mya (60, 63). The previously held conviction that certain human fossils from Java and China were perhaps early Asian representatives of *Australopithecus* or *Homo habilis* (24, 26, 70, 78) was put aside. These remains were reinterpreted as being much younger in age and within the nominal range of variation to be expected in *H. erectus* (42, 49, 135).

New Material Attributed to Plio-Pleistocene Hominidae in Asia

Due to recent fossil discoveries and the redating of older material, the contention that *H. erectus* was the first hominid to disperse into Eurasia, and at a relatively late date, has itself come under scrutiny. The most significant revision concerns reevaluation of the age of early human fossils from Sangiran and Perning in Java, which have again been dated to the Plio-Pleistocene transition (77). This time, however, the redated remains include not only specimens attributed to the supposedly *H. habilis*–like taxon *Homo modjokertensis* (78), but others that have long been considered typical examples of *H. erectus*. In addition to this material, several very poorly preserved gnathic and cranial remains, attributed by some to an enigmatic australopithecine-like taxon, *Meganthropus palaeojavanicus,* have been found in similarly ancient deposits. These fossils seemingly fall outside the morphological parameters set elsewhere by *H. erectus* (24, 79). The situation has, consequently, reverted to one that prevailed two decades ago, when a diversity of specimens representing multiple grades or clades of hominid were tentatively recognized from the earliest Pleistocene of Java. Then as now, however, there is no agreement about the true age and actual affinities of all the Javan material (Figure 1).

Additional finds on the Eurasian mainland have also come to light that argue for an older age for early hominids in Asia. The distinctive Dmanisi mandible from the Republic of Georgia, on the southwestern flank of Asia, has been dated to 1.8 mya (25), while a hominid-like lower jaw fragment from Wushan in Sichuan has recently been dated to 1.8–2.0 mya (35). Two hominid incisors from Yuanmou in Yunnan, known since the 1960s (32), have also been dated to the basal Pleistocene (64). In addition to the above paleontologi-

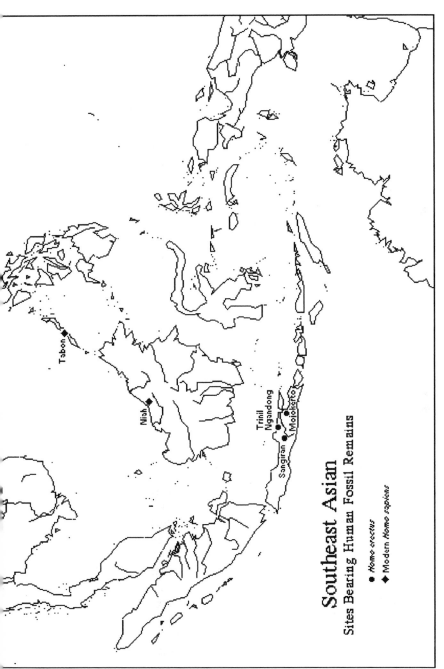

Figure 1   Important Southeast Asian sites bearing human fossil remains (All sites in Java, Indonesia, except Niah, Borneo, and Tabon, Palawan, Philippines).

cal specimens, archeological remains from Riwat in Pakistan have been dated to the late Pliocene (18), while Xiaochangliang in the Nihewan basin of Hebei and other early Paleolithic sites in north central China have been dated to the earliest Pleistocene (1.6 mya) (38).

Although critics maintain that evidence of the sort enumerated above is qualitatively no better than in the past, and hence does not warrant reconsideration, there seems at present a much greater willingness to accept all or most of it. Africanists, who have long resisted the idea of a Plio-Pleistocene human presence in Asia, have acquiesced in the hope that evidence for a dispersal of early *Homo* into Asia before the advent of more advanced forms in Africa will buttress their claim that its likely descendant, Asian *H. erectus,* was a side-branch on the human evolutionary tree uninvolved in the African origins of later human beings (17). Asianists are more than happy to accept the new evidence, as it confirms their long-held belief that Asia, like Africa, was from the outset a major theater of human evolution and that perhaps *H. erectus,* after all, really did evolve in Asia, eventually spreading back to Africa to replace the australopithecines and other assorted early hominids (103). Nevertheless, what all these remains in Java, China, and elsewhere actually represent, and how they relate to the emergence of the genus *Homo* worldwide, still requires much further study and the recovery of much more complete material.

Evidence for Early-Pleistocene Homo erectus in China

GONGWANGLING, LANTIAN, SHAANXI   Other than the Wushan and Yuanmou specimens mentioned above, a damaged partial cranium from Gongwangling, Lantian county, Shaanxi (96), is the earliest substantial hominid specimen known from China. An early-Pleistocene age of 1.15 mya, recently proposed by An & Ho (2), based on correlation of the local loess/paleosol column at the hominid-bearing site with the worldwide oxygen isotope scale, is consistent with both the cranium's faunal associates and the morphological character of the specimen. In its preserved morphology, especially its small cranial capacity ($\sim$780 cm^3), the robusticity and double-arched shape of its supraorbital torus, its high degree of postorbital constriction, the oblique orientation of its inferior zygomaxillary border, and low placement of the root of the zygomatic process, the Gongwangling cranium appears to be quite similar to material attributed to early *H. erectus* (also called *Homo ergaster* by some) from the early Pleistocene of East Africa (102), Java (77, 79), and perhaps Western Europe (7), and to deviate significantly from the more derived pattern of classic *H. erectus* seen at Zhoukoudian (23, 122).

FOSSIL EVIDENCE FOR MIDDLE-PLEISTOCENE *HOMO ERECTUS* IN CHINA

Distribution in Space and Time

The fossil record of middle-Pleistocene *H. erectus* in China has been amply supplemented since the early 1960s when the only known remains were the lost but not forgotten fossils from Zhoukoudian (Chou Kou Tien), i.e. the original Peking Man material (39). Middle-Pleistocene specimens of *H. erectus* are now known to occur not only at Zhoukoudian, but at Chenjiawo in Lantian county, Shaanxi; Quyuan River Mouth in Yunxian county, Hubei; numerous other localities in the hilly regions west of the Central China Plain in western Hubei and southwestern Henan and Shaanxi; Qizianshan in Yiyuan county, Shandong; Longtandong in Hexian county, Anhui; and perhaps at Tangshan on the outskirts of Nanjing, Jiangsu, although this latter material is still under study and may represent a premodern form of *Homo sapiens* (Figure 2). The dating of the remains mentioned above shows that the temporal range of *H. erectus* in China was considerable, spanning at least 700,000 years (see Table 1 for list of specimens and dates).

All the above discoveries go a long way toward helping to elucidate parameters of variation within *H. erectus,* as well as the magnitude of evolutionary transformation that affected this hominid lineage during its long history in East Asia. It is in the context of this more complete record of *H. erectus* in China that its status and relationships to other middle-Pleistocene human beings in various parts of the Old World should be evaluated. What follows is a more detailed look at some of the sites and specimens mentioned above.

Major Sites of Middle-Pleistocene Homo erectus in China

ZHOUKOUDIAN, BEIJING   Since 1949 great advances have been made in study of the Zhoukoudian site. These advances culminated in the late 1970s and early 1980s with extensive geochronological and geomorphological work carried out by various institutes of the Academia Sinica (113). Syntheses of the geochronological studies indicate that the site was intermittently inhabited by groups of *H. erectus* from ~440-580 kya and perhaps as late as 240 kya (33, 140, but see 1).

Between 1921 and 1966, a total of 6 complete or near-complete skull-caps, 12 cranial fragments, 15 mandibular pieces and 157 teeth (including 84 socketed and 73 isolated) were recovered at Zhoukoudian. Postcranial finds included seven femoral pieces, one fragment of a distal tibia, three humeral pieces, one clavicular fragment, a fragment of an atlas, and one lunate. Nearly all this material was lost during World War II, although an excellent set of casts still survives (53). The only known existing specimens of *H. erectus*

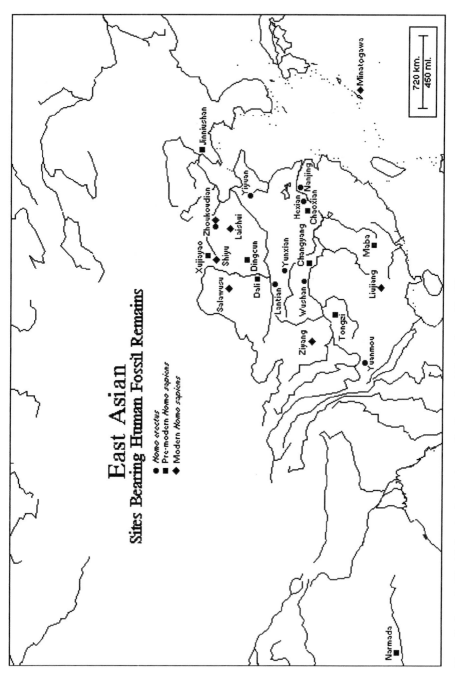

Figure 2   Important East Asian sites bearing human fossil remains (All sites located in China except Narmada, India, and Minatogawa, Okinawa, Japan).

Table 1 Important hominid fossil remains from China[a]

Site name, county, province	Attribution	Fossil specimens	Age × 10³
Longgupo, Wushan, Sichuan	Early *Homo*?	Mand. frag., upper incisor	1,800–2,000
Danawu, Yuanmou, Yunnan	*H. erectus*	Two incisors, tibial diaphysis	700–1,700
Gongwangling, Lantian, Shaanxi	*H. erectus*	Partial cranium	700–1,150
Longgudong, Jianshi, Hubei	*H. erectus*?	Teeth	700?
Donghecun, Luonan, Shaanxi	*H. erectus*	Tooth	700–1,150
Quyuanhekou, Yunxian, Hebei	*H. erectus*	Two crania	600–800
Chenjiawo, Lantian, Shaanxi	*H. erectus*	Mandible	~660
Longgushan, Yunxian, Hubei	*H. erectus*	Assorted teeth	~550
Bailongdong, Yunxi, Hubei	*H. erectus*	Assorted teeth	~550
Xinghuashan, Nanzhao, Henan	*H. erectus*	Assorted teeth	~550
Loc. 1, Zhoukoudian, Beijing	*H. erectus*	Five crania, mandibles, teeth, postcrania	220–580
Qizianshan, Yiyuan, Shandong	*H. erectus*	Cranial frags., teeth	~440
Longtandong, Hexian, Anhui	*H. erectus*	Calvaria, cranial frags, mand. frag., teeth	190–300
Tangshan, Nanjing, Jiangsu	*H. erectus*	Two partial crania	200–400
Jinniushan, Yingkou, Liaoning	Premodern *H. sapiens*	Cranium, partial skeleton	230–280
Tianshuigou, Dali, Shaanxi	Premodern *H. sapiens*	Cranium	180–230
Wanlongdong, Changyang, Hubei	Premodern *H. sapiens*	Maxilla	170–220
Dingcun, Xiangfen, Shanxi	Premodern *H. sapiens*	Assorted teeth, infant parietal	160–210
Yanshan, Chaoxian, Anhui	Premodern *H. sapiens*	Occipital, maxilla	160–220
New Cave, Zhoukoudian, Beijing	Premodern *H. sapiens*	Tooth	135–175
Miaohoushan, Benxi, Liaoning	Premodern *H. sapiens*	Teeth, femoral shaft	130–290
Shiziyan, Maba, Guangdong	Premodern *H. sapiens*	Partial cranium	120–140
Yanhuidong, Tongzi, Guizhou	Premodern *H. sapiens*	Assorted teeth	102–191
Xujiayao, Yanggao, Shanxi	Premodern *H. sapiens*	Cranial elements, max., teeth, mand. frag.	100–125
Wuguidong, Jiande, Zhejiang	Premodern *H. sapiens*	Tooth	90–117
Salawusu, Inner Mongolia	Modern *H. sapiens*	Cranial elements, mandible, postcrania	35–65
Laishui, Hebei	Modern *H. sapiens*	Skull and skeleton	28
Shiyu, Shuoxian, Shanxi	Modern *H. sapiens*	Occipital	28
Upper Cave, Zhoukoudian, Beijing	Modern *H. sapiens*	Three crania, mandible, postcrania	11–29
Tongtianyan, Liujiang, Guangxi	Modern *H. sapiens*	Cranium, partial skeleton	10–67
Huangshanxi, Ziyang, Sichuan	Modern *H. sapiens*	Partial cranium	7–39

[a]Attribution is by author. Dates include all recently published figures. See text for details and references. All other fossil material of modern *H. sapiens* in China is dated to the terminal Pleistocene—early Holocene (~8–12 kya).

from Zhoukoudian include a few teeth retained from the original excavations; a limb bone fragment, teeth, and a lower jaw found in the 1950s (97, 98); and a frontal and occipital found in 1966 (66), which fit a previously known skull-cap collected in 1934.

There is such an extensive and detailed literature on *H. erectus* from Zhoukoudian, written by both Davidson Black (4) and Franz Weidenreich (84–87, 89, 90), that only a brief review of the site's human fossils can be attempted in these pages. It is important, however, to summarize some of their salient morphological features as they have long been the standard of comparison for middle-Pleistocene hominids worldwide (see Figure 3).

Overall, the cranium is characterized by an endocranial volume approximately two thirds that of modern human beings, great cortical bone thickness, low cranial vault height, and a broad cranial base. The frontal bone has massive, horizontally oriented supraorbital tori; a distinct trough-like posttoral sulcus; pronounced postorbital constriction; and a sloping forehead. The parietals are foreshortened and slope sharply toward the midline of the skull, which produces a narrow interparietal distance. This, in combination with the massively built basicranial superstructures, produces a bell-shaped transverse cranial vault contour. The temporal bone is rhomboid-shaped with a low, straight superior border and well-developed crests and ridges on, and superior to, the mastoid process. The occipital bone is sharply angulated with a low, long, and broad plane for the attachment of the nuchal musculature and a constricted upper squamous portion. The cranium's greatest length extends from glabella to the midpoint of the transverse occipital torus, which in turn extends laterally to the supramastoid region. The lower jaw is robust, well buttressed, and chinless with a strongly everted gonial angle, a broad ascending ramus, and a well-excavated masseteric fossa. Other distinctive features of the cranial vault and base include a well-developed system of bumps and ridges on the external surface of the cranium; a thick, elongate, and tubular tympanic bone oriented perpendicular to the midline of the skull; a deep, narrow mandibular fossa; and a low degree of basicranial flexure. There are also distinctive dental traits (most significantly the shoveling of the upper incisors) and postcranial features (robust limb bones characterized by thick walls and platymeria, that is, by transverse flattening of the bone shaft), all of which have come to characterize the specimens from Zhoukoudian and serve as benchmarks for defining *H. erectus*.

In retrospect, however, the remains of *H. erectus* at Zhoukoudian are relatively homogeneous when compared with more recently discovered specimens of middle-Pleistocene Chinese hominid, which tend to differ to a greater or lesser extent from the pattern described above. Actually only the *H. erectus* material from Yiyuan in Shandong province (52), which includes cranial,

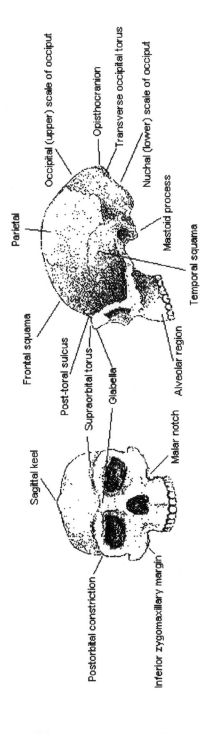

Figure 3   Reconstructed cranium of Zhoukoudian *Homo erectus* (female) showing some key features that have entered into the discussion of the relationship between archaic Asians and other middle-Pleistocene human ancestors.

postcranial, and dental remains, shows pervasive, all-around similarity to specimens of *H. erectus* known from Zhoukoudian. All the features mentioned above do appear, however, to one extent or another, in many other Chinese fossils that both pre- and postdate the Zhoukoudian site (23).

QUYUAN RIVER MOUTH, YUNXIAN, HUBEI   The two new Yunxian crania (44), recently dated by paleomagnetism and ESR to the late early or early middle Pleistocene (~600–800 kya) (8, 127), are very important, being the most complete specimens of *H. erectus* ever found on the Asian mainland. In a number of features—primarily their extremely large cranial and facial dimensions, lack of well-expressed ectocranial buttressing features, elevation of the upper margin of the temporal squama, swept-back orientation of the supraorbital tori, and reduced postorbital constriction—they are quite distinct from Zhoukoudian *H. erectus* and recall Western archaics. They preserve, however, many other features common to *H. erectus* at Zhoukoudian, including the overall shape of the cranial vault (it is very long, low, and pinched to the rear), a long and broad occipital nuchal plane, the low placement of greatest cranial breadth, and the discrete morphology of the cranial base, which is structurally indistinguishable from that of classic *H. erectus* and quite different from that found in archaic *H. sapiens* and later more modern-looking human beings (see Figures 3 and 4; 23, 44, 45). In keeping with the presence of the above *erectus*-like characteristics, the Yunxian crania lack many features thought to be diagnostic of Western archaics, such as a gracilized and flexed cranial base, transverse parietal expansion, opening up of the posterior occipital angle, constriction of the lower scale and expansion of the upper scale of the occiput, and elevation of the point of greatest cranial breadth up the cranial sidewall to the level of the parietals, which produce a more rounded and globular transverse cranial vault contour. Further distinguishing Yunxian from Western archaics is the presence of flat, anteriorly oriented, laterally flaring and elevated cheek bones; a horizontally oriented inferolateral zygomaxillary border; and a canine fossa. The above facial features represent a trait complex universally seen in fossil and modern Asians (43, 56, 61, 62, 100). Middle-Pleistocene Western archaics such as Petralona, Arago, and Atapuerca in Europe, and Bodo and Kabwe (Broken Hill) in Africa exhibit a very different facial morphology characterized by a low origin of the zygomatic root, parasagittal orientation of the zygomaxillary facies, an oblique inferolateral zygomaxillary border, and lack of a canine fossa. These features of Western archaics are later elaborated upon by Neandertals, which produced a facial topography that is at the opposite extreme from the overall morphological pattern seen in East Asia.

    The amalgam of features seen in the Yunxian crania opens up a new window on human variation during the middle Pleistocene of Asia. In some

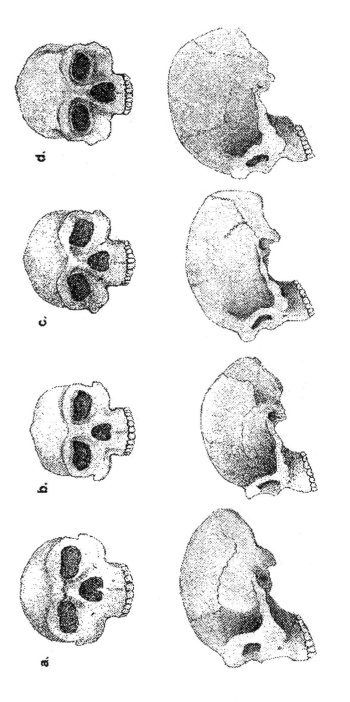

Figure 4 Hypothetical and idealized, tentative reconstruction of important hominid cranial specimens from China; above, facial aspect; below, lateral aspect. (A) Yunxian (*H. erectus*, EV 9002, male), (B) Zhoukoudian Locality 1 (*H. erectus*, composite reconstruction of Skull IX and facial fragments I–III, female), (C) Dali (premodern *H. sapiens*, Skull 101, male), (D) Zhoukoudian Upper Cave (early modern *H. sapiens*, Skull 101, male).

ways this amalgam tends to narrow the morphological gap between eastern *H. erectus* and Western archaics. In other ways the Yunxian material clearly aligns with specimens of Asian *H. erectus* and all later Asian people. Given their unexpected mix of features, the Yunxian crania also raise questions vis à vis the long-standing practice of using the Zhoukoudian remains as the sole yardstick for defining the morphology of *H. erectus* (for examples, see 3, 74, 101, 137). In addition, Yunxian's early geochronological age, confirmed by the archaic nature of its prolific associated fauna, combined with its in situ archeological remains, makes it one of the most important and unique paleoanthropological sites in all Asia.

CAVE AND OPEN-AIR SITES OF CENTRAL CHINA   The Quyuan River Mouth, Yunxian, hominid site is not an isolated occurrence. Dental remains from nearby sites in central China have also been attributed to *H. erectus* (65, 67, 111, 114, 126, 135). These, plus the Lantian mandible from Chenjiawo (95), seem to predate or slightly overlap in time material recovered at Zhoukoudian (2, 80). While closely akin morphologically to homologous remains from Zhoukoudian, many of the isolated teeth found in Hubei share the same large size associated with dental remains from the Quyuan River Mouth and Hexian sites. All these finds tend to extend the range of variation of both metric and nonmetric dental and gnathic features of *H. erectus* in China.

LONGTANDONG, HEXIAN, ANHUI   The Hexian skull-cap and associated fragmentary cranial, mandibular, and dental remains (36, 105, 112), while basically similar to those from Zhoukoudian, differ in some clear ways. The dentition is extremely large, far outstripping homologues from Zhoukoudian in overall size. The skull-cap differs from Zhoukoudian specimens in details of supraorbital construction, less well-expressed ectocranial buttressing, the high curvature of the temporal squama, a significant increase in greatest cranial breadth, and a reduction in postorbital constriction, all features somewhat analogous to those seen in Yunxian and such Javanese crania as Sambungmachan.

It has been assumed by most investigators that the cranial features enumerated above are progressive in nature, although the appearance of similar traits in the reportedly more ancient Yunxian crania suggest they may be more readily attributed to intraspecific variation. The original assumption that the Hexian skull-cap represents an advanced form of *H. erectus* was based on its seemingly late age and similarity in certain respects to Skull 5 from the upper layers at Zhoukoudian, Locality 1 (66), also considered to be relatively younger in age than other *H. erectus* fossils recovered in China. Both could, however, be older than initially suggested. The Hexian site has recently been dated to 300 kya by ESR (34), while a new set of Uranium-series assays date the upper layers at Zhoukoudian to ~400 kya (72). Other tests at both sites, however, record younger ages in the neighborhood of 200 to 250 kya (10, 33, 130, 140). If the younger dates are accepted there is the possibility that late-occurring *H. erectus* in China may in fact overlap in time early premodern *H. sapiens* as known from Yingkou (Jinniushan) in Liaoning and perhaps elsewhere (9, 11). A more conservative viewpoint is that there was a relatively swift, yet mosaic, transition from *H. erectus* to premodern human beings in China, the timing of which can not yet be resolved by available dating techniques (20). In this case it would be virtually impossible, as well as counterproductive, to sort widely variable hominid specimens into arbitrary time successive taxa (i.e. *H. erectus* vs premodern *H. sapiens*).

TANGSHAN, NANJING, JIANGSU   The most recent human fossil discovery in China consists of two partial crania, initially attributed to *H. erectus,* excavated in March 1993 from Huludong, a karst cave on the slope of Tangshan Hill on the eastern outskirts of Nanjing, Jiangsu. This is the first such discovery south of the Changjiang (Yangtze) River. The first cranium, currently under study by Prof. Lü Zun'e of Peking University, is reported on below. No information is yet available on the second.

The specimen preserves a complete frontal, the two parietals, both nasals, and a disassociated portion of the occipital. The left orbit is preserved intact, as are portions of the left maxilla and zygomatic. It is described as very similar in many features to *H. erectus* from Zhoukoudian (54). The cranium has a low, flat forehead and a continuous, horizontally oriented supraorbital torus with a distinct posttoral sulcus. The occipital bone has a short upper scale and long lower scale, a conservative *H. erectus*-like trait. Both meet at a relatively acute angle. There is a clearly delimited, horizontally oriented occipital torus surmounted by an indistinct supratoral sulcus. Cortical bone is much thicker (~10 mm) than in modern human beings. As in other archaic Chinese crania the cheek bones are anteriorly oriented and laterally flaring. The cranium is thought to represent a young adult female based on its overall size, the degree of sutural closure, and the relative weakness of the supraorbital and other ectocranial structures.

The mammalian fossils associated with the human remains represent a typical northern Chinese middle-Pleistocene fauna similar to that recovered at Zhoukoudian, Locality 1 (125). It differs from the nearby Hexian fauna in lacking common southern Chinese elements such as *Ailuropoda* (giant panda) and *Megatapirus* (giant tapir). The fauna apparently represents a southward dispersal of Palaearctic elements during a cold, glacial phase or subphase of the middle Quaternary. The morphological character of the human cranium likewise suggests closer affinities to *H. erectus* as known from Zhoukoudian rather than Hexian, even though the Hexian locality is much closer (~100 km).

Given the increased sampling of *H. erectus* in China over the past two decades it appears that no simple evolutionary trend is discernible (but see 136). Rather than resolving the argument for or against stasis in *H. erectus* during its long career in Asia (69, 91a), the new evidence seems to hint at much greater between-group variation than was initially perceived. Further study is surely warranted on whether discernible local variants of *H. erectus* can be recognized in East Asia and on the implications of this possibility for our understanding the course of human evolution during the middle Pleistocene in China.

FOSSIL EVIDENCE FOR PREMODERN *HOMO SAPIENS* IN CHINA

It was only with the resumption of paleoanthropological research in China in 1949—after the loss of the Zhoukoudian fossils during World War II—that the fossil record of premodern *H. sapiens* in East Asia began to accumulate. In 1953 the first trace of a fossil hominid more advanced than *H. erectus* but not fully modern was found at Dingcun, Xiangfen county, Shanxi province (59). While archeological and faunal remains recovered at Dingcun were relatively abundant, the fossil hominid material consisted of only three teeth—the upper right incisors and a lower right M2 of a juvenile. In 1956 additional, meager remains of premodern *H. sapiens* were recovered at Wanlongdong, Changyang county, Hubei, with the retrieval of a maxillary fragment retaining P3 and M1 (12). This was followed relatively quickly by the discovery of a partial cranium at Maba, Qujiang county, Guangdong, in 1958 (99). It was not until 1976, however, that more material of premodern *H. sapiens* was forthcoming from China, with the discovery of the important but little heralded Xujiayao remains from Yanggao county, Shanxi (14, 104, 107). This was followed in the 1980s by the excavation of a nearly complete fossil cranium from Tianshuigou, Dali county, Shaanxi (117); a cranium and partial skeleton from Jinniushan, Yingkou county, Liaoning (50, 51, 110); and cranial remains from Yanshan, Chaoxian county, Anhui (123, 124). In addition to the relatively complete specimens enumerated above, several teeth attributed to premodern *H. sapiens* or a late-occurring form of *H. erectus* are known from Yanhuidong, Tongzi county, Guizhou (106, 109). Isolated dental remains have also been produced from the New Cave (Xindong) at Zhoukoudian (28); Miaohoushan, Benxi county, Liaoning (55); and Wuguidong, Jiande county, Zhejiang (30).

The above material, when coupled with the expanded record of *H. erectus* and early modern *H. sapiens* that has accumulated in China over the past two decades, begins to lay the basis for a more thorough understanding of the course of human evolution in East Asia throughout the Pleistocene.

The Timing of Premodern Homo sapiens in China

The transition in China from *H. erectus* to what has been called "early" *H. sapiens* by Chinese workers, but which I prefer to call premodern *H. sapiens*, seems to have commenced ~300 kya, somewhat later than the first occurrence of archaic *H. sapiens* in Europe and Africa and somewhat earlier than the appearance of Neandertals in Europe and the Near East. Fragmentary remains of premoderns persist until ~100 kya when there is an abrupt decline.

With the recovery of the specimens mentioned above, the fossil record of late middle-Pleistocene to early late-Pleistocene premoderns in China is now nearly as dense as the record of middle-Pleistocene archaics in Europe and Africa. Moreover, many of the fossil-bearing sites have been dated by Uranium-series assays (10), and the dates so obtained can serve as a broad schema for placing them into a coherent geochronological framework. Problems attendant to Uranium-series dating must, however, be considered when evaluating the results (71) (see Table 1 for list of specimens and dates).

The Morphological Character of Premodern Homo sapiens in China

The post–*H. erectus*/premodern *H. sapiens* fossil human material from China is of a mixed character (see Figure 4). There is clearly a more modern overall pattern to the cranial remains known from Dali, Jinniushan, Chaoxian, Xujiayao, and Maba when compared with any of the *H. erectus* skulls discussed earlier. This is reflected primarily in cranial features such as transverse parietal expansion, resulting in a more rounded, globular braincase; a robust but fully modern temporal morphology (i.e. a high, arcuate squamosal border and a deep parietal notch); thinning and anteroposterior foreshortening of the tympanic plate; presence of a fully ossified styloid process; development of a highly flexed cranial base; and a rounding of the posterior portion of the skull associated with a diminution of the occipital torus and the separation of opisthocranion (the point of greatest posterior cranial projection) from the toral midpoint. These important aspects of cranial morphology now appear more similar to specimens of archaic *H. sapiens* known from Europe and Africa (115, 120, 121). In other features, including various facial and cranial vault dimensions and indices, Chinese premoderns are clearly transitional between *H. erectus* and modern *H. sapiens*. Premodern crania in China, nevertheless, also preserve a number of broadly archaic characteristics such as robust and laterally continuous brow ridges, sloping foreheads, and low cranial vault height in association with distinctly *erectus*-like traits, such as a well-expressed system of ectocranial buttresses (in particular the development of frontal bossing), and many discrete characters of the cranial base (e.g. the shape and size of the mandibular fossa in Dali, the morphology of the petrous pyramid in Xujiayao, etc), showing a clear derivation from predecessor populations of East Asia (22). Moreover, according to dentition and postcranial anatomy there seems to have been little if any change from the pattern established by *H. erectus* (86, 89).

Dental similarities are exemplified by remains from Tongzi in Guizhou (106, 109), Miaohoushan in Liaoning (55), Xujiayao in Shanxi (14), and Chenggong in Yunnan (68)—all dated to the late middle or early late Pleistocene—that are virtually indistinguishable from those of *H. erectus* as known from Zhoukoudian and other sites in China. Of even greater significance, however, is the study of the evolutionary history of Asian dentitions pioneered by Turner (78b) who recognizes an East Asian "sinodont dental pattern" characterized by a number of discrete traits (including shovel-shaped upper incisors, reduction or loss of M3, and deflecting wrinkle on lower M1s, etc) said to have evolved from a simpler southeast Asian "sundadont pattern," which lacks these features. Turner hypothesizes that the sinodont pattern emerged only within the past 30,000 years, following dispersal of sundadont populations into the Chinese heartland. This theory is, however, contradicted by the high incidence of strong maxillary central incisor shoveling, a key sinodont feature, and the common occurrence of nearly all other characteristic sinodont traits, in Chinese fossils that extend as far back in time as *H. erectus* (47a). Sinodonty therefore has deep roots in Asian prehistory. Rather than being a relatively recent phenomenon it is actually one of the most persuasive pieces of evidence for local evolutionary continuity in East Asia.

East Asian postcranial remains of premodern *H. sapiens* from Jinniushan (50, 51), and early modern *H. sapiens* from late-Pleistocene sites such as Qingshantou in Jilin (128), Liujiang in Guangxi (94), Minatogawa in Okinawa (41b), and Laishui in Hebei (ZE Lü, personal communication) also exhibit features of local evolutionary continuity. Specimens from all these sites retain the overall characteristics of limb bones seen in Chinese *H. erectus* (89) in contrast to the postcrania of early moderns from the Near Eastern sites of Qafzeh and Skhul and the Australian site of Kow Swamp (in Australia), which are essentially modern in overall appearance (41a, 78a).

Premodern and early modern Chinese are closely linked in many other ways besides dentition and postcrania. For instance, archaic cranial features such as extreme vault thickness, a robust but relatively modern-looking tympanic, a recurved but strongly flexed occipital, and a simple pattern of blood supply to the brain, are retained in many early modern and even Holocene specimens from China (138). Examples include the Shiyu occipital from Shanxi (13), dated to ~28 kya, which is very similar in construction to homologous material from Xujiayao; parietals from Hetao in Inner Mongolia, dated to 35+ kya (10), which retain an archaic meningeal pattern similar to that seen in

Chinese *H. erectus* and premodern *H. sapiens* (93); and the archaic character of the frontal associated with the 28,000-year-old Laishui cranium, to be discussed below.

On the other hand, the Jinniushan cranium shows derived features associated with later *H. sapiens,* particularly in the thinning of the cranial vault bones and an increase in cranial capacity ($\sim$1390 cm^3). In fact, as in Africa, a mosaic transition from archaic to premodern and later early modern people can be documented in China, with individual specimens differentially preserving various heritage features of East Asian *H. erectus* in combination with derived features that presage later more modern *H. sapiens* (22, 23).

FOSSIL EVIDENCE FOR MODERN *HOMO SAPIENS* IN CHINA

Between approximately 25 and 100 kya, a crucial period in human evolution when modern *H. sapiens* became established throughout the Old World, the trend of incremental accretion of more and more modern features in the Chinese fossil human record continues unabated. During this period, recognizable differences between northern and southern Chinese also become apparent (21), although how far back in time this division may go is at present unclear.

Fossil Evidence for Late-Pleistocene Human Evolution in Northern China

The earliest modern human remains in northern China come from Salawusu (Sjara-osso-gol) in the Hetao (Ordos) region of Inner Mongolia, known since the 1920s for a late Paleolithic culture characterized by minuscule flaked tools made on small pebbles (47). Human fossil-bearing sites in the region have recently been dated to between 35 and 65 kya by Uranium-series assays (10). The human specimens include two complete frontal bones; frontal, parietal, and occipital fragments; two partial mandibles; and an assortment of limb bones (19, 93). The frontals, both representing juvenile individuals, are fully modern in appearance, with gracile brows and rounded superior orbital margins. They have, however, a frontal curvature index intermediate between modern Chinese and *H. erectus* from Zhoukoudian, which indicates a relatively sloping forehead. The parietals are moderately thick with cortical bone rather than diplöe making the greater contribution, similar to the condition in more archaic Chinese and at variance to that seen in modern human beings. In overall proportions, however, they approach the parietals of modern Chinese to a greater degree than do those from Xujiayao. The more complete of the lower jaws is that of a juvenile. It is robust and well-buttressed with a poorly developed chin. As there are no well-preserved mandibles of premodern *H. sapiens* yet known from China, it can only be compared with those of *H.*

erectus. In this respect the jaw is said to possess discrete traits and overall proportions similar to those seen in specimens from Lantian, Zhoukoudian, and Hexian, although none of these falls beyond the known range of modern human variation (19). All in all, the Hetao remains, although without question fully modern, retain a number of plesiomorphic (i.e. ancestral) features that help establish their phylogenetic relatedness to earlier more archaic Asians.

A nearly complete hominid skeleton from Laishui, Hebei, discovered in 1988—briefly mentioned above and currently under study by Lü Zun'e—will undoubtedly play a significant role in discussions of human evolution in China when fully described. A cast of the specimen is on public display at Peking University's Sackler Museum of Archeology. The skull is considerably more robust than the Salawusu remains, particularly in regard to its projecting supraorbitals, which preserve an essentially archaic morphology. These are associated with a relatively sloping forehead and a cranial vault, base, and face that are otherwise comparatively modern. Dated to 28 kya, this material helps fill in the gap between late premoderns such as Xujiayao and late early moderns, such as the Upper Cave specimens from Zhoukoudian (88, 116). Future discoveries of this sort will assuredly further document the in situ evolution of archaic Asians toward a more modern morphology. Other recent finds dated to the late-Pleistocene of northern China, including a partial cranium from Xujiafenshan in Huanglong county, Shaanxi (82); portions of a skull cap from Niujiagou, Jingchuan county, Gansu (48); and an occipital fragment from Shiyu, Shanxi (13), differentially preserve a number of archaic features such as extreme vault thickness, mounding of bone along the sagittal suture, a flexed occipital angle, and a salient occipital torus that harken back to earlier more archaic human remains from China.

It has been argued by some that the specimens discussed above show closer affinities to early Western moderns than to living Chinese (75), which suggests that the racial differentiation of extant East Asians began after the arrival of *H. sapiens* from further west. It is thus intimated that earlier, more archaic people from China had little or no direct impact on the evolution of the modern Chinese morphotype. For instance, Skull 101 from the Upper Cave at Zhoukoudian has been shown by multivariate, morphometric analysis to be an outlier when compared with modern Asian populations (41) and most similar to early Holocene crania from Kenya (5, 31), and crania such as Huanglong are said to show closer metric affinities to early moderns in Europe than to living Chinese (81). This is, however, also the case among late-Pleistocene moderns in other parts of the world. Border Cave, an early modern specimen from South Africa, and the late-Pleistocene Omo 1 cranium from Ethiopia, when compared multivariately with modern Africans, likewise appear to be outliers, showing no demonstrable affinities to any extant African population (15), while late-Pleistocene Australians ally with contemporaries from Europe and North Africa (29). This phenomenon is almost certainly a function of the general robusticity of the specimens under consideration and their retention of plesiomorphic traits lost in their more derived descendants. The studies mentioned above certainly demonstrate that early moderns in China show overall "grade" affinities to early moderns in Europe and Africa, as should be expected. What the northern Chinese specimens discussed above also clearly demonstrate is the morphological continuity between archaic and modern human beings in China. This continuity, moreover, is not solely contingent on the persistence of discrete regional traits through time but rests on the documentation of a series of mosaic transformations that show a steady temporal progression, i.e. a process of sapienization from *H. erectus* to premodern *H. sapiens* and across the phylogenetic Rubicon to early modern human beings in Asia.

Fossil Evidence for Late-Pleistocene Human Evolution in Southern China

The Ziyang cranium from Sichuan discovered in 1951 at Huangshanxi was the first major fossil human find in China following the cessation of hostilities on the mainland in 1949 (57, 58, 92). Unfortunately, it is poorly provenienced, and its dating is problematical. A Paleolithic site in the immediate vicinity, however, has been dated to ~30 kya (46), an appropriate age given the relatively archaic nature of the Ziyang specimen. The cranium, associated with an upper jaw showing advanced periodontal disease, is small but high-vaulted with a fairly well-rounded forehead and is thought to represent an older female. Archaic features of the skull include noticeable sagittal keeling; an elongated frontal and foreshortened parietals; a distinct angular torus at the mastoid angle of the parietal; a relatively thick, robust occipital with a moderately well-expressed chignon; well-developed brows surmounted by a distinct ophryonic groove; and various cranial indices intermediate in value between premodern and recent Chinese.

A number of other sites in southern China have yielded relatively complete cranial specimens. The best preserved of these is the well-known Liujiang cranium from Guangxi that was discovered together with a nearly complete axial skeleton in 1957 (94). A Uranium-series date of 67 kya, based on associated fauna, is often quoted for these remains (6), but once again questions of provenience make this age assignment questionable. A more likely association is with the lower cultural levels at the nearby Bailiandong cave site, dated to ~30 kya, which has yielded a faunal assemblage similar to that seen at Liujiang, as well as some isolated human teeth (40).

The Liujiang cranium, while fully modern, is relatively robust and retains a number of archaic features in comparison with recent Chinese. The vault is low, bregma is situated posteriorly, the forehead slopes moderately backward, and the brow is well expressed. As in nearly all recently discovered late-Pleistocene Chinese crania, there is a relatively well-developed occipital chignon. Racially, Liujiang shows typical Mongoloid features in the forward rotation of the anterolateral surface of the frontal process of the zygoma, a low simotic (nasal bridge) index, and possession of shovel-shaped incisors. Various other facial and nasal indices further ally the cranium with southern vs northern Chinese (139).

Recently a number of crania from the terminal Pleistocene or earliest Holocene have been recovered from Lijiang (131), Mengzi (134), Yaoguan (132), and Tanzigou (27) in Yunnan; Puding (Chuandong) in Guizhou (37, 108, 129); and Longlin (133) and Dalongtan (139) in Guangxi. The crania from Yunnan and Guizhou preserve many features similar to those seen at Ziyang, while the Guangxi material is highly reminiscent of Liujiang, which suggests that the preneolithic populations of southern China maintained a conservative cranial morphology until relatively recent times. Cluster analysis allies the Liujiang and Dalongtan crania with later southern Chinese Neolithic samples from Hemudu in Zhejiang, Hedong in Guangdong, Zengpiyan in Guangxi, and Tanshishan in Fujian (139), and clearly differentiates them from more northerly Neolithic samples, which indicates continuity between late-Pleistocene and more recent populations in southern China. Similarities in nasal shape and indices and measures of overall craniometric distance indicate the close affinities of this southern Chinese complex to late-Pleistocene remains from Minatogawa in Okinawa; Tabon in the Philippines; Niah Cave in Kalimantan, Borneo; and Wadjak in Java (118, 119), which suggests that the populations of southern China maintained genetic contact with Australasian people until relatively recently.

To sum up this section, there is at present no reason to suspect that the course of human evolution in China was fundamentally different from that observed for Africa, a region where modern human beings are postulated by many to have arisen. As in Africa, Chinese fossils that span the time from *H. erectus* to modern *H. sapiens* display a mosaic of transitional features that speak to a continual human presence in their continent of origin, uninterrupted by any major replacement of archaic by more modern people. In addition, there are a set of primitive features that, while not unique to East Asia, tend to link archaic, premodern, and early modern Chinese. Thus early modern specimens from China differentially preserve plesiomorphic cranial features such as laterally continuous supraorbitals (Laishui), an angular torus (Ziyang), thick vault bones, sagittal keeling (Huanglong), etc, not generally seen in early modern specimens from other regions of the world. This, in combination with the universal retention of derived midfacial and dental features from *H. erectus* to modern human beings in East Asia, is persuasive evidence for continuity in human evolution in China. It is unlikely, however, that East Asia was an isolated evolutionary cul-de-sac, cut off from contact with the outside world. Periodic increases in genetic contact between eastern and western people during the Pleistocene may in fact have been of decisive importance in triggering the evolutionary changes that led to major transformations in the human fossil record both in China and in other parts of the Old World.

CONCLUSIONS

Human evolution in the East and West did not follow the same exact trajectory. Middle-Pleistocene hominids in China exhibit derived facial features considered by Smith et al (73) to be diagnostic of modern human beings (i.e. the frontal orientation of the medial part of the zygomatic and its lateral facies, a horizontal inferolateral zygomaticoalveolar margin, and a canine fossa), before their common occurrence further west. On the other hand, the modernization of the cranial vault and base seems to have occurred first in Africa and Europe. Approximately 300 kya these "Western" cranial vault and basicranial features, generally considered to be diagnostic of archaic *H. sapiens,* begin to appear in Chinese fossils, signaling the transition from *H. erectus* to premodern *H. sapiens* in East Asia. Somewhat later, the modern facial features mentioned above begin to appear in Near Eastern and African late archaic *H. sapiens.* What is being documented is the mosaic, incremental emplacement of modern characters into both the East Asian and West Asian/African gene pools, most likely the result of increased gene flow between these two central areas of human occupation during the middle-Pleistocene/late-Pleistocene transition.

The retention in East Asia of the diagnostic facial and dental features mentioned above, which are characteristic of all living and fossil Asians, refutes the notion that the transition from *H. erectus* to premodern *H. sapiens* in China was due to a simple replacement event, while the fact that such a transition occurred at all negates the idea that Asian *H. erectus* was distinct at the "species" level and far removed phylogenetically from other contemporaneous hominid lineages. The distinction between Asian *H. erectus* and Western archaic *H. sapiens* is hence a false dichotomy. Middle-Pleistocene hominids should all be referred to *H. erectus,* or the latter taxon should be sunk into *H. sapiens* (91). In the vernacular, middle-Pleistocene hominids from both the East and West can be simply called "archaic humans."

Demonstration of continuity in human evolution in Asia is not contingent on the persistence of discrete regional traits through time but on the documentation of a series of mosaic, morphological transformations, i.e. a process of sapienization from archaic to premodern and early modern human beings. Proponents of an African origin for modern human beings (75, 76) base their claim on similar evidence, as well as the lack of Neandertal-like traits (i.e. autapomorphies) in the African material and the identification of certain fragmentary specimens as geochronologically early representatives of anatomically modern *H. sapiens*. East Asians likewise lack Neandertal-like autapomorphies but in contrast with Africa, evolutionary continuity in Asia is further supported by the persistence of regional traits, particularly in facial and dental features. Coupled with new genetic evidence suggesting that human populations have as deep roots in Asia as in Africa (83), there seems to be no reason to have a one-sided focus on one region or another as the sole area of origination for modern people. It appears more likely that during the late middle–early late Pleistocene transition a central "zone of sapienization" extended from Africa through the Middle East to East Asia. However, as in the case for early-Pleistocene Asian hominids, the supposition that Asia played a major role in modern human origins must be put to the paleontological litmus test of future fossil discoveries. Given the recent history of recovery of fossil human specimens in China, this may not be long in coming.

ACKNOWLEDGMENTS

I take this opportunity to express my sincere thanks to Prof. Li Tianyuan for allowing me to participate in the study of the Yunxian crania. Profs. J. D. Clark, F. C. Howell, and T. D. White made much of my research possible, and I thank them for their support. I greatly appreciate the many opportunities I have had to exchange views with Chinese colleagues, including Profs. Jia Lanpo, Lü Zun'e, Wei Qi, Wu Rukang, Wu Xinzhi, Zhang Yinyun, and Zhou Guoxing, among many others. I thank Prof. Milford Wolpoff for his useful comments on drafts of this chapter. I would also like to acknowledge the financial support of the Committee for Scholarly Communication with China, the National Science Foundation (Grant # INT-9419529), the Henry Luce Foundation, the L. S. B. Leakey Foundation, and the Lowie Fund of the University of California, Berkeley, for support of travel and research related to the writing of this article. Special thanks are extended to Xu Yanna and Doug Beckner for graphics.

Literature Cited

1. Aigner JS. 1986. The age of Zhoukoudian Locality 1: the newly proposed O18 correspondences. *Anthropos* (Brno) 23:157–73
2. An ZS, Ho CK. 1989. New magnetostratigraphic dates of Lantian *Homo erectus*. *Quat. Res.* 32:213–21
3. Andrews P. 1984. An alternative interpretation of the characters used to define *Homo erectus. Cour. Forsh. -Inst. Senck.* 69: 167–75
4. Black D. 1931. On an adolescent skull of *Sinanthropus pekinensis* in comparison

with an adult skull of the same species and with other hominid skulls, recent and fossil. *Palaeontol. Sin. Ser. D* 7(2):1–145

5. Bräuer G. 1992. The origins of modern Asians: by regional evolution or by replacement? In *The Evolution and Dispersal of Modern Humans in Asia*, ed. T Akazawa, K Aoki, T Kimura, pp. 401–13. Tokyo: Hokusen-Sha

6. Brooks AS, Wood B. 1990. Paleoanthropology: the Chinese side of the story. *Nature* 344:288–98

7. Carbonell E, Bermúdez de Castro JM, Arsuaga JL, Díez JC, Rosas A, et al. 1995. Lower Pleistocene hominids and artifacts from Atapuerca-TD6 (Spain). *Science* 269: 826–30

8. Chen TM, Yang Q, Hu Y, Li TY. 1996. ESR dating of hominid fossil strata at Yunxian, Hubei. *Acta Anthropol. Sin.* In press

9. Chen TM, Yang Q, Wu E. 1994. Antiquity of *Homo sapiens* in China. *Nature* 368: 55–56

10. Chen TM, Yuan SX. 1988. Uranium-series dating of bones and teeth from Chinese Palaeolithic sites. *Archaeometry* 30: 59–76

11. Chen TM, Zhang YY. 1991. Palaeolithic chronology and possible co-existance of *H. erectus* and *H. sapiens* in China. *World Archeol.* 23:147–54

12. Chia LP (see also Jia LP). 1957. Notes on the human and some other mammalian remains from Changyang, Hupei. *Vertebr. PalAsiat.* 1:247–58 (In Chinese, Engl. Abstr.)

13. Chia LP, Gai P, You YL. 1972. Report of excavation in Shi Yu, Shanxi: a Palaeolithic site. *Acta Archaeol. Sin.* 1:39–60 (In Chinese)

14. Chia LP, Wei Q, Li CR. 1979. Report on the excavation of Hsuchiayao Man site in 1976. *Vertebr. PalAsiat.* 17:277–93 (In Chinese, Engl. Abstr.)

15. Corruccini R. 1992. Metrical consideration of the Skhul-IV and Skhul-IX and Border Cave 1 crania in the context of modern human origins. *Am. J. Phys. Anthropol.* 87: 433–45

16. Cronin JE, Boaz NT, Stringer CB, Rak Y. 1981. Tempo and mode in hominid evolution. *Nature* 292:113–22

17. Culotta E. 1995. Asian hominids grow older. *Science* 270:1116–17

18. Dennell R, Hailwood E. 1988. Late Pliocene artefacts from northern Pakistan. *Curr. Anthropol.* 29:495–98

19. Dong G, Gao S, Li B. 1982. New discovery of the fossil Ordos Man. *Chin. Sci. Bull.* 27:754–58 (Engl. ed.)

20. Etler DA. 1990. A case study of the "erectus"-"sapiens" transition in Asia: hominid remains from Hexian and Chaoxian counties, Anhui province, China. *Kroeber Anthropol. Soc. Pap.* 71/72:1–19

21. Etler DA. 1992 Recent developments in the study of human biology in China: a review. *Hum. Biol.* 64:567–85

22. Etler DA. 1994. *The Chinese Hominidae: New Finds, New Interpretations.* PhD thesis. Univ. Calif., Berkeley. 471 pp.

23. Etler DA, Li TY. 1994. New archaic human fossil discoveries in China and their bearing on hominid species definition during the middle Pleistocene. In *Integrative Paths to the Past: Paleoanthropological Advances in Honor of F. Clark Howell*, ed. R Corruccini, D Ciochon, pp. 639–76. New York: Prentice Hall

24. Franzen JL. 1985. Asian australopithecines? In *Hominid Evolution: Past, Present and Future*, ed. E Delson, pp. 253–63. New York: Liss

25. Gabunia L, Vekua A. 1995. A Plio-Pleistocene hominid from Dmanisi, East Georgia, Caucasus. *Nature* 373:509–12

26. Gao J. 1975. Australopithecine teeth associated with *Gigantopithecus*. *Vertebr. PalAsiat.* 13:81–87 (In Chinese, Engl. Abstr.)

27. Gen DM, Zhang XY. 1992. Tanzigou culture and its archeological significance. See Ref. 131a, pp. 42–48

28. Gu YM. 1978. The New Cave Man of Zhoukoudian and his living environments. *IVPP Coll. Pap. Palaeoanthropol.*, pp. 158–74 (In Chinese)

29. Habgood P. 1989. The origin of modern humans in East Asia and Australia. In *Hominidae: Proc. 2nd Int. Congr. Hum. Paleontol.*, ed. G Giacobini, pp. 431–35. Milan: Jaca Book

30. Han DF, Zhang SS. 1978. A hominid canine and mammalian material from the Pleistocene of Zhejiang. *Vertebr. PalAsiat.* 16: 255–63 (In Chinese)

31. Howells WW. 1989. Skull shapes and the map: craniometric analysis in the dispersion of modern *Homo*. *Pap. Peabody Mus. Harvard Univ.* 79:1–189

32. Hu CZ. 1973. Ape-man teeth from Yuanmou, Yunnan. *Acta Geol. Sin.* 1:65–71 (In Chinese, Engl. Abstr.)

33. Huang PH, Jin SZ, Peng ZC, Liang RY, Lu ZJ, et al. 1993. ESR dating of tooth enamel: comparison with U-series, FL and TL dating at the Peking Man site. *Appl. Radiat. Isot.* 44:239–42

34. Huang PH, Zheng L, Jin G, Liang RY, Xu Y, et al. 1994. Initial research results of ESR dating of the Hexian Man site. *Sci. Bull.* (Kexue Tongbao) 39:1919–20 (In Chinese)

35. Huang WP, Ciochon R, Gu YM, Larick R, Fang QR, et al. 1995. Early *Homo* and associated artifacts from Asia. *Nature* 378: 275–78

36. Huang WP, Fang DS, Ye YX. 1982. Preliminary study on the fossil hominid skull and fauna from Hexian, Anhui. *Vertebr. PalAsiat.* 20(3):248–56 (In Chinese, Engl. Abstr.)

37. Huang X. 1989. A fossil *Homo sapiens* cranium unearthed at Chuandong, Pu'ding, Guizhou. *Acta Anthropol. Sin.* 8:379–81 (In Chinese)

38. Jia LP (see also Chia LP). 1985. China's earliest Palaeolithic assemblages. In *Palaeoanthropology and Palaeolithic Archaeology in the People's Republic of China*, ed. RK Wu, JW Olsen, pp. 135–46. Orlando: Academic

39. Jia LP, Huang WW. 1990. *The Story of Peking Man.* London: Oxford

40. Jiang YJ, Chen GK. 1994. Concerning some problems about Liujiang Man. See Ref. 138a, pp. 114–19

41. Kamminga J, Wright RVS. 1988. The Upper Cave at Zhoukoudian and the origins of the Mongoloids. *J. Hum. Evol.* 17:739–67

41a. Kennedy G. 1984. Are the Kow Swamp hominids 'archaic'? *Am. J. Phys. Anthropol.* 65:163–68

41b. Kimura T, Takahashi H. 1990. Cross-sectional geometry of Minatogawa limb bones. *Univ. Tokyo Symp.: The Evolution and Dispersal of Modern Humans in Asia,* p. 18 (Abstr.)

42. Kramer A. 1994. A critical analysis of claims for the existence of Southeast Asian australopithecines. *J. Hum. Evol.* 26:3–22

43. Lahr MM. 1994. The multiregional model of modern human origins: a reassessment of its morphological basis. *J. Hum. Evol.* 26:23–56

44. Li TY, Etler DA. 1992. New middle Pleistocene hominid crania from Yunxian in China. *Nature* 357:404–7

45. Li TY, Etler DA. 1995. Further discussion of the morphological features of the Yunxian crania. *Jianghan Archeol.* 55:1–6 (In Chinese)

46. Li XN, Zhang SS. 1984. Paleoliths discovered in Ziyang Man Locality B. *Acta Anthropol. Sin.* 3:215–24 (In Chinese, Engl. Abstr.)

47. Licent E, Teilhard de Chardin P, Black D. 1926. On a presumably Pleistocene human tooth from the Sjara-osso-gol deposits. *Bull. Geol. Soc. China* 5:285–90

47a. Liu W. 1995. The dental morphology of Neolithic humans in north China and its relationship with modern Chinese origins. *Acta Anthropol. Sin.* 14:360–80 (In Chinese, Engl. Abstr.)

48. Liu YL, Huang WW, Lin YP. 1984. Human fossil and Paleolithic remains from Jingchuan, Gansu. *Acta Anthropol. Sin.* 3:11–18 (In Chinese, Engl. Abstr.)

49. Lovejoy CO. 1970. The taxonomic status of the *Meganthropus* mandibular fragments from the Djetis beds of Java. *Man* 5:228–36

50. Lü ZE. 1989. On the age of Jinniushan man and its evolutionary position. *Liaohai Cult. Relics J.* 1:44–55 (In Chinese)

51. Lü ZE. 1989. Discovery and significance of the human fossils at Jinniushan. In *Papers on Primitive Cultures of China*, ed. C Tian, X Shi, pp. 35–39. Beijing: Cult. Relics (In Chinese)

52. Lü ZE, Huang YP, Li PS, Meng ZY. 1989. Yiyuan fossil man. *Acta Anthropol. Sin.* 8:301–13 (In Chinese, Engl. Abstr.)

53. Mann A. 1981. The significance of the *Sinanthropus* casts and some paleodemographic notes. In *Homo erectus: Papers in Honor of Davidson Black*, ed. BA Sigmon, JS Cybulski, pp. 41–61. Toronto: Univ. Tor. Press

54. Mu XN, Xu HK, Mu DC, Zhong SL, Xu QQ, Zhang H. et al. 1993. Discovery of *Homo erectus* remains from Tangshan, Nanjing, and its significance. *Acta Palaeont. Sin.* 32(4):393–99 (In Chinese, Engl. Abstr.)

55. Museum of Liaoning. 1986. *Miaohoushan: An Early Paleolithic Site in Benxi County, Liaoning.* Beijing: Cult. Relics (In Chinese, Engl. summ.)

56. Oschinsky L. 1962. Facial flatness and cheekbone morphology in Arctic Mongoloids. *Anthropologica* ns 4:349–77

57. Pei WC. 1952. Report on the excavation of the Tzeyang Man remains and associated faunal remains from the Huangshanhsi in Szechuan. *Chin. Sci. Bull.* 3:7–13 (In Chinese)

58. Pei WC, Woo JK. 1957. Tzeyang Man. *Mem. Inst. Vertebr. Palaeontol. Palaeoanthropol. Ser.* A 1:1–71 (In Chinese, Engl. summ.)

59. Pei WC, Woo JK, Chia LP, Chow MC, Liu X, et al. 1958. Report on the excavation of Palaeolithic sites at Ting-tsun, Hsiangfenhsien, Shansi province, China. *Mem. Inst. Vertebr. Palaeontol. Palaeoanthropol. Ser.* A 2:1–111 (In Chinese, Engl. summ.)

60. Pope GG. 1983. Evidence of the age of the Asian Hominidae. *Proc. Natl. Acad. Sci. USA* 80:4988–92

61. Pope GG. 1991. Evolution of the zygomaxillary region in the genus *Homo* and its relevance to the origin of modern humans. *J. Hum. Evol.* 21:189–213

62. Pope GG. 1992. Craniofacial evidence for the origin of modern humans in China. *Yearb. Phys. Anthropol.* 35:243–98

63. Pope GG, Cronin JE. 1984. The Asian Hominidae. *J. Hum. Evol.* 13:377–96

64. Qian F. 1985. On the age of "Yuanmou Man": a discussion with Liu Tung-sheng et

al. *Acta Anthropol. Sin.* 4:324–31 (In Chinese, Engl. Abstr.)

65. Qin Li. 1983. Discovery of additional *Homo erectus* teeth in Bailongdong, Yunxi county, Hubei. *Acta Anthropol. Sin.* 2:203 (In Chinese)

66. Qiu ZL, Gu YM, Zhang YY, Chang SS. 1973. Newly discovered *Sinanthropus* remains and stone artifacts at Choukoutien. *Vertebr. PalAsiat.* 11:109–31 (In Chinese)

67. Qiu ZL, Xu CH, Zhang WH, Wang RL, Wang JZ, Zhao CF. 1982. A human fossil tooth and fossil mammals from Nanzhao, Henan. *Acta Anthropol. Sin.* 1:109–17 (In Chinese, Engl. Abstr.)

68. Qiu ZL, Zhang YY, Hu SJ. 1985. Human tooth and paleoliths found at locality 2 of Longtanshan, Chenggong, Kunming. *Acta Anthropol. Sin.* 4:233–41 (In Chinese, Engl. Abstr.)

69. Rightmire GP. 1990. *The Evolution of Homo erectus: Comparative Anatomical Studies of an Extinct Human Species.* Cambridge: Cambridge Univ. Press

70. Robinson JT. 1953. *Meganthropus*, australopithecines and hominids. *Am. J. Phys. Anthropol.* 11:1–38

71. Schwarcz HP. 1993. Uranium-series dating and the origin of modern man. In *The Origin of Modern Humans and the Impact of Chronometric Dating*, ed. MJ Aitken, CB Stringer, PA Mellars, pp. 12–26. Princeton, NJ: Princeton Univ. Press

72. Shen G, Jin L. 1991. Restudy of the upper age limit of Beijing Man site. *Acta Anthropol. Sin.* 10:273–77 (In Chinese, Engl. Abstr.)

73. Smith FH, Falsetti AB, Donnelly SM. 1989. Modern human origins. *Yearb. Phys. Anthropol.* 32:35–68

74. Stringer CB. 1984. The definition of *Homo erectus* and the existence of the species in Africa and Europe. *Cour. Forsh. -Inst. Senck.* 69:131–43

75. Stringer CB. 1991. Replacement, continuity and the origin of *Homo sapiens*. In *Continuity or Replacement: Controversies in Homo sapiens Evolution*, ed. G Bräuer, F Smith, pp. 9–24. Rotterdam: Balkema

76. Stringer CB, Bräuer G. 1994. Methods, misreading, and bias. *Am. Anthropol.* 96: 416–24

77. Swisher CC, Curtis GH, Jacob T, Getty AG, Suprijo A. 1994. Age of the earliest known hominids in Java, Indonesia. *Science* 263: 1118–21

78. Tobias P, von Koeningswald G. 1964. A comparison between the Olduvai hominines and those of Java, and some implications for hominid phylogeny. *Nature* 204: 515–18

78a. Trinkhaus E. 1990. Unusual characteristics of the middle Paleolithic humans from Qafzeh and Skhul. *Univ. Tokyo Symp.: The Evolution and Dispersal of Modern Humans in Asia*, pp. 40–42. (Abstr.)

78b. Turner CG. 1990. Major features of sundadonty and sinodonty including suggestions about east Asian microevolution, population history, and late Pleistocene relationships with Australian aboriginals. *Am. J. Phys. Anthropol.* 82:295–317

79. Tyler DE. 1995. The current picture of hominid evolution in Java. *Acta Anthropol. Sin.* 14:313–23

80. Wang LH. 1989. Chronology in Chinese paleoanthropology. In *Early Humankind in China*, ed. RK Wu, XZ Wu, SS Zhang, pp. 392–409. Beijing: Science (In Chinese)

81. Wang LH, Bräuer G. 1984. A multivariate comparison of the human calva from Huanglong county, Shaanxi province. *Acta Anthropol. Sin.* 3:313–21 (In Chinese, Engl. Abstr.)

82. Wang LH, Li Y. 1983. On a fossil human calva unearthed from Huanglong County, Shaanxi Province. *Acta Anthropol. Sin.* 2: 314–19 (In Chinese, Engl. Abstr.)

83. Ward R. 1990. On the origin and dispersion of the Asian phylogenies of *Homo sapiens*: a molecular perspective. *Univ. Tokyo Symp.: The Evolution and Dispersal of Modern Humans in Asia*, pp. 46–47 (Abstr.)

84. Weidenreich F. 1936. The mandibles of *Sinanthropus pekinensis*: a comparative study. *Palaeontol. Sin. Ser. D* 7:1–162

85. Weidenreich F. 1936. Observations on the form and proportions of the endocranial casts of *Sinanthropus pekinensis*, other hominids, and the great apes: a comparative study of brain size. *Palaeontol. Sin. Ser. D* 7:1–50

86. Weidenreich F. 1937. The dentition of *Sinanthropus pekinensis*: a comparative odontography of the hominids. *Palaeontol. Sin.* (NS D) 1:1–180

87. Weidenreich F. 1939. Six lectures on *Sinanthropus pekinensis* and related problems. *Bull. Geol. Soc. China* 19:1–110

88. Weidenreich F. 1939. On the earliest representatives of modern mankind recovered on the soil of East Asia. *Bull. Nat. Hist. Soc. Peking* 13:161–74

89. Weidenreich F. 1941. The extremity bones of *Sinanthropus pekinensis*. *Palaeontol. Sin.* (NS D) 5:1–150

90. Weidenreich F. 1943. The skull of *Sinanthropus pekinensis*: a comparative study on a primitive hominid skull. *Palaeontol. Sin.* (NS D) 10:1–484

91. Wolpoff MH, Thorne AG, Jelmnek J, Zhang YY. 1993. The case for sinking *Homo erectus*: 100 years of *Pithecanthro-*

pus is enough! *Cour. Forsh. -Inst. Senck.*
171:341–61

91a. Wolpoff MH, Wu XZ, Thorne AG. 1984.
Modern *Homo sapiens* origins: a general
theory of hominid evolution involving the
fossil evidence from East Asia. In *The Origins of Modern Humans: A World Survey of the Fossil Evidence*, ed. FH Smith, F Spencer, pp. 411–84. New York: Academic

92. Woo JK (see also Wu RK). 1958. Tzeyang
Paleolithic Man: earliest representative of
modern man in China. *Am. J. Phys. Anthropol.* 16:459–71

93. Woo JK. 1958. Fossil human parietal bone
and femur from Ordos, Inner Mongolia.
Vertebr. PalAsiat. 2:208–12 (In Chinese,
Engl. Abstr.)

94. Woo JK. 1959. Human fossils found in
Liukiang, Kwangzi, China. *Palaelovertebr.
Palaeoanthropol.* 1:97–104

95. Woo JK. 1964. Mandible of *Sinanthropus
lantianensis. Curr. Anthropol.* 5:98–99

96. Woo JK. 1966. The skull of Lantian man.
Curr. Anthropol. 7:83–86

97. Woo JK, Chao TK. 1959. New discovery of
Sinanthropus mandible from Choukoutien.
Vertebr. PalAsiat. 3:169–72

98. Woo JK, Chia LP. 1954. New discoveries
about *Sinanthropus pekinensis* in Choukoutien. *Acta Palaeontol. Sin.* 2:267–88

99. Woo JK, Peng RC. 1959. Fossil human
skull of early Paleoanthropic stage found at
Mapa, Shaokuan, Kwangtung province.
Palaeovertebr. Palaeoanthropol. 1:159–64
(In Chinese)

100. Woo TL, Morant G. 1934. A biometric
study of the "flatness" of the facial skeleton
in man. *Biometrika* 26:196–50

101. Wood B. 1984. The origins of *Homo erectus. Cour. Forsch. -Inst. Senck.* 69:99–112

102. Wood B. 1992. Origin and evoultion of the
genus *Homo. Nature* 355:783–90

103. Wood B, Turner A. 1995. Out of Africa and
into Asia. *Nature* 378:239–40

104. Wu ML. 1980. Human fossils discovered at
Xujiayao site in 1977. *Vertebr. PalAsiat.*
18:229–38 (In Chinese, Engl. Abstr.)

105. Wu ML. 1983. *Homo erectus* from Hexian,
Anhui found in 1981. *Acta Anthropol. Sin.*
2:109–15 (In Chinese, Engl. Abstr.)

106. Wu ML. 1984. New discoveries of human
fossil in Tongzi, Guizhou. *Acta Anthropol.
Sin.* 3:195–201 (In Chinese, Engl. Abstr.)

107. Wu ML. 1986. Study of the temporal bone
of Xujiayao Man. *Acta Anthropol. Sin.* 5:
20–26 (In Chinese, Engl. Abstr.)

108. Wu ML, Cao ZT. 1983. The first discovery
of the fossil bone of the ancient mankind in
Guizhou Province. *J. Guiyang Teach. Coll.*
3:11–14 (In Chinese)

109. Wu ML, Wang LH, Zhang YY, Zhang SS.
1975. Fossil human teeth and associated

fauna from northern Guizhou. *Vertebr.
PalAsiat.* 13:14–23 (In Chinese)

110. Wu RK (see also Woo JK). 1988. The reconstruction of the fossil human skull from
Jinniushan, Yingkou, Liaoning province
and its main features. *Acta Anthropol. Sin.*
7:97–101 (In Chinese, Engl. Abstr.)

111. Wu RK, Dong XR. 1980. The teeth from
Yunxian, Hubei. *Vertebr. PalAsiat.* 18:
142–49 (In Chinese, Engl. Abstr.)

112. Wu RK, Dong XR. 1982. Preliminary study
of *Homo erectus* remains from Hexian, Anhui. *Acta Anthropol. Sin.* 1:2–13 (In Chinese, Engl. Abstr.)

113. Wu RK, Lin SL. 1983. Peking man. *Sci.
Am.* 248:86–94

114. Wu RK, Wu XZ. 1982. Human fossil teeth
from Xichuan, Henan. *Vertebr. PalAsiat.*
20:1–9 (In Chinese, Engl. Abstr.)

115. Wu RK, Wu XZ. 1982. Comparison of
Tautavel Man with *Homo erectus* and early
Homo sapiens in China. *Congr. Int. Paleontol. Hum.* 1:605–16. Nice: Pretirage

116. Wu XZ (see also Woo XZ). 1961. Study on
the Upper Cave Man of Choukoutien. *Vertebr. PalAsiat.* 3:181–211 (In Chinese,
Engl. Abstr.)

117. Wu XZ. 1981. The well-preserved cranium
of an early *Homo sapiens* from Dali,
Shaanxi. *Scient. Sin.* 2:200–6 (In Chinese,
Engl. Abstr.)

118. Wu XZ. 1987. Relation between upper Paleolithic man in China and their southern
neighbors in Niah and Tabon. *Acta Anthropol. Sin.* 6:180–83 (In Chinese, Engl.
Abstr.)

119. Wu XZ. 1988. The relationship between
upper Paleolithic human fossils of China
and Japan. *Acta Anthropol. Sin.* 7:235–38
(In Chinese, Engl. Abstr.)

120. Wu XZ. 1988. Comparative study of early
Homo sapiens from China and Europe.
Acta Anthropol. Sin. 7:287–93 (In Chinese,
Engl. Abstr.)

121. Wu XZ, Bräuer G. 1993. Morphological
comparison of archaic *Homo sapiens* between China and Africa. *Z. Morphol. Anthropol.* 79:241–59

122. Wu XZ, Poirier FE. 1995. *Human Evolution in China: A Morphometric Description
of Fossils and a Review of the Sites.* New
York: Oxford Univ. Press

123. Xu CH, Zhang YY, Chen CD, Fang DS.
1984. Human occipital bone and mammalian fossils from Chaoxian, Anhui. *Acta Anthropol. Sin.* 3:202–9 (In Chinese, Engl.
Abstr.)

124. Xu CH, Zhang YY, Fang DS. 1986. Human
fossil newly discovered at Chaoxian, Anhui. *Acta Anthropol. Sin.* 5:305–10 (In Chinese, Engl. Abstr.)

125. Xu QQ, Mu XN, Xu HK, Zhong SL, Mu
DC. 1993. Discovery of middle Pleistocene

mammalian fauna from Tangshan, Nanjing and its significance. *Chin. Sci. Bull.* 38: 1403–6 (In Chinese, Engl. Abstr.)

126. Xue XX. 1987. Human fossil tooth from Luonan, Shaanxi and its geological age. *Acta Anthropol. Sin.* 6:284–88 (In Chinese, Engl. Abstr.)

127. Yan GL. 1993. A preliminary study on magnetic stratigraphy of the geological section with the fossil bed of Yunxian *Homo* of Hubei. *Earth Sci. J. China Univ. Geosci.* 18:221–26 (In Chinese, Engl. Abstr.)

128. You YZ, Zhang ZB, Li Y, Li SK, Zhang PL. 1984. Human fossils from Changanpao, Qianguo, Jilin and paleoecology. *Prehistory* 6:70–74 (In Chinese)

129. Yu J. 1984. Preliminary research on the human fossils and culture from Chuandong, Pu'ding, Guizhou. *J. Nanjing Univ.: Nat. Sci.* 1:145–55 (In Chinese)

130. Yuan SX, Chen TM, Gao S. 1991. Study on Uranium-series dating of fossil bones and teeth from Zhoukoudian site. *Acta Anthropol. Sin.* 10:189–93 (In Chinese, Engl. Abstr.)

131. Yunnan Provincial Museum. 1977. Note on Lijiang Man's skull from Yunnan. *Vertebr. PalAsiat.* 15:157–61 (In Chinese)

131a. Zhang XY, ed. 1992. *Prehistoric Archeology of Baoshan.* Kunming: Yunnan Sci. Technol. (In Chinese)

132. Zhang XY, Cao F, Yue Q. 1992. A preliminary study on the human skull fossil of Yaoguan, Shitian. See Ref. 131a, pp. 80–89

133. Zhang XY, Li C. 1982. Fossil hominid discovered at Longlin, Guangxi. *Acta Anthropol. Sin.* 1:199 (In Chinese)

134. Zhang XY, Zheng L, Yang L, Bao L. 1990. Human fossil and cultural remains from Mengzi, Yunnan. *Yunnan Soc.* 2:60–64 (In Chinese)

135. Zhang YY. 1984. The "*Australopithecus*" of west Hubei and some early Pleistocene hominids of Indonesia. *Acta Anthropol. Sin.* 3:85–92 (In Chinese, Engl. Abstr.)

136. Zhang YY. 1991. An examination of temporal variation in the hominid dental sample from Zhoukoudian Locality 1. *Acta Anthropol. Sin.* 10:85–95 (In Chinese, Engl. Abstr.)

137. Zhang YY. 1995. Fossil human crania from Yunxian: morphological comparison with *Homo erectus* crania from Zhoukoudian. *Acta Anthropol. Sin.* 14:1–7 (In Chinese, Engl. Abstr.)

138. Zhang ZB. 1988. An analysis of the physical characteristics of modern Chinese. *Acta Anthropol. Sin.* 7:314–23 (In Chinese, Engl. Abstr.)

138a. Zhou GX, ed. 1994. *Int. Symp.: Relationship Between Chinese and Japanese Ancient Men and Their Prehistoric Cultures.* Beijing: China Int. Radio (In Chinese, Engl. Abstr.)

139. Zhou GX, Zhang ZB. 1994. Study on the skeleton at the Dalongtan site with comments on the relation between Minatogawa Man and ancient men of the late Pleistocene-the early Holocene in southern China. See Ref. 138a, pp. 59–88

140. Zhou MZ, Ho CK. 1990. History of the dating of *Homo erectus* at Zhoukoudian. *Geol. Soc. Am. Spec. Pap.* 242:69–74

Annu. Rev. Anthropol. 1996. 25:303–28

ANTHROPOLOGICAL RESEARCH ON HAZARDS AND DISASTERS

Anthony Oliver-Smith

Department of Anthropology, University of Florida, Gainesville, Florida 32611

KEY WORDS: response, change, risk, political economy, applied anthropology, theory

ABSTRACT

Recent perspectives in anthropological research define a disaster as a process/event involving the combination of a potentially destructive agent(s) from the natural and/or technological environment and a population in a socially and technologically produced condition of vulnerability. From this basic understanding three general topical areas have developed: (*a*) a behavioral and organizational response approach, (*b*) a social change approach, and (*c*) a political economic/environmental approach, focusing on the historical-structural dimensions of vulnerability to hazards, particularly in the developing world. Applied anthropological contributions to disaster management are discussed as well as research on perception and assessment of hazard risk. The article closes with a discussion of potentials in hazard and disaster research for theory building in anthropology, particularly in issues of human-environment relations and sociocultural change.

INTRODUCTION

The increasing frequency and severity of natural and technological disasters particularly, but not exclusively, in the developing world place them in the center of debates on human-environment relations and issues of development and sustainability. Disasters occur at the interface of society, technology, and environment and are fundamentally the outcomes of the interactions of these features. In very graphic ways, disasters signal the failure of a society to adapt successfully to certain features of its natural and socially constructed environment in a sustainable fashion.

0084-6570/96/1015-0303$08.00

Basically, the increase in number and severity of natural and technological disasters constitutes one of the clearest tests available of the lack of resilience and sustainability of many current human environmental adaptations. Any account of human environmental adaptation in the past or present that fails to consider the interaction of the social, technological, and natural processes of hazards and disasters is far from complete. Although awareness of the centrality of these phenomena in human-environment interaction is now emerging in the social sciences, until quite recently there has been a general failure to consider the interaction of the social, technological, and natural processes that produce hazards and disasters in our accounts of human environmental adaptation. Recent concerns about global warming in producing and intensifying hazards and disasters reflect an enhanced understanding of hazards and disasters as indicators of societal adaptation.

ENVIRONMENT, SOCIETY, AND DISASTER

Since about fifteen years ago, however, a new perspective has emerged that views hazards as basic elements of environments and as constructed features of human systems rather than as extreme and unpredictable events, as they were traditionally perceived. When hazards and disasters are viewed as integral parts of environmental and human systems, they become a formidable test of societal adaptation and sustainability. In effect, if a society cannot withstand without major damage and disruption a predictable feature of its environment, that society has not developed in a sustainable way.

When disaster strikes, whether it is the slow onset of drought, exposure to hidden toxic waste, or the sudden impact of an earthquake or chemical leak, it tends to be a totalizing event or process, affecting eventually most aspects of community life. Indeed, disasters have variously been considered a "natural laboratory" or a *crise revelatrice,* as the fundamental features of society and culture are laid bare in stark relief by the reduction of priorities to basic social, cultural, and material necessities (119). In that sense, then, there is a fundamental congruence between the analytical requirements posed by disaster studies and the distinctive approach of cultural and social anthropology (74, 140). The holistic, developmental, and comparative perspectives of anthropological research placing specifics against larger societal wholes and concerned with issues of social change and evolution are particularly congruent with the totalizing nature of disasters (139).

Anthropological disaster research has taken place predominantly outside the Euro-American context, which has been the site of most disaster research by the other social sciences. The numbers of high-impact technological and natural events are increasing much more rapidly now in the non-Euro-American context, where anthropologists have traditionally worked.[1] In early anthropological writing, hazards were considered fundamentally systemic dimensions of the total environment to which traditional peoples established reasonably effective adaptations, which allowed them to maintain long-term stability and viable lifeways in difficult conditions (140). In general, anthropology has added significant breadth and ethnographic solidity to a field that, until recently, focused almost entirely on immediate responses and organizational adjustments in first-world contexts (17).[2]

MAJOR TRENDS IN ANTHROPOLOGICAL RESEARCH ON DISASTERS

Recent perspectives in anthropological research define a disaster as a process/event involving a combination of a potentially destructive agent(s) from the natural and/or technological environment and a population in a socially and technologically produced condition of environmental vulnerability. The combination of these elements produces damage or loss to the major social organizational elements and physical facilities of a community to the degree that the essential functions of the society are interrupted or destroyed, which results in individual and group stress and social disorganization of varying severity. From this basic understanding, three general perspectives on hazards and disasters have developed in anthropology: (*a*) a behavioral response approach, (*b*) a social change approach, and (*c*) a political economic/environmental approach. However, discussion of these three overarching themes as separate entities is fundamentally artificial in that they address issues that are related causally, developmentally and conceptually.

THE BEHAVIORAL RESPONSE APPROACH

A continuing tradition in disaster research in general and in anthropology specifically has tended to view hazards and disasters as challenges to the structure and organization of society and has focused on the behavior of individuals and groups in the various stages of disaster impact and aftermath. The emergence, adjustments, and interactions of individuals, groups, and organizations to the stress of warning, impact, and immediate aftermath have been the central themes developed by this research.

---

[1] Due to space limitations, it is not possible to discuss in depth the research now emerging on hazards and disasters by anthropologists from developing nations particularly, but not exclusively, in Latin America (76, 76a). The literature discussed here is limited to work appearing in English.

[2] More complete discussions of the evolution of disaster research in anthropology are available (91, 95a, 140).

Individual and Organizational Responses to Disaster

Several closely drawn profiles of immediate responses to disaster impact focus on institutional adjustments in religion and ritual, technology, economy, politics, and patterns of cooperation and conflict as they emerged both at impact and in subsequent stages. The responses of organizations in several American disasters have been carefully analyzed (71). As in normal times, differentiating factors such as race, ethnicity, class, age, and gender are key variables in the emergence of patterns of consensus and conflict (6, 7, 17, 48, 59, 76, 85, 87, 92, 94, 113, 116, 131, 151, 156, 160, 162, 164). The factors of race, ethnicity, class, gender, and age are also significant in differentiating impact (2, 6–8, 17, 20, 25, 29, 47, 54, 55, 60, 71, 76, 85, 86, 94, 102, 106, 116, 137, 141, 144, 156, 164. A minimum degree of community integration is seen as a basis for initial steps toward recovery and rebuilding, which suggests that early positive responses to disasters should be based on greater local understanding of social and physical environments for the reduction of both short- and long-term losses (42, 47, 68, 79, 91). The quality of interaction between victims and aid personnel, particularly the appearance of a contentious we-they dichotomy, and the impact of postdisaster aid on the fabric and quality of social relations in the aftermath are recurrent themes (55, 79, 87). Also explored are the potentials in these conflictive relations for mobilization of community resources for improved relief and reconstruction efforts (60, 79, 87, 94). The social responses of vulnerable populations, particularly the elderly (45, 47, 48, 125, 126) and children (42, 73, 131), have also received attention.

Predisaster systems of social relationships associated with specific institutions are explored both for the nature of postdisaster response, interaction, and the distribution of aid and other resources (17). Preexisting morally and religiously sanctioned patterns of social inequality, for example, are held responsible for further discrimination and deprivation in circumstances of famine in India (144). Davis highlighted the importance of the Russian Orthodox Church among the Pacific Eskimos after the 1964 Alaskan earthquake in the adjustment and subsequent reconstruction of five heavily damaged villages (21). Wiedman's analysis of a university in a hurricane disaster shows how educational institutions confront major threats, adapt by immediate organizational responses, and avoid major structural alterations (155). The responses to the so-called social disaster of the Oklahoma City bombing provide insights into developing tensions in value orientations within the medical profession (130). Zaman suggested that a simple behavioral approach to social responses to flood and riverbank erosion in Bangladesh is insufficient because it often ignores broader sociopolitical and historical structural factors that influence the decisions underlying adjustment to natural hazards (50, 51, 162, 163, 165, 166).

The startling increase in number and severity of technological disasters in the past decade has generated several significant anthropological studies of social responses (10, 32, 67–69, 78, 103, 117, 131–133). Recent anthropological research on the Exxon-Valdez oil spill in Alaska was prefaced by Omohundro's analysis of the social impacts of an earlier oil spill (99). Much of Alaskan research explores the impact of the stress of the spill on the social fabric of affected communities. In an examination of social solidarity, conflict, emergent groups, and potential recovery efforts from the spill, Button questioned the sociological assertion that chronic technological disasters inhibit the formation and continuity of emergent groups because they erode social cohesiveness and provoke conflict particularly over interpretations of the event (10). Loughlin's work on representation, interpretation, and activism after the Bhopal, India, pesticide leak also constitutes a major challenge to this perspective (66–68). Furthermore, the emergence of the environmental justice movement has been stimulated in large measure by technological hazard risk and impact (56, 115).

The particular social vulnerability of natural resource–dependent communities has generated an alternative conceptual model called the Natural Resource Community (NRC) (32, 108). Defined as a population living within a bounded area whose primary cultural existence is based on the utilization of renewable natural resources, the viability of NRCs is threatened when there is a disruption of the natural resource base such as contamination after a technological disaster like the oil spill. The NRC model may prove useful for social impact assessment and planning for restoration and recovery programs, especially after technological disasters that impact natural resources. Picou et al (108) questioned the lack of ecological considerations that has characterized the study of technological disasters. Employing the ecological-symbolic approach (58), Picou et al substantiated the unique cultural and economic vulnerability of natural resource communities to resource contamination and the long-term social disruption in NRCs by technological disasters as a consequence of the disruption of the relationship between human communities and their biophysical environments (108).

Relative to issues of differential response, a number of anthropological studies have focused on sociopsychological questions about vulnerability, victimization, and aid in disasters. Dudasik proposed four categories of victims for the 1970 Peruvian earthquake: event victims (direct physical victims), context victims (traumatized by postimpact physical and sociocultural conditions), peripheral victims (nonresidents suffering losses), and entry victims (volunteers and assistance agents, suffering postdisaster physical conditions and psychological stresses) (29). Research in American disasters such as the Whittier Narrows Earthquake and the Baldwin Hills Fire in California found significant linkages between impact and posttraumatic stress symptoms (71–73). Russell found that PTSD was more prevalent among Natives than non-Natives and females than males and also found significant associations between PTSD and exposure to the Exxon-Valdez oil spill (117). Further research suggests that the impact of the oil spill on the psychosocial environment was as significant as it was on the physical environment (103). A study of the Shetland Island oil spill links control of information flow to increased anxiety and suspicion among victims (12).

The cultural expression of postdisaster sociopsychological stress has also received anthropological attention (103). Examining the association between disaster exposure with both "standard" symptomatology and folk illness categories reveals the popular illness category "ataque de nervios" (nervous attacks) as a significant organizing feature of peoples' responses to the 1985 landslide disaster in Puerto Rico, which highlights the importance of predisaster cultural knowledge for appropriate assistance responses in the aftermath (46). Oliver-Smith noted the differential impact of assistance on individuals and groups after the 1970 Peruvian earthquake, arguing that disaster aid may compound the psychological trauma of the disaster by undermining the autonomy of survivors and potentiating a debilitating dependency syndrome (94). Bode's research after the same earthquake on explanation and meaning formulation explored cultural expressions of grief and mourning and culturally acceptable forms of explanation for the disaster for regaining emotional stability (4, 5).

Culture and Catastrophe

Anthropologists have long explored the construction of cultural meanings and world views and the means and contexts in which such constructions are enacted and concretized. It is frequently in extreme conditions, particularly those characterized by loss and change, that human beings find themselves confronted with difficult existential questions. The responses of disaster-stricken peoples invariably involve the moral and ethical core of the belief system and include a deep delving into concepts of both social and cosmic justice, sin and retribution, causality, the relationship of the secular to the sacred, and the existence and nature of the divine (4, 5, 71, 89).

Relocation or resettlement of disaster-stricken populations is a common strategy pursued by planners in reconstruction efforts. Recent research emphasizes importance of place in the construction of individual and community identities, in the encoding and contextualization of time and history, and in the politics of interpersonal, community, and intercultural relations (1, 43, 90, 94, 164). Such place attachments mean that the loss or removal of a community from its "ground" by disaster may be profoundly traumatic (90).

The search for explanation and meaning for tragic losses and radical change has been a concern of disaster research (5, 71, 94). Following a disaster in Cyprus from which recovery was very slow, important shifts in attitudes and values took place in key institutions such as marriage, in which serious commitment changed to a desperate grasp at security in uncertain conditions (65). Oliver-Smith (94) and Bode (4, 5) documented the shifts in religious belief, symbols, and rituals in the aftermath of the 1970 earthquake in Peru.

The need to grieve and mourn properly is another major theme in cultural anthropological research on disasters. In addition to individual losses, severe disasters often destroy whole communities, which occasions grief for lost homes, social contexts, and culturally significant places and structures. When these elements are destroyed, they must be grieved for in ways similar to bereavement for a loved one (152). The loss of formal public places, informal gathering places, and other physical features symbolic of community identity must be mourned (5, 94). Survivors may place enormous importance on fidelity to cultural tradition as well as on the need to bear witness to suffering and the tragedy as experienced (94). Bode's extraordinary exploration of grief, mourning, and meaning formulation after the 1970 Peruvian earthquake is embedded in analysis of myths and legends as well as the religious symbols and rituals that sustained individual and cultural identity (5). The cultural supports and hindrances for grief and mourning are explored in a variety of disaster and crisis contexts (5, 54, 94, 130).

Finally, meaning construction is problematic for the disaster survivor and the disaster researcher, not only existentially but politically. The multiplicity of meanings generated out of the diverse voices in the rapid sequence of events creates an arena in which interpretation becomes a very contested field. In this arena of contestation, the power of representation is particularly crucial in the politics of defining the occurrence and extent of disaster and aid distribution (3, 118). Determining when a disaster has occurred and how much and for how long aid is necessary are functions of the politics of its representation (11, 31, 67, 69).

Politics and Power

Two related themes characterize much anthropological research on political factors in disasters: (*a*) disaster as both opportunity and cause for local political socialization and mobilization, and (*b*) disaster-caused alterations in relations with the state. For both themes, examining how disasters shape, maintain, destabilize, or destroy both political organizations and relations is central (57). Disasters create contexts in which power relations and arrangements can be more clearly perceived and confronted, which transforms political consciousness, shapes individual actions, and strengthens or dissolves institutional power arrangements (10, 57, 95, 122).

Disasters are seen as contexts for creation of political solidarity, activism, new agendas, and developing new power relations. Robinson et al (113) demonstrated that the 1985 Mexico City earthquakes created the political space for emergent groups to seize major roles in aid and assistance, thereby mobilizing a significant threat to the party in power. The reigning party only recovered its hegemony by appropriating and manipulating aid distribution, particularly of housing, after more than 300,000 people were left homeless by the disaster (113). After the 1989 Loma Prieta earthquake, the local Mexican population in Watsonville, California, learned from relatives or from their own experience of the 1985 Mexico City earthquake about the politics of aid, which enabled them, as it did the Mexican survivors, to focus public and media attention on the issue of affordable housing by invading public land (57). Laird's research on the same disaster probed the ideological implications of challenges to local political hegemony brought about by mobilization of minority groups (59). Both Button (10) and Mason (77) explored the political socialization and subsequent mobilization of individuals, groups, and communities afflicted by the Exxon-Valdez oil spill. The degree to which the groups and organizations formed out of the disaster subsequently broadened their agendas to embrace issues external to the disaster is central to such research (6).

Conversely, disasters may also have inhibiting effects on local political processes. Doughty's long-term research in Peru revealed that disaster impact may combine with major political change to compound the severity of effects on community integration and recovery by subverting "normal" political processes, particularly in the acquisition of aid (24). Davis found that over the long term, the 1964 Alaskan earthquake and subsequent assistance were major factors in increased integration and contact with the state among Native American villages (22). Chairetakis, in her research on development and reconstruction after the 1980 earthquake in Campania and Basilicata in Italy, saw the entire process as reinforcing the political and economic interests of the Christian Democratic party, dominant in southern Italy for the past forty years (17). Johnston & Schulte (57), comparing the sociopolitical dynamics of the Loma Prieta earthquake in California and Hurricane Hugo in the Virgin Islands, found that disasters create opportunities to reorganize power relations. The reconstruction process may become an arena of contestation that can affect predisaster power structures and relations (57, 85–88, 105). Disasters and reconstruction often create opportunities for the entrance of new groups into the political or economic process, which promotes change and evokes or mobilizes resistance in sectors supporting status quo arrangements (17). However, the costs of rebuilding physical infrastructure also constrain opportunities for empowerment, which in the Virgin Islands, for example, intensified dependency relations (57).

Disasters and Economics

Disasters are often perceived as primarily material events. That is, disasters cause destruction to a physical environment and to the material resources of a society, including the people, occupying that environment. Furthermore, in inflicting damage, disasters create urgent material needs, eliciting flows of material goods and services. When people speak of disasters as "the best of times and the worst of times," they are often referring to the behavior of human beings toward material resources during crisis. In disasters, certain fundamental economic assumptions or questions about human behavior such as altruism, rational choice models (self interest), private property, competition, reciprocity, distribution, contracts, trust, and the tension between social norms and economic self-interest are often highlighted (38). Indeed, many of these issues are central in an Oak Ridge National Laboratory project investigating the social and economic mechanisms needed to reestablish rational market mechanisms of distribution and exchange after a nuclear war or other major societal disaster (13).

In times of material scarcity, particularly those associated with famine, a breakdown may occur in the structure of morality that dictates food and resource distribution (23). Torry maintains that many traditional societies are highly inegalitarian, and crisis subjects certain groups to severe privation or even death. In India, Torry argued, patterns of structured inequality based on religiously sanctioned differentiation (castes primarily), which in normal circumstances produce marked inequalities in resource access, result in times of crisis in a morally justified inequitable distribution of relief (144).

In technological disasters the question of the morality of access to resources often is raised in regard to employment related to the disaster. Sharply divided moral and ethical stands were maintained concerning acceptance of employment and the extremely high wages Exxon was offering for the oil spill cleanup (10). Some research suggests that the morality of resource allocation changes with the stages of the disaster. In the immediate aftermath of the 1970 Peruvian earthquake, class and ethnic lines blurred. Concepts of private property disappeared as owners of animals donated them to the common good. However, over time, the solidarity became strained and conflicts broke out over the use of private resources for the public good. When aid arrived, old schisms reemerged and differential access to resources was not only sanctioned, it was demanded (87, 94). Disasters create a highly charged environment in which the moral order of society and individual rational choice or self interest are both thrown into high relief and potential contradiction.

The convergence of people of all sorts, from emergency workers to the merely curious, on the disaster site is well documented. An equally well-documented economic phenomenon is the convergence of material aid. Improved communications technologies alert the world community much more rapidly and graphically than ever before. Modern air transport can put a major relief effort in place in a very few days and maintain a virtual air bridge of continual supplies for extended periods of time (44). In effect, a disaster can almost overnight turn a region characterized by customary scarcity into a "disaster boom economy" (30). Relief agencies enter the disaster zone not only with material goods, but more significantly, often with employment, which creates high-paying jobs (10, 103). Postdisaster aid after the 1970 Peruvian earthquake produced a number of economic effects, including a new population of relatively prosperous consumers (disaster relief and reconstruction personnel), new consumer goods, new forms of housing, new urban design, all of which generally overwhelmed local capacities and distorted the local economy (30).

POSTDISASTER SOCIAL CHANGE AND DEVELOPMENT

Disasters can also be important factors in social and cultural change. In the sense that a disaster damages or destroys a society's ability to provide, however differentially, for the needs of its members, new adjustments or arrangements may have to be formulated for it to continue functioning. Therefore, disaster research inevitably addresses the issue, or at least the potential, of change. Despite the focus on social change in the earliest social scientific discussion of disasters, the issue of long-term social change has received significantly less attention than more immediate behavioral and organizational issues. Through its tradition of lengthy field research and emphasis on social and cultural process from a developmental perspective, anthropology has perhaps devoted more attention to the implications of disasters for long-term social change than other social sciences. In some archeological research, disasters figure prominently as explanations of certain forms of cultural evolution (80, 83, 84, 127, 128).

Although nonanthropological disaster research has generally portrayed traditional societies as vulnerable and unable to cope, more or less fatalistically living under a continual reign of terror from the environment, anthropology has demonstrated the resilient and adaptive capacities with which traditional peoples respond (137). Moreover, in traditional contexts indigenous adaptations probably allowed for reasonably effective responses to hazards (96, 165, 166). However, the transformations imposed on traditional societies and their environments by the industrialized world have increased the potential of disasters for change in the traditional world. Nonetheless, the scale of change potentially introduced by disasters needs to be addressed. In some cases imposed changes have exacerbated vulnerabilities to hazards, which results in major destruction of local societies (20). In other cases disasters have produced or accentuated stresses or forces with long-term structural implications (85, 86). Anthropological findings also tend to confirm the general conclusion that disasters are likely to accelerate changes that were underway before the disaster. Such accelerations may have implications for shifts in political economic power relations in the long-term as well as for reinterpretations of both the structure and process of development.

Disaster management and anthropological disaster research in the third world have been central in recent attempts to reorient the process of reconstruction in the developed world from replacement to development goals that address predisaster community problems (59, 93, 97, 98). Much social and economic change may occur in disasters during the reconstruction phase. When disaster strikes, very few places must now reconstruct themselves. Disasters commonly result in rapid local, state, national, or international aid. This convergence of people and goods, often foreign or strange to the local population, may ultimately be as great a source of stress and change as the disaster agent and destruction themselves (10, 17, 30, 85, 116). In large-scale devastation the reconstruction process may last almost indefinitely, often evolving into development programs, and the experts and their work become permanent fixtures in the social landscape.

Disaster reconstruction is fraught with ambivalence. On the one hand, people whose lives have been disrupted need to reestablish some form of stability and continuity with the past to recontinue their lives. For some individuals and groups the status quo ante was extremely favorable, and they count on its reconstruction. On the other hand, the disaster may have revealed areas where change is much needed. Consequently, reconstruction entails significant contention over means and goals involving persistence or change (10, 17, 94, 113, 116).

Reconstruction after the 1970 Peruvian earthquake stimulated certain social changes that produced greater freedom of action for oppressed indigenous people (85, 87). Significant changes in social and political consciousness were reported among all groups in the disaster zone about the social hierarchy of mestizos and Indians (5). However, reconstruction generally produced urban and housing patterns that tended to reinforce traditional social hierarchies (97). Moreover, although disaster and recovery efforts over a 15-year period produced some significant new infrastructure, Doughty reported no major alterations in the patterns of sociocultural behavior (24).

Postdisaster reconstruction and development after the Campania-Basilicata earthquake of 1980 were totally controlled by the dominant Christian Democratic Party to reinforce their 40-year political control over the region. The result was a retrenchment of traditional forms of development with significantly fewer benefits for the region and substantial rewards for external interests. Relief and reconstruction were seen as far more destructive to the social, moral, economic, and environmental fabric of the Sele valley than the damage done by the earthquake (17, 116).

In research after the 1964 Alaskan earthquake, Davis saw increased political awareness and an enhanced sense of identity balanced by increased dependence on government agencies in two north Pacific Alaskan villages (22). In Mexico in a climate of political mobilization, the 1985 earthquake and reconstruction stimulated the formation of militant neighborhood and student organizations that momentarily challenged governmental authority and control over relief and reconstruction. Although eventually the government asserted control, the earthquake accelerated the climate of mobilization and protest and added to new demands for accountability (113). Thus, the potential for social change inherent in the reconstruction process resides in organizational and cultural changes in political awareness at the community level. However, the potential for sound social and infrastructural development inherent in the reconstruction process has not been realized in most cases studied by anthropologists.

DEVELOPMENT AND THE POLITICAL ECONOMY OF VULNERABILITY

Since the early 1980s, many anthropologists and cultural geographers, following the growth of both cultural ecological and political economic perspectives in those disciplines, began to reconsider disasters less as the result of geophysical extremes such as storms, earthquakes, avalanches, droughts, etc and more as functions of an ongoing social order, of this order's structure of human-environment relations, and of the larger framework of historical and structural processes, such as colonialism and underdevelopment, that have shaped these phenomena (53). Disaster research from this perspective becomes essentially the analysis of the social creation of vulnerability (96a). For example, Morren asserted that (*a*) hazards emerge directly from human activity; (*b*) the severity of damage is related to the intensity of human environmental intervention; (*c*) development, encouraging dependency and specialization in individuals and communities, actually reduces both normal coping capacities and the ability to respond to hazards; and (*d*) outside disaster aid may convert a short-lived local problem into a long-term one (80a, 82).

This perspective has been used in anthropology since the early days of the discipline. Ethnographic research, as noted above, has traditionally discussed hazards as a known part of a total environment to which traditional peoples had to adapt (139, 140). For example, modes of subsistence, social organization, and population densities of nomadic and transhumant pastoralists in Africa represent rational adaptations to marginal environments, yet economic pressures have produced overstocking and overpopulation, which make both people and land vulnerable to cyclic droughts (77a, 147).

Colonial governments and their successors, responding to nonindigenous pressures and forces, imposed systems of production, urban and rural settlement, and limits on population mobility that severely undermined indigenous hazard management (140). Zaman doubted the effectiveness of high cost, large-scale engineering efforts at flood control and recommended instead the promotion and use of indigenous ways of living with flood (164). Oliver-Smith, noting that little pre-Columbian archeological evidence of disaster-caused mortality exists to equal the 65,000 deaths caused by the 1970 earthquake in Peru, concluded that general and specific adaptations of pre-Columbian Andean cultures to their hazard-prone environment were reasonably effective (96). Furthermore, the high mortality produced in the 1970 earthquake could be traced in part to Spanish-induced changes in building materials, urban design, and settlement patterns, which may have produced a socially created pattern of vulnerability to hazards (96).

Increasing vulnerability to hazard continues relatively unabated today, largely because of the undermining of indigenous adaptations, based on long-term experience in local environments, through direct government policies or political economic forces creating production systems inappropriate to local culture and environmental conditions. Large-scale economic interventions such as mining, forestry, irrigation, hydroelectric, and industrial enterprises are creating hazardous conditions around the globe. Government economic policies designed to enhance growth are setting in motion processes with dangerous, potentially catastrophic ecological consequences. For example, governmental promotion of Amazonian colonization schemes of small producers has produced short-term survival strategies that contribute to soil erosion, declining yields, and ultimately loss of land to large-scale ranching interests that in turn magnify the deterioration of soil resources and environmental destruction (19, 120). Governmental policy or economic forces have promoted similar inappropriate forms of production in many parts of the world, which set in motion processes of soil erosion, desertification, and deforestation and produce conditions of extreme environmental vulnerability to natural hazards. In effect, such processes are creating both vulnerability and the preconditions of a disaster agent (55a, 61a, 80a).

Other processes associated with economic growth such as industrialization and urbanization have led to the concentration of populations in areas with vulnerable conditions (82, 141). Many people on the social and territorial periphery of the global economic system are made more vulnerable by unequal economic relationships that do not allow them access to the basic resources of land, food, and shelter (76). In general, in earlier disaster research it was assumed that people lived in dangerous circumstances because they lacked knowledge of disasters or were uninformed about risks. However, recent research shows that individuals and groups may be fully aware of risks but have no choice other than to live in dangerous areas such as floodplains or unstable hillsides. This predicament is not due to lack of information or inefficient land-use planning but to the control of land by market forces that do not permit low-income groups access to safe land for residence (76). The danger of vulnerable residence sites is frequently compounded in urban areas by pollution and poor toxic-waste disposal, contaminated water, lack of sanitary services, and unsafe housing stock (97, 141).

Torry, however, questioned explanations that express disaster solely in terms of "ultimate causation" according to systemic or structural causes such as underdevelopment or dependency (145). While praising dependency explanations for debunking the view that famines result from a lack of rainfall, Torry highlighted internal proximate factors of local social stratification that result in inequalities of risk bearing and resource allocations as important to understanding famine impact and mitigation (144, 145).

To date, the famines ravaging various regions in Africa in the past twenty years can serve as the prototype of the kind of disaster we are creating. That these famines are the direct result of human intervention, largely alien to the people and environments experiencing them, is confirmed. Turton points to the irony in a situation in which the environmental destruction wrought by pastoralists is deplored and maximum limits on animal and human populations are recommended by experts enjoying a standard of living characterized by an ethic of uninhibited maximization and maintained at the cost of massive industrial pollution (147).

While most disasters today are closely linked to models and patterns of development as they intersect with the environment, few demonstrate as tragically as famine the devastating effects that environmental processes and forces combined with the historical processes of socioeconomic systems can have on large populations. Fundamentally a third-world phenomenon, famine is considered by some to be the inevitable result of the disruption of indigenous coping mechanisms by the institutions of colonialism and the penetration of the international market (20). Due in part to the coincidence between famine locations and a tradition of research sites, as well as the extended fieldwork entailed in anthropological research and the gradual onset of famine processes compared with other forms of disaster, anthropological famine research has an identity different from other disaster research and constitutes a field and a literature that in many senses stand alone. The reader interested in famine is referred to the 1990 *Annual Review of Anthropology* (129).

APPLIED ANTHROPOLOGY AND DISASTER MANAGEMENT

Similar to most disaster research in other fields, anthropological research has an implicit applied perspective. Virtually all research is in some measure directed at the problems individuals, communities, and societies confront in disaster. There is, however, a corpus of literature in anthropological disaster research that addresses applied problems and methods explicitly.

People and communities confront a wide range of issues that vary with the scope and time frame of the total phenomenon of a disaster. Warnings are particularly problematic. The response to threats and the necessity of developing adequate warning systems have been studied (142, 146). In terms of preparedness and mitigation, Torry concluded that development planners must factor hazards into projects to avoid creating greater vulnerability (143). Traditional adaptations to environments and indigenous technical knowledge have been suggested as sources for innovative approaches to problems of mitigation and vulnerability (51, 96, 147, 162). Housing safety education in Jamaica after Hurricane Gilbert has been explored as a mitigation strategy (98). Greater linkages between reconstruction, mitigation, and development have recently been stressed (95, 143).

Early response and emergency relief operations have received some attention from anthropologists. Morren claimed that local people, usually the first responders anyway, can be effective in limiting short- and long-term losses (81). Torry assessed government food distribution programs in drought-caused emergencies in India (142). Laird has explored the efforts of local people to rechannel earthquake relief after the Loma Prieta earthquake (59). Analyses of victim and agency discourse patterns demonstrate that each party constructs the relief and reconstruction process differently (55, 79). The specific problems of different groups, such as those based on age, gender, race, or ethnicity, within communities have received considerable attention (54, 85, 92, 122, 144, 156, 160, 161).

Anthropological research on international famine relief focuses on the inefficiencies, delays, and dehumanizing effects of this relief on recipients (138, 146). Although some successes have been noted (36), much aid, particularly that involving resettlement, has created or compounded dependency as well exacerbated the disruption suffered by local people. Shipton concluded that more applied research on the functioning of and programs used by aid organizations and agencies is sorely needed to improve performance in famine relief (129).

The general process of reconstruction has received some scrutiny, particularly concerning class and ethnic differentials (97, 160) and leadership patterns (17, 27, 28, 116). Postdisaster housing has garnered attention. Patterns of discrimination in housing provision (17, 92, 116, 160), relative effectiveness of different housing provision methods (70), housing changes and vulnerability (2), and specific housing problems in US disasters (6–8) have all been explored by anthropologists.

The problems associated with postdisaster settlement and resettlement planning have received some anthropological scrutiny. Glittenberg detailed the relative success of different organizational formats of settlements after the 1976 Guatemalan earthquake (40). The frequent resettlement due to seasonal floods in Bangladesh has produced considerable anthropological criticism of technological approaches to flood adjustment (50, 51, 125, 126, 162–166). Others have explored the general problems of postdisaster resettlement (93) and specific cases in varying contexts such as Peru (90), the New Hebrides (136), and Guatemala (40). Goldman's critique of postdisaster planning in Peru from sociocultural and socioeconomic perspectives is particularly enlightening (41).

Anthropological research on relief, housing, resettlement, and other assistance issues is also linked to assessments of the organization and character of assistance agencies, particularly in these agencies' implications for development. Analyses of bureaucratic structure and decision-making processes in disaster situations as well as the management of food relief have been undertaken by anthropologists (24, 85, 94, 138, 142, 146). Further, the quality and quantity of aid itself are assessed in different disaster contexts (17, 24, 25, 85, 94). Serious criticism has been leveled at postdisaster aid that is so culturally inappropriate as to be both useless and insulting (94, 139). Doughty's revealing comparative analysis of differential aid patterns for war and disaster in Latin America focuses on cultural concepts of victimhood and deservedness (25).

The applied anthropological study of disasters has also been informed by related fields in important ways. The fields of resettlement research, refugee research, and conservation and development research in particular have informed the specifically applied aspects of the discipline. Research in involuntary resettlement, particularly stemming from development projects, has provided disaster research with comparative and theoretical material on the impacts of dislocation on individuals, families, and communities (15, 49, 104, 124). Refugee studies has informed disaster research on issues about appropriate forms of aid and issues of victim empowerment (52, 75). Finally, conservation and development and political ecological research has provided perspectives on traditional and modern systems of human-environment interactions and environmental damage with potential for disastrous consequences (18, 109, 121).

The ethical dimensions of research in crisis situations have been applied to whether questionnaires are appropriate instruments for research on people under stress, which has evoked criticism of the reification of victims and their experiences. More dialogic, open-ended methods are suggested as both ethically more appropriate and methodologically more effective (9, 89).

PERCEPTION AND ASSESSMENT OF HAZARD RISK

Hazard risk is a highly contentious issue in many social and scientific contexts. Epistemologically, risk is problematical in that it is subject to differential construction by the various parties involved. Traditionally the purview of engineers, health physicists, statisticians, and epidemiologists, risk is defined probabilistically according to "real" risk, determined scientifically and objectively, vs "perceived" risk by the public, assumed to be uninformed, false, illusory, or irrational (61–63, 158). In contrast, anthropologists entering the field have tended to emphasize nonprobabilistic approaches, conceptualizing risk in its sociocultural context (158).

The major anthropological contribution to the field to date is Douglas & Wildavsky's *Risk and Culture,* a coauthored effort by an anthropologist and a political scientist, which views risk perception as primarily a sociocultural phenomenon affected by social organization and values that guide behavior and affect judgments about what is to be considered "dangerous." Douglas & Wildavsky hypothesize that different characteristics of social life, primarily related to degrees of integration and group power relations, elicit different responses to danger (26).

Risk perception and assessment issues in anthropological research focus largely, though not exclusively, on technological hazards, including groundwater contamination (35), the coincidence of toxic-waste disposal sites and minority communities (9), radioactive contamination and knowledge systems (100), radioactive contamination and social and economic impacts (107), high-level radioactive waste transport and storage (64, 110), global warming due to the greenhouse effect (39), technology acceptance (111), risk communication (157–159), and risk perception and exposure to technology (114, 123, 134–135a), risk perception, negotiation and acceptance (14, 61), and disaster-prone industry and culture (153). Themes common to many of these contributions include the social effects of risk perceptions, the conflicts between expert opinion and local knowledge, the role of culture in the formation of expert opinion, methodological difficulties in anthropological fieldwork about risk perception, and the conflicts between development goals and environmental protection. Risk perception and assessment are grounded in the cultural norms and values that both govern and are embedded in the relationships that human communities have with their physical and social environments. In that sense, risk perception studies address both problems of immediate concern to specific communities but address theoretical questions about cultural and social constructions of reality. Risk perception research engages cultural theory directly in its focus on ideologies and constructions of social, physical, and cosmological environments.

DISASTERS: A NATURAL LABORATORY FOR ANTHROPOLOGICAL THEORY

Despite the frequent characterization of disasters as natural laboratories for the testing of hypotheses and theories on society and culture, theoretical work in disaster research has been limited. However, there have been some excursions into hypothesis testing and theory formulation about disaster stress and sociocultural responses and sociocultural evolution.

In addition to Douglas & Wildavsky's work on risk, a major contribution to social theory is Wallace's work on responses to sociocultural disorganization (148–152). Wallace's disaster research, which includes a tornado study (150), a theory of behavior in cultural crisis (151, 152), and his landmark paper on revitalization movements (149), links the issues of disaster, cultural crisis, and response and social change in one of the major contributions to middle-range theory in the social sciences of the past fifty years.

Wallace has criticized anthropology for adhering too much to its traditional mission of explaining the internal logic of traditional or non-Western cultural systems, which, he claimed, produces single-minded emphasis on normal patterns of behavior (148). Wallace saw the emphasis on normality as ignoring the opportunity that W Lloyd Warner discerned in those moments when "all hell breaks loose," when the innermost workings of communities are revealed (154).

Rossi's recent book on postearthquake reconstruction in southern Italy is the only recent work in disaster research with an explicitly theoretical goal (116). Employing quantitative and qualitative data from damaged and destroyed communities, his theoretical project is to reformulate the current discussion on "structure" and "agency" in dialectic terms and to contextualize it in empirical data. This goal alone establishes Rossi's work as the most theoretically ambitious in contemporary disaster research. Rossi's book also contains valuable methodological insights about the use of quantitative data in theory confirmation as well as important findings on reconstruction in rural communities. The 1980 southern Italian earthquake has also stimulated further theoretical speculation on crisis and cultural response in complex societies (16).

Attempts have been made to integrate disasters into theories of response to environmental change. Loughlin & Brady (66) hypothesized that adaptive infrastructure under stress conditions will integrate constraints on social action and coordinate them with recursive environmental changes. Disasters are seen as fostering theories on response hierarchies and cost/risk assessments as well as framing and testing hypotheses about environmental change and human behavior (61a,b,c). Resource scarcity—or its threat because of potential or actual impact on food supply by natural disasters—is hypothesized as a central cause of warfare in nonstate societies (33, 34).

Archeologists have considered the role of disasters as engines of sociocultural transformation. Volcanic eruptions are important in triggering large migrations and other changes (127, 128). Most recently, it has been hypothesized that tectonic uplift, seismic activity, and cyclic El Niño events have played major roles in the emergence and decline of agricultural regimes and cultural horizons in Andean state prehistory (83, 84). An exploration of "catastrophe theory" probed its potential for explaining sudden discontinuities in social evolution according to smoothly changing control variables (37, 112, 167). Renfrew's dismissal of the relevance of catastrophe theory in explaining the effects of natural cataclysms on human societies ignores the inherence of hazards to socioenvironmental systems and seems premature given the contradictions between society and environment revealed in current discussions of general ecology and sustainability.

Paine's recent call (101) for anthropological research on issues "beyond routine" responds to Wallace's earlier criticism of anthropology's emphasis on normality and more recent calls for greater understanding of cultural praxis. By encouraging an understanding of how people faced with the accidents of history undertake the remaking of themselves through remakings in culture, Paine issues a challenge in which anthropological disaster research could realize its theoretical potential.

CONCLUSION

Currently, there is a tendency toward sharing methods, theoretical perspectives, and research questions among the social sciences. For example, anthropology has embraced quantitative methods (3a) while political scientists have used ethnographic research methods to great effect (123a). Anthropologists, sociologists, geographers, and political scientists have all shared research in-

terests and theoretical perspectives on such varied themes as structural adjustment, peasant political movements, drug use, and involuntary migration and
resettlement, as well as disasters. This tendency is in part due to the increasing
urgency of a number of research issues, disasters among them, with broad
theoretical and practical significance. Consequently, general and scientific
concern in disaster research for increasing levels of vulnerability and destruction, linked particularly to environmental degradation, uncontrolled development, technological breakdown, and societal conflict, have created contexts for
common interests, sharing of methods and perspectives, and greater cross-disciplinary communication and collaboration. Thus anthropologists, cultural geographers, sociologists, social psychologists, political scientists, planners, architects, and engineers are now drawing on one another's work and are developing both theoretical perspectives and research projects that reflect the
all-encompassing quality of disaster processes and events. The global nature
of environmental and social problems contributing to the expansion of conditions of vulnerability and resulting in more frequent and more severe natural
and technological disasters places the entire problem squarely within the purview of an anthropology that chooses to address holistically the issue of
human-environment interactions for both practical and theoretical purposes.

Literature Cited

1. Altman I, Low S. 1992. *Place Attachment:
Human Behavior and Environment: Ad-
vances in Theory and Research,* Vol. 8.
New York: Plenum. 314 pp.
2. Bates F, Farrell T, Glittenberg JAK. 1979.
Some changes in housing characteristics in
Guatemala following the February 1976
earthquake and their implications for future
earthquake vulnerability. *Mass Emerg.* 4:
121–33
3. Benthall J. 1993. *Disasters, Relief and the
Media.* London: Tauris. 267 pp.
3a. Bernard HR. 1994. *Research Methods in
Cultural Anthropology: Qualitative and
Quantitative Approaches.* Thousand Oaks,
CA: Sage. 585 pp. 2nd ed.
4. Bode B. 1977. Disaster, social structure and
myth in the Peruvian Andes: the genesis of
an explanation. *Ann. NY Acad. Sci.* 293:
246–74
5. Bode B. 1989. *No Bells to Toll: Destruction
and Creation in the Andes.* New York:
Scribners. 559 pp.
6. Bolin R, Stanford L. 1990. Shelter and

housing issues in Santa Cruz County. In
*The Loma Prieta Earthquake: Studies of
Short Term Impacts,* ed. R Bolin, pp.
99–108. Boulder, CO: Inst. Behav. Sci.
Univ. Colo.
7. Bolin R, Stanford L. 1990. Shelter, housing
and recovery: a comparison of U. S. Disasters. *Disasters* 15:24–34
8. Bolton P, Liebow EB, Olson JL. 1993.
Community context and uncertainty following a damaging earthquake: low-income Latinos in Los Angeles, California.
Environ. Prof. 15:240–48
9. Button GV. 1991. *Ethical dilemmas confronting researchers of chronic technological disasters.* Presented at Annu. Meet.
Soc. Appl. Anthropol., 50th, Charleston,
SC
10. Button GV. 1992. *Social conflict and emergent groups in a technological disaster: the
Homer area community and the Exxon-Valdez oil spill.* PhD thesis. Brandeis Univ. 403
pp.
11. Button GV. 1995. "What You Don't Know

Can't Hurt You": the right to know and the Shetland Islands oil spill. *Hum. Ecol.* 23: 241–57

12. Button GV. 1995. *"The Disaster that Wasn't": the press response to the Braer oil spill in the Shetland Islands.* Presented at Annu. Meet. Am. Anthropol. Assoc., 94th, Washington, DC

13. Cantor RA, Henry S, Rayner S. 1989. *Markets, Distribution and Exchange after Societal Cataclysm (ORNL-6384).* Oak Ridge, TN: Oak Ridge Nat. Lab. 141 pp.

14. Cantor RA, Schoepfle M. 1993. Risk, rationality, and community: psychology, ethnography, and transactions in the risk management process. *Environ. Prof.* 15: 293–303

15. Cernea M. 1990. Internal refugee flows and development induced population displacement. *J. Refug. Stud.* 3:320–29

16. Chairetakis A. 1995. *The two-sided mirror: a theory of culture and crisis response in complex societies.* Presented at Annu. Meet. Am. Anthropol. Assoc., 94th, Washington, DC

17. Chairetakis A. 1991. *The past in the present: community variation and earthquake recovery in the Sele Valley, southern Italy, 1980–1989.* PhD thesis. Columbia Univ. 471 pp.

18. Clay J. 1988. *Indigenous Peoples and Tropical Forests: Models of Land Use and Management from Latin America.* Cambridge, MA: Cult. Surv. 116 pp.

19. Collins JL. 1986. Smallholder settlement of tropical South America: the social causes of ecological destruction. *Hum. Organ.* 45: 1–10

20. Copans J. 1983. The Sahelian drought: social sciences and the political economy of underdevelopment. See Ref. 53, pp. 83–97

21. Davis NY. 1970. The role of the Russian orthodox church in five Pacific Eskimo villages as revealed by the earthquake. In *The Great Alaska Earthquake of 1964. Human Ecology.* Washington, DC: Comm. Earthq. Nat. Acad. Sci.

22. Davis NY. 1986. Earthquake, tsunami, resettlement and survival in two north Pacific Alaskan native villages. See Ref. 91a, pp. 123–54

23. Dirks R. 1980. Social responses during severe food shortages and famine. *Curr. Anthropol.* 21:21–44

24. Doughty PL. 1986. Decades of disaster: promise and performance in the Callejon de Huaylas, Peru. See Ref. 91a, pp. 35–80

25. Doughty PL. 1990. *Comparing disasters: wars and earthquakes in Latin America.* Presented at Annu. Meet. Soc. Appl. Anthropol., 49th, York, England

26. Douglas M, Wildavsky A. 1982. *Risk and Culture: An Essay on the Selection of Technical and Environmental Dangers,* Berkeley, CA: Univ. Calif. Press. 221 pp.

27. D'Souza F. 1982. Recovery following the South Italian earthquake: two contrasting examples. *Disasters* 6:101–9

28. D'Souza F. 1986. Recovery following the Gediz earthquake: a study of four villages in western Turkey. *Disasters* 10:35–52

29. Dudasik S. 1980. Victimization in natural disaster. *Disasters* 4:329–38

30. Dudasik S. 1982. Unanticipated repercussions of international disaster relief. *Disasters* 4:329–38

31. Dyer CL. 1995. *An analysis of the variability of institutional and cultural reaction to the impact of Hurricane Andrew on the fisheries of Florida versus Louisiana.* Presented at Annu. Meet. Am. Anthropol. Assoc., 94th, Washington, DC

32. Dyer CL, Gill DA, Picou JS. 1992. Social disruption and the Valdez oil spill: Alaskan natives in a natural resource community. *Soc. Spectr.* 12:105–26

33. Ember C, Ember M. 1992. Resource predictability, mistrust, and war. *J. Confl. Resolut.* 36:242–62

34. Ember M, Ember C. 1988. *Fear of disasters as an engine of history: resource crises, warfare and interpersonal aggression.* Presented at Multidiscip. Conf. "What is the Engine of History?" Tex. A&M Univ., College Station, TX

35. Fitchen J. 1988. Anthropology and environmental problems in the US: the case of groundwater contamination. *Pract. Anthropol.* 10:5,18–20

36. Fleuret A. 1988. Food aid and development in rural Kenya. In *Anthropology of Development and Change in East Africa,* ed. D Brokensha, P Little, pp. 77–98. Boulder, CO: Westview

37. Friedman J. 1982. Catastrophe and continuity in social evolution. See Ref. 112a, pp. 175–96

38. Gerlach LP. 1993. Crises are for using: the 1988 drought in Minnesota. *Environ. Prof.* 15:274–87

39. Gerlach LP, Rayner S. 1988. Culture and the common management of global risks. *Pract. Anthropol.* 10:15–18

40. Glittenberg JAK. 1982. Reconstruction in four urban post-disaster settlements. In *Recovery, Change, and Development: A Longitudinal Study of the 1976 Guatemalan Earthquake,* ed. FL Bates, 2:634–707. Athens: Univ. Ga. Press

41. Goldman RE. 1985. *Planning and development in a postdisaster situation: the reconstruction of Yungay, Peru.* MA thesis. Univ. Florida. 211 pp.

42. Gordon NS, Farberow NL, Maida CA. 1996. *Children and Disasters.* New York: Brunner/Mazel. In press

43. Gordon NS, Maida CA, Farberow NL, Fidell L. 1995. Residential loss and displacement among survivors of the 1993 Altadena fire. *Nat. Hazards Res. Appl. Inf. Cent. Quick Response Rep.* 8:1–13
44. Green S. 1977. *International Disaster Relief: Toward a Responsive System.* New York: McGraw-Hill. 101 pp.
45. Greenamyre E. 1991. *Those in need and those who get: two distinct disaster categories.* Presented at Annu. Meet. Soc. Appl. Anthropol., 50th, Charleston, SC
46. Guarnaccia P. 1991. *Culture's role in shaping psychosocial responses to disaster.* Presented at Annu. Meet. Soc. Appl. Anthropol., 50th, Charleston, SC
47. Guillette E. 1991. *The impact of recurrent disaster on the aged of Botswana.* Presented at Annu. Meet. Soc. Appl. Anthropol., 50th, Charleston, SC
48. Guillette E. 1993. *The role of the aged in community recovery following Hurricane Andrew.* Boulder, CO: *Nat. Hazards Res. Appl. Inf. Cent. Quick Response Rep. 56.* 6 pp.
49. Hansen A, Oliver-Smith A, eds. 1982. *Involuntary Migration and Resettlement: The Problems and Responses of Dislocated People,* Boulder, CO: Westview. 333 pp.
50. Haque CE, Zaman MQ. 1989. Coping with riverbank erosion hazard and displacement in Bangladesh. *Disasters* 13:300–14
51. Haque CE, Zaman MQ. 1993. Human responses to riverine hazards in Bangladesh: a proposal for sustainable development. *World Dev.* 21:93–107
52. Harrell-Bond B. 1986. *Imposing Aid: Emergency Assistance for African Refugees.* Oxford: Oxford Univ. Press. 440 pp.
53. Hewitt K, ed. 1983. *Interpretations of Calamity.* New York: Allen & Unwin. 304 pp.
54. Hoffman SM. 1994. Up from the embers: a disaster survivor's story. *Natl. Cent. Posttrauma. Stress Disord. Clin. Q.* Spring: 15–16
55. Hoffman SM. 1995. *Culture deep and custom old: the reappearance of a traditional cultural grammar in the aftermath of the Oakland-Berkeley Firestorm.* Presented at Annu. Meet. Am. Anthropol. Assoc., 94th, Washington, DC
55a. Horowitz M, Salem-Murdock M. 1987. The political economy of desertification in White Nile Province, Sudan. In *Lands at Risk in the Third World: Local Level Perspectives,* ed. P Little, M Horowitz, R Nyerges, 1:95–114. Boulder, CO: Westview. 416 pp.
56. Johnston BR. 1994. *Who Pays the Price? The Sociocultural Context of Environmental Crisis.* Washington, DC: Island. 249 pp.

57. Johnston BR, Schulte J. 1992. *Natural power and power plays in Watsonville, California, and the US Virgin Islands.* Presented at Annu. Meet. Soc. Appl. Anthropol., 51st, Memphis, TN
58. Kroll-Smith JS, Couch SR. 1990. *The Real Disaster is above Ground.* Lexington: Univ. Ky. Press. 200 pp.
59. Laird R. 1991. *Rechanneling relief: nontraditional response to disaster.* Presented at Annu. Meet. Soc. Appl. Anthropol., 50th, Charleston, SC
60. Laird R. 1992. *Private troubles and public issues: the politics of disaster.* Presented at Annu. Meet. Am. Anthropol. Assoc., 91st, San Francisco
61. Laksono PM. 1988. Perception of volcanic hazards: villagers versus government officials in central Java. In *The Real and Imagined Role of Culture in Development,* ed. MR Dove, pp. 183–99. Honolulu: Univ. Hawaii Press
61a. Lees SH. 1980. The "Hazards" approach to development research: recommendations for Latin American drylands. *Hum. Organ.* 69:372–76
61b. Lees SH. 1988. Algae: a minor disaster in the Jezreel Valley, Israel. See Ref. 91a, pp. 155–76
61c. Lees SH, Bates DG. 1990. The ecology of cumulative change. In *The Ecosystem Approach in Anthropology,* ed. EF Moran, 1:247–78. Ann Arbor: Univ. Mich. Press. 476 pp.
62. Liebow EB. 1993. Who is expert at interpreting environmental hazards? *Environ. Prof.* 15:288–92
63. Liebow EB, Wolfe AK. 1993. Communities at risk: communication and choice of environmental hazards. *Environ. Prof.* 15: 237–39
64. Liebow EB. 1988. Permanent storage for nuclear power plant waste: comparing risk judgments and their social effects. *Pract. Anthropol.* 10:10–12
65. Loizos P. 1977. A struggle for meaning: reactions to disaster among Cypriot refugees. *Disasters* 1:231–39
66. Loughlin CD, Brady IA. 1978. *Extinction and Survival in Human Populations.* New York: Columbia Univ. Press. 327 pp.
67. Loughlin K. 1995. Rehabilitating science, imagining Bhopal. In *Late Editions 2: Technoscientific Imaginaries,* ed. G Marcus, pp. 277–302. Chicago: Univ. Chicago Press
68. Loughlin K. 1995. *Locating Corporate Environmentalism: The Bhopal Case.* Presented at Adv. Sem. "Power/Knowledge Shifts in America's Fin-de-Siecle," Sch. Am. Res., Santa Fe, NM
69. Loughlin K. 1996. Representing Bhopal. In *Late Editions 3: The Net, News and Vide-*

otape, ed. G Marcus. Chicago: Univ. Chicago Press

70. Low S. 1988. Housing, organization and social change: a comparison of programs for urban reconstruction in Guatemala. *Hum. Organ.* 47:15–24

71. Maida CA. 1996. *Crisis and Compassion in a World of Strangers*. New Brunswick, NJ: Rutgers Univ. Press. In press

72. Maida CA, Gordon NS, Steinberg A, Gordon G. 1989. Psychosocial impact of disasters: victims of the Baldwin Hills fire. *J. Trauma. Stress* 2:37–48

73. Maida CA, Gordon NS, Strauss G. 1993. Child and parent reactions to the Los Angeles area Whittier Narrows earthquake. *J. Soc. Behav. Pers.* 8:421–36

74. Malinowski B. 1922. *Argonauts of the Western Pacific*. New York: Dutton. 527 pp.

75. Manz B. 1988. *Refugees of a Hidden War*. Albany: State Univ. NY Press. 283 pp.

76. Maskrey A. 1989. *Disaster Mitigation: A Community Based Approach*. Oxford: Oxfam. 100 pp. 3rd ed.

76a. Maskrey A, ed. 1993. *Los Desastres No Son Naturales*. Bogotá: Tercer Mundo Editores. 166 pp.

77. Mason R. 1992. *The awakening of local environmental advocacy following the Exxon-Valdez oil spill in Kodiak, Alaska*. Presented at Annu. Meet. Soc. Appl. Anthropol., 51st, Memphis, TN

77a. McCabe JT. 1988. Drought and recovery: livestock dynamics among the Ngissonyoka Turkana of Kenya. *Hum. Ecol.* 15: 371–90

78. McNabb S. 1991. *Comparative analysis of spill impacts in ten communities*. Presented at Annu. Meet. Soc. Appl. Anthropol., 50th, Charleston, SC

79. McSpadden LA. 1991. *Case management versus bureaucratic needs: earthquake response in California*. Presented at Annu. Meet. Soc. Appl. Anthropol., 50th, Charleston, SC

80. Minnis P. 1985. *Social Adaptation to Food Stress: A Prehistoric Southwestern Example*. Chicago: Univ. Chicago Press. 239 pp.

80a. Morren G. 1980. The rural ecology of British drought 1975–76. *Hum. Ecol.* 8:33–63

81. Morren GEB. 1983. The Bushmen and the British: problems of the identification of drought and response to drought. See Ref. 53, pp. 44–66

82. Morren GEB. 1983. A general approach to the identification of hazards and responses. See Ref. 53, pp. 284–97

83. Moseley ME, Feldman RA, Ortloff CR. 1981. Living with crises: human perceptions of process and time. In *Biotic Crises in Ecological and Evolutionary Time*, ed.

MH Nitecki, pp. 231–67. Princeton, NJ: Princeton Univ. Press

84. Moseley ME, Richardson JB. 1992. Doomed by disaster. *Archaeology* 45: 44–45

85. Oliver-Smith A. 1977. Disaster rehabilitation and social change in Yungay, Peru. *Hum. Organ.* 36:491–509

86. Oliver-Smith A. 1977. Traditional agriculture, central places and post-disaster urban relocation in Peru. *Am. Ethnol.* 3: 102–16

87. Oliver-Smith A. 1979. Post-disaster consensus and conflict in a traditional society: the avalanche of Yungay, Peru. *Mass Emerg.* 4:39–52

88. Oliver-Smith A. 1979. The Yungay avalanche of 1970: anthropological perspectives on disaster and social change. *Disasters* 3:95–101

89. Oliver-Smith A. 1979. The crisis dyad: culture and meaning in medicine. In *Nourishing the Humanistic: Essays in the Dialogue Between the Social Sciences and Medicine*, ed. WR Rogers, D Barnard, pp. 73–93. Pittsburgh: Univ. Pittsburgh Press

90. Oliver-Smith A. 1982. Here there is life: the social and cultural dynamics of successful resistance to resettlement in post-disaster Peru. See Ref. 49, pp. 85–104

91. Oliver-Smith A. 1986. Disaster context and causation: an overview of changing perspectives in disaster research. See Ref. 91a, pp. 1–35

91a. Oliver-Smith A, ed. 1986. *Natural Disasters and Cultural Responses*. Williamsburg, VA: Coll. William & Mary

92. Oliver-Smith A. 1990. Postdisaster housing reconstruction and social inequality: a challenge to policy and practice. *Disasters* 14: 7–19

93. Oliver-Smith A. 1991. Success and failure in post-disaster resettlement. *Disasters* 15: 12–24

94. Oliver-Smith A. 1992. *The Martyred City: Death and Rebirth in the Peruvian Andes*. Prospect Heights, IL: Waveland. 280 pp. 2nd ed.

95. Oliver-Smith A. 1992. Disasters and development. *Environ. Urban Issues* 20:1–3

95a. Oliver-Smith A. 1993. Anthropological perspectives in disaster research. *Proc. US–Former USSR Seminar on Social Science Research on Mitigation and Recovery from Disasters and Large Scale Hazards*, pp. 94–117. Newark, NJ: Disaster Res. Cent.

96. Oliver-Smith A. 1994. Peru's five hundred year earthquake: vulnerability in historical context. In *Disasters, Development, and Environment*, ed. A Varley, pp. 3–48. London: Wiley

96a. Oliver-Smith A. 1996. Lima, Peru: underdevelopment and vulnerability in the city of the kings. In *Disasters in Megacities*, ed. JK Mitchell. Tokyo: United Nations Univ. Press. In press

97. Oliver-Smith A, Goldman RE. 1988. Planning goals and urban realities: post-disaster reconstruction in a third world city. *City Soc.* 2:105–26

98. Oliver-Smith A, Parker JW. 1992. *"Da Roof Migrate widout a Visa": A Decade of Initiatives for Safer Housing in Jamaica.* Silver Springs, MD: Basic Health Manage. 37 pp.

99. Omohundro J. 1982. The impacts of an oil spill. *Hum. Organ.* 4:17–25

100. Paine R. 1992. Chernobyl reaches Norway: the accident, science, and the threat to cultural knowledge. *Public Underst. Sci.* 1: 261–80

101. Paine R. 1992. Anthropology beyond routine: cultural alternatives for the handling of the unexpected. *Int. J. Moral Soc. Stud.* 7:183–203

102. Palinkas LA. 1990. *Ethnic differences in coping and depression after the Exxon-Valdez oil spill.* Presented at Annu. Meet. Am. Anthropol. Assoc., 89th, New Orleans

103. Palinkas LA, Downs MA, Petterson J, Russell J. 1993. Social, cultural and psychological impacts of the Exxon-Valdez oil spill. *Hum. Organ.* 52:1–13

104. Partridge W. 1989. Involuntary resettlement in development projects. *J. Refug. Stud.* 2:373–84

105. Peacock WG, Morrow BH, Gladwin H. 1996. The reshaping of Miami? Disasters and social change. See Ref. 105a. In press

105a. Peacock WG, Morrow BH, Gladwin H, eds. 1996. *Ethnicity, Gender and the Political Ecology of Disasters: Hurricane Andrew and the Reshaping of a City.* Gainesville, FL: Univ. Florida Press. In press

106. Peacock WG, Ragsdale AK. 1996. Ethnic and racial inequalities in disaster damage and insurance settlements. See Ref. 105a. In press

107. Petterson J. 1988. The reality of perception: demonstrable effects of perceived risk in Goiania, Brazil. *Pract. Anthropol.* 10:8–12

108. Picou JS, Gill DA, Dyer C, Curry EW. 1992. Disruption and stress in an Alaskan fishing community: initial and continuing impacts of the Exxon-Valdez oil spill. *Ind. Crisis Q.* 6:235–57

109. Posey D, Balee W. 1989. *Resource Management in Amazonia: Indigenous and Folk Strategies,* Vol. 7. New York: NY Bot. Gard. 287 pp.

110. Prado R. 1991. *Beauty betrayed: risk perception at a nuclear reactor site in Brazil.* Presented at Annu. Meet. Am. Anthropol. Assoc., 89th, New Orleans, LA

111. Rayner S, Cantor R. 1987. How fair is safe

enough? The cultural approach to societal technology choice. *Risk Anal.* 7:3–9

112. Renfrew C. 1978. Trajectory discontinuity and morphogenesis: the implications of catastrophe theory for archeology. *Am. Antiq.* 43:203–2

112a. Renfrew C, Rowlands MJ, Seagraves BA, eds. 1982. *Theory and Explanation in Archaeology.* New York: Academic

113. Robinson S, Hernandez Franco Y, Mata Castrejon R, Bernard HR. 1986. See Ref. 91a, pp. 81–123

114. Rosenberg H. 1990. The kitchen and the multinational corporation. In *Through the Kitchen Window: The Politics of Home and Family,* ed. M Luxton, H Rosenberg, S Arat-Koc, pp. 57–80. Toronto: Garamond

115. Rosenberg H. 1995. From trash to treasure: housewife activists and the environmental justice movement. In *Articulating Hidden Histories: Exploring the Influence of Eric Wolf,* ed. J Schneider, R Rapp, pp. 190–204. Berkeley: Univ. Calif. Press

116. Rossi I. 1993. *Community Reconstruction after an Earthquake.* Westport, CT/London: Preager. 185 pp.

117. Russell J. 1991. *Cultural and exposure variables in the expression of PTSD as an outcome of the Exxon-Valdez oil spill and cleanup.* Presented at Annu. Meet. Soc. Appl. Anthropol., 50th, Charleston, SC

118. Russell J. 1992. *The culture of chaos: the moral discourse in disaster events.* Presented at Annu. Meet. Am. Anthropol. Assoc., 91st, San Francisco

119. Sahlins M. 1972. *Stone Age Economics.* Chicago: Aldine. 348 pp.

120. Schmink M. 1982. Land conflicts in Amazonia. *Am. Ethnol.* 9:341–57

121. Schmink M, Wood C. 1984. *Frontier Expansion in Amazonia.* Gainesville, FL: Univ. Florida Press. 387 pp.

122. Schulte J. 1991. *The politics of disaster: an examination of class and ethnicity in the struggle for power following the 1989 Loma Prieta earthquake in Watsonville, California.* MA thesis. Calif. State Univ., Sacramento. 152 pp.

123. Schweitzer M, Wolfe AK, Braid RB. 1993. Studying technology intrusion in linear communities: the case of Air Force low altitude training routes. *Environ. Prof.* 15: 304–15

123a. Scott JC. 1990. *Domination and the Arts of Resistance.* New Haven, CT: Yale Univ. Press. 251 pp.

124. Scudder T, Colson E. 1982. From welfare to development: a conceptual framework for the analysis of dislocated people. See Ref. 49, pp. 267–87

125. Shaw R. 1989. Living with floods in Bangladesh. *Anthropol. Today* 5:11–13

126. Shaw R. 1992. 'Nature', culture and disas-

ters: floods and gender in Bangladesh. In *Bush Base: Forest Farm: Culture, Environment and Development*, ed. E Croll, D Parkin, pp. 200–17. London: Routledge

127. Sheets PD. 1994. *Archaeology, Volcanism and Remote Sensing in the Arenal Region, Costa Rica*. Austin: Univ. Tex. Press. 350 pp.

128. Sheets PD, Grayson DK, eds. 1979. *Volcanic Activity and Human Ecology*. New York: Academic. 644 pp.

129. Shipton P. 1990. African famines and food security: anthropological perspectives. *Annu. Rev. Anthropol.* 19:353–94

130. Stein HF. 1995. Reflections on the Oklahoma City bombing: war, mourning and the brief mercies of plenty. *Mind Hum. Interact.* 6:186–99

131. Stephens S. 1995. "Cultural fallout" of Chernobyl radiation in Sami regions: implications for children. In *Children and the Politics of Culture*, ed. S Stephens, pp. 292–321. Princeton, NJ: Princeton Univ. Press

132. Stephens S. 1995. Physical and social reproduction in a post-Chernobyl Norwegian Sami (Lapp) community. In *Conceiving the New World Order: The Global Politics of Reproduction*, ed. R Rapp, F Ginsburg, pp. 270–89. Berkeley: Univ. Calif. Press

133. Stephens S. 1995. Social consequences of Chernobyl in Norway: an anthropological perspective. In *Biomedical and Psychosocial Consequences of Radiation from Man-Made Radionuclides in the Biosphere*, ed. B Hemmingsen, pp. 181–202. Trondheim: R. Nor. Soc. Sci. Lett.

134. Stoffle RW, Stone JV, Heeringa SG. 1993. Mapping risk perception shadows: defining the locally affected population for a low-level radioactive waster facility in Michigan. *Environ. Prof.* 15:316–34

135. Stoffle RW, Traugott MW, Harshbarger CL, Jensen FV, Evans MJ, Drury P. 1988. Risk perception shadows: the superconducting super collider in Michigan. *Pract. Anthropol.* 10:6–7

135a. Stoffle RW, Traugott MW, Stone JV, McIntyre PD, Jensen FV, Davidson CD. 1991. Risk perception mapping: using ethnography to define the locally affected population for a low-level radioactive waste storage facility in Michigan. *Am. Anthropol.* 93:611–35

136. Tonkinson R. 1979. The paradox of permanency in a resettled New Hebridean community. *Mass Emerg.* 4:105–16

137. Torry WI. 1978. Natural disasters, social structure and change in traditional societies. *J. Asian Afr. Stud.* 13:167–83

138. Torry WI. 1978. Bureaucracy, community and natural disasters. *Hum. Organ.* 37: 302–8

139. Torry WI. 1979. Anthropology and disaster research. *Disasters* 3:43–52

140. Torry WI. 1979. Anthropological studies in hazardous environments: past trends and new horizons. *Curr. Anthropol.* 20: 517–41

141. Torry WI. 1980. Urban earthquake hazard in developing countries: squatter settlements and the outlook for Turkey. *Urban Ecol.* 4:317–27

142. Torry WI. 1986. Drought and the government village emergency food distribution system in India. *Hum. Organ.* 45:11–23

143. Torry WI. 1986. Drought and desertification as constraints on the agricultural development of the Western Sudan. See Ref. 91a, pp. 201–6

144. Torry WI. 1986. Morality and harm: Hindu peasant adjustments to famines. *Soc. Sci. Inf.* 25:125–60

145. Torry WI. 1986. Economic development, drought and famine: some limitations of dependency explanations. *Geojournal* 12: 5–18

146. Torry WI. 1988. Famine early warning systems: the need for an anthropological dimension. *Hum. Organ.* 47:273–81

147. Turton D. 1977. Response to drought: the Mursi of southwestern Ethiopia. *Disasters* 1:275–87

148. Wallace AFC. 1956. *Human Behavior in Extreme Situations*. Washington, DC: Natl. Acad. Sci. Natl. Res. Counc. 35 pp.

149. Wallace AFC. 1956. Rivitalization movements. *Am. Anthropol.* 58:204–81

150. Wallace AFC. 1956. *Tornado in Worcester: An Exploratory Study of Individual and Community Behavior in an Extreme Situation*. Washington, DC: Natl. Acad. Sci. Natl. Res. Counc. 98 pp.

151. Wallace AFC. 1956. Mazeway resynthesis: a bio-cultural theory of religious inspiration. *Trans. NY Acad. Sci.* 18:626–38

152. Wallace AFC. 1957. Mazeway disintegration: the individual's perception of sociocultural disorganization. *Hum. Organ.* 16: 23–27

153. Wallace AFC. 1987. *St. Clair: A Nineteenth-Century Coal Town's Experience with a Disaster Prone Industry*. New York: Knopf. 519 pp.

154. Warner WL. 1947. *The Social System of the Modern Factory*. Oxford: Oxford Univ. Press. 245 pp.

155. Wiedman D. 1993. *Organizational responses to Hurricane Andrew: a university in crisis*. Presented at Annu. Meet. Soc. Appl. Anthropol., 52nd, San Antonio, TX

156. Wiest RE, Mocellin JSP, Motsisi DT. 1992. *The Needs of Women and Children in Disasters and Emergencies*. Winnipeg: Univ. Manit. 86 pp.

157. Wolfe AK. 1993. Risk communication in

social context: improving effective communication. *Environ. Prof.* 15:248–55

158. Wolfe AK. 1988. Environmental risk and anthropology. *Pract. Anthropol.* 10:1

159. Wolfe AK. 1988. Risk communication: Who's educating whom? *Pract. Anthropol.* 10:13–14

160. Yelvington K. 1996. Coping in a temporary way: the tent cities. See Ref. 105a. In press

161. Yelvington K, Kerner D. 1993. *Ethnic relations and ethnic conflict in Tent City: understanding Andrew's aftermath.* Presented at Annu. Meet. Soc. Appl. Anthropol., 52nd, San Antonio, TX

162. Zaman MQ. 1986. The role of social relations in the response to riverbank erosion hazards and population resettlement in Bangladesh. See Ref. 91a, pp. 117–200

163. Zaman MQ. 1989. The social and political context of adjustment to riverbank erosion hazard and population resettlement in Bangladesh. *Hum. Organ.* 48:196–205

164. Zaman MQ. 1991. The displaced poor and resettlement policies in Bangladesh. *Disasters* 15:117–25

165. Zaman MQ. 1994. Ethnography of disasters: making sense of flood and erosion in Bangladesh. *East. Anthropol.* 47:129–55

166. Zaman MQ, Haque CE. 1991. Coping with riverbank erosion hazard and displacement hazard in Bangladesh: survival strategies and adjustment. *Disasters* 13:300–14

167. Zeeman EC. 1982. Decision making and evolution. See Ref. 112a, pp. 375–46

Annu. Rev. Anthropol. 1996. 25:329–52

ANTHROPOLOGY AND THE CONSERVATION OF BIODIVERSITY

Benjamin S. Orlove

Division of Environmental Studies, University of California, Davis, California 95616

Stephen B. Brush

Department of Human & Community Development, University of California, Davis, California 95616

KEY WORDS: biodiversity, conservation, genetic resources, indigenous people, protected areas

ABSTRACT

Conservation programs for protected areas and plant genetic resources have evolved in similar ways, beginning with a focus on single species and expanding to ecosystem strategies that involve the participation of local people. Anthropologists have described the increasing importance of the participation of local people in conservation programs, both of local populations in protected area management and of farmers in plant genetic resources. Both protected areas and plant genetic resources link local populations, national agencies, and international organizations. Anthropological research (*a*) documents local knowledge and practices that influence the selection and maintenance of crop varieties and the conservation of rare and endangered species in protected areas, and (*b*) clarifies the different concerns and definitions of biodiversity held by local populations and international conservationists. In addition, anthropologists operate in nongovernmental organizations (NGOs) and international agencies, participating in policy debates and acting as advocates and allies of local populations of farmers and indigenous peoples.

INTRODUCTION

The loss of biological diversity has become an important scientific and political issue since 1970 and is increasingly addressed by anthropologists. Biological diversity is defined in the Convention on Biological Diversity as "the

0084-6570/96/1015-0329$08.00

329

variability among living organisms from all sources including, inter alia, terrestrial, marine and other aquatic ecosystems and the ecological complexities of which they are part; this includes diversity within species, between species and of ecosystems" (130). While most biological diversity is comprised of undomesticated plants and animals, an important subset involves the diversity among domesticated organisms. The loss of biological diversity appears to be accelerating because of habitat alteration, rapid population growth, and technological change (48). The cultural value of biodiversity and the importance of genetic resources in agriculture and medicine have added urgency to conserving diversity.

This review focuses on the relation between anthropology and conservation in protected areas and in genetic resources of crops. Anthropologists have also contributed to conservation elsewhere, including in forest and marine ecosystems and in pastoralism and range management. Anthropologists are involved in both protected area and agricultural resource conservation as researchers on indigenous knowledge and management, as practitioners in managing conservation programs, and as advocates for indigenous peoples' rights.

Strategies for managing protected areas and conserving crop diversity have evolved in similar ways, from an initial emphasis on preserving single species, to habitat protection, to ecosystem conservation involving the participation of local people. Parallel sets of national and international institutions address linkages among local people, biological resources, and policy for conservation in protected areas and for agricultural resources.

PROTECTED AREAS

Although states and other political entities have protected wildlife and forests through the establishment of reserves for many centuries, large-scale expansion of protected areas has occurred in the past 25 years, often in settings with long-established human populations. These areas were set up to conserve biodiversity through the protection of the habitat in which undomesticated plant and animal species live. Similarly, while the anthropological literature on this topic draws on well-established themes in the field, it has burgeoned recently as well. The first writings appeared in the mid-1980s, and they have expanded greatly since 1990.

The Growth of Protected Areas

The historical antecedents of protected areas can be located in royal game and forest preserves in Europe and Asia (33) and in colonial policies in Africa and Asia, which established forest preserves for the management of timber resources (115) and game preserves for recreational hunting by colonial officials

(93). In more recent decades, the threat of species extinction has become more palpable, as seen in the decline of temperate-zone songbirds, which provided the title to a major 1962 book, *Silent Spring* (28), and in the diminishing of populations of large tropical mammals. The concern for the protection of biodiversity became a key element of national and international environmental movements, especially as a consequence of the growing awareness of the extent and impact of the clearing of tropical forests. The measure of success of conservation is generally taken in the prevention of species extinction. Many conservationists also seek to maintain genetic diversity within particular species, especially the protection of subspecies, as necessary to reduce the risk of species extinction.

Conservation policy includes efforts on three levels. The first targets individual species, often by limiting or preventing hunting and harvesting. The second focuses on the protection of the habitat in which the populations of endangered species live. The third manages entire assemblies of ecosystems. For example, the first would protect spotted owls, the second would protect the forests in which spotted owls live (thus also protecting other species that inhabit these forests), and the third would manage the complex of forests, meadows, agricultural lands, and other zones. The first is oriented directly to the species; the second establishes protected areas as reserves; and the third enacts systems of reserves—managing or reducing gaps in sets of fragmented protected areas (132) or treating protected areas as cores surrounded by buffers and linked through corridors (68). In ecological terms, the first is associated with population ecology, the second with ecosystem ecology, and the third with landscape ecology. A number of conservation policies, distinct from the establishment of protected areas, continue with this first phase, which includes zoos for captive breeding programs, prohibitions on international ivory trade, and limits on commercial whaling. Because of the expansion of protected ecosystems and landscapes into settled zones, conservationists have reconsidered resident and neighboring human groups, leading many to view them as potential participants in conservation rather than as poachers of wildlife or destroyers of habitat (97, 98, 119, 158).

Before the 1970s, many terms, such as national parks, nature reserves, and wildlife sanctuaries, were used to designate conservation units. The need for a single term became apparent in international conferences, and in 1978 the International Union for the Conservation of Nature established "protected area" as the cover term. A typology of eight categories of protected areas, distinguished by management objectives and practices, was codified in 1985 (see Table 1) and has become the standard international classification (97). These eight are ranked in an order of decreasing strictness—the higher the number, the fewer the restrictions on human activity and the greater the array

Table 1   Categories and management objective of protected areas

IUCN[a] category number	Category name	Management objectives
I	Scientific reserve/strict nature reserve	To protect nature and maintain natural processes in an undisturbed state to permit scientific study, environmental monitoring, education, and the maintenance of genetic resources
II	National park	To protect natural and scenic areas of national or international significance for scientific research, education and recreation
III	National monument/ natural landmark	To protect and preserve nationally significant natural features because of their special interest or unique characteristics
IV	Managed natural reserve/ wildlife sanctuary	To protect nationally significant species, groups of species, biotic communities, or physical features of the environment where these require human manipulation for their perpetuation
V	Protected landscapes	To maintain nationally significant natural landscapes that are characteristic of the harmonious interaction of man and land while providing opportunities for public enjoyment through recreation and tourism
VI	Resource reserve	To protect natural resources for future use and to prevent or contain development activities that could affect the resource pending the establishment of further management objectives
VII	Natural biotic area/ anthropological reserve	To allow the way of life of societies living in harmony with the environment to continue undisturbed by modern technology
VIII	Multiple-use management area/managed resource area	To provide for the sustained production of water, timber, wildlife, pasture, and outdoor recreation

[a]International Union for the Conservation of Nature

of goals, such as education, recreation, and resource extraction, which are added to preservation of biodiversity. Of these eight, only the five most stringent are included in most discussions of protected areas, because higher levels of resource extraction are permitted in the other three. When we look only at these five categories, the expansion of protected areas in the past 25 years is evident. Of the nearly 150,000,000 km^2 in such areas in 1992—6.27% of the earth's land surface—only 24% had been established by 1971, with 38% established between 1971 and 1982, and 38% established between 1982 and 1992 (97).

The Emergence of Anthropological Research on Protected Areas

Anthropological antecedents of the study of protected areas include the theme of adaptation in ecological anthropology of the 1960s and 1970s (62, 111). Studies of local management of common property resources, especially by maritime anthropologists, demonstrated the ability of some local populations to keep resource extraction at sustainable levels in specific areas (88, 96). Political anthropologists have long-standing interests in competing claims over territory, in the relations between states and local populations, and in social movements (148). Detailed examination of policy issues is well-developed in applied anthropology, and advocacy anthropologists have been closely involved with indigenous and minority movements, often linked to the politics of protected areas.

ANTHROPOLOGICAL INVOLVEMENTS   As protected areas have emerged as an institution of great importance, anthropologists of diverse theoretical backgrounds have undertaken to study them. Turner's interest in kinship, symbolism, and the body (142–144), Stearman's research in cultural and environmental history (139, 140), and Marks's cultural ecology (92) have all converged on the environmental politics of protected areas (93, 141, 145, 146).

Several distinctive features of anthropology make it particularly well-suited for studying protected areas: the commitment to long-term field studies in the relatively isolated regions in which protected areas are established; the exposure to biology in four-field departments; and the willingness to study not only local populations but also reserve managers, international conservationists, biologists, government officials, and staff of nongovernmental organizations (NGOs). Moreover, environmentalism itself became an object of study for anthropologists interested in discourse, ideology, and postmodernism. In addition to conducting scholarly research, anthropologists have also engaged in the debates over protected areas in other ways: as advocates for indigenous rights organizations such as Cultural Survival (30), as policy-makers in international institutions such as the World Bank (40) and the World Wildlife Fund (153), as cultural intermediaries who arrange for the publication of interviews with local inhabitants of protected areas (78), and as expert witnesses in court cases in which indigenous land claims are adjudicated (100). In both academic and advocacy roles, anthropologists have argued strongly for the participation of local populations in the planning and management of protected areas. These arguments are sometimes based on social justice claims (55)—that the often poor and marginal inhabitants of protected areas should not bear the costs of conservation—or on human rights claims, in which local populations have entitlements as citizens of the states that administer the protected areas, as native or indigenous peoples with specific claims to sovereignty over their territories, and as human beings who participate in the planet-wide interactions among different species (75, 76). In other cases, these arguments are based on pragmatic grounds. Without the consent of the local populations, protected areas cannot be managed effectively (54, 65). This applied and advocacy work is rendered difficult by the contrast between the temporary nature of successes and the permanence of failures (All species extinctions and most displacements of local populations are irreversible).

METHODS   Anthropologists use several methods in the study of protected areas. The most common is the interview-based longitudinal case study of local populations and their interactions with organizations such as national and international agencies, NGOs, indigenous rights organizations, international conservation organizations, and national and international media. These case studies depict complex processes of accommodation and conflict. The resulting accounts are often organized into narratives, each stage of which is marked by specific actions of governments and NGOs and by local responses. Other anthropologists, drawing on research methods in economic and ecological anthropology, conduct surveys of samples of individuals or households to report on interactions with plant and animal populations within reserves. Particular attention has been paid to hunting (3, 4), herding (68), and forest management (45, 115, 125).

PUBLICATIONS   With some recent exceptions (4, 34, 87, 112), this work has tended to appear in applied journals such as *Human Organization* and *Society and Natural Resources,* advocacy journals such as *Cultural Survival Quarterly,* broad-circulation environmental policy journals such as *Ambio* and *The Ecologist,* and conservation journals such as *Conservation Biology.* Much of the work is published in edited volumes, often by environmentally oriented publishing firms such as Sierra Club Books (78) and Island Press (75, 132, 155), or in applied science monograph series by university presses (125, 154). Research results also often appear in the "gray literature" of commissioned reports for international and national agencies and NGOs. These edited volumes and reports often contain a number of position papers and programmatic statements. In this rapidly changing and highly politicized field, researchers often take strongly opposed positions on specific programs (45, 102).

Natives, Locals, and Conservationists

As protected areas expanded after 1970, it became evident that the North American model of uninhabited national parks could not be applied worldwide. One effort to render compatible the goals of preserving endangered species and including resident populations was what Conklin & Graham termed "the contemporary equation of indigenous resource management practices with Western environmentalism" (34:2). This equation has given rise to the stereotype that Redford has termed "the ecologically noble savage" (128; cf 1, 126, 127). Standing in complementary opposition to this image is the notion of "pristine wilderness" (55) held by many biologists—that ecosystems can exist in, or return to, a state free from disturbance from all human beings, including native peoples.

The terms of this debate reflect the importance of indigenous peoples in early anthropological studies of protected areas. In these studies, conducted in such diverse settings as Australia, Arctic North America, the Amazon Basin, and pastoral zones of East Africa, the resident populations of protected areas are all minority native peoples. Although indigenous peoples and endangered species are often found in remote areas, there are many protected areas whose residents are not indigenous, such as Spanish-speaking Mexican mestizos (77), other nonindigenous minorities such as Afro-Colombians (49), and members of other nations, such as Cameroon, without clear majority populations (69). Because these cases make it difficult to claim that each protected area can be identified with a specific indigenous population, we use the terms "local" and "resident" to refer generally to the inhabitants of protected areas, and restrict "indigenous" and "native" to the minority peoples for whom this term is widely recognized and accepted (39).

INITIAL POSITIONINGS   The claims that indigenous peoples live in harmony with nature—and hence do not threaten the continued existence of plant and animal species—rest in part on long-standing traditions in Western thought (33, 34). These claims are justified by four sorts of evidence: (a) the long history of presence of human populations throughout virtually all of the earth's surface, which suggests that the threats to species do not come from small-scale native populations (155); (b) the rich detail of indigenous environmental knowledge (108); (c) specific management practices, based on this knowledge, that maintain animal and plant populations (87); and (d) religious beliefs about and ritual uses of plants and animals, which assure indigenous commitment to the conservation of these species (105, 106). Of particular importance to supporting this notion of native stewardship are studies of the selective tending and controlled burning of wild plants, and of the limitation of access to fishing grounds. In contrast, studies of hunters have tended to show a great concern for optimizing short-term returns rather than for ensuring long-term conservation (A Stearman, personal communication). However, the strong claims that all indigenous people are by nature conservationists can easily be attacked by counterexamples—species extinctions due to human hunting in the prehistoric past (138) and indigenous peoples who grant large timber cutting or mining concessions on their lands (145). Moreover, indigenous peoples themselves take a variety of positions on these claims (16, 37).

RECENT PRAGMATISM   Though some individuals still take polar positions in favor of (122) or against (116) this notion of the "ecologically noble savage," more recent writings take a less absolute and more pragmatic stance that stresses the practicality and urgency of coordinating resident populations and conservationists. This pragmatism is based on several grounds. The first can be termed "the scale of threats." Consider Alaska, for example: Native peoples would be likely to rank protected-area managers as less severe threats to their well-being and autonomy than recreational and commercial hunters and fishermen, who in turn are less severe than the firms that extract petroleum. Likewise, one could rank the threats to wildlife, in which native subsistence hunters and fishermen are less severe than recreational and commercial hunters and fishermen, who in turn are less severe than petroleum firms (29, 120, 136). Similar rankings could be established for many other regions of the world. From this perspective, an association between resident peoples and conservationists—what Conklin & Graham, discussing the Amazon, called "the Indian-environmentalist alliance" (34)— becomes what can be called a "second-best option" for both sides. That is, though both resident populations and protected area managers might consider their best option would be full autonomy to control their territories on their own, without any need to take other groups, organizations, or institutions into account, they would still nonetheless consider this alliance better than their other options, especially since these other options usually include considerable pressure from other outside groups, organizations, or institutions, often committed to short-term exploitation of these territories. The research on this alliance has focused on the forms of coordination within such alliances, on the advantages to both sides that these alliances represent, and on the obstacles to establishing and maintaining these alliances.

Cooperative management   Resident populations and conservation managers coordinate their efforts to monitor and protect wild plant and animal species. The Mapimí Biosphere Reserve in north-central Mexico, run jointly by the United Nations and Mexican agencies to protect an endangered tortoise species, is particularly interesting in the thoroughness of its documentation of the cooperative management and in that the local population of small-scale cattle ranchers are Spanish-speaking and very different from the populations in Mexico that are usually identified as indigenous. Local ranchers have developed dense social ties with reserve managers and scientists. Each group exchanges favors with the other. Of particular importance is the former's assistance to the latter in preventing tortoise hunting and in monitoring populations, and the latter's assistance to the former in negotiations with representatives of the national government (77). In the Yukon-Delta National Wildlife Refuge in Alaska, a similarly cooperative arrangement has been established between conservationists and the local Yup'ik Eskimo, for whom protected caribou herds are a major source of food. Having learned in earlier periods of crisis that a lack of cooperation creates serious difficulties, both groups coordinate in establishing the level and timing of hunting seasons, and in allocating the number of hunted animals among villages and households (136). In Kakadu National Park in Australia, the National Park Service and local aboriginal groups became allied in the face of threats by provincial government and business interests to open a remote area to settlement and extensive mining operations. They now manage the park jointly, establishing policies for visitors, removing introduced plants undesirable to both groups, and restoring wetlands whose capacity to support native wildlife had been reduced by introduced buffalo (67, 150). A specific benefit of cooperative management that has attracted much attention is the prevention and limitation of incursions into protected areas (137). This alliance has postponed petroleum drilling in the Arctic National Wildlife Refuge in Alaska (29). It has also stemmed colonization by agricultural migrants in hill zones in Nepal (65) and some valley zones in Zimbabwe (102). Such examples have generated much enthusiasm in policy-making circles, who term these arrangements "co-management" (118) and "community-based conservation" (155). In these cases, local populations produce most or all of their food locally and obtain cash from small-scale, long-established sale of complementary products—crops, livestock, game, or fish.

In addition to the protection of land tenure and of customary economic activities, cooperative management has often been organized around newer income-generating activities, often called Integrated Conservation and Development Programs (ICDPs) (18, 153). In the second phase of conservation, linked to habitat protection, two common forms have been ecotourism and the establishment of extractive reserves from which selected wild plants and animals are harvested on a limited and controlled basis. Despite some reported successes, often due to highly specific local circumstances (15, 16, 102, 153), both of these had mixed results, since both ecotourism (54, 64, 152, 153) and extractive reserves (47, 53) often generate severe environmental problems and provide income for local groups that is lower, less reliable, or more unevenly distributed across households or between genders than anticipated. Others have hoped for a kind of "pharmaceutical prospecting" for new medicines based on forest plants, though few such projects have generated concrete results (6). The third phase of conservation, linked to the management of reserves, buffers, and corridors, has sought to reduce human activity within core reserves by promoting new activities in buffers. The difficulty with such efforts is that the inherent ambiguity of such an intermediate category leads to widely diverging goals and expectations, as shown with particular clarity in the case of the Maasai displaced from a core zone, the Serengeti National Park in Tanzania, into the buffer zone, the Ngorongoro Conservation Area (68, 95).

Limits to cooperative management   Many anthropologists have balanced the often overblown projections of proposals for cooperative management and ICDPs by showing the structural limitations these arrangements face. They have stressed organizational and communicative incompatibilities between local populations and conservationists.

First, there are organizational incompatibilities between the centralized, bureaucratic structures of state agencies, international conservation organizations, and NGOs on the one hand, and the more decentralized patterns of local populations. Conservationists often do not know how to coordinate with age-sets in East Africa (68), with Amazonian natives whose leaders exhort rather than command (34), and with Andean peasants who demand village-by-village assemblies for even minor decisions (112, 113), while the residents do not trust the conservationists, who often come for brief periods and rarely remain in particular positions for more than a few years. In addition, indigenous leaders who establish ties with conservationists face "liabilities of leadership," (34) becoming alienated from their communities without gaining strong support from national and international conservationists, much as reserve managers who are seen as "going native" can become vulnerable to challenges from both sides. Moreover, further organizational dilemmas arise in some protected areas, such as those in eastern Paraguay; different indigenous groups compete for access to specific protected areas (129). Even when such alliances are strong, powerful groups may oppose both conservationists and resident populations alike. In Brazil, the tie between indigenous residents and international conservationists has created a "nationalist backlash" (34) against both groups.

Second, there are communicative incompatibilities between local populations and conservationists that stem from the differences between national and minority languages or from the gulf between sets of ecological, economic, and social categories (46, 51). In the Lake Titicaca National Reserve in Peru, reserve managers maintain sharp distinctions between groups who live in the reserve and those who live on its borders and between subsistence and commercial forms of harvesting plants. Although these categories seem self-evident to government officials and conservationists, they make little sense to the local peasants and fishermen, whose notions of social and spatial boundaries and economic activities are distinct (43, 88, 112). Similar difficulties plague even the most successful cases of cooperative management. In Mapimí, conservationists and local ranchers divide the reserve into different sets of zones (77). In Kakadu, where both sides agree that fire—a long-standing feature of Australian ecosystems (123)—is a key to maintaining a diversity of habitats within the park, great differences separate the managers (who want to plan in advance a system of "controlled burns" based on the calendar, the moisture content of key plants, other features measured by instruments and their academic study of other regimes of fire management) from the aborigines (whose decisions that the bush has become "dirty" and needs burning rest on many rules of thumb and on their ongoing travels through the Park) (89).

Summary

During the past 25 years, as the loss of animal and plant species has become an issue of broad concern, the protected areas of the world have quadrupled in size, and they have come to be a topic of research by anthropologists. Examining the interactions of human populations that reside in and near protected areas with their natural environments, anthropologists have shown that customary practices of resource extraction usually, but not inevitably, are compatible with the goals of conservation of endangered species. Examining the interactions of these populations with conservationists, NGOs, government agencies, and large-scale commercial interests, anthropologists have shown that these populations and conservationists can sometimes, but not always, establish alliances to protect endangered species and limit the degradation of habitat. Both of these findings suggest the importance of local populations as participants in conservation programs, a theme anthropologists have supported through applied research and advocacy work as well as through academic study. As the following section shows, anthropological research on plant genetic resources parallels this work on protected areas.

PLANT GENETIC RESOURCES

Biological diversity of plants includes species not used directly by human beings, others that are exploited but not cultivated, and domesticated plants (99, 157). The term "plant genetic resources" has been generally used in reference to varieties of crop species, especially since the organization in 1974 of the International Board on Plant Genetic Resources (renamed International Plant Genetic Resources Institute) (32). Anthropologists (99, 103, 107, 124) have advocated that human knowledge be included as a component of plant genetic resources for species directly managed and manipulated by people.

There are four types of plant genetic resources: (*a*) landraces of crop species, (*b*) semidomesticated (weedy) crop relatives, (*c*) wild crop relatives, and (*d*) nondomesticated perennial species. Human ecology, ethnobiology, and conservation methods differ for each type. Landraces are managed and dependent on human activity and are therefore a focus of anthropological research. An example of a weedy crop relative is teosinte (*Zea mexicana*), which easily crosses with maize (*Zea mays*) (156). The proximity and similarity of weedy crop relatives to cultivars form bases for their recognition in folk nomenclature. Folk nomenclatures often categorize wild relatives within the same family as the cultivars, for example "atoqpa papa" ("fox's potato") of the

Andes (20). Perennial species, such as tree species and medicinal plants, are often exploited as nondomesticates, although they may be protected by the people who use them (99, 126). Like other plants, there is a positive relation between how much these species are used and the detail about their variants in folk nomenclature (10).

Landraces are mixed populations of local crop varieties, and among the four types of plant genetic resources they are the most diverse in folk nomenclatures, collections, and scientific description (22, 60). The terms "traditional" or "ancestral," frequently used to describe landraces, obscure the fact that these crop populations undergo continuous selection and evolution (72). Landraces are arguably the world's most important genetic resource because they are directly linked to humankind's primary food supply. Landraces have a number of distinguishing characteristics. Although some crops are comprised of several species (often polyploids, e.g. wheat, potato), the greatest diversity of landraces is infraspecific (that is, within rather than between species). Landraces are associated with cradle areas of crop domestication, although diversity and region of domestication are not synonymous (60). Landraces are also associated with marginal agricultural zones (106) and highly heterogeneous environments (160), "traditional" farming systems characterized by small-scale farms and subsistence production (31, 110), poverty (90), and ethnic minorities (107). In contrast with crop varieties used in industrial agriculture, landraces tend to be locally rather than broadly adapted, and they are managed as mixed populations rather than as distinct pure lines (23).

The loss of biodiversity resulting from clearing tropical rain forests (81, 157) is also experienced in farming systems, as extensive cropping patterns are replaced by intensive ones (60). Underlying this conversion are such fundamental causes as human population growth, cultural change, and the expansion of the market economy and spatial integration of different regions (115). Genetic resources have increased in value because of potential scarcity and the development of biotechnology (114). Value is also increased by the food and medicine needs of the large human population, reliance on yield gains rather than more land or irrigation water to increase production (109), and the potential of climate change from carbon emissions (70).

Anthropological Perspectives on Plant Genetic Resources

Speculation about the origin and value of crop diversity dates back to antiquity, and it forcefully emerged in the nineteenth century as a concern of naturalists such as De Candolle (42) and Darwin (38). Themes that have guided research on agricultural diversity include locating the place and processes of domestication of cultivated crops, identifying their wild progenitors, and reconstructing crop evolution. These are enduring themes in botany (63), geography (61), agronomy (60, 147), and anthropology (71). Since 1970, new themes about agricultural biodiversity have emerged: the ethnobiology of this diversity, its cultural ecology, participatory conservation, and the politics of genetic resources.

THE ETHNOBIOLOGY OF AGRICULTURAL DIVERSITY   The varietal or infraspecific level is one of the six regular ethnobiological ranks. This level is common to many ethnobotanical systems (10), and elaborate varietal classification is conspicuous in many folk systems. Despite the acknowledged importance of landraces and their lexical prominence, most ethnobiologists have avoided the systematic analysis of the infraspecific variation of crops. Folk varietal classification may be regarded as unfit for systematic botanical taxonomy because it rests on relatively few and often superficial plant characteristics (27)—an aversion that seems to prevail among ethnobiologists (26), who may be vexed by the inconsistency and complexity of varietal names in their quest to describe universal building blocks of folk taxonomy (10). Nevertheless, the richness of folk varietal names and the importance of varietal distinctions to cultivators have not escaped the attention of ethnobiologists (14, 99).

The ethnobiology of varietal taxa begins with the observation and studies of the great numbers of varieties of single crop species that are recognized in some farming cultures. Classic cases in the anthropological literature include classification of 92 rice varieties by the Hanunoo (35) and 200 potato names among Aymara peasants of the Lake Titicaca basin (82). Though ethnobiologists have frequently noted that varietal classification is associated with culturally important plants, there are relatively few extended studies of folk classification at this level. Exceptions are studies of manioc classification among the Aguaruna Jívaro (11–14) and potato classification among Andean farmers (20, 124).

Four topics dominate the current ethnobiology of plant genetic resources. The first is the perception of varietal differences. Darwin's (38) observation that plant parts most used by people present the greatest amount of difference is reflected in the ethnobiological rule that cultural importance is positively related to lexical differentiation (10). Thus, varietal differences usually emphasize the part of the plant that is directly used: the rice panicle (83, 131), potato tubers (20, 124), maize ears (8), and so forth. Other plant characteristics may be noted, such as plant height or flower color, but these are generally secondary criteria in folk taxonomies of crops. The second topic is the consistency of folk naming of crop varieties. Inconsistency among informants is reported in several studies (44, 84), but this variability is not always the case (13, 124). Women have been found to be both more knowledgeable and more consistent than men (14, 103).

A third theme in the ethnobiology of agricultural biodiversity is the utilitarian vs cognitive basis of folk nomenclature (10, 101). Logically, we might expect the diversity of cultivars and its nomenclature to be driven by use factors. In some crops, it is clear that infraspecific variation has a utilitarian basis, for instance in the agronomic distinctions between maize varieties in Chiapas (7–9) and the water-depth tolerance of different rice varieties (83). Nevertheless, a nonutilitarian basis for diversity in form and name seems to apply elsewhere (14, 20, 72).

Related to the utilitarian/cognitive theme is the fourth theme: the relation of folk nomenclature to botanical differences. As pointed out by Bulmer (26), folk nomenclature should logically be related to biological criteria that might be used by "scientific" taxonomists. Yet the infraspecific level is tenuous and often assumed to be overclassified (27). Nevertheless, intensive systematic research on crop varieties does show a relatively high correspondence between folk classification and underlying genetic differences (91, 124), although this finding is not universal (85). The cognitive aspects of biodiversity are logically connected to genetic resources, and this link is recognized in "indigenous knowledge systems" and decision-making research (17, 24, 73). The study of knowledge systems has tended to be descriptive or focused on linguistic issues such as taxonomic structure of language.

THE CULTURAL ECOLOGY OF PLANT GENETIC RESOURCES   Cultural ecology differs from ethnobiology in that its unit of analysis is behavior in relation to the biophysical realm. Farmer behavior and decision-making about crop variety selection has been extensively studied (50), and the connection between farmer behavior and genetic resources has been studied for some crops (7, 9, 20, 25, 44, 91, 159). The association between cultural diversity and agricultural biodiversity is evident in cuisine (66, 151) and social identity (44, 74, 107).

Determining the biological (evolutionary and genetic) significance of diverse farming systems and their persistence under changing conditions requires social and biological data and interdisciplinary analysis by anthropologists, economists, geneticists, and ecologists. A seldom reached goal is to describe how human changes, such as population growth or cultural change, affect specific biotic factors such as crop populations (22, 131, 160). The challenge is to avoid essentializing the stewardship of biological resources as ecological nobility or the processes of change as misguided technology adoption. Ethnobiologists must be attentive to the complexity of plant populations in dynamic and patchy social contexts. Farmers do not often practice conservation for its own sake, but they do give social value to local resources, an issue that ethnobiology can illuminate. Since the days of carrying capacity research, cultural ecologists have struggled with the need to confront both biological and socioeconomic complexity and to avoid treating either side as a black box. The lack of diachronic data is an obstacle, but this is surmountable by qualitative or quantitative methods that use cross-sectional analysis (25). Relating localized cultural ecology research to spatially dispersed biotic factors is possible through geographic information systems (GIS).

Diversity and stability are commonly associated in theory (31, 117), although this is criticized as "folk ecology" (56) rather than as a scientific axiom. Low-input farming systems might be especially subject to genetic vulnerability because of pests and tropical conditions, weak infrastructure, and economic marginality (109). Anthropologists and others (2, 31, 110) have argued that crop genetic diversity is a primary way to protect production in low-input farming systems, so that decreasing diversity may leave peasant cultivators more vulnerable. Loss of diversity in national agricultural sectors has also been associated with vulnerability (5, 109). Fluctuation in production and yield over time is given but may be exacerbated by modern conditions in several ways: genetic vulnerability, input supply problems, market instability (5). Agricultural instability at the local and national level must also be distinguished. Instability may not be caused by less diversity per se but rather by eliminating the buffering effects of isolation or weak integration into a larger system, so market synchronization and covariation among dispersed regions can increase the national coefficients of variation of production or yield, even though they are unchanged at the local level (5).

Testing the diversity/stability hypothesis is difficult, and the most convincing efforts are the longitudinal national studies of grain production that reduce the noise of short-term and local environmental fluctuations or supply problems (5, 134). Cereal production in both developed and underdeveloped countries is now generally more unstable than before 1965—albeit with important exceptions (134)—but instability results not from the loss of genetic diversity but from the breakdown of agricultural and economic isolation and the subsequent increase of covariation (5, 134). The major National Research Council report (109) on genetic resources concluded that genetic vulnerability in less developed nations has actually been decreased by the availability of disease-resistant modern varieties.

PARTICIPATORY CONSERVATION   The observation that crop populations are more diverse in "premodern" farming systems and therefore are endangered by modernization dates to the early decades of this century (59). During the Green Revolution, concern was raised about "genetic erosion" caused by the diffusion of modern and high-yielding crop varieties (63). Undoubtedly, the decrease of the area planted in landraces and their elimination from some regions have caused genetic erosion, but we do not have a formal assessment of the amount of genetic diversity lost or remaining in farmers' fields. Methodological complexities of such an assessment are staggering and can only be solved by interdisciplinary research at the case-study level.

The response to genetic erosion was to collect landraces for storage in gene banks (ex situ conservation) (32). The advantages of these collections are their relative stability, inclusion of most genes (alleles) from crop populations, and accessibility to crop breeders for crop improvement. However, these collections are vulnerable and not the sole solution to the need to conserve plant genetic resources. Gene banks do not preserve the ecosystem that generates crop germplasm (22); they are subject to genetic drift (58, 135); they do not include diversity that arises after collection; and gene banks do not conserve farmer knowledge, which is part of the resource base of crops (24, 31, 41).

To broaden the base of conservation, biological and social scientists have argued that conservation efforts should include farmers in centers of crop diversity, so that in situ can complement ex situ conservation (2, 19, 110). The feasibility of in situ conservation is suggested by the persistence of landraces in farming systems that have undergone technological change (22). Conservation may be encouraged through formal efforts directed to encourage on-farm conservation by increasing the value of local crop resources. Methods to reinforce in situ conservation include developing markets for local crops, increased nonmarket valuation through education and information, and participatory breeding efforts that rely on local crop resources, farmer selection, and on-farm research (41, 103). The need for farmer participation, especially in marginal zones and low-input agriculture, is well documented for agricultural development (41, 103), but whether genetic conservation can be stimulated is untested.

THE POLITICS OF GENETIC RESOURCES   Landraces have strong economic value for plant breeding and biotechnology, but they are undervalued by farmers as genetic resources. Because genetic resources are public goods and treated as common property, farmers who cultivate them do not benefit directly from their genetic value, and society has a tendency to underinvest in their conservation (94, 133, 149). Wealth differences between areas producing genetic resources and industrial nations using them are compounded by markets and private property (52, 80, 104). Intellectual property rights for crop breeders, in the form of plant variety protection and patents, are available for whole plants and gene sequences in industrial nations, while genetic resources in the forest or in farmers' fields are customarily defined as public goods or common heritage (24, 79). Theoretically, it is conceivable that seed companies in industrial countries might claim ownership of seed varieties that are little different from those that farmers provided freely. More importantly, the lack of economic valuation for genetic resources managed by farmers means that they have no incentive to conserve them.

A heated political debate on intellectual property, farmers' and indigenous rights, and conservation has gone on for nearly two decades (52, 79, 104).

Anthropologists have recently entered into this debate (21, 24, 57, 121). Compensation cannot address historic inequities, because it focuses on only one exchange out of a multiplicity of flows of technology, knowledge, and capital, and a "balance sheet" of benefits that flow between countries is all but impossible to construct. Genetic resources are public goods, because collection of seed samples in no way decreases their availability, and the origin of much germplasm in storage is unknown or ambiguous. Genetic resources are usually a product of collective invention, often involving different regions and nations. Compensation to one farmer, community, or nation may arbitrarily ignore the contributions of others. Finally, payment does not necessarily address the future or create a lasting incentives for conservation.

Nevertheless, it is widely argued that some form of compensation to farmers for genetic resources is needed, especially to encourage conservation. However, what type of compensation to extend to farmers is much debated (24, 57, 79). Compensation may be either direct, in the form of subsidies (79, 130), or indirect, in the form of investment in economic and agricultural development (21). One proposition is to extend intellectual property protection to indigenous knowledge and farmers' varieties (57, 121), and another is to use contracts (130).

The costs of in situ conservation of agricultural genetic resources are now borne unfairly by farmers, but compensating for these costs by any means is problematic (21, 24, 86). Intellectual property and contracts that include royalties depend on a market in genetic resources. Whether such a market can operate and its impact on local farm communities or indigenous groups are unknown. High transaction costs, reliance on state legal systems, and limited duration bedevil the use of intellectual property to compensate farmers and indigenous people (21). Contracts that include royalty agreements are an alternative to intellectual property, but these affect few farmers and provide only short-term compensation (86, 130). Indirect compensation through investment in agricultural development can aim for both in situ conservation and benefits to farmers (2, 19, 31, 36, 110), but this is a diffuse method. In situ conservation persists in areas where agricultural development programs such as the Green Revolution have limited impacts, which suggests that compensation through indirect means is difficult.

CONCLUSIONS

Conservation programs for protected areas and plant genetic resources have evolved in similar ways, beginning with a focus on single species and expanding to ecosystem strategies that involve the participation of local people. Ecosystem conservation, such as watershed management with mixed land uses, has an analogy in in situ conservation of plant genetic resources. This expansion is a response to (*a*) the realization that the needs of conserving biological diversity exceed the ability to establish and maintain biological reserves or gene banks and to (*b*) the recognition of the rights and interests of the people who live close to protected areas and who manage plant genetic resources. Anthropological research on protected areas and plant genetic resources emerged in the 1970s and draws on a diversity of approaches, including cultural ecology, ethnobiology, political economy, and interpretative anthropology. This research has influenced the evolving strategies to conserve biodiversity.

Common Themes in Protected Areas and Plant Genetic Resources

PARTICIPATION   Anthropologists have described the increasing importance of the participation of local people in conservation programs, both of local populations in protected area management and of farmers in plant genetic resources. This participation is justified by two sorts of reasons. The first, linked to issues of social justice, is a recognition of the rights that come from long histories of residence in protected areas or of cultivation and maintenance of crop varieties. The second, linked to pragmatic concerns of reducing or preventing loss of biodiversity, stems from the effectiveness of participation in conservation by local populations, based on their detailed knowledge and management practices, on their commitments to local ecosystems and forms of agriculture, and on the high costs of excluding them from conservation management. These two reasons are connected with broader political and cultural concerns: the first with new debates over citizenship in the post–Cold War era, with renewed debates over nationalism and multiculturalism, the second with the strongly economic language of a neoliberal era of growth-oriented discourse and of privatization of state enterprises. This economic language frames many of the debates over anthropology and conservation. Protected areas and crop varieties are described as kinds of property (whether territorial or intellectual) and as kinds of resources whose value can be measured, managed, and distributed.

ORGANIZATION   Both protected areas and plant genetic resources involve the conservation of biodiversity at several spatial, social, and political scales. They link local populations, national agencies, and international organizations. The concern for biodiversity at a global scale, the planetary scale of threats to biodiversity (habitat modification, population increase, intensification of resource use, growing international trade, climate change) (48), and the development of international environmental NGOs and environmental organizations within the United Nations have made international organizations especially important. Here, some differences in scale may be noted. Debates over plant genetic resources concentrate at the international level (due to the large-scale international trade in plant genetic material and to the existence of a single key international organization, the International Plant Genetic Resources Institute, within the framework of international agricultural research institutes). Debates over protected areas are often at the national level (due to the association between nation-states and territorial sovereignty, and to the development of nation-specific laws and regulations for land use and ownership). This contrast also demonstrates one of the surprising shifts in global politics in the past 25 years: Organizations and movements that represent indigenous and native peoples have grown in strength, while peasant cultivators' and farmers' have become weaker.

POSITIONS OF AND FOR ANTHROPOLOGISTS   Within universities and research institutions, anthropologists continue well-established traditions of scholarly research, especially in two areas: (*a*) documenting local knowledge and practices that influence the selection and maintenance of crop varieties and the conservation of rare and endangered species in protected areas, and (*b*) clarifying the different concerns and definitions of biodiversity held by local populations and international conservationists. In addition, anthropologists operate in other arenas—NGOs, international agencies, social movements—participating in policy debates and acting as advocates and allies of local populations of farmers, indigenous peoples, and other subordinate groups. These multiple roles and forms of engagement are one of the promising features of the involvement of anthropologists with biodiversity and conservation.

ACKNOWLEDGMENTS
We thank Jim Hafner for his work as a research assistant. We also appreciate the comments from Andrea Kaus, Melissa Nelson, Joe Spaeder, Allyn Stearman, Brent Berlin, Brien Meilleur, and Terry Turner.

Literature Cited

1. Alcorn JB. 1993. Indigenous peoples and conservation. *Conserv. Biol.* 7:424–26
2. Altieri MA, Merrick LC. 1987. In situ conservation of crop genetic resources through maintenance of traditional farming systems. *Econ. Bot.* 41:86–96
3. Alvard M. 1993. Testing the 'ecologically noble savage' hypothesis: interspecific prey choice by Piro hunters of Amazonian Peru. *Hum. Ecol.* 21(4):355–87
4. Alvard M. 1995. Intraspecific prey choice by amazonian hunters. *Curr. Anthropol.* 36(5):789–818
5. Anderson JR, Hazell PBR. 1989. *Variabil-*

ity in Grain Yields: Implications for Agricultural Research and Policy in Developing Countries. Baltimore: Johns Hopkins Univ. Press

6. Balick MJ, Elisabetsky E, Laird SA. 1995. Medicinal Resources of the Tropical Forest: Biodiversity and Its Importance to Human Health. New York: Columbia Univ. Press

7. Bellon MR. 1991. The ethnoecology of maize variety management: a case study from Mexico. Hum. Ecol. 19:389–418

8. Bellon MR, Brush SB. 1994. Keepers of maize in Chiapas, Mexico. Econ. Bot. 48: 196–209

9. Bellon MR, Taylor JE. 1993. Farmer soil taxonomy and technology adoption. Econ. Dev. Cult. Change 41:764–86

10. Berlin B. 1992. Ethnobiological Classification: Principles of Categorization of Plants and Animals in Traditional Societies. Princeton, NJ: Princeton Univ. Press

11. Boster JS. 1983. A comparison of the diversity of Jivaroan gardens with that of the tropical forest. Hum. Ecol. 11:47–68

12. Boster JS. 1984. Inferring decision making from preferences and behavior: an analysis of Aguaruna Jívaro manioc selection. Hum. Ecol. 12:343–58

13. Boster JS. 1985. 'Requiem for the omniscient informant': there's life in the old girl yet. In Directions in Cognitive Anthropology, ed. J Dougherty, pp. 177–97. Urbana: Univ. Ill. Press

14. Boster JS. 1985. Selection for perceptual distinctiveness: evidence from Aguaruna cultivars. Econ. Bot. 39:310–25

15. Brandon KE, Wells MP. 1992. Planning for people and parks: design dilemmas. World Dev. 20(4):557–70

16. Breslin P, Chapin M. 1988. Conservation Kuna-style. In Direct to the Poor: Grassroots Development in Latin America, ed. S Annis, P Hakim, pp. 73–82. Boulder, CO: Rienner

17. Brokensha DW, Warren DM, Werner O, eds. 1980. Indigenous Knowledge Systems and Development. Washington, DC: Univ. Press Am.

18. Brownrigg LA. 1985. Native cultures and protected areas: management options. In Culture and Conservation: The Human Dimension in Environmental Planning, ed. DC Pitt, JA McNeely, pp. 33–44. London: Croom Helm

19. Brush SB. 1991. A farmer-based approach to conserving crop germplasm. Econ. Bot. 45:153–65

20. Brush SB. 1992. Ethnoecology, biodiversity, and modernization in Andean potato agriculture. J. Ethnobiol. 12:161–85

21. Brush SB. 1993. Indigenous knowledge of biological resources and intellectual property rights: the role of anthropology. Am. Anthropol. 95:653–86

22. Brush SB. In situ conservation of landraces in centers of crop diversity. Crop Sci. 35: 346–54

23. Brush SB, Kesseli R, Ortega R, Cisneros P, Zimmerer KS, Quiros C. 1995. Potato diversity in the Andean Center of crop domestication. Conserv. Biol. 9:1189–98

24. Brush SB, Stabinsky DF, eds. 1995. Valuing Local Knowledge: Indigenous People and Intellectual Property Rights. Washington, DC: Island

25. Brush SB, Taylor JE, Bellon MR. 1992. Biological diversity and technology adoption in Andean potato agriculture. J. Dev. Econ. 39:365–87

26. Bulmer R. 1970. Which came first, the chicken or the egg-head? In Echanges et Communications, ed. J Pouillon, P Miranda, pp. 1069–91. The Hague: Mouton

27. Burtt BL. 1970. Infraspecific categories in flowering plants. Biol. J. Linn. Soc. 2: 233–38

28. Carson R. 1962. Silent Spring. Boston: Houghton Mifflin

29. Childers RA. 1994. Cultural protection: a link to tradition. Forum Appl. Res. Public Policy 9(4):79–83

30. Clay JW. 1988. Indigenous Peoples and Tropical Forests: Models of Land Use and Management from Latin America. Cambridge, MA: Cult. Surv.

31. Cleveland DA, Soleri D, Smith SE. 1994. Do folk crop varieties have a role in sustainable agriculture? BioScience 44: 740–51

32. Cohen JI, Williams JT, Plucknett DL, Shands H. 1991. Ex situ conservation of plant genetic resources: global development and environmental concerns. Science 253:866–72

33. Colchester M. 1994. Salvaging Nature: Indigenous Peoples, Protected Areas and Biodiversity Conservation. Geneva: U. N. Res. Inst. Soc. Dev.

34. Conklin DA, Graham LR. 1995. The shifting middle ground: Amazonian indians and eco-politics. Am. Anthropol. 97(4):1–17

35. Conklin HC. 1957. Hanunoo Agriculture. FAO For. Dev. Pap. No. 12. Rome: Food Agric. Organ.

36. Cooper D, Vallvé R, Hobbelink H, eds. 1992. Growing Diversity: Genetic Resources and Local Food Security. London: Intermed. Technol.

37. Coordinadora de las Organizaciones Indígenas de la Cuenca Amazónica. 1989. Two agendas on Amazon development. Cult. Surv. Q. 13(4):75–87

38. Darwin C. 1875. The Variation of Plants and Animals Under Domestication, 2 Vols. London: Murray. 2nd ed.

39. Dasmann RF. 1984. The relationship between protected areas and indigenous people. See Ref. 98, pp. 667–71

40. Davis S. 1988. Indigenous peoples, environmental protection and sustainable development. *World Bank Off. Environ. Sci. Affairs Occas. Pap.* Washington, DC: World Bank

41. de Boef W, Amanor K, Wellard K, Bebbington A, eds. 1993. *Cultivating Knowledge: Genetic Diversity, Farmer Experimentation and Crop Research.* London: Intermed. Technol.

42. De Candolle A. 1882. *Origine des Plantes Cultivées.* Paris: Germer Bailliere

43. Dejoux C, Iltis A, eds. 1992. *Lake Titicaca: A Synthesis of Limnological Knowledge.* Boston: Kluwer

44. Dennis JV. 1987. *Farmer management of rice variety diversity in northern Thailand.* PhD thesis. Cornell Univ., Ithaca, NY

45. Derman B. 1995. Environmental NGOs, dispossession, and the state: the ideology and praxis of African nature and development. *Hum. Ecol.* 23(2):199–215

46. Dove MR. 1986. Practical reason of weeds in Indonesia: peasant vs state views of *Imperata* and *Chromolaena. Hum. Ecol.* 14(2):163–90

47. Dove MR. 1993. A revisionist view of tropical deforestation and development. *Environ. Conserv.* 20(1):17–25

48. Durham WH. 1995. Political ecology and environmental destruction in Latin America. In *The Social Causes of Environmental Destruction in Latin America,* ed. M Painter, WH Durham, pp. 249–64. Ann Arbor: Univ. Mich. Press

49. Escobar A. 1996. Cultural politics and biological diversity: state, capital, and social movements in the Pacific Coast of Colombia. In *Cultures of Protest: Dissent and Direct Action in the Late Twentieth Century,* ed. R Fox, O Starn. New Brunswick, NJ: Rutgers Univ. Press

50. Feder G, Just RE, Zilberman D. 1985. Adoption of agricultural innovations in developing countries: a survey. *Econ. Dev. Cult. Change* 33:255–98

51. Forbes AA. 1993. Heirs to the land: mapping the future of the Makalu-Barun. *Appalachia* 26(1):78–91

52. Fowler C, Mooney PR. 1990. *Shattering: Food, Politics and the Loss of Genetic Diversity.* Tucson: Univ. Ariz. Press

53. Gann B. 1995. Heartburn of darkness. *Sierra* 80(6):56–57

54. Gibson CC, Marks SA. 1995. Transforming rural hunters into conservationists: an assessment of community-based wildlife management programs in Africa. *World Dev.* 23(6):941–57

55. Gómez-Pompa A, Kaus A. 1992. Taming the wilderness myth. *BioScience* 42(4): 271–79

56. Goodman D. 1975. The theory of diversity-stability relationships in ecology. *Q. Rev. Biol.* 50:237–66

57. Greaves T. 1994. *A Sourcebook on Intellectual Property and Indigenous Knowledge.* Washington, DC: Soc. Appl. Anthropol.

58. Hamilton MB. 1994. Ex situ conservation of wild plant species: time to reassess the genetic assumptions and implications of seed banks. *Conserv. Biol.* 8:39–49

59. Harlan JR. 1975. Our vanishing genetic resources. *Science* 188:618–21

60. Harlan JR. 1992. *Crops and Man.* Madison, WI: Am. Soc. Agron. Crop Sci. Soc. Am. 2nd ed.

61. Harris DR, Hillman GC, eds. 1989. *Foraging and Farming: The Exploration of Plant Exploitation.* London: Unwin Hyman

62. Harris M. 1968. *The Rise of Anthropological Theory: A History of Theories of Culture.* New York: Crowell

63. Hawkes JG. 1983. *The Diversity of Crop Plants.* Cambridge, MA: Harvard Univ. Press

64. Heinen JT, Kattel B. 1992. Parks, people, and conservation: a review of management issues in Nepal's protected areas. *Popul. Environ.* 14(1):49–84

65. Heinen JT, Yonzon PB. 1994. A review of conservation issues and programs in Nepal: from a single species focus toward biodiversity protection. *Mount. Res. Dev.* 14(1): 61–76

66. Hernandez XE. 1985. Maize and man in the greater Southwest. *Econ. Bot.* 39: 416–30

67. Hill MA, Press AJ. 1994. Kakadu National Park: an Australian experience in comanagement. See Ref. 155, pp. 135–57

68. Homewood KM, Rodgers WA. 1991. *Maasailand Ecology: Pastoralist Development and Wildlife Conservation in Ngorongoro, Tanzania.* Cambridge: Cambridge Univ. Press

69. Infield M. 1989. Hunters claim a stake in the forest. *New Sci.* 124(4):52–54

70. Jackson MT, Ford-Lloyd BV, Parry ML. 1990. *Climatic Change and Plant Genetic Resources.* London: Belhaven

71. Johannessen S, Hastorf CA, eds. 1994. *Corn and Culture in the Prehistoric New World.* Boulder CO: Westview

72. Johns T, Keen SL. 1986. Ongoing evolution of the potato on the altiplano of western Bolivia. *Econ. Bot.* 40:409–24

73. Johnson A. 1974. Ethnoecology and planting practices in a swidden agricultural system. *Am. Ethnol.* 1:87–101

74. Johnsson M. 1986. *Food and Culture Among the Bolivian Aymara: Symbolic Expressions of Social Relations.* Upps. Stud.

Cult. Anthropol. 7. Stockholm: Almqvist & Wiksell

75. Johnston BR, ed. 1994. *Who Pays the Price?: The Sociocultural Context of Environmental Crisis.* Washington, DC: Island

76. Johnston BR. 1995. Human rights and the environment. *Hum. Ecol.* 23(2):111–23

77. Kaus A. 1993. Environmental perceptions and social relations in the Mapimí Biosphere Reserve. *Conserv. Biol.* 7(2): 398–406

78. Kemf E, ed. 1993. *The Law of the Mother: Protecting Indigenous Peoples in Protected Areas.* San Francisco: Sierra Club Books

79. Kloppenburg JR, ed. 1988. *Seeds and Sovereignty: The Use and Control of Plant Genetic Resources.* Durham NC: Duke Univ. Press

80. Kloppenburg JR, Kleinman DL. 1987. The plant germplasm controversy. *BioScience* 37:190–98

81. Krattiger AF, McNeely JA, Lesser WH, Miller KR, Hill YS, Senanayake R, eds. 1994. *Widening Perspectives on Biodiversity.* Gland, Switz.: Int. Union Conserv. Nat.

82. LaBarre W. 1947. Potato taxonomy among the Aymara Indians of Bolivia. *Acta Am.* 5:83–103

83. Lambert DH. 1985. *Swamp Rice Farming: An Indigenous Pahang Malay Agricultural System.* Boulder, CO: Westview

84. Laughlin R. 1975. *The Great Tzotzil Dictionary of San Lorenzo Zinacantán.* Washington, DC: Smithson. Inst.

85. Lebot V, Meilleur BA, Manshardt RM. 1994. Genetic diversity in eastern Polynesian Eumusa bananas. *Pac. Sci.* 48:16–31

86. Lesser WH, Krattiger AF. 1994. The complexities of negotiating terms for germplasm collection. *Diversity* 10:6–10

87. Levieil DP, Orlove BS. 1990. Local control of aquatic resources: community and ecology in Lake Titicaca, Peru. *Am. Anthropol.* 92(2):18–38

88. Levieil DP, Orlove BS. 1992. Socioeconomic importance of macrophytes. See Ref. 43, pp. 505–10

89. Lewis HT. 1989. Ecologial and technological knowledge of fire: aborigines versus park rangers in Northern Australia. *Am. Anthropol.* 91(4):940–61

90. Lipton M, Longhurst R. 1985. *Modern Varieties, International Agricultural Research, and the Poor.* Consult. Group Int. Agric. Res. Stud. Pap. 2. Washington, DC: World Bank

91. Louette D. 1994. *Gestion Traditionnelle de Variétés de Maïs dans la Reserve de la Biosphere Sierra de Manantlán et Conservation in situ des Ressources Génétiques de*

Plantes Cultivées. PhD thesis. Éc. Natl. Supér. Agron., Montpellier

92. Marks SA. 1976. *Large Mammals and a Brave People: Subsistence Hunters in Zambia.* Seattle: Univ. Wash. Press

93. Marks SA. 1984. *The Imperial Lion: Human Dimensions of Wildlife Management in Central Africa.* Boulder, CO: Westview

94. Mayer E. 1992. *La Chacra de Papa: Economía y Ecología.* Lima: Cent. Peru. Estud. Soc.

95. McCabe JT, Perkins S, Schofield C. 1992. Can conservation and development be coupled among pastoral people: an examination of the Maasai of the Ngorongoro Conservation Area, Tanzania. *Hum. Organ.* 51(4):353–36

96. McCay BJ, Acheson JM, eds. 1987. *The Question of the Commons: The Culture and Ecology of Communal Resources.* Tucson, AZ: Univ. Ariz. Press

97. McNeely JA, Harrison J, Dingwall PR, eds. 1994. *Protecting Nature: Regional Reviews of Protected Areas.* Gland, Switz.: Int. Union Conserv. Nat.

98. McNeely JA, Miller KR, eds. 1984. *National Parks, Conservation, and Development: The Role of Protected Areas in Sustaining Society. Proc. World Congr. Natl. Parks.* Bali, Indonesia. Washington, DC: Smithson. Inst.

99. Meilleur BA. 1994. In search of "keystone societies." In *Eating on the Wild Side: The Pharmacologic, Ecologic, and Social Implications of Using Noncultigens,* ed. NL Etkin, pp. 259–79. Tucson, AZ: Univ. Ariz. Press

100. Merlan F. 1991. The limits of cultural constructionism: the case of Coronation Hill. *Oceania* 61:341–52

101. Messer E. 1991. Systematic and medicinal reasoning in Mitla folk botany. *J. Ethnopharmacol.* 33:107–28

102. Metcalfe S. 1994. The Zimbabwe Communal Areas Management Programme for Indigenous Resources (CAMPFIRE). See Ref. 155, pp. 161–92

103. Moock JL, Rhoades RE, eds. 1992. *Diversity, Farmer Knowledge, and Sustainability.* Ithaca, NY: Cornell Univ. Press

104. Mooney PR. 1980. *Seeds of the Earth: A Private or Public Resource?* London: Int. Coalit. Dev. Action

105. Nabhan GP. 1985. *Gathering the Desert.* Tucson, AZ: Univ. Ariz. Press

106. Nabhan GP. 1985. Native crop diversity in aridoamerica: conservation of regional gene pools. *Econ. Bot.* 39:387–99

107. Nabhan GP. 1989. *Enduring Seeds: Native American Agriculture and Wild Plant Conservation.* San Francisco: North Point

108. Nabhan GP, Rea AM, Reichhardt KL, Mellink E, Hutchinson CP. 1982. Papago influ-

ences on habitat and biotic diversity: Quitovac oasis ethnoecology. *J. Ethnobiol.* 2(2):124–43

109. National Research Council. 1993. *Managing Global Genetic Resources: Agricultural Crop Issues and Policies.* Washington, DC: Nat. Acad. Sci.

110. Oldfield ML, Alcorn JB. 1987. Conservation of traditional agroecosystems. *BioScience* 37:199–208

111. Orlove BS. 1980. Ecological anthropology. *Annu. Rev. Anthropol.* 9:235–73

112. Orlove BS. 1991. Mapping reeds and reading maps: the politics of representation in Lake Titicaca. *Am. Ethnol.* 18(1):3–38

113. Orlove BS, Levieil DP, Treviño HP. 1992. Social and economic aspects of the Lake Titicaca fisheries. See Ref. 43, pp. 500–4

114. Pearce D, Moran D. 1994. *The Economic Value of Biodiversity.* London: Earthscan

115. Peluso NL. 1992. *Rich Forests, Poor People: Resource Control and Resistance in Java.* Berkeley: Univ. Calif. Press

116. Peres CA. 1994. Indigenous reserves and nature conservation in Amazonian forests. *Conserv. Biol.* 8(2):586–88

117. Pimm SL. 1986. Community stability and structure. In *Conservation Biology*, ed. ME Soulé, pp. 309–29. Sunderland, MA: Sinauer Assoc.

118. Pinkerton E. 1989. *Cooperative Management of Local Fisheries: New Directions for Improved Management and Community Development.* Vancouver: Univ. Br. Columbia Press

119. Pitt DC, McNeely JA, eds. 1985. *Culture and Conservation: The Human Dimension in Environmental Planning.* London: Croom Helm

120. Poole PJ. 1993. Indigenous peoples and biodiversity protection. In *The Social Challenge of Biodiversity Conservation*, ed. S Davis. Washington, DC: Glob. Environ. Facil.

121. Posey DA. 1990. Intellectual property rights and just compensation for indigenous knowledge. *Anthropol. Today* 6: 13–16

122. Posey DA. 1992. Interpreting and applying the "reality" of indigenous concepts: What is necessary to learn from the natives? See Ref. 126, pp. 21–34

123. Pyne SJ. 1991. *Burning Bush: A Fire History of Australia.* New York: Holt

124. Quiros CF, Brush SB, Douches DS, Zimmerer KS, Huestes G. 1990. Biochemical and folk assessment of variability of Andean cultivated potatoes. *Econ. Bot.* 44: 254–66

125. Redford KH. 1990. The ecologically noble savage. *Orion Nature Q.* 9(3):25–29

126. Redford KH, Padoch C, eds. 1992. *Conservation of Neotropical Forests: Working*

from Traditional Resource Use. New York: Columbia Univ. Press

127. Redford KH, Stearman AM. 1993. Forest-dwelling native Amazonians and the conservation of biodiversity: interests in common or in collision? *Conserv. Biol.* 7(2): 248–55

128. Redford KH, Stearman AM. 1993. On common ground? Response to Alcorn. *Conserv. Biol.* 7(2):427–28

129. Reed RK. 1995. *Prophets of Agroforestry: Guaraní Communities and Commercial Gathering.* Austin: Univ. Tex. Press

130. Reid WV, Laird SA, Meyer C, Gámez R, Sittenfeld A, et al. 1993. *Biodiversity Prospecting: Using Resources for Sustainable Development.* Washington, DC: World Resour. Inst.

131. Richards P. 1985. *Indigenous Agricultural Revolution: Ecology and Food Production in West Africa.* Boulder, CO: Westview

132. Schelhas J, Greenberg R, eds. 1996. *Forest Patches in Tropical Landscapes.* Washington, DC: Island

133. Sedjo RA. 1992. Property rights, genetic resources, and biotechnological change. *J. Law Econ* 35:199–213

134. Singh AJ, Byerlee D. 1990. Relative variability in wheat yields across countries and over time. *J. Agric. Econ.* 41:21–32

135. Soleri D, Smith SE. 1995. Morphological and phenological comparisons of two Hopi maize varieties conserved in situ and ex situ. *Econ. Bot.* 49:56–77

136. Spaeder J. 1995. *The Qavilnguut (Kilbuck) Caribou Herd: An Alaskan Example of Cooperative Management.* Rep. to the 18 participating Yup'ik villages and the Alsk. Dept. Fish Game and US Fish Wildlife Serv., Davis, CA

137. Staver C, Simeone R, Stocks A. 1994. Land resource management and forest conservation in central Amazonian Peru: regional, community, and farm-level approaches among native peoples. *Mount. Res. Dev.* 14(2):147–57

138. Steadman DW. 1995. Prehistoric extinctions of Pacific island birds: biodiversity meets zooarchaeology. *Science* 267: 1123–31

139. Stearman AM. 1984. Yuquí connection: another look at Siriono deculturation. *Am. Anthropol.* 86(3):630–50

140. Stearman AM. 1989. Yuquí foragers in the Bolivian Amazon: subsistence strategies, prestige, and leadership in an acculturating society. *J. Anthropol. Res.* 45(2):219–44

141. Stearman AM, Redford KH. 1995. Game management and cultural survival: the Yuquí Ethnodevelopment Project in lowland Bolivia. *Oryx* 29(1):29–34

142. Turner T. 1984. Dual opposition, hierarchy and value: moiety structure and symbolic

polarity in central Brazil and elsewhere. In *Différences, Valeurs, Hiérarchie: Textes Offerts à Louis Dumont*, ed. JC Galey, pp. 335–70. Paris: Ed. Éc. Ht. Étud. Sci. Soc.

143. Turner T. 1986. Production, exploitation and social consciousness in the "peripheral situation." *Soc. Anal.* (19):91–115

144. Turner T. 1991. Representing, resisting, rethinking: historical transformations of Kayapó culture and anthropological consequences. In *Colonial Situations: Essays on the Contextualization of Ethnographic Knowledge*, ed. GW Stocking, pp. 285–313. Madison, WI: Univ. Wis. Press

145. Turner T. 1993. The role of indigenous peoples in the environmental crisis: the example of the Kayapó of the Brazilian Amazon. *Perspect. Biol. Med.* 36(3):526–47

146. Turner T. 1995. An indigenous people's struggle for socially equitable and ecologically sustainable production: the Kayapó revolt against extractivisim. *J. Lat. Am. Anthropol.* 1(1):98–121

147. Vavilov N. 1926. *Studies on the Origin of Cultivated Plants*. Leningrad: Inst. Appl. Bot. Plant Improv.

148. Vincent J. 1990. *Anthropology and Politics: Visions, Traditions, and Trends*. Tucson, AZ: Univ. Ariz. Press

149. Vogel JH. 1994. *Genes for Sale: Privatization as a Conservation Policy.* New York: Oxford Univ. Press

150. Weaver S. 1991. The role of Aboriginals in the management of Australia's Cobourg (Gurig) and Kakadu National Parks. See

Ref. 154, pp. 311–32

151. Weismantel MJ. 1988. *Food, Gender and Poverty in the Ecuadorian Andes*. Philadelphia: Univ. Pa. Press

152. Wells MP. 1994. A profile and interim assessment of the Annpurna Conservation Area Project, Nepal. See Ref. 155, pp. 261–81

153. Wells MP, Brandon K, Hannah LJ, eds. 1992. *People and Parks: Linking Protected Area Management with Local Communities*. Washington, DC: World Bank/World Wildl. Fund/US Agency Int. Dev.

154. West PC, Brechin SR, eds. 1991. *Resident Peoples and National Parks: Social Dilemmas and Strategies in International Conservation*. Tucson: Univ. Ariz. Press

155. Western D, Wright RM, Strum SC, eds. 1994. *Natural Connections: Perspectives in Community-Based Conservation*. Washington, DC: Island

156. Wilkes HG. 1985. Teosinte: the closest relative of maize revisited. *Maydica* 30: 209–23

157. Wilson EO, ed. 1988. *Biodiversity*. Washington, DC: Natl. Acad. Sci.

158. World Commission on Environment and Development. 1987. *Our Common Future*. Oxford/New York: Oxford Univ. Press

159. Zimmerer KS. 1991. Managing diversity in potato and maize fields of the Peruvian Andes. *J. Ethnobiol.* 11:23–49

160. Zimmerer KS. 1991. The regional biogeography of native potato cultivars in highland Peru. *J. Biogeogr.* 18:165–78

Annu. Rev. Anthropol. 1996. 25:353–82

LANGUAGE AND SPACE

Stephen C. Levinson

Max Planck Institute for Psycholinguistics, P.O. Box 310, 6500 AH Nijmegen, The Netherlands

KEY WORDS: space, cognition and language, linguistic relativity

ABSTRACT

This review describes some recent, unexpected findings concerning variation in spatial language across cultures, and places them in the context of the general anthropology of space on the one hand, and theories of spatial cognition in the cognitive sciences on the other. There has been much concern with the symbolism of space in anthropological writings, but little on concepts of space in practical activities. This neglect of everyday spatial notions may be due to unwitting ethnocentrism, the assumption in Western thinking generally that notions of space are universally of a single kind. Recent work shows that systems of spatial reckoning and description can in fact be quite divergent across cultures, linguistic differences correlating with distinct cognitive tendencies. This unexpected cultural variation raises interesting questions concerning the relation between cultural and linguistic concepts and the biological foundations of cognition. It argues for more sophisticated models relating culture and cognition than we currently have available.

THE ANTHROPOLOGY OF SPACE AND THE NEGLECT OF "EVERYDAY" SPATIAL CONCEPTS

The title of this chapter conjoins two of the perduring objects of Western intellectual inquiry: language and space (for historical reviews, see 37, 74). The review focuses on the intersection—the language *of* space.[1] Apart from drawing attention to some important new findings about spatial language, it

---

[1] One topic omitted here is "language in space," i.e. the large literature on the distribution of language types and families (see 120 and references therein). For correlations with archaeology, see 135, and with population genetics, see 22.

353

shows how the study of the language of space might play a fundamental role in the anthropology of space more generally.

The use of space, patterns of settlement, and above all, the symbolism of spatial arrangements are classical issues in sociocultural anthropology (36) and archaeology (136). The recent literature on the anthropology of space is now so large that it would resist even book-length review. However, a few inadequate pointers may still be helpful. The traditional focus on cosmological schemes is only somewhat abated by postmodernist scruples about the basis of anthropological knowledge. It is even being resuscitated by ethnoarchaeologists, e.g. in the Mayan culture area where there is an extensive ethnographic literature (see 47 and references therein). Abstract cosmological themes and their instantiation in grandiose architectural schemes, e.g. in the Asian civilizations, are as interesting to archaeologists, architects, and geographers (154) as to ethnographers (151). A related traditional focus on the symbolism of domestic space, with classics such as Bourdieu (8:90), Hugh-Jones (70), Littlejohn (109), and Tambiah (151:176ff), also continues to flourish, but now with much closer documentation (45, 163), and a concern with social identity, such as with gender and access (2, 115). The anthropology of the "built environment" has received its own excellent review in the current format (92). A new line here is the study of the interactional use of domestic and public spaces, where the homology between linguistic forms and spatial arrangements is beginning to be explored, especially with respect to formal/informal speech registers (35, 81, 154, 174). This line of work, unusually rich in its study of cross-modal symbolism, builds of course on kinesics and interaction analysis (49, 85).

Another traditional line giving birth to new offspring is the spatial mapping of the nature-culture dichotomy, with a new interest in landscape and its associations and symbolism, a development to be found in both sociocultural anthropology (69) and archaeology (152). Landscape in turn ties in to the thriving field of ethnoecology (see 34, 172). All these themes are so well-woven into current anthropological thinking that it is hard to find a good contemporary ethnography that does not dwell at length on spatial matters, although it is much more unusual to find careful attention paid also to spatial language (as in 164).

These references are no more than inadequate bibliographical leads to a vast literature, but one that although multifaceted, has a fundamental gap. The focus has been on collective representations, on cosmologies and the symbolic uses and associations of space, with little mention of the kind of notions in daily use to solve spatial problems (4). One might have expected to find this in the study of hunting or herding and transhumance. Although there are fine studies of navigational lore and practice in the Oceanic world that have sparked much cross-disciplinary interest [see 40, 72; see also Frake's (46) studies of medieval European navigation], this literature stands isolated. There seems to be astonishingly little of substance about how, for example, hunter-gatherers find their way in deserts and tundras. Real studies of Australian Aboriginal way-finding appear to reduce to those done by a sailor-explorer (107, 108), a seconded Indian policeman (87), and some recent notes by Nash (118).

Another way to study the everyday use of spatial concepts is to investigate the language of spatial description. How do people refer to places, describe spatial arrangements, say where someone is going, and so forth? This is the focus of this review. Even for the anthropologist with relatively little interest in language, this may be a rewarding area, because frequently one can see direct connections between classical questions of cosmology, aesthetics and art style, practical activities like hunting or herding, and the linguistic resources used to make spatial distinctions in different cultures.

Meanwhile, especially in other disciplines,[2] there has been extensive recent interest in "language and space," with four international conferences within the past year or so. The reasons for the recent concentration of effort are various and include (*a*) developments within the cognitive sciences, which suggest rich innate bases for spatial cognition of all sorts; (*b*) a set of expectations from cognitive linguistics, based on assumed commonalities of human experience; (*c*) a series of "neo-Whorfian" findings within linguistics and psychology that suggest far more cultural variation in spatial language and cognition than expected by either (*a*) or (*b*).[3]

It is this high tension between different orders of "hard facts," e.g. the neuropsychological and the linguistic, as well as between theories of various kinds, that makes the area so interesting. This review tries to lay out the background to this concentration of intellectual activity.[4]

I attempt below to draw attention to the way the new findings in (*c*) have upset the applecart. But for fear of losing the essentials in the details, I have

---

[2] The disciplines are those that have found common ground under the rubric of the "cognitive sciences," notably philosophy, linguistics, psychology, and the brain sciences. The philosophical literature is hardly referred to here, but see Eilan et al (38) for some papers in the analytical tradition and Casey (21) for the continental tradition.

[3] For reconsiderations of the Whorfian issues in general, see Gumperz & Levinson (51) and Hill & Mannheim (68). Incidentally, cross-cultural psychologists have, since the time of the Torres Straits expedition at the turn of the century, reported significant cross-cultural variation in spatial acuities. See Berry et al (5).

[4] The following standard linguistic conventions are employed: Linguistic forms are in italics; when treated as utterances, they are within double quotes. Glosses of actual forms or of a range of forms across languages are in single quotes, while capital letters are employed for hypothetical semantic primes.

listed some of the dashed hypotheses and the contradicting findings in advance:

1. *Hypothesis:* Learning spatial language essentially involves mapping the local expressions onto the antecedently given, largely innate, stock of spatial concepts (24, 114, 142). Thus our cognitive categories determine our linguistic categories.

   Contradicting facts: 1. Languages simply do not use the same or even similar spatial concepts (see e.g. 15). 2. Children can be shown to be oriented from their earliest language comprehension to the local culture-specific semantic distinctions (e.g. 23). 3. Where languages encode spatial concepts different from our familiar ones, speakers of those languages can be shown to use correspondingly different spatial concepts in nonlinguistic reasoning; in short, language may determine the cognitive categories rather than the other way around (18, 127).

2. *Hypothesis:* Our conceptions of space are everywhere essentially relativistic and body centered, anthropomorphic and egocentric (24, 114). Thus all cultures make symbolic use of the primordial opposition between 'left' and 'right' (66, 119).

   Contradicting fact: Many languages do not use the planes through the body to derive spatial coordinates, i.e. they have no left/right/front/back spatial terms (e.g. 16, 99). Such cultures may have no symbolic associations with left and right hands (105).

The anthropological contribution to these debates could be massive. Unfortunately the anthropology of space, though rich in its own right, is largely unconnected, a result of the relative neglect of how people think and talk about spatial notions in everyday life. This review therefore concentrates on the low-level, fundamental, everyday spatial notions as discoverable, in both their generalities and cultural specificities, through analyzing language. A central theme is that linguistic patterns point to some systematic differences in the *cognitive style* with which individuals of different cultures deal with space, and that it is these underlying cognitive specializations that may help us to integrate diverse spatial features within a culture, from cosmology to domestic architecture down to the details of aesthetic preference and material culture. In short, cognition is the intermediate variable that promises to explain cultural propensities in spatial behavior, and language may offer us more than just privileged access to it. It will be helpful then to begin with some brief reference to the picture of spatial cognition offered to us by the cognitive sciences, and return later to the same theme to show how cultural variation needs to be brought into the picture.

SPATIAL COGNITION IN COGNITIVE SCIENCE

Human beings think spatially. Not exclusively, but it is no doubt one of the fundamental tricks of human cognition. Casting nonspatial problems into spatial thinking gives us literacy, geometry, diagrams, mandala, dream-time landscapes, measures of close and distant relatives and of high and low social groups, and much more. Just as maps stand in an abstract spatial relation to real spatial terrain,[5] so spatial arrangements can give us symbolic "maps" to other domains. They can even give us maps of the mind, as exploited in the classical and medieval art of memory (176). From what the cognitive advantage thus accrued derives is not satisfactorily explained, but it is perhaps not fanciful to imagine that it is just another way that ancient brain structures (to do, for example, with navigation) are put to new uses in the extended symbolic world that human beings inhabit.

Spatial cognition has been intensively studied in the twentieth century by sciences as diverse as ethology, cognitive and behaviorist psychology, the study of child development, neurology, and the brain sciences generally. There is for example a wondrous literature on animal way-finding and orientation (138, 162), and it is striking how much less is known about human (and primate) cognition and behavior. Nevertheless, the information on human spatial abilities and their neurophysiological basis is enormous, and there is no room here even for the mention of highlights. What is worth drawing attention to is a consistent bias in this research toward a focus on egocentric, anthropomorphic, relativistic spatial concepts and abilities, as opposed to allocentric, abstract, absolute spatial information. The attitude is summed up by Poincaré (133:257): "Absolute space is nonsense, and it is necessary for us to begin by referring space to a system of axes invariably bound to the body."

Take as an example the study of how spatial information is handled in the primate brain. The picture that emerges is one of great complexity, with multiple systems of egocentric coordinates for each sensory mode (125). Thus, when we pick up a coffee cup, the visual system processes the two-dimensional retinal arrays to extract, partly by stereopsis, partly by the analysis of properties of the array itself, a model that includes partial depth information from a particular viewpoint (112). Next we abstract and recognize three-dimensional objects, perhaps by matching them with an inventory of three-dimensional models, thus recognizing the cup and its orientation and placement in depth from the retina. This information then drives the reaching mechanism, first through shoulder-centered coordinates and then (through different neural pathways) the hand-based coordinates that achieve a grasp on the object seen

---

[5] Another topic neglected here: See References 46, 56, and 156 for maps across time and culture.

(76). How the retinal coordinates are translated into shoulder- and hand-based ones remains a matter of contention: Perhaps information is translated into a general spatial model and then out again, or perhaps specialized dedicated translation processes are involved (144). Apparently there are two independent neural pathways involved in the perception of space, called the "what" and "where" systems, the one controlling, for example, our perception of what things are and the other their location in egocentric space (113, 157). Findings like this are potentially highly relevant to our topic of the language of space: Landau & Jackendoff (89) have speculated that the what/where distinction shows up directly as a universal of language, giving us object-names specialized for shape on the one hand, and closed-class spatial morphemes (like our spatial prepositions) on the other.[6] This general emphasis on egocentric, relativistic concepts of space has been rarely effectively challenged—most effectively by O'Keefe & Nadel (123; see also 122), who claim that absolute spatial concepts, mental maps of terrain, are encoded in the hippocampus.

Although the notion of mental maps in psychology is half a century old (153), the same bias toward the study of egocentric spatial information and coordination is also to be found in psychology. Thus, for example, in the study of children's spatial abilities, it is suspected that allocentric behavior is actually generated by operations on egocentric information [for a review, see Pick (131)]. In the psychology of language, it has been repeatedly asserted that human spatial language is a direct reflection of our egocentric, anthropomorphic, and relativistic spatial concepts (24, 114). Rooted in this tradition is the prediction that all languages use the planes through the human body to give us, as Kant (78) put it (see 159), our first grounds for intuitions about space, in terms of 'up' and 'down', 'left' and 'right', 'back' and 'front'. This prediction turns out to be false, as we shall see, and raises the possibility that this entire tradition partly reflects the linguistic prejudices of the Indo-European tongues.

THE LANGUAGE OF SPACE[7]

Space as a Natural Domain

Space is not a restricted semantic domain like (arguably) color or kinship. As a pretheoretical notion it covers at least location and motion, and arguably shape as well—in fact much of what we talk about. What follows uses this unanalyzed notion, itself partly a product of our own cultural preoccupations no doubt, which may conceivably cross-cut emic notions reflected in various languages. Probably few languages have lexicalized the abstract superordinate

---

[6] Critique can be found in the commentary to Landau & Jackendoff (89) and in Brown (14, 15).

[7] For how to collect information about spatial language, see References 98, 139, 169.

concept 'space' itself in the way that the European ones have (although for the contrary assumption, see 48).[8] It is therefore worth asking whether there is cross-linguistic evidence for a superordinate domain here. There is at least this evidence: As far as we know (158), all languages have 'where' questions, literal answers to which are spatial descriptions. Not all languages, however, have one superordinate question form: Many distinguish 'whence', 'whereto', and 'where', others 'where (location)' from 'where (motion to/from)', although mostly such forms show morphological relatedness one to another.

There are reasons to think that the spatial domain has internal natural cleavages, according to the intellectual problems posed by the need to describe different kinds of spatial arrays or events. It will be useful to introduce the terminology, following Talmy (149), whereby the thing to be located is the "figure," and the thing with respect to which it is to be located is called the "ground" (alternative fully equivalent terminologies are, respectively, theme vs relatum, trajector vs landmark). (Where the ground or landmark object is the speaker, or another speech event participant, the normal appellation for such descriptions is *deictic,* but deictic elements of meaning creep into all sorts of spatial descriptions.) Then, restricting ourselves to static spatial arrays, we may distinguish different classes of descriptive problem:

1. No coordinate systems employed:
    a. prototype deixis: e.g. F is 'here' near speaker
    b. contiguity: "topological" relations: e.g. F is 'on' G
    c. named locations
2. Coordinate systems or "frames of reference" employed:
    a. Horizontal
        i. Intrinsic,
        ii. Relative
        iii. Absolute
    b. Vertical

One may look at these as different strategies that may be employed to locate a referent (or describe its movement). In the first major class, no coordinate system is employed to specify the figure's location with respect to the ground. That is, no angular specification is given: *The orange is here* fails to specify an angular location from the deictic center, here presumably the speaker, and in the same way *The orange is in the bowl* does not specify an angle with respect

---

[8] For example, there is no obvious locution for 'place' in Tzeltal, although there is a lexicalized concept for 'the place in which an object belongs or is properly kept'. Similarly, although there can be few cultures more preoccupied with places than the traditional Australian ones, the notion of 'place' encoded linguistically is usually restricted to sacred sites (as in Guugu Yimithirr) or to socially "owned" locations [as in Arrernte (55:306, fn 4)]. On the distinction between 'space' and 'place' in Western thought, see Casey (21).

to the bowl in anything like the way *The orange is to the left of the bowl* does. The strategy for location reference is here 'choose a ground or landmark object in close contiguity with the object to be located'.

A different strategy is to choose a prominent ground object at some remove from the figure or object to be located, and then to specify a search-domain from the ground by specifying an angle from that landmark, as in *The orange is to the left of the bowl, Amsterdam is north of Utrecht,* or *The statue by Giambologna is in front of the cathedral.* Here the possibilities grow complex, and languages make different resources available.

One may also talk similarly of *The bird above the tree,* using the vertical angle overdetermined by gravity, our upright stance and normally upright head position. The vertical dimension is special in various ways and is an angular specification that creeps into essentially nonangular topological specifications, as illustrated by *The orange on the table* (about which more later).

I now describe something of what we know of cultural and linguistic variation on these different parameters. Note that this way of carving up the pie (though indebted to many predecessors and colleagues) is my own (for more justification, see 102), and the reader interested in other treatments should see References 6, 65, 114, 147, 149, 160. One advantage of the present scheme is that it handles extensive and intensive field data from a score of non-Indo-European languages under investigation at the Max Planck Institute for Psycholinguistics—data that other schemes are likely to founder on. Incidentally I treat motion and static location in parallel. Talmy (149) has influentially argued that motion is primary, static description derived, sometimes as "fictive motion"—I believe this itself to be a cross-linguistic variable (103).

Deixis

Deixis is the way parameters of the speech event enter into the interpretation of linguistic expressions (for elementary exposition, see 97, 101; for complexities, see 75, 110; and for good cross-linguistic surveys, see 1, 165; see also 32). Such parameters can enter into spatial expressions in different ways:

1. Central: In deictic demonstrative pronouns like *this* or adverbs like *here,* what is denoted depends largely on the contextual parameters (crudely, one might gloss *here* as 'the contextually appropriate area including the speaker'). Similarly for motion, *come* denotes motion toward the deictic center, usually the speaker.

2. Compositional: when one adds a deictic to an already well-formed spatial description (cf *The cup is at the side of the table* with *The cup is at this side of the table*).

3. As optional origo: where a speech participant is used as a center or origin for a coordinate system (often incidentally), as in *The ball is to the left of*

the tree (from where I am standing), or *It's thirty miles north (from where we are now)*.

This discussion is restricted to the central cases, like deictic adverbs and demonstratives, and motion verbs like *come* and *go*. There is well-known cross-linguistic variation in the size and structure of inventories of deictic demonstratives, which have been ably reviewed elsewhere (see especially 1 and references therein), and I note only the kinds of variation involved. First, one needs to distinguish between speaker-centric systems (where a distal demonstrative glosses as, for example, 'that, away from speaker') and systems organized around other participants as well (where, for example, a distal demonstrative might gloss as 'that, near you', which may even be opposed to another 'that, near him'). This opposition should be of fundamental sociological importance, but little has been done on the actual usage of systems of the latter kind (but see 26). Second, additional spatial parameters are often built into demonstrative series. For example, some Papuan languages, in addition to marking horizontal distance from speaker and addressee, also indicate vertical location relative to the speaker (thus providing terms glossing e.g. 'that far away up there' vs 'that far away on the level' vs 'that far away below'). Other Papuan languages build in geographic features, with forms glossing 'that north' or 'that there inland' (see 43:75–77). The Eskimo languages are justly renowned for their enormous demonstrative series, sometimes incorporating shape distinctions, geographical distinctions (e.g. along coast, away from coast, upriver, downriver), visibility conditions, and the like (44, 73).

Sociological reasons for variation in demonstrative inventories have been the focus of various speculations, e.g. by Kay (80), Denny (32, 33), and most recently by Perkins (129). A leading idea is that in small-scale speech communities without literacy, language use is fundamentally more contextually dependent than in complex speech communities. Using a sample of 49 languages, Perkins claims that deictic distinctions are indeed more numerous and more grammaticalized in small-scale speech communities (but see 25 for critique). In fact such global speculations are unlikely to be reflected directly in the size of demonstrative series. For one, indexical language is at the heart of all language socialization (121); for another, context-dependence is a feature that is found in many other areas of vocabulary. A more promising general line of investigation, which attempts to relate sociocultural factors to systems of demonstratives and their grammatical properties, is exemplified by Hanks's work (53, 54; see also 26).

Seen as one kind of strategy for locating objects in space, deictic demonstratives (at least those that do not incorporate geographical or orientational features) may pragmatically succeed in indicating distance but fail to indicate angular location on the horizontal. It is for that reason, presumably, that they are often accompanied by gesture. The study of gesture has in recent years blossomed, but there still remains relatively little good observation of pointing gestures and their interpretation. A notable exception is the work of Haviland (59, 60). Haviland's work makes clear that here again is an area ripe for ethnographic investigation: Far from being the self-evident "roots of reference" (in Lyons's phrase), the very opacity of a pointing gesture in another culture indicates just how complex and socioculturally dependent are the grounds for deictic interpretation.

Deictic verbs of motion have received less attention. In some languages, e.g. the Mayan ones, they belong to an elaborate series of motion verbs, many of which incorporate deictic parameters (e.g. 'arriving here' vs 'arriving there') (see e.g. 58 on Tzotzil; 13). On grounds of systematicity and parsimony one might suspect that verbs of motion should reflect the kinds of distinction made in demonstrative series. This is sometimes the case, so that Palauan, for example, which has demonstratives glossing as 'this near speaker', 'that near addressee', and 'that near neither speaker nor addressee' has corresponding motion verbs 'come toward speaker', 'go toward hearer', 'go away from both speaker and addressee' (1:279). However, recent work suggests that 'go' verbs rarely actually encode 'motion away from deictic center'—rather, they are unmarked for deictic distinctions, and only by opposition to the deictically specified 'come' verbs pick up a Gricean conversational implicature of 'motion away' (168). It could be that distal deictics like 'that' and 'there' are similarly unmarked, and it is for this reason that their usage is notoriously difficult to pin down.

"Topological" Notions

In a work that has had tremendous, though often indirect and unrecognized, impact on the study of spatial concepts, Piaget & Inhelder (130) argued that the child passes through a series of stages of spatial reasoning: At first it grasps only topological notions, then much later grasps Euclidean notions of metric distance and angle, and finally grasps projective geometrical notions.[9] Topology, sometimes described as "rubber-sheet geometry," is the study of geometrical properties that remain constant under transformation or "deformation." Thus a sphere and a cube are topologically equivalent, and together they are distinct from a doughnut or a bicycle tire. Piaget discovered that children less than four will, under the right circumstances, conflate circles, ellipses, and squares, while distinguishing objects with holes in them. Children's drawings, in their disregard for the order and location of eyes, nose, and mouth also seem

---

[9] For anthropological work that attempts to build directly on these Piagetian stages, see Hallpike (52) on "primitive thought" and Wynn (175) on hominid spatial competence as expressed in tools.

to follow topological principles.[10] Spatial relations between two objects of undistinguished shape and size are limited to primitive kinds: Piaget listed proximity, order, enclosure, and continuity. Thus semantic notions like NEAR, AT, BETWEEN, IN, etc have been called topological. Children do learn linguistic terms for these notions earlier than other kinds of spatial vocabulary, at least in those European languages whose acquisition has been intensively studied (77, 142). This may differ for other languages (see below).

Much analytic and descriptive work has been done on this kind of spatial language, which is often encoded in closed-class morphemes, e.g. prepositions or local cases. A review of this work lies beyond the present scope, but see Miller & Johnson-Laird (114) for semantic treatment; Herskovits (65:127–56) for a careful consideration of the range of uses of English *at, in, on;* Vande-loise (160) for corresponding French expressions; Talmy (149) for ideas about the relation between topological notions and closed-class grammatical mor-phemes; and Landau & Jackendoff (89) for alleged neurophysiological bases.

Some more recent developments should be reported. One is the now con-siderable work on the diachronic "evolution" of (largely topological) spatial morphemes (especially pre- and post-positions) from other sources, for which see Heine et al (64) and Svorou (147) and references therein. This literature makes clear that body parts are a frequent source for such closed-class items, and it has been claimed that this mapping of body to world is an essentially metaphorical process (19, 88), an analysis critiqued for at least one language in Levinson (100).

Much of the cross-linguistic comparison of spatial expressions has been done on the basis of existing grammatical descriptions. This is a perilous enterprise, since there is rarely any proper description of the meanings of these expressions in grammars, and instead an assumption that the English gloss 'in', 'at', 'on', etc, map one-to-one to the foreign language. More careful comparisons reveal substantial differences even across closely related lan-guages like English and Dutch. Looking just at IN and ON notions, Bowerman & Pederson (9, 12) have shown that one way to look at the variation is to make a list of different situations that may be covered by an 'in' or 'on' expression (expressions that include prototypical containment and vertical support situ-ations), and then see whether any cross-linguistic patterns emerge. They find that the situations covered form an implicational hierarchy, so that, for exam-ple, any language that extends the prototypical horizontal 'on' relation such

---

[10] Piaget's work has been heavily criticized in the light of recent studies of infant cognition. Babies apparently know things Piaget has been thought to think they don't. However, the criticism often neglects the careful distinction he made between perceptual and cognitive or "repre-sentational" faculties, the former being by his own account fully in place by twelve months.

that it considers a ring to be 'on' a finger will certainly consider a spider to be 'on' the ceiling.

However, such orderly variation is only part of the picture. Some languages simply fail to exhibit any direct coding of IN, ON, or AT notions. This is sometimes because they fractionate these meanings as it were, so that, for example, in the Mayan language Tzeltal, IN-notions are distributed across a range of locative predicates specialized to differently shaped containers (15). Or sometimes they fail to encode them altogether. Thus in the Australian language Guugu Yimithirr the vertical dimension is a major axis that has no topological, contact-only expression: ABOVE and ON are not distinguished and IN is expressed by metaphor, while AT notions are expressed primarily by the locative case, which also has rather broader meanings.

The corresponding motion events, such as 'put in' or 'enter', also show fundamental cross-linguistic variations. Talmy (150) noted a tendency for languages to adopt one of two major lexicalization strategies: to package the spatial *path* with the verb (as in *enter, exit, insert*) or instead to package the path separately as a *satellite,* i.e. particle or adverb (as in *go in, go out, put in,* etc). English favors the latter lexicalization pattern, while borrowing some exemplars of the other pattern from the Romance languages. Slobin (143) has explored how children acquire these patterns and how they come to constitute a way of "thinking for speaking," therefore patterning the construction of discourse as well. This typology, however, which turns out to be somewhat leaky, should not distract from the very different ways that languages construe path distinctions in the first place. In an important comparative study of language acquisition, Choi & Bowerman (23; see also 9) showed that Korean classifies 'putting in' or 'putting on' situations in quite different ways than English: In Korean the relevant distinction is not 'in' vs 'on' but 'tight fit' vs 'loose fit'. A close look at the linguistic development of children raised in Dutch-, English-, Tzotzil-, and Korean-speaking homes shows that children do not start from a common conceptual core, given say by innate presumption or biological endowment, but from the earliest point of language production already make distinctions more like adult speakers of their own languages (10). Recent work by the same authors shows that children are already sensitive to the language-specific distinctions in comprehension before they are able to produce the relevant expressions at all (11). As Bowerman (9:170) concluded with respect to the production evidence, "there was little evidence that [the children] had strong prelinguistic biases for classifying space differently from the way introduced by their language. This leaves the door open to the possibility that, after all, spatial thought—undeniably one of our most basic cognitive capacities—bears the imprint of language."

Named Locations

A final solution to spatial description that avoids substantial Euclidean geometry is to proliferate named locations. One can then state that the figure is 'at' the named location. Of course there are many ad hoc locutions that can be employed here, but speech communities do also standardize place names to a greater or lesser extent. The study of toponyms has, of course, been long of interest to historians, and the patterns in the Old World are extensively documented, but the scientific study of place-names from a sociolinguistic or anthropological point of view is in its infancy. Hunn (71) has made provocative suggestions for such a study, noting that the density of place names in hunter-gatherer societies follows certain laws, and that the nomenclature, like ethnobotanical nomenclature, systematically varies from monolexemes to descriptive phrases according to taxonomic hierarchy and cultural importance (see also 79). My own field experience in village Tamilnadu, where fields had individual names that also came to designate their owners in colloquial parlance, suggests a rich sociology here. With growing interest in indigenous land rights, it is likely that this is an area of study that will prove of increasing interest.

SPECIFYING LOCATION WITH COORDINATE SYSTEMS OR FRAMES OF REFERENCE

It has long been noted that *The cat is behind the truck* is ambiguous based on a reading where the cat is at the truck's rear and a reading where the truck is between the speaker and the cat, regardless of the orientation of the truck. This ambiguity draws attention to the existence of different *frames of reference,* as they were called in Gestalt psychology half a century ago, in effect different coordinate systems. In the first *intrinsic* reading, we employ a coordinate system based on the truck, use the truck's asymmetries and functions to find a named side, and project out a search domain from that named side, within which the cat is to be found. In the second deictic or (as I prefer) *relative* reading, we employ coordinates based on the speaker (or some other viewer), find a truck, and project out a search domain on the occluded side of the truck such that the cat may be found within it. (This is actually an oversimplified description; see below.)

Although fairly complex geometrical notions, involved with coordinate systems, search domains, and the like are involved in each case, evidence shows that the intrinsic system is in some sense simpler. Children learn the intrinsic uses of 'front' and 'back' notions earlier than the deictic or relative ones (77). Indeed there seems to be an implicational universal that if a language has deictic/relative notions of this kind, it will have intrinsic ones, but not necessarily vice-versa. Finally, there are logical asymmetries: The intrinsic notions are binary relations, the relative ones are covertly ternary; the intrinsic notions fail to support spatial inferences, the relative ones do so (94, 102).

The standard references either fail to note or downplay the existence of a third frame of reference, which I shall call the *absolute,* most obviously exemplified by cardinal directions like north, south, east, and west. Languages and cultures in which this kind of coordinate system forms the central means for specifying locations, regardless of scale or context, have been documented only recently.

Before proceeding to these three systems, it should be noted that there is some unclarity in the literature over whether frames of reference are a *linguistic* matter at all. Because we can use the same words, say *The cat is behind the truck,* for two different construals, perhaps *behind* is semantically nonspecific with regard to reference frames, just as *big* in *That book is big* is nonspecific with regard to which dimensions are large. Psychologists have found this tempting (see e.g. 20), and linguists have encouraged them by assuming the same expressions can always be used across reference frames (see e.g. 147: 23). In fact, although there is a tendency for some ambiguity across reference frames, there are often entirely distinct terms associated with each. A second general issue is whether the typology of reference frames across languages is more a matter of contexts of preferred usage (so that, for example, we prefer relative expressions like *in front of* for visually perceived arrays, but *north of* for geographical scale references) than of grammatical stipulation. Although there is some room for dispute here, the evidence suggests that there are languages that scarcely use at all one or more of these frames of reference; that is, the linguistic resources are simply absent in some cases. (In other cases, the linguistic resources may be present, but the cognitive abilities necessary for their correct use largely absent: It is not unusual to find cultures that supply linguistic terms for left and right, but where the speakers are confused about how to use them, or cultures like the European ones whose languages have good cardinal direction terms like *north,* but scarcely anyone knows where north is.)

We may now proceed to details.

The Intrinsic Frame of Reference

In the intrinsic frame of reference the figure object is located with respect to what are often called *intrinsic* or *inherent* features of the ground object. The locutions are bad because there is often nothing intrinsic, and everything is culturally imposed and assigned in the isolation and designation of these features. Consider for example the phrases *in front of the TV, in front of the steps, in front of the church, in front of the ship, in the front of the book,* etc (in the relevant nonrelative or "nondeictic" sense[11]). Clearly the notion 'front' of an object is not an inherent property: In the case of the TV it is based on canonical viewing position, in the case of the steps on the direction they are ascended and not descended, in the case of the Church the west end regardless of the ordinary entrance, in the case of the book the first few pages, in the case of the ship the direction of canonical movement, etc. Various underlying principles may be discerned, and their relative priorities observed. Thus, direction of motion is secondary to direction of sense organs as shown by the designated fronts of crabs (41; 114:402–5). Although the designation of English *front* is such a complex amalgam of orientational, perceptual, functional, and other cultural factors, the correct use of the word is not merely a matter of rote learning: Two-year-olds can assign *fronts* to objects by a generally correct algorithm of some kind (96).

The English intrinsic system can be thought of as a six-sided box-like armature that is imposed on objects. The cubic armature is oriented by gravity, so the *top* side of an object is uppermost, and the *bottom* the underneath facet. *Front* and *back* are found in the way sketched in the previous paragraph, by taking "perceptual apparatus" (as with animals, cameras, etc), canonical direction of motion, canonical direction of use, etc into account. The two remaining facets are the *sides.* If the object is animate, it may have its own *left* and *right side,* if not, it may inherit its left and right from the human beings who wear it or drive it or sit in it. If human beings characteristically confront it, as they do with desks, cupboards, and mirrors, the *left* side is transferred from the closest human left side (114). Objects can obviously resist these assignments, if like cubes and balls they lack both inherent and functional asymmetries.

Although a fair bit of work has been done on corresponding notions cross-linguistically (see e.g. 147 and references therein), it mostly fails to examine the actual semantics of the systems, making them appear cross-linguistically more similar than they actually are. For example, Tzeltal has body-part terms that at first sight look a bit like English 'front', 'back', 'sides', and so on. Yet the system works in a totally different way (see 28 for a similar Tzotzil system, 111 for a contrasting Zapotec system, 106 for a quite different Totonac one). There is no fixed armature at all, and certainly no fixed orientation (of the kind that gives us English *top*). Instead, the system is driven by an axial geometry together with an analysis of shapes, which scarcely refers at all to human use or orientation. Thus the 'face', 'back', 'stomach', 'nose' of a stone or novel object are assigned regardless of its orientation, its use, or any viewing angle.

---

[11] Note that the intrinsic reading is often forced by the definite article, which in turn constrains the preposition: thus *at the front of the TV,* but *in the front of the book.* There has been relatively little work on the way these collocations select interpretations, perhaps because things look messy—for example, the definite article in *to the left of Bill* fails to resolve the ambiguity.

This is consistent with other aspects of Tzeltal spatial description, in which, despite appearances, the human frame plays almost no part in the actual concepts employed (100). Another kind of cross-linguistic variation occurs in the perception of asymmetries: English may assign a top and a bottom to a cube or a sphere, but the Tzeltal body part terms resist this. English considers a tree to lack intrinsic fronts and backs, but Chamus considers otherwise (63). The way in which objects are partitioned into named facets is related in some way, not yet fully clear, to the ways in which they are assigned dimensions [of the 'length', 'width', 'height' type (7)], on which subject there is just beginning some cross-linguistic comparison (see 90, 145 and references therein).

These details may seem of little interest to the nonlinguist but in fact they can have important cultural corrolates. For example, consider the labeling of the interior sides of a building. For us, the front of a church or cinema is the side to which the audience is oriented, and audience left determines building left. This is so for the Pohnpeians as well. Like many peoples, they value the right side. When the high chief sits in the assembly hall facing the commoners, should lesser chiefs sit on his left, or on his right to the building's left? In choosing the latter solution, which allows, for example, a uniform left-side-of-building alignment for women, Pohnpeians opt for the intrinsic orientation of the containing building, thus perhaps symbolizing the coherence of the entire social system (82, 83).

The intrinsic frame of reference can also be used to describe motion. Thus *The truck is moving backwards,* or *It's turning right* (not in the sense of 'right from my viewpoint') uses the truck's assigned intrinsic facets to indicate directional characteristics of motion. Perhaps one might gloss *It's turning right* in terms of the truck being at location L1 at t1 and at L2 at t2, such that L2 is at the right side of the truck at t1. It is interesting to note that motion allows objects that would otherwise resist the assignment of intrinsic facets to now acquire them. Thus, if a cube is sliding down an inclined plane, its leading edge can be called its *front,* and it could now be said to veer to its *left.* Perhaps we should think about the path itself as having intrinsic properties assigned to it, which then determine the named facets of the moving object. If the truck is reversing and is said to be *turning right,* my intuition is that the truck's intrinsic left and right are now reversed. If so, this suggests that facets assigned on the basis of motion can overrule those based on other intrinsic criteria. When we give route directions, we typically use these intrinsic sorts of locutions: *go forward, turn to the left, then take the next right,* and so on. We can describe abstract diagrams and patterns in the same terms, using fictive motion or an imaginary tour (95).

The intrinsic frame of reference is close to linguistic bedrock. Although there are languages, such as the Australian language Guugu Yimithirr (57, 99), that use it minimally, most have fairly elaborate systems of one kind or another. There are also languages that almost exclusively rely on it [e.g. Mopan (27)]. Children appear to acquire it earlier than other systems (77). All this is puzzling because the principles for assignment of intrinsic facets are culture-specific and often highly complex, as illustrated above. The puzzlement increases when one considers the logical properties of intrinsic expressions, which are incapable of supporting any sustained spatial inference (94). The explanation for the prominence of the intrinsic frame of reference is probably that the relations are conceptually simple in one respect: They are binary, unlike the covertly ternary relations in the relative frame of reference.

The Relative (So-Called Deictic) Frame of Reference

One reading of *The cat is behind the truck* is similar to *The cat is behind the tree;* namely it has the truck or tree between speaker or viewer on the one hand, and the cat on the other. This is clearly a ternary relationship between points: viewer, truck, cat. Many languages, English among them of course, have 'front', 'back', 'left', and 'right' expressions with this kind of ternary relation, but they are also often ambiguous between this and a binary intrinsic relation of the kind just reviewed. Piaget correctly predicted that the ternary relation should be hard for children to learn, and in fact the 'left'/'right' uses may not be fully acquired until age 11 or 12. Nevertheless, it is this system that many authors from Kant (78) onward have considered fundamental to human spatial cognition.

The complexity of these systems is such that the correct analysis of such ternary 'left', 'right', 'front', 'back' systems is still, despite considerable work, quite unclear. The problem is that whereas an intrinsic left, right, front, back system, in its descriptions of the regions around myself, has my right clockwise from my front, a relative ternary system like the English one (there are others mentioned below) has the right of the tree anticlockwise from its front! Here is one explanation (24; 65:156–92): We assimilate the tree to the "canonical encounter" where speakers face each other, hence the front of the tree is toward us; but we fail to make the rotation of 'left' and 'right' because that is too conceptually complex. The problem with this account, however, is that, apart from cultural variability in preferred positions for verbal interaction, children in fact learn to make the rotation to others' lefts and rights by age five or six, long before they master this mixed-up system! Another explanation is that the terms *front* and *back* in this usage have nothing to do with 'front' and 'back': *in front of* in *The cat is in front of the tree* simply means 'between me and', while *behind* in *The cat is behind the tree* means 'is occluded from my viewpoint by' or something similar (114:399–400). Such a brute-force solution hardly satisfies our feelings about what kinds of notions are lexicalized in natural languages, but a more serious objection is that on this account there is no explanation for the frequent ambiguity in many languages of 'front'/'back' terms between an intrinsic and relative interpretation, for there would be simply nothing in common between the relevant semantical notions.

I believe that the correct solution is that these relative ternary relations often introduce a secondary coordinate system. In English, the primary coordinate system is based on the viewer, so that *The cat is to the left of the tree* could be glossed as something like 'from this viewpoint, the cat is further left in the visual field than the tree'. But for the *front/back* terms we map a secondary coordinate system onto the tree under 180 degree rotation (following the canonical encounter idea if you like), so that the tree is now assigned a 'front' and a 'back'. Now *The cat is in front of the tree* means just what it says: The cat will be found in a region projected from the front of the tree, where 'front' is found by a 180 degree rotation of the viewer's front about the tree.

It may be objected that this results in a fundamental difference between the 'left'/'right' terms (which don't involve a secondary coordinate system) and the 'front'/'back' terms (which do). But for many languages, this is probably correct. Thus Hausa prefers an interpretation under which 'in front of' means what English 'behind' means. The secondary coordinates are translated but not rotated. However, Hausa also allows a less-favored English-like interpretation of the 'front'/'back' terms. In either case, the 'left'/'right' terms stay constant (67). The same appears to be true of actual Japanese usage in spatial tasks (K Inoue, personal communication). This potential independent flexibility of the 'front'/'back' terms would depend on the variable mapping of the secondary coordinates. In some languages, the 'left'/'right' terms may also rotate with the variable assignment of 'front'/'back' terms. Thus, in Tamil both an English and Hausa-like assignment of 'front' and 'back' are possible, but 'left' and 'right' may then flip too. In this case, 'left' and 'right' are also determined by a secondary coordinate system.

The use of primary and secondary coordinate systems makes the details of these relative systems complex. Why have peoples and languages bothered to develop such systems? One answer is that intrinsic systems alone appear fairly inadequate. First, not all useful landmark objects (like rocks or trees) will necessarily offer distinguishable facets by the local intrinsic criteria. Second, relative systems do support proper logical inferences: If A is to left of B, and B to the left of C, then A is to the left of C (94). A third potential advantage of these systems is that they hook up to visual experience in a very direct way. A visual memory of a scene provides all the information that I need to describe it in relative terms. Actually, the degree to which such systems are visually defined may itself be an interesting cross-linguistic variable (e.g. Does 'behind' require partial occlusion?).

Relative systems of spatial description build in a viewpoint and are thus essentially "subjective." For this reason they have been called deictic, although it is important to see that such descriptions are not necessarily egocentric: The viewpoint need not be the speaker (*It's to the left of the tree from where you are sitting*), nor any participant in the speech event (as in *The goalkeeper deflected the ball to the left of the goal*). The nondeictic uses may be thought of in terms of a relativization to text (1, 42) or in terms of Bühler's "transpositions" (53, 60). Alternatively, one could think about the deictic uses as just special (if normal) uses of a viewpoint-dependent system, which is itself not essentially deictic.

Such systems allow the description not only of static arrays but also of motion events (as in *The squirrel ran behind the tree*). In such descriptions the viewpoint is normally held constant. One reason is that their logical structure has the same contextual dependency as deictic inferences generally. Just as *I am taller than you, you are taller than Bill, so I am taller than Bill* fails as an inference if the speaker and addressee change midway, so logical inferences of the kind *if A is to left of B, and B to the left of C, then A is to the left of C* fail if the viewpoint changes. By holding the viewpoint constant, we can describe not only motions, but also describe patterns as fictive motions, as in *The line runs up, then left, then up, then right* (95). This holding static of the viewpoint limits the utility for the description, for example, of long and complex journeys, and as suggested above route directions are usually given using intrinsic 'left', 'right', 'front', 'back' notions.[12]

The Absolute Frame of Reference

Many speech communities make extensive use of fixed bearings, or absolute coordinates, like north, south, east, and west. Conceptually, cardinal directions are very abstract notions. A notion like 'north' cannot be thought of as a proximate place or landmark, because then if we moved sideways the bearing would change. Rather, it defines an infinite sequence of parallel lines—a conceptual "slope"—across the environment. Nor does it matter what defines the slope, just so long as everybody in the speech community agrees: These are cultural conventions, not "natural" directions, whatever basis there may be in the environment. The sun's rising and setting cannot directly determine fixed bearings of any accuracy due to solstitial variation, and cultures seem to settle

---

[12] How would one know? Suppose that the route to be described had a shape approximating a capital P without the final join between the loop and the upright. A relative description might go *Go straight ahead, turn right, then come back this way, then left*, while a more natural intrinsic route description would go *Go straight, turn right, then straight, then right again* (95). It will be harder to distinguish the two systems when the relative system is successively transposed or deictically shifted to each step of the journey, but then we would expect the ternary relations presupposed by locutions such as *Take the alley to the left of the gas-station*.

on fixed bearings that are abstracted from varied additional sources, from seasonal winds, to mountain inclines, to coastal alignments, to river drainage directions, to star-setting points. Given these varied sources, there is no need for such systems to give us quadrants or orthogonal axes, although many cardinal direction systems have those properties.

Absolute direction systems give us external bearings on an array, but without employing viewpoints. They are "allocentric" systems. Local landmarks can give us some of the same properties, especially within a restricted territory, but they do not have the same abstract properties as notions like 'north'. The point is made vivid by many Austronesian island languages, which fix an East-West absolute axis by reference to the monsoons but use a 'mountain'-'sea' axis to contrast with it. As one moves around such islands the one axis remains constant, the other rotates (124). Truly intermediate cases may be the riverine systems of Alaska, which operate as abstract systems within a vast drainage area but are reset when crossing into another drainage system (93). Many systems that take their terminology from local landmark features are in fact fully abstracted. For example, Tenejapan Tzeltal abstracts a north/south axis from the mountain incline of the local environment, but the axis remains constant outside the territory (17). In fact, the very wide distribution of systems of these sorts may have been missed because the terminology, in terms of hillsides, river directions, coastal features, and so on, may have appeared directly referential.[13]

Absolute systems yield elegant spatial descriptions of all sorts and scales of spatial arrangements. Just like relative 'left', absolute 'north' is an implicitly comparative relation (cf 'bigger than') that allows complex spatial inferences. Thus if A is north of B, and B is north of C, A is north of C. But an absolute system has the logical superiority that the validity of such inferences is not relative to a fixed viewpoint, as it is with 'left' or 'right' (or 'in front'/'behind'). In fact it is by far the most elegant solution to the problem of angular descriptions on the horizontal. There are just two catches: (a) Such systems do not catch egocentric constancies—e.g it is impossible to give a general recipe for setting the table in such terms, with forks on the left and knives on the right; (b) to use such systems speakers and addressees must be constantly and correctly oriented to the local fixed bearings (more below). These difficulties might lead one to expect that such systems would be learned late by children, but apparently they are learned earlier than relative expressions (29, 30).

Motion descriptions are as natural in these systems as are location specifications. Some languages even use cardinal directions as verb roots [e.g.

---

[13] For this reason, among others, I doubt the generalization that cardinal direction terms are frequently derived from body-part terms (see 14).

Kayardild (39)]. One special feature of absolute motion descriptions is that they allow the specification of direction without any reference to places: One can talk happily of birds heading north, ships sailing east, winds blowing west, and so on, without reference to sources and goals, which are often thought to be essential to the description of motion events. Similarly, one can specify alignments, e.g. of mountains or rivers, without reference to locations.

Such systems are of special interest when they occur without a corresponding relative system of 'left', 'right', 'front', 'back' terms. Then descriptions of most spatial arrays, even in small-scale space, must use absolute terminology. Such descriptions classify spatial arrays in a very different way than our own relative sort of system. For us, a cup to the left of a bottle becomes a cup to the right of a bottle when we walk around to the other side of the table, but in an absolute system the cup remains, say, north of the bottle from any viewpoint. On the other hand, constancies that we have built into our cultural environment, such as gear-stick to right of steering wheel, are constantly varying assemblages under absolute descriptions. Cultures favoring absolute frames of reference may build cultural environments that have constancies that may be "invisible" to our kind of cultural description [e.g. windbreaks to the east (118)].

THE VERTICAL DIMENSION

Our three frames of reference can equally be distinguished on the vertical axis. Suppose a fly hovers above an upright bottle. The three frames of reference coincide—the fly is in line with the top of the bottle (intrinsic), it appears above the bottle in my visual field (relative), and it is higher in the axis defined by gravity (absolute). However, if the bottle is on its side and the fly is vertically above, the intrinsic frame has the fly by the side, not above the bottle. In English, the intrinsic frame of reference is now eclipsed, although if you lie down with the fly in the same axis as your trunk, "The fly is above your head" may be acceptable (20). If I, the speaker, lie on my side, it gets better still. Because intrinsic tops, relative viewpoints, and gravitational fields normally align, we scarcely notice the possibilities that the frames of reference may fail to coincide. Therefore, the vertical dimension is usually massively overdetermined and unproblematic (and always ripe for symbolic exploitation). Perhaps because of that, elements of vertical meaning intrude into intrinsic descriptions, so that in English the top of the bottle is that part that is canonically vertical. Absolute systems often build the vertical dimension into the relevant linguistic system, so that in Australian languages, for example, 'up' and 'down' are often the same specialized part of speech as 'north', 'south', 'east', and 'west'. In fact, some Mayan languages may have systematically collapsed 'up' and, for example, 'south' for symbolic purposes (17, 146).

LANGUAGE AND COGNITION: WHORFIAN EFFECTS?

Linguistic details are, so it may appear, matters for linguists. However, when those details correlate with larger things, they come to have a much broader interest. The language of space correlates with many other realms of experience; for example, with details of the symbolism of values, with kinesics, and with material culture and aesthetics. The connecting linkage, the intermediate variable, is of course cognition. There are at least some grounds for thinking that language plays a causal role in the relevant cognitive specializations.

Every linguistic distinction must be supported by the relevant conceptual distinctions, perceptual acuities and mental algorithms. For example, take the intrinsic frame of reference: one can usually apply 'front', 'back', 'side' appellations to asymmetric objects, however novel (although in English one may need to know something about functional properties of the object). There must be an algorithm to achieve this (see e.g. the sketch in 114:403). To apply the Tzeltal body part system to novel objects, one needs to carry out a specialized geometrical analysis, but no ancillary functional information is needed (100). The application of the relative frame of reference requires instant access to knowledge of left and right, a notoriously fallible procedure, despite endless practice and systematic skewings in our constructed environments. Where the conventions allow mappings of secondary coordinates under both rotation and translation, as in Hausa and Tamil, there have to be procedures for determining which mapping is pertinent.

Most obviously of all, to use an absolute frame of reference on a range of scales, e.g. the table top in front of you, one needs to have instant access to the relevant fixed bearings. If you ask a European to point to north, she is likely to be flummoxed, which shows that her system of cardinal directions is more about the orientation of paper than of places. Speakers of languages that use the absolute frame of reference where we would use a relative one can be shown to be always oriented. Indeed, knowing where 'north' is will not be sufficient. One also needs to know the correct bearings from one's current location of all other locations to which one may want to refer; in short, one needs to "dead reckon," keeping track not only of directions but also of metric distances. Some direct evidence for this ability is available for speakers of relevant Australian languages (99, 107, 108), a Mayan language [Tzeltal (SC Levinson, unpublished data)], and a Khoisan language (166:209–27), but apart from a handful of such observations, and despite the interest in hunter-gather exploitation systems, there is an amazing gap in systematic study here. Knowing that such computations are unconsciously and routinely carried out (as explored by surprise tests) does not tell us how it is done. In the Guugu Yimithirr case the native exegesis points to many environmental clues, but how these are integrated in constant background computation is unknown (99).

To explore the cognitive background to the use of frames of reference in language, one can devise a simple set of field experiments (3). These exploit various logical and rotational properties of the three main frames of reference mentioned above. For example, imagine a mouse facing a block of cheese, both on a bread board. In the intrinsic frame of reference, if this is coded as 'cheese in front of mouse', the description will remain true when the observer wanders around the board, or even when the board is rotated. The absolute description 'mouse north of cheese' will remain true as the observer wanders around, but not if the board is rotated. The relative description 'mouse to left of cheese' will become false when the viewer walks around to the other side, or when he stays constant and the board rotates. Thus conceptual codings in each of the different frames of reference have different tolerances to (or different truth conditions under) rotations of these kinds (102).

These properties can then be exploited to explore aspects of memory, inference, and other cognitive operations. For example, persons facing a table can be asked to memorize an arrow facing to their left, and as it happens, south. They can then be rotated 180 degrees and asked to recognize which arrow they saw before from two on another table, one facing to their left and north, the other facing to their right and south. If they choose the arrow that preserves the left-facing property, we can be fairly sure they are using a relative frame of reference to memorize spatial arrays. If they choose the arrow that preserves the south-facing property (hence the rightwards-pointing one), we can be fairly sure they are using an absolute frame of reference. We can elaborate this methodology to explore different kinds of psychological capacity (18, 127, 140).

There are two ways to explore the relation between language and cognition in this way. One is to predict that if a language or speech community employs specific frames of reference to describe arrays of certain sorts, then members of that speech community will use the same frames of reference in nonlinguistic tasks, i.e. in memory or inference and in spatial thinking generally. (Note that the predictions are only clear where the language in question excludes certain frames of reference.) Languages and their speakers can then be typed, the predictions made and tested over a wide range of languages. The results obtained suggest that this is indeed a reliable prediction: We think spatially in the frames of reference that our languages make prominent (3, 126, 127, 161). Another way to explore the linkage between language and cognition is to explore the linguistic systems and cognitive repercussions in depth in particular field sites. This has been done for example in Tenejapan Tzeltal (18, 102, 104), where it is possible to show that the linguistic use of an absolute frame of reference is correlated with the use of the same frame of reference in recall, recognition, inference, and even gesture.

These findings show that specializations in spatial language correlate with nonlinguistic coding strategies or cognitive styles. Although proper caution is in order before presuming causality from correlation, it seems inescapable that language plays a crucial role in forming and standardizing such cognitive styles within a speech community.[14]

LANGUAGE, COGNITION, AND CULTURE

It was suggested above that cognition is the intermediate variable between language and other aspects of culture. Thus we would expect specializations in cognitive style correlated with spatial language to surface in other cultural manifestations. As yet, the work that would show this has scarcely been begun. But consider the following examples.

Tenejapan Tzeltal uses no relative frame of reference, and thus no 'left', 'right', 'front', 'back' terms for spatial reference in that frame. Although Tenejapans have terms for left and right hands, they do not extend these freely even to other parts of the body, let alone to spatial regions (105). Nor do they, contrary to the predictions of Hertz (66) and Needham (119), subscribe to the allegedly universal symbolism of 'left' and 'right'. Their material culture, from domestic architecture to weaving, favors symmetry, and they have difficulty distinguishing figures reflected about a vertical axis. Instead, in line with their emphasis on the absolute frame of reference based on their sloping territory, they subscribe to a cosmology of the inclined plane, with the ceremonial center south and upward, and the corral of the souls in the lowlands. Time is conceived of as stretching up to the south. This localization of time and space, mythic and real, allows gestural depiction. This picture contrasts with some other Mayan cultures, e.g. the Mopan, where an intrinsic frame of reference is predominant, a frame of reference that defeats extended spatial inferences, like transitivity. The associated complex of features seems to run way beyond spatial thinking altogether, into details of the kinship system for example (27).[15]

---

[14] Incidentally, the fact that peoples of similar material culture and ecology, even related cultural history, can vary fundamentally in their preferences for frames of reference will rule out any simple ecological determinism here.

[15] For a collection on spatial description in the Mayan languages see Haviland & Levinson (62), and for Mesoamerican languages more generally, see de León & Levinson (31). Incidentally, such regional comparisons can be most revealing; there is plenty of material but no synthesis for the Australian cultures and languages yet available. For the Austronesian languages, see Senft (141), supplemented by Barnes (4), Fox (45), and Toren (154). For the Himalayan region, see B Bickel & M Gaenszle (in preparation). The circumpolar cultures would also promise a rich comparative project (44). For particular cultures, see work on the Navajo, where there is excellent spatial material (50, 132, 173), and on Bali, where there is rich ethnography, and where Wassmann & Dasen (161) have now done some of the linguistic and cognitive work.

It is a commonplace of the Australianist ethnography that landscape and locality are the media on which cultural knowledge and social history are written. Spatial orientation is the key to understanding myth, art, camping arrangements, gesture—almost every aspect of social life (117, 134, 137, 148). The languages (mainly) emphasize the absolute frame of reference (59–61, 91, 167, 170). Cognition follows suit (86, 99, 104, 107, 108). Gesture and language (59) and handsign and sand-drawing (84, 116, 171) are deeply intertwined. Although the complete picture has yet to be painted, there is little doubt that the key to understanding much of this intricate cultural detail, and the way it coheres, is the spatialization of thought and language in a predominantly absolute frame of reference.

This field of research thus promises to yield a new kind of synthesis of cultural and social observations of many different kinds, from the details of ecological exploitation to the preference for object shapes, domestic architecture, cosmological systems, and kinesic patterns. It is a branch of cognitive anthropology that has been very much underexploited. In this review, I have attempted to make the more technical background accessible to the general reader, in the hope that its promise may be better appreciated and built upon.

ACKNOWLEDGMENTS

I am indebted to Elizabeth Keating, Gunter Senft, and David Wilkins for comments.

Literature Cited

1. Anderson S, Keenan E. 1985. Deixis. See Ref. 141a, pp. 259-307
2. Ardener S, ed. 1993. *Women and Space: Ground Rules and Social Maps.* Oxford: Berg
3. Baayen H, Danziger E, eds. 1994. *Annual Report of the MPI for Psycholinguistics 1993.* Nijmegen: Max Planck Inst. Psycholinguist.
4. Barnes RH. 1993. Everyday space: some considerations on the representation and use of space in Indonesia. In *Alltagswissen,* ed. J Wassmann, P Dasen, pp. 159–80. Freiburg: Universitätsverlag
5. Berry JW, Irvine SH, Hunt EB. 1988. *Indigenous Cognition: Functioning in Cultural Context.* Dordrecht: Nijhoff
6. Bickel B. 1996. Spatial operations in deixis, cognition, and culture: where to ori-
ent oneself in Belhare. In *With Language in Mind: The Relationship Between Linguistic and Conceptual Representation,* ed. J Nuyts, E Pederson. Cambridge: Cambridge Univ. Press
7. Bierwisch M, Lang E, eds. 1989. *Dimensional Adjectives: Grammatical Structure and Conceptual Interpretation.* Berlin: Springer-Verlag
8. Bourdieu P. 1977. *Outline of a Theory of Practice.* Cambridge: Cambridge Univ. Press
9. Bowerman M. 1996. The origins of children's spatial semantic categories: cognitive versus linguistic determinants. See Ref. 51, pp. 145–76
10. Bowerman M, de León L, Choi S. 1995. Verbs, particles, and spatial semantics: learning to talk about spatial actions in

topologically different languages. In *Proc. 27th Annu. Child Lang. Res. Forum,* ed. EV Clark, pp. 101–10, Stanford, CA: CSLI

11. Bowerman M, Levinson SC, eds. 1996. Language acquisition and conceptual development. Cambridge: Cambridge Univ. Press

12. Bowerman M, Pederson E. 1992. *Crosslinguistic perspectives on topological spatial relations.* Presented at Annu. Meet. Am. Anthropol. Assoc., 91st, San Francisco

13. Brown P. 1991. Spatial conceptualization in Tzeltal. *Work. Pap. No. 6,* Cogn. Anthropol. Res. Group, Nijmegen

14. Brown P. 1993. The role of shape in the acquisition of Tzeltal locatives: a preliminary report. In *Proc. 25th Child Lang. Res. Forum,* ed. EV Clark, pp. 211–20. Stanford, CA: CSLI/Univ. Chicago Press

15. Brown P. 1994. The INs and ONs of Tzeltal locative expressions: the semantics of static descriptions of location. See Ref. 62, pp. 743–90

16. Brown P, Levinson SC. 1992. 'Left' and 'right' in Tenejapa: investigating a linguistic and conceptual gap. See Ref. 31, pp. 590–611

17. Brown P, Levinson SC. 1993. "Uphill" and "downhill" in Tzeltal. *J. Linguist. Anthropol.* 3(1):46–74

18. Brown P, Levinson SC. 1993. Linguistic and nonlinguistic coding of spatial arrays: explorations in Mayan cognition. *Work. Pap. No. 24,* Cogn. Anthropol. Res. Group, Nijmegen

19. Brugman C. 1983. The use of body-part terms as locatives in Chalcatongo Mixtec. *Surv. Calif. Other Indian Lang.* 4:235–90

20. Carlson-Radvansky LA, Irwin DA. 1993. Frames of reference in vision and language: Where is above? *Cognition* 46:223–44

21. Casey ES. 1993. *Getting Back into Place: Toward a Renewed Understanding of the Place-World.* Bloomington: Indiana Univ. Press

22. Cavalli-Sforza L, Piazza A, Menozzi P, Mountain J. 1988. Reconstruction of human evolution: bringing together genetic, archaeological and linguistic data. *Proc. Natl. Acad. Sci. USA* 85(16):6002–6

23. Choi S, Bowerman M. 1991. Learning to express motion events in English and Korean: the influence of language-specific lexicalization patterns. *Cognition* 41: 83–121

24. Clark HH. 1973. Space, time, semantics, and the child. In *Cognitive Development and the Acquisition of Language,* ed. TE Moore, pp. 28–64. New York: Academic

25. Danziger E. 1993. Review of Perkins: "Deixis, Grammar and Culture." *Linguistics* 31:977–80

26. Danziger E. 1994. Out of sight, out of mind: person, perception and function in Mopan Maya spatial deixis. See Ref. 62, pp. 885–907

27. Danziger E. 1996. Parts and their counterparts: social and spatial relationships among the Mopan Maya. *J. R. Anthropol. Inst. Man* 2(1):67–82

28. de León L. 1993. Shape, geometry and location: the case of Tzotzil body part terms. In *CLS 29: Papers from the Parasession on Conceptual Representations,* ed. K Beals, G Cooke, D Kathman, S Kita, KE McCullough, et al, pp. 77–90. Chicago: Univ. Chicago Press

29. de León L. 1994. Explorations in the acquisition of location and trajectory in Tzotzil. See Ref. 62, pp. 857–84

30. de León L. 1996. The development of geocentric location in young speakers of Guugu Yimithirr. *Work. Pap. No. 33,* Cogn. Anthropol. Res. Group, Nijmegen

31. de León L, Levinson SC, eds. 1992. Space in Mesoamerican languages. *Z. Phon. Sprachwiss. Kommun.forsch.* 45(6): 570– 89. Berlin: Akademie Verlag

32. Denny JP. 1978. Locating the universals in lexical systems for spatial deixis. In *CLS 14: Papers from the Parasession on the Lexicon,* ed. D Farkas, WM Jacobsen, KW Todrys, pp. 71–84. Chicago: Univ. Chicago Press

33. Denny JP. 1988. Contextualization and differentiation in cross-cultural cognition. See Ref. 5, pp. 213–29

34. Descola P. 1994. *In the Society of Nature: A Native Ecology in Amazonia.* Cambridge: Cambridge Univ. Press

35. Duranti A. 1994. *From Grammar to Politics.* Berkeley: Univ. Calif. Press

36. Durkheim E, Mauss M. 1963/1903. *Primitive Classification,* ed./transl. R Needham. Chicago: Univ. Chicago Press (From French)

37. Earman J. 1989. *World Enough and Space-Time: Absolute Versus Relational Theories of Space and Time.* Cambridge, MA: MIT Press

38. Eilan N, McCarthy R, Brewer B, eds. 1993. *Spatial Representation: Problems in Philosophy and Psychology.* Oxford: Blackwell

39. Evans N. 1995. *A Grammar of Kayardild.* Berlin: Mouton Grammar Libr.

40. Feinberg R. 1988. *Polynesian Seafaring and Navigation.* Kent, OH: Kent State Univ. Press

41. Fillmore C. 1975. *Santa Cruz Lectures on Deixis.* Mimeo, Indiana Univ. Linguist. Club

42. Fillmore C. 1982. Towards a descriptive framework for spatial deixis. See Ref. 75, pp. 31–60

43. Foley WA. 1986. *The Papuan Languages of New Guinea.* Cambridge: Cambridge Univ. Press
44. Fortescue M. 1988. Eskimo orientation systems. *Medd. Grønl.: Man Soc.* 11:3–30
45. Fox J, ed. 1993. *Inside Austronesian houses.* Canberra: Aust. Nat. Univ. Press
46. Frake C. 1985. Cognitive maps of time and tide among medieval seafarers. *Man (NS)* 20:254–70
47. Freidel D, Schele L, Parker J. 1993. *Maya Cosmos.* New York: Morrow
48. Goddard C, Wierzbicka A, eds. 1994. *Semantic and Lexical Universals.* Amsterdam, Philadelphia: Benjamins
49. Goodwin C. 1981. *Conversational Organization: Interaction Between Speakers and Hearers.* New York: Academic
50. Griffin-Pierce T. 1992. *Earth Is My Mother, Sky Is My Father: Space, Time and Astronomy in Navajo Sandpainting.* Albuquerque: Univ. N. M. Press
51. Gumperz JJ, Levinson SC, eds. 1996. *Rethinking Linguistic Relativity.* Cambridge: Cambridge Univ. Press
52. Hallpike CR. 1979. *Foundations of Primitive Thought.* Oxford: Clarendon
53. Hanks W. 1990. *Referential Practice: Language and Lived Space in a Maya Community.* Chicago: Univ. Chicago Press
54. Hanks W. 1996. Language form and communicative practices. See Ref. 51, pp. 232–70
55. Harkins J, Wilkins DP. 1994. Mparntwe Arrernte and the search for lexical universals. See Ref. 48, pp. 285–310
56. Harley JB, Woodward D, eds. 1987. *The History of Cartography,* 3 Vols. Chicago: Univ. Chicago Press
57. Haviland JB. 1979. Guugu Yimidhirr. In *Handbook of Australian Languages,* ed. RMW Dixon, B Blake, pp. 27–182. Canberra: Aust. Nat. Univ. Press
58. Haviland JB. 1991. The grammaticalization of motion (and time) in Tzotzil. *Work. Pap. No. 2,* Cogn. Anthropol. Res. Group, Nijmegen
59. Haviland JB. 1993. Anchoring, iconicity and orientation in Guugu Yimithirr pointing gestures. *J. Linguist. Anthropol.* 3(1):3–45
60. Haviland JB. 1996. Projections, transpositions, and relativity. See Ref. 51, pp. 269–323
61. Haviland JB. 1996. Guugu Yimithirr cardinal directions. In *My Space or Yours: Beyond the Individual in the Cognitive Study of Language,* ed. E Danziger. *Ethos: J. Soc. Psychol. Anthropol.* In press
62. Haviland JB, Levinson SC, eds. 1994. *Space in Mayan Languages. Linguistics* 32 (4/5)
63. Heine B. 1989. Adpositions in African languages. *Linguist. Afr.* 2:77–127
64. Heine B, Claudi U, Hünnemeyer F. 1991. *Grammaticalization: A Conceptual Framework.* Chicago: Univ. Chicago Press
65. Herskovits A. 1986. *Language and Spatial Cognition: An Interdisciplinary Study of the Prepositions in English.* Cambridge: Cambridge Univ. Press
66. Hertz R. 1960/1909. The pre-eminence of the right hand: a study in religious polarity. In *'Death' and 'the Right Hand,'* ed./ transl. R Needham, C Needham, pp. 89-113. London: Cohen & West
67. Hill C. 1982. Up/down, front/back, left/right: a contrastive study of Hausa and English. See Ref. 165, pp. 11–42
68. Hill JH, Mannheim B. 1992. Language and world view. *Annu. Rev. Anthropol.* 21: 381–406
69. Hirsch E, O'Hanlon M, eds. 1995. *The Anthropology of Landscape.* Oxford: Clarendon
70. Hugh-Jones S. 1979. *The Palm and the Pleiades: Ritual and Cosmology in Northwest Amazonia.* Cambridge: Cambridge Univ. Press
71. Hunn E. 1993. Columbia Plateau Indian place names: what can they teach us? *J. Linguist. Anthropol.* 6(1):3–26
72. Hutchins E. 1983. Understanding Micronesian navigation. In *Mental Models,* ed. D Gentner, A Stevens, pp. 191–225. Hillsdale, NJ: Erlbaum
73. Jacobson SA. 1984. Semantics and morphology of demonstratives in Central Yupík Eskimo. *Etudes/Inuit/Stud.* 8:185–92
74. Jammer M. 1954. *Concepts of Space: The History of Theories of Space in Physics.* Cambridge, MA: Harvard Univ. Press
75. Jarvella R, Klein W, eds. 1982. *Speech, Place and Action: Studies in Deixis and Related Topics.* New York: Wiley
76. Jeannerod M. 1988. *The Neural and Behavioural Organisation of Goal-Directed Movements.* Oxford: Clarendon
77. Johnston JR, Slobin D. 1978. The development of locative expressions in English, Italian, Serbo-Croatian and Turkish. *J. Child Lang.* 6:529–45
78. Kant I. 1991/1768. Von dem ersten Grunde des Unterschiedes der Gegenden im Raume [On the first ground of the distinction of regions in space]. In *The Philosophy of Right and Left: Incongruent Counterparts and the Nature of Space,* ed./transl. J Van Cleve, RE Frederick, pp. 27–34. Dordrecht: Kluwer
79. Kari J. 1989. Some principles of Alaskan Athabaskan toponymic knowledge. In *General and Amerindian Ethnolinguistics,* ed. MR Key, H Hoenigswald, pp. 129–50. Berlin: Mouton
80. Kay P. 1977. Language evolution and speech style. In *Sociocultural Dimensions*

of Language Change, ed. B Blount, M Sanchez, pp. 21–34. New York: Academic
81. Keating E. 1995. Spatial conceptions of social hierarchy in Pohnpei, Micronesia. In *Spatial Information Theory: Theoretical Basis for GIS,* ed. AU Frank, W Kuhn, pp. 463–74. Berlin: Springer-Verlag
82. Keating E. 1995. *Power sharing: language, rank, gender and social space in Pohnpei, Micronesia.* PhD thesis. Univ. Calif., Los Angeles. 310 pp.
83. Keating E. 1996. The social valuing of left and right in Pohnpei: linking status, space and cognition. *Work. Pap. No. 35,* Cogn. Anthropol. Res. Group, Nijmegen
84. Kendon A. 1988. *Sign Languages of Aboriginal Australia.* Cambridge: Cambridge Univ. Press
85. Kendon A. 1991. *Conducting Interaction.* Cambridge: Cambridge Univ. Press
86. Klich LZ. 1983. Re-directions in cognitive research with Australian Aborigines. *Aust. Aborig. Stud.* 1:38–42
87. Lahiri TK. 1965. *Tracking techniques of Australian Aborigines.* Canberra: Aust. Inst. Aborig./Torres Strait Islander Stud.
88. Lakoff G. 1987. *Women, Fire and Other Dangerous Things.* Chicago: Univ. Chicago Press
89. Landau B, Jackendoff R. 1993. "What" and "where" in spatial language and spatial cognition. *Behav. Brain Sci.* 16:217–65
90. Lang E. 1995. Basic dimension terms: a first look at universal features and typological variation. *Forsch.schwerpkt. Allg. Sprachwiss. Work. Pap. No. 1,* Berlin
91. Laughren M. 1978. Directional terminology in Warlpiri. *Work. Pap. Lang. Linguist.,* 1:1–16. Launceston, Aust: Tasman. Coll. Adv. Educ.
92. Lawrence DL, Low SM. 1990. The built environment and spatial form. *Annu. Rev. Anthropol.* 19:453–505
93. Leer J. 1989. Directional systems in Athabaskan and Na-Dene. In *Trends in Linguistics,* ed. E Cook, KD Rice, 15:575–622. Berlin: Mouton
94. Levelt WJM. 1984. Some perceptual limitations on talking about space. In *Limits in Perception,* ed. AJ van Doorn, WA van der Grind, JJ Koenderink, pp. 323–58. Utrecht: Ver. Ned. Uitg. Sci. Press
95. Levelt WJM. 1996. Perspective taking and ellipsis in spatial descriptions. In *Language and Space,* ed. P Bloom, M Peterson, L Nadel, M Garrett. Cambridge, MA: MIT Press
96. Levine SC, Carey S. 1982. Up front: the acquisition of a concept and a word. *J. Child Lang.* 9:645–57
97. Levinson SC. 1983. *Pragmatics.* Cambridge: Cambridge Univ. Press
98. Levinson SC. 1992. Primer for the field investigation of spatial description and conception. *Pragmatics* 2(1):5–47
99. Levinson SC. 1992. Language and cognition: cognitive consequences of spatial description in Guugu Yimithirr. *Work. Pap. No. 13,* Cogn. Anthropol. Res. Group, Nijmegen
100. Levinson SC. 1994. Vision, shape and linguistic description: Tzeltal body-part terminology and object description. See Ref. 62, pp. 791–855
101. Levinson SC. 1994. Deixis. In *Encyclopedia of Language and Linguistics,* ed. RE Asher, 2:853–57. Oxford: Pergamon
102. Levinson SC. 1996. Frames of reference and Molyneux's question: cross-linguistic evidence. In *Language and Space,* ed. P Bloom, M Peterson, L Nadel, M. Garrett. Cambridge, MA: MIT Press
103. Levinson SC. 1996. Relativity in spatial conception and description. See Ref. 51
104. Levinson SC. 1996. Studying Spatial Conceptualization across Cultures. In *My Space or Yours: Beyond the Individual in the Cognitive Study of Language,* ed. E Danziger. *Ethos: J. Soc. Psychol. Anthropol.* In press
105. Levinson SC, Brown P. 1994. Immanuel Kant among the Tenejapans: anthropology as empirical philosophy. *Ethos* 22(1):3–41
106. Levy P. 1994. How shape becomes grammar: on the semantics of part morphemes in Totonac. *Work. Pap. No. 29,* Cogn. Anthropol. Res. Group, Nijmegen
107. Lewis D. 1976. Observations on route finding and spatial orientation among the aboriginal peoples of the Western Desert Region of Central Australia. *Oceania* 46(4): 249–82
108. Lewis D. 1976. Route finding by desert aborigines in Australia. *J. Navig.* 29:21–38
109. Littlejohn J. 1960. The Temne house. *Sierra Leone Stud.* 14:63–79
110. Lyons J. 1977. *Semantics,* Vols. 1, 2. Cambridge: Cambridge Univ. Press
111. MacLaury R. 1989. Zapotec body-part locatives: prototypes and metaphoric extensions. *Int. J. Am. Linguist.* 55(2):119–54
112. Marr D. 1982. *Vision.* New York: Freeman
113. McCarthy R. 1993. Assembling routines and addressing representations: an alternative conceptualization of 'what' and 'where' in the human brain. See Ref. 38, pp. 373–99
114. Miller G, Johnson-Laird PN. 1976. *Language and Perception.* Cambridge, MA: Harvard Univ. Press
115. Moore H. 1986. *Space, Text and Gender: An Anthropological Study of the Marakwet of Kenya.* Cambridge: Cambridge Univ. Press
116. Munn N. 1986. *Walbiri Iconography.* Ithaca, NY: Cornell Univ. Press

117. Myers F. 1986. *Pintupi Country, Pintupi Self.* Canberra: Aust. Inst. Aborig. Torres Strait Isl. Stud.

118. Nash D. 1993. *Notes on way-finding in Australia's deserts by Warlpiri and their neighbours.* Presented at Conf. Spat. Represent., Max Planck Inst. Psycholinguist., Nijmegen

119. Needham R. 1973. *Left and Right.* Chicago: Univ. Chicago Press

120. Nichols J. 1992. *Linguistic Diversity in Space and Time.* Chicago: Univ. Chicago Press

121. Ochs E. 1996. Linguistic resources for socializing humanity. See Ref. 51, pp. 407–37

122. O'Keefe J. 1993. Kant and the sea-horse: an essay in the neurophilosophy of space. See Ref. 38, pp. 43–64

123. O'Keefe J, Nadel L. 1978. *The Hippocampus as a Cognitive Map.* Oxford: Clarendon

124. Ozanne-Rivierre F. 1987. L'expression linguistique de l'espace: quelques exemples oceaniens. *Cah. Lacito* 2:129–55

125. Paillard J, ed. 1991. *Brain and Space.* Oxford: Oxford Sci.

126. Pederson E. 1993. Geographic and manipulable space in two Tamil linguistic systems. In *Spatial Information Theory,* ed. AU Frank, I Campari, pp. 294–311. Berlin: Springer-Verlag

127. Pederson E. 1995. Language as context, language as means: spatial cognition and habitual language use. *Cogn. Linguist.* 6(1):33–62

128. Pederson E. 1996. Review of S Svorou's "The grammar of space." In *Sprachtypol. Universal.forsch.* 49(2):37–41

129. Perkins RD. 1992. *Deixis, Grammar and Culture.* Amsterdam, Philadelphia: Benjamins

130. Piaget J, Inhelder B. 1956. *The Child's Conception of Space.* London: Routledge/Kegan Paul

131. Pick HL Jr. 1993. Organization of spatial knowledge in children. See Ref. 38, pp. 31–42

132. Pinxten R, van Dooren I, Harvey F. 1983. *Anthropology of Space: Explorations into the Natural Philosophy and Semantics of the Navajo.* Philadelphia: Univ. Pa. Press

133. Poincaré H. 1946. *The Foundations of Science.* Transl. GB Halsted. Lancaster, PA: Science Press

134. Rapoport A. 1975. Australian aboriginals and the definition of place. In *Shelter, Sign & Symbol,* ed. P Oliver, pp. 38–51. London: Barrie & Jenkins

135. Renfrew C. 1987. *Archaeology and Language.* Cambridge: Cambridge Univ. Press

136. Renfrew C, Zubrow EBW, eds. 1994. *The Ancient Mind: Elements of Cognitive Archaeology.* Cambridge: Cambridge Univ. Press

137. Rumsey A. 1994. The dreaming, human agency and inscriptive practice. *Oceania* 65:116–30

138. Schöne H. 1984. *Spatial Orientation.* Princeton, NJ: Princeton Univ. Press

139. Senft G. 1994. Ein Vorschlag, wie man standardisiert Daten zum Thema 'Sprache, Kognition und Konzeption des Raums' in verschiedenen Kulturen erheben kann. *Linguist. Ber.* 154:413–29

140. Senft G. 1995. Sprache, Kognition und Konzepte des Raumes in verschiedenen Kulturen. *Kognitionswiss.* 4:166–70

141. Senft G, ed. 1996. *Classificatory Particles in Kilivila.* Oxford: Oxford Univ. Press. 337 pp.

141a. Shopen T, ed. 1985. *Language Typology and Syntactic Description,* Vol. 3, *Grammatical Categories and the Lexicon.* Cambridge: Cambridge Univ. Press

142. Slobin DI. 1985. Cross-linguistic evidence for the language-making capacity. In *The Cross-Linguistic Study of Language Acquisition,* ed. DI Slobin, pp. 1157–256. Hillsdale, NJ: Erlbaum

143. Slobin DI. 1996. From "thought and language" to "thinking for speaking." See Ref. 51, pp. 70–96

144. Stein JF. 1992. The representation of egocentric space in the posterior parietal cortex. *Behav. Brain Sci.* 15(4):691–700

145. Stolz C. 1995. *Spatial dimensions and orientation of objects in Yucatec Maya.* PhD thesis. Univ. Bielefeld

146. Stross B. 1991. Classic Maya directional glyphs. *J. Linguist. Anthropol.* 1(1):97–114

147. Svorou S. 1994. *The Grammar of Space.* Amsterdam: Benjamins

148. Swain T. 1993. *A Place for Strangers: Towards a History of Australian Aboriginal Being.* Cambridge: Cambridge Univ. Press

149. Talmy L. 1983. How language structures space. In *Spatial Orientation: Theory, Research and Application,* ed. H Pick, L Acredolo, pp. 225–82. New York: Plenum

150. Talmy L. 1985. Lexicalization patterns: semantic structure in lexical forms. See Ref. 141a, pp. 56–149

151. Tambiah S. 1985. *Culture, Thought and Social Action.* Cambridge, MA: Harvard Univ. Press

152. Tilley C. 1994. *A Phenomenology of Landscape: Places, Paths and Monuments.* Oxford: Berg

153. Tolman EC. 1948. Cognitive maps in rats and men. *Psychol. Rev.* 55(4):109–45

154. Toren C. 1990. *Making Sense of Hierarchy: Cognition as Social Process in Fiji.* London: Athlone

155. Tuan Y-F. 1977. *Space and Place: The Perspective of Experience.* Minneapolis: Univ. Minn. Press

156. Turnbull D. 1993. *Maps Are Territories:*

Science Is an Atlas: A Portfolio of Exhibits. Chicago: Univ. Chicago Press

157. Ulltan R. 1978. Some general characteristics of interrogative systems. In *Universals of Human Language,* ed. J Greenberg, 4:211–48. Stanford, CA: Stanford Univ. Press

158. Ungerleider LG, Mishkin M. 1982. Two cortical visual systems. In *Analysis of Visual Behavior,* ed. DJ Ingle, MA Goodale, RJW Mansfield, pp. 549–86. Cambridge, MA: MIT Press

159. Van Cleve J, Frederick RE, eds. 1991. *The Philosophy of Right and Left.* Dordrecht: Kluwer

160. Vandeloise C. 1991. *Spatial Prepositions: A Case Study from French.* Chicago: Univ. Chicago Press

161. Wassmann J, Dasen P. 1996. Une combination de methodes ethnographiques et psychologiques dans l'étude des processus cognitifs à Bali. In *Théorie et Pratique de l'Interculturel,* ed. B Krewer. Paris: L'Harmattan. In press

162. Waterman TH. 1989. *Animal Navigation.* Sci. Am. Libr.

163. Waterson R. 1991. *The Living House: An Anthropology of Architecture in South East Asia.* Singapore: Oxford Univ. Press

164. Weiner JF. 1991. *The Empty Space: Poetry, Space and Being Among the Foi of Papua New Guinea.* Bloomington: Indiana Univ. Press

165. Weissenborn J, Klein W, eds. 1982. *Here and There: Cross-Linguistic Studies on Deixis and Demonstration.* Amsterdam: Benjamins

166. Widlok T. 1994. *The social relationships of changing Hai//om hunter/gatherers in* northern Namibia, 1990–1994. PhD thesis. Univ. London

167. Wilkins D. 1991. The semantics, pragmatics and diachronic development of 'associated motion' in Mparnte Arrernte. *Buffalo Pap. Linguist.* 1:207–57

168. Wilkins D, Hill D. 1995. When 'GO' means 'COME': questioning the basicness of basic motion verbs. *Cogn. Linguist.* 6:209–59

169. Wilkins D, Senft G. 1994. *A man, a tree, and forget about the pigs: space games, spatial reference and an attempt to identify functional equivalents across languages.* Presented at 19th Linguist. Agency Univ. Duisburg Conf., Duisburg

170. Wilkins DP. 1989. *Mparntwe Arrernte (Aranda): the structure and semantics of an Australian language.* PhD thesis. Aust. Nat. Univ., Canberra. 621 pp.

171. Wilkins DP. 1996. *Handsigns and hyperpolysemy: exploring the cultural foundations of semantic association.* Pacific Linguistics. In press

172. Williams N, Baines G, eds. 1993. *Traditional Ecological Knowledge.* Canberra Cent. Resour. Environ. Stud., Aust. Nat. Univ.

173. Witherspoon G. 1992. *Language and Art in the Navajo Universe.* Ann Arbor: Univ. Mich. Press

174. Wolfowitz C. 1991. *Language Style and Social Space: Stylistic Choice in Suriname Javanese.* Urbana: Univ. Ill. Press

175. Wynn T. 1989. *The Evolution of Spatial Competence.* Urbana-Champaign: Univ. Ill. Press

176. Yates FA. 1966. *The Art of Memory.* Chicago: Univ. Chicago Press

Annu. Rev. Anthropol. 1996. 25:383–409
Copyright © 1996 by Annual Reviews Inc. All rights reserved

THE ANTHROPOLOGY OF CITIES:
Imagining and Theorizing the City

Setha M. Low

PhD Programs in Psychology (Environmental) and Anthropology, Graduate School and University Center of the City University of New York, 33 West 42nd Street, New York, NY 10036

KEY WORDS: urban theory, urban anthropology, globalization, deindustrialization, racism

ABSTRACT

This review considers the following questions: Why is the city undertheorized in anthropology? Why is an anthropological voice rarely heard in the urban studies and urban policy discourse? Anthropological literature published since 1989 is reviewed, with an emphasis on contributions to urban theory and the locating of anthropological studies within the broader context of urban studies. The city is found not to be absent in anthropological theory, but it has had no major theoretical impact. The images of the ethnic city, divided city, deindustrialized city, and global city have been most influential, as has research in the areas of racism, migration, poststructural studies of conflict and resistance, and critiques of architecture and urban planning. The literature continues to focus on the links between the experience of individuals and sociopolitical and economic processes as well as on the cultural meaning of the urban environment. The newest areas of inquiry include the study of urban space and time, metropolitan knowledge, and ethnoaesthetics.

INTRODUCTION

Why has the city been undertheorized in anthropology? Urban analysis has been left to a group of scholars who draw from architecture, history, geography, planning, sociology, and economics (33, 43, 79, 80, 210, 216, 222, 224, 254), bringing their unique interdisciplinary skills to the study of the city. These interdisciplinary analyses are quite broad in scope and focus on the city as part of a critical theoretical discourse. Anthropologists, however, have been more concerned with everyday urban processes, so although the city is present in anthropology, it has not had a major impact.

In addition, why is an anthropological voice rarely heard in the urban studies discourse, even though many anthropologists have contributed actively to the urban poverty, immigration, architecture, and planning literature? Stack (227), Bourgois (20), Susser (232), and Newman (160) argue that while anthropological data are essential to understanding urban problems, anthropologists have hesitated to participate in urban public policy debates.

I address the above queries concerning the city and anthropology by (*a*) reviewing the anthropological literature on the city published since 1989, (*b*) identifying organizing images and metaphors as well as concepts and issues, (*c*) highlighting anthropological contributions, (*d*) positioning anthropological studies within the broader discourse of urban studies and urban policy, and (*e*) offering suggestions for future research.

In earlier reviews, Fox (58, 59), Jackson (88), and Gulick (73) advocated an anthropology *of* the city, rather than *in* the city. They argued that the distinction "is not trivial or hairsplitting" (73:xiv), yet their perspective has been criticized as essentializing the city as an institution and identifying it through population density, unique physical qualities or appearance, and styles of social interaction (136). I am not arguing for an essentialism of the city but favor attending to the social relations, symbols, and political economies manifest in the city, and view the "urban" as a process rather than as a type or category.

Theorizing the city is a necessary part of understanding the changing postindustrial, advanced capitalist, postmodern moment in which we live. The city as a site of everyday practice provides valuable insights into the linkages of macroprocesses with the texture and fabric of human experience. The city is not the only place where these linkages can be studied, but the intensification of these processes—as well as their human outcomes—occurs and can be understood best in cities. Thus, the "city" is not a reification but the focus of cultural and sociopolitical manifestations of urban lives and everyday practices.

An eclectic set of materials selected from recently written field-based ethnographies and articles within anthropology, as well as monographs and articles from the cognate fields of geography, sociology, history, urban planning, and political science, are included. Kemper (106) has indexed and summarized urban anthropology dissertations, and Sanjek (208) and Kemper (105) have covered urban work published through 1990. Therefore, I focus mainly on works published since that date. Books were selected from both fieldwork and nonfieldwork-based monographs, and articles were selected from English-language anthropology journals. The selections from other disciplines include books and articles drawn from major journals and bibliographies in the urban studies and urban policy fields. Of course, some research was excluded, including that on urbanization, urban applied anthropology, urban historical archaeology, urban medical anthropology, and urban linguistics. Research on poverty and homelessness is covered by Susser in this volume of the *Annual Review of Anthropology*.

HISTORICAL OVERVIEW

With the emergence of the Chicago School in the 1920s and 1930s and the development of an urban ecological perspective (173), the city is viewed as made up of adjacent ecological niches occupied by human groups in a series of concentric rings surrounding a central core. Class, occupation, world view, and life experiences are coterminous with an inhabitant's location within these niches. Social change occurs through socioeconomic transitions, with each group replacing the next in an outward spiral. Research strategies focus on participant observation to uncover and explain the adaptations and accommodations of urban populations to these microenvironments. The contemporary sociologists Anderson (5) and Wacquant (238), both of whom trained at the University of Chicago and studied the African-American ghetto experience in Chicago, continue to draw upon this work for theoretical and methodological inspiration.

A second major influence on how we view the city was the Institute of Community Studies (in Bethal Green, London) program of policy and planning research on slum clearance and replacement of housing in London, England, and Lagos, Nigeria. From the 1950s to the present, Young & Willmott (250), Marris (143, 144), and their colleagues conceived of the city as a series of urban "communities" based on extended family relations and kinship networks. Bott's (19) research on the social networks of middle-class English families drew upon discussions with anthropologists at the University of Manchester (66). Network analysis, used to study the social organization of city residents, was also used to understand the rapidly urbanizing populations of Africa (156) and Latin America (128), and employed by North American researchers to study the interconnections and interdependencies of family and household relationships among the urban poor (226, 227). Network analyses are now more elaborate and quantitative, and they still provide an important methodological strategy and theoretical model for urban research (96, 115, 123).

Planned physical and social change in Latin-American low-income residential neighborhoods (126, 127) as well as the planning and design of new towns such as Ciudad Guayana (174) and Brasília (51) provided further ethnographic examples of local as well as national/international conflict over planning goals. Peattie (175) identified foreign capital investment and Rabinow (186) identified the power/knowledge of the technologies of planning and architecture as antithetical to producing a humane environment for local populations and workers. Studies of urban renewal (68) and community rebuilding after natural disasters (167) further examined how redevelopment processes exclude the psychosocial needs of residents. Conflicts emerge among government institutions, planning experts, and local communities that set the stage for contemporary poststructural analyses of urban struggles for land tenure rights (10, 84) and adequate housing (129) as well as critiques of planning and architecture as instruments of social control (133, 148, 181).

Another theoretical force has been Leeds's cumulative work (119), recently published in a posthumous volume (209). Although Leeds concentrated on supralocal and local linkages and the nation/state level of analysis, his fieldwork dealt predominantly with the city as the point of articulation in these complex relationships. Leeds's model of the flow of goods, cash, labor, and services between metropole and countryside continues to be used in analyses of the city (70, 71).

The most important transition in the anthropological study of the city, however, occurred in the 1980s with the introduction of political economy. Susser's (231) landmark ethnography of a Brooklyn working-class neighborhood, Hannerz's monograph (75), and Mullings's (157) critique of urban anthropology in the United States ushered in a decade of ethnographies that document how structural forces shape urban experience. The examination of the social effects of industrial capitalism and deconstruction of the confusion of urbanism with inequality and alienation produced a new urban paradigm (157, 168).

The final development in this trajectory includes the notion of "representational cities" (89)—an approach in which messages encoded in the environment are read as texts. Jacobs argues that "ethnographic studies were commonly prescribed the role of rendering more real the exotic and marginalized, but were seen to have little value in terms of the modern project of theory-building" (89:828). Radicalized urban ethnography, however, links everyday practices and the broader processes of class formation. According to Jacobs (89), new cities require new forms of analysis in which the urban built environment becomes a discursive realm. The representational approach is reflected in Holston's (82) analysis of the planning and architecture of Brasília read as an ideological tract of an imagined socialist utopia, and in Dorst's (49) postmodern ethnography of the re-creation of the history and landscape of Chadd's Ford, Pennsylvania.

The coincidence of geographical region with theoretical geneology has resulted in research continuities within culture areas. The tradition of British social anthropology in Africa has generated a series of ethnographies of social relations in the city—exchanges, political alliances, market relationships, and network analyses that form the core of contemporary African urban analyses (11, 137, 156, 176). Other continuities include the examination of favelas, shantytowns, and turgurios in the urban periphery, and the informal economy in Latin America (99, 207); Japanese ethnographies that focus on work organization (17, 74, 110, 230); and Chinese studies that emphasize urban hierarchies (72, 92).

The historical development of an anthropology of cities has produced many approaches drawn upon to this day, including urban ecology models; community, family, and network analyses; critiques of the power/knowledge of planning and architecture; supralocal/local linkage analyses; and political economic, representational, and discursive models of the city.

IMAGINING THE CITY: METAPHORS AND IMAGES

The contemporary literature is much more diverse and does not fall neatly into the categories presented above; it is therefore best presented through a series of images and metaphors. These images of the city are meant to be heuristic and illuminating and should not be confused with previous evolutionary schemes or the development of urban typologies (59, 73). They are a guide to the diverse ideas, concepts, and frameworks used to analyze and write about the city, and they are different lenses that offer the reader as well as the writer different ways to communicate about an often elusive and discursively complex subject.

Social Relations

THE ETHNIC CITY   As illustrated by the protagonist's difficulties in the movie *Little Odessa* (1994), which is set in the Russian immigrant community of Brighton Beach, Brooklyn, it is often impossible to escape the pressures of one's cultural group when one remains in the community. However, trying to leave can lead to unexpected and sometimes unfortunate circumstances. *Little Odessa* presents a mythic image of an East-Coast ethnic city. This image of the ethnic city, which has deep historical roots, focuses on ethnic politics and ethnically based urban social movements. Edited volumes addressing the many immigrant groups coexisting in large US cities (36, 56, 116, 235) and ethnographies that portray the differences in the structure of opportunity (103), access to power by generation (100), location of headquarters and subsidiary relations (114), and self-conscious creation of collective identities (124, 244) define the parameters of group success and failure in this urban model.

There are two dominant streams of research: (a) studies of the ethnic city as a mosaic of enclaves economically, linguistically, and socially self-contained as a strategy of political and economic survival (183, 252); and (*b*) studies of ethnic groups that may or may not function as enclaves but that are defined by their location in the occupational structure (141), their position in the local immigrant social structure (142), their degree of marginality (139), or their historical and racial distinctiveness as the basis of discrimination and oppression (37, 57, 113). The ethnic enclave has been criticized as often assumed rather than empirically verified (180). Nonetheless, it has generated a productive stream of research (182, 184). Studies of urban ethnic communities provide important insights into collective ethnic politics.

One book that has received considerable attention is Portes & Stepick's *City on the Edge* (183), a study of the development of Miami, Florida, a city of competing ethnic enclaves. Historically dominated by the white middle class, the cultural hegemony of Miami has more recently shifted to Cuban-born immigrants, and Spanish has become the lingua franca of commerce and sociopolitical networks. Cuban-born immigrants have been singularly successful in manipulating the local power structure and media to create a new kind of ethnic politics in which the oppressed have become the oppressor.

Probably the most ambitious research program has been Lamphere's (116) project on the changing relations between established residents and newcomers in Miami; Chicago; Houston; Philadelphia; Monterey Park, California; and Garden City, Kansas, which identifies quite different strategies in the development of ethnic politics. Horton (87) discussed the "voluntary construction of ethnicity" (87:234) of the Chinese majority and Latino newcomers in Monterey Park, California. Stull (228, 229) emphasized class-based perceptions of ethnic identity in Garden City, Kansas. And Goode & Schneider (67) framed their study in terms of racial as well as ethnic divisions in Philadelphia.

Goode & Schneider's (67) depiction of Philadelphia is particularly noteworthy in that it assesses the political and economic processes that segregate Philadelphia's neighborhoods. Although Goode & Schneider use the term racially "divided city," their research suggests that new immigrants settling in older divided communities are in fact reconfiguring the city into ethnically diverse neighborhoods. An ethnically based real estate market has developed, as well as speciality shopping areas, local ethnic associations, and a proliferation of ethnic festivals. Philadelphia is interesting in that it draws upon two complementary images: It is a historically diverse city known for its neighborhoods dotted with churches and synagogues that mark ethnic differences, and it is a city divided into racial territories of black and white (111).

THE DIVIDED CITY   The divided city conjures up images of the Berlin Wall (18) or the Danube, which divides Buda from Pest. Within anthropology it evokes hidden barriers of race and class encoded in metaphors of uptown and downtown, upscale and ghetto, and particularly in the United States, of black and white. McDonogh (149) interpreted the experience of being black and Catholic in the divided city of Savannah, Georgia, as "characterized by a continuous tension among discourses that sustain stereotypes, delimit social groups, and shape the activities of citizens who participate in urban cultures" (149:65). Keith & Cross (102), however, argued that the divided city has restored the cultural primacy of the urban as a culture and cash nexus or "city as playground." The division here is between the white cultural playgrounds and the abandoned black residential areas so clearly seen in cities such as Washington, Los Angeles, and New York City.

The processes producing the divided city have been studied primarily in US cities. Studies focus on different aspects of racism and racial segregation (246). Williams's (247) exploration of the displacement of blacks through gentrification and other real estate activities and Greenbaum's (68) examination of housing abandonment provide ethnographic explanations for the more theoretical overviews of American residential apartheid (27, 147). According to Massey & Denton (147), the continued high level of urban residential segregation exemplifies racial prejudice and discriminatory real estate practices and mortgage structures designed to insulate whites from blacks. Gregory (69) noted that a shift from race-based to class-based politics is even separating the residences of low-income blacks in Queens, New York City, from middle-class blacks who are increasingly adopting the political values of white homeowners.

Further explorations of the economic, social, and political consequences of racism include Page's (170) concept of "white public space" to analyze how white institutions control even the production of "blackness." Here efforts by black entrepreneurs to serve their own people and culture are coopted by the white power structure that dominates the economic and communication systems used by the black community. Sacks (206) explained race, class, and gender relations through the metaorganization of capitalism, which she defined as a materially based and state-reinforced social and cultural construction. Fernandez-Kelly (104) explained the divided city through the unequal distribution of "cultural capital"—the symbolic repertory whose meanings individuals learn and use as members of particular social networks—and "social capital"—the relations of reciprocity between individuals and groups. Cultural and social capital are defined by physical vectors such as urban space and by collective constructions such as social class, race, and gender, and thus are toponomical, dependent on physical and social location.

Unequal distribution of material resources and urban services is also identified as a reflection of the "major cleavage between those able to augment their basic needs through labor market participation at a wage high enough to insulate them from the vagaries of state budget crises and those who remain on state services just to survive" (94:112). Susser (232, 233) pointed to the separation of mothers and male children as perpetuating the dismantling of the black family and as increasing the vulnerability of black male children, while Jones (93, 95) demonstrated that although mothers want their children to achieve, the material bases for social reproduction are not available to support such desires. Ogbu (166) and George (61) identified city schools' failure to provide educational environments that affirm and allow black and other minority student achievements.

The most extreme image of the divided city is Wacquant's (238) concept of the hyperghetto, a racially and socioeconomically segregated section of the inner city characterized by the "depacification" of everyday life, "desertification" of organizations and institutions, social "dedifferentiation," and "informalization" of the economy. Wacquant (237) compared the stigma and racial division of South Side Chicago's Black Belt with the Parisian Red Belt of the urban periphery, which "highlights the distinctively racial dimension of inner city poverty in the United States" (237:380). Mingione (153) commented on the "Americanization" of poverty in European cities to describe the increasing racialization and ghettoization of the European poor.

Other researchers, however, argue that the South Side of Chicago is a special case, and that New York's Harlem and Los Angeles's South Central are not experiencing these desertification and depacification processes. Newman (160, 162, 163) and George (61) refute the generalizations of Wacquant & Wilson (240) and identified instead an increase in the number of local churches, the development of new Afrocentric schools, and a reappropriation of identity politics based on positive black images.

THE GENDERED CITY   The city has been perceived primarily as a male place in which women, "along with minorities, children, the poor, are still not full citizens in the sense that they have never been granted full and free access to the streets…and they have survived and flourished in the interstices of the city, negotiating the contradictions of the city in their own particular way" (248:8). The life within these interstices makes up the gendered city, seen by feminists (48, 80, 146, 225, 248) as a place of work, struggle, and strife.

Anthropological studies have focused on women's work and workplaces in the informal sphere: the market (38, 78), homework, (245), and domestic service (64, 190). With the increasing feminization of key sectors of the informal economy and the informalization of economic and political processes in third world cities, more women are supporting their children as street vendors ("higglers") in Jamaica (78), market women in West Africa (38), pieceworkers in urban Turkey (245), and domestic workers in Bolivia (64). Repak (190) argued that the structural forces in El Salvador of no rural jobs, low marriage rates, and multiple partners have produced a gender-specific migration of women as a low-wage labor source of domestics for Washington, DC, households. This historical-structural theory of "gendered labor recruitment" explains why single women come to cities, but it is their newly acquired values of freedom, growth, and individual achievement that explain why they stay.

Another way of conceptualizing the gendered city has been to document and analyze women's urban protests against their "silencing" in urban public high schools (54), their exclusion from the sites of knowledge acquisition in Sudan and New York (101), and their control by traditional and Western hegemonies in Cairo (138). Hayden (80) is particularly concerned about the absence of physical and spatial markers of women's contributions and designs monuments to the forgotten histories of women who built and nourished Los Angeles. Redevelopment schemes erase the cultural, architectural, and spatial remains of ordinary people and leave an urban landscape that provides no "place memories" for women, immigrants, and other minorities (23, 80, 132, 164).

THE CONTESTED CITY   The West Indian Labor Day Parade in Brooklyn, New York (100); the Halloween Parade in Greenwich Village, New York (112); and Las Fallas in Valencia (117)—events that temporarily invert the urban power structure through symbolic control of the streets—are well-known images of "the contested city." The growing attention to the masquerade politics of urban cultural movements (39) and to earlier work on urban social movements (9, 32) has broadened contemporary concepts of urban struggle and resistance. Poststructural analyses describe the city as a site of ongoing urban conflicts about the material basis for social reproduction reflected in a concern for the quality of life (94), access to land (12, 83), and neighborhood control of affordable housing (13). Historical studies of Central Park in New York City (192a) and of Barcelona (98) also record the solidarity of class and gender in the struggle to control land and labor.

Resistance, however, is not always a process of active contestation (165). Pred (185) and Banck (8) emphasized how simply naming streets can be an act of political struggle. In urban high schools, resistance has been explored through the concept of "silencing," a vehicle for understanding how it is that "language, representations, and even the forms of resistance permitted or not" (53) shape patterns of social injustice.

The contested city also provides a site for methodological innovation. Burawoy (28) used the "modern metropolis" as a laboratory for students who produced ethnographies looking at issues of power and resistance. Abu-Lughod's (3) "collective ethnography" of New York City's Lower East Side is another effort "to capture the economic and social complexities found in our newest forms of inner-city neighborhoods" (3:5). These inner-city neighborhoods have become arenas for struggle with developers and city government officials, but also sites of conflict for the subgroups that live within them.

Economics

THE DEINDUSTRIALIZED CITY   Michael Moore's underground film *Roger and Me* (1989) tells the story of the closing of the General Motors automobile factory in Flint, Michigan, and the resulting unemployment of workers, disinvestment in the community, declining standard of living, and subsequent deterioration of family and personal life. The story is a common one: deterioration of a city because of the closing or relocation of industries that were the sole employers in working-class towns. The forces of globalization, new forms of flexible capital, and new venues of cheap labor have accelerated the number of these closings and their socially deleterious effects.

The consequences of deindustrialization on the lives of working-class men and women have been described by Pappas (171), who focused on the effects of the closing of the Seiberling plant of the Firestone Tire and Rubber company in the midwestern industrial town of Barberton, Ohio. His ethnography sensitively depicts the reaction of displaced workers who once had a modicum of affluence and security. Nash (159), in her comprehensive historical-structural analysis of the economic and social decline of Pittsfield, Massachusetts, sees the response to deindustrialization in terms of the construction of community and corporate hegemony. When General Electric announced downsizing and the subsequent closing of local plants, the discourse between employees and management began to change, and issues of corporate responsibility, social contract, and community welfare took on new meaning. Nash (159:324) concluded that:

> General Electric consciously used the threat and actual practice of moving production elsewhere when they recognized the strength of nationally organized unions....Their growing global investments were as much an attempt to control the labor movement in their domestic plants as to take advantage of cheap labor in export processing plants or branches within low-wage countries.

Related research looks at the costs of deindustrialization according to its impact on residents in New York City suburbs (161), immigrants in Philadelphia (111), and African-Americans in Chicago's ghettos (240). Deindustrialization has contributed to the hyperghettoization of the city (240) and to the "withering" of the middle-class American dream (161). The consequences of urban deindustrialization also are found in the poverty and homelessness literature.

THE GLOBAL CITY   New York, Tokyo, and London are cited as the preeminent global cities—centers of technology, financial production, and support services (210) in which translocal economic forces have more weight than local policies in shaping urban economies (211). These three cities have "undergone massive and *parallel* changes in their economic base, spatial organization, and social structure" (210:4) to accommodate their "command post" functions as key locations for markets, finance and special services, and sites of production and innovation. The resulting polarization of the city and the economy, the internationalization and "casualization" of labor, and deterritorialization of the social organization of work and community are products of the same post-Fordist forces that have reshaped the deindustrialized city. Global forces are also reshaping regional systems of cities and the formation of transnational identities and communities (212). For example, along the US-Mexico border a distinct category, the "border metropolis," has arisen that is characterized by commuting populations and transnational character (7, 81).

"World city" has also been used to describe the changing economies of large, central cities from a world systems perspective (241). Friedmann (60), summing up a decade of research, argued that world cities: (*a*) articulate local economies in a global economy, (*b*) provide a space for capital accumulation that excludes the world as a whole, (*c*) are locations of intense economic and social interaction, (*d*) are hierarchically arranged within the world system order, and (*e*) constitute a social class—the transnational capitalist class. Another manifestation is the "dual city" (155), comprised of upper-class and upper-middle-class professionals who act as a group in pursuing their own political ends and who effectively diffuse the political influence of more pluralistic neighborhoods.

The consequences of globalization have been examined in the creation of the third world "global factory" (199), the transformation of the Tsukji wholesale fish market in Tokyo (17), and the reinterpretation of Hong Kong's economic past and future within a global framework (220). Anthropological contributions, however, have primarily focused on transnational perspectives of migration (215) in which issues of race, class, ethnicity, and nationalism are reconsidered (35, 62, 121, 169). Everything from drug trafficking by gangs (77) to selling hats in Harlem made in Africa emblazoned with Malcolm's "X" (40) is transformed by international capitalism. Transnational forces are also changing the "social, territorial, and cultural reproduction of group identity" (6:191) in such a way that landscapes of group identity are deterritorialized. The shifting terrain of public culture is constantly redefining the local according to the global. This new world of cultural ebb and flow, however, has probably been captured more adequately in the media-based image of the informational city.

THE INFORMATIONAL CITY   In *The Informational City,* Castells (33) described another kind of dual city, one in which space flows supersede the meaning of the space of places. Space flows, however, are organized on the principles of information-processing activities, rather than on the everyday spaces of living and working. The resulting meaninglessness of everyday places and political institutions is resented and resisted through a variety of individual and collective strategies. People attempt to reaffirm their cultural identity, often in territorial terms, by "mobilizing to achieve their demands, organizing their communities, and staking out their places to preserve meaning, to restore whatever limited control they can over work and residence" (33:350).

Castells (34) further outlined his theory of the informational society as a world in which control over knowledge and information decides who holds power in society. Communications technology and media control of images, representations, and public opinion, as well as the increasing ability of computer networks to allow the individual to create personal images, illustrate the growing tension between globalization and individualization. Individuals react by representing their values and interests through the reassertion of primary identities of self-identified communities, which results in the rejection of other communities, increasing racism and xenophobia. In response, Martin (145) suggested that the emphasis on adaptive, continuous change is creating an everyday concept of the "flexible body"; that new forms of inequality—in poverty, education, immigrant experience, and communication—are being produced (234); and that the dynamics of the new identity-making are, in fact, dialectical rather than unidimensional processes (132).

Hannerz (76), in *Cultural Complexity,* offered another version of an informational society based on cultural flows organized according to states, markets, and movements. Here the city is the center of cultural growth, the place where the interplay of the centralizing agencies of culture—schools and media—and the decentralizing forces of the diversity of subcultures are located. Hannerz, in contrast with Castells, emphasized the linkages between local experience and these global cultural flows.

Urban Planning and Architecture

THE MODERNIST CITY   Brasília is the archetypal modernist city. It is based on CIAM's (Congrès Internationaux d'Architecture Moderne's) premise of social transformation and executed by the force of a strong central government. The design of Brasília was supposed to integrate the disparate classes and colors of Brazil's complex social structure while simultaneously revitalizing the economy through the creation of new jobs and industries in the central region. Brasília was conceived by President Kubitschek as an attempt to celebrate Brazil's arrival as a modern country ready to take its proper place in the world system and global economy. As a symbolic statement it was successful, but as a city its abstract architecture and idealist plan conflicted with the needs and desires of its people. This story is the substrate of Holston's (82) architectural ethnography, which provides an effective critique of Brasília's plan and architecture as well as of the underlying cultural assumptions of the monumental urban project. Holston's (84) critique of modernist planning has led him to search for a new social imagination, one that provides "spaces of insurgent citizenship" as sources of legitimation and political participation (85).

"The colonial city," another urban image recently reviewed by King (108), is often critiqued from a modernist perspective in the sense that the "modern technologies" of planning and architecture are employed to build these new societies and indoctrinate citizens within the spatial confines of rationally planned towns (249). Mitchell's (154) *Colonizing Egypt* and Rabinow's (186) *French Modern* both examined the building and "enframing" of power relations reflected in colonial spatial configurations and visual perspectives. Low (130, 131) explored the impact of the Spanish colonial system of spatial organization on the urban landscape. Pellow (177) investigated the British control of land and political power in the space accorded local peoples in Accra, Ghana, while King (107) linked colonialism with the broader issues of urbanism and the world economy. The analysis of the role of planning agencies and of vested local interests has become a critical part of any study of urbanization and the politics of modernization in third world countries such as Ghana (31) and China (45).

THE POSTMODERN CITY   The movie *Pulp Fiction* (1994) reflects the space-time compression proposed by Harvey (79) and Giddens (63) as a feature of contemporary social life. Jameson (90) argued that late capitalism has a distinctive cultural logic that is reshaping the form and functioning of the city (224a). Boyer (23) calls it the "city of illusion," Zukin (254) the "city of cultural consumption," and Rutheiser (203) the "nonplace urban realm" where the packaging of cities as commodities creates the "city of scenographic sites" (23).

Dorst's (49) extraordinary analysis of Chadd's Ford, Pennsylvania, as an image, idea, ideological discourse, and assemblage of texts—a written suburb—and of the preservation of Chadd's Ford as a representative display of a place that exists putatively only in Andrew Wyeth's paintings, demonstrates the theoretical power of ethnography when applied to a postmodern site. Dorst employed the concept of postmodern hyperspaces constructed to behave like depthless surfaces to explain the visual impact of the mirror-glass surface of the Brandywine Museum and its enframed scenes (49:108).

Conversely, Fjellman (55) considers the ultimate city of illusion: Walt Disney World in Orlando, Florida. He argued that Walt Disney World has become the major middle-class pilgrimage center in the United States, "partly because of the brilliance of its cross-referential marketing and partly because its utopian aspects appeal strongly to real peoples' real needs in late capitalist society" (55:10). The cinema structures one's experience there, with activities constructed as movie scenes: Thus, all experience is composed of surfaces similar to the "veneer" and "vignette" of Dorst's Chadd's Ford.

Another approach has been to document the "imagineering" of the post-modern city, as in Rutheiser's (204) study of how Atlanta's nondistinctive identity was "repackaged" for the 1996 Olympics into an image of "traditional urbanity" (203), and McDonogh's (148) exploration of the ideological impact of Olympics planning on the reconstitution of public space and citizenship in Barcelona. Sieber (219) showed how postindustrial port cities use the revitalization of the waterfront to create downtown tourist sites with middle-class images of housing complexes and shopping malls, while Cooper (41) traced the transformation of spatial ideologies for imagining the Toronto waterfront. Ruble (200) also critiqued the reshaping of the image of a provincial Russian city in the postsocialist transition. In each of these revitalization schemes, histories and monuments of public memory are manipulated to create a seamless presentation of the city's revalorized cultural heritage (22, 164, 218).

Hong Kong has also been identified as an important site of postmodernity. The four eroding ecologies of the merchant city, the industrial city, the financial city, and the capital city have created colonial spaces with working-class conditions adjacent to commodity spaces with new towns and high-rise buildings (44). The contradictions of these spaces can be seen on any Sunday when groups of Filipina domestic workers picnic on blankets, filling the cement sidewalks and streets because the city will not provide public parks and recreation; while during the week a staggering number of street hawkers sell their wares next to transnational corporate buildings (221). The skyscraper architecture of Hong Kong derives from modernist ideas of town planning, but these buildings are transformed by the hyperdensity of the site (1). Dovey (50) argued that these corporate towers are produced by the forces of creative destruction that are emblematic of the condition of postmodernity (79).

THE FORTRESS CITY   Imagine private police guarding New York City's wealthy Upper East Side, or private highways running along the median strip of Los Angeles's freeways (163a). Remember the fortified encampments of futuristic films such as *Road Warrior* (1982) and *Mad Max* (1980) or the underground prison of the recent film *Twelve Monkeys* (1996). These are all images of the fortress city, conceived of by Davis (46) and modeled on Los Angeles.

Davis's fortress city is drawn from his radical history of the development of Los Angeles, in which he traces the control of media, seizure of land, busting of unions, rigging of water rights, and exclusion of minorities from political participation, all of which has resulted in the destruction of public space. Davis explains that the resulting militarization (47) took a long time to develop, with many periods of working-class and minority resistance producing minor successes. However, the riots in South Central Los Angeles and movies such as *Boyz in the 'Hood* (1991) suggest that unequal social relations solidified with the continued infusion of capital from movie-making businesses and Pacific rim financial services that accelerated land speculation, development, and rising housing prices.

The social production of the fortress city is explained in Fainstein's study of the logic of large development projects in such cities as New York and London (52:1):

> This built environment forms contours which structure social relations, causing commonalities of gender, sexual orientation, race, ethnicity, and class to assume spatial identities. Social groups, in turn, imprint themselves physically on the urban structure through the formation of communities, competition for territory, and segregation—in other words, through clustering, the erection of boundaries, and establishing distance.

Large mixed commercial and residential development projects reinforce the segregation of the divided city, further cutting off communities by visual boundaries, growing distances, and ultimately, walls. Merry (151) argued that in middle-class and upper-middle-class urban neighborhoods residents seek privacy because they desire peace and can afford it. Such neighborhoods are marked by patterns of avoidance of social contact: building fences, cutting off relationships, and moving out in response to problems and conflicts. Government simultaneously expands its regulatory role: "Zoning laws, local police departments, ordinances about dogs, quiet laws, laws against domestic and interpersonal violence, all provide new forms of regulation of family and neighborhood life" (152:87).

In the fortress city, youth gangs and homeless youth are part of the new social imaginaries: "[N]ew social subjects are created and create themselves in and through the social space of the city" (201). Space takes on the ability to confirm identity (132), and gangs compete for limited urban spaces (91), as institutional and private forces increasingly constrain and structure the lives of street addicts and other marginalized groups within the public arena (242).

Within this context, acts of violence and crime are increasingly feared. Anderson (5) discussed the "streetwise" behavior of Philadelphians: in which residents cross the street when faced with oncoming young black males. Wacquant (239) portrayed the perceived isolation of families in Chicago's Black Belt, where the streets are deserted and no longer patrolled by police. Bourgois (21) described the fear and sense of vulnerability experienced by El Barrio residents and by anthropologists faced with the everyday violence of those who sell crack in East Harlem, New York City. African-American adolescents in Baltimore perceive this violence as both within and against their communities (97), while suburbanites and the black and Latino urban-working poor do not accept a structural economic analysis of criminality but instead blame crime on individual actors rather than on social forces (20).

Most studies of the fortress city focus on Los Angeles, Chicago, and New York, even though the United States does not have a monopoly on this type of social and physical development. Brazil offers examples of fortification and urban violence that match any US venue (213). Banck (8) documented growing fear with the increased differentials of consumption by class. Linger (125) has written an ethnography about *brigas,* violent confrontations that are a kind of cultural performance occurring during Carnival. Caldeira (30) described the increasing fear of street crime and building of fortified enclaves in São Paulo, and Low's research in Caracas, Venezuela, is informed by the fear middle-class residents experience when they leave their gated compounds. The fortress city is on the horizon as a new built form and device of social control that should be studied as part of our inquiry into growing urban economic inequality.

Religion and Culture

THE SACRED CITY   Levy's (122) insightful account of Hinduism and the organization of the traditional Newar city of Bhaktapur presents the city as a "mesocosm," an essential middle world that symbolically mediates between the cosmological universe and the experience of everyday life. Bhaktapur is said to be an archaic city, one that uses "marked" symbols to solve the problem of cultural communication among many people, and Levy provided an analysis of how these symbolic forms, such as sacrifice, festival calendars, and the pantheon of divinities, work to order a very large and complex city. Civic life is a "choreographed ballet" (122:17) of religious observance and practice. Parish (172), also working in Bhaktapur, reiterated that the city is a sacred setting for collective ritual, "a mandala of shrines" (172:21) that embodies the Hindu religious system and cosmology within which individuals locate and create moral selves. Lynch (136) also examined the construction of identity, but in the Hindu city of Mathura, where ancestral place becomes a metaphor for the self-identity of the Chaubes, a community of priests who act as guides and ritual specialists performing the necessary rites for pilgrims at Krishna's birthplace.

The image of the sacred city is analyzed through its symbolic form in Hindu (122, 136, 172) and Islamic cities (2, 189), but there are other aspects of sacredness. Research on religion as a basis of urban resistance movements (29, 189, 243), as a basis of class politics (236), as an expression of gay identity (217), and as a vehicle of immigrant survival (26) suggests that religion plays a variety of roles in the lives of urban residents. Reeves (189) in particular argued that religion as a form of resistance goes unnoticed in Northern Egypt and therefore is not controlled or countered. Burdick's (29) work in Brazil, however, suggests that there are many religious discourses in the arena, some of which produce strong counterreactions.

THE TRADITIONAL CITY   Several studies of cities in Japan, India, and China consider the maintenance of tradition within the urban context. While not contributing directly to a theory of the city, these studies investigate dimensions of urban life often overlooked by other researchers.

Bestor's (14, 15) work on a shitamachi neighborhood in Tokyo and Robertson's (191) study of newcomers in a small Japanese city portray urban experience as a struggle for balance between the maintenance of tradition and the pressures of rapid social change. Kondo (110), however, examined the relationship of work and self-concept, in which a person's occupational status may come into conflict with traditional values and sex-role obligations. Japanese urban studies also consider the maintenance of traditional forms of status privilege and status recognition, in business (74, 230) and among the nobility (118). A fascinating study of a Mongol city in China focuses on the many details of urban social hierarchies and provides insights into the management of marriage and romance within this traditional setting (92).

Indigenous studies of urban processes provide an important window into indigenous conceptualizations of problems and culturally significant themes. Edited volumes by indigenous authors on urban anthropology in China (72) and on urban sociology in India (187, 188) include a number of articles emphasizing ongoing conflicts between the desire to preserve cultural traditions in the face of rapid social change.

Images of the city, however, are not the only contribution that anthropologists have been making to an anthropology of cities, and the final section of this review discusses how anthropologists have approached the city through the concepts of space, time, knowledge, and aesthetics.

THEORIZING THE CITY: SPACE, KNOWLEDGE, TIME, AND AESTHETICS

The view that contemporary cities not only pose problems intrinsic to the metropolitan experience, but that they also underscore and transform many of the most traditional concerns of the discipline—the social organization of space; the meanings of knowledge, group, and power; and the intricacies of commodity, exchange, and political economy—has been taken up by a group of scholars involved in the theoretical revitalization of the field (for a similar undertaking, see also 135, 251). The concern has been to articulate understandings of particular cities—Vienna; Barcelona; Valencia; Savannah; Atlanta; New York; Toronto; Accra; Shanghai; Tokyo; Belize City; and San José, Costa Rica—with broader anthropological concepts of space, knowledge, time, and identity. The inquiry began not with imagining the city as a metaphorical object but with imagining urbanites: residents, homeless people, planners, municipal bureaucrats, and architects experiencing the city through the social relations, political economic, and planning processes outlined in the previous section.

The Cultural Meaning of Urban Space (197) reflects an attempt to understand "the meaning of urban spaces through the knowledge of the people who live within them" (197:xi). The studies are characterized by the search for the underlying social and cultural values and power politics that give form and meaning to the cityscape and the built urban environment. McDonogh's (150) ethnography of "emptiness" provides an evocative theoretical category that marks not an absence of urbanness but a zone of intense competition that betrays the imposition of urban power. Low (130) focuses on the historical emergence of spatial meanings of power relations in the Spanish American plaza, while others are concerned with the symbolic mapping of contested arenas of urban social interaction such as privacy (178), neighborhood (16), and schooling (202). Research on the design of housing (42, 134) and place attachment to urban space (4) also contribute to this ongoing venture.

Setting Boundaries (179) is more concerned with boundaries and perimeters, that is, the way in which "physical and conceptual boundaries are integrally tied to the creation, maintenance, transformation and definition of social and societal relations—of socio-cultural behavior and action" (179:3). In these chapters the concept of boundary is dealt with both spatially and metaphorically, which links the materialist and metaphorical analyses of social and spatial demarcation (for a similar concept within cultural geography, see 223).

Many of the ideas explored in these volumes have been further elaborated by asking how meaning is created through both the social production of space and the social construction of space (133, 192), and how power is represented in the history and evolution of the built forms (117, 120, 131, 195). An ethnographic approach to the study of urban space including four areas of spatial/cultural analysis—historical emergence, sociopolitical and economic structuring, patterns of social use, and experiential meanings—is one means of working out this theoretical agenda (133).

Rotenberg has also proposed a second project, that of identifying other forms of metropolitan knowledge as a "subset of the knowledge people gain from their lived experience and value socialization" (197:xii). City dwellers share the knowledge because they live in dense and specialized concentrations of people, information, built form, and economic activity. Rotenberg (194) speaks of the "salubrity of sites" as a way to understand how metropolitan knowledge is made manifest on the urban landscape. For example, in *Landscape and Power in Metropolitan Vienna* (195), he elaborated this idea by tracing the history of open spaces and gardens in Vienna and documenting how these spaces have become a spatial template of urban symbolic communication.

An additional project, the study of time, directs urban researchers to consider how schedules coordinate the circulation of people in the city as a means for studying embedded power relations. Rutz argued that "a *politics* of time is concerned with the *appropriation* of the time of others, the *institutionalization* of a dominant time, and the *legitimation* of power by means of the control of time" (205:7). Rotenberg's (193) study of Viennese urban schedules, Lovell's (128a) study of street time in New York City, and Gounis's (67a) documentation of the daily homeless shelter routine in New York City demonstrate the tyranny of urban schedules over individuals subject to their control. Local control of both time and space are critical to the survival of homeless people who live in urban public spaces (86).

The most recent contribution to this urban dialogue is Rotenberg's (196) contention that the identity of the city also structures residents' urban experience, adding urban identity to place and time as universal sources of metropolitan knowledge. This proposal resonates with Sennett's (216) interest in embodied urban experience. These universal characterizations bring us temptingly close to earlier essentializing discourses but also provide provocative material for perceiving how the city as a set of processes links experience and structure.

One other promising project is the study of ethnoaesthetics. Although much of this literature focuses on indigenous media and aesthetic and political sensibilities (65), the implications of this work transform our notions of the urban, global, transnational, and marginal. In the city, where culture-making often occurs, "performing aboriginality" takes on new aesthetic and identity meanings (158). Bright & Bakewell (25) in *Looking High and Low* also attempted to reposition art and ethnoaesthetics to redefine notions of cultural identity. Urban murals and low-rider cars provide examples of how the city constitutes an important dimension of the aesthetic (24). Although relatively undeveloped as part of the urban discourse, the study of ethnoaesthetics and cultural identity and the demystification of art and artistic creation (140) are useful in analyzing the culture of cities (109, 254).

CONCLUSIONS

The anthropological literature on the city published since 1989 has incorporated a number of models and paradigms from other disciplines. The influence of political economy, architectural and planning theory, cultural studies, urban sociology, and cultural geography can be seen in the increasing attention to economic, political, and discursive models of the city. However, poststructural and postmodern epistemologies have resulted in a recasting of the questions and modes of inquiry used to study the city. The dominant research trends in anthropology appear to be poststructural studies of race, class, and gender in the urban context; political economic studies of transnational culture; and symbolic and social production studies of urban space and planning.

A number of theoretically useful images and metaphors of the city organize this inquiry. Some—the ethnic city, divided city, deindustrialized city, and global city—have had an impact on the body of research and have encouraged ongoing projects. For instance, the ethnic city has encouraged discussion of assimilation and the development of ethnic politics, and the global city has focused attention on the unique roles of cities in the development of transnational cultures. Other images suggest future research endeavors: The symbolic structure of the sacred city suggests further inquiry into the symbolic structure of secular cities and the study of the relationship between public symbols and the organization and meaning of everyday urban life. The contested city is a powerful image for poststructural studies that enriches the investigation of conflict and resistance in both the public and private urban realms. The promise of the informational city is already reflected in the growing number of studies on the hegemony of media and information technologies, and the image of the fortress city has influenced research on social inequality and residential segregation.

Some areas of research have been particularly influential within the broader field of urban studies and urban policy. The anthropological twist on globalization has focused attention on the transnational aspects of migration, culture-making, and identity management, and on the shifting cultural environments and meanings that contextualize (and decontextualize) behavior. Ethnographies offer an experience-near critique of inner-city life that provides a more complex understanding of the differences between cities' and residents' responses to racial segregation and class inequality such that research based on one city—Chicago—is held suspect. Anthropological critiques of planning and design projects provide a methodology and framework for decoding the ideological intentions and material consequences of architectural plans and landscape designs, while radicalized fieldwork retains the power to demonstrate the how, why, and when of urban processes.

ACKNOWLEDGMENTS

I thank Dolores Hayden, Joel Lefkowitz, Deborah Pellow, Robert Rotenberg, Carol Stack, Ida Susser, Laurel Wilson, and the editors of the *Annual Review of Anthropology* for their thoughtful comments and suggestions. I also thank the members of my Anthropology of Cities graduate seminar for their critique of readings and insightful discussions that helped to clarify certain points in this review.

Any *Annual Review* chapter, as well as any article cited in an *Annual Review* chapter, may be purchased from the Annual Reviews Preprints and Reprints service. 1-800-347-8007; 415-259-5017; email: arpr@class.org

Literature Cited

1. Abbas A. 1994. Building on disappearance: Hong Kong architecture and the city. *Public Cult.* 6:441–59
2. Abu-Lughod JL. 1987. The Islamic city: historic myth, Islamic essence, and contemporary relevance. *Int. J. Middle East. Stud.* 19:155–76
3. Abu-Lughod JL. 1994. *From Urban Village to East Village: The Battle for New York's Lower East Side.* Oxford: Blackwell
4. Altman I, Low SM. 1992. *Place Attachment.* New York: Plenum
5. Anderson E. 1990. *Streetwise: Race, Class and Change in an Urban Community.* Chicago: Chicago Univ. Press
6. Appadurai A. 1991. Global ethnoscapes: notes and queries for a transnational anthropology. In *Recapturing Anthropology,* ed. R Fox, pp. 191–210. Santa Fe, NM: Sch. Am. Res.
7. Arreola DD, Curtis JR. 1993. *The Mexican Border Cities.* Tucson: Univ. Ariz. Press
8. Banck GA. 1993. Signifying urban space: Vitória, Brazil. In *Urban Symbolism,* ed. PJM Nas, pp. 104–15. Lieden: Brill
9. Banck GA. 1994. Mass consumption and urban contest in Brazil: some reflections on lifestyle and class. *Bull. Lat. Am. Res.* 13: 45–60
10. Banck GA, Doimo AM. 1989. Between utopia and strategy: a case study of a Brazilian urban social movement. In *Urban Social Movements in the Third World,* ed. F Schuurman, RV Naerssen, pp. 125–50. London: Routledge
11. Barnes S. 1986. *Patrons and Power: Creating a Political Community in Metropolitan Lagos.* Bloomington: Indiana Univ. Press
12. Barriga MD. 1995. The politics of urban expansion in Mexico City: of *ejido* urbanization in the Ajusco foothills, 1938–1990. *Urban Anthropol.* 24:363–96
13. Beck S. 1992. *Manny Almeida's Ringside Lounge: The Cape Verdean's Struggle for this Neighborhood.* Providence, RI: Gávea-Brown
14. Bestor TC. 1989. *Neighborhood Tokyo.* Stanford, CA: Stanford Univ. Press
15. Bestor TC. 1992. Conflict, legitimacy, and tradition in a Tokyo neighborhood. In *Japanese Social Organization,* ed. T Sugiyama, pp. 23–47. Honolulu: Univ. Hawaii Press
16. Bestor TC. 1993. Rediscovering shitamachi: subculture, class and Tokyo's "traditional" urbanism. See Ref. 197, pp. 47–60
17. Bestor TC. 1997. *Tokyo's Marketplace: Culture and Trade in the Tsukji Wholesale Fish Market.* Stanford, CA: Stanford Univ. Press. In press
18. Borneman J. 1991. *After the Wall: East Meets West in the New Berlin.* New York: Basic Books
19. Bott E. 1957. *Family and Social Network: Roles, Norms and External Relationships in Ordinary Urban Families.* London: Tavistock
20. Bourgois P. 1995. *In Search of Respect: Selling Crack in El Barrio.* Cambridge: Cambridge Univ. Press
21. Bourgois P. 1996. Confronting anthropology, education, and inner-city apartheid: ethnographic vulnerability in El Barrio. *Am. Anthropol.* 98(2):1–10
22. Boyer MC. 1992. Cities for sale: merchandising history at South Street Seaport. See Ref. 224a, pp. 181–204
23. Boyer MC. 1994. *The City of Collective Memory.* Cambridge, MA: MIT Press
24. Bright BJ. 1995. Remappings: Los Angeles low riders. See Ref. 27, pp. 89–123
25. Bright BJ, Bakewell L, eds. 1995. *Looking High and Low: Art and Cultural Identity.* Tucson: Univ. Ariz. Press
26. Brown KM. 1991. *Mama Lola: A Vodou Priestess in Brooklyn.* Berkeley: Univ. Calif. Press
27. Bullard RD, Grigsby JE III, Lee C. 1994. *Residential Apartheid: The American Legacy.* Los Angeles: CAAS Urban Policy Ser.
28. Burawoy M, Burton A, Ferguson AA, Fox KJ, Gamson J. 1991. *Ethnography Unbound: Power and Resistance in the Modern Metropolis.* Berkeley: Univ. Calif. Press

29. Burdick J. 1993. *Looking for God in Brazil: The Progressive Catholic Church in Urban Brazil's Religious Arena.* Berkeley: Univ. Calif. Press
30. Caldeira T. 1996. Fortified communities. *Public Cult.* 8(2):303–28
31. Campbell J. 1995. Urbanization, culture, and the politics of urban development in Ghana, 1875–1980. *Urban Anthropol.* 23: 409–50
32. Castells M. 1983. *The City and the Grassroots.* Berkeley: Univ. Calif. Press
33. Castells M. 1989. *The Informational City: Information Technology, Economic Restructuring and the Urban-Regional Process.* Oxford: Blackwell
34. Castells M. 1996. The Net and the self: working notes for a critical theory of the informational society. *Crit. Anthropol.* 16(1):9–38
35. Charles C. 1992. Transnationalism in the construct of Haitian migrants' racial categories of identity in New York City. See Ref. 215, pp. 101–24
36. Chavez LR. 1990. Immigrants in US Cities. *Urban Anthropol.* 19:1–184
37. Chen HS. 1992. *Chinatown No More: Taiwan Immigrants in Contemporary New York.* Ithaca, NY: Cornell Univ. Press
38. Clark G. 1994. *Onions Are my Husband: Survival and Accumulation by West African Market Women.* Chicago: Univ. Chicago Press
39. Cohen A. 1993. *Masquerade Politics: Explorations in the Structure of Urban Cultural Movements.* Berkeley: Univ. Calif. Press
40. Coombe R, Stoller P. 1994. X marks the spot: the ambiguities of African trading in the commerce of the Black public sphere. *Public Cult.* 7:249–74
41. Cooper M. 1994. Spatial discourses and social boundaries: re-imagining the Toronto waterfront. *City Soc. Annu. Rev.* 1994:93–117
42. Cooper M, Rodman MC. 1992. *New Neighbours: A Case Study of Cooperative Housing.* Toronto: Univ. Toronto Press
43. Cronon W. 1991. *Nature's Metropolis: Chicago and the Great West.* New York: Norton
44. Cuthbert A. 1995. Under the volcano: postmodern space in Hong Kong. In *Postmodern Cities and Spaces,* ed. S Watson, K Gibson, pp. 138–48. Oxford: Blackwell
45. Davis DS, Kraus R, Naughton B, Perry J. 1995. *Urban Spaces in Contemporary China: The Potential for Autonomy and Community in Post-Mao China.* Cambridge: Cambridge Univ. Press
46. Davis M. 1990. *City of Quartz: Excavating the Future in Los Angeles.* London: Verso
47. Davis M. 1992. Fortress Los Angeles: the militarization of urban space. See Ref. 224a, pp. 154–80
48. di Leonardo M. 1993. What a difference political economy makes: feminist anthropology in the postmodern era. *Anthropol. Q.* 66:76–80
49. Dorst JD. 1989. *The Written Suburb: An American Site; An Ethnographic Dilemma.* Philadelphia: Univ. Pa. Press
50. Dovey K. 1992. Corporate towers and symbolic capital. *Environ. Plan. B: Plan. Des.* 19:173–88
51. Epstein D. 1973. *Brasília, Plan and Reality: A Study of Planned and Spontaneous Urban Development.* Berkeley: Univ. Calif. Press
52. Fainstein SS. 1994. *City Builders: Property, Politics and Planning in London and New York.* Oxford: Blackwell
53. Fine M. 1991. *Framing Dropouts: Notes on the Politics of an Urban Public High School.* Albany: South. Univ. NY Press
54. Fine M. 1992. *Disruptive Voices: The Possibilities of Feminist Research.* Ann Arbor: Univ. Mich. Press
55. Fjellman SM. 1992. *Vinyl Leaves: Walt Disney World and America.* Boulder, CO: Westview
56. Foner N. 1987. *New Immigrants in New York.* New York: Columbia Univ. Press
57. Fong TP. 1995. *The First Suburban Chinatown: The Remaking of Monterey Park, California.* Philadelphia: Temple Univ. Press
58. Fox R. 1972. Rational and romance in urban anthropology. *Urban Anthropol.* 1: 205–33
59. Fox R. 1977. *Urban Anthropology: Cities in Their Cultural Settings.* Englewood Cliffs, NJ: Prentice Hall
60. Friedmann J. 1995. Where we stand: a decade of world city research. In *World Cities in a World System,* ed. PL Knox, PJ Taylor, pp. 21–47. Cambridge: Cambridge Univ. Press
61. George L. 1992. *No Crystal Stair: African-Americans in the City of the Angels.* London: Verso
62. Georges E. 1992. Gender, class, and migration in the Dominican Republic: women's experiences in a transnational community. See Ref. 215, pp. 81–100
63. Giddens A. 1990. *The Consequences of Modernity.* Stanford, CA: Stanford Univ. Press
64. Gill L. 1994. *Precarious Dependencies: Gender, Class and Domestic Service in Bolivia.* New York: Columbia Univ. Press
65. Ginsburg F. 1991. Indigenous media: Faustian bargain or global village? *Cult. Anthropol.* 6:95–114
66. Gluckman M. 1971. Preface to 2nd edition. In *Family and Social Network,* by E Bott, pp. xiii–xxx. New York: Free Press

67. Goode J, Schneider JA. 1994. *Reshaping Ethinic and Racial Relations in Philadelphia: Immigrants in a Divided City.* Philadelphia: Temple Univ. Press

67a. Gounis K. 1992. Temporality and the domestication of homelessness. See Ref. 205, pp. 127-49

68. Greenbaum SD. 1993. Housing abandonment in inner-city black neighborhoods: a case study of the effects of the dual housing market. See Ref. 197, pp. 139-56

69. Gregory S. 1992. The changing significance of race and class in an African-American community. *Am. Ethnol.* 19: 255-74

70. Guildin GE. 1989. The invisible hinterland: Hong Kong's reliance on Southern Guangdong Province. *City Soc.* 3:23-39

71. Guildin GE. 1992. *Urbanizing China.* New York: Greenwood Press

72. Guildin GE, Southall A. 1993. *Urban Anthropology in China.* Leiden: Brill

73. Gulick J. 1989. *The Humanity of Cities: An Introduction to Urban Societies.* Granby, MA: Bergin & Garvey

74. Hamabata MM. 1990. *Crested Kimono: Power and Love in the Japanese Business Family.* Ithaca: Cornell Univ. Press

75. Hannerz U. 1980. *Exploring the City.* New York: Columbia Univ. Press

76. Hannerz U. 1992. *Cultural Complexity: Studies in the Social Organization of Meaning.* New York: Columbia Univ. Press

77. Harrison FV. 1989. Drug trafficking in world capitalism: a perspective on Jamaican posses in the US. *Soc. Justice* 16: 115-31

78. Harrison FV. 1991. Women in Jamaica's urban informal economy: insights from a Kingston slum. In *Third World Women and the Politics of Feminism,* ed. CT Mohanty, A Russo, L Torres, pp. 173-96. Bloomington: Indiana Univ. Press

79. Harvey D. 1990. *The Condition of Postmodernity: An Enquiry into the Origins of Cultural Change.* Cambridge: Blackwell

80. Hayden D. 1995. *The Power of Place.* Cambridge, MA: MIT Press

81. Herzog LA. 1991. The transfrontier organization of space along the US-Mexico border. *Geoforum* 22:255-69

82. Holston J. 1989. *The Modernist City: An Anthropological Critique of Brasília.* Chicago: Chicago Univ. Press

83. Holston J. 1991. The misrule of law: land and usurpation in Brazil. *Comp. Stud. Soc. Hist.* 33:695-725

84. Holston J. 1995. Spaces of insurgent citizenship. *Plan. Theory* 13:35-51

85. Holston J, Appadurai A. 1996. Cities and citizenship. *Public Cult.* 8:187-204

86. Hopper K. 1991. Symptoms, survival and the redefinition of public space. *Urban Anthropol.* 20:155-75

87. Horton J. 1995. *The Politics of Diversity: Immigration, Resistance and Change in Monterey Park, California.* Philadelphia: Temple Univ. Press

88. Jackson P. 1985. Urban ethnography. *Prog. Hum. Geogr.* 10:157-76

89. Jacobs J. 1993. The city unbound: qualitative approaches to the city. *Urban Stud.* 30:827-48

90. Jameson F. 1984. Post-modernism, or the cultural logic of late capitalism. *New Left Rev.* 146:53-92

91. Jankowski MS. 1991. *Islands in the Street: Gangs and American Urban Society.* Berkeley: Univ. Calif. Press

92. Jankowiak W. 1993. *Sex, Death, and Hierarchy in a Chinese City.* New York: Columbia Univ. Press

93. Jones DJ. 1993. The culture of achievement among the poor: the case of mothers and children in a Head Start program. *Crit. Anthropol.* 13:247-66

94. Jones DJ, Turner JT. 1989. Housing and the material basis of social reproduction: political conflict and the quality of life in New York city. See Ref. 134, pp. 13-42

95. Jones DJ, Turner JT, Montbach J. 1992. Declining social services and the threat to social reproduction: an urban dilemma. *City Soc.* 6:99-114

96. Kadushin C, Jones DJ. 1992. Social networks and urban neighborhoods in New York City. *City Soc.* 6:58-75

97. Kaljee LM, Stanton B, Ricardo I, Whitehead TL. 1995. Urban African American adolescents and their parents: perceptions of violence within and against their communities. *Hum. Organ.* 54:363-72

98. Kaplan T. 1992. *Red City, Blue Period: Social Movements in Picasso's Barcelona.* Berkeley: Univ. Calif. Press

99. Kasarda J, Crenshaw EM. 1991. Third world urbanization: dimensions, theories, and determinants. *Annu. Rev. Sociol.* 17: 467-501

100. Kasinitz P. 1992. *Caribbean New York: Black Immigrants and the Politics of Race.* Ithaca, NY: Cornell Univ. Press

101. Katz C. 1993. Growing girls/closing circles: limits on the spaces of knowing in rural Sudan and United States cities. In *Full Circles: Geographies of Women over the Life Course,* ed. C Katz, J Monk, pp. 88-106. London: Routledge

102. Keith M, Cross M. 1993. *Race, the City and the State.* New York: Routledge

103. Kelly MPF. 1993. Rethinking citizenship in the global village: reflections on immigrants and the underclass. New York: Russell Sage Found. Work. Pap. 38

104. Kelly MPF. 1993. Towanada's triumph: unfolding the meanings of adolescent pregnancy in the Baltimore ghetto. New York: Russell Sage Found. Work. Pap. 40

105. Kemper RV. 1991. Trends in urban anthropological research: an analysis of the journal *Urban Anthropology. Urban Anthropol.* 10:373–503

106. Kemper RV. 1993. Urban anthropology: an analysis of trends in US and Canadian dissertations. *Urban Anthropol.* 22:1–215

107. King AD. 1990. *Urbanism, Colonialism and the World Economy: Culture and Spatial Foundations of the Urban World System.* New York: Routledge

108. King AD. 1995. Writing colonial space: a review article. *Comp. Stud. Soc. Hist.* 37: 541–54

109. King AD. 1996. *Re-presenting the City.* London: Macmillan

110. Kondo D. 1990. *Crafting Selves: Power, Gender, and Discourse.* Chicago: Univ. Chicago Press

111. Koptiuch K. 1991. Third worldizing at home. *Soc. Text* 9:87–99

112. Kugelmass J. 1994. *The Greenwich Village Halloween Parade.* New York: Columbia Univ. Press

113. Kwong P. 1987. *The New Chinatown.* New York: Hill & Wang

114. Laguerre MS. 1994. Headquarters and subsidiaries: Haitian immigrant family households in New York City. In *Families in the United States: A Multicultural Perspective,* ed. RL Taylor, pp. 47–61. Englewood Cliffs, NJ: Prentice-Hall

115. Laguerre MS. 1994. *The Informal City.* New York: St. Martin's Press

116. Lamphere L. 1992. *Structuring Diversity: Ethnographic Perspectives on the New Immigration.* Chicago: Univ. Chicago Press

117. Lawrence D. 1992. Transcendence of place: the role of La Placeta in Valencia's Las Fallas. See Ref. 4, pp. 211–30

118. Lebra RS. 1993. *Above the Clouds: Status Culture of the Modern Japanese Nobility.* Berkeley: Univ. Calif. Press

119. Leeds A. 1973. Locality power in relation to supralocal power institutions. In *Urban Anthropology,* ed. A Southall, pp. 15–41. New York: Oxford Univ. Press

120. Leone MP. 1995. A historical archaeology of capitalism. *Am. Anthropol.* 97:251–68

121. Lessinger J. 1992. Investing or going home? A transnational strategy among Indian immigrants in the United States. See Ref. 215, pp. 53–80

122. Levy R. 1990. *Mesocosm: Hinduism and the Organization of a Traditional Newar City in Nepal.* Berkeley: Univ. Calif. Press

123. Liebow EB. 1989. Category or community? Measuring urban Indian social cohesion with network sampling. *J. Ethn. Stud.* 16:76–100

124. Liebow EB. 1991. Urban Indian institutions in Phoenix: transformation from headquarters city to community. *J. Ethn. Stud.* 18:1–27

125. Linger DT. 1992. *Dangerous Encounters: Meanings of Violence in a Brazilian City.* Stanford, CA: Stanford Univ. Press

126. Lobo S. 1983. *A House of my Own: Social Organization in the Squatter Settlements of Lima, Peru.* Tucson: Univ. Ariz. Press

127. Logan K. 1984. *Haciendo Pueblo: The Development of a Guadalajaran Suburb.* University: Univ. Ala. Press

128. Lomnitz LA. 1977. *Networks and Marginality: Life in a Mexican Shantytown.* New York: Academic

128a. Lovell A. 1992. Seizing the moment: power, contingency, and the temporality in street life. See Ref. 205, pp. 86–107

129. Low SM. 1988. Housing organization and social change: a comparison of programs for urban reconstruction in Guatemala City. *Hum. Organ.* 47:15–24

130. Low SM. 1993. Cultural meaning of the plaza: the history of the Spanish American gridplan-plaza urban design. See Ref. 197, pp. 75–94

131. Low SM. 1995. Indigenous architecture and the Spanish American Plaza in Mesoamerica and the Caribbean. *Am. Anthropol.* 97:748–62

132. Low SM. 1996. A response to Castells: an anthropology of the city. *Crit. Anthropol.* 16:57–62

133. Low SM. 1996. Spatializing culture: the social production and social construction of public space. *Am. Ethnol.* In press

134. Low SM, Chambers E. 1989. *Housing, Culture, and Design: A Comparative Perspective.* Philadelphia: Univ. Pa. Press

135. Lynch O. 1994. Urban anthropology, postmodernist cities, and perspectives. *City Soc. Annu. Rev.* 1994:35–52

136. Lynch O. 1996. Contesting and contested identities: Mathura's chaubes. In *Narratives of Agency: Self-making in China, India and Japan,* ed. W Dissanayake, pp. 74–103. Minneapolis: Univ. Minn. Press

137. MacGaffey J. 1987. *Entrepreneurs and Parasites: The Struggle for Indigenous Capitalism in Zaire.* Cambridge: Cambridge Univ. Press

138. Macleod AE. 1991. *Accommodating Protest: Working Women, the New Veiling and Change in Cairo.* New York: Columbia Univ. Press

139. Mahler SJ. 1995. *American Dreaming: Immigrant Life on the Margins.* Princeton, NJ: Princeton Univ. Press

140. Marcus G, Myers FR. 1995. *The Traffic in Culture: Refiguring Art and Anthropology.* Berkeley: Univ. Calif. Press

141. Margolis ML. 1994. *Little Brazil: An Ethnography of Brazilian Immigrants in New*

York City. Princeton, NJ: Princeton Univ. Press

142. Markowitz F. 1993. *A Community in Spite of Itself: Soviet Jewish Emigre in New York.* Washington, DC: Smithson. Inst. Press

143. Marris P. 1962. *Family and Social Change in an African City: A Study of Rehousing in Lagos.* Boston: Northwestern Univ. Press

144. Marris P. 1995. Knowledge and persuasion: research at ICS. In *Young at Eighty: The Prolific Public Life of Michael Young,* ed. G Gench, T Flower, K Gavron, pp. 75–83. Manchester: Carcanet

145. Martin E. 1996. Flexible bodies in a society of flows. *Crit. Anthropol.* 16:49–56

146. Massey D. 1994. *Space, Place, and Gender.* Minneapolis: Univ. Minn. Press

147. Massey D, Denton N. 1993. *American Apartheid: Segregation and the Making of the Underclass.* Cambridge, MA: Harvard Univ. Press

148. McDonogh GW. 1991. Discourses of the city: urban problems and urban planning. *City Soc.* 5:40–63

149. McDonogh GW. 1993. *Black and Catholic in Savannah, Georgia.* Knoxville: Univ. Tenn Press

150. McDonogh GW. 1993. The geography of emptiness. See Ref. 197, pp. 3–16

151. Merry S. 1990. *Getting Justice and Getting Even.* Chicago: Univ. Chicago Press

152. Merry S. 1993. Mending walls and building fences: constructing the private neighborhood. *J. Leg. Plur.* 33:71–90

153. Minigione E. 1993. The new urban poverty and the underclass. *Int. J. Urban Reg. Res.* 17:319–428

154. Mitchell T. 1988. *Colonizing Egypt.* Cambridge: Cambridge Univ. Press

155. Mollenkopf J, Castells M. 1991. *Dual City: Restructuring New York.* New York: Russell Sage Found.

156. Moore SF. 1994. *Anthropology and Africa: Changing Perspectives on a Changing Scene.* Charlottesville/London: Univ. Press Va.

157. Mullings L. 1987. *Cities of the United States: Studies in Urban Anthropology.* New York: Columbia Univ. Press

158. Myers F. 1994. Culture-making: performing aboriginality at the Asia society gallery. *Am. Ethnol.* 21:679–99

159. Nash J. 1989. *From Tank Town to High Tech: The Clash of Community and Industrial Cycles.* Albany: South. Univ. NY Press

160. Newman KS. 1992. Culture and structure in *The Truly Disadvantaged. City Soc.* 6: 3–25

161. Newman KS. 1993. *Declining Fortunes: The Withering of the American Dream.* New York: Basic Books

162. Newman KS. 1996. Working poor: low wage employment in the lives of Harlem youth. In *Transitions through Adolescence: Interpersonal Domains and Context,* ed. JJ Graber, A Peterson. New York: Erlbaum

163. Newman KS. 1996. Place and race: midlife experience in Harlem. In *The Idea of Middle Age,* ed. R Shweder. Chicago: Univ. Chicago Press

163a. *New York Times.* 1996. A toll road in California offers a high-tech answer to traffic. Jan. 2, pp. A1, C33

164. Norkunas M. 1993. *The Politics of Public Memory.* Albany: South. Univ. NY Press

165. O'Connor RA. 1990. Place, power and discourse in the Thai image of Bangkok. *J. Siam Soc.* 78:61–73

166. Ogbu J. 1991. *Minority Status and Schooling.* New York: Garland

167. Oliver-Smith A. 1986. *The Martyred City: Death and Rebirth in the Andes.* Albuquerque: Univ. NM Press

168. Ong A. 1987. *Spirits of Resistance and Capitalist Discipline.* Albany: South. Univ. NY Press

169. Ong A. 1992. Limits to cultural accumulation: Chinese capitalists on the American Pacific Rim. See Ref. 215, pp. 125–44

170. Page H, Thomas RB. 1994. White public space and the construction of white privilege in US health care: fresh concepts and a new model of analysis. *Med. Anthropol. Q.* 81:109–16

171. Pappas G. 1989. *The Magic City: Unemployment in a Working-Class Community.* Ithaca, NY: Cornell Univ. Press

172. Parish SM. 1994. *Moral Knowing in a Hindu Sacred City: An Exploration of Mind, Emotion, and Self.* New York: Columbia Univ. Press

173. Park R, Burgess E. 1974. *The City.* Chicago: Univ. Chicago Press

174. Peattie LR. 1972. *The View from the Barrio.* Ann Arbor: Univ. Mich. Press

175. Peattie LR. 1987. *Planning: Rethinking Ciudad Guyana.* Ann Arbor: Univ. Mich. Press

176. Peil M. 1991. *Lagos: The City is the People.* Boston: Hall

177. Pellow D. 1991. Chieftaincy and the evolution of an Accra *zongo. Ethnohistory* 38: 414–50

178. Pellow D. 1993. Chinese privacy. See Ref. 197, pp. 31–46

179. Pellow D. 1996. *Setting Boundaries: The Anthropology of Spatial and Social Organization.* Amherst: Bergin & Garvey

180. Pessar P. 1995. The elusive enclave: ethnicity, class and nationality among Latino entrepreneurs in greater Washington, DC. *Hum. Organ.* 54:383–92

181. Plotnicov L. 1987. The political economy of skyscrapers: an anthropological intro-

duction to advanced industrial cities. *City Soc.* 1:35–51

182. Portes A, Schauffler R. 1994. Language and the second generation: bilingualism yesterday and today. *Int. Migr. Rev.* 28: 641–61

183. Portes A, Stepick A. 1993. *City on the Edge: The Transformation of Miami.* Berkeley: Univ. Calif. Press

184. Portes A, Zhou M. 1993. The new second generation: segmented assimilation and its variants. *Ann. Am. Acad. Polit. Soc. Sci.* 530:74–96

185. Pred A. 1992. Languages of everyday practice and resistance: Stockholm at the end of the nineteenth century. In *Reworking Modernity,* ed. A Pred, M Watts, pp. 118–54. New Brunswick, NJ: Rutgers Univ. Press

186. Rabinow P. 1989. *French Modern: Norms and Forms of Missionary and Didactic Pathos.* Cambridge, MA: MIT Press

187. Ram N. 1995. *Beyond Ambedkar: Essays on Dalits in India.* New Delhi: Har-Anand

188. Rao MSA, Bhatt C, Khadekar LN. 1991. *A Reader in Urban Sociology.* Delhi: Orient Longman. 2nd ed.

189. Reeves EB. 1995. Power, resistance and the cult of Muslim saints in a northern Egyptian town. *Am. Ethnol.* 22:306–23

190. Repak TA. 1995. *Waiting on Washington: Central American Workers in the Nation's Capital.* Philadelphia: Temple Univ. Press

191. Robertson J. 1991. *Native and Newcomer: Making and Remaking a Japanese City.* Berkeley: Univ. Calif. Press

192. Rodman MC, Cooper M. 1995. Housing cultural difference: questions of power and space in developing Canadian nonprofits and co-ops. *Can. J. Urban Res.* June

192a. Rosenzweig R, Blackmar E. 1992. *The Park and the People: A History of Central Park.* Ithaca, NY: Cornell Univ. Press

193. Rotenberg R. 1992. *Time and Order in Metropolitan Vienna.* Washington, DC: Smithson. Inst. Press

194. Rotenberg R. 1993. On the salubrity of sites. See Ref. 197, pp. 17–30

195. Rotenberg R. 1995. *Landscape and Power in Metropolitan Vienna.* Baltimore: Johns Hopkins Press

196. Rotenberg R. 1996. The metropolis and everyday life. In *Urban Life,* ed. G Gmelch, WP Zenner, pp. 60–81. Prospect Heights, IL: Waveland

197. Rotenberg R, McDonogh GW. 1993. *The Cultural Meaning of Urban Space.* Westport, CT: Bergin & Garvey

198. Deleted in proof

199. Rothstein FA, Blim ML. 1991. *Anthropology and the Global Factory: Studies of the New Industrialization in the Late Twentieth Century.* New York: Bergin & Garvey

200. Ruble B. 1992. Reshaping the city: the politics of property in a provincial Russian city. *Urban Anthropol.* 21:203–33

201. Ruddick S. 1996. *Young and Homeless in Hollywood: Mapping Social Identities.* New York: Routledge

202. Rutheiser C. 1993. Mapping contested terrains: schoolrooms and streetcorners in urban Belize. See Ref. 197, pp. 103–20

203. Rutheiser C. 1996. Making public space in a nonplace urban realm: "re-vitalizing" Olympia Atlanta. *Urban Anthropol.* In press

204. Rutheiser C. 1996. *Imagineering Atlanta: The Politics of Place in the City of Dreams.* New York: Verso

205. Rutz HJ, ed. 1992. *The Politics of Time.* Washington, DC: Am. Anthropol. Assoc.

206. Sacks KB. 1996. *Race, Class, Gender and the Jewish Question.* New Brunswick, NJ: Rutgers Univ. Press

207. Safa HI. 1986. Urbanization, the informal economy, and state policy in Latin America. *Urban Anthropol.* 15:135–63

208. Sanjek R. 1990. Urban anthropology in the 1980's: a world view. *Annu. Rev. Anthropol.* 19:151–86

209. Sanjek R. 1994. *Cities, Classes, and the Social Order: Anthony Leeds.* Ithaca, NY: Cornell Univ. Press

210. Sassen S. 1991. *The Global City: New York, London, Tokyo.* Princeton, NJ: Princeton Univ. Press

211. Sassen S. 1995. The state and the global city: notes towards a conception of place-centered governance. *Compet. Change* 1: 31–50

212. Sassen S. 1996. Whose city is it? Globalization and the formation of new claims. *Public Cult.* 8:205–24

213. Scheper-Hughes N. 1992. *Death Without Weeping: The Violence of Everyday Life in Brazil.* Berkeley: Univ. Calif. Press

214. Deleted in proof

215. Schiller NG, Basch L, Blanc-Szanton C. 1992. *Towards a Transnational Perspective on Migration: Race, Class, Ethnicity and Nationalism Reconsidered.* New York: NY Acad. Sci.

216. Sennett R. 1994. *Flesh and Stone: The Body and the City in Western Civilization.* New York: Norton

217. Shokeid M. 1995. *Gay Synagogue in New York.* New York: Columbia Univ. Press

218. Sieber RT. 1990. Selecting a new past: emerging definitions of heritage in Boston Harbor. *J. Urban Cult. Stud.* 1:101–22

219. Sieber RT. 1991. Waterfront revitalization in postindustrial port cities of North America. *City Soc.* 5:120–36

220. Smart A. 1995. Hong Kong's slums and squatters areas: a development perspective. In *Housing the Urban Poor,* ed. BC

Aldrich, RS Sandhu, pp. 97–111. New Delhi: Staar
221. Smart J. 1989. *The Political Economy of Street Hawkers in Hong Kong.* Hong Kong: Cent. Asian Stud.
222. Smith N. 1984. *Uneven Development: Nature, Capital and the Production of Space.* Oxford: Blackwell
223. Smith N, Katz C. 1993. Grounding metaphor: towards a spatialized politics. In *Place and the Politics of Identity,* ed. M Keith, S Pile, pp. 67–83. London: Routledge
224. Soja E. 1989. *Postmodern Geographies: The Reassertation of Space in Critical Social Theory.* New York: Verso
224a. Sorkin M, ed. 1992. *Variations on a Theme Park.* New York: Noonday
225. Spain D. 1992. *Gendered Spaces.* Chapel Hill: Univ. NC Press
226. Stack C. 1974. *All Our Kin: Strategies for Survival in a Black Community.* New York: Harper & Row
227. Stack C. 1996. *Call to Home: African Americans Reclaim the Rural South.* New York: Basic Books
228. Stull D. 1990. When the packers came to town: changing ethnic relations in Garden City, Kansas. *Urban Anthropol.* 19: 303–425
229. Stull D, Broadway MJ, Griffith D. 1995. *Any Way You Cut It: Meat Processing and Small-Town America.* Lawrence: Univ. Kans. Press
230. Sumihara N. 1993. A case study of cross-cultural interaction in a Japanese multinational corporation in the United States. In *Diversity and Differences in Organizations,* ed. RR Sims, RF Denneby, pp. 136–47. Westport, CT: Quorum Books
231. Susser I. 1982. *Norman Street.* New York: Oxford Univ. Press
232. Susser I. 1991. The separation of mothers and children. See Ref. 156, pp. 207–24
233. Susser I. 1993. Creating family forms: the exclusion of men and teenage boys in the New York City shelter system 1987–1991. *Crit. Anthropol.* 13:267–85
234. Susser I. 1996. Anthropological perspectives on the informational society. *Crit. Anthropol.* 16:39–48
235. Sutton CR, Chaney EM. 1987. *Caribbean Life in New York City.* Staten, NY: Cent. Migr. Stud.
236. Taylor C. 1994. *The Black Churches in Brooklyn.* New York: Columbia Univ. Press
237. Wacquant LJD. 1993. Urban outcastes: Sigman and division in the black American ghetto and the French urban periphery. *Int. J. Urban Reg. Res.* 17:366–83

238. Wacquant LJD. 1994. The new urban color line: the state and fate of the ghetto in postfordist America. In *Social Theory and the Politics of Identity,* ed. C Calhoun, pp. 231–76. Oxford: Blackwell
239. Wacquant LJD. 1995. Dangerous places: violence and isolation in Chicago's black belt and the Parisian red belt. In *Urban Poverty and Family Life in Chicago's Inner City,* ed. WJ Wilson. Oxford: Oxford Univ. Press
240. Wacquant LJD, Wilson WJ. 1989. The cost of racial and class exclusion in the inner city. *Ann. Am. Acad. Polit. Soc. Sci.* 501: 8–25
241. Wallerstein I. 1990. Culture as the ideological battleground of the modern world-system. *Theory Cult. Soc.* 7:31–56
242. Waterson A. 1993. *Street Addicts in the Political Economy.* Philadelphia: Temple Univ. Press
243. Watts M. 1996. Islamic modernities? Citizenship, civil society and Islamism in a Nigerian city. *Public Cult.* 8:251–90
244. Weibel-Orlando J. 1991. *Indian Country, L.A.: Maintaining Ethnic Community in Complex Society.* Urbana: Univ. Ill. Press
245. White J. 1994. *Money Makes Us Relatives: Women's Labor in Urban Turkey.* Austin: Univ. Tex. Press
246. Williams B. 1992. Poverty among African Americans in the urban United States. *Hum. Organ.* 51:164–74
247. Williams B. 1996. "There goes the neighborhood": gentrification, displacement and homelessness in Washington, DC. In *There's No Place Like Home: Poverty and Homelessness in America,* ed. AL deHavenon, pp. 172–91. Westport, CT/London: Bergin & Garvey
248. Wilson E. 1991. *The Sphinx in the City: Urban Life, the Control of Disorder, and Women.* Berkeley: Univ. Calif. Press
249. Wright G. 1991. *The Politics of Design in French Colonial Urbanism.* Chicago: Univ. Chicago Press
250. Young M, Willmott P. 1957. *Family and Kinship in East London.* Middlesex: Penguin
251. Zenner W. 1994. Nominalism and essentialism in urban anthropology. *City Soc. Annu. Rev.* 1994:53–66
252. Zhou M. 1992. *Chinatown: The Socioeconomic Potential of an Urban Enclave.* Philadelphia: Temple Univ. Press
253. Zukin S. 1991. *Landscapes of Power: From Detroit to Disney World.* Berkeley: Univ. Calif. Press
254. Zukin S. 1995. *The Cultures of Cities.* Cambridge: Blackwell

Annu. Rev. Anthropol. 1996. 25:411–35

THE CONSTRUCTION OF POVERTY AND HOMELESSNESS IN US CITIES

I. Susser

Anthropology Department, Hunter College, City University of New York, 695 Park Avenue, New York, NY, 10021

KEY WORDS: underclass, increasing inequality, poor households, gender conflict, inner city

ABSTRACT

The review focuses on analyses of the creation of culture among poor populations in the United States whose lives have been structured by residing at the center of the global economy. Literature is examined concerning the changing construction of labor, space, time, and identity in the new poverty. Throughout, the review examines the generation of poverty and questions of gender, race, political mobilization, and resistance. This outline of current research provides a framework for an analysis of the violence and conflict generated by the lowering of wages and the reduction of leisure time.

Introduction

As poverty increases worldwide and the gap between rich and poor grows ever greater, the poor have become invisible, marginalized, or excluded from public view. This change has been little considered in the anthropological literature (156, 245). While there has been some significant research in the field (see below), the level of interest has yet to reflect the increasing inequality and poverty generated within the global economy of advanced capitalism.

While the immiseration of the American worker, deindustrialization, and the shift to service industries are everywhere reported, theory about growing poor populations in the midst of corporate wealth is less common. As large populations in Africa, Latin America, and other areas are consigned to sweat-shop conditions; below-subsistence wages; and a decline in already inadequate health, sanitation, and social services, theories of advanced capitalism have

0084-6570/96/1015-0411$08.00

411

focused on the growth of cyberspace, tourism and shifting worlds, identities, and perceptions. While identifying these issues as theoretical challenges, anthropologists have rarely viewed the increasing poverty among both urban and rural populations as requiring the same level of analysis.

Homeless populations in the United States are not large, according to the general census (26, 87, 89–91, 96, 123). However, they are one of the few highly visible and public signs of the increasing poverty of millions of Americans. They have emerged as a symbol of the new poverty in the United States (84–86, 141, 201, 247). Political concern for housing the homeless, or at least removing them from the streets and subways, stems from the need to make the increasing inequality to which the majority of the residents are subject invisible, individual, and private (141, 142, 201). Consequently, studies of the homeless in the United States address how poverty is represented as well as how the poor are treated and the way they live their lives.

Recent concerns about the so-called underclass must be viewed in the same context. While the underclass constitutes only about 11% of the poor population of the United States (33), literature about the underclass by sociologists, psychologists, political scientists, educators, social workers, and health providers constitutes by far the largest proportion of research about poverty in this country in the past decade (4, 33, 41, 44, 97–99, 101, 103, 105, 106, 134, 156, 172, 219, 234–237, 245, 246, 249, 253). Once again, this group may be more visible and more subject to public scrutiny. Almost by definition members of the underclass are in direct conflict with public institutions, either through substance abuse, the criminal justice system, mental institutions, foster care, vagrancy and homelessness, or at the very least in their need for public assistance (4, 33, 219). Other poor people who manage to avoid interaction with public institutions are labeled the "deserving" poor and are left out of discussions of the underclass. This distinction between the deserving and the undeserving poor is an old one and can be traced back several hundred years (175, 234). In social science its roots may be found in familiar categories such as the "hardliving" poor, whose lives contrast with those apparently able to maintain middle-class norms more successfully (95, 179). Such disparaging contrasts were criticized in ethnographies of the late 1960s and early 1970s that demonstrated the situational basis for "hustling" and many of the other characteristics described as "hardliving" norms (121, 203, 231).

Concerning poverty in the global economy and its place in current theories of advanced capitalism, we can identify two opposing conceptualizations of the poor in the postmodern world, or the new world "disorder" (30). First, there is the view that the poor are irrelevant to the global economy. Not only are the poor invisible, but their labor is no longer viewed as necessary. Deindustrialization in the core countries is a reflection of a decreasing need for manual workers worldwide, which presages a reduction in the needed work force to fewer, more highly educated people who will be involved in the new informational technology. Low-skilled service workers will still be necessary but not in the numbers of the previously industrialized work force. The export of industry to poorer countries represents not only a search for cheaper labor but also an overall reduction in the central importance of that labor within world capitalism. Thus, from this theoretical perspective, the structural adjustment policies of the International Monetary Fund and similar policies pursued in the United States and Europe result from an abandonment of populations whose labor and health is no longer necessary to production in the global economy (29, 30, 186, 221).

The opposing view is that labor in industrial production is still crucial and central to the global economy. However, the export of production from the center to the less media-visible periphery, and the development of the informational service economy, is an outright assault on working-class populations. The departure of industry from the strongly unionized welfare states that constituted the core of modern capitalism represents the ongoing search for cheaper, weaker, unorganized labor associated with less regulated state intervention. This is one more step in the battle for control of production and the extraction of profit (16, 68, 69). In addition, the shift to hiring more women, as well as the creation of an uneven post-Fordist work force in the United States and parts of Europe, can be incorporated into this argument (13, 82, 153, 178).

While the first view implies that many workers are no longer needed and that massive populations of poverty are a drain on and a threat to nation-states and the world economy, the second view suggests a massive reserve army of labor—the poor—that depresses all workers' wages. This reserve army is available to be integrated into the work force and then to be discarded in relation to the needs of the global economy (234).

To assess the adequacy of these two views, we need to consider what in fact constitutes an effective reserve work force at different historical periods with different effects on inequality, poverty, and social welfare (15, 195, 225). Nation-states, employers, and working-class movements define differently over time the categories of people available to work. As social programs and regulations shift, so too do the people who can be viewed as reserve labor. For certain historical periods in the United States, women, children, and the elderly have been legislated out of the work force. At other times they have been recruited to fill employment needs. Such changes can be perceived in the history of laws about child labor, in protective legislation for women, and in the conflicting and historically fluid approaches of feminists, unions, and the state to such regulation (107, 140, 182). Massive social upheaval by people demanding work and security for the aged during the Great Depression led to the introduction of mandatory retirement through the Social Security Act of 1935 (157). The abolition of mandatory retirement in the 1990s and current incentives for early retirement in the face of downsizing of corporations and other institutions such as hospitals and universities illuminate how broader political issues interact with the characterization of a work force.

Changing patterns of prisons, military recruitment strategies, the enforcement of immigration laws, and societal handling of the mentally ill and definitions of mental illness, institutional labor, slavery, indentured servitude, and racial discrimination are other areas where the availability of labor and its cost are periodically redefined (38, 46, 69, 84–86, 103, 165, 170, 171, 244, 245). Thus, cultural definitions of available labor are historically produced by nation-states, class conflict, and social movements. Such constructions of legitimate dependency and community responsibility, institutionalized in state regulation and cultural expectations of age, gender, and other social identities, constrain the ability of industries to lower wages by hiring indiscriminately the least-protected workers.

Consequently, we can view the departure of industries from core industrialized countries not according to problematic ethnocentric notions of deindustrialization but as an expansion of the industrial work force. Workers in areas previously restricted to agriculture and the extraction of raw materials have been recategorized as candidates for industrial employment. In particular, these new developments target women as industrial workers. These women are some of the least-protected workers in international labor. They are frequently subordinated, sometimes assaulted in their own households, historically excluded from most forms of paid employment and education, and situated in the poorest regions of the world (13, 47, 50, 154, 158, 178, 208). This massive expansion in the incorporation of global labor, the breakdown of household definitions of gendered labor (75, 117, 157, 205, 217), and the increasing gender-specific patterns of immigration from poorer countries to the core (54, 58, 226) must be carefully considered before theorists accept arguments based on a reduction in the need for labor as a result of the informational technology of advanced capitalism.

Since the early twentieth century, the routines of Fordism included the concept of a "fair day's wage." Fordism was predicated on the maintenance of a presumed nuclear household, the reinforcement of specific gendered interactions, and enforcement of segmented hiring patterns that traced and retraced ethnic and racial hierarchies (1, 60, 70, 71, 82, 114, 144, 145, 165, 171). Class conflict under Fordism produced unions that fought successfully for an expanded social wage, job security, occupational safety, health benefits, and seniority policies. Nevertheless, industrial unions were themselves threaded with the racial and sexual presuppositions of corporate hegemony, as well as refutations of such ideology (7, 31, 37, 78, 176, 177, 182). Today we find flexible accumulation accompanied by a growing informal economy, enfeebled unions, less security for most workers [including middle-income professionals (155)], the shrinking of the welfare state, and escalating poverty (82, 101, 120, 128, 166, 187, 236). Under these conditions the hegemonic construction of the white male worker that was encoded as part of the charter of industrial unions has collapsed. Unions were weakened by their own failure to incorporate different visions of race, gender, and the poor of the developed and underdeveloped worlds into the voices of class conflict (6, 31, 60, 82, 83, 182). The definition of who could work was changed by the export of industry, and the work force was expanded to include women and members of poor third-world nations. As a result, unions centered in the urban heartland of capitalism and based on the gendering and racial discrimination of Fordism were unequipped to fight the destruction of their standard of living. This is the context in which poverty becomes central to workers in core countries and the periphery in the twenty-first century.

Theoretical Approaches to Reinvention of the Social Order

What concepts have social researchers and more specifically, anthropologists offered in understanding the new social order and poverty and homelessness? Within the metropoles there are ethnographic studies of the effects of deindustrialization and the shift to a service economy (151, 159, 202, 211). Some of the most graphic and penetrating studies of the new poverty concern health and disease in the United States (10, 108, 118, 160, 196, 198, 210). Among third-world workers there are studies of the new industries, which are often situated in marginal environments—borderlands—outside the regulatory control of specific nation-states and which are thus able to avoid established patterns of class conflict and state compromise (13, 50, 153, 154, 158, 178, 212, 218, 233). Studies of transnationalism and migration both locally and transcontinentally, as well as the postmodern emphasis on shifting populations and travel, connect these two parallel examinations of poverty (106a, 116, 188, 205).

Recent research has promoted and stimulated a reexamination of the role of the ethnographer and his/her differentiation from those studied under currently shifting postmodern conditions both within anthropology and within the global economy, which are as many have noted, directly related (152). Finally, ethnographers have endeavored to represent the voices of the poor in the contemporary context.

Labor Shifts in the New Global Economy

The significance of low-paid employment and US deindustrialization in the creation of poverty and homelessness is well established (16, 45, 94, 102, 163,

237, 245). This perspective is frequently stated at the beginning and end of ethnographies about homelessness and urban poverty. However, because participant observation conducted over one to several years captures only immediate processes, it tends also to contribute to the reification of the instant in terms of identities and categories that occupy the space and time of the fieldwork. Poor people appear poor rather than unemployed or underemployed. Homeless people appear homeless rather than displaced. Even when the departure of industry can be documented and the rise in real estate costs traced, ethnographers seldom capture the before and after effects.

Several ethnographies document what might be termed the making of poverty in the United States: *From Tank Town to High Tech* (151), *Norman Street* (211), and *The Magic City* (159). These monographs describe the reduction of "stable" working-class households to poverty through the departure of industry and capture the impact of such changes on local politics, health, and general living conditions.

Poor communities are also forming among migrants without access to capital. New Asian immigrants, similar to Haitians, Mexicans, and others, are being recruited to fill the low-paid employment created by the new global economy (50, 67, 111, 115, 116, 168, 239, 250, 252, 253).

The shift toward hiring women service workers is also addressed in recent ethnographic research. *Caring by the Hour* documents the experiences of poor black women workers in a North Carolina city (181). Sacks documented the breadth of the women's work requirements, the limited options for promotion, and the participation of such previously excluded groups in political mobilization. Other ethnographies of the new low-paid service workers (162, 183, 202) portray a work force with reduced control, fewer benefits, and less security than is found in ethnographies of US labor from the 1950s through the 1970s (25). However, they belie earlier theories that women, because of the dual work day and their household responsibilities, would be unable or unwilling to mobilize around work concerns (7, 17, 215).

The core of the new US work force has become the low-paid worker outside the unions who lives either in the "postmodern" family or alone and also subordinated by gender, minority, and immigrant status (182). The potential of these groups for unionization or political mobilization constitutes one of the central questions in determining the directions of the new global economy.

Poverty and the Construction of Space in the New Global Economy

Global changes have not only affected the work place but the construction of space in the global economy as well. Class conflict in the United States since the 1950s has taken place in battles over the boundaries, services, and maintenance of working-class communities. Real estate decisions, housing discrimination, gentrification, and urban development policies structure the visibility of poverty and the experiences of the poor (130, 199, 200). As has been extensively demonstrated, poor neighborhoods reflect mortgage restrictions and a losing battle for scarce public services such as schools, road repair, and health care (27, 28, 150). The spatial construction of poverty is manifest in the division of communities. The destruction of housing for the building of expressways, the bypassing of public transportation, and the creation of suburban loans, enclosed shopping malls, and recreational centers epitomized by the much analyzed Disneyland/World phenomena separate middle-income purchasers from the poor (34, 193, 194, 256; see S Low, this volume). All of these semipublic environments marginalize the poor and represent areas of contestation over the resegregation of social interaction by class and income (2, 49, 184, 193, 194, 199, 241, 256).

Urban renewal policies followed by gentrification in the 1970s and 1980s have isolated the urban poor in enclosed and practically invisible communities (130, 200). Such invisible and relatively powerless communities concomitantly become sites of last resort for methadone clinics, housing for the mentally ill, and—partially as a consequence of the well-known phenomenon of Not In My Backyard (NIMBY)—industrial waste disposal plants (200). The separation of the poor has occurred more slowly in minority communities but may be increasing as minority members of the middle class find ways to enter better-off suburbs and city neighborhoods (235–237, 245).

Homeless people in the United States are significant not for their numbers but because they represent the incursions of increasing impoverishment into public space—particularly space occupied or desired by middle-income and even wealthy people (11, 12, 124, 125, 141, 142, 201). Homeless people frequent railroad stations, public parks, and public transportation. In New York City, they have set up covered shelters outside the United Nations. In Los Angeles, they congregate on the beaches of Venice (247). Unlike in Martin Luther King Jr's time, when the Poor People's March built a shantytown outside the White House, the homeless people in central tourist spots in Washington, DC; New York City; and San Francisco are not constructing their shelters to make a political point. The political point emerges from their visible need.

The poor have been generally excluded from cyberspace (29, 30, 79, 201, 222). As informational technology enwebs the household into the wider net of the corporation (29), the poor and homeless drop below the threshold of societal communications. However, the overall impact of these changes remains to be evaluated; some poor people have adapted new technologies to their own purposes (30, 79). Artists address the irony of homeless people in cyberspace in the creation of Poliscar, a vehicle for a homeless person to park on the street and live in that is equipped with information technology (201).

Time Out and Out of Time in the New Global Economy of Poverty

People's experience of time has changed in the new global economy. The categorization of time under capitalism was first raised by EP Thompson in his classic paper on nineteenth-century England (227). Since Thompson and others relate the defining of time precisely to emerging industrial employment, the changing forms of employment under post-Fordism might be expected to change the concepts and usage of time for the 1990s (48, 61, 82, 180).

Concepts and uses of time have become social markers in a class-stratified society. Oscar Lewis, in his culture of poverty description, discussed present orientation (119, 230), and others have used similar markers to define the underclass (4, 245). Such discussions also appear in the AIDS prevention literature: Homeless people's evaluation of their lifespan may be shorter and may reduce their commitment to efforts at HIV prevention through safer sex and clean needles (32, 196, 198, 223). Similarly, time is the ultimate issue in debates about teenage pregnancy and class-based fertility patterns (59, 207, 214).

Researchers argue that time created for and by homeless people takes on different meanings for the homeless than for the rest of the population. Poor people must keep institutional time requirements, yet when they arrive they must wait. This embodies the unequal power relationship between the poor and service providers (118, 211, 224, 230). Because poor women are the mediators between their households and institutional services, their experience of waiting and unequal control over time may be much greater than men's. In addition, since women are frequently responsible for the transport and needs of children and the organization of reciprocal kin networks based on the needs of many people with conflicting time requirements, they become less able to meet the time schedules of institutions whether they be employers, schools, or the welfare office (118, 211, 224, 230).

For the homeless, time is not usually determined by a regular work schedule, yet it is clearly constricted and defined by institutional events (72, 74, 124, 248). A reversal of time occurs among homeless people dependent on institutionalized work schedules for food and shelter. Many services for homeless people are staffed by employees who only work weekdays. On weekends, finding food and shelter is much more problematic, and homeless people are frequently alone, cold, and hungry, waiting for weekdays to restart their social life (72). A similar reversal occurs between night and day. Public places, lobbies, and hallways are used in the daytime by those with homes as they go to work or enter various commercial establishments. At night, homeless people repopulate coveted niches in the deserted central city (124). In another reversal, "seizing the moment" becomes more important for homeless people than maintaining reliable routines (124). Without routine employment and a paycheck, people must continually be ready to react to each random or unscheduled opportunity as it arises. As a result, institutional routines are flaunted, and homeless people are categorized by service-agency providers as unreliable and without concepts of time. As is so often the case, the social creation of behavior among the poor is treated as evidence of individual unworthiness. People who are homeless reconfigure both time and space as they negotiate survival (180, 238). Thus the new urban poverty carries with it time hierarchies, time resistance, and time restatement as part of the re-creation of class and inequality under global capitalism.

Re-Creating Gender in the Context of the Poverty and Homelessness of the New Global Economy

Poverty and homelessness are clearly gendered (71, 161, 192, 213, 215–219, 221–223). However, it is once again important to remain cautious of static and reified conceptions. Gender among US poor people in the 1990s is an area of open battle sometimes resulting in fatalities. Both men and women have restated, re-created, and resisted the stereotypical portraits of earlier periods.

Because employment, public assistance, social security, and credit differentiate experiences by gender, poverty and homelessness have always differed between men and women (1, 3, 71, 107, 140, 203, 205). However, entitlements, employment, and institutional constraints have also altered dramatically since the 1970s. The past two decades have witnessed crucial change and struggle in the definitions of gendered responsibilities by the state, in the expectations between men and women, and in the structuring of households.

Poor men and women share poverty and the responsibilities for households and children. While they may find common ground and common interest in relation to employment and state policies, even in these areas their opportunities and losses differ: Women may benefit from housing programs, while men may have more access to job training. In addition, men and women battle and are battered in struggles over household structure and control of children and resources. Relations between men and women are important determinants of the experiences of poverty and homelessness and need to be examined. We have to analyze the conflicts that run from the state through the household and the intensifying of those conflicts in the 1990s.

It is no longer sufficient to talk of male or female domination or subordination among poor people in the United States. Arenas of power for men are contradicted by other arenas of power or access to resources for women. The complexity of the interactions, rather than equalizing relations between men and women, often leads to escalating conflict.

Decades of Change: The Feminization of Poverty or the Disappearance of Men?

In the mid-1980s problems began to be formulated in terms of the "feminization of poverty" (192). As single-headed households became more common, the fact that working women earned less than men who might previously have supported the household, combined with the failure of many men to actually pay child support, resulted in a majority of households headed by women below the poverty line (44, 96, 245, 255). Concomitantly, there was an increase in the proportion of children being reared in poverty.

Along with the recognition of the feminization of poverty arose a focus on violence against women. A leading and rising cause of injury and death for women 15 years and older was violence from their male partners (77a). Ethnographies of the 1980s and 1990s document violence and fear, both of which need to be analyzed more systematically according to the changing experiences of men and women and changing expectations of gender (22, 136–138, 171, 189, 190, 205).

By the 1990s, concern began to center around the exclusion and disappearance of poor men (38, 161, 219). Rapidly increasing incarceration rates for poor and minority men, as well as growing disease and homicide rates, contributed to this formulation. Figures suggested that while men battered and brutalized women, men were more likely to kill one another. In addition, it became clear that poor men were excluded from public assistance funds, less likely to find employment, and less likely than poor and minority women to finish school.

Although the gendering of poverty was evident, the lives of poor men and women were so interconnected that the experience of each bore directly on the other. From the 1980s, as more men were excluded from employment and public assistance or disappeared through incarceration or death, more women became responsible for poor households (38, 96, 148, 245). In the light of these points of strain, domestic violence between men and women became a growing issue.

As noted above, it is not enough in the context of the new poverty to speak of one gender hierarchy. Eligibility for public assistance, housing subsidies, and low-paid service employment often favors women over men (161, 203, 211, 224). While men have lost some of the advantages that used to accrue from access to better paid industrial employment, they may still have access to more forms of income in manufacturing, the informal economy, and the illegal drug world, as well as more freedom from the costs, responsibilities, and possible entrapment of child care (22, 51, 117, 250). Just as with concepts of time and space, concepts of gender have to be reworked to fit the circumstances of the new poverty within different sectors of the global economy.

Homelessness is also experienced differently according to gender (35–40, 66, 161, 217, 219). Women lucky enough to keep their children from foster care are more likely to be assigned private rooms and services available in a rundown hotel (109, 219). Men and women without children or separated from them find themselves assigned to large sex-segregated shelters (217, 219, 223). As a result, homeless women without children excluded from services for women with children are likely to be the most brutalized group of all. They are subject to the miseries, deprivations, and dangers of homelessness and, above and beyond this, to assault by men if they spend time alone on the streets (66, 122).

Even children experience poverty differently by gender. Jagna Sharff in her research on the Lower East Side of Manhattan developed an early analysis of gendered poverty in discussing the experience of poor Latino children. She suggested that poor boys find themselves recruited into the illegal and frequently fatally attractive world of the drug trade because it is the only viable occupation for providing income for an extremely needy household. That is, early on, boys in poor households are expected to and try to live up to the male role of provider. Poor girls, Sharff argued, are more likely to be kept home to do domestic tasks and are channeled into schooling. They are less likely to be drawn into the competitive and dangerous territory of drug dealing (189). Women may use the drugs, but they do not as readily profit from them and are therefore less likely to be killed in battles over control of trade (189, 240, 243).

Sharff's formulations were originally stated according to child-rearing patterns and reinforcements for gender differentiation within poor households, which reflected limited options available in the wider society. She also argued that some young boys might be allowed to adopt less aggressive strategies to avoid high-risk assigned roles. She did not address behavior of girls wishing to broaden their options in this constrained environment, but it might be fair to view early pregnancy as one method available to girls in this situation. The originality and challenge of Sharff's analysis was marred by a possible interpretation that perhaps families chose these routes for their children and encouraged the criminality of boys, or that poor families did not desire the same professional routes of advancement for their children as middle-class families (for a different view, see 98, 100). In contrast, when Sharff's research is viewed as a description of systematic channeling through both pressures on poor families and societal expectations and opportunities for boys and girls, her analysis is supported by work concerning the gendering of childhood experience in homeless shelters (219) and opens important avenues for further study.

A more textured analysis of variations in opportunities by gender and their impact on the construction of households and child rearing would appear to be the next challenge confronting research on poverty in the United States. As Castells noted, the restructuring of gender in the global economy is one of the central features of the informational society (30). However, gender is being rewritten differently according to class within this new society, which we need to rethink (30, 217, 219, 222).

Identity, Race, Class, and Gender

The political economy of poverty of the 1980s focused on "class, race, and gender." Similarly, within cultural studies race and gender were characterized as significant identities. However, in an examination of the literature of urban poverty and homelessness, we find somewhat separate traditions of analysis for gender and for race. We find parallel historical analyses of employment segregation, as in views of the segmented work force of Fordism. Both women and minorities were excluded from the higher paying, unionized jobs that carried seniority, security, and benefits (44, 70, 78, 80, 114, 140, 250).

However, the impact of such exclusions on households and class experience was very different by gender and by race. Women were not excluded from housing or from providing a future for their children until the proliferation of single-headed families and the so-called feminization of poverty. Only an analysis that ignores identity, community, household, and social movements beyond the work place and in fact ignores the gendering of social life can view race and gender as parallel identity processes operating in similar ways within a class-based society. As Anna Tsing noted in an entirely different context, "This work rejects the notion that gender asymmetries are parallel to those of race, class, and nationality, for race, class and national hierarchies are themselves everywhere constructed in gendered ways, and gender divisions are established with 'communal' materials" (229:18). However, while they are not parallel processes or similar hierarchies, race and gender interact within a class system and as some have argued the existence of both complex hierarchies in combination has contributed to the maintenance of inequalities (80, 148, 182, 208).

Race

There is the issue of race (63, 76, 77, 81, 103, 129). Then there is the gendering of race (43, 62, 148, 149), and then there is the issue of a racial and gendered system in relation to class dynamics. All these issues bear directly on analyses of urban poverty and homelessness of the 1990s.

In terms of race, analyses of the underclass, of homelessness, and of urban poverty document the disproportion of people of color who find themselves in these populations. However, in terms of numbers, as has often been mentioned but rarely remembered, most poor people in the United States are not people of color. Nevertheless, as with the homeless, race has become a visible and politically useful metaphor for the new poverty.

Some studies of poverty simply identify the racial composition or racial identity of the people studied and move from there to the circumstances of poverty or homelessness with little attention to the impact of color on the experience (other than perhaps to refer to the history of racial discrimination in the United States). One might consider those researchers to be using race as a shorthand classification for probable history or opportunities without providing an analysis of race itself (11, 218, 219).

Other studies of poverty focus on the racial hostilities in poor neighborhoods and the experiences of racial discrimination of certain populations. While such studies do not focus specifically on the concept and experience of race, they begin to examine the cross-cutting issues of race and poverty in a more dynamic, analytical way (19, 136, 137, 203, 205, 209, 211). For example, Mercer Sullivan compared the experiences of teenage men in three neighborhoods. He documented the intersecting forces of neighborhood segregation, social networks, racial discrimination in employment, and the structure of the drug economy to explain why young white men find their way out of adolescent criminal behavior while minority adolescents find themselves trapped and defined by the records of their youth (209).

Steve Gregory and Roger Sanjek's edited collection on race is a recent effort to confront and "historicize" the concept of race in Western capitalism. They provide a political economy of identity by including articles on Jews, Egyptians, and other groups associated with contested racial categories (76). Other researchers have focused on the significance of the gendering of poverty and race (148, 149).

Perhaps conceptualization of the interplay of poverty, gender, and race can be advanced through a more detailed examination of four ethnographies that address poverty among men and women in different contexts: Philippe Bourgois's recent research among young men in East Harlem, New York City (22–24); Jay MacLeod's research among working-class teenagers (127); Elijah Anderson's perspective on young men in a Northeast city (4, 5); and Jagna Sharff's analysis of women and men's lives on the Lower East Side of New York City (189, 190).

These ethnographies together force us to confront central questions concerning the ethnographic enterprise among the poor of US urban cities. It is difficult to document the misery of the poor in the contemporary United States without falling into the problem of either romanticizing or minimizing the devastation or of painting such distress, victimization, and brutalization that the description becomes fuel for political assaults upon the poor themselves. Sharff's description of young men dealing and dying in the drug trade on the lower East Side of Manhattan in the 1970s and Bourgois's descriptions of the sale of crack in El Barrio, East Harlem (in northern Manhattan) in the 1990s are similarly graphic and disturbing. Such works might be assailed for presenting the worst and neglecting positive portraits of hardworking or politically active people in the same neighborhoods. However, the struggle to portray people involved in the most condemned activities of our society in human and comprehensible ways must also be recognized as one of the strengths of the anthropological method in both research sites (22).

Each ethnography rewrites gender such that simplistic stereotypes disintegrate in the light of the research. Bourgois described one woman who shot her partner and then became a crack dealer with power largely because, just as with the men, people believe that she will act if double-crossed (22). She does not have to fear violence because, like a man, she has established that she can fight back. This adoption of the "macho role" and its reflection also in her relationship with her new partner can be viewed as a reversal of gender expectations. This woman does not represent most women in El Barrio. However, her experience dramatically demonstrates the situational nature of gender roles as well as illuminates through contradiction a material basis for the continuity and power of machismo.

Sharff outlined women adopting stereotypic roles as they go out dancing, dressed in sophisticated middle-class styles with the explicit intentions of hypergamy. Later, she describes one such woman finally acquiring unionized work and no longer forced to depend on such futile strategies to support her five children (190). Once again, the manipulation of gender roles as situational strategy emerges from descriptions of women's struggle to support households, rear children, and survive in poverty in the urban United States (14, 228). Nowhere in these ethnographies do we find the stereotypic portrait of the modest Latina woman, trapped by traditional values and unable to change to confront the dangers of poverty and mortality facing herself and her kin. In fact, we find in some descriptions women empowered by organizing in their neighborhoods, fighting for more services, or simply trying to maintain what they have (14, 132, 212, 213, 215, 218, 228).

Anderson, a sociologist, wrote about young men and women and the expectations and behavior of youth in poverty (4, 5). While he provided direct quotes, his work does not fit the methodological and ethnographic model of much anthropological research (25a, 232), which leaves room to doubt the conclusions. Many perceptions from outsiders, such as older residents, are quoted as substantiation for generalizations about cause and effect. Generalizations such as: "Often...teenagers lack interest in school, and in time they may drop out in favor of spending time with their street-oriented peers" (5:92) contrast dramatically with descriptions of the humiliation and misery of school experiences that provide a less pat explanation for the same phenomenon (22, 110, 127). Bourgois, Sharff, and MacLeod (22, 127) are careful to describe individuals, follow situations, trace events creating a body of literature and thick description clearly judged by anthropological standards. Anderson's adoption of participant observation follows no such disciplinary tenets. He summarizes and quotes without describing in their full context and varied interconnections the people and events from which his evaluations are derived.

Despite methodological differences, Anderson identified some reversal of gender roles: Young women look for young men by whom to become pregnant and then leave them and set up independent households on the public assistance check (5:126). He quotes some men as saying such "new" women are "just out to use you" (5:126). The young women described by Anderson as trapped by their middle-class dreams are similar to those described by Ruth Sidel (191), and they support Delmos Jones's emphasis on achievement aspirations among the poor (98, 100). However, generalizations, as well as lack of context or discussion of resistance and agency, tend to fuel discussions that blame the victim or emphasize the individual problems of the poor without sufficient attention to the structural constraints of unemployment and racism within which people create their lives.

Jay MacLeod (127) used the concept of habitus to conceptualize the social reproduction of race and class (18, 65). This approach differs from the approach of Anderson and others because it allows for variation, agency, and resistance. In terms of issues of social reproduction, MacLeod argued that class is not enough because "the way in which individuals and groups respond to structures of domination is open-ended" (127:139). In discussing the lives of two friendship sets of teenage boys, one black and one white, MacLeod argued: "[A]lthough social class is of primary importance, there are intermediate factors at work that, as constitutive of the habitus, shape the subjective responses of the two groups of boys and produce quite different expectations and actions." (127:140). Is the concept of habitus necessary? Does it mean more or less than socialization, social context, or environment? MacLeod discussed the complex interaction between hegemonic ideas of gender (differentiated by class, although he did not discuss this), structural unemployment, and individual and family history. This he calls habitus. Whatever the label, such conceptualizations allow for more flexibility and difference than a simple class analysis. They avoid laying the blame on families implied in theories of the underclass and the culture of poverty without neglecting the accumulation of social or cultural capital or lack thereof that children acquire from family experiences.

In discussing unemployed white teenage youth, MacLeod emphasized the significance of gender in providing the macho image that allows young boys to build respect among their own group and to validate violence and marginality according to that societal standard. The image of mother is one area in which young girls can find validation no matter how they fare at school or in the job market (127). Thus, gender again frames the options also defined by poverty and race. In response to similar conditions of school failure and unemployment, young men can opt for validation in the macho image while young girls can see motherhood as a route to success.

Political controversy surrounds ethnographies of poverty, race, and gender because of the implications of the research for the possibilities of social change (5, 22, 127, 190). Not only do ideologies of family and gender vary by class (169, 203, 217, 219), they are also associated with different forms of political mobilization. They reflect varying conceptualizations of inequality, race, nationalism, sexual orientation, and resistance, (17, 62, 149, 213, 215, 251). For example, Leith Mullings noted that for African Americans an integrationist approach to race relations in the United States incorporates the ideologies of middle-class nuclear families (although since this is contested among men and women of the US middle class, we must wonder which concept of gender roles in the nuclear family may be adopted). Nationalist or Afrocentric mobilization against racial discrimination involves an idealization of past traditions that invokes the complementarity of male and female roles and reinforces a male/female gender hierarchy. A transformative or revolutionary approach seeks to change society and the basis for class inequality as well as that of race and gender and attempts to combat gender hierarchies along with discrimination by race (149). The representation of gender in ethnography cannot be seen apart from the political impact of such analysis and is clearly contested terrain.

As this review of recent ethnographies of poverty indicates, the transformation of gender as it interacts with the historically changing construction of poverty and race, shifting gender hierarchies, and escalating gender conflict are marked features of the global economy in the 1990s.

Collapsing Time and Space: Relocating Populations and Shifting Identities Among the Poor and Homeless in the New Global Economy

In line with the growth of the global economy, not only resident minorities are poor but also many migrant populations. Members of many new immigrant groups are poor, work for below minimum wage, have little access to benefits, and live in inner cities (55, 67, 111, 115, 116, 252, 253).

Studies of US poverty such as Carol Stack's *Call to Home* (205) discuss return migration among African Americans. Other studies describe children being sent back to Puerto Rico for discipline and other reasons (22, 190). Many discussions of international migration focus on similar phenomena (54,

188, 226). Studies of the homeless also portray a constantly shifting population, as people move across streets, shelters, cities, mental institutions, detoxification centers, and jails and are then relocated in apartments in new neighborhoods (124, 125, 220, 248). In connecting the experiences of poor immigrants with discussion of urban poverty issues, we can begin to capture the complex and conflicted movement of the poor and the working class associated with the integration of the global economy (115).

Movement across nations, between nations, and through urban areas, as depicted in the homeless literature, must be incorporated into views of the "postmodern" poor and working class. This is true whether one perceives such movement and flexibility according to the flexible economy and the associated flexible bodies (82, 131), the informational society (29, 30), or whether one accepts the prevailing paradigm of an unstructured, unexplainable, constantly shifting and jumbled postmodern world.

The Voices of the Poor and the Creation of Culture in the New Global Economy

Discussions of the culture of the poor have been controversial since the culture of poverty debates of the 1960s (101, 119, 134, 147, 216). However, ethnographies of the US urban poor echo with the voices of suffering and defeat as well as with defiance, resistance, and agency. As Setha Low has noted, neighborhood residents still rally to religious festivals and local parades (126). Women and men still mobilize to protect or demand homes, work, and services for themselves and their children (14, 126, 133, 135, 205, 211–213, 215, 218, 228). Nevertheless, a consistency emerges in the experiences described and the struggles of poverty in the 1990s. Women describe the miseries of raising children in poverty, with little help and many problems. Children report on their own brutalizing experiences at home, in school, and on the streets. Men describe their efforts to work and go straight and the losses of respect and future that underlay their turn to street life. Whether the ethnographer is Anderson, Bourgois, Sharff, MacLeod, or Stack, many of the experiences and the descriptions cry out in similar ways. The ethnographers' differences surface in the focus on agency and community resistance (14, 126, 132, 205, 211, 213, 215, 218, 228), self-destructive resistance (22, 127), and survival (190) versus misery and defeat (5). No ethnography leaves any doubt about the daily suffering in US inner cities.

Reflections and Mirrors in Ethnography in the New Global Economy

As Carol Stack wrote in a discussion of feminist ethnography, "[W]e are accountable for the consequences of our writing, fully cognizant that the story we construct is our own" (206). Ethnographers of poverty of the 1990s have similarly reexamined their own histories and interactions with the people they describe. Stack, contrasting her work of the 1970s with that of the 1990s, claims a sense of liberation. No longer constrained to locate logical sequences and objective reports, she is able to identify the contradictions in daily life and to enter her discussions from a variety of perspectives.

June Nash suggests that the hesitancy of contemporary anthropologists to conduct fieldwork almost inevitably results in objectification. Other ethnographers begin to reconsider the construction of their own white and female identities (42, 56, 152, 182). Patricia Zavella noted the difficulties of being partly of one group and partly of others and always in a hierarchical relation with informants. While *in* a group, as a middle-class academic she is not *of* that group. She wrote about the cross-cutting identities of sexual orientation and the way in which this structures her Latina, feminist, middle-class discourse (251).

However, as ethnographers grapple with the issues of reflexivity and the incorporation of voices, the hierarchies of "otherness," and the imposition and creation of identities of color, gender, nation, and foreignness, certain messages emerge clearly.

Current research has yielded visions of the ongoing assault on the lives of the poor and working class in US society as well as the resilience and humanity of those hidden from view in the new global economy. With all the imperfections of representation, the voices that emerge from these works need desperately to be heard. Perhaps they can be heard more fully and in all their contradictions when the anthropologist constructs herself/himself in the same text. However, with the increasing assault upon the living standards and employment security of working people, in which academics are also included, the idea of the other may not be as salient as many fear. The question that Kim Hopper, Kostas Gounis, Stack, Merrill Singer, and others rightfully ask is not whether we can describe the lives of the poor but how we can fight against the misery we see created (73, 88, 92, 93, 197, 206).

Literature Cited

1. Abramovitz M. 1988. *Regulating the Women*. Boston: South End
2. Abu-Lughod J. 1994. *From Urban Village to East Village*. Oxford: Blackwell
3. Adler JS. 1992. Streetwalkers, degraded outcasts, and good-for-nothing huzzies:
women and the dangerous class in antebellum St. Louis. *J. Soc. Hist.* 25(4):737–55
4. Anderson E. 1989. Sex codes and family life among poor inner city youths. *Ann. Am. Acad. Polit. Soc. Sci.* 501:59–78
5. Anderson E. 1990. *Streetwise: Race, Class*

and Change in an Urban Community. Chicago: Univ. Chicago Press

6. Anglin M. 1992. A question of loyalty: national and regional identity in narratives of Appalachia. *Anthropol. Q.* 65(3): 105–16

7. Anglin M. 1993. Engendering the struggle: women's labor and traditions of resistance in rural southern Appalachia. In *Fighting Back in Appalachia,* ed. S Fisher, pp. 263–81. Philadelphia: Temple Univ. Press

8. Deleted in proof

9. Bailey T, Waldinger R. 1991. The changing ethnic/racial division of labor. See Ref. 143, pp. 43–79

10. Balshem M. 1991. Cancer control and causality: talking about cancer in a working class community. *Am. Ethnol.* 18(1): 152–73

11. Basch L, Schiller N, Szanton C. 1994. *Nations Unbound: Transnational Projects, Postcolonial Predicaments, and Deterritorialized Nation States.* Langhorne, PA: Gordon & Breach

12. Baxter E, Hopper K. 1981. *Private Lives/ Public Spaces: Homeless Adults on the Streets of New York, New York.* New York: Commun. Serv. Soc. NY

13. Benaria L, Roldan M. 1987. *The Crossroads of Class and Gender.* Chicago: Univ. Chicago Press

14. Benmayor R, Torruellas R, Juarbe A. 1991. *Puerto Rican Women and a Culture of Empowerment.* Presented at the NY Acad. Sci., April, New York City

15. Blim M. 1996. Cultures and the problems of capitalisms. *Crit. Anthropol.* 16(1): 79–93

16. Bluestone D, Harrison B. 1982. *The Deindustrialization of America.* New York: Basic Books

17. Bookman A, Morgen S, eds. 1988. *Women and the Politics of Empowerment.* Philadelphia: Temple Univ. Press

18. Bourdieu P. 1977. *Outline of a Theory of Practice.* Cambridge: Cambridge Univ. Press

19. Bourgois P. 1989. If you're not black you're white: a history of ethnic relations in St. Louis. *City Soc.* 3(2):106–31

20. Deleted in proof

21. Deleted in proof

22. Bourgois P. 1995. *In Search of Respect: Selling Crack in El Barrio.* Cambridge: Cambridge Univ. Press

23. Bourgois P. 1995. The political economy of resistance and self-destruction in the crack economy: an ethnographic perspective. *Ann. NY Acad. Sci.* 749:97–118

24. Bourgois P, Dunlap E. 1993. Exorcising sex-for-crack: an ethnographic perspective from Harlem. In *Crack Pipe as Pimp: An Ethnographic Investigation of Sex-for-*

Crack Exchange. New York: Lexington Books

25. Burawoy M. 1979. The anthropology of industrial work. *Annu. Rev. Anthropol.* 8: 231–66

25a. Burawoy M, ed. 1993. *Ethnography Unbound.* Berkeley: Univ. Calif. Press

26. Burt MR. 1992. *Over the Edge: The Growth of Homelessness in the 80's.* New York: Russell Sage Found.

27. Castells M. 1977. *The Urban Question.* London: Arnold

28. Castells M. 1983. *The City and the Grassroots.* Berkeley: Univ. Calif. Press

29. Castells M. 1989. *The Informational City.* London: Blackwell

30. Castells M. 1996. The net and the self: working notes for a critical theory of the informational society. *Crit. Anthropol.* 16(1):In press

31. Cohen L. 1990. *Making a New Deal.* Cambridge: Cambridge Univ. Press

32. Connors M. 1992. Risk perception, risk taking and risk management among intravenous drug users: implications for AIDS prevention. *Soc. Sci. Med.* 34:591–601

33. Corcoran M, Duncan GJ, Gurin G, Gurin P. 1985. Myth and reality: the causes and persistence of poverty. *J. Policy Anal. Manage.* 4(4):516–36

34. Davis M. 1990. *City of Quartz: Excavating the Future in Los Angeles.* New York: Verso

35. Dehavenon A. 1989–1990. Charles Dickens meets Franz Kafka: the maladministration of New York City's public assistance programs. *Rev. Law Soc. Change* 17(2): 231–54

36. Dehavenon A. 1990. *The Tyranny of Indifference.* New York: Action Res. Proj. Hunger, Homelessness, Fam. Health

37. Dehavenon A. 1992. *Promises! Promises! Promises! The Failed Hopes of New York City's Homeless Families in 1992.* New York: Action Res. Proj. Hunger, Homelessness, Fam. Health

38. Dehavenon A. 1993. Not enough to go around: an etic model for the cross-cultural study of the causes of matrifocality. In *Where Did All the Men Go? Female-Headed Households Cross-Culturally,* ed. J Mencher, A Okongwu, pp. 53–69. Boulder, CO: Westview

39. Dehavenon A. 1995. A retrospective on two and a half decades of East Harlem research. *Ann. NY Acad. Sci.* 749:137–51

40. Dehavenon A. 1995. *Out in the Cold: The Social Exclusion of New York City's Homeless Families in 1995.* New York: Action Res. Proj. Hunger, Homelessness, Fam. Health

41. di Leonardo M. 1992. White lies: rape, race, and the myth of the Black underclass. *Village Voice* 38:1–7

42. di Leonardo M. 1994. White ethnicities, identity, and Baby Bear's chair. *Soc. Text* 41:165–91
43. Dill B. 1988. "Making your job good yourself": domestic service and the construction of personal dignity. See Ref. 17, pp. 33–53
44. Eggers ML, Massey DS. 1992. A longitudinal analysis of urban poverty: blacks in US metropolitan areas between 1970–1980. *Soc. Sci. Res.* 21(2):175–203
45. Erickson J, Wilhelm C, eds. 1986. *Housing the Homeless.* New Brunswick, NJ: Cent. Urban Res.
46. Estroff S. 1981. *Making It Crazy.* Berkeley: Univ. Calif. Press
47. Etienne M, Leacock E, eds. 1980. *Women and Colonization.* Hadley, MA: South Press/Bergin & Garvey
48. Fabian J. 1983. *Time and the Other.* New York: Columbia Univ. Press
49. Fainstein S. 1994. *City Builders.* Oxford: Blackwell
50. Fernandez-Kelly P. 1981. *For We are Sold Me and My People.* Albany: State Univ. NY Press
51. Fernandez-Kelly P. 1990. Delicate transactions: gender, home, and employment among Hispanic women. In *Uncertain Terms: Negotiating Gender in American Culture,* ed. F Ginsburg, A Lowenhaupt-Tsing, pp. 183–95. Boston: Beacon
52. Deleted in proof
53. Deleted in proof
54. Foner N. 1987. *New Immigrants in New York.* New York: Columbia Univ. Press
55. Foner N. 1995. Contemporary immigration: issues and perspectives. See Ref. 52, pp. 245–52
56. Frankenberg R. 1995. Whiteness and Americanness: examining constructions of race, culture and nation in white women's life narratives. See Ref. 77, pp. 62–77
57. Deleted in proof
58. Gailey C. 1992. A good man is hard to find: overseas migration and the decentered family in the Tongan Islands. *Crit. Anthropol.* 12(1):47–74
59. Geronimus AT. 1992. Clashes of common sense: on the previous child care experience of teenage mothers-to-be. *Hum. Organ.* 51:318–29
60. Gerstle G, Frazier S. 1989. *The Rise and Fall of the New Deal Order.* Princeton, NJ: Princeton Univ. Press
61. Giddens A. 1981. *A Contemporary Critique of Historical Materialism.* Berkeley: Univ. Calif. Press
62. Gilkes CT. 1988. Building in many places: multiple commitments and ideologies in black women's community work. See Ref. 17, pp. 53–77
63. Gilroy P. 1993. *Black Atlantic: Modernity and Double Consciousness.* Cambridge, MA: Harvard Univ. Press
64. Deleted in proof
65. Giroux H. 1983. *Theory and Resistance in Education.* London: Heinemann
66. Golden S. 1990. Lady versus low creature: old roots of current attitudes toward homeless women. *Frontiers* 11(2–3):1–7
67. Goode J, Schneider J. 1994. *Reshaping Ethnic and Racial Relations in Philadelphia: Immigrants in a Divided City.* Philadelphia: Temple Univ. Press
68. Gordon D. 1978. Capitalist development and the history of American cities. In *Marxism and the Metropolis,* ed. W Tabb, L Sawers, pp. 25–63. New York: Oxford Univ. Press
69. Gordon D. 1988. The global economy: new edifice or crumbling foundations. *New Left Rev.* 172:14–64
70. Gordon D, Edwards R, Reich M. 1982. *Segmented Work, Divided Workers.* Cambridge: Cambridge Univ. Press
71. Gordon L. 1994. *Pitied but Not Entitled.* New York: Free Press
72. Gounis K. 1992. Temporality and the domestication of homelessness. See Ref. 180, pp. 127–49
73. Gounis K. 1996. Urban marginality and ethnographic practice: ethical dilemmas and political implications. *City Soc. Annu. Rev.* In press
74. Gounis K, Susser E. 1990. Shelterization and its implications for mental health services. In *Psychiatry Takes to the Street,* ed. N Cohen, pp. 231–55. New York: Guilford
75. Grasmuck S, Pessar P. 1991. *Between Two Islands: Dominican International Migration.* Berkeley: Univ. Calif. Press
76. Gregory S. 1992. The changing significance of race and class in an African American Community. *Am. Ethnol.* 19(2):255–75
77. Gregory S, Sanjek R, eds. 1994. *Race.* New Brunswick, NJ: Rutgers Univ. Press
77a. Grisso J, Schwarz D, Miles C, Holmes J. 1996. Injuries among inner-city minority women: a population-based longitudinal study. *Am. J. Public Health* 86(1):67–70
78. Gutman H. 1976. *Work, Culture and Society in Industrializing America.* New York: Vintage
79. Hakken D, Andrews B. 1993. *Computing Myths, Class Realities.* Boulder, CO: Westview
80. Harris M. 1987. *Why Nothing Works: The Anthropology of Daily Life.* New York: Simon & Schuster
81. Harrison FV. 1995. The persistant power of "race" in the cultural and political economy of racism. *Annu. Rev. Anthropol.* 24:47–74
82. Harvey D. 1990. *The Condition of Postmodernity.* Cambridge, MA: Harvard Univ. Press

83. Hobsbawm E. 1964. *Laboring Men.* Garden City, NJ: Anchor
84. Hopper K. 1987. The public response to homelessness in New York City: the last hundred years. In *On Being Homeless: Historical Perspectives,* ed. R Beard. New York: Mus. City NY
85. Hopper K. 1989. The ordeal of shelter: continuities and discontinuities in the public response to homelessness. *Notre Dame J. Law Ethics Public Policy* 4(2):301–23
86. Hopper K. 1990. Public shelter as "a hybrid institution": homeless men in historical perspective. *J. Soc. Issues* 46(4):13–29
87. Hopper K. 1991. Homelessness old and new: the matter of definition. *Housing Policy Debate* 2:757–813
88. Hopper K. 1991. Research for what? Lessons from the study of homelessness. *Bull. Am. Acad. Arts Sci.* 44:13–31
89. Hopper K. 1991. Symptoms, survival, and the redefinition of public space: a feasability study of homeless people at a metropolitan airport. *Urban Anthropol.* 20:155–75
90. Hopper K. 1992. Counting the homeless: s-night in New York. *Eval. Rev.* 16(4):376–88
91. Hopper K. 1995. Definitional quandaries and other hazards in counting the homeless: an invited commentary. *Am. J. Orthopsychiatry* 65:340–46
92. Hopper K, Baumohl J. 1994. Held in abeyance: rethinking homelessness and advocacy. *Am. Behav. Sci.* 37:522–52
93. Hopper K, Cox L. 1982. Litigation in advocacy for the homeless: the case of New York City. *Dev. Seeds Change* (2):57–62
94. Hopper K, Susser E, Conover S. 1987. Economics of makeshift: deindustrialization and homelessness in New York City. *Urban Anthropol.* (14):183–236
95. Howell J. 1973. *Hard Living on Clay Street.* New York: Anchor
96. Jencks C. 1994. *The Homeless.* Cambridge, MA: Harvard Univ. Press
97. Jencks C, Peterson PE. 1991. *The Urban Underclass.* Washington, DC: Brookings Inst.
98. Jones DJ. 1993. The culture of achievement among the poor: the case of mothers and children in a Headstart program. *Crit. Anthropol.* 13(3):247–67
99. Jones DJ. 1994. Culture, domination and social complexity. *High Plains Anthropol.* 14(2):19–33
100. Jones DJ. 1995. The anthropology of lower income urban enclaves. *Ann. NY Acad. Sci.* 749:189–203
101. Jones DJ, Susser I, eds. 1993. The widening gap between rich and poor. *Crit. Anthropol.* 13(3):211–15
102. Jones DJ, Turner J, Montbach J. 1992. Declining social services and the threat to social reproduction: an urban dilemma. *City Soc.* 6(2):99–114
103. Jones J. 1992. *The Dispossessed: America's Underclasses from the Civil War to the Present.* New York: Basic Books
104. Deleted in proof
105. Katz M. 1989. *The Undeserving Poor.* New York: Pantheon
106. Katz M. 1993. *The "Underclass" Debate: Views from History.* Princeton, NJ: Princeton Univ. Press
106a. Kearney M. 1995. The local and the global: the anthropology of globalization and transnationalism. *Annu. Rev. Anthropol.* 24:547–65
107. Kessler-Harris A. 1982. *Out to Work.* New York: Oxford Univ. Press
108. Koegel P. 1992. Understanding homelessness: an ethnographic approach. In *Homelessness: A Prevention-Oriented Approach,* ed. RJ Jahiel. Baltimore: John Hopkins Univ. Press
109. Kozol J. 1988. *Rachel and Her Children.* New York: Crown
110. Kozol J. 1992. *Savage Inequalities.* New York: Harper Collins
111. Kwong P. 1987. *The New Chinatown.* New York: Hill & Wang
112. Deleted in proof
113. Deleted in proof
114. Lamphere L. 1987. *From Working Daughters to Working Mothers.* Ithaca, NY: Cornell Univ. Press
115. Lamphere L, ed. 1992. *Structuring Diversity: Ethnographic Perspectives on the New Immigration.* Chicago: Univ. Chicago Press
116. Lamphere L, Stepick A, Grenier G. 1994. *Newcomers in the Workplace: Immigrants and the Restructuring of the US Economy.* Philadelphia: Temple Univ. Press
117. Lamphere L, Zavella P, Gonzalez F, Evans P. 1993. *Sunbelt Working Mothers.* Ithaca, NY: Cornell Univ. Press
118. Lazarus E. 1990. Falling through the cracks: contradictions and barriers to care in a prenatal clinic. *Med. Anthropol.* 12:269–87
119. Lewis O. 1966. The culture of poverty. *Sci. Am.* 215:19–25
120. Lichter D, Eggebeen DJ. 1992. Child poverty and the changing rural family. *Rural Sociol.* 57(2):151–72
121. Liebow E. 1967. *Tally's Corner.* Boston: Little Brown
122. Liebow E. 1993. *Tell Them Who I Am: The Lives of Homeless Women.* New York: Free Press
123. Link BG, Susser E, Stueve A, Phelan J, Moore RE, Struening E. 1994. Lifetime and five-year prevalence of homelessness in the U. S. *Am. J. Public Health* 84:1907–12
124. Lovell A. 1992. Seizing the moment:

power, contingency, and temporality in street life. See Ref. 180, pp. 86–107

125. Lovell A. 1994. The dispersed city: homelessness, mental illness, and urban space. *Courr. CNRS* 81:170–72

126. Low SM. 1996. A response to Castells: an anthropology of the city. *Crit. Anthropol.* 16(1):In press

127. MacLeod J. 1987. *Ain't No Making It: Leveled Aspirations in a Low-Income Neighborhood.* Boulder, CO: Westview

128. Mann C, Albelda R. 1988. Jobs, fathers and the states: welfare policy and the new federalism. *Rev. Radical Polit. Econ.* 20 (2–3):61–67

129. Marable M. 1995. *Beyond Black and White.* London: Verso

130. Marcuse P. 1985. Gentrification, abandonment and displacement: connections, causes and policy responses in New York City. *J. Urban Contemp. Law* (28):193–240

131. Martin E. 1996. The society of flows and the flows of culture: reading Castells in the light of cultural accounts of the body, health and complex systems. *Crit. Anthropol.* 16(1):49–57

132. Mathieu A. 1990. *Parents on the move.* PhD thesis. New School Soc. Res., New York

133. Maxwell A. 1988. The anthropology of poverty in black communities: a critique and systems alternative. *Urban Anthropol.* 17(2–3):171–91

134. Maxwell A. 1993. The underclass, social isolation and concentration effects: "the culture of poverty" revisited. *Crit. Anthropol.* 13(3):231–45

135. Maxwell A. 1996. A home by any means necessary: government policy and squatting in the housing projects of a mid-Atlantic city. In *There's No Place Like Home: Homelessness and the New Faces of U. S. Poverty,* ed. A Dehavenon. Hadley, MA: Bergin & Garvey

136. Merry S. 1981. Defensible space undefended: social factors in crime control through environmental design. *Urban Aff. Q.* 16(4):397–422

137. Merry S. 1981. *Urban Danger: Life in a Neighborhood of Strangers.* Philadelphia: Temple Univ. Press

138. Merry S. 1995. Gender violence and legally engendered selves. *Identities* 2(1–2):49–73

139. Deleted in proof

140. Milkman R. 1987. *Gender at Work.* Chicago: Univ. Ill. Press

141. Mitchell D. 1992. Iconography and locational conflict from the underside: free speech, People's Park, and the politics of homelessness in Berkeley, California. *Polit. Geogr.* 11(2):152–69

142. Mitchell D. 1995. The end of public space? People's Park, definitions of the public, and

democracy. *Ann. Assoc. Am. Geogr.* 85(1): 108–33

143. Mollenkopf J, Castells M, eds. 1991. *The Dual City.* New York: Russell Sage Found.

144. Montgomery D. 1979. *Workers Control in America.* Cambridge: Cambridge Univ. Press

145. Montgomery D. 1987. *The Fall of the House of Labor.* Cambridge: Cambridge Univ. Press

146. Deleted in proof

147. Mullings L. 1989. Gender and the application of anthropological knowledge to public policy in the United States. In *Gender and Anthropology,* ed. S Morgan, pp. 360–82. Washington, DC: Am. Anthropol. Assoc.

148. Mullings L. 1995. Households headed by women: the politics of race, class and gender. In *Conceiving the New World Order,* ed. F Ginzburg, R Rapp, pp. 122–39. Berkeley: Univ. Calif. Press

149. Mullings L. 1996. *On Our Own Terms.* New York: Routledge

150. Mullings L, Susser I. 1992. *Harlem Research and Development Report.* New York: Manhattan Borough Pres. Off.

151. Nash J. 1989. *From Tank Town to High Tech.* Albany: South. Univ. NY Press

152. Nash J. 1995. The anthropology of stranger and native. *Ann. NY Acad. Sci.* 749: 205–16

153. Nash J, Fernandez-Kelly P. 1984. *Women, Men and the International Division of Labor.* Albany: South. Univ. NY Press

154. Nash J, Safa H. 1986. *Women and Change in Latin America.* South Hadley, MA: Bergin & Garvey

155. Newman K. 1988. *Falling from Grace.* New York: Free Press

156. Newman K. 1992. Culture and structure in *The Truly Disadvantaged. City Soc.* 6:3–25

157. Olson L. 1982. *The Political Economy of Aging.* New York: Columbia Univ. Press

158. Ong A. 1987. *Spirits of Resistance and Capitalist Discipline.* Albany: South. Univ. NY Press

159. Pappas G. 1989. *The Magic City.* Ithaca, NY: Cornell Univ. Press

160. Pappas G, Queen S, Hadden W, Fisher G. 1993. The increasing disparity of mortality between socioeconomic groups in the United States: 1960–1986. *N. Engl. J. Med.* 329(2):103–9

161. Passaro J. 1996. *Men on the Street, Women in Their Place: Homelessness, Race and "Family Values."* New York: Routledge

162. Paules GF. 1991. *Dishing It Out.* Philadelphia: Temple Univ. Press

163. Perlo V. 1988. Deterioration of black economic conditions. *Rev. Rad. Polit. Econom.* 20(2/3):55–59

164. Deleted in proof

165. Piven F, Cloward R. 1971. *Regulating the Poor*. New York: Vintage
166. Portes A, Castells M, Benton L, eds. 1989. *The Informal Economy*. Baltimore: Johns Hopkins Univ. Press
167. Deleted in proof
168. Portes A, Zhou M. 1993. The new second generation: segmented assimilation and its variants. *Ann. Am. Acad. Polit. Soc. Sci.* 530:74–96
169. Rapp R. 1987. Urban kinship in contemporary America: families, classes and ideology. In *Cities of the United States*, ed. L Mullings, pp. 219–43. New York: Columbia Univ. Press
170. Rhodes L. 1991. *Emptying Beds*. Berkeley: Univ. Calif. Press
171. Richie E. 1995. *Compelled to Crime*. New York: Routledge
172. Ricketts E, Sawhill I. 1988. Defining and measuring the underclass. *J. Policy Anal. Manage.* 7(2):316–25
173. Deleted in proof
174. Deleted in proof
175. Rosner D. 1982. Health care and the "truly needy": 19th century origins of the concept. *Milbank Mem. Fund Q.* 60:355
176. Rosner D, Markowitz G. 1987. *Dying for Work: Worker's Safety and Health in Twentieth-Century America*. Indianapolis: Indiana Univ. Press
177. Rosner D, Markowitz G. 1991. *Deadly Dust*. Princeton, NJ: Princeton Univ. Press
178. Rothstein F, Blim M, eds. 1992. *Anthropology and the Global Factory*. New York: Bergin & Garvey
179. Rubin L. 1976. *Worlds of Pain*. New York: Basic Books
180. Rutz H, ed. 1992. *The Politics of Time. Ethnol. Soc. Monogr. Ser. 4*. Washington, DC: Am. Anthropol. Assoc.
181. Sacks K. 1988. *Caring by the Hour.* Chicago: Univ. Ill. Press
182. Sacks K. 1996. *Race, Class, Gender and the Jewish Question*. New Brunswick, NJ: Rutgers Univ. Press
183. Sacks K, Remy D. 1984. *Our Troubles Are Going to Have Trouble with Us*. New Brunswick, NJ: Rutgers Univ. Press
184. Samson C. 1994. The three faces of privatization. *Sociology* 28(1):79–97
185. Deleted in proof
186. Sassen S. 1991. *The Global City*. Princeton, NJ: Princeton Univ. Press
187. Sassen S. 1991. The informal economy. See Ref. 143, pp. 79–103
188. Schiller N, Basch L, Blanc-Szanton C, eds. 1992. *Towards a Transnational Perspective on Migration*. New York: NY Acad. Sci.
189. Sharff J. 1987. The underground economy of a poor neighborhood. In *Cities in the United States*, ed. L Mullings, pp. 19–50. New York: Columbia Univ. Press
190. Sharff J. 1996. *King Kong on 4th Street*. Boulder, CO: Westview
191. Sidel R. 1990. *On Her Own: Growing Up in the Shadow of the American Dream*. New York: Viking
192. Sidel R. 1992. *Women and Children Last*. New York: Basic Books
193. Sieber RT. 1990. Selecting a new past: emerging definitions of heritage in Boston Harbor. *J. Urban Cult. Stud.* 1:101–22
194. Sieber RT. 1991. Waterfront revitalization in postindustrial port cities of North America. *City Soc.* 5:120–36
195. Silver H. 1993. National conceptions of new urban poverty: social structural change in Britain, France and the United States. *Int. J. Urban Reg. Res.* 17(3):336–54
196. Singer M. 1994. AIDS and the health crisis of the US urban poor: the perspective of critical medical anthropology. *Soc. Sci. Med.* 39(7):931–48
197. Singer M. 1995. Beyond the ivory tower: critical praxis in medical anthropology. *Med. Anthropol. Q.* 9:80–106
198. Singer M, Flores D, Davison L, Burke G, Castillo Z, et al. 1990. SIDA: the economic, social and cultural context of AIDS among Latinos. *Med. Anthropol. Q.* 4:73–117
199. Smith N. 1992. New city, new frontier: the lower east side as wild, wild west. In *Variations on a Theme Park*, ed. M Sorkin, pp. 61–93. New York: Noonday
200. Smith N. 1996. *The New Urban Frontier: Gentrification and the Revanchist City*. London: Routledge
201. Smith N. 1996. Spaces of vulnerability: the space of flows and the politics of scale. *Crit. Anthropol.* 16(1):63–79
202. Stacey J. 1990. *Brave New Families*. New York: Basic Books
203. Stack C. 1974. *All Our Kin*. New York: Harper & Row
204. Deleted in proof
205. Stack C. 1996. *Call to Home: African Americans Reclaim the Rural South*. New York: Basic Books
206. Stack C. 1996. Writing ethnography: feminist critical practice. In *Feminist Dilemmas in Fieldwork*, ed. D Wolf, pp. 96–106. Boulder, CO: Westview
207. Stein Z. 1985. A woman's age. *Am. J. Epidemiol.* 121:327–42
208. Stoler A. 1989. Making an empire respectable: the politics of race and sexual morality in the twentieth century colonial cultures. *Am. Ethnol.* 16:634–60
209. Sullivan M. 1990. *Getting Paid*. Ithaca, NY: Cornell Univ. Press
210. Susser E, Valencia E, Conover S. 1993. Prevalence of HIV infection among psychiatric patients in a large men's shelter. *Am. J. Public Health* 83:568–70
211. Susser I. 1982. *Norman Street: Poverty and*

Politics in an Urban Neighborhood. New York: Oxford Univ. Press

212. Susser I. 1985. Union Carbide and the community surrounding it: the case of a community in Puerto Rico. *Int. J. Health Serv.* 15(4):561–83

213. Susser I. 1986. Political activity among working class women in a U. S. city. *Am. Ethnol.* 13(1):108–117

214. Susser I. 1986. Work and reproduction in sociologic context. In *Reproduction and the Workplace, Occupational Medicine: State of the Art Rev.* 1(3):517–39. Philadelphia: Hanley & Belfus

215. Susser I. 1988. Working class women, social protest and changing ideologies. See Ref. 17, pp. 257–72

216. Susser I. 1989. Gender in the anthropology of the United States. In *Gender and Anthropology,* ed. S Morgen, pp. 343–60. Washington, DC: Am. Anthropol. Assoc.

217. Susser I. 1991. The separation of mothers and children. See Ref. 143, pp. 207–25

218. Susser I. 1992. Women as political actors in rural Puerto Rico: continuity and change. See Ref. 178, pp. 206–20

219. Susser I. 1993. Creating family forms: the exclusion of men and teenage boys from families in the New York City shelter system, 1987–91. *Crit. Anthropol.* 13(3): 267–85

220. Susser I. 1995. *Fear and violence in dislocated communities.* Presented at Annu. Meet. Am. Anthropol. Assoc., 94th, Washington, DC

221. Susser I, ed. 1996. *Special Issue on Anthropological Perspectives on the Informational Society. Crit. Anthropol.* 16(1)

222. Susser I. 1996. The shaping of conflict in the space of flows. *Crit. Anthropol.* 16(1): 39–49

223. Susser I, Gonzalez M. 1992. Sex, drugs and videotape: the prevention of AIDS in a New York City shelter for homeless men. *Med. Anthropol.* 14:307–22

224. Susser I, Kreniske J. 1987. The welfare trap: a public policy for deprivation. In *Cities in the United States,* ed. L Mullings, pp. 51–68. New York: Columbia Univ. Press

225. Susser M. 1993. Health as a human right: an epidemiologist's perspective on the public health. *Am. J. Public Health* 83:418–26

226. Sutton C, Chaney E, eds. 1987. *Caribbean Life in New York.* New York: Cent. Migr. Stud.

227. Thompson EP. 1969. Time, work-discipline and industrial capitalism. *Past Present* 38:56–97

228. Torruellas RM. 1995. "Mi Sacrificio Bien Pago": Puerto Rican women on welfare and family values. *Ann. NY Acad. Sci.* 749:177–87

229. Tsing A. 1993. *In the Realm of the Diamond Queen.* Princeton, NJ: Princeton Univ. Press

230. Urciuoli B. 1992. Time, talk and class: New York Puerto Ricans as temporal and linguistic others. See Ref. 180, pp. 108–26

231. Valentine B. 1978. *Hustling and Other Hard Work.* New York: Free Press

232. Van Velsen J. 1969. The extended-case method and situational analysis. In *The Craft of Social Anthropology,* ed. A Epstein, pp. 129–49. London: Soc. Sci. Paperback

233. Vélez-Ibàñez CG. 1995. The challenge of funds of knowledge in urban arenas: another way of understanding the learning resources of poor Mexicano households in the U. S. Southwest and their implications for national contexts. *Ann. NY Acad. Sci.* 749:253–80

234. Vincent J. 1993. Framing the underclass. *Crit. Anthropol.* 13(3):215–31

235. Wacquant L. 1994. The new urban color line: the state and fate of the ghetto in postfordist America. In *Social Theory and the Politics of Identity,* ed. C Calhoun, pp. 231–76. Oxford: Blackwell

236. Wacquant L. 1996. Red Belt, Black Belt: racial division, class inequality and the state in the French urban periphery and the American ghetto. In *The New Poverty and the Underclass in Advanced Societies,* ed. E Mingione, pp. 234–74. Oxford: Blackwell

237. Wacquant L, Wilson W. 1989. The cost of racial and class exclusion in the inner city. *Ann. Am. Acad. Polit. Soc. Sci.* 501:8–25

238. Wagner D. 1993. *Checkerboard Square.* Boulder, CO: Westview

239. Waldinger R. 1986–1987. Changing ladders and musical chairs: ethnicity and opportunity in post-industrial New York. *Polit. Soc.* 15:369–402

240. Waterston A. 1993. *Street Addicts in the Political Economy.* Philadelphia: Temple Univ. Press

241. Williams B. 1988. *Upscaling Downtown: Stalled Gentrification in Washington, D. C.* Ithaca, NY: Cornell Univ. Press

242. Deleted in proof

243. Williams T. 1989. *The Cocaine Kids: The Inside Story of a Teenage Drug Ring.* Reading, MA: Addison-Wesley

244. Wilson WJ. 1980. *The Declining Significance of Race.* Chicago: Univ. Chicago Press

245. Wilson WJ. 1987. *The Truly Disadvantaged.* Chicago: Univ. Chicago Press

246. Wilson WJ. 1991. Another look at the truly disadvantaged. *Polit. Sci. Q.* 106:639–57

247. Wolch J, Dear M. 1993. *Malign Neglect.* San Francisco: Jossey-Bass. 378 pp.

248. Wolch J, Rowe S. 1992. On the streets:

mobility paths of the urban homeless. *City Soc.* 6(2)115–40

249. Wright SE. 1993. Blaming the victim, blaming society or blaming the discipline: fixing responsibility for poverty and homelessness. *Soc. Q.* 34(1):1–16

250. Zavella P. 1987. *Women's Work and Chicano Families*. Ithaca, NY: Cornell Univ. Press

251. Zavella P. 1994. Reflections on diversity among Chicanos. See Ref. 77, pp. 199–212

252. Zavella P. 1996. Living on the edge: everyday lives of poor Chicano/Mexicano families. In *Mapping Multiculturalism?* ed. A

Gordon, C Newfield. Minneapolis: Univ. Minn. Press. In press

253. Zavella P. 1996. The tables are turned: immigration, poverty, and social conflict in California communities. In *The New Nativism*, ed. J Perea. New York: NY Univ. Press. In press

254. Deleted in proof

255. Zinn M. 1989. Family, race and poverty in the eighties. *Signs* 14(4):856–74

256. Zukin S. 1991. *Landscapes of Power: From Detroit to Disneyworld*. Berkeley: Univ. Calif. Press

AUTHOR INDEX

SUBJECT INDEX

CUMULATIVE INDEXES

CONTRIBUTING AUTHORS, VOLUMES 17–25

CHAPTER TITLES, VOLUMES 17–25

479

LINGUISTICS AND COMMUNICATIVE PRACTICES

CHAPTER TITLES 483